LINCOLN CHRISTIAN COLLEGE AND SEMINARY

D0661043

SELECTED WRITINGS
OF
GERTRUDE STEIN

SELECTED WRITINGS

OF

GERTRUDE STEIN

Edited, with an Introduction and Notes, by
CARL VAN VECHTEN

and with an Essay on Gertrude Stein by
F. W. DUPEE

VINTAGE BOOKS

A Division of Random House, New York

Copyright, 1945, 1946, © *1962, by Random House, Inc. Copyright, 1933, 1934, by Gertrude Stein. Copyright, 1934, 1935, by Modern Library, Inc. Copyright, 1940, by Atlantic Monthly, Inc. Copyright, 1945, by Random House, Inc. Copyright renewed, 1936, by Gertrude Stein. Copyright renewed, 1945, by Conde Nast Publications, Inc. Copyright renewed, 1960, 1961, 1962, by Alice B. Toklas.*

All rights reserved under International and Pan-American Copyright Conventions. Published in the United States by Random House, Inc., New York, and simultaneously in Canada by Random House of Canada Limited, Toronto. Originally published by The Modern Library in 1962.

ISBN: 0-394-71710-4

The editor and publishers acknowledge their indebtedness to the Hogarth Press for *Composition as Explanation* and *Preciosilla;* to *Vanity Fair* for *Have They Attacked Mary. He Giggled. (A Political Caricature);* to *The Atlantic Monthly* for *The Winner Loses.*

Manufactured in the United States of America

Vintage Books Edition, May, 1972

6789B

CONTENTS

A MESSAGE FROM GERTRUDE STEIN

I always wanted to be historical, from almost a baby on, I felt that way about it, and Carl was one of the earliest ones that made me be certain that I was going to be. When I was around fourteen I used to love to say to myself those awful lines of George Eliot, May I be one of those immortal something or other, I havent the poem here and although I knew then how it went I do not now, and then later when they used to ask me when I was going back to America, not until I am a lion, I said, I was not completely certain that I was going to be but now here I am, thank you all. How terribly exciting each one of these were, first there was the doing of them, the intense feeling that they made sense, then the doubt and then each time over again the intense feeling that they did make sense. It was Carl who arranged for the printing of *Tender Buttons,* he knew and what a comfort it was that there was the further knowing of the printed page, so naturally it was he that would choose and introduce because he was the first that made the first solemn contract and even though the editor did disappear, it was not before the edition was printed and distributed, wonderful days, and so little by little it was built up and all the time Carl wrote to me and I wrote to him and he always knew, and it was always a comfort and now he has put down all his knowledge of what I did and it is a great comfort. Then there was my first publisher who was commercial but who said he would print and he would publish even if he did not understand and if he did not make money, it sounds like a fairy tale but it is true, Bennett said, I will print a book of yours a year whatever it is and he has, and often I have worried but he always said there was nothing to worry about and there wasnt. And now I am pleased here are the selected writings and naturally I wanted more, but I do and can say that all that are here are those that I wanted the most, thanks and thanks again.

Paris. June 18, 1946   GERTRUDE STEIN

GENERAL INTRODUCTION

There used to be something known to all readers as "Steinese." Steinese was the peculiar literary idiom invented by Gertrude Stein around 1910 and made familiar to a large American public by her admirers and nonadmirers alike. Gnomic, repetitive, illogical, sparsely punctuated, this idiom became a scandal and a delight, lending itself equally to derisory parody and fierce denunciation. It had a formidable currency in writing and conversation throughout the teens, twenties, and thirties. "A rose is a rose is a rose" and "Pigeons on the grass alas" were encountered as frequently—almost—as the "Yes, we have no bananas," a nonsense phrase—later a song —of popular origin which may actually have been inspired by Steinese. "My little sentences have gotten under their skins," Gertrude Stein was at last able to say, with the pride of someone who craved recognition the more that she got mere notoriety. In other words, her little sentences, originally quoted in scorn, had come in time to be repeated from something like affection; and thus the very theory that underlay her technique of reiteration was proved: what people loved they repeated, and what people repeated they loved.

Simple-minded as she sounded to the public, Gertrude Stein did have her theories—few writers of note have had more stringent ones. If she was "the Mother Goose of Montparnasse," as someone said (such attempts to characterize her in a witty phrase were constantly repeated, too), she was a Mother Goose with a mind. She had studied psychology with William James at Radcliffe; conducted laboratory experiments there with Hugo Münsterberg; come close to getting an M.D. at Johns Hopkins; and then, settling in Paris with her brother Leo, communed with Picasso in his Paris studio where a different kind of experiment was in progress: the plastic analysis of spatial relations which gave rise to Cubist painting.

Thus, behind the popular image of Gertrude Stein there

came to be, as we all know by now, a woman of immense
purpose, equipped with astonishing powers of assimilation,
concentration and hard work—as well as, to be sure, relaxation (she liked to lie in the sun and stare right into it). Her
meeting with Picasso was in itself purely fortuitous; such a
meeting might have befallen any tourist with a mildly quest-
ing spirit and enough money to buy paintings which, in any
event, went almost begging. Gertrude Stein converted this
meeting into the basis of a vocation and a life. It became for
her the major case—her acquaintance with William James
was another—of genius by association. Her scientific interests
now fused with a passion, at last fully awakened, for art and
literature. Out of this union of the laboratory and the studio
came a body of theory and writing like none before or after
it. There were elements in it of the Naturalism that was just
then (*ca.* 1900) taking root in American literature. So far as
these elements alone went, Gertrude Stein might have been
a Dreiser *manqué*—except that, with her Cubist predilections,
she became, as it were, post-Dreiser. Like Dreiser and other
Naturalists she held quasi-scientific conceptions of race and
individual character; life expressed itself best in forms of
"struggle" (the word was frequently hers, as it was that of
Dreiser's generation: "the class struggle," "the struggle for
existence"). Her first mature work, *Three Lives*, was a triple
portrait of the servant, a type of oppressed individual with a
special appeal for the Naturalist novelist; in addition, her
trio, two Germans and a Negro girl, belonged to ethnic
minorities, another staple Naturalist subject. *Three Lives*
proved to be a study in the language, syntax, and rhythms
of consciousness rather than in the effects of oppression, social or cosmic. Here her aesthetic predilections checkmated
and partially transformed the Dreisserian elements. *Three
Lives* remains her most widely admired book.

The American writer who most attracted her was not
Dreiser or any of his school, but Henry James. And there may
have been personal as well as aesthetic reasons for her refusal
of Naturalist pessimism and protest. Gertrude Stein felt no
urgent identification with the oppressed; life was a struggle
that she could very probably win. Her grandparents had been

German-Jewish immigrants, but they had prospered in the United States; her parents, prospering too, had been beguiled by art, languages, and educational theory; as children, Gertrude Stein and her sister and brothers, like the young Jameses at an earlier period, had been transported to Europe for a prolonged stay in some of its great cities. Thus the impression left by the elder Steins, at least on Gertrude Stein, was that of people who, if they were not exactly free spirits, had to a degree done as they liked and made themselves at home equally in America and Europe. No doubt their example, as she conceived of it, fortified her own determination to do the same, do even better. Hence the impulse, so patiently and passionately followed by her, to root herself in a profession, in the city of Paris, in a society of her choosing. The consequences for her personality were, again, astonishing. In her maturity, she gave the impression, not merely of doing what she liked but of *being* almost anything she wanted to be. She seemed, as the many surviving likenesses of her suggest, at once female and male, Jew and non-Jew, American *pur sang* and European peasant, artist and public figure, and so on. She did not, however, create this intricate unity and sustain it without showing evidences of great strain. Her magnetic, almost magical, self-mastery was buttressed by frank self-indulgence and advertised to the world by a good deal of unashamed self-congratulation. A regular system of compensations characterized her life. Inclusions entailed exclusions in a virtually mechanical perfection of balance. For almost every idea she embraced, almost every person she befriended, there was some idea that remained pointedly alien to her, some person who was an outsider. Henry James had played something like this drama too, though with more compunction, it seems, and with himself often cast as the outsider. Gertrude Stein, never the outsider, seems not to have risen—or sunk—to the level of James's flexibility. Thus her combined residence, salon, and art gallery in the rue de Fleurus, where she presided with the aid of the devoted Miss Toklas, presented the aspects, now of an infinitely charming refuge, now of a bristling fortress. The former aspect predominated; the wariest visitor was apt to be struck by things about Gertrude Stein which were more literally magical than her self-mastery—things that were not to be fully accounted for by will, intelligence, or the principle of genius by association: her magnificent head and features, her appealing voice, her elementally refreshing laugh.

But Gertrude Stein's family background was not the only source, or even the principal one, of her prodigious and largely good-humored will to power. The same background failed to supply her brother Leo with any such determination to make himself at home in the world. Brilliant, erratic, eternally unfulfilled, Leo Stein became an early advocate and perennial patient of psychoanalysis, finding a sort of father-land only in Freud. In Gertrude Stein's case, obviously, it was her involvement in the profession of literature, and the exacting mysteries attending it, that made the difference. The profession was the more engrossing because of the variety of influences she brought to bear on it. If her conception of liter-ature included elements of Naturalism, it also anticipated the literary Modernism that was to culminate in the chief works of Joyce, Eliot, Yeats, and others. To her as to them (up to a point), literature in the twentieth century presented itself as a problem in the reconstruction of form and language. But where the solution of this problem was a means to an end for these writers, it became, for her, on the whole, a pursuit worthy in itself of her best efforts. She had no quarrel, as they did, with culture, with history, with the self. Culture in her terminology becomes "composition," an aggregate of institu-tions, technologies, and human relations which the artist, as artist, accepts as it is, eliciting its meanings primarily through eye and ear rather than through mind, memory, or imagina-tion. And words, like the other materials of the literary medium, become useful to the artist, assume a character purely aesthetic, in proportion as they can be converted from bearers of established meaning and unconscious association into plastic entities.

Such was the theoretical basis of her work, a basis to which she added many refinements as she sought to find literary equivalents for the various experiments conducted by the

Cubists. Her theories have been admirably expounded and criticized in a number of recent books. The usual conclusion is the common-sense one. Literature is a temporal art rather than, like painting, a spatial one; and in using words as plastic entities, as things in themselves, words become not more but less alive, indeed peculiarly inert. Mr. Kenneth Burke has called Gertrude Stein's practice "art by subtraction," a phrase that expresses well the literal and merely negative aspect of her work at its least effective. Mr. B L. Reid has made Burke's phrase the title of a hostile study of Gertrude Stein; and Mr. John Malcolm Brinnin, in *The Third Rose*, the best biography of her, sums up his investigations into her methods as follows:

> Language is plastic, but its plasticity must be informed and determined by the philosophy or, at least, by the information it conveys. In her earlier works, Gertrude Stein operated under this injunction naturally; but as she continued, her attraction to painting led her to wish for the same plastic freedom for literature, and eventually to write as though literature *were* endowed with such freedom. "The painter," said Georges Braque, "knows things by sight; the writer, who knows them by name, profits by a prejudice in his favor." This was the profit Gertrude Stein threw away.

All this applies to darkest Stein. Mr. Brinnin and many others, including the present writer, find this territory difficult of access. Nor, of course, is one helped by having learned one's way around in, say, *Finnegans Wake* and *Four Quartets*. On the contrary, a knowledge of Joyce's or Eliot's methods sets one to looking in Gertrude Stein for meanings and values according to the principle of association. But this is the wrong principle to apply to, for example, *Tender Buttons*. Gertrude Stein was insistent that she was not practicing "automatic writing" or working in any literary convention, such as Surrealism, related to automatic writing. No release of unconscious impulses, her own or those of fictional characters, is intended. She must, in fact, have devoted

much labor to eliminating such suggestions. Thus the body
of her theory and writing at its most advanced occupies an
anomalous position among the various modern schools.

The usual theoretical objections to her work are per-
suasive; yet between them and her work there is always a
certain accusing margin of doubt. Poets have found her work
exciting, however inexplicably so, as if words in themselves
might in certain circumstances appeal to some receptive
apparatus in man that is comparable to what people call
extrasensory perception. This is not, on the whole, the experience of the present writer in the farther reaches of Gertrude
Stein. Yet, read aloud, certain passages in, say, *Tender Buttons,* do make their effect, especially if read in the company
of people prepared to laugh. The silent reader expects
familiar rewards for his efforts. The *viva voce* reader is more
apt to take what comes and make the most of it. To the ear,
when it is lent freely to a given passage, the contrast stands
out between, on the one hand, the perpetual flow of *non
sequiturs* in the passage and, on the other, the air of conviction conveyed by the very definite words, the pregnant
pauses, the pat summary phrases ("This is this," "It is surely
cohesive," "It is not the same."); and the mingling of ap-
parent conviction with transparent nonsense throughout such
a passage takes on its own kind of momentary sense, giving
rise (if the reader is lucky) to a wondering laugh. As one of
her pat phrases suggests, "It shows shine." Does it also *show
Stein*? If so, reading these tongue-twisting words aloud helps
to bring the pun to light. So too with the occasional rhymes
and jingles strewn through this prose: they also come alive
better when spoken.

Tender Buttons is probably Gertrude Stein's most "private"
performance. The verbal still-lifes in that book defy even Mr.
Donald Sutherland, the critic who, in *Gertrude Stein: A
Biography of Her Work,* has made more headway than anyone else in interpreting her. Here is a passage, surely very
beautiful, from "Lend a Hand or Four Religions" (published
in *Useful Knowledge,* 1928), followed by Mr. Sutherland's
comment:

First religion   She is feeling that the grasses grow
four times yearly and does she furnish a house as
well. . . . Let her think of a stable man and a stable
can be a place where they care for the Italians every
day. And a mission of kneeling there where the water
is flowing kneeling, a chinese christian, and let her
think of a stable man and wandering and a repetition
of counting. Count to ten. He did. He did not. Count
to ten. And did she gather the food as well. Did she
gather the food as well. Did she separate the green
grasses from one another. They grow four times
yearly. Did she see some one as she was advancing
and did she remove what she had and did she lose
what she touched and did she touch it and the water
there where she was kneeling where it was flowing.
And are stables a place where they care for them as
well.

One might say that the essence of this passage is
the phrase "as well"—a sort of welcome to anything
that is there to come into the composition, such a
welcome being the genius of France and as often as
not of America. The coherence of the passage, which
consists in a sort of melodic progress of consideration,
is between the rational French discursiveness and the
rambling American sympathy as Whitman had it.
But more important is the kind of existence expressed
here. The existence of the woman in the passage is
intimately involved with the existence, growth, and
movement of things in the landscape. Her kneeling
and the water flowing and the grass growing four
times yearly and the caring for Italians are all part
of the same slow natural living of the place and the
world.

In serious literary circles, as distinguished from the large
public, Gertrude Stein's real accomplishments were always

known. There, her influence was at one time considerable, though it worked in very different ways and degrees on different individuals. It was known that her writing had influenced, in certain respects, Sherwood Anderson and, later, Hemingway. It was supposed that Steinese had found echoes in Don Marquis' *archy and mehitabel* as well as in the difficult poetry of Wallace Stevens, who once wrote "Twenty men crossing a bridge,/ Into a village,/ Are/ Twenty men crossing a bridge/ Into a village." Her insistence on the primacy of phenomena over ideas, of the sheer magnificence of unmediated reality, found a rapturous response in Stevens, a quiet one in Marianne Moore. In *Axel's Castle,* Edmund Wilson's discriminating study of modern literature published as early as 1931, she had a chapter to herself, as had, in each case, Yeats, Valéry, Eliot, Proust, and Joyce. *Axel's Castle* was a decisive event in the history of modern reputations. Wilson had some doubts as to Gertrude Stein's readableness in certain books but few doubts as to her general importance. Steinese and its inventor had become reputable.

By the time she died, in 1946, at the age of 72, Gertrude Stein had become something she wanted still more to be, historical (see "A Message from Gertrude Stein," which precedes). Beginning with *The Autobiography of Alice B. Toklas* (written in 1932) she had developed unsuspected capacities for writing intelligibly and charmingly. The universal surprise at this fact, combined with the intrinsic fascination of the book, made it a best seller. And dire though the *Autobiography* is with special pleading, it remains one of the best memoirs in American literature.

The improvement in her literary status disturbed for a while her firm sense of herself and her place in the world. "Money is funny," she said quizzically as the royalties poured in. But she soon embraced her new role and played it with good-humored dignity. Returning to America for the first time since 1903, she lectured to sizable audiences across the country. And following World War II she became a kind of oracle and motherly hostess to American military personnel in liberated Paris. Just before her death her sayings and doings over there were much in the news in America, and her later writings, cast in a much modified Steinese, were sought by the popular magazines. The present volume, edited by Mr. Carl Van Vechten, her friend for over thirty years, was in the press when she died and was published later in the same year. Its aim was to make examples of her more difficult writing available along with examples of that more popular writing, and thus to demonstrate, as far as possible, the unity of her life and work. She seems to have died at peace with herself, her natural craving for recognition to some extent satisfied. At least she died firmly in character, having delivered from her hospital bed the last specimen, and one of the most searching and comical specimens, of Steinese. "What is the answer?" she inquired, and getting no answer said, laughing, "In that case, what is the question?"

February, 1962   F. W. DUPEE

A STEIN SONG

Gertrude Stein rings bells, loves baskets, and wears handsome waistcoats. She has a tenderness for green glass and buttons have a tenderness for her. In the matter of fans you can only compare her with a motion-picture star in Hollywood and three generations of young writers have sat at her feet. She has influenced without coddling them. In her own time she is a legend and in her own country she is with honor. Keys to sacred doors have been presented to her and she understands how to open them. She writes books for children, plays for actors, and librettos for operas. Each one of them is one. For her a rose is a rose and how!

I composed this strictly factual account of Miss Stein and her activities for a catalogue of the Gotham Book Mart in 1940, but all that I said then seems to be truer than ever today. Gertrude Stein currently is not merely a legend, but also a whole folklore, a subject for an epic poem, and the young GIs who crowded into her Paris apartment on the rue Christine during and after the Greater War have augmented the number of her fans until their count is as hard to reckon as that of the grains of sand on the shore by the sea. During the war I frequently received letters from soldiers and sailors who, with only two days' furlough at their disposal and a long way to travel, sometimes by jeep, spent all of their free hours in Paris with the author of *Tender Buttons*. Other GIs bore her away on a flying tour of Germany and still others carried her by automobile to Belgium to speak to their comrades there. In Paris she gave public talks to groups of them too large to fit into her apartment. *Life* and the *New York Times Magazine* contracted for articles from her pen. Her play of existence in occupied France, *Yes Is for a Very Young Man*, was presently produced at the Community Playhouse in Pasadena, California. Some of these tributes, naturally, were due to her personality and charm, but most of them stem directly from the library shelves which hold her collected works. Furthermore, as she once categorically informed Alfred Harcourt, it is to her so-called "difficult" works that she owes her world-wide celebrity.

There is more direct testimony regarding her experiences with the GIs in her letters to me. On November 26, 1944, after the coming of the Americans, an event excitingly described in this Collection, she cabled me: "Joyous Days. Endless Love." In 1945, she wrote, "How we love the American army we never do stop loving the American army one single minute." If you will recall Alexandre Dumas's motto, *J'aime qui m'aime,* you will be certain they loved her too. Still later she wrote me: "Enclosed is a description of a talk I gave them which did excite them, they walked me home fifty strong after the lecture was over and in the narrow streets of the quarter they made all the automobiles take side streets, the police looked and followed a bit but gave it up." Captain Edmund Geisler, her escort on the Belgian excursion, said to me, "Wherever she spoke she was frank and even belligerent. She made the GIs awfully mad, but she also made them think and many ended in agreement with her."

II

In *Everybody's Autobiography,* Gertrude Stein confesses: "It always did bother me that the American public were more interested in me than in my work." Perhaps this statement may be affirmed justifiably of the anonymous masses, but it would be incorrect to apply it generally to the critics, novelists, and reviewers who frequently have considered her writings worth discussing seriously. It has occurred to me that a brief summary of the opinions of a few of these distinguished gentlemen might serve to reassure the reading world at large and Miss Stein herself on this controversial point.

André Maurois, for example, says of her: "In the universal confusion (the war years and after) she remains intelligent: she has kept her poetic sense and even her sense of humor." Of *Wars I Have Seen* he writes: "The originality of the ideas, the deliberate fantasy of the comparisons, the naïveté of the tone, combined with the profundity of the thought, the repetitions, the absence of punctuation, all that first irritates the reader finally convinces him so that more orthodox styles appear insipid to him. Gertrude Stein is believed to be a difficult writer. This is false. There is not a single phrase in this book that cannot be comprehended by a schoolgirl of sixteen years."

Here is Ben Ray Redman's testimony: "Few writers have ever dared to be, or have ever been able to be, as simple as she, as simple as a child, pointing straight, going straight to the heart of a subject, to its roots; pointing straight, when and where adults would take a fancier way than pointing because they have learned not to point. . . . In the past, perhaps wilfully, she has often failed to communicate, and it was either her misfortune or her fun, depending on her intention."

Or perhaps you would prefer Virgil Thomson's capsule definition: "To have become a Founding Father of her century is her own reward for having long ago, and completely, dominated her language."

An earlier, sympathetic, and highly descriptive view is that of Sherwood Anderson: "She is laying word against word, relating sound to sound, feeling for the taste, the smell, the rhythm of the individual word. She is attempting to do something for the writers of our English speech that may be better understood after a time, *and she is not in a hurry.* . . . There is a thing one might call 'the extension of the province of his art' one wants to achieve. One works with words and one would like words that have a taste on the lips, that have a perfume to the nostrils, rattling words one can throw into a box and shake, making a sharp jingling sound, words that, when seen on the printed page, have a distinct arresting effect upon the eye, words that when they jump out from under the pen one may feel with the fingers as one might caress the cheeks of his beloved. And what I think is that these books of Gertrude Stein do in a very real sense recreate life in words."

William Carlos Williams's opinion is correlated to the above: "Having taken the words to her choice, to emphasize further what she has in mind she has completely unlinked them (in her most recent work: 1930) from their former relationships to the sentence. This was absolutely essential and unescapable. Each under the new arrangement has a quality of its own, but not conjoined to carry the burden science, philosophy, and every higgledy-piggledy figment of law and order have been laying upon them in the past. They are like a crowd at Coney Island, let us say, seen from an airplane. . . . She has placed writing on a plane where it may deal unhampered with its own affairs, unburdened with scientific and philosophic lumber."

Edmund Wilson feels compelled to admit: "Whenever we pick up her writings, however unintelligible we may find them, we are aware of a literary personality of unmistakable originality and distinction."

Julian Sawyer contends: "If the name of anything or everything is dead, as Miss Stein has always rightly contested, the only thing to do to keep it alive is to rename it. And that is what Miss Stein did and does."

Pursuing these commentators, I fall upon Thornton Wilder who asserts: "There have been too many books that attempted to flatter or woo or persuade or coerce the reader. Miss Stein's theory of the audience insists on the fact that the richest rewards for the reader have come from those works in which the authors admitted no consideration of an audience into their creating mind."

And as a coda, allow me to permit Joseph Alsop, Jr., to speak: "Miss Stein is no out-pensioner upon Parnassus; no crank; no seeker after personal publicity; no fool. She is a remarkably shrewd woman, with an intelligence both sensitive and tough, and a single one of her books, *Three Lives*, is her sufficient ticket of admission to the small company of authors who have had something to say and have known how to say it."

III

If Picasso is applauded for painting pictures which do not represent anything he has hitherto seen, if Schoenberg can

pen a score that sounds entirely new even to ears accustomed
to listen to modern music, why should an employer of English
words be required to form sentences which are familiar in
meaning, shape, and sound to any casual reader? Miss Stein
herself implies somewhere that where there is communication
(or identification) there can be no question of creation. This
is solid ground, walked on realistically, as anyone who has
been exposed to performances of music by Reger, for example,
can readily testify. However, it must be borne in mind that
composers and painters are not always inspired to *absolute*
creation: Schoenberg wrote music for *Pelléas et Mélisande*
and the tuneful *Verklaerte Nacht,* while Picasso had his rose
and blue and classic periods which are representational. Like
the composer and painter Miss Stein has her easier moments
(*The Autobiography of Alice B. Toklas,* for instance, is
written in imitation of Miss Toklas's own manner) and even
in her more "difficult" pages there are variations, some of
which are in the nature of experiment. One of the earliest of
her inventions was her use of repetition which she describes
as "insistence." "Once started expressing this thing, expressing
anything there can be no repetition because the essence of
that expression is insistence, and if you insist you must each
time use emphasis and if you use emphasis it is not possible
while anybody is alive that they should use exactly the same
emphasis. . . . It is exactly like a frog hopping he cannot
ever hop exactly the same distance or the same way of hopping at every hop. A bird's singing is perhaps the nearest
thing to repetition but if you listen they too vary their insistence." Then she began to find new names for things, names
which were not nouns, if possible, and, renaming things, became so enchanted sometimes with her own talent and the
music of the words as they dropped that she became
enamored of the magic of the mere sounds, but quickly she
sensed this was an impasse and began more and more to
strive to express her exact meaning with pronouns, conjunc-
tions, and participial clauses. After a while she came back to
nouns, realizing that nouns, the names of things, make poetry,
"When I said, A rose is a rose is a rose, and then later made
that into a ring, I made poetry and what did I do I caressed

completely caressed and addressed a noun." She had another period of exciting discovery when she found that paragraphs are emotional and sentences are not. Finally, it came
to her that she could condense and concentrate her meaning
into one word at a time, "even if there were always one after
the other." "I found," she has told us, "that any kind of book
if you read with glasses and somebody is cutting your hair
and so you cannot keep the glasses on and you use your
glasses as a magnifying glass and so read word by word
reading word by word makes the writing that is not anything
be something. . . . So that shows to you that a whole thing
is not interesting because as a whole well as a whole there
has to be remembering and forgetting, but one at a time, oh
one at a time is something oh yes definitely something." But
do not get the idea that her essential appeal is to the ear or
the subconscious. "It is her eyes and mind that are important
and concerned in choosing." Perhaps the most concrete explanation of her work that she has ever given us is the
following (from *The Autobiography of Alice B. Toklas*):
"Gertrude Stein, in her work, has always been possessed by
the intellectual passion for exactitude in the description of
inner and outer reality. She has produced a simplification by
this concentration, and as a result the destruction of associational emotion in poetry and prose. She knows that beauty,
music, decoration, the result of emotion should never be the
cause, even events should not be the cause of emotion nor
should emotion itself be the cause of poetry or prose. They
should consist of an exact reproduction of either an outer or
inner reality." She says again, this time in *What Are Masterpieces*, "If you do not remember while you are writing, it may
seem confused to others but actually it is clear and eventually
that clarity will be clear that is what a masterpiece is, but
if you remember while you are writing it will seem clear at
the time to any one but the clarity will go out of it that is
what a masterpiece is not."

In whatever style it pleases Miss Stein to write, however,
it is her custom to deal almost exclusively with "actualities,"
portraits of people she *knows*, descriptions of places, objects,
and events which surround her and with which she is im-

mediately concerned. This quality, true of almost all of her
writing since *Three Lives* and *The Making of Americans,*
her perpetual good humor, and her sense of fun, which leads
her occasionally into intentional obscurantism, all assist in
keeping part of her prospective audience at a little distance
behind her. There is, for instance, in *Four Saints* at the close
of the celebrated *Pigeons on the Grass* air (an air the meaning
of which has been elucidated both by Miss Stein and Julian
Sawyer) a passage which runs *Lucy Lily Lily Lucy,* etc.,
beautifully effective as sung to the music in Virgil Thomson's
score. Those who believe this to be meaningless embroidery,
like *Hey, nonny nonny* in an Elizabethan ballad, are perfectly sane. Miss Stein enjoyed the sound of the words, *but*
the words did not come to her out of thin air, as is evidenced
by a discovery I made recently. Lucy Lily Lamont is a girl
who lives on page 35 of *Wars I Have Seen* and from the
context one might gather that Miss Stein knew her a long
time ago. Another example of this bewildering kind of refer-
ence is the "October 15" paragraph in *As a Wife Has a Cow*
in the current collection. In my note to that idyl I have
referred the reader to the probable origin of this passage.
The books of this artist are indeed full of these sly references to matters unknown to their readers and only someone
completely familiar with the routine, and roundabout, ways
of Miss Stein's daily life would be able to explain every line
of her prose, but without even mentioning Joyce's *Ulysses* or
Eliot's *The Waste Land,* could not the same thing be said
truthfully of Shakespeare's Sonnets?

No wonder Miss Stein exclaims pleasurably somewhere or
other: "Also there is why is it that in this epoch the only
real literary thinking has been done by a woman."

IV

The material I have selected for this Collection contains at
least a sample of practically every period and every manner
in Gertrude Stein's career from the earliest to the latest. Her
five earliest works (with the exception of *Cultivated Motor
Automatism,* which she wrote as a student) are included, all

but one complete, and it is significant that none of them resembles its neighbor in style. *Melanctha,* in manner, differs from *The Making of Americans* and the same may be said of *Tender Buttons,* the *Portrait of Mable Dodge at the Villa Curonia,* and the portraits of Matisse and Picasso published in *Camera Work* in 1912. Definite dates do not mark her various modes into periods as they do those of Picasso. Her very latest books, *Wars I Have Seen* and *Brewsie and Willie,* are not written in perplexing prose. I have, I think, included a sample of most of the forms in which she has worked. Not only the famous *Four Saints,* but also two other plays from an earlier period are to be discovered herein. Examples of her poetry, of her lectures, and essays may be examined in these pages. Lack of space has prevented me from including either of her novels, *Ida* or *Lucy Church Amiably. Miss Furr and Miss Skeene* and *Melanctha,* however, give sufficient indication of her talent for fiction. Of her two books for children, *The World Is Round* and the unpublished (except in French translation) *First Reader,* nothing is offered either. On the other hand, every element of her so-called "difficult" manner is represented together with two essays attempting to explain this manner and, of course, *The Autobiography of Alice B. Toklas* explains pretty nearly everything to everybody. Dear Gertrude, may I do a little caressing myself and say truthfully A Collection is a Collection is a Collection?

Carl Van Vechten

New York, April 11, 1946

My introduction to this volume was written, and sent to the printer, a little over three months before Gertrude Stein's death in Paris, July 27, 1946, but I feel that it is wiser, for both sentimental and practical reasons, to let it stand unchanged.

C. V. V.

THE AUTOBIOGRAPHY OF
ALICE B. TOKLAS

Written in 1932, published by Harcourt Brace and Co., in 1933. An abridged version had appeared previously in the ATLANTIC MONTHLY. In EVERYBODY'S AUTOBIOGRAPHY Gertrude Stein wrote: "Well anyway it was a beautiful autumn in Bilignin and in six weeks I wrote THE AUTOBIOGRAPHY OF ALICE B. TOKLAS and it was published and it became a best seller. . . . I bought myself a new eight-cylinder Ford car and the most expensive coat made to order by Hermes and fitted by the man who makes horse covers for race horses for Basket the white poodle and two collars studded for Basket. I had never made any money before in my life and I was most excited."

BEFORE I CAME TO PARIS

I was born in San Francisco, California. I have in consequence always preferred living in a temperate climate but it is difficult, on the continent of Europe or even in America, to find a temperate climate and live in it. My mother's father was a pioneer, he came to California in '49, he married my grandmother who was very fond of music. She was a pupil of Clara Schumann's father. My mother was a quiet charming woman named Emilie.

My father came of polish patriotic stock. His grand-uncle raised a regiment for Napoleon and was its colonel. His father left his mother just after their marriage, to fight at the barricades in Paris, but his wife having cut off his supplies, he soon returned and led the life of a conservative well to do land owner.

I myself have had no liking for violence and have always enjoyed the pleasures of needlework and gardening. I am fond of paintings, furniture, tapestry, houses and flowers and even vegetables and fruit-trees. I like a view but I like to sit with my back turned to it.

I led in my childhood and youth the gently bred existence of my class and kind. I had some intellectual adventures at this period but very quiet ones. When I was about nineteen years of age I was a great admirer of Henry James. I felt that The Awkward Age would make a very remarkable play and I wrote to Henry James suggesting that I dramatise it. I had from him a delightful letter on the subject and then, when I felt my inadequacy, rather blushed for myself and did not keep the letter. Perhaps at that time I did not feel that I was justified in preserving it, at any rate it no longer exists.

Up to my twentieth year I was seriously interested in music. I studied and practised assiduously but shortly then it seemed futile, my mother had died and there was no unconquerable sadness, but there was no real interest that led me on. In the story Ada in Geography and Plays Gertrude Stein has given a very good description of me as I was at that time.

From then on for about six years I was well occupied. I led a pleasant life, I had many friends, much amusement many interests, my life was reasonably full and I enjoyed it but I was not very ardent in it. This brings me to the San Francisco fire which had as a consequence that the elder brother of Gertrude Stein and his wife came back from Paris to San Francisco and this led to a complete change in my life.

I was at this time living with my father and brother. My father was a quiet man who took things quietly, although he felt them deeply. The first terrible morning of the San Francisco fire I woke him and told him, the city has been rocked by an earthquake and is now on fire. That will give us a black eye in the East, he replied turning and going to sleep again. I remember that once when my brother and a comrade had gone horse-back riding, one of the horses returned riderless to the hotel, the mother of the other boy began to make a terrible scene. Be calm madam, said my father, perhaps it is my son who has been killed. One of his axioms I always remember, if you must do a thing do it graciously. He also told me that a hostess should never apologise for any failure in her household arrangements, if there is a hostess there is insofar as there is a hostess no failure.

As I was saying we were all living comfortably together and there had been in my mind no active desire or thought of change. The disturbance of the routine of our lives by the fire followed by the coming of Gertrude Stein's older brother and his wife made the difference.

Mrs. Stein brought with her three little Matisse paintings, the first modern things to cross the Atlantic. I made her acquaintance at this time of general upset and she showed them to me, she also told me many stories of her life in Paris.

Gradually I told my father that perhaps I would leave San Francisco. He was not disturbed by this, after all there was at that time a great deal of going and coming and there were many friends of mine going. Within a year I also had gone and I had come to Paris. There I went to see Mrs. Stein who had in the meantime returned to Paris, and there at her house I met Gertrude Stein. I was impressed by the coral brooch she wore and by her voice. I may say that only three times in my life have I met a genius and each time a bell within me rang and I was not mistaken, and I may say in each case it was before there was any general recognition of the quality of genius in them. The three geniuses of whom I wish to speak are Gertrude Stein, Pablo Picasso and Alfred Whitehead. I have met many important people, I have met several great people but I have only known three first class geniuses and in each case on sight within me something rang. In no one of the three cases have I been mistaken. In this way my new full life began.

2

MY ARRIVAL IN PARIS

This was the year 1907. Gertrude Stein was just seeing through the press Three Lives which she was having privately printed, and she was deep in The Making of Americans, her thousand page book. Picasso had just finished his portrait of her which nobody at that time liked except the painter and the painted and which is now so famous, and he had just begun his strange complicated picture of three women, Matisse had just finished his Bonheur de Vivre, his first big composition which gave him the name of fauve or a zoo. It was the moment Max Jacob has since called the heroic age of cubism. I remember not long ago hearing Picasso and Gertrude Stein talking about various things that had happened at that time, one of them said but all that could not have happened in that one year, oh said the other, my dear you forget we were young then and we did a great deal in a year.

There are a great many things to tell of what was happening then and what had happened before, which led up to then, but now I must describe what I saw when I came.

The home at 27 rue de Fleurus consisted then as it does now of a tiny pavillon of two stories with four small rooms, a kitchen and bath, and a very large atelier adjoining. Now the atelier is attached to the pavillon by a tiny hall passage added in 1914 but at that time the atelier had its own entrance, one rang the bell of the pavillon or knocked at the door of the atelier, and a great many people did both, but more knocked at the atelier. I was privileged to do both. I had been invited to dine on Saturday evening which was the evening when everybody came, and indeed everybody did come. I went to dinner. The dinner was cooked by Hélène. I must tell a little about Hélène.

Hélène had already been two years with Gertrude Stein and her brother. She was one of those admirable bonnes in other words excellent maids of all work, good cooks thoroughly occupied with the welfare of their employers and of themselves, firmly convinced that everything purchasable was far too dear. Oh but it is dear, was her answer to any question. She wasted nothing and carried on the household at the regular rate of eight francs a day. She even wanted to include guests at that price, it was her pride, but of course that was difficult since she for the honour of her house as well as to satisfy her employers always had to give every one enough to eat. She was a most excellent cook and she made a very good soufflé. In those days most of the guests were living more or less precariously, no one starved, some one always helped but still most of them did not live in abundance. It was Braque who said about four years later when they were all beginning to be known, with a sigh and a smile, how life has changed we all now have cooks who can make a soufflé.

Hélène had her opinions, she did not for instance like Matisse. She said a frenchman should not stay unexpectedly to a meal particularly if he asked the servant beforehand what there was for dinner. She said foreigners had a perfect right to do these things but not a frenchman and Matisse had once done it. So when Miss Stein said to her, Monsieur Matisse is staying for dinner this evening, she would say, in that case I will not make an omelette but fry the eggs. It takes the same number of eggs and the same amount of butter but it shows less respect, and he will understand.

Hélène stayed with the household until the end of 1913. Then her husband, by that time she had married and had a little boy, insisted that she work for others no longer. To her great regret she left and later she always said that life at home was never as amusing as it had been at the rue de Fleurus. Much later, only about three years ago, she came back for a year, she and her husband had fallen on bad times and her boy had died. She was as cheery as ever and enormously interested. She said isn't it extraordinary, all those people whom I knew when they were nobody are now always mentioned in the newspapers, and the other night over the radio they mentioned the name of Monsieur Picasso. Why they even speak in the newspapers of Monsieur Braque, who used to hold up the big pictures to hang because he was the strongest, while the janitor drove the nails, and they are putting into the Louvre, just imagine it, into the Louvre, a picture by that little poor Monsieur Rousseau, who was so timid he did not even have courage enough to knock at the door. She was terribly interested in seeing Monsieur Picasso and his wife and child and cooked her very best dinner for him, but how he has changed, she said, well, said she, I suppose that is natural but then he has a lovely son. We thought that really Hélène had come back to give the young generation the once over. She had in a way but she was not interested in them. She said they made no impression on her which made them all very sad because the legend of her was well known to all Paris. After a year things were going better again, her husband was earning more money, and she once more remains at home. But to come back to 1907.

Before I tell about the guests I must tell what I saw. As I said being invited to dinner I rang the bell of the little pavillon and was taken into the tiny hall and then into the small dining room lined with books. On the only free space, the doors, were tacked up a few drawings by Picasso and Matisse. As the other guests had not yet come Miss Stein took me into the atelier. It often rained in Paris and it was always difficult to go from the little pavillon to the atelier door in the rain in evening clothes, but you were not to mind such things as the hosts and most of the guests did not. We went into the atelier which opened with a yale key the only yale key in the quarter at that time, and this was not so much for safety, because in those days the pictures had no value, but because the key was small and could go into a purse instead of being enormous as french keys were. Against the walls were several pieces of large italian renaissance furniture and in the middle of the room was a big renaissance table, on it a lovely inkstand, and at one end of it note-books neatly arranged, the kind of note-books french children use, with pictures of earthquakes and explorations on the outside of them. And on all the walls right up to the ceiling were pictures. At one end of the room was a big cast iron stove that Hélène came in and filled with a rattle, and in one corner of the room was a large table on which were horseshoe nails and pebbles and little pipe cigarette holders which one looked at curiously but did not touch, but which turned out later to be accumulations from the pockets of Picasso and Gertrude Stein. But to return to the pictures. The pictures were so strange that one quite instinctively looked at anything rather than at them just at first. I have refreshed my memory by looking at some snap shots taken inside the atelier at that time. The chairs in the room were also all italian renaissance, not very comfortable for short-legged people and one got the habit of sitting on one's legs. Miss Stein sat near the stove in a lovely high-backed one and she peacefully let her legs hang, which was a matter of habit, and when any one of the many visitors came to ask her a question she lifted herself up out of this chair and usually replied in french, not just now. This usually referred to some-thing they wished to see, drawings which were put away, some german had once spilled ink on one, or some other not to be fulfilled desire. But to return to the pictures. As I say they completely covered the white-washed walls right up to the top of the very high ceiling. The room was lit at this time by high gas fixtures. This was the second stage. They had just been put in. Before that there had only been lamps, and a stalwart guest held up the lamp while the others looked. But gas had just been put in and an ingenious american painter named Sayen, to divert his mind from the birth of his first child, was arranging some mechanical contrivance that would light the high fixtures by themselves. The old land-lady extremely conservative did not allow electricity in her houses and electricity was not put in until 1914, the old land-lady by that time too old to know the difference, her house agent gave permission. But this time I am really going to tell about the pictures.

It is very difficult now that everybody is accustomed to

everything to give some idea of the kind of uneasiness one felt when one first looked at all these pictures on these walls. In those days there were pictures of all kinds there, the time had not yet come when there were only Cézannes, Renoirs, Matisses and Picassos, nor as it was even later only Cézannes and Picassos. At that time there was a great deal of Matisse, Picasso, Renoir, Cézanne but there were also a great many other things. There were two Gauguins, there were Manguins, there was a big nude by Valloton that felt like only it was not like the Odalisque of Manet, there was a Toulouse-Lautrec. Once about this time Picasso looking at this and greatly daring said, but all the same I do paint better than he did. Toulouse-Lautrec had been the most important of his early influences. I later bought a little tiny picture by Picasso of that epoch. There was a portrait of Gertrude Stein by Valloton that might have been a David but was not, there was a Maurice Denis, a little Daumier, many Cézanne water colours, there was in short everything, there was even a little Delacroix and a moderate sized Greco. There were enormous Picassos of the Harlequin period, there were two rows of Matisses, there was a big portrait of a woman by Cézanne and some little Cézannes, all these pictures had a history and I will soon tell them. Now I was confused and I looked and I looked and I was confused. Gertrude Stein and her brother were so accustomed to this state of mind in a guest that they paid no attention to it. Then there was a sharp tap at the atelier door. Gertrude Stein opened it and a little dark dapper man came in with hair, eyes, face, hands and feet all very much alive. Hullo Alfy, she said, this is Miss Toklas. How do you do Miss Toklas, he said very solemnly. This was Alfy Maurer an old habitué of the house. He had been there before there were these pictures, when there were only japanese prints, and he was among those who used to light matches to light up a little piece of the Cézanne portrait. Of course you can tell it is a finished picture, he used to explain to the other american painters who came and looked dubiously, you can tell because it has a frame, now whoever heard of anybody framing a canvas if the picture isn't finished. He had followed, followed, followed always humbly always sincerely. it was he who selected the first lot of pictures for the famous Barnes collection some years later faithfully and enthusiastically. It was he who when later Barnes came to the house and waved his cheque-book said, so help me God, I didn't bring him. Gertrude Stein who has an explosive temper, came in another evening and there were her brother, Alfy and a stranger. She did not like the stranger's looks. Who is that, said she to Alfy. I didn't bring him, said Alfy. He looks like a Jew, said Gertrude Stein, he is worse than that, says Alfy. But to return to that first evening. A few minutes after Alfy came in there was a violent knock at the door and, dinner is ready, from Hélène. It's funny the Picassos have not come, said they all, however we won't wait at least Hélène won't wait. So we went into the court and into the pavillon and dining room and began dinner. It's funny, said Miss Stein, Pablo is always promptness itself, he is never early and he is never late, it is his pride that punctuality is the politeness of kings, he even makes Fernande punctual. Of course he often says yes when he has no intention of doing what he says yes to, he can't say no, no is not in his vocabulary and you have to know whether his yes means yes or means no, but when he says a yes that means yes and he did about tonight he is always punctual. These were the days before automobiles and nobody worried about accidents. We had just finished the first course when there was a quick patter of footsteps in the court and Hélène opened the door before the bell rang. Pablo and Fernande as everybody called them at that time walked in. He, small, quick moving but not restless, his eyes having a strange faculty of opening wide and drinking in what he wished to see. He had the isolation and movement of the head of a bull-fighter at the head of their procession. Fernande was a tall beautiful woman with a wonderful big hat and a very evidently new dress, they were both very fussed. I am very upset, said Pablo, but you know very well Gertrude I am never late but Fernande had ordered a dress for the vernissage tomorrow and it didn't come. Well here you are anyway, said Miss Stein, since it's you Hélène won't mind. And we all sat down. I was next to Picasso who was silent and then gradually became peaceful. Alfy paid compliments

to Fernande and she was soon calm and placid. After a little
while I murmured to Picasso that I liked his portrait of Gertrude Stein. Yes, he said, everybody says that she does not
look like it but that does not make any difference, she will,
he said. The conversation soon became lively it was all about
the opening day of the salon indépendant which was the
great event of the year. Everybody was interested in all the
scandals that would or would not break out. Picasso never
exhibited but as his followers did and there were a great many
stories connected with each follower the hopes and fears
were vivacious.

While we were having coffee footsteps were heard in the
court quite a number of footsteps and Miss Stein rose and
said, don't hurry, I have to let them in. And she left.

When we went into the atelier there were already quite a
number of people in the room, scattered groups, single and
couples all looking and looking. Gertrude Stein sat by the
stove talking and listening and getting up to open the door
and go up to various people talking and listening. She usually
opened the door to the knock and the usual formula was,
de la part de qui venez-vous, who is your introducer. The
idea was that anybody could come but for form's sake and
in Paris you have to have a formula, everybody was supposed
to be able to mention the name of somebody who had told
them about it. It was a mere form, really everybody could
come in and as at that time these pictures had no value and
there was no social privilege attached to knowing any one
there, only those came who really were interested. So as I say
anybody could come in, however, there was the formula. Miss
Stein once in opening the door said as she usually did by
whose invitation do you come and we heard an aggrieved
voice reply, but by yours, madame. He was a young man
Gertrude Stein had met somewhere and with whom she had
had a long conversation and to whom she had given a cordial
invitation and then had as promptly forgotten.

The room was soon very very full and who were they all.
Groups of hungarian painters and writers, it happened that
some hungarian had once been brought and the word had
spread from him throughout all Hungary, any village where

there was a young man who had ambitions heard of 27 rue
de Fleurus and then he lived but to get there and a great
many did get there. They were always there, all sizes and
shapes, all degrees of wealth and poverty, some very charming, some simply rough and every now and then a very
beautiful young peasant. Then there were quantities of germans, not too popular because they tended always to want
to see anything that was put away and they tended to break
things and Gertrude Stein has a weakness for breakable objects, she has a horror of people who collect only the unbreak-
able. Then there was a fair sprinkling of americans, Mildred
Aldrich would bring a group or Sayen, the electrician, or
some painter and occasionally an architectural student would
accidentally get there and then there were the habitués,
among them Miss Mars and Miss Squires whom Gertrude
Stein afterwards immortalised in her story of Miss Furr and
Miss Skeene. On that first night Miss Mars and I talked of
a subject then entirely new, how to make up your face. She
was interested in types, she knew that there were femme
décorative, femme d'intérieur and femme intrigante; there
was no doubt that Fernande Picasso was a femme décorative,
but what was Madame Matisse, femme d'intérieur, I said,
and she was very pleased. From time to time one heard the
high spanish whinnying laugh of Picasso and gay contralto
outbreak of Gertrude Stein, people came and went, in and
out. Miss Stein told me to sit with Fernande. Fernande was
always beautiful but heavy in hand. I sat, it was my first
sitting with a wife of a genius.

Before I decided to write this book my twenty-five years
with Gertrude Stein, I had often said that I would write,
The wives of geniuses I have sat with. I have sat with so
many. I have sat with wives who were not wives, of geniuses
who were real geniuses. I have sat with real wives of geniuses
who were not real geniuses. I have sat with wives of geniuses,
of near geniuses, of would be geniuses, in short I have sat
very often and very long with many wives and wives of many
geniuses.

As I was saying Fernande, who was then living with Picasso
and had been with him a long time that is to say they were

all twenty-four years old at that time but they had been together a long time, Fernande was the first wife of a genius I
sat with and she was not the least amusing. We talked hats.
Fernande had two subjects hats and perfumes. This first day
we talked hats. She liked hats, she had the true french feeling about a hat, if a hat did not provoke some witticism
from a man on the street the hat was not a success. Later on
once in Montmartre she and I were walking together. She
had on a large yellow hat and I had on a much smaller blue
one. As we were walking along a workman stopped and called
out, there go the sun and the moon shining together. Ah, said
Fernande to me with a radiant smile, you see our hats are a
success.

Miss Stein called me and said she wanted to have me meet
Matisse. She was talking to a medium sized man with a
reddish beard and glasses. He had a very alert although
slightly heavy presence and Miss Stein and he seemed to be
full of hidden meanings. As I came up I heard her say, Oh
yes but it would be more difficult now. We were talking, she
said, of a lunch party we had in here last year. We had just
hung all the pictures and we asked all the painters. You know
how painters are, I wanted to make them happy so I placed
each one opposite his own picture, and they were happy so
happy that we had to send out twice for more bread, when
you know France you will know that that means that they
were happy, because they cannot eat and drink without bread
and we had to send out twice for bread so they were happy.
Nobody noticed my little arrangement except Matisse and
he did not until just as he left, and now he says it is a proof
that I am very wicked, Matisse laughed and said, yes I
know Mademoiselle Gertrude, the world is a theatre for you,
but there are theatres and theatres, and when you listen so
carefully to me and so attentively and do not hear a word I
say then I do say that you are very wicked. Then they both
began talking about the vernissage of the independent as
every one else was doing and of course I did not know what
it was all about. But gradually I knew and later on I will
tell the story of the pictures, their painters and their followers
and what this conversation meant.

Later I was near Picasso, he was standing meditatively. Do you think, he said, that I really do look like your president Lincoln. I had thought a good many things that evening but I had not thought that. You see, he went on, Gertrude, (I wish I could convey something of the simple affection and confidence with which he always pronounced her name and with which she always said, Pablo. In their long friendship with all its sometimes troubled moments and its complications this has never changed.) Gertrude showed me a photograph of him and I have been trying to arrange my hair to look like his, I think my forehead does. I did not know whether he meant it or not but I was sympathetic. I did not realise then how completely and entirely american was Gertrude Stein. Later I often teased her, calling her a general, a civil war general of either or both sides. She had a series of photographs of the civil war, rather wonderful photographs and she and Picasso used to pore over them. Then he would suddenly remember the spanish war and he became very spanish and very bitter and Spain and America in their persons could say very bitter things about each other's country. But at this my first evening I knew nothing of all this and so I was polite and that was all.

And now the evening was drawing to a close. Everybody was leaving and everybody was still talking about the vernissage of the independent. I too left carrying with me a card of invitation for the vernissage. And so this, one of the most important evenings of my life, came to an end.

I went to the vernissage taking with me a friend, the invitation I had been given admitting two. We went very early. I had been told to go early otherwise we would not be able to see anything, and there would be no place to sit, and my friend liked to sit. We went to the building just put up for this salon. In France they always put things up just for the day or for a few days and then take them down again. Gertrude Stein's elder brother always says that the secret of the chronic employment or lack of unemployment in France is due to the number of men actively engaged in putting up and taking down temporary buildings. Human nature is so permanent in France that they can afford to be as temporary

as they like with their buildings. We went to the long low
certainly very very long temporary building that was put up
every year for the independents. When after the war or just
before, I forget, the independent was given permanent
quarters in the big exposition building, the Grand Palais,
it became much less interesting. After all it is the adventure
that counts. The long building was beautifully alight with
Paris light.

In earlier, still earlier days, in the days of Seurat, the independent had its exhibition in a building where the rain
rained in. Indeed it was because of this, that in hanging
pictures in the rain, poor Seurat caught his fatal cold. Now
there was no rain coming in, it was a lovely day and we felt
very festive. When we got in we were indeed early as nearly
as possible the first to be there. We went from one room to
another and quite frankly we had no idea which of the pictures the Saturday evening crowd would have thought art
and which were just the attempts of what in France are
known as the Sunday painters, workingmen, hair-dressers and
veterinaries and visionaries who only paint once a week when
they do not have to work. I say we did not know but yes
perhaps we did know. But not about the Rousseau, and there
was an enormous Rousseau there which was the scandal of
the show, it was a picture of the officials of the republic,
Picasso now owns it, no that picture we could not know as
going to be one of the great pictures, and that as Hélène
was to say, would come to be in the Louvre. There was also
there if my memory is correct a strange picture by the same
douanier Rousseau, a sort of apotheosis of Guillaume Apollinaire with an aged Marie Laurencin behind him as a muse.
That also I would not have recognized as a serious work of
art. At that time of course I knew nothing about Marie
Laurencin and Guillaume Apollinaire but there is a lot to tell
about them later. Then we went on and saw a Matisse. Ah
there we were beginning to feel at home. We knew a Matisse
when we saw it, knew at once and enjoyed it and knew that
it was great art and beautiful. It was a big figure of a woman
lying in among some cactuses. A picture which was after the
show to be at the rue de Fleurus. There one day the five

sweetly, Gertrude has told me of your desire, it would give me great pleasure to give you lessons, you and your friend, I will be the next few days very busy installing myself in my new apartment. Gertrude is coming to see me the end of the week, if you and your friend would accompany her we could then make all arrangements. Fernande spoke a very elegant french, some lapses of course into montmartrois that I found difficult to follow, but she had been educated to be a schoolmistress, her voice was lovely and she was very very beautiful with a marvellous complexion. She was a big woman but not too big because she was indolent and she had the small round arms that give the characteristic beauty to all french women. It was rather a pity that short skirts ever came in because until then one never imagined the sturdy french legs of the average french woman, one thought only of the beauty of the small rounded arms. I agreed to Fernande's proposal and left her.

On my way back to where my friend was sitting I became more accustomed not so much to the pictures as to the people. I began to realise there was a certain uniformity of type. Many years after, that is just a few years ago, when Juan Gris whom we all loved very much died, (he was after Pablo Picasso Gertrude Stein's dearest friend) I heard her say to Braque, she and he were standing together at the funeral, who are all these people, there are so many and they are so familiar and I do not know who any of them are. Oh, Braque replied, they are all the people you used to see at the vernissage of the independent and the autumn salon and you saw their faces twice a year, year after year, and that is the reason they are all so familiar.

Gertrude Stein and I about ten days later went to Montmartre, I for the first time. I have never ceased to love it. We go there every now and then and I always have the same tender expectant feeling that I had then. It is a place where you were always standing and sometimes waiting, not for anything to happen, but just standing. The inhabitants of Montmartre did not sit much, they mostly stood which was just as well as the chairs, the dining room chairs of France, did not tempt one to sit. So I went to Montmartre and I

began my apprenticeship of standing. We first went to see
Picasso and then we went to see Fernande. Picasso now
never likes to go to Montmartre, he does not like to think
about it much less talk about it. Even to Gertrude Stein he
is hesitant about talking of it, there were things that at that
time cut deeply into his spanish pride and the end of his
Montmartre life was bitterness and disillusion, and there is
nothing more bitter than spanish disillusion.

But at this time he was in and of Montmartre and lived
in the rue Ravignan.

We went to the Odéon and there got into an omnibus, that
is we mounted on top of an omnibus, the nice old horse-
pulled omnibuses that went pretty quickly and steadily across
Paris and up the hill to the place Blanche. There we got out
and climbed a steep street lined with shops with things to
eat, the rue Lepic, and then turning we went around a corner
and climbed even more steeply in fact almost straight up and
came to the rue Ravignan, now place Emile-Goudeau but
otherwise unchanged, with its steps leading up to the little
flat square with its few but tender little trees, a man carpentering in the corner of it, the last time I was there not very
long ago there was still a man carpentering in a corner of
it, and a little café just before you went up the steps where
they all used to eat, it is still there, and to the left the low
wooden building of studios that is still there.

We went up the couple of steps and through the open door
passing on our left the studio in which later Juan Gris was
to live out his martyrdom but where then lived a certain
Vaillant, a nondescript painter who was to lend his studio
as a ladies dressing room at the famous banquet for Rousseau, and then we passed a steep flight of steps leading down
where Max Jacob had a studio a little later, and we passed
another steep little stairway which led to the studio where
not long before a young fellow had committed suicide,
Picasso painted one of the most wonderful of his early pictures of the friends gathered round the coffin, we passed all
this to a larger door where Gertrude Stein knocked and
Picasso opened the door and we went in.

He was dressed in what the french call the singe or monkey

costume, overalls made of blue jean or brown, I think his was blue and it is called a singe or monkey because being all of one piece with a belt, if the belt is not fastened, and it very often is not, it hangs down behind and so makes a monkey. His eyes were more wonderful than even I remembered, so full and so brown, and his hands so dark and delicate and alert. We went further in. There was a couch in one corner, a very small stove that did for cooking and heating in the other corner, some chairs, the large broken one Gertrude Stein sat in when she was painted and a general smell of dog and paint and there was a big dog there and Picasso moved her about from one place to another exactly as if the dog had been a large piece of furniture. He asked us to sit down but as all the chairs were full we all stood up and stood until we left. It was my first experience of standing but afterwards I found that they all stood that way for hours. Against the wall was an enormous picture, a strange picture of light and dark colours, that is all I can say, of a group, an enormous group and next to it another in a sort of a red brown, of three women, square and posturing, all of it rather frightening. Picasso and Gertrude Stein stood together talking. I stood back and looked. I cannot say I realised anything but I felt that there was something painful and beautiful there and oppressive but imprisoned. I heard Gertrude Stein say, and mine. Picasso thereupon brought out a smaller picture, a rather unfinished thing that could not finish, very pale almost white, two figures, they were all there but very unfinished and not finishable. Picasso said, but he will never accept it. Yes, I know, answered Gertrude Stein. But just the same it is the only one in which it is all there. Yes, I know, he replied and they fell silent. After that they continued a low toned conversation and then Miss Stein said, well we have to go, we are going to have tea with Fernande. Yes, I know, replied Picasso. How often do you see her, she said, he got very red and looked sheepish. I have never been there, he said resentfully. She chuckled, well anyway we are going there, she said, and Miss Toklas is going to have lessons in french. Ah the Miss Toklas, he said, with small feet like a spanish woman and earrings like a gypsy and a father who is king of Poland like the Poniatowskis, of course she will take lessons. We all laughed and went to the door. There stood a very beautiful man, oh Agero, said Picasso, you know the ladies. He looks like a Greco, I said in english. Picasso caught the name, a false Greco, he said. Oh I forgot to give you these, said Gertrude Stein handing Picasso a package of newspapers, they will console you. He opened them up, they were the Sunday supplement of american papers, they were the Katzenjammer kids. Oh oui, Oh oui, he said, his face full of satisfaction, merci thanks Getrude, and we left.

We left then and continued to climb higher up the hill. What did you think of what you saw, asked Miss Stein. Well I did see something. Sure you did, she said, but did you see what it had to do with those two pictures you sat in front of so long at the vernissage. Only that Picassos were rather awful and the others were not. Sure, she said, as Pablo once remarked, when you make a thing, it is so complicated making it that it is bound to be ugly, but those that do it after you they don't have to worry about making it and they can make it pretty, and so everybody can like it when the others make it.

We went on and turned down a little street and there was another little house and we asked for Mademoiselle Belle-vallée and we were sent into a little corridor and we knocked and went into a moderate sized room in which was a very large bed and a piano and a little tea table and Fernande and two others.

One of them was Alice Princet. She was rather a madonna like creature, with large lovely eyes and charming hair. Fernande afterwards explained that she was the daughter of a workingman and had the brutal thumbs that of course were a characteristic of workingmen. She had been, so Fernande explained, for seven years with Princet who was in the government employ and she had been faithful to him in the fashion of Montmartre, that is to say she had stuck to him through sickness and health but she had amused herself by the way. Now they were to be married. Princet had become the head of his small department in the government service and it would be necessary for him to invite other heads of departments to his house and so of course he must regularise the relation. They were actually married a few months afterward and it was apropos of this marriage that Max Jacob made his famous remark, it is wonderful to long for a woman for seven years and to possess her at last. Picasso made the more practical one, why should they marry simply in order to divorce. This was a prophecy.

No sooner were they married than Alice Princet met Derain and Derain met her. It was what the french call un coup de foudre, or love at first sight. They went quite mad about each other. Princet tried to bear it but they were married now and it was different. Beside he was angry for the first time in his life and in his anger he tore up Alice's first fur coat which she had gotten for the wedding. That settled the matter, and within six months after the marriage Alice left Princet never to return. She and Derain went off together and they have never separated since. I always liked Alice Derain. She had a certain wild quality that perhaps had to do with her brutal thumbs and was curiously in accord with her madonna face.

The other woman was Germaine Pichot, entirely a different type. She was quiet and serious and spanish, she had the square shoulders and the unseeing fixed eyes of a spanish woman. She was very gentle. She was married to a spanish painter Pichot, who was rather a wonderful creature, he was long and thin like one of those primitive Christs in spanish churches and when he did a spanish dance which he did later at the famous banquet to Rousseau, he was awe inspiringly religious.

Germaine, so Fernande said, was the heroine of many a strange story, she had once taken a young man to the hospital, he had been injured in a fracas at a music hall and all his crowd had deserted him. Germaine quite naturally stood by and saw him through. She had many sisters, she and all of them had been born and bred in Montmartre and they were all of different fathers and married to different nationalities, even to turks and armenians. Germaine, much later, was very ill for years and she always had around her a devoted coterie. They used to carry her in her armchair to the nearest cinema and they, and she in the armchair, saw the performance through. They did this regularly once a week. I imagine they are still doing it.

The conversation around the tea table of Fernande was not lively, nobody had anything to say. It was a pleasure to meet, it was even an honour, but that was about all. Fernande complained a little that her charwoman had not adequately dusted and rinsed the tea things, and also that buying a bed and a piano on the instalment plan had elements of unpleasantness. Otherwise we really none of us had much to say.

Finally she and I arranged about the french lessons, I was to pay fifty cents an hour and she was to come to see me two days hence and we were to begin. Just at the end of the visit they were more natural. Fernande asked Miss Stein if she had any of the comic supplements of the american papers left. Gertrude Stein replied that she had just left them with Pablo.

Fernande roused like a lioness defending her cubs. That is a brutality that I will never forgive him, she said. I met him on the street, he had a comic supplement in his hand, I asked him to give it to me to help me to distract myself and he brutally refused. It was a piece of cruelty that I will never forgive. I ask you, Gertrude, to give to me myself the next copies you have of the comic supplement. Gertrude Stein said, why certainly with pleasure.

As we went out she said to me, it is to be hoped that they will be together again before the next comic supplements of the Katzenjammer kids come out because if I do not give them to Pablo he will be all upset and if I do Fernande will make an awful fuss. Well I suppose I will have to lose them or have my brother give them to Pablo by mistake.

Fernande came quite promptly to the appointment and we proceeded to our lesson. Of course to have a lesson in french one has to converse and Fernande had three subjects, hats, we had not much more to say about hats, perfumes, we had something to say about perfumes. Perfumes were Fernande's really great extravagance, she was the scandal of Montmartre because she had once bought a bottle of perfume named Smoke and had paid eighty francs for it at that time sixteen dollars and it had no scent but such wonderful colour, like real bottled liquid smoke. Her third subject was the categories of furs. There were three categories of furs, there were first category, sables, second category ermine and chinchilla, third category martin fox and squirrel. It was the most suprising thing I had heard in Paris. I was surprised. Chinchilla second, squirrel called fur and no seal skin.

Our only other conversation was the description and names of the dogs that were then fashionable. This was my subject and after I had described she always hesitated, ah yes, she would say illuminated, you wish to describe a little belgian dog whose name is griffon.

There we were, she was very beautiful but it was a little heavy and monotonous, so I suggested we should meet out of doors, at a tea place or take walks in Montmartre. That was better. She began to tell me things. I met Max Jacob. Fernande and he were very funny together. They felt themselves to be a courtly couple of the first empire, he being le vieux marquis kissing her hand and paying compliments and she the Empress Josephine receiving them. It was a caricature but a rather wonderful one. Then she told me about a mysterious horrible woman called Marie Laurencin who made noises like an animal and annoyed Picasso. I thought of her as a horrible old woman and was delighted when I met the young chic Marie who looked like a Clouet. Max Jacob read my horoscope. It was a great honour because he wrote it down. I did not realise it then but I have since and most of all very lately, as all the young gentlemen who nowadays so much admire Max are so astonished and impressed that he wrote mine down as he has always been supposed never to write them but just to say them off hand. Well anyway I have mine and it is written.

Then she also told me a great many stories about Van Dongen and his dutch wife and dutch little girl. Van Dongen broke into notoriety by a portrait he did of Fernande. It was in that way that he created the type of almond eyes that were later so much the vogue. But Fernande's almond eyes were natural, for good or for bad everything was natural in Fernande.

Of course Van Dongen did not admit that this picture was a portrait of Fernande, although she had sat for it and there was in consequence much bitterness. Van Dongen in these days was poor, he had a dutch wife who was a vegetarian and they lived on spinach. Van Dongen frequently escaped from the spinach to a joint in Montmartre where the girls paid for his dinner and his drinks.

The Van Dongen child was only four years old but terrific. Van Dongen used to do acrobatics with her and swing her around his head by a leg. When she hugged Picasso of whom she was very fond she used almost to destroy him, he had a great fear of her.

There were many other tales of Germaine Pichot and the circus where she found her lovers and there were tales of all the past and present life of Montmartre. Fernande herself had one ideal. It was Evelyn Thaw the heroine of the moment. And Fernande adored her in the way a later generation adored Mary Pickford, she was so blonde, so pale, so nothing and Fernande would give a heavy sigh of admiration.

The next time I saw Gertrude Stein she said to me suddenly, is Fernande wearing her earrings. I do not know, I said. Well notice, she said. The next time I saw Gertrude Stein I said, yes Fernande is wearing her earrings. Oh well, she said, there is nothing to be done yet, it's a nuisance because Pablo naturally having nobody in the studio cannot stay at home. In another week I was able to announce that Fernande was not wearing her earrings. Oh well it's alright then she has no more money left and it is all over, said Gertrude Stein. And it was. A week later I was dining with Fernande and Pablo at the rue de Fleurus.

I gave Fernande a chinese gown from San Francisco and Pablo gave me a lovely drawing.

And now I will tell you how two americans happened to be in the heart of an art movement of which the outside world at that time knew nothing.

GERTRUDE STEIN IN PARIS—1903-1907

During Gertrude Stein's last two years at the Medical School, Johns Hopkins, Baltimore, 1900-1903, her brother was living in Florence. There he heard of a painter named Cézanne and saw paintings by him owned by Charles Loeser. When he and his sister made their home in Paris the following year they went to Vollard's the only picture dealer who had Cézannes for sale, to look at them.

Vollard was a huge dark man who lisped a little. His shop was on the rue Laffitte not far from the boulevard. Further along this short street was Durand-Ruel and still further on almost at the church of the Martyrs was Sagot the ex-clown. Higher up in Montmartre on the rue Victor-Massé was Mademoiselle Weill who sold a mixture of pictures, books and bric-à-brac and in entirely another part of Paris on the rue Faubourg-Saint-Honoré was the ex-café keeper and photographer Druet. Also on the rue Laffitte was the confectioner Fouquet where one could console oneself with delicious honey cakes and nut candies and once in a while instead of a picture buy oneself strawberry jam in a glass bowl.

The first visit to Vollard has left an indelible impression on Gertrude Stein. It was an incredible place. It did not look like a picture gallery. Inside there were a couple of canvases turned to the wall, in one corner was a small pile of big and little canvases thrown pell mell on top of one another, in the center of the room stood a huge dark man glooming. This was Vollard cheerful. When he was really cheerless he put his huge frame against the glass door that led to the street, his arms above his head, his hands on each upper corner of the portal and gloomed darkly into the street. Nobody thought then of trying to come in.

They asked to see Cézannes. He looked less gloomy and became quite polite. As they found out afterward Cézanne was the great romance of Vollard's life. The name Cézanne was to him a magic word. He had first learned about Cézanne from Pissarro the painter. Pissarro indeed was the man from whom all the early Cézanne lovers heard about Cézanne. Cézanne at that time was living gloomy and embittered at Aix-en-Provence. Pissarro told Vollard about him, told Fabry, a Florentine, who told Loeser, told Picabia, in fact told everybody who knew about Cézanne at that time.

There were Cézannes to be seen at Vollard's. Later on Gertrude Stein wrote a poem called Vollard and Cézanne, and Henry McBride printed it in the New York Sun. This was the first fugitive piece of Gertrude Stein's to be so printed and it gave both her and Vollard a great deal of pleasure. Later on when Vollard wrote his book about Cézanne, Vollard at Gertrude Stein's suggestion sent a copy of the book to Henry McBride. She told Vollard that a whole page of one of New York's big daily papers would be devoted to his book. He did not believe it possible, nothing like that had ever happened to anybody in Paris. It did happen and he was deeply moved and unspeakably content. But to return to that first visit.

They told Monsieur Vollard they wanted to see some Cézanne landscapes, they had been sent to him by Mr. Loeser of Florence. Oh yes, said Vollard looking quite cheerful and he began moving about the room, finally he disappeared behind a partition in the back and was heard heavily mounting the steps. After a quite long wait he came down again and had in his hand a tiny picture of an apple with most of the canvas unpainted. They all looked at this thoroughly, then they said, yes but you see what we wanted to see was a landscape. Oh yes, sighed Vollard and he looked even more cheerful, after a moment he again disappeared and this time came back with a painting of a back, it was a beautiful painting there is no doubt about that but the brother and sister were not yet up to a full appreciation of Cézanne nudes and so they returned to the attack. They wanted to see a landscape. This time after even a longer wait he came back with a very large canvas and a very little fragment of a landscape painted on it. Yes that was it, they said, a landscape but what they wanted was a smaller canvas but one all covered. They said, they thought they would like to see one like that. By this time the early winter evening of Paris was closing in and just at this moment a very aged charwoman came down the same back stairs, mumbled, bon soir monsieur et madame, and quietly went out of the door, after a moment another old charwoman came down the same stairs, murmured, bon soir messieurs et mesdames and went quietly out of the door. Gertrude Stein began to laugh and said to her brother, it is all nonsense, there is no Cézanne. Vollard goes upstairs and tells these old women what to paint and he does not understand us and they do not understand him and they paint something and he brings it down and it is a Cézanne. They both began to laugh uncontrollably. Then they recovered and once more explained about the landscape. They said what they wanted was one of those marvellously yellow sunny Aix landscapes of which Loeser had several examples. Once more Vollard went off and this time he came back with a wonderful small green landscape. It was lovely, it covered all the canvas, it did not cost much and they bought it. Later on Vollard explained to every one that he had been visited by two crazy americans and they laughed and he had been much annoyed but gradually he found out that when they laughed most they usually bought something so of course he waited for them to laugh.

From that time on they went to Vollard's all the time. They had soon the privilege of upsetting his piles of canvases and finding what they liked in the heap. They bought a tiny little Daumier, head of an old woman. They began to take an interest in Cézanne nudes and they finally bought two tiny canvases of nude groups. They found a very very small Manet painted in black and white with Forain in the foreground and bought it, they found two tiny little Renoirs. They frequently bought in twos because one of them usually liked one more than the other one did, and so the year wore on. In the spring Vollard announced a show of Gauguin and they for the first time saw some Gauguins. They were rather awful but they finally liked them, and bought two Gauguins. Gertrude Stein liked his sun-flowers but not his figures and her brother preferred the figures. It sounds like a great deal now but in those days these things did not cost much. And so the winter went on.

There were not a great many people in and out of Vollard's but once Gertrude Stein heard a conversation there that pleased her immensely. Duret was a well known figure in Paris. He was now a very old and a very handsome man. He had been a friend of Whistler, Whistler had painted him in evening clothes with a white opera cloak over his arm. He was at Vollard's talking to a group of younger men and one of them Roussel, one of the Vuillard, Bonnard, the post impressionist group, said something complainingly about the lack of recognition of himself and his friends, that they were not even allowed to show in the salon. Duret looked at him kindly, my young friend, he said, there are two kinds of art, never forget this, there is art and there is official art. How can you, my poor young friend, hope to be official art. Just look at yourself. Supposing an important personage came to France, and wanted to meet the representative painters and have his portrait painted. My dear young friend, just look at yourself, the very sight of you would terrify him. You are a nice young man, gentle and intelligent, but to the important personage you would not seem so, you would be terrible. No they need as representative painter a medium sized, slightly stout man, not too well dressed but dressed in the fashion of his class, neither bald or well brushed hair and a respectful bow with it. You can see that you would not do. So never say another word about official recognition, or if you do look in the mirror and think of important personages. No, my dear young friend there is art and there is official art, there always has been and there always will be.

Before the winter was over, having gone so far Gertrude Stein and her brother decided to go further, they decided to buy a big Cézanne and then they would stop. After that they would be reasonable. They convinced their elder brother that this last outlay was necessary, and it was necessary as will soon be evident. They told Vollard that they wanted to buy a Cézanne portrait. In those days practically no big Cézanne portraits had been sold. Vollard owned almost all of them. He was enormously pleased with this decision. They now were introduced into the room above the steps behind the partition where Gertrude Stein had been sure the old charwoman painted the Cézannes and there they spent days deciding which portrait they would have. There were about eight to choose from and the decision was difficult. They had often to go and refresh themselves with honey cakes at Fouquet's. Finally they narrowed the choice down to two, a portrait of a man and a portrait of a woman, but this time they could not afford to buy twos and finally they chose the portrait of the woman.

Vollard said of course ordinarily a portrait of a woman always is more expensive than a portrait of a man but, said he looking at the picture very carefully, I suppose with Cézanne it does not make any difference. They put it in a cab and they went home with it. It was this picture that Alfy Maurer used to explain was finished and that you could tell that it was finished because it had a frame.

It was an important purchase because in looking and looking at this picture Gertrude Stein wrote Three Lives.

She had begun not long before as an exercise in literature to translate Flaubert's Trois Contes and then she had this Cézanne and she looked at it and under its stimulus she wrote Three Lives.

The next thing that happened was in the autumn. It was the first year of the autumn salon, the first autumn salon that had ever existed in Paris and they, very eager and excited, went to see it. There they found Matisse's picture afterwards known as La Femme au Chapeau.

This first autumn salon was a step in official recognition of the outlaws of the independent salon. Their pictures were to be shown in the Petit Palais opposite the Grand Palais where the great spring salon was held. That is, those outlaws were to be shown there who had succeeded enough so that they began to be sold in important picture shops. These in collaboration with some rebels from the old salons had created the autumn salon.

The show had a great deal of freshness and was not alarming. There were a number of attractive pictures but there was one that was not attractive. It infuriated the public, they tried to scratch off the paint.

Gertrude Stein liked that picture, it was a portrait of a woman with a long face and a fan. It was very strange in its colour and in its anatomy. She said she wanted to buy it. Her brother had in the meantime found a white-clothed woman on a green lawn and he wanted to buy it. So as usual they decided to buy two and they went to the office of the secretary of the salon to find out about prices. They had never been in the little room of a secretary of a salon and it was very exciting. The secretary looked up the prices in his catalogue. Gertrude Stein has forgotten how much and even whose it was, the white dress and dog on the green grass, but the Matisse was five hundred francs. The secretary explained that of course one never paid what the artist asked, one suggested a price. They asked what price they should suggest. He asked them what they were willing to pay. They said they did not know. He suggested that they offer four hundred and he would let them know. They agreed and left.

The next day they received word from the secretary that Monsieur Matisse had refused to accept the offer and what did they want to do. They decided to go over to the salon and look at the picture again. They did. People were roaring with laughter at the picture and scratching at it. Gertrude Stein could not understand why, the picture seemed to her perfectly natural. The Cézanne portrait had not seemed natural, it had taken her some time to feel that it was natural but this picture by Matisse seemed perfectly natural and she could not understand why it infuriated everybody. Her brother was less attracted but all the same he agreed and they bought it. She then went back to look at it and it upset her to see them all mocking at it. It bothered her and angered her because she did not understand why because to her it was so alright, just as later she did not understand why since the writing was all so clear and natural they mocked at and were enraged by her work.

And so this was the story of the buying of La Femme au Chapeau by the buyers and now for the story from the seller's point of view as told some months after by Monsieur and Madame Matisse. Shortly after the purchase of the picture they all asked to meet each other. Whether Matisse wrote and asked or whether they wrote and asked Gertrude Stein does not remember. Anyway in no time they were knowing each other and knowing each other very well.

The Matisses lived on the quay just off the boulevard Saint-Michel. They were on the top floor in a small three-roomed apartment with a lovely view over Notre Dame and the river. Matisse painted it in winter. You went up and up the steps. In those days you were always going up stairs and down stairs. Mildred Aldrich had a distressing way of dropping her key down the middle of the stairs where an elevator might have been, in calling out goodbye to some one below, from her sixth story, and then you or she had to go all the way up or all the way down again. To be sure she would often call out, never mind, I am bursting open my door. Only americans did that. The keys were heavy and you either forgot them or dropped them. Sayen at the end of a Paris summer when he was congratulated on looking so well and sun-burned, said, yes it comes from going up and down stairs.

Madame Matisse was an admirable housekeeper. Her place was small but immaculate. She kept the house in order, she was an excellent cook and provider, she posed for all of Matisse's pictures. It was she who was La Femme au Chapeau, lady with a hat. She had kept a little millinery shop to keep them going in their poorest days. She was a very straight dark woman with a long face and a firm large loosely hung mouth like a horse. She had an abundance of dark hair. Gertrude Stein always liked the way she pinned her hat to her head and Matisse once made a drawing of his wife making this characteristic gesture and gave it to Miss Stein. She always wore black. She always placed a large black hat-pin well in the middle of the hat and the middle of the top of her head and then with a large firm gesture, down it came. They had with them a daughter of Matisse, a daughter he had had before his marriage and who had had diphtheria and had had to have an operation and for many years had to wear a black ribbon around her throat with a silver button. This Matisse put into many of his pictures. The girl was exactly like her father and Madame Matisse, as she once explained in her melodramatic simple way, did more than her duty by this child because having read in her youth a novel in which the heroine had done so and been consequently much loved all her life, had decided to do the same. She herself had had two boys but they were neither of them at that time living with them. The younger Pierre was in the south of France on the borders of Spain with Madame Matisse's father and mother, and the elder Jean with Monsieur Matisse's father and mother in the north of France on the borders of Belgium.

Matisse had an astonishing virility that always gave one an extraordinary pleasure when one had not seen him for some time. Less the first time of seeing him than later. And one did not lose the pleasure of this virility all the time he was with one. But there was not much feeling of life in this virility. Madame Matisse was very different, there was a very profound feeling of life in her for any one who knew her.

Matisse had at this time a small Cézanne and a small Gauguin and he said he needed them both. The Cézanne had been bought with his wife's marriage portion, the Gauguin with the ring which was the only jewel she had ever owned. And they were happy because he needed these two pictures. The Cézanne was a picture of bathers and a tent, the Gauguin the head of a boy. Later on in life when Matisse became a very rich man, he kept on buying pictures. He said he knew about pictures and had confidence in them and he did not know about other things. And so for his own pleasure and as the best legacy to leave his children he bought Cézannes. Picasso also later when he became rich bought pictures but they were his own. He too believed in pictures and wants to leave the best legacy he can to his son and so keeps and buys his own.

The Matisses had had a hard time. Matisse had come to

Paris as a young man to study pharmacy. His people were
small grain merchants in the north of France. He had become
interested in painting, had begun copying the Poussins at the
Louvre and become a painter fairly without the consent of
his people who however continued to allow him the very
small monthly sum he had had as a student. His daughter was
born at this time and this further complicated his life. He had
at first a certain amount of success. He married. Under the
influence of the paintings of Poussin and Chardin he had
painted still life pictures that had considerable success at the
Champ-de-Mars salon, one of the two big spring salons. And
then he fell under the influence of Cézanne, and then under
the influence of negro sculpture. All this developed the
Matisse of the period of La Femme au Chapeau. The year
after his very considerable success at the salon he spent the
winter painting a very large picture of a woman setting a
table and on the table was a magnificent dish of fruit. It had
strained the resources of the Matisse family to buy this fruit,
fruit was horribly dear in Paris in those days, even ordinary
fruit, imagine how much dearer was this very extraordinary
fruit and it had to keep until the picture was completed and
the picture was going to take a long time. In order to keep
it as long as possible they kept the room as cold as possible,
and that under the roof and in a Paris winter was not difficult,
and Matisse painted in an overcoat and gloves and he painted
at it all winter. It was finished at last and sent to the salon
where the year before Matisse had had considerable success,
and there it was refused. And now Matisse's serious troubles
began, his daughter was very ill, he was in an agonising
mental struggle concerning his work, and he had lost all
possibility of showing his pictures. He no longer painted at
home but in an atelier. It was cheaper so. Every morning
he painted, every afternoon he worked at his sculpture, late
every afternoon he drew in the sketch classes from the nude,
and every evening he played his violin. These were very dark
days and he was very despairful. His wife opened a small
millinery shop and they managed to live. The two boys
were sent away to the country to his and her people and they
continued to live. The only encouragement came in the atelier

where he worked and where a crowd of young men began to gather around him and be influenced by him. Among these the best known at that time was Manguin, the best known now Derain. Derain was a very young man at that time, he enormously admired Matisse, he went away to the country with them to Collioure near Perpignan, and he was a great comfort to them all. He began to paint landscapes outlining his trees with red and he had a sense of space that was quite his own and which first showed itself in a landscape of a cart going up a road bordered with trees lined in red. His paintings were coming to be known at the independent.

Matisse worked every day and every day and every day and he worked terribly hard. Once Vollard came to see him. Matisse used to love to tell the story. I have often heard him tell it. Vollard came and said he wanted to see the big picture which had been refused. Matisse showed it to him. He did not look at it. He talked to Madame Matisse and mostly about cooking, he liked cooking and eating as a frenchman should, and so did she. Matisse and Madame Matisse were both getting very nervous although she did not show it. And this door, said Vollard interestedly to Matisse, where does that lead to, does that lead into a court or does that lead on to a stairway. Into a court, said Matisse. Ah yes, said Vollard. And then he left.

The Matisses spent days discussing whether there was anything symbolic in Vollard's question or was it idle curiosity. Vollard never had any idle curiosity, he always wanted to know what everybody thought of everything because in that way he found out what he himself thought. This was very well known and therefore the Matisses asked each other and all their friends, why did he ask that question about that door. Well at any rate within the year he had bought the picture at a very low price but he bought it, and he put it away and nobody saw it, and that was the end of that.

From this time on things went neither better nor worse for Matisse and he was discouraged and aggressive. Then came the first autumn salon and he was asked to exhibit and he sent La Femme au Chapeau and it was hung. It was derided and attacked and it was sold.

Matisse was at this time about thirty-five years old, he was depressed. Having gone to the opening day of the salon and heard what was said of his picture and seen what they were trying to do to it he never went again. His wife went alone. He stayed at home and was unhappy. This is the way Madame Matisse used to tell the story.

Then a note came from the secretary of the salon saying that there had been an offer made for the picture, an offer of four hundred francs. Matisse was painting Madame Matisse as a gypsy holding a guitar. This guitar had already had a history. Madame Matisse was very fond of telling the story. She had a great deal to do and she posed beside and she was very healthy and sleepy. One day she was posing, he was painting, she began to nod and as she nodded the guitar made noises. Stop it, said Matisse, wake up. She woke up, he painted, she nodded and the guitar made noises. Stop it, said Matisse, wake up. She woke up and then in a little while she nodded again the guitar made even more noises. Matisse furious seized the guitar and broke it. And added Madame Matisse ruefully, we were very hard up then and we had to have it mended so he could go on with the picture. She was holding this same mended guitar and posing when the note from the secretary of the autumn salon came. Matisse was joyful, of course I will accept, said Matisse. Oh no, said Madame Matisse, if those people (ces gens) are interested enough to make an offer they are interested enough to pay the price you asked, and she added, the difference would make winter clothes for Margot. Matisse hesitated but was finally convinced and they sent a note saying he wanted his price. Nothing happened and Matisse was in a terrible state and very reproachful and then in a day or two when Madame Matisse was once more posing with the guitar and Matisse was painting, Margot brought them a little blue telegram. Matisse opened it and he made a grimace. Madame Matisse was terrified, she thought the worst had happened. The guitar fell. What is it, she said. They have bought it, he said. Why do you make such a face of agony and frighten me so and perhaps break the guitar, she said. I was winking at you, he said, to tell you, because I was so moved I could not speak.

And so, Madame Matisse used to end up the story triumphantly, you see it was I, and I was right to insist upon the original price, and Mademoiselle Gertrude, who insisted upon buying it, who arranged the whole matter.

The friendship with the Matisses grew apace. Matisse at that time was at work at his first big decoration, Le Bonheur de Vivre. He was making small and larger and very large studies for it. It was in this picture that Matisse first clearly realised his intention of deforming the drawing of the human body in order to harmonise and intensify the colour values of all the simple colours mixed only with white. He used his distorted drawing as a dissonance is used in music or as vinegar or lemons are used in cooking or egg shells in coffee to clarify. I do inevitably take my comparisons from the kitchen because I like food and cooking and know something about it. However this was the idea. Cézanne had come to his unfinishedness and distortion of necessity, Matisse did it by intention.

Little by little people began to come to the rue de Fleurus to see the Matisses and the Cézannes, Matisse brought people, everybody brought somebody, and they came at any time and it began to be a nuisance, and it was in this way that Saturday evenings began. It was also at this time that Gertrude Stein got into the habit of writing at night. It was only after eleven o'clock that she could be sure that no one would knock at the studio door. She was at that time planning her long book, The Making of Americans, she was struggling with her sentences, those long sentences that had to be so exactly carried out. Sentences not only words but sentences and always sentences have been Gertrude Stein's life long passion. And so she had then and indeed it lasted pretty well to the war, which broke down so many habits, she had then the habit of beginning her work at eleven o'clock at night and working until the dawn. She said she always tried to stop before the dawn was too clear and the birds were too lively because it is a disagreeable sensation to go to bed then. There were birds in many trees behind high walls in those days, now there are fewer. But often the birds and the dawn caught her and she stood

in the court waiting to get used to it before she went to bed.
She had the habit then of sleeping until noon and the beating
of the rugs into the court, because everybody did that in those
days, even her household did, was one of her most poignant
irritations.

So the Saturday evenings began.

Gertrude Stein and her brother were often at the Matisses
and the Matisses were constantly with them. Madame Matisse
occasionally gave them a lunch, this happened most often
when some relation sent the Matisses a hare. Jugged hare
prepared by Madame Matisse in the fashion of Perpignan was
something quite apart. They also had extremely good wine, a
little heavy, but excellent. They also had a sort of Madeira
called Roncio which was very good indeed. Maillol the
sculptor came from the same part of France as Madame
Matisse and once when I met him at Jo Davidson's, many
years later, he told me about all these wines. He then told
me how he had lived well in his student days in Paris for
fifty francs a month. To be sure, he said, the family sent me
homemade bread every week and when I came I brought
enough wine with me to last a year and I sent my washing
home every month.

Derain was present at one of these lunches in those early
days. He and Gertrude Stein disagreed violently. They discussed philosophy, he basing his ideas on having read the
second part of Faust in a french translation while he was
doing his military service. They never became friends. Gertrude Stein was never interested in his work. He had a sense
of space but for her his pictures had neither life nor depth
nor solidity. They rarely saw each other after. Derain at that
time was constantly with the Matisses and was of all Matisse's
friends the one Madame Matisse liked the best.

It was about this time that Gertrude Stein's brother happened one day to find the picture gallery of Sagot, an ex-
circus clown who had a picture shop further up the rue
Laffitte. Here he, Gertrude Stein's brother, found the paintings of two young spaniards, one, whose name everybody
has forgotten, the other one, Picasso. The work of both of
them interested him and he bought a water colour by the

forgotten one, a café scene. Sagot also sent him to a little
furniture store where there were some paintings being shown
by Picasso. Gertrude Stein's brother was interested and
wanted to buy one and asked the price but the price asked
was almost as expensive as Cézanne. He went back to Sagot
and told him. Sagot laughed. He said, that is alright, come
back in a few days and I will have a big one. In a few days
he did have a big one and it was very cheap. When Gertrude
Stein and Picasso tell about those days they are not always
in agreement as to what happened but I think in this case
they agree that the price asked was a hundred and fifty
francs. The picture was the now well known painting of a
nude girl with a basket of red flowers.

Gertrude Stein did not like the picture, she found something rather appalling in the drawing of the legs and feet,
something that repelled and shocked her. She and her brother
almost quarrelled about this picture. He wanted it and she
did not want it in the house. Sagot gathering a little of the
discussion said, but that is alright if you do not like the legs
and feet it is very easy to guillotine her and only take the
head. No that would not do, everybody agreed, and nothing
was decided.

Gertrude Stein and her brother continued to be very
divided in this matter and they were very angry with each
other. Finally it was agreed that since he, the brother, wanted
it so badly they would buy it, and in this way the first Picasso
was brought into the rue de Fleurus.

It was just about this time that Raymond Duncan, the
brother of Isadora, rented an atelier in the rue de Fleurus.
Raymond had just come back from his first trip to Greece and
had brought back with him a greek girl and greek clothes.
Raymond had known Gertrude Stein's elder brother and his
wife in San Francisco. At that time Raymond was acting as
advance agent for Emma Nevada who had also with her Pablo
Casals the violoncellist, at that time quite unknown.

The Duncan family had been then at the Omar Khayyám
stage, they had not yet gone greek. They had after that gone
italian renaissance, but now Raymond had gone completely
greek and this included a greek girl. Isadora lost interest in

him, she found the girl too modern a greek. At any rate Raymond was at this time without any money at all and his wife was enceinte. Gertrude Stein gave him coal and a chair for Penelope to sit in, the rest sat on packing cases. They had another friend who helped them, Kathleen Bruce, a very beautiful, very athletic English girl, a kind of sculptress, she later married and became the widow of the discoverer of the South Pole, Scott. She had at that time no money to speak of either and she used to bring a half portion of her dinner every evening for Penelope. Finally Penelope had her baby, it was named Raymond because when Gertrude Stein's brother and Raymond Duncan went to register it they had not thought of a name. Now he is against his will called Menalkas but he might be gratified if he knew that legally he is Raymond. However that is another matter.

Kathleen Bruce was a sculptress and she was learning to model figures of children and she asked to do a figure of Gertrude Stein's nephew. Gertrude Stein and her nephew went to Kathleen Bruce's studio. There they, one afternoon, met H. P. Roché. Roché was one of those characters that are always to be found in Paris. He was a very earnest, very noble, devoted, very faithful and very enthusiastic man who was a general introducer. He knew everybody, he really knew them and he could introduce anybody to anybody. He was going to be a writer. He was tall and red-headed and he never said anything but good good excellent and he lived with his mother and his grandmother. He had done a great many things, he had gone to the austrian mountains with the austrians, he had gone to Germany with the germans and he had gone to Hungary with hungarians and he had gone to England with the english. He had not gone to Russia although he had been in Paris with russians. As Picasso always said of him, Roché is very nice but he is only a translation.

Later he was often at 27 rue de Fleurus with various nationalities and Gertrude Stein rather liked him. She always said of him he is so faithful, perhaps one need never see him again but one knows that somewhere Roché is faithful. He did give her one delightful sensation in the very early days of their acquaintance. Three Lives, Gertrude Stein's first book was just then being written and Roché who could read english was very impressed by it. One day Gertrude Stein was saying something about herself and Roché said good good excellent that is very important for your biography. She was terribly touched, it was the first time that she really realised that some time she would have a biography. It is quite true that although she has not seen him for years somewhere Roché is probably perfectly faithful.

But to come back to Roché at Kathleen Bruce's studio. They all talked about one thing and another and Gertrude Stein happened to mention that they had just bought a picture from Sagot by a young spaniard named Picasso. Good good excellent, said Roché, he is a very interesting young fellow, I know him. Oh do you, said Gertrude Stein, well enough to take somebody to see him. Why certainly, said Roché. Very well, said Gertrude Stein, my brother I know is very anxious to make his acquaintance. And there and then the appointment was made and shortly after Roché and Gertrude Stein's brother went to see Picasso.

It was only a very short time after this that Picasso began the portrait of Gertrude Stein, now so widely known, but just how that came about is a little vague in everybody's mind. I have heard Picasso and Gertrude Stein talk about it often and they neither of them can remember. They can remember the first time that Picasso dined at the rue de Fleurus and they can remember the first time Gertrude Stein posed for her portrait at rue Ravignan but in between there is a blank. How it came about they do not know. Picasso had never had anybody pose for him since he was sixteen years old, he was then twenty-four and Gertrude Stein had never thought of having her portrait painted, and they do not either of them know how it came about. Anyway it did and she posed to him for this portrait ninety times and a great deal happened during that time. To go back to all the first times.

Picasso and Fernande came to dinner, Picasso in those days was, what a dear friend and schoolmate of mine, Nellie Jacot, called, a good-looking bootblack. He was thin dark, alive with big pools of eyes and a violent but not rough way. He was sitting next to Gertrude Stein at dinner and she took

up a piece of bread. This, said Picasso, snatching it back with
violence, this piece of bread is mine. She laughed and he
looked sheepish. That was the beginning of their intimacy.

That evening Gertrude Stein's brother took out portfolio
after portfolio of japanese prints to show Picasso, Gertrude
Stein's brother was fond of japanese prints. Picasso solemnly
and obediently looked at print after print and listened to the
descriptions. He said under his breath to Gertrude Stein,
he is very nice, your brother, but like all americans, like
Haviland, he shows you japanese prints. Moi j'aime pas ça,
no I don't care for it. As I say Gertrude Stein and Pablo
Picasso immediately understood each other.

Then there was the first time of posing. The atelier of
Picasso I have already described. In those days there was
even more disorder, more coming and going, more red-hot
fire in the stove, more cooking and more interruptions. There
was a large broken armchair where Gertrude Stein posed.
There was a couch where everybody sat and slept. There was
a little kitchen chair upon which Picasso sat to paint, there
was a large easel and there were many very large convases.
It was at the height of the end of the Harlequin period when
the canvases were enormous, the figures also, and the groups.

There was a little fox terrier there that had something the
matter with it and had been and was again about to be taken
to the veterinary. No frenchman or frenchwoman is so poor or
so careless or so avaricious but that they can and do constantly take their pet to the vet.

Fernande was as always, very large, very beautiful and very
gracious. She offered to read La Fontaine's stories aloud to
amuse Gertrude Stein while Gertrude Stein posed. She took
her pose, Picasso sat very tight on his chair and very close
to his canvas and on a very small palette which was of a uniform brown grey colour, mixed some more brown grey and
the painting began. This was the first of some eighty or
ninety sittings.

Toward the end of the afternoon Gertrude Stein's two
brothers and her sister-in-law and Andrew Green came to
see. They were all excited at the beauty of the sketch and

Andrew Green begged and begged that it should be left as it was. But Picasso shook his head and said, non.

It is too bad but in those days no one thought of taking a photograph of the picture as it was then and of course no one of the group that saw it then remembers at all what it looked like any more than do Picasso or Gertrude Stein.

Andrew Green, none of them knew how they had met Andrew Green, he was the great-nephew of Andrew Green known as the father of Greater New York. He had been born and reared in Chicago but he was a typical tall gaunt new englander, blond and gentle. He had a prodigious memory and could recite all of Milton's Paradise Lost by heart and also all the translations of chinese poems of which Gertrude Stein was very fond. He had been in China and he was later to live permanently in the South Sea islands after he finally inherited quite a fortune from his great-uncle who was fond of Milton's Paradise Lost. He had a passion for oriental stuffs. He adored as he said a simple centre and a continuous design. He loved pictures in museums and he hated everything modern. Once when during the family's absence he had stayed at the rue de Fleurus for a month, he had outraged Hélène's feelings by having his bed-sheets changed every day and covering all the pictures with cashmere shawls. He said the pictures were very restful, he could not deny that, but he could not bear it. He said that after the month was over that he had of course never come to like the new pictures but the worst of it was that not liking them he had lost his taste for the old and he never again in his life could go to any museum or look at any picture. He was tremendously impressed by Fernande's beauty. He was indeed quite overcome. I would, he said to Gertrude Stein, if I could talk french, I would make love to her and take her away from that little Picasso. Do you make love with words, laughed Gertrude Stein. He went away before I came to Paris and he came back eighteen years later and he was very dull.

This year was comparatively a quiet one. The Matisses were in the South of France all winter, at Collioure on the Mediterranean coast not far from Perpignan, where Madame Matisse's people lived. The Raymond Duncans had disappeared after having been joined first by a sister of Penelope who was a little actress and was very far from being dressed greek, she was as nearly as she possible could be a little Parisian. She had accompanying her a very large dark greek cousin. He came in to see Gertrude Stein and he looked around and he announced, I am greek, that is the same as saying that I have perfect taste and I do not care for any of these pictures. Very shortly Raymond, his wife and baby, the sister-in-law and the greek cousin disappeared out of the court at 27 rue de Fleurus and were succeeded by a german lady.

This german lady was the niece and god-daughter of german field-marshals and her brother was a captain in the german navy. Her mother was english and she herself had played the harp at the bavarian court. She was very amusing and had some strange friends, both english and french. She was a sculptress and she made a typical german sculpture of little Roger, the concierge's boy. She made three heads of him, one laughing, one crying and one sticking out his tongue. all three together on one pedestal. She sold this piece to the royal museum at Potsdam. The concierge during the war often wept at the thought of her Roger being there, sculptured, in the museum at Potsdam. She invented clothes that could be worn inside out and taken to pieces and be made long or short and she showed these to everybody with great pride. She had as an instructor in painting a weird looking frenchman one who looked exactly like the pictures of Huckleberry Finn's father. She explained that she employed him out of charity, he had won a gold medal at the salon in his youth and after that had had no success. She also said that she never employed a servant of the servant class. She said that decayed gentlewomen were more appetising and more efficient and she always had some widow of some army officer or functionary sewing or posing for her. She had an austrian maid for a while who cooked perfectly delicious austrian pastry but she did not keep her long. She was in short very amusing and she and Gertrude Stein used to talk to each other in the court. She always wanted to know what Gertrude Stein thought of everybody who came in and out. She wanted to know if she came to her conclusions by deduc tion, observation, imagination or analysis. She was amusing and then she disappeared and nobody thought anything about her until the war came and then everybody wondered if after all there had not been something sinister about this german woman's life in Paris.

Practically every afternoon Gertrude Stein went to Montmartre, posed and then later wandered down the hill usually walking across Paris to the rue de Fleurus. She then formed the habit which has never left her of walking around Paris, now accompanied by the dog, in those days alone. And Saturday evenings the Picassos walked home with her and dined and then there was Saturday evening.

During these long poses and these long walks Gertrude Stein meditated and made sentences. She was then in the middle of her negro story Melanctha Herbert, the second story of Three Lives and the poignant incidents that she wove into the life of Melanctha were often these she noticed in walking down the hill from the rue Ravignan.

It was at that time that the hungarians began their pilgrimages to the rue de Fleurus. There were strange groups of americans then, Picasso unaccustomed to the virginal quality of these young men and women used to say of them, ils sont pas des hommes, ils sont pas des femmes, ils sont des américains. They are not men, they are not women, they are americans. Once there was a Bryn Mawr woman there, wife of a well known portrait painter, who was very tall and beautiful and having once fallen on her head had a strange vacant expression. Her, he approved of, and used to call the Empress. There was a type of american art student, male, that used very much to afflict him, he used to say no it is not he who will make the future glory of America. He had a characteristic reaction when he saw the first photograph of a sky-scraper. Good God, he said, imagine the pangs of jealousy a lover would have while his beloved came up all those flights of stairs to his top story studio.

It was at this time that a Maurice Denis, a Toulouse-Lautrec and many enormous Picassos were added to the collection. It was at this time also that the acquaintance and friendship with the Vallotons began.

Vollard once said when he was asked about a certain painter's picture, oh ça c'est un Cézanne pour les pauvres, that is a Cézanne for the poor collector. Well Valloton was a Manet for the impecunious. His big nude had all the hardness, the stillness and none of the quality of the Olympe of Manet and his portraits had the aridity but none of the elegance of David. And further he had the misfortune of having married the sister of an important picture-dealer. He was very happy with his wife and she was a very charming woman but then there were the weekly family reunions, and there was also the wealth of his wife and the violence of his step-sons. He was a gentle soul, Valloton, with a keen wit and a great deal of ambition but a feeling of impotence, the result of being the brother-in-law of picture dealers. However for a time his pictures were very interesting. He asked Gertrude Stein to pose for him. She did the following year. She had come to like posing, the long still hours followed by a long dark walk intensified the concentration with which she was creating her sentences. The sentences of which Marcel Brion, the french critic has written, by exactitude, austerity, absence of variety in light and shade, by refusal of the use of the subconscious Gertrude Stein achieves a symmetry which has a close analogy to the symmetry of the musical fugue of Bach.

She often described the strange sensation she had as a result of the way in which Valloton painted. He was not at that time a young man as painters go, he had already had considerable recognition as a painter in the Paris exposition of 1900. When he painted a portrait he made a crayon sketch and then began painting at the top of the canvas straight across. Gertrude Stein said it was like pulling down a curtain as slowly moving as one of his swiss glaciers. Slowly he pulled the curtain down and by the time he was at the bottom of the canvas, there you were. The whole operation took about two weeks and then he gave the canvas to you. First however he exhibited it in the autumn salon and it had considerable notice and everybody was pleased.

Everybody went to the Cirque Médrano once a week, at least, and usually everybody went on the same evening. There the clowns had commenced dressing up in misfit clothes instead of the old classic costume and these clothes later so well known on Charlie Chaplin were the delight of Picasso and all his friends in Montmartre. There also were the english jockeys and their costumes made the mode that all Montmartre followed. Not very long ago somebody was talking about how well the young painters of to-day dressed and what a pity it was that they spent money in that way. Picasso laughed. I am quite certain, he said, they pay less for the fashionable complet, their suits of clothes, than we did for our rough and common ones. You have no idea how hard it was and expensive it was in those days to find english tweed or a french imitation that would look rough and dirty enough. And it was quite true one way and another the painters in those days did spend a lot of money and they spent all they got hold of because in those happy days you could owe money for years for your paints and canvases and rent and restaurant and practically everything except coal and luxuries.

The winter went on. Three Lives was written. Gertrude Stein asked her sister-in-law to come and read it. She did and was deeply moved. This pleased Gertrude Stein immensely, she did not believe that any one could read anything she wrote and be interested. In those days she never asked any one what they thought of her work, but were they interested enough to read it. Now she says if they can bring themselves to read it they will be interested.

Her elder brother's wife has always meant a great deal in her life but never more than on that afternoon. And then it had to be typewritten. Gertrude Stein had at that time a wretched little portable typewriter which she never used. She always then and for many years later wrote on scraps of paper in pencil, copied it into french school note-books in ink and then often copied it over again in ink. It was in connection with these various series of scraps of paper that her elder brother once remarked, I do not know whether Gertrude has more genius than the rest of you all, that I know nothing about, but one thing I have always noticed, the rest of you paint and write and are not satisfied and throw it away or tear it up, she does not say whether she is satisfied or not, she copies it very often but she never throws away any piece of paper upon which she has written.

Gertrude Stein tried to copy Three Lives on the typewriter but it was no use, it made her nervous, so Etta Cone came to the rescue. The Miss Etta Cones as Pablo Picasso used to call her and her sister. Etta Cone was a Baltimore connection of Gertrude Stein's and she was spending a winter in Paris. She was rather lonesome and she was rather interested.

Etta Cone found the Picassos appalling but romantic. She was taken there by Gertrude Stein whenever the Picasso finances got beyond everybody and was made to buy a hundred francs' worth of drawings. After all a hundred francs in those days was twenty dollars. She was quite willing to indulge in this romantic charity. Needless to say these drawings became in very much later years the nucleus of her collection.

Etta Cone offered to typewrite Three Lives and she began. Baltimore is famous for the delicate sensibilities and conscientiousness of its inhabitants. It suddenly occurred to Gertrude Stein that she had not told Etta Cone to read the manuscript before beginning to typewrite it. She went to see her and there indeed was Etta Cone faithfully copying the manuscript letter by letter so that she might not by any indiscretion become conscious of the meaning. Permission to read the text having been given the typewriting went on.

Spring was coming and the sittings were coming to an end. All of a sudden one day Picasso painted out the whole head. I can't see you any longer when I look, he said irritably. And so the picture was left like that.

Nobody remembers being particularly disappointed or particularly annoyed at this ending to the long series of posings. There was the spring independent and then Gertrude Stein and her brother were going to Italy as was at that time their habit. Pablo and Fernande were going to Spain, she for the first time, and she had to buy a dress and a hat and perfumes and a cooking stove. All french women in those days when they went from one country to another took along a french oil stove to cook on. Perhaps they still do. No matter where they were going this had to be taken with them. They always paid a great deal of excess baggage, all french women who went travelling. And the Matisses were back and they had to meet the Picassos and to be enthusiastic about each other, but not to like each other very well. And in their wake, Derain met Picasso and with him came Braque.

It may seem very strange to every one nowadays that before this time Matisse had never heard of Picasso and Picasso had never met Matisse. But at that time every little crowd lived its own life and knew practically nothing of any other crowd. Matisse on the Quai Saint-Michel and in the indépendant did not know anything of Picasso and Montmartre and Sagot. They all, it is true, had been in the very early stages bought one after the other by Mademoiselle Weill, the bric-à-brac shop in Montmartre, but as she bought everybody's pictures, pictures brought by any one, not necessarily by the painter, it was not very likely that any painter would, except by some rare chance, see there the paintings of any other painter. They were however all very grateful to her in later years because after all practically everybody who later became famous had sold their first little picture to her.

As I was saying the sittings were over, the vernissage of the independent was over and everybody went away.

It had been a fruitful winter. In the long struggle with the portrait of Gertrude Stein, Picasso passed from the Harlequin, the charming early italian period to the intensive struggle which was to end in cubism. Gertrude Stein had written the story of Melanctha the negress, the second story of Three Lives which was the first definite step away from the nineteenth century and into the twentieth century in literature. Matisse had painted the Bonheur de Vivre and had created the new school of colour which was soon to leave its mark on everything. And everybody went away. That summer the Matisses came to Italy. Matisse did not care about it very much, he preferred France and Morocco but Madame Matisse was deeply touched. It was a girlish dream fulfilled. She said, I say to myself all the time, I am in Italy. And I say it to Henri all the time and he is very sweet about it, but he says, what of it.

The Picassos were in Spain and Fernande wrote long letters describing Spain and the spaniards and earthquakes.

In Florence except for the short visit of the Matisses and a short visit from Alfy Maurer the summer life was in no way related to the Paris life.

Gertrude Stein and her brother rented for the summer a villa on top of the hill at Fiesole near Florence, and there they spent their summers for several years. The year I came to Paris a friend and myself took this villa, Gertrude Stein and her brother having taken a larger one on the other side of Fiesole, having been joined that year by their elder brother, his wife and child. The small one, the Casa Ricci, was very delightful. It had been made livable by a Scotch woman who born Presbyterian became an ardent Catholic and took her old Presbyterian mother from one convent to another. Finally they came to rest in Casa Ricci and there she made for herself a chapel and there her mother died. She then abandoned this for a larger villa which she turned into a retreat for retired priests and Gertrude Stein and her brother rented the Casa Ricci from her. Gertrude Stein delighted in her landlady who looked exactly like a lady-in-waiting to Mary Stuart and with all her trailing black robes genuflected before every Catholic symbol and would then climb up a precipitous ladder and open a little window in the roof to look at the stars. A strange mingling of Catholic and Protestant exaltation.

Hélène the french servant never came down to Fiesole. She had by that time married. She cooked for her husband during the summer and mended the stockings of Gertrude Stein and her brother by putting new feet into them. She also made jam. In Italy there was Maddalena quite as important in Italy as Hélène in Paris, but I doubt if with as much appreciation for notabilities. Italy is too accustomed to the famous and the children of the famous. It was Edwin Dodge who apropos of these said, the lives of great men oft remind us we should leave no sons behind us.

Gertrude Stein adored heat and sunshine although she always says that Paris winter is an ideal climate. In those days it was always at noon that she preferred to walk. I, who have and had no fondness for a summer sun, often accompanied her. Sometimes later in Spain I sat under a tree and wept but she in the sun was indefatigable. She could even lie in the sun and look straight up into a summer noon sun, she said it rested her eyes and head.

There were amusing people in Florence. There were the Berensons and at that time with them Gladys Deacon, a well known international beauty, but after a winter of Montmartre Gertrude Stein found her too easily shocked to be interesting. Then there were the first russians, von Heiroth and his wife, she who afterwards had four husbands and once pleasantly remarked that she had always been good friends with all her husbands. He was foolish but attractive and told the usual russian stories. Then there were the Thorolds and a great many others. And most important there was a most excellent english lending library with all sorts of strange biographies which were to Gertrude Stein a source of endless pleasure. She once told me that when she was young she had read so much, read from the Elizabethans to the moderns, that she was terribly uneasy lest some day she would be without anything to read. For years this fear haunted her but in one way and another although she always reads and reads she seems always to find more to read. Her eldest brother used to complain that although he brought up from Florence every day as many books as he could carry, there always were just as many to take back.

It was during this summer that Gertrude Stein began her great book, The Making of Americans.

It began with an old daily theme that she had written when at Radcliffe,

"Once an angry man dragged his father along the ground through his own orchard. 'Stop!' cried the groaning old man at last. 'Stop! I did not drag my father beyond this tree.'

"It is hard living down the tempers we are born with. We all begin well. For in our youth there is nothing we are more intolerant of than our own sins writ large in others and we fight them fiercely in ourselves; but we grow old and see that these our sins are of all sins the really harmless ones to own, nay that they give a charm to any character, and so our struggle with them dies away." And it was to be the history of a family. It was a history of a family but by the time I came to Paris it was getting to be a history of all human beings, all who ever were or are or could be living.

Gertrude Stein in all her life has never been as pleased with anything as she is with the translation that Bernard Faÿ and Madame Seillière are making of this book now. She has just been going over it with Bernard Faÿ and as she says, it is wonderful in english and it is even as wonderful in french. Elliot Paul, when editor of transition once said that he was certain that Gertrude Stein could be a best-seller in France. It seems very likely that his prediction is to be fulfilled.

But to return to those old days in the Casa Ricci and the first beginnings of those long sentences which were to change the literary ideas of a great many people.

Gertrude Stein was working tremendously over the beginning of The Making of Americans and came back to Paris under the spell of the thing she was doing. It was at this time that working every night she often was caught by the dawn coming while she was working. She came back to a Paris fairly full of excitement. In the first place she came back to her finished portrait. The day he returned from Spain Picasso sat down and out of his head painted the head in without having seen Gertrude Stein again. And when she saw it he and she were content. It is very strange but neither can remember at all what the head looked like when he painted it out. There is another charming story of the portrait.

Only a few years ago when Gertrude Stein had had her hair cut short, she had always up to that time worn it as a crown on top of her head as Picasso has painted it, when she had had her hair cut, a day or so later she happened to come into a room and Picasso was several rooms away. She had a hat on but he caught sight of her through two doorways and approaching her quickly called out, Gertrude, what is it, what is it. What is what, Pablo, she said. Let me see, he said. She let him see. And my portrait, said he sternly. Then his face softening he added, mais, quand même tout y est, all the same it is all there.

Matisse was back and there was excitement in the air. Derain, and Braque with him, had gone Montmartre. Braque

was a young painter who had known Marie Laurencin when
they were both art students, and they had then painted each
other's portraits. After that Braque had done rather geographical pictures, rounded hills and very much under the colour
influence of Matisse's independent painting. He had come to
know Derain, I am not sure but that they had known each
other while doing their military service, and now they knew
Picasso. It was an exciting moment.

They began to spend their days up there and they all
always ate together at a little restaurant opposite, and Picasso
was more than ever as Gertrude Stein said the little bull-
fighter followed by his squadron of four, or as later in her
portrait of him, she called him, Napoleon followed by his
four enormous grenadiers. Derain and Braque were great big
men, so was Guillaume a heavy set man and Salmon was not
small. Picasso was every inch a chief.

This brings the story to Salmon and Guillaume Apollinaire,
although Gertrude Stein had known these two and Marie
Laurencin a considerable time before all this was happening.

Salmon and Guillaume Apollinaire both lived in Montmartre in these days. Salmon was very lithe and alive but
Gertrude Stein never found him particularly interesting. She
liked him. Guillaume Apollinaire on the contrary was very
wonderful. There was just about that time, that is about the
time when Gertrude Stein first knew Apollinaire, the excitement of a duel that he was to fight with another writer.
Fernande and Pablo told about it with so much excitement
and so much laughter and so much Montmartre slang, this
was in the early days of their acquaintance, that she was
always a little vague about just what did happen. But the
gist of the matter was that Guillaume challenged the other
man and Max Jacob was to be the second and witness for
Guillaume. Guillaume and his antagonist each sat in their
favourite café all day and waited while their seconds went
to and fro. How it all ended Gertrude Stein does not know
except that nobody fought, but the great excitement was the
bill each second and witness brought to his principal. In these
was itemised each time they had a cup of coffee and of course
they had to have a cup of coffee every time they sat down at

one or other café with one or other principal, and again when
the two seconds sat with each other. There was also the question under what circumstances were they under the absolute
necessity of having a glass of brandy with the cup of coffee.
And how often would they have had coffee if they had not
been seconds. All this led to endless meetings and endless
discussion and endless additional items. It lasted for days,
perhaps weeks and months and whether anybody finally was
paid, even the café keeper, nobody knows. It was notorious
that Apollinaire was parted with the very greatest difficulty
from even the smallest piece of money. It was all very absorbing.

Apollinaire was very attractive and very interesting. He
had a head like one of the late roman emperors. He had a
brother whom one heard about but never saw. He worked
in a bank and therefore he was reasonably well dressed.
When anybody in Montmartre had to go anywhere where
they had to be conventionally clothed, either to see a relation
or attend to a business matter, they always wore a piece of
a suit that belonged to the brother of Guillaume.

Guillaume was extraordinarily brilliant and no matter what
subject was started, if he knew anything about it or not, he
quickly saw the whole meaning of the thing and elaborated
it by his wit and fancy carrying it further than anybody
knowing anything about it could have done, and oddly
enough generally correctly.

Once, several years later, we were dining with the Picassos,
and in a conversation I got the best of Guillaume. I was very
proud, but, said Eve (Picasso was no longer with Fernande),
Guillaume was frightfully drunk or it would not have happened. It was only under such circumstances that anybody
could successfully turn a phrase against Guillaume. Poor
Guillaume. The last time we saw him was after he had come
back to Paris from the war. He had been badly wounded in
the head and had had a piece of his skull removed. He looked
very wonderful with his bleu horizon and his bandaged head.
He lunched with us and we all talked a long time together.
He was tired and his heavy head nodded. He was very serious
almost solemn. We went away shortly after, we were work-

ing with the American Fund for French Wounded, and never saw him again. Later Olga Picasso, the wife of Picasso, told us that the night of the armistice Guillaume Apollinaire died, that they were with him that whole evening and it was warm and the windows were open and the crowd passing were shouting, à bas Guillaume, down with William and as every one always called Guillaume Apollinaire Guillaume, even in his death agony it troubled him.

He had really been heroic. As a foreigner, his mother was a pole, his father possibly an italian, it was not at all necessary that he should volunteer to fight. He was a man of full habit, accustomed to a literary life and the delights of the table, and in spite of everything he volunteered. He went into the artillery first. Every one advised this as it was less dangerous and easier than the infantry, but after a while he could not bear this half protection and he changed into the infantry and was wounded in a charge. He was a long time in hospital, recovered a little, it was at this time that we saw him, and finally died on the day of the armistice.

The death of Guillaume Apollinaire at this time made a very serious difference to all his friends apart from their sorrow at his death. It was the moment just after the war when many things had changed and people naturally fell apart. Guillaume would have been a bond of union, he always had a quality of keeping people together, and now that he was gone everybody ceased to be friends. But all that was very much later and now to go back again to the beginning when Gertrude Stein first met Guillaume and Marie Laurencin.

Everybody called Gertrude Stein Gertrude, or at most Mademoiselle Gertrude, everybody called Picasso Pablo and Fernande Fernande and everybody called Guillaume Apollinaire Guillaume and Max Jacob Max but everybody called Marie Laurencin Marie Laurencin.

The first time Gertrude Stein ever saw Marie Laurencin, Guillaume Apollinaire brought her to the rue de Fleurus, not on a Saturday evening, but another evening. She was very interesting. They were an extraordinary pair. Marie Laurencin was terribly near-sighted and of course she never wore eye-glasses, no french woman and few frenchmen did in those days. She used a lorgnette.

She looked at each picture carefully that is, every picture on the line, bringing her eye close and moving over the whole of it with her lorgnette, an inch at a time. The pictures out of reach she ignored. Finally she remarked, as for myself, I prefer portraits and that is of course quite natural, as I myself am a Clouet. And it was perfectly true, she was a Clouet. She had the square thin build of the mediaeval french women in the french primitives. She spoke in a high pitched beautifully modulated voice. She sat down beside Gertrude Stein on the couch and she recounted the story of her life, told that her mother who had always had it in her nature to dislike men had been for many years the mistress of an important personage, had borne her, Marie Laurencin. I have never, she added, dared let her know Guillaume although of course he is so sweet that she could not refuse to like him but better not. Some day you will see her.

And later on Gertrude Stein saw the mother and by that time I was in Paris and I was taken along.

Marie Laurencin, leading her strange life and making her strange art, lived with her mother, who was a very quiet, very pleasant, very dignified woman, as if the two were living in a convent. The small apartment was filled with needlework which the mother had executed after the designs of Marie Laurencin. Marie and her mother acted toward each other exactly as a young nun with an older one. It was all very strange. Later just before the war the mother fell ill and died. Then the mother did see Guillaume Apollinaire and liked him.

After her mother's death Marie Laurencin lost all sense of stability. She and Guillaume no longer saw each other. A relation that had existed as long as the mother lived without the mother's knowledge now that the mother was dead and had seen and liked Guillaume could no longer endure. Marie against the advice of all her friends married a german. When her friends remonstrated with her she said, but he is the only one who can give me a feeling of my mother.

Six weeks after the marriage the war came and Marie had

to leave the country, having been married to a german. As she told me later when once during the war we met in Spain, naturally the officials could make no trouble for her, her passport made it clear that no one knew who her father was and they naturally were afraid because perhaps her father might be the president of the french republic.

During these war years Marie was very unhappy. She was intensely french and she was technically german. When you met her she would say, let me present to you my husband a boche, I do not remember his name. The official french world in Spain with whom she and her husband occasionally came in contact made things very unpleasant for her, constantly referring to Germany as her country. In the meanwhile Guillaume with whom she was in correspondence wrote her passionately patriotic letters. It was a miserable time for Marie Laurencin.

Finally Madame Groult, the sister of Poiret, coming to Spain, managed to help Marie out of her troubles. She finally divorced her husband and after the armistice returned to Paris, at home once more in the world. It was then that she came to the rue de Fleurus again, this time with Erik Satie. They were both Normans and so proud and happy about it.

In the early days Marie Laurencin painted a strange picture, portraits of Guillaume, Picasso, Fernande and herself. Fernande told Gertrude Stein about it. Gertrude Stein bought it and Marie Laurencin was so pleased. It was the first picture of hers any one had ever bought.

It was before Gertrude Stein knew the rue Ravignan that Guillaume Apollinaire had his first paid job, he edited a little pamphlet about physical culture. And it was for this that Picasso made his wonderful caricatures, including one of Guillaume as an exemplar of what physical culture could do.

And now once more to return to the return from all their travels and to Picasso becoming the head of a movement that was later to be known as the cubists. Who called it cubist first I do not know but very likely it was Apollinaire. At any rate he wrote the first little pamphlet about them all and illustrated it with their paintings.

I can so well remember the first time Gertrude Stein took

me to see Guillaume Apollinaire. It was a tiny bachelor's apartment on the rue des Martyrs. The room was crowded with a great many small young gentlemen. Who, I asked Fernande, are all these little men. They are poets, answered Fernande. I was overcome. I had never seen poets before, one poet yes but not poets. It was on that night too that Picasso, just a little drunk and to Fernande's great indignation persisted in sitting beside me and finding for me in a spanish album of photographs the exact spot where he was born. I came away with rather a vague idea of its situation.

Derain and Braque became followers of Picasso about six months after Picasso had, through Gertrude Stein and her brother, met Matisse. Matisse had in the meantime introduced Picasso to negro sculpture.

At that time negro sculpture had been well known to curio hunters but not to artists. Who first recognised its potential value for the modern artist I am sure I do not know. Perhaps it was Maillol who came from the Perpignan region and knew Matisse in the south and called his attention to it. There is a tradition that it was Derain. It was also very possible that it was Matisse himself because for many years there was a curio-dealer in the rue de Rennes who always had a great many things of this kind in his window and Matisse often went up the rue de Rennes to go to one of the sketch classes.

In any case it was Matisse who first was influenced, not so much in his painting but in his sculpture, by the african statues and it was Matisse who drew Picasso's attention to it just after Picasso had finished painting Gertrude Stein's portrait.

The effect of this african art upon Matisse and Picasso was entirely different. Matisse through it was affected more in his imagination than in his vision. Picasso more in his vision than in his imagination. Strangely enough it is only very much later in his life that this influence has affected his imagination and that may be through its having been re-enforced by the Orientalism of the russians when he came in contact with that through Diaghilev and the russian ballet.

In these early days when he created cubism the effect of

the african art was purely upon his vision and his forms, his imagination remained purely spanish. The spanish quality of ritual and abstraction had been indeed stimulated by his painting the portrait of Gertrude Stein. She had a definite impulse then and always toward elemental abstraction. She was not at any time interested in african sculpture. She always says that she liked it well enough but that it has nothing to do with europeans, that it lacks naïveté, that it is very ancient, very narrow, very sophisticated but lacks the elegance of the egyptian sculpture from which it is derived. She says that as an american she likes primitive things to be more savage.

Matisse and Picasso then being introduced to each other by Gertrude Stein and her brother became friends but they were enemies. Now they are neither friends nor enemies. At that time they were both.

They exchanged pictures as was the habit in those days. Each painter chose the one of the other one that presumably interested him the most. Matisse and Picasso chose each one of the other one the picture that was undoubtedly the least interesting either of them had done. Later each one used it as an example, the picture he had chosen, of the weaknesses of the other one. Very evidently in the two pictures chosen the strong qualities of each painter were not much in evidence.

The feeling between the Picassoites and the Matisseites became bitter. And this, you see, brings me to the independent where my friend and I sat without being aware of it under the two pictures which first publicly showed that Derain and Braque had become Picassoites and were definitely not Matisseites.

In the meantime naturally a great many things had happened.

Matisse showed in every autumn salon and every independent. He was beginning to have a considerable following. Picasso, on the contrary, never in all his life has shown in any salon. His pictures at that time could really only be seen at 27 rue de Fleurus. The first time as one might say that he had ever shown at a public show was when Derain and

Braque, completely influenced by his recent work, showed theirs. After that he too had many followers.

Matisse was irritated by the growing friendship between Picasso and Gertrude Stein. Mademoiselle Gertrude, he explained, likes local colour and theatrical values. It would be impossible for any one of her quality to have a serious friendship with any one like Picasso. Matisse still came frequently to the rue de Fleurus but there was no longer any frankness of intercourse between them all. It was about this time that Gertrude Stein and her brother gave a lunch for all the painters whose pictures were on the wall. Of course it did not include the dead or the old. It was at this lunch that as I have already said Gertrude Stein made them all happy and made the lunch a success by seating each painter facing his own picture. No one of them noticed it, they were just naturally pleased, until just as they were all leaving Matisse, standing up with his back to the door and looking into the room suddenly realised what had been done.

Matisse intimated that Gertrude Stein had lost interest in his work. She answered him, there is nothing within you that fights itself and hitherto you have had the instinct to produce antagonism in others which stimulated you to attack. But now they follow.

That was the end of the conversation but a beginning of an important part of The Making of Americans. Upon this idea Gertrude Stein based some of her most permanent distinctions in types of people.

It was about this time that Matisse began his teaching. He now moved from the Quai Saint-Michel, where he had lived ever since his marriage, to the boulevard des Invalides. In consequence of the separation of church and state which had just taken place in France the french government had become possessed of a great many convent schools and other church property. As many of these convents ceased to exist, there were at that time a great many of their buildings empty. Among others a very splendid one on the boulevard des Invalides.

These buildings were being rented at very low prices because no lease was given, as the government when it docided how to use them permanently would put the tenants out without warning. It was therefore an ideal place for artists as there were gardens and big rooms and they could put up with the inconveniences of housekeeping under the circumstances. So the Matisses moved in and Matisse instead of a small room to work in had an immense one and the two boys came home and they were all very happy. Then a number of those who had become his followers asked him if he would teach them if they organised a class for him in the same building in which he was then living. He consented and the Matisse atelier began.

The applicants were of all nationalities and Matisse was at first appalled at the number and variety of them. He told with much amusement as well as surprise that when he asked a very little woman in the front row, what in particular she had in mind in her painting, what she was seeking, she replied, Monsieur je cherche le neuf. He used to wonder how they all managed to learn french when he knew none of their languages. Some one got hold of some of these facts and made fun of the school in one of the french weeklies This hurt Matisse's feelings frightfully. The article said, and where did these people come from, and it was answered, from Massachusetts. Matisse was very unhappy.

But in spite of all this and also in spite of many dissensions the school flourished. There were difficulties. One of the hungarians wanted to earn his living posing for the class and in the intervals when some one else posed go on with his painting. There were a number of young women who protested, a nude model on a model stand was one thing but to have it turn into a fellow student was another. A hungarian was found eating the bread for rubbing out crayon drawings that the various students left on their painting boards and this evidence of extreme poverty and lack of hygiene had an awful effect upon the sensibilities of the americans. There were quite a number of americans. One of these americans under the plea of poverty was receiving his tuition for nothing and then was found to have purchased for himself a tiny Matisse and a tiny Picasso and a tiny Seurat. This was not only unfair, because many of the others wanted and could not afford to own a picture by the master and they were paying their tuition, but, since he also bought a Picasso, it was treason. And then every once in a while some one said something to Matisse in such bad french that it sounded like something very different from what it was and Matisse grew very angry and the unfortunate had to be taught how to apologise properly. All the students were working under such a state of tension that explosions were frequent. One would accuse another of undue influence with the master and then there were long and complicated scenes in which usually some one had to apologise. It was all very difficult since they themselves organised themselves.

Gertrude Stein enjoyed all these complications immensely. Matisse was a good gossip and so was she and at this time they delighted in telling tales to each other.

She began at that time always calling Matisse the C.M. or cher maître. She told him the favourite Western story, pray gentlemen, let there be no bloodshed. Matisse came not unfrequently to the rue de Fleurus. It was indeed at this time that Hélène prepared him the fried eggs instead of an omelet.

Three Lives had been typewritten and now the next thing was to show it to a publisher. Some one gave Gertrude Stein the name of an agent in New York and she tried that. Nothing came of it. Then she tried publishers directly. The only one at all interested was Bobbs-Merrill and they said they could not undertake it. This attempt to find a publisher lasted some time and then without being really discouraged she decided to have it printed. It was not an unnatural thought as people in Paris often did this. Some one told her about the Grafton Press in New York, a respectable firm that printed special historical things that people wanted to have printed. The arrangements were concluded, Three Lives was to be printed and the proofs to be sent.

One day some one knocked at the door and a very nice very american young man asked if he might speak to Miss Stein. She said, yes come in. He said, I have come at the request of the Grafton Press. Yes, she said. You see, he said slightly hesitant, the director of the Grafton Press is under the impression that perhaps your knowledge of english. But

I am an american, said Gertrude Stein indignantly. Yes yes I understand that perfectly now, he said, but perhaps you have not had much experience in writing. I suppose, said she laughing, you were under the impression that I was imperfectly educated. He blushed, why no, he said, but you might not have had much experience in writing. Oh yes, she said, oh yes. Well it's alright. I will write to the director and you might as well tell him also that everything that is written in the manuscript is written with the intention of its being so written and all he has to do is to print it and I will take the responsibility. The young man bowed himself out.

Later when the book was noticed by interested writers and newspaper men the director of the Grafton Press wrote Gertrude Stein a very simple letter in which he admitted he had been surprised at the notice the book had received but wished to add that now that he had seen the result he wished to say that he was very pleased that his firm had printed the book. But this last was after I came to Paris.

GERTRUDE STEIN BEFORE SHE
CAME TO PARIS

Once more I have come to Paris and now I am one of the habitués of the rue de Fleurus. Gertrude Stein was writing The Making of Americans and she had just commenced correcting the proofs of Three Lives. I helped her correct them.

Gertrude Stein was born in Allegheny, Pennsylvania. As I am an ardent californian and as she spent her youth there I have often begged her to be born in California but she has always remained firmly born in Allegheny, Pennsylvania. She left it when she was six months old and has never seen it again and now it now longer exists being all of it Pittsburgh. She used however to delight in being born in Allegheny, Pennsylvania when during the war, in connection with war work, we used to have papers made out and they always immediately wanted to know one's birth-place. She used to say if she had been really born in California as I wanted her to have been she would never have had the pleasure of seeing the various french officials try to write, Allegheny, Pennsylvania.

When I first knew Gertrude Stein in Paris I was surprised never to see a french book on her table, although there were always plenty of english ones, there were even no french newspapers. But do you never read french, I as well as many other people asked her. No, she replied, you see I feel with my eyes and it does not make any difference to me what language I hear. I don't hear a language, I hear tones of voice and rhythms, but with my eyes I see words and sentences and there is for me only one language and that is english. One of the things that I have liked all these years is to be surrounded by people who know no english. It has left me more intensely alone with my eyes and my english. I do not know if it would have been possible to have english be so all in all to me otherwise. And they none of them could read a word I wrote, most of them did not even know that I did write. No, I like living with so very many people and being all alone with english and myself.

One of her chapters in The Making of Americans begins: I write for myself and strangers.

She was born in Allegheny, Pennsylvania, of a very respectable middle class family. She always says that she is very grateful not to have been born of an intellectual family, she has a horror of what she calls intellectual people. It has always been rather ridiculous that she who is good friends with all the world and can know them and they can know her, has always been the admired of the precious. But she always says some day they, anybody, will find out that she is of interest to them, she and her writing. And she always consoles herself that the newspapers are always interested. They always say, she says, that my writing is appalling but they always quote it and what is more, they quote it correctly, and those they say they admire they do not quote. This at some of her most bitter moments has been a consolation. My sentences do get under their skin, only they do not know that they do, she has often said.

She was born in Allegheny, Pennsylvania, in a house, a twin house. Her family lived in one and her father's brother's family lived in the other one. These two families are the families described in The Making of Americans. They had lived in these houses for about eight years when Gertrude Stein was born. A year before her birth, the two sisters-in-law who had never gotten along any too well were no longer on speaking terms.

Gertrude Stein's mother as she describes her in The Making of Americans, a gentle pleasant little woman with a quick temper, flatly refused to see her sister-in-law again. I don't know quite what had happened but something. At any rate the two brothers who had been very successful business partners broke up their partnership, the one brother went to New York where he and all his family after him became very rich and the other brother, Gertrude Stein's family, went to Europe. They first went to Vienna and stayed there until Gertrude Stein was about three years old. All she remembers of this is that her brother's tutor once, when she was allowed to sit with her brothers at their lessons, described a tiger's snarl and that that pleased and terrified her. Also that in a picture-book that one of her brothers used to show her there was a story of the wanderings of Ulysses who when sitting sat on bent-wood dining room chairs. Also she remembers that they used to play in the public gardens and that often the old Kaiser Francis Joseph used to stroll through the gardens and sometimes a band played the austrian national hymn which she liked. She believed for many years that Kaiser was the real name of Francis Joseph and she never could come to accept the name as belonging to anybody else.

They lived in Vienna for three years, the father having in the meanwhile gone back to America on business and then they moved to Paris. Here Gertrude Stein has more lively memories. She remembers a little school where she and her elder sister stayed and where there was a little girl in the corner of the school yard and the other little girls told her not to go near her, she scratched. She also remembers the bowl of soup with french bread for breakfast and she also remembers that they had mutton and spinach for lunch and as she was very fond of spinach and not fond of mutton she used to trade mutton for spinach with the little girl opposite. She also remembers all of her three older brothers coming to see them at the school and coming on horse-back. She also remembers a black cat jumping from the ceiling of their house at Passy and scaring her mother and some unknown person rescuing her.

The family remained in Paris a year and then they came back to America. Gertrude Stein's elder brother charmingly describes the last days when he and his mother went shopping and bought everything that pleased their fancy, seal skin coats and caps and muffs for the whole family from the mother to the small sister Gertrude Stein, gloves dozens of gloves, wonderful hats, riding costumes, and finally ending up with a microscope and a whole set of the famous french history of zoology. Then they sailed for America.

This visit to Paris made a very great impression upon Gertrude Stein. When in the beginning of the war, she and I having been in England and there having been caught by the outbreak of the war and so not returning until October, were back in Paris, the first day we went out Gertrude Stein said, it is strange, Paris is so different but so familiar. And then reflectively, I see what it is, there is nobody here but the french (there were no soldiers or allies there yet), you can see the little children in their black aprons, you can see the streets because there is nobody on them, it is just like my memory of Paris when I was three years old. The pavements smell like they used (horses had come back into use), the smell of french streets and french public gardens that I remember so well.

They went back to America and in New York, the New York family tried to reconcile Gertrude Stein's mother to her sister-in-law but she was obdurate.

This story reminds me of Miss Etta Cone, a distant connection of Gertrude Stein, who typed Three Lives. When I first met her in Florence she confided to me that she could forgive but never forget. I added that as for myself I could forget but not forgive. Gertrude Stein's mother in this case was evidently unable to do either.

The family went west to California after a short stay in Baltimore at the home of her grandfather, the religious old man she describes in The Making of Americans, who lived in an old house in Baltimore with a large number of those cheerful pleasant little people, her uncles and her aunts.

Gertrude Stein has never ceased to be thankful to her mother for neither forgetting or forgiving. Imagine, she has said to me, if my mother had forgiven her sister-in-law and my father had gone into business with my uncle and we had lived and been brought up in New York, imagine, she says, how horrible. We would have been rich instead of being reasonably poor but imagine how horrible to have been brought up in New York.

I as a californian can very thoroughly sympathise.

And so they took the train to California. The only thing Gertrude Stein remembers of this trip was that she and her sister had beautiful big austrian red felt hats trimmed each with a beautiful ostrich feather and at some stage of the trip her sister leaning out of the window had her hat blown off. Her father rang the emergency bell, stopped the train, got the hat to the awe and astonishment of the passengers and the conductor. The only other thing she remembers is that they had a wonderful hamper of food given them by the aunts in Baltimore and that in it was a marvellous turkey. And that later as the food in it diminished it was renewed all along the road whenever they stopped and that that was always exciting. And also that somewhere in the desert they saw some red indians and that somewhere else in the desert they were given some very funny tasting peaches to eat.

When they arrived in California they went to an orange grove but she does not remember any oranges but remembers filling up her father's cigar boxes with little limes which were very wonderful.

They came by slow stages to San Francisco and settled down in Oakland. She remembers there the eucalyptus trees seeming to her so tall and thin and savage and the animal life very wild. But all this and much more, all the physical life of these days, she has described in the life of the Hersland family in her Making of Americans. The important thing to tell about now is her education.

Her father having taken his children to Europe so that they might have the benefit of a european education now insisted that they should forget their french and german so that their american english would be pure. Gertrude Stein had prattled in german and then in french but she had never read until she read english. As she says eyes to her were more important than ears and it happened then as always that english was her only language.

Her bookish life commenced at this time. She read any-

thing that was printed that came her way and a great deal
came her way. In the house were a few stray novels, a few
travel books, her mother's well bound gift books Wordsworth
Scott and other poets, Bunyan's Pilgrim's Progress a set of
Shakespeare with notes, Burns, Congressional Records en-
cyclopedias etcetera. She read them all and many times. She
and her brothers began to acquire other books. There was
also the local free library and later in San Francisco there
were the mercantile and mechanics libraries with their excellent sets of eighteenth century and nineteenth century
authors. From her eighth year when she absorbed Shakespeare to her fifteenth year when she read Clarissa Harlowe,
Fielding, Smollett etcetera and used to worry lest in a few
years more she would have read everything and there would
be nothing unread to read, she lived continuously with the
english language. She read a tremendous amount of history,
she often laughs and says she is one of the few people of
her generation that has read every line of Carlyle's Frederick
the Great and Lecky's Constitutional History of England
besides Charles Grandison and Wordsworth's longer poems.
In fact she was as she still is always reading. She reads anything and everything and even now hates to be disturbed
and above all however often she has read a book and however foolish the book may be no one must make fun of it or
tell her how it goes on. It is still as it always was real to her.

The theatre she has always cared for less. She says it goes
too fast, the mixture of eye and ear bothers her and her
emotion never keeps pace. Music she only cared for during
her adolescence. She finds it difficult to listen to it, it does
not hold her attention. All of which of course may seem
strange because it has been so often said that the appeal of
her work is to the ear and to the subconscious. Actually it
is her eyes and mind that are active and important and concerned in choosing.

Life in California came to its end when Gertrude Stein
was about seventeen years old. The last few years had been
lonesome ones and had been passed in an agony of adolescence. After the death of first her mother and then her father
she and her sister and one brother left California for the

East. They came to Baltimore and stayed with her mother's people. There she began to lose her lonesomeness. She has often described to me how strange it was to her coming from the rather desperate inner life that she had been living for the last few years to the cheerful life of all her aunts and uncles. When later she went to Radcliffe she described this experience in the first thing she ever wrote. Not quite the first thing she ever wrote. She remembers having written twice before. Once when she was about eight and she tried to write a Shakespearean drama in which she got as far as a stage direction, the courtiers making witty remarks. And then as she could not think of any witty remarks gave it up.

The only other effort she can remember must have been at about the same age. They asked the children in the public schools to write a description. Her recollection is that she described a sunset with the sun going into a cave of clouds. Anyway it was one of the half dozen in the school chosen to be copied out on beautiful parchment paper. After she had tried to copy it twice and the writing became worse and worse she was reduced to letting some one else copy it for her. This, her teacher considered a disgrace. She does not remember that she herself did.

As a matter of fact her handwriting has always been illegible and I am very often able to read it when she is not. She has never been able or had any desire to indulge in any of the arts. She never knows how a thing is going to look until it is done, in arranging a room, a garden, clothes or anything else. She cannot draw anything. She feels no relation between the object and the piece of paper. When at the medical school, she was supposed to draw anatomical things she never found out in sketching how a thing was made concave or convex. She remembers when she was very small she was to learn to draw and was sent to a class. The children were told to take a cup and saucer at home and draw them and the best drawing would have as its reward a stamped leather medal and the next week the same medal would again be given for the best drawing. Gertrude Stein went home, told her brothers and they put a pretty cup and saucer before her and each one explained to her how to draw it. Nothing happened. Finally one of them drew it for her. She took it to the class and won the leather medal. And on the way home in playing some game she lost the leather medal. That was the end of the drawing class.

She says it is a good thing to have no sense of how it is done in the things that amuse you. You should have one absorbing occupation and as for the other things in life for full enjoyment you should only contemplate results. In this way you are bound to feel more about it than those who know a little of how it is done.

She is passionately addicted to what the french call métier and she contends that one can only have one métier as one can only have one language. Her métier is writing and her language is english.

Observation and construction make imagination, that is granting the possession of imagination, is what she has taught many young writers. Once when Hemingway wrote in one of his stories that Gertrude Stein always knew what was good in a Cézanne, she looked at him and said, Hemingway, remarks are not literature.

The young often when they have learnt all they can learn accuse her of an inordinate pride. She says yes of course. She realises that in english literature in her time she is the only one. She has always known it and now she says it.

She understands very well the basis of creation and therefore her advice and criticism is invaluable to all her friends. How often have I heard Picasso say to her when she has said something about a picture of his and then illustrated by something she was trying to do, racontez-moi cela. In other words tell me about it. These two even to-day have long solitary conversations. They sit in two little low chairs up in his apartment studio, knee to knee and Picasso says, expliquez-moi cela. And they explain to each other. They talk about everything, about pictures, about dogs, about death, about unhappiness. Because Picasso is a spaniard and life is tragic and bitter and unhappy. Gertrude Stein often comes down to me and says, Pablo has been persuading me that I am as unhappy as he is. He insists that I am and with as much cause. But are you, I ask. Well I don't think I look it, do I, and she laughs. He says, she says, that I don't look it because I have more courage, but I don't think I am, she says, no I don't think I am.

And so Gertrude Stein having been in Baltimore for a winter and having become more humanised and less adolescent and less lonesome went to Radcliffe. There she had a very good time.

She was one of a group of Harvard men and Radcliffe women and they all lived very closely and very interestingly together. One of them, a young philosopher and mathematician who was doing research work in psychology left a definite mark on her life. She and he together worked out a series of experiments in automatic writing under the direction of Münsterberg. The result of her own experiments, which Gertrude Stein wrote down and which was printed in the Harvard Psychological Review was the first writing of hers ever to be printed. It is very interesting to read because the method of writing to be afterwards developed in Three Lives and Making of Americans already shows itself.

The important person in Gertrude Stein's Radcliffe life was William James. She enjoyed her life and herself. She was the secretary of the philosophical club and amused herself with all sorts of people. She liked making sport of question asking and she liked equally answering them. She liked it all. But the really lasting impression of her Radcliffe life came through William James.

It is rather strange that she was not then at all interested in the work of Henry James for whom she now has a very great admiration and whom she considers quite definitely as her forerunner, he being the only nineteenth century writer who being an american felt the method of the twentieth century. Gertrude Stein always speaks of America as being now the oldest country in the world because by the methods of the civil war and the commercial conceptions that followed it America created the twentieth century, and since all the other countries are now either living or commencing to be living a twentieth century life, America having begun the creation of the twentieth century in the sixties of the nineteenth century is now the oldest country in the world.

In the same way she contends that Henry James was the first person in literature to find the way to the literary methods of the twentieth century. But oddly enough in all of her formative period she did not read him and was not interested in him. But as she often says one is always naturally antagonistic to one's parents and sympathetic to one's grandparents. The parents are too close, they hamper you, one must be alone. So perhaps that is the reason why only very lately Gertrude Stein reads Henry James.

William James delighted her. His personality and his teaching and his way of amusing himself with himself and his students all pleased her. Keep your mind open, he used to say, and when some one objected, but Professor James, this that I say, is true. Yes, said James, it is abjectly true.

Gertrude Stein never had subconscious reactions, nor was she a successful subject for automatic writing. One of the students in the psychological seminar of which Gertrude Stein, although an undergraduate was at William James' particular request a member, was carrying on a series of experiments on suggestions to the subconscious. When he read his paper upon the result of his experiments, he began by explaining that one of the subjects gave absolutely no results and as this much lowered the average and made the conclusion of his experiments false he wished to be allowed to cut this record out. Whose record is it, said James. Miss Stein's, said the student. Ah, said James, if Miss Stein gave no response I should say that it was as normal not to give a response as to give one and decidedly the result must not be cut out.

It was a very lovely spring day, Gertrude Stein had been going to the opera every night and going also to the opera in the afternoon and had been otherwise engrossed and it was the period of the final examinations, and there was the examination in William James' course. She sat down with the examination paper before her and she just could not. Dear Professor James, she wrote at the top of her paper. I am so sorry but really I do not feel a bit like an examination paper in philosophy to-day, and left.

The next day she had a postal card from William James

saying, Dear Miss Stein, I understand perfectly how you feel I often feel like that myself. And underneath it he gave her work the highest mark in his course.

When Gertrude Stein was finishing her last year at Radcliffe, William James one day asked her what she was going to do. She said she had no idea. Well, he said, it should be either philosophy or psychology. Now for philosophy you have to have higher mathematics and I don't gather that that has ever interested you. Now for psychology you must have a medical education, a medical education opens all doors, as Oliver Wendell Holmes told me and as I tell you. Gertrude Stein had been interested in both biology and chemistry and so medical school presented no difficulties.

There were no difficulties except that Gertrude Stein had never passed more than half of her entrance examinations for Radcliffe, having never intended to take a degree. However with considerable struggle and enough tutoring that was accomplished and Gertrude Stein entered Johns Hopkins Medical School.

Some years after when Gertrude Stein and her brother were just beginning knowing Matisse and Picasso, William James came to Paris and they met. She went to see him at his hotel. He was enormously interested in what she was doing, interested in her writing and in the pictures she told him about. He went with her to her house to see them. He looked and gasped. I told you, he said, I always told you that you should keep your mind open.

Only about two years ago a very strange thing happened. Gertrude Stein received a letter from a man in Boston. It was evident from the letter head that he was one of a firm of lawyers. He said in his letter that he had not long ago in reading in the Harvard library found that the library of William James had been given as a gift to the Harvard library. Among these books was the copy of Three Lives that Gertrude Stein had dedicated and sent to James. Also on the margins of the book were notes that William James had evidently made when reading the book. The man then went on to say that very likely Gertrude Stein would be very interested in these notes and he proposed, if she wished, to copy them out for her as he had appropriated the book, in other words taken it and considered it as his. We were very puzzled what to do about it. Finally a note was written saying that Gertrude Stein would like to have a copy of William James' notes. In answer came a manuscript the man himself had written and of which he wished Gertrude Stein to give him an opinion. Not knowing what to do about it all, Gertrude Stein did nothing.

After having passed her entrance examinations she settled down in Baltimore and went to the medical school. She had a servant named Lena and it is her story that Gertrude Stein afterwards wrote as the first story of the Three Lives.

The first two years of the medical school were alright. They were purely laboratory work and Gertrude Stein under Llewelys Barker immediately betook herself to research work. She began a study of all the brain tracts, the beginning of a comparative study. All this was later embodied in Llewelys Barker's book. She delighted in Doctor Mall, professor of anatomy, who directed her work. She always quotes his answer to any student excusing himself or herself for anything. He would look reflective and say, yes that is just like our cook. There is always a reason. She never brings the food to the table hot. In summer of course she can't because it is too hot, in winter of course she can't because it is too cold, yes there is always a reason. Doctor Mall believed in everybody developing their own technique. He also remarked, nobody teaches anybody anything, at first every student's scalpel is dull and then later every student's scalpel is sharp, and nobody has taught anybody anything.

These first two years at the medical school Gertrude Stein liked well enough. She always liked knowing a lot of people and being mixed up in a lot of stories and she was not awfully interested but she was not too bored with what she was doing and besides she had quantities of pleasant relatives in Baltimore and she liked it. The last two years at the medical school she was bored, frankly openly bored. There was a good deal of intrigue and struggle among the students, that she liked, but the practice and theory of medicine did not interest her at all. It was fairly well known among all her teachers that she was bored, but as her first two years of scientific work had given her a reputation, everybody gave her the necessary credits and the end of her last year was approaching. It was then that she had to take her turn in the delivering of babies and it was at that time that she noticed the negroes and the places that she afterwards used in the second of Three Lives stories, Melanctha Herbert, the story that was the beginning of her revolutionary work.

As she always says of herself, she has a great deal of inertia and once started keeps going until she starts somewhere else.

As the graduation examinations drew near some of her professors were getting angry. The big men like Halstead, Osler etcetera knowing her reputation for original scientific work made the medical examinations merely a matter of form and passed her. But there were others who were not so amiable. Gertrude Stein always laughed, and this was difficult. They would ask her questions although as she said to her friends, it was foolish of them to ask her, when there were so many eager and anxious to answer. However they did question her from time to time and as she said, what could she do, she did not know the answers and they did not believe that she did not know them, they thought that she did not answer because she did not consider the professors worth answering. It was a difficult situation, as she said, it was impossible to apologise and explain to them that she was so bored she could not remember the things that of course the dullest medical student could not forget. One of the professors said that although all the big men were ready to pass her he intended that she should be given a lesson and he refused to give her a pass mark and so she was not able to take her degree. There was great excitement in the medical school. Her very close friend Marion Walker pleaded with her, she said, but Gertrude Gertrude remember the cause of women, and Gertrude Stein said, you don't know what it is to be bored.

The professor who had flunked her asked her to come to see him. She did. He said, of course Miss Stein all you have to do is to take a summer course here and in the fall naturally you will take your degree. But not at all, said Gertrude Stein, you have no idea how grateful I am to you. I have so much inertia and so little initiative that very possibly if you had not kept me from taking my degree I would have, well, not taken to the practice of medicine, but at any rate to pathological psychology and you don't know how little I like pathological psychology, and how all medicine bores me. The professor was completely taken aback and that was the end of the medical education of Gertrude Stein.

She always says she dislikes the abnormal, it is so obvious. She says the normal is so much more simply complicated and interesting.

It was only a few years ago that Marion Walker, Gertrude Stein's old friend, came to see her at Bilignin where we spend the summer. She and Gertrude Stein had not met since those old days nor had they corresponded but they were as fond of each other and disagreed as violently about the cause of women as they did then. Not, as Gertrude Stein explained to Marion Walker, that she at all minds the cause of women or any other cause but it does not happen to be her business.

During these years at Radcliffe and Johns Hopkins she often spent the summers in Europe. The last couple of years her brother had been settled in Florence and now that everything medical was over she joined him there and later they settled down in London for the winter.

They settled in lodgings in London and were not uncomfortable. They knew a number of people through the Berensons, Bertrand Russell, the Zangwills, then there was Willard (Josiah Flynt) who wrote Tramping With Tramps, and who knew all about London pubs, but Gertrude Stein was not very much amused. She began spending all her time in the British Museum reading the Elizabethans. She returned to her early love of Shakespeare and the Elizabethans, and became absorbed in Elizabethan prose and particularly in the prose of Greene. She had little note-books full of phrases that pleased her as they had pleased her when she was a child. The rest of the time she wandered about the London streets and found them infinitely depressing and dismal. She never really got over this memory of London and never wanted to go back there, but in nineteen hundred and twelve she went over to see John Lane, the publisher and then living a very pleasant life and visiting very gay and pleasant people she forgot the old memory and became very fond of London.

She always said that that first visit had made London just like Dickens and Dickens had always frightened her. As she says anything can frighten her and London when it was like Dickens certainly did.

There were some compensations, there was the prose of Greene and it was at this time that she discovered the novels of Anthony Trollope, for her the greatest of the Victorians. She then got together the complete collection of his work some of it difficult to get and only obtainable in Tauchnitz and it is of this collection that Robert Coates speaks when he tells about Gertrude Stein lending books to young writers. She also bought a quantity of eighteenth century memoirs among them the Creevy papers and Walpole and it is these that she loaned to Bravig Imbs when he wrote what she believes to be an admirable life of Chatterton. She reads books but she is not fussy about them, she cares about neither editions nor make-up as long as the print is not too bad and she is not even very much bothered about that. It was at this time too that, as she says, she ceased to be worried about there being in the future nothing to read, she said she felt that she would always somehow be able to find something.

But the dismalness of London and the drunken women and children and the gloom and the lonesomeness brought back all the melancholy of her adolescence and one day she said she was leaving for America and she left. She stayed in America the rest of the winter. In the meantime her brother also had left London and gone to Paris and there later she joined him. She immediately began to write. She wrote a short novel.

The funny thing about this short novel is that she completely forgot about it for many years. She remembered herself beginning a little later writing the Three Lives but this first piece of writing was completely forgotten, she had never mentioned it to me, even when I first knew her. She must have forgotten about it almost immediately. This spring just two days before our leaving for the country she was looking for some manuscript of The Making of Americans that she wanted to show Bernard Faÿ and she came across these two carefully written volumes of this completely forgotten first novel. She was very bashful and hesitant about it, did not really want to read it. Louis Bromfield was at the house that evening and she handed him the manuscript and said to him, you read it.

5

1907-1914

And so life in Paris began and as all roads lead to Paris, all of us are now there, and I can begin to tell what happened when I was of it.

When I first came to Paris a friend and myself stayed in a little hotel in the boulevard Saint-Michel, then we took a small apartment in the rue Notre-Dame-des-Champs and then my friend went back to California and I joined Gertrude Stein in the rue de Fleurus.

I had been at the rue de Fleurus every Saturday evening and I was there a great deal beside. I helped Gertrude Stein with the proofs of Three Lives and then I began to typewrite The Making of Americans. The little badly made french portable was not strong enough to type this big book and so we bought a large and imposing Smith Premier which at first looked very much out of place in the atelier but soon we were all used to it and it remained until I had an american portable, in short until after the war.

As I said Fernande was the first wife of a genius I was to sit with. The geniuses came and talked to Gertrude Stein and the wives sat with me. How they unroll, an endless vista through the years. I began with Fernande and then there were Madame Matisse and Marcelle Braque and Josette Gris and Eve Picasso and Bridget Gibb and Marjory Gibb and Hadley and Pauline Hemingway and Mrs. Sherwood Anderson and Mrs. Bravig Imbs and the Mrs. Ford Madox Ford and endless others, geniuses, near geniuses and might be geniuses, all having wives, and I have sat and talked with them all all the wives and later on, well later on too, I have sat and talked with all. But I began with Fernande.

I went too to the Casa Ricci in Fiesole with Gertrude Stein and her brother. How well I remember the first summer I stayed with them. We did charming things. Gertrude Stein and I took a Fiesole cab, I think it was the only one and drove in this old cab all the way to Siena. Gertrude Stein had once walked it with a friend but in those hot italian days I preferred a cab. It was a charming trip. Then another time we went to Rome and we brought back a beautiful black renaissance plate. Maddalena, the old italian cook, came up to Gertrude Stein's bedroom one morning to bring the water for her bath. Gertrude Stein had the hiccoughs. But cannot the signora stop it, said Maddalena anxiously. No, said Gertrude Stein between hiccoughs. Maddalena shaking her head sadly went away. In a minute there was an awful crash. Up flew Maddalena, oh signora, signora, she said, I was so upset because the signora had the hiccoughs that I broke the black plate that the signora so carefully brought from Rome. Gertrude Stein began to swear, she has a reprehensible habit of swearing whenever anything unexpected happens and she always tells me she learned it in her youth in California, and as I am a loyal californian I can then say nothing. She swore and the hiccoughs ceased. Maddalena's face was wreathed in smiles. Ah the signora, she said, she has stopped hiccoughing. Oh no I did not break the beautiful plate, I just made the noise of it and then said I did it to make the signora stop hiccoughing.

Gertrude Stein is awfully patient over the breaking of even her most cherished objects, it is I, I am sorry to say who usually break them. Neither she nor the servant nor the dog do, but then the servant never touches them, it is I who dust them and alas sometimes accidentally break them. I always beg her to promise to let me have them mended by an expert before I tell her which it is that is broken, she always replies she gets no pleasure out of them if they are mended but alright have it mended and it is mended and it gets put away. She loves objects that are breakable, cheap objects and valuable objects, a chicken out of a grocery shop or a pigeon out of a fair, one just broke this morning, this time it was not I who did it, she loves them all and she remembers them all but she knows that sooner or later they will break and she says that like books there are always more to find. However to me this is no consolation. She says she likes what she has and she likes the adventure of a new one. That is what she always says about young painters, about anything, once everybody knows they are good the adventure is over. And adds Picasso with a sigh, even after everybody knows they are good not any more people really like them than they did when only the few knew they were good.

I did have to take one hot walk that summer. Gertrude Stein insisted that no one could go to Assisi except on foot. She has three favourite saints, Saint Ignatius Loyola, Saint Theresa of Avila and Saint Francis. I alas have only one favourite saint, Saint Anthony of Padua because it is he who finds lost objects and as Gertrude Stein's elder brother once said of me, if I were a general I would never lose a battle, I would only mislay it. Saint Anthony helps me find it. I always put a considerable sum in his box in every church I visit. At first Gertrude Stein objected to this extravagance but now she realises its necessity and if I am not with her she remembers Saint Anthony for me.

It was a very hot italian day and we started as usual about noon, that being Gertrude Stein's favourite walking hour, because it was hottest and beside presumably Saint Francis had walked it then the oftenest as he had walked it at all hours. We started from Perugia across the hot valley. I gradually undressed, in those days one wore many more clothes than one does now, I even, which was most unconventional in those days, took off my stockings, but even so I dropped a few tears before we arrived and we did arrive. Gertrude Stein was very fond of Assisi for two reasons, because of Saint Francis and the beauty of his city and because the old women used to lead instead of a goat a little pig up and down the hills of Assisi. The little black pig was always decorated with a red ribbon. Gertrude Stein had always liked little pigs and she always said that in her old age she expected to wander up and down the hills of Assisi with a little black pig. She now wanders about the hills of the Ain with a large white dog and a small black one, so I suppose that does as well.

She was always fond of pigs, and because of this Picasso made and gave her some charming drawings of the prodigal son among the pigs. And one delightful study of pigs all by themselves. It was about this time too that he made for her the tiniest of ceiling decorations on a tiny wooden panel and it was an hommage à Gertrude with women and angels bringing fruits and trumpeting. For years she had this tacked to the ceiling over her bed. It was only after the war that it was put upon the wall.

But to return to the beginning of my life in Paris. It was based upon the rue de Fleurus and the Saturday evenings and it was like a kaleidoscope slowly turning.

What happened in those early years. A great deal happened.

As I said when I became an habitual visitor at the rue de Fleurus the Picassos were once more together, Pablo and Fernande. That summer they went again to Spain and he came back with some spanish landscapes and one may say that these landscapes, two of them still at the rue de Fleurus and the other one in Moscow in the collection that Stchoukine founded and that is now national property, were the beginning of cubism. In these there was no african sculpture influence. There was very evidently a strong Cézanne influence, particularly the influence of the late Cézanne water colours, the cutting up the sky not in cubes but in spaces.

But the essential thing, the treatment of the houses was essentially spanish and therefore essentially Picasso. In these pictures he first emphasised the way of building in spanish villages, the line of the houses not following the landscape but cutting across and into the landscape, becoming undistinguishable in the landscape by cutting across the landscape. It was the principle of the camouflage of the guns and the ships in the war. The first year of the war, Picasso and Eve, with whom he was living then, Gertrude Stein and myself, were walking down the boulevard Raspail a cold winter evening. There is nothing in the world colder than the Raspail on a cold winter evening, we used to call it the retreat from Moscow. All of a sudden down the street came some big cannon, the first any of us had seen painted, that is camouflaged. Pablo stopped, he was spell-bound. C'est nous qui avons fait ça, he said, it is we that have created that, he said. And he was right, he had. From Cézanne through him they had come to that. His foresight was justified.

But to go back to the three landscapes. When they were first put up on the wall naturally everybody objected. As it happened he and Fernande had taken some photographs of the villages which he had painted and he had given copies of these photographs to Gertrude Stein. When people said that the few cubes in the landscapes looked like nothing but cubes, Gertrude Stein would laugh and say, if you had objected to these landscapes as being too realistic there would be some point in your objection. And she would show them the photographs and really the pictures as she rightly said might be declared to be too photographic a copy of nature. Years after Elliot Paul at Gertrude Stein's suggestion had a photograph of the painting by Picasso and the photographs of the village reproduced on the same page in transition and it was extraordinarily interesting. This then was really the beginning of cubism. The colour too was characteristically spanish, the pale silver yellow with the faintest suggestion of green, the colour afterwards so well known in Picasso's cubist pictures, as well as in those of his followers.

Gertrude Stein always says that cubism is a purely spanish conception and only spaniards can be cubists and that the only real cubism is that of Picasso and Juan Gris. Picasso created it and Juan Gris permeated it with his clarity and his exaltation. To understand this one has only to read the life and death of Juan Gris by Gertrude Stein, written upon the death of one of her two dearest friends, Picasso and Juan Gris, both spaniards.

She always says that americans can understand spaniards. That they are the only two western nations that can realise abstraction. That in americans it expresses itself by disembodiedness, in literature and machinery, in Spain by ritual so abstract that it does not connect itself with anything but ritual.

I always remember Picasso saying disgustedly apropos of some germans who said they liked bull-fights, they would, he said angrily, they like bloodshed. To a spaniard it is not bloodshed, it is ritual.

Americans, so Gertrude Stein says, are like spaniards, they are abstract and cruel. They are not brutal they are cruel. They have no close contact with the earth such as most europeans have. Their materialism is not the materialism of existence, of possession, it is the materialism of action and abstraction. And so cubism is spanish.

We were very much struck, the first time Gertrude Stein and I went to Spain, which was a year or so after the beginning of cubism, to see how naturally cubism was made in Spain. In the shops in Barcelona instead of post cards they had square little frames and inside it was placed a cigar, a real one, a pipe, a bit of handkerchief etcetera, all absolutely the arrangement of many a cubist picture and helped out by cut paper representing other objects. That is the modern note that in Spain had been done for centuries.

Picasso in his early cubist pictures used printed letters as did Juan Gris to force the painted surface to measure up to something rigid, and the rigid thing was the printed letter. Gradually instead of using the printed thing they painted the letters and all was lost, it was only Juan Gris who could paint with such intensity a printed letter that it still made the rigid contrast. And so cubism came little by little but it came.

It was in these days that the intimacy between Braque and Picasso grew. It was in these days that Juan Gris, a raw rather effusive youth came from Madrid to Paris and began to call Picasso cher maître to Picasso's great annoyance. It was apropos of this that Picasso used to address Braque as cher maître, passing on the joke, and I am sorry to say that some foolish people have taken this joke to mean that Picasso looked up to Braque as a master.

But I am once more running far ahead of those early Paris days when I first knew Fernande and Pablo.

In those days then only the three landscapes had been painted and he was beginning to paint some heads that seemed cut out in planes, also long loaves of bread.

At this time Matisse, the school still going on, was really beginning to be fairly well known, so much so that to everybody's great excitement Bernheim jeune, a very middle class firm indeed, was offering him a contract to take all his work at a very good price. It was an exciting moment.

This was happening because of the influence of a man named Fénéon. Il est très fin, said Matisse, much impressed by Fénéon. Fénéon was a journalist, a french journalist who had invented the thing called a feuilleton en deux lignes, that is to say he was the first one to hit off the news of the day in two lines. He looked like a caricature of Uncle Sam made french and he had been painted standing in front of a curtain in a circus picture by Toulouse-Lautrec.

And now the Bernheims, how or wherefor I do not know, taking Fénéon into their employ, were going to connect themselves with the new generation of painters.

Something happened, at any rate this contract did not last long, but for all that it changed the fortunes of Matisse. He now had an established position. He bought a house and some land in Clamart and he started to move out there. Let me describe the house as I saw it.

This home in Clamart was very comfortable, to be sure the bath-room, which the family much appreciated from long contact with americans, although it must be said that the Matisses had always been and always were scrupulously neat and clean, was on the ground floor adjoining the dining room. But that was alright, and is and was a french custom, in french houses. It gave more privacy to a bath-room to have it on the ground floor. Not so long ago in going over the new house Braque was building the bath-room was again below, this time underneath the dining room. When we said, but why, they said because being nearer the furnace it would be warmer.

The grounds at Clamart were large and the garden was

what Matisse between pride and chagrin called un petit
Luxembourg. There was also a glass forcing house for flowers.
Later they had begonias in them that grew smaller and
smaller. Beyond were lilacs and still beyond a big demount-
able studio. They liked it enormously. Madame Matisse with
simple recklessness went out every day to look at it and pick
flowers, keeping a cab waiting for her. In those days only
millionaires kept cabs waiting and then only very occasionally.

They moved out and were very comfortable and soon the
enormous studio was filled with enormous statues and enormous pictures. It was that period of Matisse. Equally soon he
found Clamart so beautiful that he could not go home to it,
that is when he came into Paris to his hour of sketching from
the nude, a thing he had done every afternoon of his life ever
since the beginning of things, and he came in every afternoon.
His school no longer existed, the government had taken over
the old convent to make a Lycée of it and the school had
come to an end.

These were the beginning of very prosperous days for the
Matisses. They went to Algeria and they went to Tangiers
and their devoted german pupils gave them Rhine wines and
a very fine black police dog, the first of the breed that any of
us had seen.

And then Matisse had a great show of his pictures in Berlin.
I remember so well one spring day, it was a lovely day and
we were to lunch at Clamart with the Matisses. When we
got there they were all standing around an enormous packing
case with its top off. We went up and joined them and there
in the packing case was the largest laurel wreath that had
ever been made, tied with a beautiful red ribbon. Matisse
showed Gertrude Stein a card that had been in it. It said on
it, To Henri Matisse, Triumphant on the Battlefield of Berlin,
and was signed Thomas Whittemore. Thomas Whittemore was
a bostonian archeologist and professor at Tufts College, a great
admirer of Matisse and this was his tribute. Said Matisse,
still more rueful, but I am not dead yet. Madame Matisse,
the shock once over said, but Henri look, and leaning down
she plucked a leaf and tasted it, it is real laurel, think how

good it will be in soup. And, said she still further brightening, the ribbon will do wonderfully for a long time as hair ribbon for Margot.

The Matisses stayed in Clamart more or less until the war. During this period they and Gertrude Stein were seeing less and less of each other. Then after the war broke out they came to the house a good deal. They were lonesome and troubled, Matisse's family in Saint-Quentin, in the north, were within the german lines and his brother was a hostage. It was Madame Matisse who taught me how to knit woollen gloves. She made them wonderfully neatly and rapidly and I learned to do so too. Then Matisse went to live in Nice and in one way and another, although remaining perfectly good friends, Gertrude Stein and the Matisses never see each other.

The Saturday evenings in those early days were frequented by many hungarians, quite a number of germans, quite a few mixed nationalities, a very thin sprinkling of americans and practically no english. These were to commence later, and with them came aristocracy of all countries and even some royalty.

Among the germans who used to come in those early days was Pascin. He was at that time a thin brilliant-looking creature, he already had a considerable reputation as maker of neat little caricatures in Simplicissimus, the most lively of the german comic papers. The other germans told strange stories of him. That he had been brought up in a house of prostitution of unknown and probably royal birth, etcetera.

He and Gertrude Stein had not met since those early days but a few years ago they saw each other at the vernissage of a young dutch painter Kristians Tonny who had been a pupil of Pascin and in whose work Gertrude Stein was then interested. They liked meeting each other and had a long talk.

Pascin was far away the most amusing of the germans although I cannot quite say that because there was Uhde.

Uhde was undoubtedly well born, he was not a blond german, he was a tallish thin dark man with a high forehead and an excellent quick wit. When he first came to Paris he went to every antiquity shop and bric-à-brac shop in the town in order to see what he could find. He did not find much, he found what purported to be an Ingres, he found a few very early Picassos, but perhaps he found other things. At any rate when the war broke out he was supposed to have been one of the super spies and to have belonged to the german staff.

He was said to have been seen near the french war office after the declaration of war, undoubtedly he and a friend had a summer home very near what was afterward the Hindenburg line. Well at any rate he was very pleasant and very amusing. He it was who was the first to commercialise the douanier Rousseau's pictures. He kept a kind of private art shop. It was here that Braque and Picasso went to see him in their newest and roughest clothes and in their best Cirque Médrano fashion kept up a constant fire of introducing each other to him and asking each other to introduce each other.

Uhde used often to come Saturday evening accompanied by very tall blond good-looking young men who clicked their heels and bowed and then all evening stood solemnly at attention. They made a very effective background to the rest of the crowd. I remember one evening when the son of the great scholar Bréal and his very amusing clever wife brought a spanish guitarist who wanted to come and play. Uhde and his bodyguard were the background and it came on to be a lively evening, the guitarist played and Manolo was there. It was the only time I ever saw Manolo the sculptor, by that time a legendary figure in Paris. Picasso very lively undertook to dance a southern spanish dance not too respectable, Gertrude Stein's brother did the dying dance of Isadora, it was very lively, Fernande and Pablo got into a discussion about Frédéric of the Lapin Agile and apaches. Fernande contended that the apaches were better than the artists and her forefinger went up in the air. Picasso said, yes apaches of course have their universities, artists do not. Fernande got angry and shook him and said, you are witty, but you are only stupid. He ruefully showed that she had shaken off a button and she very angry said, and you, your only claim to distinction is that you are a precocious child. Things were not in those days going any too well between them, it was just about the time that they were quitting the rue Ravignan to live in an apartment in the boulevard Clichy, where they were to have a servant and to be prosperous.

But to return to Uhde and first to Manolo. Manolo was perhaps Picasso's oldest friend. He was a strange spaniard. He, so the legend said, was the brother of one of the greatest pickpockets in Madrid. Manolo himself was gentle and ad-mirable. He was the only person in Paris with whom Picasso spoke spanish. All the other spaniards had french wives or french mistresses and having so much the habit of speaking french they always talked french to each other. This always seemed very strange to me. However Picasso and Manolo always talked spanish to each other.

There were many stories about Manolo, he had always loved and he had always lived under the protection of the saints. They told the story of how when he first came to Paris he entered the first church he saw and there he saw a woman bring a chair to some one and receive money. So Manolo did the same, he went into many churches and always gave everybody a chair and always got money, until one day he was caught by the woman whose business it was and whose chairs they were and there was trouble.

He once was hard up and he proposed to his friends to take lottery tickets for one of his statues, everybody agreed, and then when everybody met they found they all had the same number. When they reproached him he explained that he did this because he knew his friends would be unhappy if they did not all have the same number. He was supposed to have left Spain while he was doing his military service, that is to say he was in the cavalry and he went across the border, and sold his horse and his accoutrement, and so had enough money to come to Paris and be a sculptor. He once was left for a few days in the house of a friend of Gauguin. When the owner of the house came back all his Gauguin souvenirs and all his Gauguin sketches were gone. Manolo had sold them to Vollard and Vollard had to give them back. Nobody minded. Manolo was like a sweet crazy religiously uplifted spanish beggar and everybody was fond of him. Moréas, the greek poet, who in those days was a very well known figure in

Paris was very fond of him and used to take him with him for company whenever he had anything to do. Manolo always went in hopes of getting a meal but he used to be left to wait while Moréas ate. Manolo was always patient and always hopeful although Moréas was as well known then as Guillaume Apollinaire was later, to pay rarely or rather not at all.

Manolo used to make statues for joints in Montmartre in return for meals etcetera, until Alfred Stieglitz heard of him and showed his things in New York and sold some of them and then Manolo returned to the french frontier, Céret and there he has lived ever since, turning night into day, he and his catalan wife.

But Uhde. Uhde one Saturday evening presented his fiancée to Gertrude Stein. Uhde's morals were not all that they should be and as his fiancée seemed a very well to do and very conventional young woman we were all surprised. But it turned out that it was an arranged marriage. Uhde wished to respectabilise himself and she wanted to come into possession of her inheritance, which she could only do upon marriage. Shortly after she married Uhde and shortly after they were divorced. She then married Delaunay the painter who was just then coming into the foreground. He was the founder of the first of the many vulgarisations of the cubist idea, the painting of houses out of plumb, what was called the catastrophic school.

Delaunay was a big blond frenchman. He had a lively little mother. She used to come to the rue de Fleurus with old vicomtes who looked exactly like one's youthful idea of what an old french marquis should look like. These always left their cards and then wrote a solemn note of thanks and never showed in any way how entirely out of place they must have felt. Delaunay himself was amusing. He was fairly able and inordinately ambitious. He was always asking how old Picasso had been when he had painted a certain picture. When he was told he always said, oh I am not as old as that yet. I will do as much when I am that age.

As a matter of fact he did progress very rapidly. He used to come a great deal to the rue de Fleurus. Gertrude Stein used to delight in him. He was funny and he painted one rather fine picture, the three graces standing in front of Paris, an enormous picture in which he combined everybody's ideas and added a certain french clarity and freshness of his own. It had a rather remarkable atmosphere and it had a great success. After that his pictures lost all quality, they grew big and empty or small and empty. I remember his bringing one of these small ones to the house, saying, look I am bringing you a small picture, a jewel. It is small, said Gertrude Stein, but is it a jewel.

It was Delaunay who married the ex-wife of Uhde and they kept up quite an establishment. They took up Guillaume Apollinaire and it was he who taught them how to cook and how to live. Guillaume was extraordinary. Nobody but Guillaume, it was the italian in Guillaume, Stella the New York painter could do the same thing in his early youth in Paris, could make fun of his hosts, make fun of their guests, make fun of their food and spur them to always greater and greater effort.

It was Guillaume's first opportunity to travel, he went to Germany with Delaunay and thoroughly enjoyed himself.

Uhde used to delight in telling how his former wife came to his house one day and dilating upon Delaunay's future career, explained to him that he should abandon Picasso and Braque, the past, and devote himself to the cause of Delaunay, the future. Picasso and Braque at this time it must be remembered were not yet thirty years old. Uhde told everybody this story with a great many witty additions and always adding, I tell you all this sans discrétion, that is tell it to everybody.

The other german who came to the house in those days was a dull one. He is, I understand a very important man now in his own country and he was a most faithful friend to Matisse, at all times, even during the war. He was the bulwark of the Matisse school. Matisse was not always or indeed often very kind to him. All women loved him, so it was supposed. He was a stocky Don Juan. I remember one big scandinavian who loved him and who would never come in on Saturday evening but stood in the court and whenever the door opened for some one to come in or go out you could see her smile in the dark of the court like the smile of the Cheshire cat. He was always bothered by Gertrude Stein. She did and bought such strange things. He never dared to criticise anything to her but to me he would say, and you, Mademoiselle, do you, pointing to the despised object, do you find that beautiful.

Once when we were in Spain, in fact the first time we went to Spain, Gertrude Stein had insisted upon buying in Cuenca a brand new enormous turtle made of Rhine stones. She had very lovely old jewellery, but with great satisfaction to herself she was wearing this turtle as a clasp. Purrmann this time was dumbfounded. He got me into a corner. That jewel, he said, that Miss Stein is wearing, are those stones real.

Speaking of Spain also reminds me that once we were in a crowded restaurant. Suddenly in the end of the room a tall form stood up and a man bowed solemnly at Gertrude Stein who as solemnly replied. It was a stray hungarian from Saturday evening, surely.

There was another german whom I must admit we both liked. This was much later, about nineteen twelve. He too was a dark tall german. He talked english, he was a friend of Marsden Hartley whom we liked very much, and we liked his german friend, I cannot say that we did not.

He used to describe himself as the rich son of a not so rich father. In other words he had a large allowance from a moderately poor father who was a university professor. Rönnebeck was charming and he was always invited to dinner. He was at dinner one evening when Berenson the famous critic of Italian art was there. Rönnebeck had brought with him some photographs of pictures by Rousseau. He had left them in the atelier and we were all in the dining room. Everybody began to talk about Rousseau. Berenson was puzzled, but Rousseau, Rousseau, he said, Rousseau was an honourable painter but why all this excitement. Ah, he said with a sigh, fashions change, that I know, but really I never thought that Rousseau would come to be the fashion for the young. Berenson had a tendency to be supercilious and so everybody let him go on and on. Finally Rönnebeck said gently, but perhaps Mr. Berenson, you have never heard of the great Rousseau, the douanier Rousseau. No, admitted Berenson, he hadn't, and later when he saw the photographs he understood less than ever and was fairly fussed. Mabel Dodge who was present, said, but Berenson, you must remember that art is inevitable. That, said Berenson recovering himself, you understand, you being yourself a femme fatale.

We were fond of Rönnebeck and beside the first time he came to the house he quoted some of Gertrude Stein's recent work to her. She had loaned some manuscript to Marsden Hartley. It was the first time that anybody had quoted her work to her and she naturally liked it. He also made a translation into german of some of the portraits she was writing at that time and thus brought her her first international reputation. That however is not quite true, Roché the faithful Roché had introduced some young germans to Three Lives and they were already under its spell. However Rönnebeck was charming and we were very fond of him.

Rönnebeck was a sculptor, he did small full figure portraits and was doing them very well, he was in love with an american girl who was studying music. He liked France and all french things and he was very fond of us. We all separated as usual for the summer. He said he had a very amusing summer before him. He had a commission to do a portrait figure of a countess and her two sons, the little counts and he was to spend the summer doing this in the home of the countess who had a magnificent place on the shores of the Baltic.

When we all came back that winter Rönnebeck was different. In the first place he came back with lots of photographs of ships of the german navy and insisted upon showing them to us. We were not interested. Gertrude Stein said, of course, Rönnebeck, you have a navy, of course, we americans have a navy, everybody has a navy, but to anybody but the navy, one big ironclad looks very much like any other, don't be silly. He was different though. He had had a good time. He had photos of himself with all the counts and there was also one with the crown prince of Germany who was a great friend of the countess. The winter, it was the winter of 1913-1914, wore on. All the usual things happened and we gave as usual some dinner parties. I have forgotten what the occasion of one was but we thought Rönnebeck would do excellently for it. We invited him. He sent word that he had to go to Munich for two days but he would travel at night and get back for the dinner party. This he did and was delightful as he always was.

Pretty soon he went off on a trip to the north, to visit the cathedral towns. When he came back he brought us a series of photographs of all these northern towns seen from above. What are these, Gertrude Stein asked. Oh, he said, I thought you would be interested, they are views I have taken of all the cathedral towns. I took them from the tip top of the steeples and I thought you would be interested because see, he said, they look exactly like the pictures of the followers of Delaunay, what you call the earthquake school, he said turning to me. We thanked him and thought no more about it. Later when during the war I found them, I tore them up in a rage.

Then we all began to talk about our summer plans. Gertrude Stein was to go to London in July to see John Lane to sign the contract for Three Lives. Rönnebeck said, why don't you come to Germany instead or rather before or immediately after, he said. Because, said Gertrude Stein, as you know I don't like germans. Yes I know, said Rönnebeck, I know, but you like me and you would have such a wonderful time. They would be so interested and it would mean so much to them, do come, he said. No, said Gertrude Stein, I like you alright but I don't like germans.

We went to England in July and when we got there Gertrude Stein had a letter from Rönnebeck saying that he still awfully wanted us to come to Germany but since we wouldn't had we not better spend the summer in England or perhaps in Spain but not as we had planned come back to Paris. That was naturally the end. I tell the story for what it is worth.

When I first came to Paris there was a very small sprinkling of americans Saturday evenings, this sprinkling grew gradually more abundant but before I tell about americans I must tell all about the banquet to Rousseau.

In the beginning of my stay in Paris a friend and I were living as I have already said in a little apartment on the rue

Notre-Dame-des-Champs. I was no longer taking french lessons from Fernande because she and Picasso were together again but she was not an infrequent visitor. Autumn had come and I can remember it very well because I had bought my first winter Paris hat. It was a very fine hat of black velvet, a big hat with a brilliant yellow fantaisie. Even Fernande gave it her approval.

Fernande was lunching with us one day and she said that there was going to be a banquet given for Rousseau and that she was giving it. She counted up the number of the invited. We were included. Who was Rousseau. I did not know but that really did not matter since it was to be a banquet and everybody was to go, and we were invited.

Next Saturday evening at the rue de Fleurus everybody was talking about the banquet to Rousseau and then I found out that Rousseau was the painter whose picture I had seen in that first independent. It appeared that Picasso had recently found in Montmartre a large portrait of a woman by Rousseau, that he had bought it and that this festivity was in honour of the purchase and the painter. It was going to be very wonderful.

Fernande told me a great deal about the menu. There was to be riz à la Valenciennes, Fernande had learnt how to cook this on her last trip to Spain, and then she had ordered, I forget now what it was that she had ordered, but she had ordered a great deal at Félix Potin, the chain store of groceries where they made prepared dishes. Everybody was excited. It was Guillaume Apollinaire, as I remember, who knowing Rousseau very well had induced him to promise to come and was to bring him and everybody was to write poetry and songs and it was to be very rigolo, a favourite Montmartre word meaning a jokeful amusement. We were all to meet at the café at the foot of the rue Ravignan and to have an apéritif and then go up to Picasso's atelier and have dinner. I put on my new hat and we all went to Montmartre and all met at the café.

As Gertrude Stein and I came into the café there seemed to be a great many people present and in the midst was a tall thin girl who with her long thin arms extended was swaying forward and back. I did not know what she was doing, it was evidently not gymnastics, it was bewildering but she looked very enticing. What is that, I whispered to Gertrude Stein. Oh that is Marie Laurencin, I am afraid she has been taking too many preliminary apéritifs. Is she the old lady that Fernande told me about who makes noises like animals and annoys Pablo. She annoys Pablo alright but she is a very young lady and she has had too much, said Gertrude Stein going in. Just then there was a violent noise at the door of the café and Fernande appeared very large, very excited and very angry. Félix Potin, said she, has not sent the dinner. Everybody seemed overcome at these awful tidings but I, in my american way said to Fernande, come quickly, let us telephone. In those days in Paris one did not telephone and never to a provision store. But Fernande consented and off we went. Everywhere we went there was either no telephone or it was not working, finally we got one that worked but Félix Potin was closed or closing and it was deaf to our appeals. Fernande was completely upset but finally I persuaded her to tell me just what we were to have had from Félix Potin and then in one little shop and another little shop in Montmartre we found substitutes, Fernande finally announcing that she had made so much riz à la Valenciennes that it would take the place of everything and it did.

When we were back at the café almost everybody who had been there had gone and some new ones had come, Fernande told them all to come along. As we toiled up the hill we saw in front of us the whole crowd. In the middle was Marie Laurencin supported on the one side by Gertrude Stein and on the other by Gertrude Stein's brother and she was falling first into one pair of arms and then into another, her voice always high and sweet and her arms always thin graceful and long. Guillaume of course was not there, he was to bring Rousseau himself after every one was seated.

Fernande passed this slow moving procession, I following her and we arrived at the atelier. It was rather impressive. They had gotten trestles, carpenter's trestles, and on them had placed boards and all around these boards were benches. At the head of the table was the new acquisition, the Rous-

seau, draped in flags and wreaths and flanked on either side
by big statues, I do not remember what statues. It was very
magnificent and very festive. The riz à la Valenciennes was
presumably cooking below in Max Jacob's studio. Max not
being on good terms with Picasso was not present but they
used his studio for the rice and for the men's overcoats. The
ladies were to put theirs in the front studio which had been
Van Dongen's in his spinach days and now belonged to a
frenchman by the name of Vaillant. This was the studio
which was later to be Juan Gris'.

I had just time to deposit my hat and admire the arrangements, Fernande violently abusing Marie Laurencin all the
time, when the crowd arrived. Fernande large and imposing,
barred the way, she was not going to have her party spoiled
by Marie Laurencin. This was a serious party, a serious
banquet for Rousseau and neither she nor Pablo would
tolerate such conduct. Of course Pablo, all this time, was
well out of sight in the rear. Gertrude Stein remonstrated,
she said half in english half in french, that she would be
hanged if after the struggle of getting Marie Laurencin up
that terrific hill it was going to be for nothing. No indeed and
beside she reminded Fernande that Guillaume and Rousseau
would be along any minute and it was necessary that every
one should be decorously seated before that event. By this
time Pablo had made his way to the front and he joined in
and said, yes yes, and Fernande yielded. She was always a
little afraid of Guillaume Apollinaire, of his solemnity and of
his wit, and they all came in. Everybody sat down.

Everybody sat down and everybody began to eat rice and
other things, that is as soon as Guillaume Apollinaire and
Rousseau came in which they did very presently and were
wildly acclaimed. How well I remember their coming. Rousseau a little small colourless frenchman with a little beard,
like any number of frenchmen one saw everywhere. Guillaume
Apollinaire with finely cut florid features, dark hair and a
beautiful complexion. Everybody was presented and everybody sat down again. Guillaume slipped into a seat beside
Marie Laurencin. At the sight of Guillaume, Marie who had
become comparatively calm seated next to Gertrude Stein,

broke out again in wild movements and outcries. Guillaume got her out of the door and downstairs and after a decent interval they came back Marie a little bruised but sober. By this time everybody had eaten everything and poetry began. Oh yes, before this Frédéric of the Lapin Agile and the University of Apaches had wandered in with his usual companion a donkey, was given a drink and wandered out again. Then a little later some italian street singers hearing of the party came in. Fernande rose at the end of the table and flushed and her forefinger staight into the air said it was not that kind of a party, and they were promptly thrown out.

Who was there. We were there and Salmon, André Salmon, then a rising young poet and journalist, Pichot and Germaine Pichot, Braque and perhaps Marcelle Bracque but this I do not remember, I know that there was talk of her at that time, the Raynals, the Ageros the false Greco and his wife, and several other pairs whom I did not know and do not remember and Vaillant, a very amiable ordinary young frenchman who had the front studio.

The ceremonies began. Guillaume Apollinaire got up and made a solemn eulogy, I do not remember at all what he said but it ended up with a poem he had written and which he half chanted and in which everybody joined in the refrain, La peinture de ce Rousseau. Somebody else then, possibly Raynal, I don't remember, got up and there were toasts, and then all of a sudden André Salmon who was sitting next to my friend and solemnly discoursing of literature and travels, leaped upon the by no means solid table and poured out an extemporaneous eulogy and poem. At the end he seized a big glass and drank what was in it, then promptly went off his head, being completely drunk, and began to fight. The men all got hold of him, the statues tottered, Braque, a great big chap, got hold of a statue in either arm and stood there holding them while Gertrude Stein's brother another big chap, protected little Rousseau and his violin from harm. The others with Picasso leading because Picasso though small is very strong, dragged Salmon into the front atelier and locked him in. Everybody came back and sat down.

Thereafter the evening was peaceful. Marie Laurencin

sang in a thin voice some charming old norman songs. The
wife of Agero sang some charming old limousin songs, Pichot
danced a wonderful religious spanish dance ending in making
of himself a crucified Christ upon the floor. Guillaume Apollinaire solemnly approached myself and my friend and asked
us to sing some of the native songs of the red indians. We did
not either of us feel up to that to the great regret of Guillaume
and all the company. Rousseau blissful and gentle played the
violin and told us about the plays he had written and his
memories of Mexico. It was all very peaceful and about three
o'clock in the morning we all went into the atelier where
Salmon had been deposited and where we had left our hats
and coats to get them to go home. There on the couch lay
Salmon peacefully sleeping and surrounding him, half chewed,
were a box of matches, a petit bleu and my yellow fantaisie.
Imagine my feelings even at three o'clock in the morning.
However, Salmon woke up very charming and very polite
and we all went out into the street together. All of a sudden
with a wild yell Salmon rushed down the hill.

Gertrude Stein and her brother, my friend and I, all in one
cab, took Rousseau home.

It was about a month later that one dark Paris winter
afternoon I was hurrying home and felt myself being followed. I hurried and hurried and the footsteps drew nearer
and I heard, mademoiselle, mademoiselle. I turned. It was
Rousseau. Oh mademoiselle, he said, you should not be out
alone after dark, may I see you home. Which he did.

It was not long after this that Kahnweiler came to Paris.
Kahnweiler was a german married to a frenchwoman and they
had lived for many years in England. Kahnweiler had been in
England in business, saving money to carry out a dream of
some day having a picture shop in Paris. The time had come
and he started a neat small gallery in the rue Vignon. He felt
his way a little and then completely threw in his lot with
the cubist group. There were difficulties at first, Picasso always suspicious did not want to go too far with him. Fernande did the bargaining with Kahnweiler but finally they
all realised the genuineness of his interest and his faith, and
that he could and would market their work. They all made

LINCOLN CHRISTIAN COLLEGE AND SEMINA

contracts with him and until the war he did everything for them all. The afternoons with the group coming in and out of his shop were for Kahnweiler really afternoons with Vasari. He believed in them and their future greatness. It was only the year before the war that he added Juan Gris. It was just two months before the outbreak of the war that Gertrude Stein saw the first Juan Gris paintings at Kahnweiler's and bought three of them.

Picasso always says that he used in those days to tell Kahnweiler that he should become a french citizen, that war would come and there would be the devil to pay. Kahnweiler always said he would when he had passed the military age but that he naturally did not want to do military service a second time. The war came, Kahnweiler was in Switzerland with his family on his vacation and he could not come back. All his possessions were sequestrated.

The auction sale by the government of Kahnweiler's pictures, practically all the cubist pictures of the three years before the war, was the first occasion after the war where everybody of the old crowd met. There had been quite a conscious effort on the part of all the older merchants, now that the war was over, to kill cubism. The expert for the sale, who was a well known picture dealer, had avowed this as his intention. He would keep the prices down as low as possible and discourage the public as much as possible. How could the artists defend themselves.

We happened to be with the Braques a day or two before the public show of pictures for the sale and Marcelle Braque, Braque's wife, told us that they had come to a decision. Picasso and Juan Gris could do nothing they were spaniards, and this was a french government sale. Marie Laurencin was technically a german, Lipschitz was a russian at that time not a popular thing to be. Braque a frenchman, who had won the croix de guerre in a charge, who had been made an officer and had won the légion d'honneur and had had a bad head wound could do what he pleased. He had a technical reason too for picking a quarrel with the expert. He had sent in a list of people likely to buy his pictures, a privilege always accorded to an artist whose pictures are to be pub-

licly sold, and catalogues had not been sent to these people.
When we arrived Braque had already done his duty. We came
in just at the end of the fray. There was a great excitement.

Braque had approached the expert and told him that he
had neglected his obvious duties. The expert had replied that
he had done and would do as he pleased and called Braque a
norman pig. Braque had hit him. Braque is a big man and
the expert is not and Braque tried not to hit hard but nevertheless the expert fell. The police came in and they were
taken off to the police station. There they told their story.
Braque of course as a hero of the war was treated with all
due respect, and when he spoke to the expert using the
familiar thou the expert completely lost his temper and his
head and was publicly rebuked by the magistrate. Just after
it was over Matisse came in and wanted to know what had
happened and was happening, Gertrude Stein told him.
Matisse said, and it was a Matisse way to say it, Braque a
raison, celui-là a volé la France, et on sait bien ce que c'est
que voler la France.

As a matter of fact the buyers were frightened off and all
the pictures except those of Derain went for little. Poor
Juan Gris whose pictures went for very little tried to be brave.
They after all did bring an honourable price, he said to Gertrude Stein, but he was sad.

Fortunately Kahnweiler, who had not fought against
France, was allowed to come back the next year. The others
no longer needed him but Juan needed him desperately and
Kahnweiler's loyalty and generosity to Juan Gris all those
hard years can only be matched by Juan's loyalty and generosity when at last just before his death and he had become
famous tempting offers from other dealers were made to him.

Kahnweiler coming to Paris and taking on commercially the
cause of the cubists made a great difference to all of them.
Their present and future were secure.

The Picassos moved from the old studio in the rue Ravignan to an apartment in the boulevard Clichy. Fernande began
to buy furniture and have a servant and the servant of course
made a soufflé. It was a nice apartment with lots of sunshine.
On the whole however Fernande was not quite as happy as

she had been. There were a great many people there and even afternoon tea. Braque was there a great deal, it was the height of the intimacy between Braque and Picasso, it was at that time they first began to put musical instruments into their pictures. It was also the beginning of Picasso's making constructions. He made still lifes of objects and photographed them. He made paper constructions later, he gave one of these to Gertrude Stein. It is perhaps the only one left in existence.

This was also the time when I first heard of Poiret. He had a houseboat on the Seine and he had given a party on it and he had invited Pablo and Fernande. He gave Fernande a handsome rose-coloured scarf with gold fringe and he also gave her a spun glass fantaisie to put on a hat, an entirely new idea in those days. This she gave to me and I wore it on a little straw pointed cap for years after. I may even have it now.

Then there was the youngest of the cubists. I never knew his name. He was doing his military service and was destined for diplomacy. How he drifted in and whether he painted I do not know. All I know is that he was known as the youngest of the cubists.

Fernande had at this time a new friend of whom she often spoke to me. This was Eve who was living with Marcoussis. And one evening all four of them came to the rue de Fleurus, Pablo, Fernande, Marcoussis and Eve. It was the only time we ever saw Marcoussis until many many years later.

I could perfectly understand Fernande's liking for Eve. As I said Fernande's great heroine was Evelyn Thaw, small and negative. Here was a little french Evelyn Thaw, small and perfect.

Not long after this Picasso came one day and told Gertrude Stein that he had decided to take an atelier in the rue Ravignan. He could work better there. He could not get back his old one but he took one on the lower floor. One day we went to see him there. He was not in and Gertrude Stein as a joke left her visiting card. In a few days we went again and Picasso was at work on a picture on which was written ma jolie and at the lower corner painted in was Gertrude Stein's visiting card. As we went away Gertrude Stein said,

Fernande is certainly not ma jolie, I wonder who it is. In a few days we knew. Pablo had gone off with Eve.

This was in the spring. They all had the habit of going to Céret near Perpignan for the summer probably on account of Manolo, and they all in spite of everything went there again. Fernande was there with the Pichots and Eve was there with Pablo. There were some redoubtable battles and then everybody came back to Paris.

One evening, we too had come back, Picasso came in. He and Gertrude Stein had a long talk alone. It was Pablo, she said when she came in from having bade him goodbye, and he said a marvellous thing about Fernande, he said her beauty always held him but he could not stand any of her little ways. She further added that Pablo and Eve were now settled on the boulevard Raspail and we would go and see them to-morrow.

In the meanwhile Gertrude Stein had received a letter from Fernande, very dignified, written with the reticence of a frenchwoman. She said that she wished to tell Gertrude Stein that she understood perfectly that the friendship had always been with Pablo and that although Gertrude had always shown her every mark of sympathy and affection now that she and Pablo were separated, it was naturally impossible that in the future there should be any intercourse between them because the friendship having been with Pablo there could of course be no question of a choice. That she would always remember their intercourse with pleasure and that she would permit herself, if ever she were in need, to throw herself upon Gertrude's generosity.

And so Picasso left Montmartre never to return.

When I first came to the rue de Fleurus Gertrude Stein was correcting the proofs of Three Lives. I was soon helping her with this and before very long the book was published. I asked her to let me subscribe to Romeike's clipping bureau, the advertisement for Romeike in the San Francisco Argonaut having been one of the romances of my childhood. Soon the clippings began to come in.

It is rather astonishing the number of newspapers that noticed this book, printed privately and by a perfectly unknown person. The notice that pleased Gertrude Stein most was in the Kansas City Star. She often asked then and in later years who it was who might have written it but she never found out. It was a very sympathetic and a very understanding review. Later on when she was discouraged by what others said she would refer to it as having given her at that time great comfort. She says in Composition and Explanation, when you write a thing it is perfectly clear and then you begin to be doubtful about it, but then you read it again and you lose yourself in it again as when you wrote it.

The other thing in connection with this her first book that gave her pleasure was a very enthusiastic note from H. G. Wells. She kept this for years apart, it had meant so much to her. She wrote to him at that time and they were often to meet but as it happened they never did. And they are not likely to now.

Gertrude Stein was at that time writing The Making of Americans. It had changed from being a history of a family to being a history of everybody the family knew and then it became the history of every kind and of every individual human being. But in spite of all this there was a hero and he was to die. The day he died I met Gertrude Stein at Mildred Aldrich's apartment. Mildred was very fond of Gertrude Stein and took a deep interest in the book's ending. It was over a thousand pages long and I was typewriting it.

I always say that you cannot tell what a picture really is or what an object really is until you dust it every day and you cannot tell what a book is until you type it or proof-read it. It then does something to you that only reading never can do. A good many years later Jane Heap said that she had never appreciated the quality of Gertrude Stein's work until she proof-read it.

When The Making of Americans was finished, Gertrude Stein began another which also was to be long and which she called A Long Gay Book but it did not turn out to be long, neither that nor one begun at the same time Many Many Women because they were both interrupted by portrait writing. This is how portrait writing began.

Hélène used to stay at home with her husband Sunday

evening, that is to say she was always willing to come but
we often told her not to bother. I like cooking, I am an extremely good five-minute cook, and beside, Gertrude Stein
liked from time to time to have me make american dishes.
One Sunday evening I was very busy preparing one of these
and then I called Gertrude Stein to come in from the atelier
for supper. She came in much excited and would not sit down.
Here I want to show you something, she said. No I said it
has to be eaten hot. No, she said, you have to see this first.
Gertrude Stein never likes her food hot and I do like mine
hot, we never agree about this. She admits that one can
wait to cool it but one cannot heat it once it is on a plate so
it is agreed that I have it served as hot as I like. In spite of
my protests and the food cooling I had to read. I can still
see the little tiny pages of the note-book written forward and
back. It was the portrait called Ada, the first in Geography
and Plays. I began it and I thought she was making fun of
me and I protested, she says I protest now about my autobiography. Finally I read it all and was terribly pleased with
it. And then we ate our supper.

This was the beginning of the long series of portraits. She
has written portraits of practically everybody she has known,
and written them in all manners and in all styles.

Ada was followed by portraits of Matisse and Picasso, and
Stieglitz who was much interested in them and in Gertrude
Stein printed them in a special number of Camera Work.

She then began to do short portraits of everybody who
came in and out. She did one of Arthur Frost, the son of A.
B. Frost the american illustrator. Frost was a Matisse pupil
and his pride when he read his portrait and found that it was
three full pages longer than either the portrait of Matisse or
the portrait of Picasso was something to hear.

A. B. Frost complained to Pat Bruce who had led Frost to
Matisse that it was a pity that Arthur could not see his way
to becoming a conventional artist and so earning fame and
money. You can lead a horse to water but you cannot make
him drink said Pat Bruce. Most horses drink. Mr. Bruce, said
A. B. Frost.

Bruce, Patrick Henry Bruce, was one of the early and most

ardent Matisse pupils and soon he made little Matisses, but
he was not happy. In explaining his unhappiness he told
Gertrude Stein, they talk about the sorrows of great artists,
the tragic unhappiness of great artists but after all they are
great artists. A little artist has all the tragic unhappiness and
the sorrows of a great artist and he is not a great artist.

She did portraits of Nadelman, also of the protégés of the
sculptress Mrs. Whitney, Lee and Russell also of Harry
Phelan Gibb, her first and best english friend. She did portraits of Manguin and Roché and Purrmann and David
Edstrom, the fat swedish sculptor who married the head of
the Christian Science Church in Paris and destroyed her.
And Brenner, Brenner the sculptor who never finished anything. He had an admirable technique and a great many ob-
sessions which kept him from work. Gertrude Stein was very
fond of him and still is. She once posed to him for weeks and
he did a fragmentary portrait of her that is very fine. He
and Cody later published some numbers of a little review
called Soil and they were among the very early ones to print
something of Gertrude Stein. The only little magazine that
preceded it was one called Rogue, printed by Allan Norton
and which printed her description of the Galérie Lafayette.
This was of course all much later and happened through Carl
Van Vechten.

She also did portraits of Miss Etta Cone and her sister
Doctor Claribel Cone. She also did portraits of Miss Mars
and Miss Squires under the title of Miss Furr and Miss
Skeene. There were portraits of Mildred Aldrich and her
sister. Everybody was given their portrait to read and they
were all pleased and it was all very amusing. All this occupied
a great deal of that winter and then we went to Spain.

In Spain Gertrude Stein began to write the things that led
to Tender Buttons.

I liked Spain immensely. We went several times to Spain
and I always liked it more and more. Gertrude Stein says
that I am impartial on every subject except that of Spain and
spaniards.

We went straight to Avila and I immediately lost my heart
to Avila, I must stay in Avila forever I insisted. Gertrude

Stein was very upset, Avila was alright but, she insisted, she needed Paris. I felt that I needed nothing but Avila. We were both very violent about it. We did however stay there for ten days and as Saint Theresa was a heroine of Gertrude Stein's youth we thoroughly enjoyed it. In the opera Four Saints written a few years ago she describes the landscape that so profoundly moved me.

We went on to Madrid and there we met Georgiana King of Bryn Mawr, an old friend of Gertrude Stein from Baltimore days. Georgiana King wrote some of the most interesting of the early criticisms of Three Lives. She was then re-editing Street on the cathedrals of Spain and in connection with this she had wandered all over Spain. She gave us a great deal of very good advice.

In these days Gertrude Stein wore a brown corduroy suit, jacket and skirt, a small straw cap, always crocheted for her by a woman in Fiesole, sandals, and she often carried a cane. That summer the head of the cane was of amber. It is more or less this costume without the cap and the cane that Picasso has painted in his portrait of her. This costume was ideal for Spain, they all thought of her as belonging to some religious order and we were always treated with the most absolute respect. I remember that once a nun was showing us the treasures in a convent church in Toledo. We were near the steps of the altar. All of a sudden there was a crash, Gertrude Stein had dropped her cane. The nun paled, the worshippers startled. Gertrude Stein picked up her cane and turning to the frightened nun said reassuringly, no it is not broken.

I used in those days of spanish travelling to wear what I was wont to call my spanish disguise. I always wore a black silk coat, black gloves and a black hat, the only pleasure I allowed myself were lovely artificial flowers on my hat. These always enormously interested the peasant women and they used to very courteously ask my permission to touch them, to realise for themselves that they were artificial.

We went to Cuenca that summer, Harry Gibb the english painter had told us about it. Harry Gibb is a strange case of a man who foresaw everything. He had been a successful

animal painter in his youth in England, he came from the
north of England, he had married and gone to Germany,
there he had become dissatisfied with what he had been doing
and heard about the new school of painting in Paris. He came
to Paris and was immediately influenced by Matisse. He then
became interested in Picasso and he did some very remarkable painting under their combined influences. Then all this
together threw him into something else something that fairly
completely achieved what the surréalists after the war tried
to do. The only thing he lacked is what the french call saveur,
what may be called the graciousness of a picture. Because of
this lack it was impossible for him to find a french audience.
Naturally in those days there was no english audience. Harry
Gibb fell on bad days. He was always falling upon bad days.
He and his wife Bridget one of the pleasantest of the wives
of a genius I have sat with were full of courage and they
faced everything admirably, but there were always very
difficult days. And then things were a little better. He found
a couple of patrons who believed in him and it was at this
time, 1912-1913, that he went to Dublin and had rather an
epoch-making show of his pictures there. It was at that time
that he took with him several copies of the portrait of Mabel
Dodge at the Villa Curonia, Mabel Dodge had had it printed
in Florence, and it was then that the Dublin writers in the
cafés heard Gertrude Stein read aloud. Doctor Gogarty, Harry
Gibb's host and admirer, loved to read it aloud himself and
have others read it aloud.

After that there was the war and eclipse for poor Harry,
and since then a long sad struggle. He has had his ups and
downs, more downs than up, but only recently there was a
new turn of the wheel. Gertrude Stein who loved them both
dearly always was convinced that the two painters of her
generation who would be discovered after they were dead,
they being predestined to a life of tragedy, were Juan Gris
and Harry Gibb. Juan Gris dead these five years is beginning
to come into his own. Harry Gibb still alive is still unknown.
Gertrude Stein and Harry Gibb have always been very loyal
and very loving friends. One of the very good early portraits

she did she did of him, it was printed in the Oxford Review and then in Geography and Plays.

So Harry Gibb told us about Cuenca and we went on a little railroad that turned around curves and ended in the middle of nowhere and there was Cuenca.

We delighted in Cuenca and the population of Cuenca delighted in us. It delighted in us so much that it was getting uncomfortable. Then one day when we were out walking, all of a sudden the population, particularly the children, kept their distance. Soon a uniformed man came up and saluting said that he was a policeman of the town and that the governor of the province had detailed him to always hover in the distance as we went about the country to prevent our being annoyed by the population and that he hoped that this would not inconvenience us. It did not, he was charming and he took us to lovely places in the country where we could not very well have gone by ourselves. Such was Spain in the old days.

We finally came back to Madrid again and there we discovered the Argentina and bull-fights. The young journalists of Madrid had just discovered her. We happened upon her in a music hall, we went to them to see spanish dancing, and after we saw her the first time we went every afternoon and every evening. We went to the bull-fights. At first they upset me and Gertrude Stein used to tell me, now look, now don't look, until finally I was able to look all the time.

We finally came to Granada and stayed there for some time and there Gertrude Stein worked terrifically. She was always very fond of Granada. It was there she had her first experience of Spain when still at college just after the spanish-american war when she and her brother went through Spain. They had a delightful time and she always tells of sitting in the dining room talking to a bostonian and his daughter when suddenly there was a terrific noise, the hee-haw of a donkey. What is it, said the young bostonian trembling. Ah, said the father, it is the last sigh of the Moor.

We enjoyed Granada, we met many amusing people english and spanish and it was there and at that time that Gertrude Stein's style gradually changed. She says hitherto she had been interested only in the insides of people, their character and what went on inside them, it was during that summer that she first felt a desire to express the rhythm of the visible world.

It was a long tormenting process, she looked, listened and described. She always was, she always is, tormented by the problem of the external and the internal. One of the things that always worries her about painting is the difficulty that the artist feels and which sends him to painting still lifes, that after all the human being essentially is not paintable. Once again and very recently she has thought that a painter has added something to the solution of this problem. She is interested in Picabia in whom hitherto she has never been interested because he at least knows that if you do not solve your painting problem in painting human beings you do not solve it at all. There is also a follower of Picabia's, who is facing the problem, but will he solve it. Perhaps not. Well anyway it is that of which she is always talking and now her own long struggle with it was to begin.

These were the days in which she wrote Susie Asado and Preciosilla and Gypsies in Spain. She experimented with everything in trying to describe. She tried a bit inventing words but she soon gave that up. The english language was her medium and with the english language the task was to be achieved, the problem solved. The use of fabricated words offended her, it was an escape into imitative emotionalism.

No, she stayed with her task, although after the return to Paris she described objects, she described rooms and objects, which joined with her first experiments done in Spain, made the volume Tender Buttons.

She always however made her chief study people and therefore the never ending series of portraits.

We came back to the rue de Fleurus as usual.

One of the people who had impressed me very much when I first came to the rue de Fleurus was Mildred Aldrich.

Mildred Aldrich was then in her early fifties, a stout vigorous woman with a George Washington face, white hair and admirably clean fresh clothes and gloves. A very striking figure and a very satisfying one in the crowd of mixed nationalities. She was indeed one of whom Picasso could say and did say, c'est elle qui fera la gloire de l'Amérique. She made one very satisfied with one's country, which had produced her.

Her sister having left for America she lived alone on the top floor of a building on the corner of the boulevard Raspail and the half street, rue Boissonnade. There she had at the window an enormous cage filled with canaries. We always thought it was because she loved canaries. Not at all. A friend had once left her a canary in a cage to take care of during her absence. Mildred as she did everything else, took excellent care of the canary in the cage. Some friend seeing this and naturally concluding that Mildred was fond of canaries gave her another canary. Mildred of course took excellent care of both canaries and so the canaries increased and the size of the cage grew until in 1914 she moved to Huiry to the Hilltop on the Marne and gave her canaries away. Her excuse was that in the country cats would eat the canaries. But her real reason she once told me was that she really could not bear canaries.

Mildred was an excellent housekeeper. I was very surprised, having had a very different impression of her, going up to see her one afternoon, finding her mending her linen and doing it beautifully.

Mildred adored cablegrams, she adored being hard up, or rather she adored spending money and as her earning capacity although great was limited, Mildred was chronically hard up. In those days she was making contracts to put Maeterlinck's Blue Bird on the american stage. The arrangements demanded endless cablegrams, and my early memories of Mildred were of her coming to our little apartment in the rue Notre-Dame-des-Champs late in the evening and asking me to lend her the money for a long cable. A few days later the money was returned with a lovely azalea worth five times the money. No wonder she was always hard up. But everybody listened to her. No one in the world could tell stories like Mildred. I can still see her at the rue de Fleurus sitting in one of the big armchairs and gradually the audience increasing around her as she talked.

She was very fond of Gertrude Stein, very interested in her work, enthusiastic about Three Lives, deeply impressed but slightly troubled by The Making of Americans, quite upset by Tender Buttons, but always loyal and convinced that if Gertrude Stein did it it had something in it that was worth while.

Her joy and pride when in nineteen twenty-six Gertrude Stein gave her lecture at Cambridge and Oxford was touching. Gertrude Stein must come out and read it to her before leaving. Gertrude Stein did, much to their mutual pleasure.

Mildred Aldrich liked Picasso and even liked Matisse, that is personally, but she was troubled. One day she said to me, Alice, tell me is it alright, are they really alright, I know Gertrude thinks so and Gertrude knows, but really is it not all fumisterie, is it not all false.

In spite of these occasional doubtful days Mildred Aldrich liked it all. She liked coming herself and she liked bringing other people. She brought a great many. It was she who brought Henry McBride who was then writing on the New York Sun. It was Henry McBride who used to keep Gertrude Stein's name before the public all those tormented years. Laugh if you like, he used to say to her detractors, but laugh with and not at her, in that way you will enjoy it all much better.

Henry McBride did not believe in worldly success. It ruins you, it ruins you, he used to say. But Henry, Gertrude Stein used to answer dolefully, don't you think I will ever have any success, I would like to have a little, you know. Think of my unpublished manuscripts. But Henry McBride was firm, the best that I can wish you, he always said, is to have no success. It is the only good thing. He was firm about that.

He was however enormously pleased when Mildred was successful and he now says he thinks the time has come when Gertrude Stein could indulge in a little success. He does not think that now it would hurt her.

It was about this time that Roger Fry first came to the house. He brought Clive Bell and Mrs. Clive Bell and later there were many others. In these days Clive Bell went along with the other two. He was rather complainful that his wife and Roger Fry took too much interest in capital works of art. He was quite funny about it. He was very amusing, later when he became a real art critic he was less so.

Roger Fry was always charming, charming as a guest and charming as a host; later when we went to London we spent a day with him in the country.

He was filled with excitement at the sight of the portrait of Gertrude Stein by Picasso. He wrote an article about it in the Burlington Review and illustrated it by two photographs side by side, one the photograph of this portrait and the other a photograph of a portrait by Raphael. He insisted that these two pictures were equal in value. He brought endless people to the house. Very soon there were throngs of englishmen, Augustus John and Lamb, Augustus John amazing looking and not too sober, Lamb rather strange and attractive.

It was about this time that Roger Fry had many young disciples. Among them was Wyndham Lewis, Wyndham Lewis, tall and thin, looked rather like a young frenchman on the rise, perhaps because his feet were very french, or at least his shoes. He used to come and sit and measure pictures. I can not say that he actually measured with a measuring-rod but he gave all the effect of being in the act of taking very careful measurement of the canvas, the lines within the canvas and everything that might be of use. Gertrude Stein rather liked him. She particularly liked him one day when he came and told all about his quarrel with Roger Fry. Roger Fry had come in not many days before and had already told all about it. They told exactly the same story only it was different, very different.

This was about the time too that Prichard of the Museum of Fine Arts, Boston and later of the Kensington Museum began coming. Prichard brought a great many young Oxford men. They were very nice in the room, and they thought Picasso wonderful. They felt and indeed in a way it was true that he had a halo. With these Oxford men came Thomas Whittemore of Tufts College. He was fresh and engaging and later to Gertrude Stein's great delight he one day said, all blue is precious.

Everybody brought somebody. As I said the character of

the Saturday evenings was gradually changing, that is to say, the kind of people who came had changed. Somebody brought the Infanta Eulalia and brought her several times. She was delighted and with the flattering memory of royalty she always remembered my name even some years after when we met quite by accident in the place Vendôme. When she first came into the room she was a little frightened. It seemed a strange place but gradually she liked it very much.

Lady Cunard brought her daughter Nancy, then a little girl, and very solemnly bade her never forget the visit.

Who else came. There were so many. The bavarian minister brought quantities of people. Jacques-Emile Blanche brought delightful people, so did Alphonse Kann. There was Lady Otoline Morrell looking like a marvellous feminine version of Disraeli and tall and strange shyly hesitating at the door. There was a dutch near royalty who was left by her escort who had to go and find a cab and she looked during this short interval badly frightened.

There was a roumanian princess, and her cabman grew impatient. Hélène came in to announce violently that the cabman would not wait. And then after a violent knock, the cabman himself announced that he would not wait.

It was an endless variety. And everybody came and no one made any difference. Gertrude Stein sat peacefully in a chair and those who could did the same, the rest stood. There were the friends who sat around the stove and talked and there were the endless strangers who came and went. My memory of it is very vivid.

As I say everybody brought people. William Cook brought a great many from Chicago, very wealthy stout ladies and equally wealthy tall good-looking thin ones. That summer having found the Balearic Islands on the map, we went to the island of Mallorca and on the little boat going over was Cook. He too had found it on the map. We stayed only a little while but he settled down for the summer, and then later he went back and was the solitary first of all the big crowd of americans who have discovered Palma since. We all went back again during the war.

It was during this summer that Picasso gave us a letter to

a friend of his youth one Raventos in Barcelona. But does he talk french, asked Gertrude Stein, Pablo giggled, better than you do Gertrude, he answered.

Raventos gave us a good time, he and a descendant of de Soto took us about for two long days, the days were long because so much of them were night. They had an automobile, even in those early days, and they took us up into the hills to see early churches. We would rush up a hill and then happily come down a little slower and every two hours or so we ate a dinner. When we finally came back to Barcelona about ten o'clock in the evening they said, now we will have an apéritif and then we will eat dinner. It was exhausting eating so many dinners but we enjoyed ourselves.

Later on much later on indeed only a few years ago Picasso introduced us to another friend of his youth.

Sabartes and he have known each other ever since they were fifteen years old but as Sabartes had disappeared into South America, Montevideo, Uruguay, before Gertrude Stein met Picasso, she had never heard of him. One day a few years ago Picasso sent word that he was bringing Sabartes to the house. Sabartes, in Uruguay, had read some things of Gertrude Stein in various magazines and he had conceived a great admiration of her work. It never occurred to him that Picasso would know her. Having come back for the first time in all these years to Paris he went to see Picasso and he told him about this Gertrude Stein. But she is my only friend, said Picasso, it is the only home I go to. Take me, said Sabartes, and so they came.

Gertrude Stein and spaniards are natural friends and this time too the friendship grew.

It was about this time that the futurists, the italian futurists, had their big show in Paris and it made a great deal of noise. Everybody was excited and this show being given in a very well known gallery everybody went. Jacques-Emile Blanche was terribly upset by it. We found him wandering tremblingly in the garden of the Tuileries and he said, it looks alright but is it. No it isn't, said Gertrude Stein. You do me good, said Jacques-Emile Blanche.

The futurists all of them led by Severini thronged around

Picasso. He brought them all to the house. Marinetti came by himself later as I remember. In any case everybody found the futurists very dull.

Epstein the sculptor came to the rue de Fleurus one evening. When Gertrude Stein first came to Paris in nineteen hundred and four, Epstein was a thin rather beautiful rather melancholy ghost who used to slip in and out among the Rodin statues in the Luxembourg museum. He had illustrated Hutchins Hapgood's studies of the ghetto and with the funds he came to Paris and was very poor. Now when I first saw him, he had come to Paris to place his sphynx statue to Oscar Wilde over Oscar Wilde's grave. He was a large rather stout man, not unimpressive but not beautiful. He had an english wife who had a very remarkable pair of brown eyes, of a shade of brown I had never before seen in eyes.

Doctor Claribel Cone of Baltimore came majestically in and out. She loved to read Gertrude Stein's work out loud and she did read it out loud extraordinarily well. She liked ease and graciousness and comfort. She and her sister Etta Cone were traveling. The only room in the hotel was not comfortable. Etta bade her sister put up with it as it was only for one night. Etta, answered Doctor Claribel, one night is as important as any other night in my life and I must be comfortable. When the war broke out she happened to be in Munich engaged in scientific work. She could never leave because it was never comfortable to travel. Everybody delighted in Doctor Claribel. Much later Picasso made a drawing of her.

Emily Chadbourne came, it was she who brought Lady Otoline Morrell and she also brought many bostonians.

Mildred Aldrich once brought a very extraordinary person Myra Edgerly. I remembered very well that when I was quite young and went to a fancy-dress ball, a Mardi Gras ball in San Francisco, I saw a very tall and very beautiful and very brilliant woman there. This was Myra Edgerly young. Genthe, the well known photographer did endless photographs of her, mostly with a cat. She had come to London as a miniaturist and she had had one of those phenomenal successes that americans do have in Europe. She had miniatured everybody, and the royal family, and she had maintained her earnest gay careless outspoken San Francisco way through it all. She now came to Paris to study a little. She met Mildred Aldrich and became very devoted to her. Indeed it was Myra who in nineteen thirteen, when Mildred's earning capacity was rapidly dwindling secured an annuity for her and made it possible for Mildred to retire to the Hilltop on the Marne.

Myra Edgerly was very earnestly anxious that Gertrude Stein's work should be more widely known. When Mildred told her about all those unpublished manuscripts Myra said something must be done. And of course something was done.

She knew John Lane slightly and she said Gertrude Stein and I must go to London. But first Myra must write letters and then I must write letters to everybody for Gertrude Stein. She told me the formula I must employ. I remember it began, Miss Gertrude Stein as you may or may not know, is, and then went on and said everything you had to say.

Under Myra's strenuous impulsion we went to London in the winter of nineteen twelve, thirteen, for a few weeks. We did have an awfully good time.

Myra took us with her to stay with Colonel and Mrs. Rogers at Riverhill in Surrey. This was in the vicinity of Knole and of Ightham Mote, beautiful houses and beautiful parks. This was my first experience of country-house visiting in England since, as a small child, I had only been in the nursery. I enjoyed every minute of it. The comfort, the open fires, the tall maids who were like annunciation angels, the beautiful gardens, the children, the ease of it all. And the quantity of objects and of beautiful things. What is that, I would ask Mrs. Rogers, ah that I know nothing about, it was here when I came. It gave me a feeling that there had been so many lovely brides in that house who had found all these things there when they came.

Gertrude Stein liked country-house visiting less than I did. The continuous pleasant hesitating flow of conversation, the never ceasing sound of the human voice speaking in english, bothered her.

On our next visit to London and when because of being

caught by the war we stayed in country houses with our friends a very long time, she managed to isolate herself for considerable parts of the day and to avoid at least one of the three or four meals, and so she liked it better.

We did have a good time in England. Gertrude Stein completely forgot her early dismal memory of London and has liked visiting there immensely ever since.

We went to Roger Fry's house in the country and were charmingly entertained by his quaker sister. We went to Lady Otoline Morrell and met everybody. We went to Clive Bell's. We went about all the time, we went shopping and ordered things. I still have my bag and jewel box. We had an extremely good time. And we went very often to see John Lane. In fact we were supposed to go every Sunday afternoon to his house for tea and Gertrude Stein had several interviews with him in his office. How well I knew all the things in all the shops near the Bodley Head because while Gertrude Stein was inside with John Lane while nothing happened and then when finally something happened I waited outside and looked at everything.

The Sunday afternoons at John Lane's were very amusing. As I remember during that first stay in London we went there twice.

John Lane was very interested. Mrs. John Lane was a Boston woman and very kind.

Tea at the John Lane's Sunday afternoons was an experience. John Lane had copies of Three Lives and The Portrait of Mabel Dodge. One did not know why he selected the people he did to show it to. He did not give either book to any one to read. He put it into their hands and took it away again and inaudibly he announced that Gertrude Stein was here. Nobody was introduced to anybody. From time to time John Lane would take Gertrude Stein into various rooms and show her his pictures, odd pictures of English schools of all periods, some of them very pleasing. Sometimes he told a story about how he had come to get it. He never said anything else about a picture. He also showed her a great many Beardsley drawings and they talked about Paris.

The second Sunday he asked her to come again to the

Bodley Head. This was a long interview. He said that Mrs. Lane had read Three Lives and thought very highly of it and that he had the greatest confidence in her judgment. He asked Gertrude Stein when she was coming back to London. She said she probably was not coming back to London. Well, he said, when you come in July I imagine we will be ready to arrange something. Perhaps, he added, I may see you in Paris in the early spring.

And so we left London. We were on the whole very pleased with ourselves. We had had a very good time and it was the first time that Gertrude Stein had ever had a conversation with a publisher.

Mildred Aldrich often brought a whole group of people to the house Saturday evening. One evening a number of people came in with her and among them was Mabel Dodge. I remember my impression of her very well.

She was a stoutish woman with a very sturdy fringe of heavy hair over her forehead, heavy long lashes and very pretty eyes and a very old fashioned coquetry. She had a lovely voice. She reminded me of a heroine of my youth, the actress Georgia Cayvan. She asked us to come to Florence to stay with her. We were going to spend the summer as was then our habit in Spain but we were going to be back in Paris in the fall and perhaps we then would. When we came back there were several urgent telegrams from Mabel Dodge asking us to come to the Villa Curonia and we did.

We had a very amusing time. We liked Edwin Dodge and we liked Mabel Dodge but we particularly liked Constance Fletcher whom we met there.

Constance Fletcher came a day or so after we arrived and I went to the station to meet her. Mabel Dodge had described her to me as a very large woman who would wear a purple robe and who was deaf. As a matter of fact she was dressed in green and was not deaf but very short sighted, and she was delightful.

Her father and mother came from and lived in Newbury-port, Massachusetts. Edwin Dodge's people came from the same town and this was a strong bond of union. When Constance was twelve years old her mother fell in love with the english tutor of Constance's youngest brother. Constance knew that her mother was about to leave her home. For a week Constance laid on her bed and wept and then accompanied her mother and her future step-father to Italy. Her step-father being an englishman Constance became passionately an english woman. The step-father was a painter who had a local reputation among the english residents in Italy.

When Constance Fletcher was eighteen years old she wrote a best-seller called Kismet and was engaged to be married to Lord Lovelace the descendant of Byron.

She did not marry him and thereafter lived always in Italy. Finally she became permanently fixed in Venice. This was after the death of her mother and father. I always liked as a californian her description of Joaquin Miller in Rome, in her younger days.

Now in her comparative old age she was attractive and impressive. I am very fond of needlework and I was fascinated by her fashion of embroidering wreaths of flowers. There was nothing drawn upon her linen, she just held it in her hands, from time to time bringing it closely to one eye, and eventually the wreath took form. She was very fond of ghosts. There were two of them in the Villa Curonia and Mabel was very fond of frightening visiting americans with them which she did in her suggestive way very effectively. Once she drove a house party consisting of Jo and Yvonne Davidson, Florence Bradley, Mary Foote and a number of others quite mad with fear. And at last to complete the effect she had the local priest in to exorcise the ghosts. You can imagine the state of mind of her guests. But Constance Fletcher was fond of ghosts and particularly attached to the later one, who was a wistful ghost of an english governess who had killed herself in the house.

One morning I went in to Constance Fletcher's bedroom to ask her how she was, she had not been very well the night before.

I went in and closed the door. Constance Fletcher very large and very white was lying in one of the vast renaissance beds with which the villa was furnished. Near the door was a very large renaissance cupboard. I had a delightful night, said Constance Fletcher, the gentle ghost visited me all night, indeed she has just left me. I imagine she is still in the cupboard, will you open it please. I did. Is she there, asked Constance Fletcher. I said I saw nothing. Ah yes, said Constance Fletcher.

We had a delightful time and Gertrude Stein at that time wrote The Portrait of Mabel Dodge. She also wrote the portrait of Constance Fletcher that was later printed in Geography and Plays. Many years later indeed after the war in London I met Siegfried Sassoon at a party given by Edith Sitwell for Gertrude Stein. He spoke of Gertrude Stein's portrait of Constance Fletcher which he had read in Geography and Plays and said that he had first become interested in Gertrude Stein's work because of this portrait. And he added, and did you know her and if you did can you tell me about her marvellous voice. I said, very much interested, then you did not know her. No, he said, I never saw her but she ruined my life. How, I asked excitedly. Because, he answered, she separated my father from my mother.

Constance Fletcher had written one very successful play which had had a long run in London called Green Stockings but her real life had been in Italy. She was more italian than the italians. She admired her step-father and therefore was english but she was really dominated by the fine italian hand of Machiavelli. She could and did intrigue in the italian way better than even the italians and she was a disturbing influence for many years in Venice not only among the english but also among the italians.

André Gide turned up while we were at the Villa Curonia. It was rather a dull evening. It was then also that we first met Muriel Draper and Paul Draper. Gertrude Stein always liked Paul very much. She delighted in his american enthusiasm, and explanation of all things musical and human. He had had a great deal of adventure in the West and that was another bond between them. When Paul Draper left to return to London Mabel Dodge received a telegram saving, pearls missing suspect the second man. She came to Gertrude Stein in great agitation asking what she should do about it

Don't wake me, said Gertrude Stein, do nothing. And then sitting up, but that is a nice thing to say, suspect the second man, that is charming, but who and what is the second man. Mabel explained that the last time they had a robbery in the villa the police said that they could do nothing because nobody suspected any particular person and this time Paul to avoid that complication suspected the second man servant. While this explanation was being given another telegram came, pearls found. The second man had put the pearls in the collar box.

Haweis and his wife, later Mina Loy were also in Florence. Their home had been dismantled as they had had workmen in it but they put it all in order to give us a delightful lunch. Both Haweis and Mina were among the very earliest to be interested in the work of Gertrude Stein. Haweis had been fascinated with what he had read in manuscript of The Making of Americans. He did however plead for commas. Gertrude Stein said commas were unnecessary, the sense should be intrinsic and not have to be explained by commas and otherwise commas were only a sign that one should pause and take breath but one should know of oneself when one wanted to pause and take breath. However, as she liked Haweis very much and he had given her a delightful painting for a fan, she gave him two commas. It must however be added that on re-reading the manuscript she took the commas out.

Mina Loy equally interested was able to understand without the commas. She has always been able to understand.

Gertrude Stein having written The Portrait of Mabel Dodge, Mabel Dodge immediately wanted it printed. She had three hundred copies struck off and bound in Florentine paper. Constance Fletcher corrected the proofs and we were all awfully pleased. Mabel Dodge immediately conceived the idea that Gertrude Stein should be invited from one country house to another and do portraits and then end up doing portraits of american millionaires which would be a very exciting and lucrative career. Gertrude Stein laughed. A little later we went back to Paris.

It was during this winter that Gertrude Stein began to

write plays. They began with the one entitled, It Happened a Play. This was written about a dinner party given by Harry and Bridget Gibb. She then wrote Ladies' Voices. Her interest in writing plays continues. She says a landscape is such a natural arrangement for a battle-field or a play that one must write plays.

Florence Bradley, a friend of Mabel Dodge, was spending a winter in Paris. She had had some stage experience and had been interested in planning a little theatre. She was vitally interested in putting these plays on the stage. Demuth was in Paris too at this time. He was then more interested in writing than in painting and particularly interested in these plays. He and Florence Bradley were always talking them over together.

Gertrude Stein has never seen Demuth since. When she first heard that he was painting she was much interested. They never wrote to each other but they often sent messages by mutual friends. Demuth always sent word that some day he would do a little picture that would thoroughly please him and then he would send it to her. And sure enough after all these years, two years ago some one left at the rue de Fleurus during our absence a little picture with a message that this was the picture that Demuth was ready to give to Gertrude Stein. It is a remarkable little landscape in which the roofs and windows are so subtle that they are as mysterious and as alive at the roofs and windows of Hawthorne or Henry James.

It was not long after this that Mabel Dodge went to America and it was the winter of the armoury show which was the first time the general public had a chance to see any of these pictures. It was there that Marcel Duchamp's Nude Descending the Staircase was shown.

It was about this time that Picabia and Gertrude Stein met. I remember going to dinner at the Picabias' and a pleasant dinner it was, Gabrielle Picabia full of life and gaiety, Picabia dark and lively, and Marcel Duchamp looking like a young norman crusader.

I was always perfectly able to understand the enthusiasm that Marcel Duchamp aroused in New York when he went there in the early years of the war. His brother had just died from the effect of his wounds, his other brother was still at the front and he himself was inapt for military service. He was very depressed and he went to America. Everybody loved him. So much so that it was a joke in Paris that when any american arrived in Paris the first thing he said was, and how is Marcel. Once Gertrude Stein went to see Braque, just after the war, and going into the studio in which there happened just then to be three young americans, she said to Braque, and how is Marcelle. The three young americans came up to her breathlessly and said, have you seen Marcel. She laughed, and having become accustomed to the inevitableness of the american belief that there was only one Marcel, she explained that Braque's wife was named Marcelle and it was Marcelle Braque about whom she was enquiring.

In those days Picabia and Gertrude Stein did not get to be very good friends. He annoyed her with his incessantness and what she called the vulgarity of his delayed adolescence. But oddly enough in this last year they have gotten to be very fond of each other. She is very much interested in his drawing and in his painting. It began with his show just a year ago. She is now convinced that although he has in a sense not a painter's gift he has an idea that has been and will be of immense value to all time. She calls him the Leonardo da Vinci of the movement. And it is true, he understands and invents everything.

As soon as the winter of the armoury show was over Mabel Dodge came back to Europe and she brought with her what Jacques-Emile Blanche called her collection des jeunes gens assortis, a mixed assortment of young men. In the lot were Carl Van Vechten, Robert Jones and John Reed. Carl Van Vechten did not come to the rue de Fleurus with her. He came later in the spring by himself. The other two came with her. I remember the evening they all came. Picasso was there too. He looked at John Reed critically and said, le genre de Braque mais beaucoup moins rigolo, Braque's kind but much less diverting. I remember also that Reed told me about his trip through Spain. He told me he had seen many strange sights there, that he had seen witches chased through the street of Salamanca. As I had been spending months in Spain and he only weeks I neither liked his stories nor believed them.

Robert Jones was very impressed by Gertrude Stein's looks. He said he would like to array her in cloth of gold and he wanted to design it then and there. It did not interest her.

Among the people that we had met at John Lane's in London was Gordon Caine and her husband. Gordon Caine had been a Wellesley girl who played the harp with which she always travelled, and who always re-arranged the furniture in the hotel room completely, even if she was only to stay one night. She was tall, rosy-haired and very good-looking. Her husband was a well known humorous english writer and one of John Lane's authors. They had entertained us very pleasantly in London and we asked them to dine with us their first night in Paris. I don't know quite what happened but Hélène cooked a very bad dinner. Only twice in all her long service did Hélène fail us. This time and when about two weeks later Carl Van Vechten turned up. That time too she did strange things, her dinner consisting of a series of hors d'œuvres. However that is later.

During dinner Mrs. Caine said that she had taken the liberty of asking her very dear friend and college mate Mrs. Van Vechten to come in after dinner because she was very anxious that she should meet Gertrude Stein as she was very depressed and unhappy and Gertrude Stein could undoubtedly have an influence for the good in her life. Gertrude Stein said that she had a vague association with the name of Van Vechten but could not remember what it was. She has a bad memory for names. Mrs. Van Vechten came. She too was a very tall woman, it would appear that a great many tall ones go to Wellesley, and she too was good-looking. Mrs. Van Vechten told the story of the tragedy of her married life but Gertrude Stein was not particularly interested.

It was about a week later that Florence Bradley asked us to go with her to see the second performance of the Sacre du Printemps. The russian ballet had just given the first performance of it and it had made a terrible uproar. All

Paris was excited about it. Florence Bradley had gotten three tickets in a box, the box held four, and asked us to go with her. In the meantime there had been a letter from Mabel Dodge introducing Carl Van Vechten, a young New York journalist. Gertrude Stein invited him to dine the following Saturday evening.

We went early to the russian ballet, these were the early great days of the russian ballet with Nijinsky as the great dancer. And a great dancer he was. Dancing excites me tremendously and it is a thing I know a great deal about. I have seen three very great dancers. My geniuses seem to run in threes, but that is not my fault, it happens to be a fact. The three really great dancers I have seen are the Argentina, Isadora Duncan and Nijinsky. Like the three geniuses I have known they are each one of a different nationality.

Nijinsky did not dance in the Sacre du Printemps but he created the dance of those who did dance.

We arrived in the box and sat down in the three front chairs leaving one chair behind. Just in front of us in the seats below was Guillaume Apollinaire. He was dressed in evening clothes and he was industriously kissing various important looking ladies' hands. He was the first one of his crowd to come out into the great world wearing evening clothes and kissing hands. We were very amused and very pleased to see him do it. It was the first time we had seen him doing it. After the war they all did these things but he was the only one to commence before the war.

Just before the performance began the fourth chair in our box was occupied. We looked around and there was a tall well-built young man, he might have been a dutchman, a scandinavian or an american and he wore a soft evening shirt with the tiniest pleats all over the front of it. It was impressive, we had never even heard that they were wearing evening shirts like that. That evening when we got home Gertrude Stein did a portrait of the unknown called a Portrait of One.

The performance began. No sooner had it commenced when the excitement began. The scene now so well known with its brilliantly coloured background now not at all extraordinary, outraged the Paris audience. No sooner did the music begin and the dancing than they began to hiss. The defenders began to applaud. We could hear nothing, as a matter of fact I never did hear any of the music of the Sacre du Printemps because it was the only time I ever saw it and one literally could not, throughout the whole performance, hear the sound of music. The dancing was very fine and that we could see although our attention was constantly distracted by a man in the box next to us flourishing his cane, and finally in a violent altercation with an enthusiast in the box next to him, his cane came down and smashed the opera hat the other had just put on in defiance. It was all incredibly fierce.

The next Saturday evening Carl Van Vechten was to come to dinner. He came and he was the young man of the soft much-pleated evening shirt and it was the same shirt. Also of course he was the hero or villain of Mrs. Van Vechten's tragic tale.

As I said Hélène did for the second time in her life make an extraordinarily bad dinner. For some reason best known to herself she gave us course after course of hors d'œuvres finishing up with a sweet omelet. Gertrude Stein began to tease Carl Van Vechten by dropping a word here and there of intimate knowledge of his past life. He was naturally bewildered. It was a curious evening.

Gertrude Stein and he became dear friends.

He interested Allan and Louise Norton in her work and induced them to print in the little magazine they founded, The Rogue, the first thing of Gertrude Stein's ever printed in a little magazine, The Galérie Lafayette. In another number of this now rare little magazine, he printed a little essay on the work of Gertrude Stein. It was he who in one of his early books printed as a motto the device on Gertrude Stein's note-paper, a rose is a rose is a rose is a rose. Just recently she has had made for him by our local potter at the foot of the hill at Belley some plates in the yellow clay of the country and around the border is a rose is a rose is a rose is a rose and in the centre is to Carl.

In season and out he kept her name and her work before
the public. When he was beginning to be well known and
they asked him what he thought the most important book
of the year he replied Three Lives by Gertrude Stein. His
loyalty and his effort never weakened. He tried to make
Knopf publish The Making of Americans and he almost succeeded but of course they weakened.

Speaking of the device of rose is a rose is a rose is a rose,
it was I who found it in one of Gertrude Stein's manuscripts
and insisted upon putting it as a device on the letter paper,
on the table linen and anywhere that she would permit that
I would put it. I am very pleased with myself for having
done so.

Carl Van Vechten has had a delightful habit all these
years of giving letters of introduction to people who he
thought would amuse Gertrude Stein. This he has done with
so much discrimination that she has liked them all.

The first and perhaps the one she has liked the best was
Avery Hopwood. The friendship lasted until Avery's death
a few years ago. When Avery came to Paris he always asked
Gertrude Stein and myself to dine with him. This custom
began in the early days of the acquaintance. Gertrude Stein
is not a very enthusiastic diner-out but she never refused
Avery. He always had the table charmingly decorated with
flowers and the menu most carefully chosen. He sent us endless petits bleus, little telegrams, arranging this affair and
we always had a good time. In these early days, holding his
head a little on one side and with his tow-coloured hair, he
looked like a lamb. Sometimes in the latter days as Gertrude
Stein told him the lamb turned into a wolf. Gertrude Stein
would I know at this moment say, dear Avery. They were
very fond of each other. Not long before his death he came
into the room one day and said I wish I could give you something else beside just dinner, he said, perhaps I could give
you a picture. Gertrude Stein laughed, it is alright, she said
to him, Avery, if you will always come here and take just
tea. And then in the future beside the petit bleu in which he
proposed our dining with him he would send another petit
bleu saying that he would come one afternoon to take just

tea. Once he came and brought with him Gertrude Atherton. He said so sweetly, I want the two Gertrudes whom I love so much to know each other. It was a perfectly delightful afternoon. Every one was pleased and charmed and as for me a californian, Gertrude Atherton had been my youthful idol and so I was very content.

The last time we saw Avery was on his last visit to Paris. He sent his usual message asking us to dinner and when he came to call for us he told Gertrude Stein that he had asked some of his friends to come because he was going to ask her to do something for him. You see, he said, you have never gone to Montmartre with me and I have a great fancy that you should to-night. I know it was your Montmartre long before it was mine but would you. She laughed and said, of course Avery.

We did after dinner go up to Montmartre with him. We went to a great many queer places and he was so proud and pleased. We were always going in a cab from one place to another and Avery Hopwood and Gertrude Stein went together and they had long talks and Avery must have had some premonition that it was the last time because he had never talked so openly and so intimately. Finally we left and he came out and put us into a cab and he told Gertrude Stein it had been one of the best evenings of his life. He left the next day for the south and we for the country. A little while after Gertrude Stein had a postal from him telling her how happy he had been to see her again and the same morning there was the news of his death in the Herald.

It was about nineteen twelve that Alvin Langdon Coburn turned up in Paris. He was a queer american who brought with him a queer english woman, his adopted mother. Alvin Langdon Coburn had just finished a series of photographs that he had done for Henry James. He had published a book of photographs of prominent men and he wished now to do a companion volume of prominent women. I imagine it was Roger Fry who had told him about Gertrude Stein. At any rate he was the first photographer to come and photograph her as a celebrity and she was nicely gratified. He did make some very good photographs of her and gave them to her and then he disappeared and though Gertrude Stein has often asked about him nobody seems ever to have heard of him since.

This brings us pretty well to the spring of nineteen fourteen. During this winter among the people who used to come to the house was the younger step-daughter of Bernard Berenson. She brought with her a young friend, Hope Mirlees and Hope said that when we went to England in the summer we must go down to Cambridge and stay with her people. We promised that we would.

During the winter Gertrude Stein's brother decided that he would go to Florence to live. They divided the pictures that they had bought together, between them. Gertrude Stein kept the Cézannes and Picassos and her brother the Matisses and Renoirs, with the exception of the original Femme au Chapeau.

We planned that we would have a little passage-way made between the studio and the little house and as that entailed cutting a door and plastering we decided that we would paint the atelier and repaper the house and put in electricity. We proceeded to have all this done. It was the end of June before this was accomplished and the house had not yet been put in order when Gertrude Stein received a letter from John Lane saying he would be in Paris the following day and would come to see her.

We worked very hard, that is I did and the concierge and Hélène and the room was ready to receive him.

He brought with him the first copy of Blast by Wyndham Lewis and he gave it to Gertrude Stein and wanted to know what she thought of it and would she write for it. She said she did not know.

John Lane then asked her if she would come to London in July as he had almost made up his mind to republish the Three Lives and would she bring another manuscript with her. She said she would and she suggested a collection of all the portraits she had done up to that time. The Making of Americans was not considered because it was too long. And so that having been arranged John Lane left.

In those days Picasso having lived rather sadly in the rue

Schœlcher was to move a little further out to Montrouge. It was not an unhappy time for him but after the Montmartre days one never heard his high whinnying spanish giggle. His friends, a great many of them, had followed him to Montparnasse but it was not the same. The intimacy with Braque was waning and of his old friends the only ones he saw frequently were Guillaume Apollinaire and Gertrude Stein. It was in that year that he began to use ripolin paints instead of the usual colours used by painters. Just the other day he was talking a long time about the ripolin paints. They are, said he gravely, la santé des couleurs, that is they are the basis of good health for paints. In those days he painted pictures and everything with ripolin paints as he still does, and as so many of his followers young and old do.

He was at this time too making constructions in paper, in tin and in all sorts of things, the sort of thing that made it possible for him afterwards to do the famous stage setting for Parade.

It was in these days that Mildred Aldrich was preparing to retire to the Hilltop on the Marne. She too was not unhappy but rather sad. She wanted us often in those spring evenings to take a cab and have what she called our last ride together. She more often than ever dropped her house key all the way down the centre of the stairway while she called good-night to us from the top story of the apartment house on the rue Boissonnade.

We often went out to the country with her to see her house. Finally she moved in. We went out and spent the day with her. Mildred was not unhappy but she was very sad. My curtains are all up, my books in order, everything is clean and what shall I do now, said Mildred. I told her that when I was a little girl, my mother said that I always used to say, what shall I do now, which was only varied by now what shall I do. Mildred said that the worst of it was that we were going to London and that she would not see us all summer. We assured her that we would only stay away a month, in fact we had return tickets, and so we had to, and as soon as we got home we would go out to see her. Anyway she was happy that at last Gertrude Stein was going to have a publisher who would publish her books. But look out for John Lane, he is a fox, she said, as we kissed her and left.

Hélène was leaving 27 rue de Fleurus because, her husband having recently been promoted to be foreman in his work shop he insisted that she must not work out any longer but must stay at home.

In short in this spring and early summer of nineteen fourteen the old life was over.

6

THE WAR

Americans living in Europe before the war never really believed that there was going to be war. Gertrude Stein always tells about the little janitor's boy who, playing in the court, would regularly every couple of years assure her that papa was going to the war. Once some cousins of hers were living in Paris, they had a country girl as a servant. It was the time of the russian-japanese war and they were all talking about the latest news. Terrified she dropped the platter and cried, and are the germans at the gates.

William Cook's father was an Iowan who at seventy years of age was making his first trip in Europe in the summer of nineteen fourteen. When the war was upon them he refused to believe it and explained that he could understand a family fighting among themselves, in short a civil war, but not a serious war with one's neighbours.

Gertrude Stein in 1913 and 1914 had been very interested reading the newspapers. She rarely read french newspapers, she never read anything in french, and she always read the Herald. That winter she added the Daily Mail. She liked to read about the suffragettes and she liked to read about Lord Roberts' campaign for compulsory military service in England. Lord Roberts had been a favourite hero of hers early in her life. His Forty-One Years in India was a book she often read and she had seen Lord Roberts when she and her brother, then taking a college vacation, had seen Edward the Seventh's coronation procession. She read the

Daily Mail, although, as she said, she was not interested in
Ireland.

We went to England July fifth and went according to
programme to see John Lane at his house Sunday afternoon.

There were a number of people there and they were talking of many things but some of them were talking about
war. One of them, some one told me he was an editorial
writer on one of the big London dailies, was bemoaning the
fact that he would not be able to eat figs in August in Pro-
vence as was his habit. Why not, asked some one. Because of
the war, he answered. Some one else, Walpole or his brother
I think it was, said that there was no hope of beating Germany as she had such an excellent system, all her railroad
trucks were numbered in connection with locomotives and
switches. But, said the eater of figs, that is all very well as
long as the trucks remain in Germany on their own lines and
switches, but in an aggressive war they will leave the
frontiers of Germany and then, well I promise you then
there will be a great deal of numbered confusion.

This is all I remember definitely on that Sunday afternoon
in July.

As we were leaving, John Lane said to Gertrude Stein
that he was going out of town for a week and he made a
rendezvous with her in his office for the end of July, to sign
the contract for Three Lives. I think, he said, in the present
state of affairs I would rather begin with that than with
something more entirely new. I have confidence in that book.
Mrs. Lane is very enthusiastic and so are the readers.

Having now ten days on our hands we decided to accept
the invitation of Mrs. Mirlees, Hope's mother, and spend a
few days in Cambridge. We went there and thoroughly enjoyed ourselves.

It was a most comfortable house to visit. Gertrude Stein
liked it, she could stay in her room or in the garden as much
as she liked without hearing too much conversation. The
food was excellent, scotch food, delicious and fresh, and it
was very amusing meeting all the University of Cambridge
dignitaries. We were taken into all the gardens and invited

into many of the homes. It was lovely weather, quantities of roses, morris-dancing by all the students and girls and generally delightful. We were invited to lunch at Newnham, Miss Jane Harrison, who had been Hope Mirlees' pet enthusiasm, was much interested in meeting Gertrude Stein. We sat up on the dais with the faculty and it was very awe inspiring. The conversation was not however particularly amusing. Miss Harrison and Gertrude Stein did not particularly interest each other.

We had been hearing a good deal about Doctor and Mrs. Whitehead. They no longer lived in Cambridge. The year before Doctor Whitehead had left Cambridge to go to London University. They were to be in Cambridge shortly and they were to dine at the Mirlees'. They did and I met my third genius.

It was a pleasant dinner. I sat next to Housman, the Cambridge poet, and we talked about fishes and David Starr Jordan but all the time I was more interested in watching Doctor Whitehead. Later we went into the garden and he came and sat next to me and we talked about the sky in Cambridge.

Gertrude Stein and Doctor Whitehead and Mrs. Whitehead all became interested in each other. Mrs. Whitehead asked us to dine at her house in London and then to spend a week end, the last week end in July with them in their country home in Lockridge, near Salisbury Plain. We accepted with pleasure.

We went back to London and had a lovely time. We were ordering some comfortable chairs and a comfortable couch covered with chintz to replace some of the italian furniture that Gertrude Stein's brother had taken with him. This took a great deal of time. We had to measure ourselves into the chairs and into the couch and to choose chintz that would go with the pictures, all of which we successfully achieved. These chairs and this couch, and they are comfortable, in spite of war came to the door one day in January, nineteen fifteen at the rue de Fleurus and were greeted by us with the greatest delight. One needed such comforting and such comfort in those days. We dined with the Whiteheads and liked them more than ever and they liked us more than ever and were kind enough to say so.

Gertrude Stein kept her appointment with John Lane at the Bodley Head. They had a very long conversation, this time so long that I quite exhausted all the shop windows of that region for quite a distance, but finally Gertrude Stein came out with a contract. It was a gratifying climax.

Then we took the train to Lockridge to spend the week end with the Whiteheads. We had a week-end trunk, we were very proud of our week-end trunk, we had used it on our first visit and now we were actively using it again. As one of my friends said to me later, they asked you to spend the week end and you stayed six weeks. We did.

There was quite a house party when we arrived, some Cambridge people, some young men, the younger son of the Whiteheads, Eric, then fifteen years old but very tall and flower-like and the daughter Jessie just back from Newnham. There could not have been much serious thought of war because they were all talking of Jessie Whitehead's coming trip to Finland. Jessie always made friends with foreigners from strange places, she had a passion for geography and a passion for the glory of the British Empire. She had a friend, a finn, who had asked her to spend the summer with her people in Finland and had promised Jessie a possible uprising against Russia. Mrs. Whitehead was hesitating but had practically consented. There was an older son North who was away at the time.

Then suddenly, as I remember, there were the conferences to prevent the war, Lord Grey and the russian minister of foreign affairs. And then before anything further could happen the ultimatum to France. Gertrude Stein and I were completely miserable as was Evelyn Whitehead, who had french blood and who had been raised in France and had strong french sympathies. Then came the days of the invasion of Belgium and I can still hear Doctor Whitehead's gentle voice reading the papers out loud and then all of them talking about the destruction of Louvain and how they must help the brave little belgians. Gertrude Stein desperately un-

happy said to me, where is Louvain. Don't you know, I said.
No, she said, nor do I care, but where is it.

Our week end was over and we told Mrs. Whitehead that
we must leave. But you cannot get back to Paris now, she
said. No, we answered, but we can stay in London. Oh no,
she said, you must stay with us until you can get back to
Paris. She was very sweet and we were very unhappy and
we liked them and they liked us and we agreed to stay. And
then to our infinite relief England came into the war.

We had to go to London to get our trunks, to cable to
people in America and to draw money, and Mrs. Whitehead
wished to go in to see if she and her daughter could do anything to help the belgians. I remember that trip so well.
There seemed so many people about everywhere, although
the train was not overcrowded, but all the stations even little
country ones, were filled with people, not people at all
troubled but just a great many people. At the junction where
we were to change trains we met Lady Astley, a friend of
Myra Edgerly's whom we had met in Paris. Oh how do you
do, she said in a cheerful loud voice, I am going to London
to say goodbye to my son. Is he going away, we said politely.
Oh yes, she said, he is in the guards you know, and is leaving
tonight for France.

In London everything was difficult. Gertrude Stein's letter
of credit was on a french bank but mine luckily small was
on a California one. I say luckily small because the banks
would not give large sums but my letter of credit was so
small and so almost used up that they without hesitation
gave me all that there was left of it.

Gertrude Stein cabled to her cousin in Baltimore to send
her money, we gathered in our trunks, we met Evelyn Whitehead at the train and we went back with her to Lockridge.
It was a relief to get back. We appreciated her kindness
because to have been at a hotel in London at that moment
would have been too dreadful.

Then one day followed another and it is hard to remember just what happened. North Whitehead was away and
Mrs Whitehead was terribly worried lest he should rashly
enlist. She must see him. So they telegraphed to him to come

at once. He came. She had been quite right. He had immediately gone to the nearest recruiting station to enlist and luckily there had been so many in front of him that the office closed before he was admitted. She immediately went to London to see Kitchener. Doctor Whitehead's brother was a bishop in India and he had in his younger days known Kitchener very intimately. Mrs. Whitehead had this introduction and North was given a commission. She came home much relieved. North was to join in three days but in the meantime he must learn to drive a motor car. The three days passed very quickly and North was gone. He left immediately for France and without much equipment. And then came the time of waiting.

Evelyn Whitehead was very busy planning war work and helping every one and I as far as possible helped her. Gertrude Stein and Doctor Whitehead walked endlessly around the country. They talked of philosophy and history, it was during these days that Gertrude Stein realised how completely it was Doctor Whitehead and not Russell who had had the ideas for their great book. Doctor Whitehead, the gentlest and most simply generous of human beings never claimed anything for himself and enormously admired anyone who was brilliant, and Russell undoubtedly was brilliant.

Gertrude Stein used to come back and tell me about these walks and the country still the same as in the days of Chaucer, with the green paths of the early britons that could still be seen in long stretches, and the triple rainbows of that strange summer. They used, Doctor Whitehead and Gertrude Stein, to have long conversations with game-keepers and mole-catchers. The mole-catcher had said, but sir, England has never been in a war but that she has been victorious. Doctor Whitehead turned to Gertrude Stein with a gentle smile. I think we may say so, he said. The game-keeper, when Doctor Whitehead seemed discouraged said to him, but Doctor Whitehead, England is the predominant nation, is she not. I hope she is, yes I hope she is, replied Doctor Whitehead gently.

The germans were getting nearer and nearer Paris. One

day Doctor Whitehead said to Gertrude Stein, they were just going through a rough little wood and he was helping her, have you any copies of your writings or are they all in Paris. They are all in Paris, she said. I did not like to ask, said Doctor Whitehead, but I have been worrying.

The germans were getting nearer and nearer Paris and the last day Gertrude Stein could not leave her room, she sat and mourned. She loved Paris, she thought neither of manuscripts nor of pictures, she thought only of Paris and she was desolate. I came up to her room, I called out, it is alright Paris is saved, the germans are in retreat. She turned away and said, don't tell me these things. But it's true, I said, it is true. And then we wept together.

The first description that any one we knew received in England of the battle of the Marne came in a letter to Gertrude Stein from Mildred Aldrich. It was practically the first letter of her book the Hilltop on the Marne. We were delighted to receive it, to know that Mildred was safe, and to know all about it. It was passed around and everybody in the neighbourhood read it.

Later when we returned to Paris we had two other descriptions of the battle of the Marne. I had an old school friend from California, Nellie Jacot who lived in Boulogne-sur-Seine and I was very worried about her. I telegraphed to her and she telegraphed back characteristically, Nullement en danger ne t'inquiète pas, there is no danger don't worry. It was Nellie who used to call Picasso in the early days a good-looking boot-black and used to say of Fernande, she is alright but I don't see why you bother about her. It was also Nellie who made Matisse blush by cross-questioning him about the different ways he saw Madame Matisse, how she looked to him as a wife and how she looked to him as a picture, and how he could change from one to the other. It was also Nellie who told the story which Gertrude Stein loved to quote, of a young man who once said to her, I love you Nellie, Nellie is your name, isn't it. It was also Nellie who when we came back from England and we said that everybody had been so kind, said, oh yes, I know that kind.

Nellie described the battle of the Marne to us. You know, she said, I always come to town once a week to shop and I always bring my maid. We come in in the street car because it is difficult to get a taxi in Boulogne and we go back in a taxi. Well we came in as usual and didn't notice anything and when we had finished our shopping and had had our tea we stood on a corner to get a taxi. We stopped several and when they heard where we wanted to go they drove on. I know that sometimes taxi drivers don't like to go out to Boulogne so I said to Marie tell them we will give them a big tip if they will go. So she stopped another taxi with an old driver and I said to him, I will give you a very big tip to take us out to Boulogne. Ah, said he laying his finger on his nose, to my great regret madame it is impossible, no taxi can leave the city limits to-day. Why, I asked. He winked in answer and drove off. We had to go back to Boulogne in a street car. Of course we understood later, when we heard about Gallieni and the taxis, said Nellie and added, and that was the battle of the Marne.

Another description of the battle of the Marne when we first came back to Paris was from Alfy Maurer. I was sitting, said Alfy at a café and Paris was pale, if you know what I mean, said Alfy, it was like a pale absinthe. Well I was sitting there and then I noticed lots of horses pulling lots of big trucks going slowly by and there were some soldiers with them and on the boxes was written Banque de France. That was the gold going away just like that, said Alfy, before the battle of the Marne.

In those dark days of waiting in England of course a great many things happened. There were a great many people coming and going in the Whiteheads' home and there was of course plenty of discussion. First there was Lytton Strachey. He lived in a little house not far from Lockridge.

He came one evening to see Mrs. Whitehead. He was a thin sallow man with a silky beard and a faint high voice. We had met him the year before when we had been invited to meet George Moore at the house of Miss Ethel Sands. Gertrude Stein and George Moore, who looked very like a prosperous Mellins Food baby, had not been interested in each other. Lytton Strachey and I talked together about Picasso and the russian ballet.

He came in this evening and he and Mrs. Whitehead discussed the possibility of rescuing Lytton Strachey's sister who was lost in Germany. She suggested that he apply to a certain person who could help him. But, said Lytton Strachey faintly, I have never met him. Yes, said Mrs. Whitehead, but you might write to him and ask to see him. Not, replied Lytton Strachey faintly, if I have never met him.

Another person who turned up during that week was Bertrand Russell. He came to Lockridge the day North Whitehead left for the front. He was a pacifist and argumentative and although they were very old friends Doctor and Mrs. Whitehead did not think they could bear hearing his views just then. He came and Gertrude Stein, to divert everybody's mind from the burning question of war or peace, introduced the subject of education. This caught Russell and he explained all the weaknesses of the american system of education, particularly their neglect of the study of greek. Gertrude Stein replied that of course England which was an island needed Greece which was or might have been an island. At any rate greek was essentially an island culture, while America needed essentially the culture of a continent which was of necessity latin. This argument fussed Mr. Russell, he became very eloquent. Gertrude Stein then became very earnest and gave a long discourse on the value of greek to the english, aside from its being an island, and the lack of value of greek culture for the americans based upon the psychology of americans as different from the psychology of the english. She grew very eloquent on the disembodied abstract quality of the american character and cited examples, mingling automobiles with Emerson, and all proving that they did not need greek, in a way that fussed Russell more and more and kept everybody occupied until everybody went to bed.

There were many discussions in those days. The bishop, the brother of Doctor Whitehead and his family came to lunch. They all talked constantly about how England had come into the war to save Belgium. At last my nerves could

bear it no longer and I blurted out, why do you say that, why
do you not say that you are fighting for England, I do not
consider it a disgrace to fight for one's country.

Mrs. Bishop, the bishop's wife was very funny on this
occasion. She said solemnly to Gertrude Stein, Miss Stein
you are I understand an important person in Paris. I think
it would come very well from a neutral like yourself to suggest to the french government that they give us Pondichéry.
It would be very useful to us. Gertrude Stein replied politely
that to her great regret her importance such as it was was
among painters and writers and not with politicians. But
that, said Mrs. Bishop, would make no difference. You should
I think suggest to the french government that they give us
Pondichéry. After lunch Gertrude Stein said to me under her
breath, where the hell is Pondichéry.

Gertrude Stein used to get furious when the english all
talked about german organisation. She used to insist that the
germans had no organisation, they had method but no organisation. Don't you understand the difference, she used to
say angrily, any two americans, any twenty americans, any
millions of americans can organise themselves to do something but germans cannot organise themselves to do anything,
they can formulate a method and this method can be put
upon them but that isn't organisation. The germans, she
used to insist, are not modern, they are a backward people
who have made a method of what we conceive as organisation, can't you see. They cannot therefore possibly win this
war because they are not modern.

Then another thing that used to annoy us deadfully was
the english statement that the germans in America would
turn America against the allies. Don't be silly, Gertrude Stein
used to say to any and all of them, if you do not realise that
the fundamental sympathy in America is with France and
England and could never be with a mediaeval country like
Germany, you cannot understand America. We are republi-
can, she used to say with energy, profoundly intensely and
completely a republic and a republic can have everything in
common with France and a great deal in common with
England but whatever its form of government nothing in

common with Germany. How often I have heard her then and since explain that americans are republicans living in a republic which is so much a republic that it could never be anything else.

The long summer wore on. It was beautiful weather and beautiful country, and Doctor Whitehead and Gertrude Stein never ceased wandering around in it and talking about all things.

From time to time we went to London. We went regularly to Cook's office to know when we might go back to Paris and they always answered not yet. Gertrude Stein went to see John Lane. He was terribly upset. He was passionately patriotic. He said of course he was doing nothing at present but publishing war-books but soon very soon things would be different or perhaps the war would be over.

Gertrude Stein's cousin and my father sent us money by the United States cruiser Tennessee. We went to get it. We were each one put on the scale and our heights measured and then they gave the money to us. How, said we to one another, can a cousin who has not seen you in ten years and a father who has not seen me for six years possibly know our heights and our weights. It had always been a puzzle. Four years ago Gertrude Stein's cousin came to Paris and the first thing she said to him was, Julian how did you know my weight and height when you sent me money by the Tennessee. Did I know it, he said. Well, she said, at any rate they had written it down that you did. I cannot remember of course, he said, but if any one were to ask me now I would naturally send to Washington for a copy of your passport and I probably did that then. And so was the mystery solved.

We also had to go to the american embassy to get temporary passports to go back to Paris. We had no papers, nobody had any papers in those days. Gertrude Stein as a matter of fact had what they called in Paris a papier de matriculation which stated that she was an american and a french resident.

The embassy was very full of not very american looking citizens waiting their turn. Finally we were ushered in to a very tired looking young american. Gertrude Stein remarked upon the number of not very american looking citizens that were waiting. The young american sighed. They are easier, he said, because they have papers, it is only the native born american who has no papers. Well what do you do about them, asked Gertrude Stein. We guess, he said, and we hope we guess right. And now, said he, will you take the oath. Oh dear, he said, I have said it so often I have forgotten it.

By the fifteenth of October Cook's said we could go back to Paris. Mrs. Whitehead was to go with us. North, her son, had left without an overcoat, and she had secured one and she was afraid he would not get it until much later if she sent it the ordinary way. She arranged to go to Paris and deliver it to him herself or find some one who would take it to him directly. She had papers from the war office and Kitchener and we started.

I remember the leaving London very little, I cannot even remember whether it was day-light or not but it must have been because when we were on the channel boat it was day-light. The boat was crowded. There were quantities of belgian soldiers and officers escaped from Antwerp, all with tired eyes. It was our first experience of the tired but watchful eyes of soldiers. We finally were able to arrange a seat for Mrs. Whitehead who had been ill and soon we were in France. Mrs. Whitehead's papers were so overpowering that there were no delays and soon we were in the train and about ten o'clock at night we were in Paris. We took a taxi and drove through Paris, beautiful and unviolated, to the rue de Fleurus. We were once more at home.

Everybody who had seemed so far away came to see us. Alfy Maurer described being on the Marne at his favourite village, he always fished the Marne, and the mobilisation locomotive coming and the germans were coming and he was so frightened and he tried to get a conveyance and finally after terrific efforts he succeeded and got back to Paris. As he left Gertrude Stein went with him to the door and came back smiling. Mrs. Whitehead said with some constraint, Gertrude you have always spoken so warmly of Alfy Maurer but how can you like a man who shows himself not only selfish but a coward and at a time like this. He thought only of saving himself and he after all was a neutral. Gertrude

Stein burst out laughing. You foolish woman, she said, didn't you understand, of course Alfy had his girl with him and he was scared to death lest she should fall into the hands of the germans.

There were not many people in Paris just then and we liked it and we wandered around Paris and it was so nice to be there, wonderfully nice. Soon Mrs. Whitehead found means of sending her son's coat to him and went back to England and we settled down for the winter.

Gertrude Stein sent copies of her manuscripts to friends in New York to keep for her. We hoped that all danger was over but still it seemed better to do so and there were Zeppelins to come. London had been completely darkened at night before we left. Paris continued to have its usual street lights until January.

How it all happened I do not at all remember but it was through Carl Van Vechten and had something to do with the Nortons, but at any rate there was a letter from Donald Evans proposing to publish three manuscripts to make a small book and would Gertrude Stein suggest a title for them. Of these three manuscripts two had been written during our first trip into Spain and Food, Rooms etcetera, immediately on our return. They were the beginning, as Gertrude Stein would say, of mixing the outside with the inside. Hitherto she had been concerned with seriousness and the inside of things, in these studies she began to describe the inside as seen from the outside. She was awfully pleased at the idea of these three things being published, and immediately consented, and suggested the title of Tender Buttons. Donald Evans called his firm the Claire Marie and he sent over a contract just like any other contract. We took it for granted that there was a Claire Marie but there evidently was not. There were printed of this edition I forget whether it was seven hundred and fifty or a thousand copies but at any rate it was a very charming little book and Gertrude Stein was enormously pleased, and it, as every one knows, had an enormous influence on all young writers and started off columnists in the newspapers of the whole country on their long campaign of ridicule. I must say that when the columnists are really funny, and they quite often are, Gertrude Stein chuckles and reads them aloud to me.

In the meantime the dreary winter of fourteen and fifteen went on. One night, I imagine it must have been about the end of January, I had as was and is my habit gone to bed very early, and Gertrude Stein was down in the studio working, as was her habit. Suddenly I heard her call me gently. What is it, I said. Oh nothing, said she, but perhaps if you don't mind putting on something warm and coming downstairs I think perhaps it would be better. What is it, I said, a revolution. The concierges and the wives of the concierges were all always talking about a revolution. The french are so accustomed to revolutions, they have had so many, that when anything happens they immediately think and say, revolution. Indeed Gertrude Stein once said rather impatiently to some french soldiers when they said something about a revolution, you are silly, you have had one perfectly good revolution and several not quite so good ones; for an intelligent people it seems to me foolish to be always thinking of repeating yourselves. They looked very sheepish and said, bien sûr mademoiselle, in other words, sure you're right.

Well I too said when she woke me, is it a revolution and are there soldiers. No, she said, not exactly. Well what is it, said I impatiently. I don't quite know, she answered, but there has been an alarm. Anyway you had better come. I started to turn on the light. No, she said, you had better not. Give me your hand and I will get you down and you can go to sleep down stairs on the couch. I came. It was very dark. I sat down on the couch and then I said, I'm sure I don't know what is the matter with me but my knees are knocking together. Gertrude Stein burst out laughing, wait a minute, I will get you a blanket, she said. No don't leave me, I said. She managed to find something to cover me and then there was a loud boom, then several more. It was a soft noise and then there was the sound of horns blowing in the streets and then we knew it was all over. We lighted the lights and went to bed.

I must say I would not have believed it was true that knees

knocked together as described in poetry and prose if it had
not happened to me.

The next time there was a Zeppelin alarm and it was not
very long after this first one, Picasso and Eve were dining
with us. By this time we knew that the two-story building of
the atelier was no more protection than the roof of the little
pavillon under which we slept and the concierge had suggested that we should go into her room where at least we
would have six stories over us. Eve was not very well these
days and fearful so we all went into the concierge's room.
Even Jeanne Poule the Breton servant who had succeeded
Hélène, came too. Jeanne soon was bored with this precau-
tion and so in spite of all remonstrance, she went back to her
kitchen, lit her light, in spite of the regulations, and proceeded
to wash the dishes. We soon too got bored with the concierge's loge and went back to the atelier. We put a candle
under the table so that it would not make much light, Eve
and I tried to sleep and Picasso and Gertrude Stein talked
until two in the morning when the all's clear sounded and
they went home.

Picasso and Eve were living these days on the rue
Schœlcher in a rather sumptuous studio apartment that
looked over the cemetery. It was not very gay. The only excitement were the letters from Guillaume Apollinaire who
was falling off of horses in the endeavour to become an
artilleryman. The only other intimates at that time were a
russian whom they called G. Apostrophe and his sister the
baronne. They bought all the Rousseaus that were in Rousseau's atelier when he died. They had an apartment in the
boulevard Raspail above Victor Hugo's tree and they were
not unamusing. Picasso learnt the russian alphabet from them
and began putting it into some of his pictures.

It was not a very cheerful winter. People came in and out,
new ones and old ones. Ellen La Motte turned up, she was
very heroic but gun shy. She wanted to go to Serbia and
Emily Chadbourne wanted to go with her but they did not
go.

Gertrude Stein wrote a little novelette about this event.

Ellen La Motte collected a set of souvenirs of the war for

her cousin Dupont de Nemours. The stories of how she got them were diverting. Everybody brought you souvenirs in those days, steel arrows that pierced horses' heads, pieces of shell, ink-wells made out of pieces of shell, helmets, some one even offered us a piece of a Zeppelin or an aeroplane, I forget which, but we declined. It was a strange winter and nothing and everything happened. If I remember rightly it was at this time that some one, I imagine it was Apollinaire on leave, gave a concert and a reading of Blaise Cendrars' poems. It was then that I first heard mentioned and first heard the music of Erik Satie. I remember this took place in some one's atelier and the place was crowded. It was in these days too that the friendship between Gertrude Stein and Juan Gris began. He was living in the rue Ravignan in the studio where Salmon had been shut up when he ate my yellow fantaisie.

We used to go there quite often. Juan was having a hard time, no one was buying pictures and the french artists were not in want because they were at the front and their wives or their mistresses if they had been together a certain number of years were receiving an allowance. There was one bad case, Herbin, a nice little man but so tiny that the army dismissed him. He said ruefully the pack he had to carry weighed as much as he did and it was no use, he could not manage it. He was returned home inapt for service and he came near starving. I don't know who told us about him, he was one of the early simple earnest cubists. Luckily Gertrude Stein succeeded in interesting Roger Fry. Roger Fry took him and his painting over to England where he made and I imagine still has a considerable reputation.

Juan Gris' case was more difficult. Juan was in those days a tormented and not particularly sympathetic character. He was very melancholy and effusive and as always clear sighted and intellectual. He was at that time painting almost entirely in black and white and his pictures were very sombre. Kahnweiler who had befriended him was an exile in Switzerland, Juan's sister in Spain was able to help him only a little. His situation was desperate.

It was just at this time that the picture dealer who after-

wards, as the expert in the Kahnweiler sale said he was going
to kill cubism, undertook to save cubism and he made contracts with all the cubists who were still free to paint. Among
them was Juan Gris and for the moment he was saved.

As soon as we were back in Paris we went to see Mildred
Aldrich. She was within the military area so we imagined
we would have to have a special permit to go and see her.
We went to the police station of our quarter and asked them
what we should do. He said what papers have you. We have
american passports, french matriculation papers, said Gertrude Stein taking out a pocket full. He looked at them all
and said and what is this, of another yellow paper. That, said
Gertrude Stein, is a receipt from my bank for the money I
have just deposited. I think, said he solemnly, I would take
that along too. I think, he added, with all those you will not
have any trouble.

We did not as a matter of fact have to show any one any
papers. We stayed with Mildred several days.

She was much the most cheerful person we knew that
winter. She had been through the battle of the Marne, she
had had the Uhlans in the woods below her, she had watched
the battle going on below her and she had become part of
the country-side. We teased her and told her she was beginning to look like a french peasant and she did, in a funny
kind of way, born and bred new englander that she was. It
was always astonishing that the inside of her little french
peasant house with french furniture, french paint and a
french servant and even a french poodle, looked completely
american. We saw her several times that winter.

At last the spring came and we were ready to go away
for a bit. Our friend William Cook after nursing a while in
the american hospital for french wounded had gone again to
Palma de Mallorca. Cook who had always earned his living
by painting was finding it difficult to get on and he had retired to Palma where in those days when the spanish exchange was very low one lived extremely well for a few
francs a day.

We decided we would go to Palma too and forget the war
a little. We had only the temporary passports that had been

given to us in London so we went to the embassy to get permanent ones with which we might go to Spain. We were first interviewed by a kindly old gentleman most evidently not in the diplomatic service. Impossible, he said, why, said he, look at me, I have lived in Paris for forty years and come of a long line of americans and I have no passport. No, he said, you can have a passport to go to America or you can stay in France without a passport. Gertrude Stein insisted upon seeing one of the secretaries of the embassy. We saw a flushed reddish-headed one. He told us exactly the same thing. Gertrude Stein listened quietly. She then said, but so and so who is exactly in my position, a native born american, has lived the same length of time in Europe, is a writer and has no intention of returning to America at present, has just received a regular passport from your department. I think, said the young man still more flushed, there must be some error. It is very simple, replied Gertrude Stein, to verify it by looking the matter up in your records. He disappeared and presently came back and said, yes you are quite correct but you see it was a very special case. There can be, said Gertrude Stein severely, no privilege extended to one american citizen which is not to be, given similar circumstances, accorded to any other american citizen. He once more disappeared and came back and said, yes yes now may I go through the preliminaries. He then explained that they had orders to give out as few passports as possible but if any one really wanted one why of course it was quite alright. We got ours in record time.

And we went to Palma thinking to spend only a few weeks but we stayed the winter. First we went to Barcelona. It was extraordinary to see so many men on the streets. I did not imagine there could be so many men left in the world. One's eyes had become so habituated to menless streets, the few men one saw being in uniform and therefore not being men but soldiers, that to see quantities of men walking up and down the Ramblas was bewildering. We sat in the hotel window and looked. I went to bed early and got up early and Gertrude Stein went to bed late and got up late and so in a way we overlapped but there was not a moment when there were not quantities of men going up and down the Ramblas.

We arrived in Palma once again and Cook met us and arranged everything for us. William Cook could always be depended upon. In those days he was poor but later when he had inherited money and was well to do and Mildred Aldrich had fallen upon very bad ways and Gertrude Stein was not able to help any more, William Cook gave her a blank cheque and said, use that as much as you need for Mildred, you know my mother loved to read her books.

William Cook often disappeared and one knew nothing of him and then when for one reason or another you needed him there he was. He went into the american army later and at that time Gertrude Stein and myself were doing war work for the American Fund for French Wounded and I had often to wake her up very early. She and Cook used to write the most lugubrious letters to each other about the unpleasantness of sunrises met suddenly. Sunrises were, they contended, alright when approached slowly from the night before, but when faced abruptly from the same morning they were awful. It was William Cook too who later on taught Gertrude Stein how to drive a car by teaching her on one of the old battle of the Marne taxis. Cook being hard up had become a taxi driver in Paris, that was in sixteen and Gertrude Stein was to drive a car for the American Fund for French Wounded. So on dark nights they went out beyond the fortifications and the two of them sitting solemnly on the driving seat of one of those old two-cylinder before-the-war Renault taxis, William Cook taught Gertrude Stein how to drive. It was William Cook who inspired the only movie Gertrude Stein ever wrote in english, I have just published it in Operas and Plays in the Plain Edition. The only other one she ever wrote, also in Operas and Plays, many years later and in french, was inspired by her white poodle dog called Basket.

But to come back to Palma de Mallorca. We had been there two summers before and had liked it and we liked it again. A great many americans seem to like it now but in those days Cook and ourselves were the only americans to inhabit the island. There were a few english, about three families there. There was a descendant of one of Nelson's captains, a Mrs. Penfold, a sharp-tongued elderly lady and her husband. It was she who said to young Mark Gilbert, an english boy of sixteen with pacifist tendencies who had at tea at their house refused cake, Mark you are either old enough to fight for your country or young enough to eat cake. Mark ate cake.

There were several french families there, the french consul, Monsieur Marchand with a charming italian wife whom we soon came to know very well. It was he who was very much amused at a story we had to tell him of Morocco. He had been attached to the french residence at Tangiers at the moment the french induced Moulai Hafid the then sultan of Morocco to abdicate. We had been in Tangiers at that time for ten days, it was during the first trip to Spain when so much happened that was important to Gertrude Stein.

We had taken on a guide Mohammed and Mohammed had taken a fancy to us. He became a pleasant companion rather than a guide and we used to take long walks together and he used to take us to see his cousin's wonderfully clean arab middle class homes and drink tea. We enjoyed it all. He also told us all about politics. He had been educated in Moulai Hafid's palace and he knew everything that was happening. He told us just how much money Moulai Hafid would take to abdicate and just when he would be ready to do it. We liked these stories as we liked all Mohammed's stories always ending up with, and when you come back there will be street cars and then we won't have to walk and that will be nice. Later in Spain we read in the papers that it had all happened exactly as Mohammed had said it would and we paid no further attention. Once in talking of our only visit to Morocco we told Monsieur Marchand this story. He said, yes that is diplomacy, probably the only people in the world who were not arabs who knew what the french government wanted so desperately to know were you two and you knew it quite by accident and to you it was of no importance.

Life in Palma was pleasant and so instead of travelling any

more that summer we decided to settle down in Palma. We
sent for our french servant Jeanne Poule and with the aid of
the postman we found a little house on the calle de Dos de
Mayo in Terreno, just outside of Palma, and we settled down.
We were very content. Instead of spending only the summer
we stayed until the following spring.

We had been for some time members of Mudie's Library
in London and wherever we went Mudie's Library books
came to us. It was at this time that Gertrude Stein read aloud
to me all of Queen Victoria's letters and she herself became
interested in missionary autobiographies and diaries. There
were a great many in Mudie's Library and she read them all.

It was during this stay at Palma de Mallorca that most of
the plays afterwards published in Geography and Plays were
written. She always says that a certain kind of landscape
induces plays and the country around Terreno certainly did.

We had a dog, a mallorcan hound, the hounds slightly
crazy, who dance in the moonlight, striped, not all one colour
as the spanish hound of the continent. We called this dog
Polybe because we were pleased with the articles in the Fig-
aro signed Polybe. Polybe was, as Monsieur Marchand said,
like an arab, bon accueil à tout le monde et fidèle à personne.
He had an incurable passion for eating filth and nothing
would stop him. We muzzled him to see if that would cure
him, but this so outraged the russian servant of the english
consul that we had to give it up. Then he took to annoying
sheep. We even took to quarrelling with Cook about Polybe.
Cook had a fox terrier called Marie-Rose and we were convinced that Marie-Rose led Polybe into mischief and then
virtuously withdrew and let him take the blame. Cook was
convinced that we did not know how to bring up Polybe.
Polybe had one nice trait. He would sit in a chair and gently
smell large bunches of tube-roses with which I always filled
a vase in the centre of the room on the floor. He never tried
to eat them, he just gently smelled them. When we left we
left Polybe behind us in the care of one of the guardians of
the old fortress of Belver. When we saw him a week after he
did not know us or his name. Polybe comes into many of the
plays Gertrude Stein wrote at that time.

The feelings of the island at that time were very mixed as to the war. The thing that impressed them the most was the amount of money it cost. They could discuss by the hour, how much it cost a year, a month, a week, a day, an hour and even a minute. We used to hear them of a summer evening, five million pesetas, a million pesetas, two million pesetas, good-night, good-night, and know they were busy with their endless calculations of the cost of the war. As most of the men even those of the better middle classes read wrote and ciphered with difficulty and the women not at all, it can be imagined how fascinating and endless a subject the cost of the war was.

One of our neighbours had a german governess and whenever there was a german victory she hung out a german flag. We responded as well as we could, but alas just then there were not many allied victories. The lower classes were strong for the allies. The waiter at the hotel was always looking forward to Spain's entry into the war on the side of the allies. He was certain that the spanish army would be of great aid as it could march longer on less food than any army in the world. The maid at the hotel took great interest in my knitting for the soldiers. She said of course madame knits very slowly, all ladies do. But, said I hopefully, if I knit for years may I not come to knit quickly, not as quickly as you but quickly. No, said she firmly, ladies knit slowly. As a matter of fact I did come to knit very quickly and could even read and knit quickly at the same time.

We led a pleasant life, we walked a great deal and ate extremely well, and were well amused by our Breton servant.

She was patriotic and always wore the tricolour ribbon around her hat. She once came home very excited. She had just been seeing another french servant and she said, imagine, Marie has just had news that her brother was drowned and has had a civilian funeral. How did that happen, I asked also much excited. Why, said Jeanne, he had not yet been called to the army. It was a great honour to have a brother have a civilian funeral during the war. At any rate it was rare. Jeanne was content with spanish newspapers, she had no trouble reading them, as she said, all the important words were in french.

Jeanne told endless stories of french village life and Gertrude Stein could listen a long time and then all of a sudden she could not listen any more.

Life in Mallorca was pleasant until the attack on Verdun began. Then we all began to be very miserable. We tried to console each other but it was difficult. One of the frenchmen, an engraver who had palsy and in spite of the palsy tried every few months to get the french consul to accept him for the army, used to say we must not worry if Verdun is taken, it is not an entry into France, it is only a moral victory for the germans. But we were all desperately unhappy. I had been so confident and now I had an awful feeling that the war had gotten out of my hands.

In the port of Palma was a german ship called the Fangturm which sold pins and needles to all the Mediterranean ports before the war and further, presumably, because it was a very big steamer. It had been caught in Palma when the war broke out and had never been able to leave. Most of the officers and sailors had gotten away to Barcelona but the big ship remained in the harbour. It looked very rusty and neglected and it was just under our windows. All of a sudden as the attack on Verdun commenced, they began painting the Fangturm. Imagine our feelings. We were all pretty unhappy and this was despair. We told the french consul and he told us and it was awful.

Day by day the news was worse and one whole side of the Fangturm was painted and then they stopped painting. They knew it before we did. Verdun was not going to be taken. Verdun was safe. The germans had given up hoping to take it.

When it was all over we none of us wanted to stay in Mallorca any longer, we all wanted to go home. It was at this time that Cook and Gertrude Stein spent all their time talking about automobiles. They neither of them had ever driven but they were getting very interested. Cook also began to wonder how he was going to earn his living when he got to Paris. His tiny income did for Mallorca but it would not

keep him long in Paris. He thought of driving horses for
Félix Potin's delivery wagons, he said after all he liked horses
better than automobiles. Anyway he went back to Paris and
when we got there, we went a longer way, by way of Madrid,
he was driving a Paris taxi. Later on he became a trier-out
of cars for the Renault works and I can remember how exciting it was when he described how the wind blew out his
cheeks when he made eighty kilometres an hour. Then later
he joined the american army.

We went home by way of Madrid. There we had a curious
experience. We went to the american consul to have our
passports visaed. He was a great big flabby man and he had
a filipino as an assistant. He looked at our passports, he
measured them, weighed them, looked at them upside down
and finally said that he supposed they were alright but how
could he tell. He then asked the filipino what he thought.
The filipino seemed inclined to agree that the consul could
not tell. I tell you what you do, he said ingratiatingly, you go
to the french consul since you are going to France and you
live in Paris and if the french consul says they are alright, why
the consul will sign. The consul sagely nodded.

We were furious. It was an awkward position that a french
consul, not an american one should decide whether american
passports were alright. However there was nothing else to do
so we went to the french consul.

When our turn came the man in charge took our passports
and looked them over and said to Gertrude Stein, when were
you last in Spain. She stopped to think, she never can remember anything when anybody asks her suddenly, and she
said she did not remember but she thought it was such and
such a date. He said no, and mentioned another year. She
said very likely he was right. Then he went on to give all
the dates of her various visits to Spain and finally he added a
visit when she was still at college when she was in Spain
with her brother just after the spanish war. It was all in a
way rather frightening to me standing by but Gertrude Stein
and the assistant consul seemed to be thoroughly interested
in fixing dates. Finally he said, you see I was for many years
in the letter of credit department of the Crédit Lyonnais in

Madrid and I have a very good memory and I remember, of course I remember you very well. We were all very pleased. He signed the passports and told us to go back and tell our consul to do so also.

At the time we were furious with our consul but now I wonder if it was not an arrangement between the two offices that the american consul should not sign any passport to enter France until the french consul had decided whether its owner was or was not desirable.

We came back to an entirely different Paris. It was no longer gloomy. It was no longer empty. This time we did not settle down, we decided to get into the war. One day we were walking down the rue des Pyramides and there was a ford car being backed up the street by an american girl and on the car it said, American Fund for French Wounded. There, said I, that is what we are going to do. At least, said I to Gertrude Stein, you will drive the car and I will do the rest. We went over and talked to the american girl and then interviewed Mrs. Lathrop, the head of the organisation. She was enthusiastic, she was always enthusiastic and she said, get a car. But where, we asked. From America, she said. But how, we said. Ask somebody, she said, and Gertrude Stein did, she asked her cousin and in a few months the ford car came. In the meanwhile Cook had taught her to drive his taxi.

As I said it was a changed Paris. Everything was changed, and everybody was cheerful.

During our absence Eve had died and Picasso was now living in a little home in Montrouge. We went out to see him. He had a marvelous rose pink silk counterpane on his bed. Where did that come from Pablo, asked Gertrude Stein. Ah ça, said Picasso with much satisfaction, that is a lady. It was a well known chilean society woman who had given it to him. It was a marvel. He was very cheerful. He was constantly coming to the house, bringing Paquerette a girl who was very nice or Irene a very lovely woman who came from the mountains and wanted to be free. He brought Erik Satie and the Princesse de Polignac and Blaise Cendrars.

It was a great pleasure to know Erik Satie. He was from

Normandy and very fond of it. Marie Laurencin comes from Normandy, so also does Braque. Once when after the war Satie and Marie Laurencin were at the house for lunch they were delightfully enthusiastic about each other as being normans. Erik Satie liked food and wine and knew a lot about both. We had at that time some very good eau de vie that the husband of Mildred Aldrich's servant had given us and Erik Satie, drinking his glass slowly and with appreciation, told stories of the country in his youth.

Only once in the half dozen times that Erik Satie was at the house did he talk about music. He said that it had always been his opinion and he was glad that it was being recognised that modern french music owed nothing to modern Germany. That after Debussy had led the way french musicians had either followed him or found their own french way.

He told charming stories, usually of Normandy, he had a playful wit which was sometimes very biting. He was a charming dinner-guest. It was many years later that Virgil Thomson, when we first knew him in his tiny room near the Gare Saint-Lazare, played for us the whole of Socrate. It was then that Gertrude Stein really became a Satie enthusiast.

Ellen La Motte and Emily Chadbourne, who had not gone to Serbia, were still in Paris. Ellen La Motte, who was an ex Johns Hopkins nurse, wanted to nurse near the front. She was still gun shy but she did want to nurse at the front, and they met Mary Borden-Turner who was running a hospital at the front and Ellen La Motte did for a few months nurse at the front. After that she and Emily Chadbourne went to China and after that became leaders of the anti-opium campaign.

Mary Borden-Turner had been and was going to be a writer. She was very enthusiastic about the work of Gertrude Stein and travelled with what she had of it and volumes of Flaubert to and from the front. She had taken a house near the Bois and it was heated and during that winter when the rest of us had no coal it was very pleasant going to dinner there and being warm. We liked Turner. He was a captain in the British army and was doing contre-espionage work very successfully. Although married to Mary Borden he did not believe in millionaires. He insisted upon giving his own

Christmas party to the women and children in the village in which he was billeted and he always said that after the war he would be collector of customs for the British in Düsseldorf or go out to Canada and live simply. After all, he used to say to his wife, you are not a millionaire, not a real one. He had british standards of millionairedom. Mary Borden was very Chicago. Gertrude Stein always says that chicagoans spend so much energy losing Chicago that often it is difficult to know what they are. They have to lose the Chicago voice and to do so they do many things. Some lower their voices, some raise them, some get an english accent, some even get a german accent, some drawl, some speak in a very high tense voice, and some go chinese or spanish and do not move the lips. Mary Borden was very Chicago and Gertrude Stein was immensely interested in her and in Chicago.

All this time we were waiting for our ford truck which was on its way and then we waited for its body to be built. We waited a great deal. It was then that Gertrude Stein wrote a great many little war poems, some of them have since been published in the volume Useful Knowledge which has in it only things about America.

Stirred by the publication of Tender Buttons many newspapers had taken up the amusement of imitating Gertrude Stein's work and making fun of it. Life began a series that were called after Gertrude Stein.

Gertrude Stein suddenly one day wrote a letter to Masson who was then editor of Life and said to him that the real Gertrude Stein was as Henry McBride had pointed out funnier in every way than the imitations, not to say much more interesting, and why did they not print the original. To her astonishment she received a very nice letter from Mr. Masson saying that he would be glad to do so. And they did. They printed two things that she sent them, one about Wilson and one longer thing about war work in France. Mr. Masson had more courage than most.

This winter Paris was bitterly cold and there was no coal. We finally had none at all. We closed up the big room and stayed in a little room but at last we had no more coal. The government was giving coal away to the needy but we did not feel justified in sending our servant to stand in line to get it. One afternoon it was bitterly cold, we went out and on a street corner was a policeman and standing with him was a sergeant of police. Gertrude Stein went up to them. Look here, she said to them, what are we to do. I live in a pavillon on the rue de Fleurus and have lived there many years. Oh yes, said they nodding their heads, certainly madame we know you very well. Well, she said, I have no coal not even enough to heat one small room. I do not want to send my servant to get it for nothing, that does not seem right. Now, she said, it is up to you to tell me what to do. The policeman looked at his sergeant and the sergeant nodded. Alright, they said.

We went home. That evening the policeman in civilian clothes turned up with two sacks of coal. We accepted thankfully and asked no questions. The policeman, a stalwart breton became our all in all. He did everything for us, he cleaned our home, he cleaned our chimneys, he got us in and he got us out and on dark nights when Zeppelins came it was comfortable to know that he was somewhere outside.

There were Zeppelin alarms from time to time, but like everything else we had gotten used to them. When they came at dinner time we went on eating and when they came at night Gertrude Stein did not wake me, she said I might as well stay where I was if I was asleep because when asleep it took more than even the siren that they used then to give the signal, to wake me.

Our little ford was almost ready. She was later to be called Auntie after Gertrude Stein's aunt Pauline who always behaved admirably in emergencies and behaved fairly well most times if she was properly flattered.

One day Picasso came in and with him and leaning on his shoulder was a slim elegant youth. It is Jean, announced Pablo, Jean Cocteau and we are leaving for Italy.

Picasso had been excited at the prospect of doing the scenery for a russian ballet, the music to be by Satie, the drama by Jean Cocteau. Everybody was at the war, life in Montparnasse was not very gay, Montrouge with even a faithful servant was not very lively, he too needed a change. He was very lively at the prospect of going to Rome. We all said goodbye and we all went our various ways.

The little ford car was ready. Gertrude Stein had learned to drive a french car and they all said it was the same. I have never driven any car, but it would appear that it is not the same. We went outside of Paris to get it when it was ready and Gertrude Stein drove it in. Of course the first thing she did was to stop dead on the track between two street cars. Everybody got out and pushed us off the track. The next day when we started off to see what would happen we managed to get as far as the Champs Elysées and once more stopped dead. A crowd shoved us to the side walk and then tried to find out what was the matter. Gertrude Stein cranked, the whole crowd cranked, nothing happened. Finally an old chauffeur said, no gasoline. We said proudly, oh yes at least a gallon, but he insisted on looking and of course there was none. Then the crowd stopped a whole procession of military trucks that were going up the Champs Elysées. They all stopped and a couple of them brought over an immense tank of gasoline and tried to pour it into the little ford. Naturally the process was not successful. Finally getting into a taxi I went to a store in our quarter where they sold brooms and gasoline and where they knew me and I came back with a tin of gasoline and we finally arrived at the Alcazar d'Eté, the then headquarters of the American Fund for French Wounded.

Mrs. Lathrop was waiting for one of the cars to take her to Montmartre. I immediately offered the service of our car and went out and told Gertrude Stein. She quoted Edwin Dodge to me. Once Mabel Dodge's little boy said he would like to fly from the terrace to the lower garden. Do, said Mabel. It is easy, said Edwin Dodge, to be a spartan mother.

However Mrs. Lathrop came and the car went off. I must confess to being terribly nervous until they came back but come back they did.

We had a consultation with Mrs. Lathrop and she sent us off to Perpignan, a region with a good many hospitals that

no american organisation had ever visited. We started. We
had never been further from Paris than Fontainebleau in the
car and it was terribly exciting.

We had a few adventures, we were caught in the snow and
I was sure that we were on the wrong road and wanted to
turn back. Wrong or right, said Gertrude Stein, we are going
on. She could not back the car very successfully and indeed I
may say even to this day when she can drive any kind of a
car anywhere she still does not back a car very well. She
goes forward admirably, she does not go backwards successfully. The only violent discussions that we have had in connection with her driving a car have been on the subject of
backing.

On this trip South we picked up our first military god-son.
We began the habit then which we kept up all through the
war of giving any soldier on the road a lift. We drove by day
and we drove by night and in very lonely parts of France and
we always stopped and gave a lift to any soldier, and never
had we any but the most pleasant experiences with these
soldiers. And some of them were as we sometimes found out
pretty hard characters. Gertrude Stein once said to a soldier
who was doing something for her, they were always doing
something for her, whenever there was a soldier or a chauffeur
or any kind of a man anywhere, she never did anything for
herself, neither changing a tyre, cranking the car or repairing
it. Gertrude Stein said to this soldier, but you are tellement
gentil, very nice and kind. Madame, said he quite simply,
all soldiers are nice and kind.

This faculty of Gertrude Stein of having everybody do anything for her puzzled the other drivers of the organisation.
Mrs. Lathrop who used to drive her own car said that nobody
did those things for her. It was not only soldiers, a chauffeur
would get off the seat of a private car in the place Vendôme
and crank Gertrude Stein's old ford for her. Gertrude Stein
said that the others looked so efficient, of course nobody
would think of doing anything for them. Now as for herself
she was not efficient, she was good humoured, she was demo-
cratic, one person was as good as another, and she knew what
she wanted done. If you are like that she says, anybody will

do anything for you. The important thing, she insists, is that you must have deep down as the deepest thing in you a sense of equality. Then anybody will do anything for you.

It was not far from Saulieu that we picked up our first military god-son. He was a butcher in a tiny village not far from Saulieu. Our taking him up was a good example of the democracy of the french army. There were three of them walking along the road. We stopped and said we could take one of them on the step. They were all three going home on leave and walking into the country to their homes from the nearest big town. One was a lieutenant, one was a sergeant and one a soldier. They thanked us and then the lieutenant said to each one of them, how far have you to go. They each one named the distance and then they said, and you my lieutenant, how far have you to go. He told them. Then they all agreed that it was the soldier who had much the longest way to go and so it was his right to have the lift. He touched his cap to his sergeant and officer and got in.

As I say he was our first military god-son. We had a great many afterwards and it was quite an undertaking to keep them all going. The duty of a military god-mother was to write a letter as often as she received one and to send a package of comforts or dainties about once in ten days. They liked the packages but they really liked letters even more. And they answered so promptly. It seemed to me, no sooner was my letter written than there was an answer. And then one had to remember all their family histories and once I did a dreadful thing, I mixed my letters and so I asked a soldier whose wife I knew all about and whose mother was dead to remember me to his mother, and the one who had the mother to remember me to his wife. Their return letters were quite mournful. They each explained that I had made a mistake and I could see that they had been deeply wounded by my error.

The most delightful god-son we ever had was one we took on in Nîmes. One day when we were in the town I dropped my purse. I did not notice the loss until we returned to the hotel and then I was rather bothered as there had been a good deal of money in it. While we were eating our dinner the waiter said some one wanted to see us. We went out and there was a man holding the purse in his hand. He said he had picked it up in the street and as soon as his work was over had come to the hotel to give it to us. There was a card of mine in the purse and he took it for granted that a stranger would be at the hotel, beside by that time we were very well known in Nîmes. I naturally offered him a considerable reward from the contents of the purse but he said no. He said however that he had a favour to ask. They were refugees from the Marne and his son Abel now seventeen years old had just volunteered and was at present in the garrison at Nîmes, would I be his god-mother. I said I would, and I asked him to tell his son to come to see me his first free evening. The next evening the youngest, the sweetest, the smallest soldier imaginable came in. It was Abel.

We became very attached to Abel. I always remember his first letter from the front. He began by saying that he was really not very much surprised by anything at the front, it was exactly as it had been described to him and as he had imagined it, except that there being no tables one was compelled to write upon one's knees.

The next time we saw Abel he was wearing the red fourragère, his regiment as a whole had been decorated with the legion of honour and we were very proud of our filleul. Still later when we went into Alsace with the french army, after the armistice, we had Abel come and stay with us a few days and a proud boy he was when he climbed to the top of the Strasbourg cathedral.

When we finally returned to Paris, Abel came and stayed with us a week. We took him to see everything and he said solemnly at the end of his first day, I think all that was worth fighting for. Paris in the evening however frightened him and we always had to get somebody to go out with him. The front had not been scareful but Paris at night was.

Some time later he wrote and said that the family were moving into a different department and he gave me his new address. By some error the address did not reach him and we lost him.

We did finally arrive at Perpignan and began visiting hospitals and giving away our stores and sending word to head-quarters if we thought they needed more than we had. At first it was a little difficult but soon we were doing all we were to do very well. We were also given quantities of comfort-bags and distributing these was a perpetual delight, it was like a continuous Christmas. We always had permission from the head of the hospital to distribute these to the soldiers themselves which was in itself a great pleasure but also it enabled us to get the soldiers to immediately write postal cards of thanks and these we used to send off in batches to Mrs. Lathrop who sent them to America to the people who had sent the comfort-bags. And so everybody was pleased.

Then there was the question of gasoline. The American Fund for French Wounded had an order from the french government giving them the privilege of buying gasoline. But there was no gasoline to buy. The french army had plenty of it and were ready to give it to us but they could not sell it and we were privileged to buy it but not to receive it for nothing. It was necessary to interview the officer in command of the commissary department.

Gertrude Stein was perfectly ready to drive the car anywhere, to crank the car as often as there was nobody else to do it, to repair the car, I must say she was very good at it, even if she was not ready to take it all down and put it back again for practice as I wanted her to do in the beginning, she was even resigned to getting up in the morning, but she flatly refused to go inside of any office and interview any official. I was officially the delegate and she was officially the driver but I had to go and interview the major.

He was a charming major. The affair was very long drawn out, he sent me here and he sent me there but finally the matter was straightened out. All this time of course he called me Mademoiselle Stein because Gertrude Stein's name was on all the papers that I presented to him, she being the driver. And so now, he said, Mademoiselle Stein, my wife is very anxious to make your acquaintance and she has asked me to ask you to dine with us. I was very confused. I hesitated. But I am not Mademoiselle Stein, I said. He almost jumped out of his chair. What, he shouted, not Mademoiselle

Stein. Then who are you. It must be remembered this was war time and Perpignan almost at the spanish frontier. Well, said I, you see Mademoiselle Stein. Where is Mademoiselle Stein, he said. She is downstairs, I said feebly, in the automobile. Well what does all this mean, he said. Well, I said, you see Mademoiselle Stein is the driver and I am the delegate and Mademoiselle Stein has no patience she will not go into offices and wait and interview people and explain, so I do it for her while she sits in the automobile. But what, said he sternly, would you have done if I had asked you to sign something. I would have told you, I said, as I am telling you now. Indeed, he said, let us go downstairs and see this Mademoiselle Stein.

We went downstairs and Gertrude Stein was sitting in the driver's seat of the little ford and he came up to her. They immediately became friends and he renewed his invitation and we went to dinner. We had a good time. Madame Dubois came from Bordeaux, the land of food and wine. And what food above all the soup. It still remains to me the standard of comparison with all the other soups in the world. Sometimes some approach it, a very few have equalled it but none have surpassed it.

Perpignan is not far from Rivesaltes and Rivesaltes is the birthplace of Joffre. It had a little hospital and we got it extra supplies in honour of Papa Joffre. We had also the little ford car showing the red cross and the A.F.F.W. sign and ourselves in it photographed in front of the house in the little street where Joffre was born and had this photograph printed and sent to Mrs. Lathrop. The postal cards were sent to America and sold for the benefit of the fund. In the meantime the U.S. had come into the war and we had some one send us a lot of ribbon with the stars and stripes printed on it and we cut this up and gave it to all the soldiers and they and we were pleased.

Which reminds me of a french peasant. Later in Nîmes we had an american ambulance boy in the car with us and we were out in the country. The boy had gone off to visit a waterfall and I had gone off to see a hospital and Gertrude Stein stayed with the car. She told me when I came back that an old peasant had come up to her and asked her what uniform the young man was wearing. That, she had said proudly, is the uniform of the american army, your new ally. Oh, said the old peasant. And then contemplatively, I ask myself what will we accomplish together, je me demande je me demande qu'est-ce que nous ferons ensemble.

Our work in Perpignan being over we started back to Paris. On the way everything happened to the car. Perhaps it had been too hot even for a ford car in Perpignan. Perpignan is below sea level near the Mediterranean and it is hot. Gertrude Stein who had always wanted it hot and hotter has never been really enthusiastic about heat after this experience. She said she had been just like a pancake, the heat above and the heat below and cranking a car beside. I do not know how often she used to swear and say, I am going to scrap it, that is all there is about it I am going to scrap it. I encouraged and remonstrated until the car started again.

It was in connection with this that Mrs. Lathrop played a joke on Gertrude Stein. After the war was over we were both decorated by the french government, we received the Reconnaissance Française. They always in giving you a decoration give you a citation telling why you have been given it. The account of our valour was exactly the same, except in my case they said that my devotion was sans relâche, with no abatement, and in her case they did not put in the words sans relâche.

On the way back to Paris we, as I say had everything happen to the car but Gertrude Stein with the aid of an old tramp on the road who pushed and shoved at the critical moments managed to get it to Nevers where we met the first piece of the american army. They were the quartermasters department and the marines, the first contingent to arrive in France. There we first heard what Gertrude Stein calls the sad song of the marines, which tells how everybody else in the american army has at sometime mutinied, but the marines never.

Immediately on entering Nevers, we saw Tarn McGrew, a californian and parisian whom we had known very slightly but he was in uniform and we called for help. He came. We told him our troubles. He said, alright get the car into the garage of the hotel and to-morrow some of the soldiers will put it to rights. We did so.

That evening we spent at Mr. McGrew's request at the Y.M.C.A. and saw for the first time in many years americans just americans, the kind that would not naturally ever have come to Europe. It was quite a thrilling experience. Gertrude Stein of course talked to them all, wanted to know what state and what city they came from, what they did, how old they were and how they liked it. She talked to the french girls who were with the american boys and the french girls told her what they thought of the american boys and the american boys told her all they thought about the french girls.

The next day she spent with California and Iowa in the garage, as she called the two soldiers who were detailed to fix up her car. She was pleased with them when every time there was a terrific noise anywhere, they said solemnly to each other, that french chauffeur is just changing gears. Gertrude Stein, Iowa and California enjoyed themselves so thoroughly that I am sorry to say the car did not last out very well after we left Nevers, but at any rate we did get to Paris.

It was at this time that Gertrude Stein conceived the idea of writing a history of the United States consisting of chapters wherein Iowa differs from Kansas, and wherein Kansas differs from Nebraska etcetera. She did do a little of it which also was printed in the book, Useful Knowledge.

We did not stay in Paris very long. As soon as the car was made over we left for Nîmes, we were to do the three departments the Gard, the Bouches-du-Rhône and the Vaucluse.

We arrived in Nîmes and settled down to a very comfortable life there. We went to see the chief military doctor in the town, Doctor Fabre and through his great kindness and that of his wife we were soon very much at home in Nîmes, but before we began our work there, Doctor Fabre asked a favour of us. There were no automobile ambulances left in Nîmes. At the military hospital was a pharmacist, a captain in the army, who was very ill, certain to die, and wanted to die in his own home. His wife was with him and would sit with him and we were to have no responsibility for him except to drive him home. Of course we said we would and we did.

It had been a long hard ride up into the mountains and it was dark long before we were back. We were still some distance from Nîmes when suddenly on the road we saw a couple of figures. The old ford car's lights did not light up much of anything on the road, and nothing along the side of the road and we did not make out very well who it was. However we stopped as we always did when anybody asked us to give them a lift. One man, he was evidently an officer said, my automobile has broken down and I must get back to Nîmes. Alright we said, both of you climb into the back, you will find a mattress and things, make yourselves comfortable. We went on to Nîmes. As we came into the city I called through the little window, where do you want to get down, where are you going, a voice replied. To the Hôtel Luxembourg, I said. That will do alright, the voice replied. We arrived in front of the Hôtel Luxembourg and stopped. Here there was plenty of light. We heard a scramble in the back and then a little man, very fierce with the cap and oak leaves of a full general and the legion of honour medal at his throat, appeared before us. He said, I wish to thank you but before I do so I must ask you who you are. We, I replied cheerfully are the delegates of the American Fund for French Wounded and we are for the present stationed at Nîmes. And I, he retorted, am the general who commands here and as I see by your car that you have a french military number you should have reported to me immediately. Should we, I said, I did not know, I am most awfully sorry. It is alright, he said aggressively, if you should ever want or need anything let me know.

We did let him know very shortly because of course there was the eternal gasoline question and he was kindness itself and arranged everything for us.

The little general and his wife came from the north of France and had lost their home and spoke of themselves as refugees. When later the big Bertha began to fire on Paris and one shell hit the Luxembourg gardens very near the rue de Fleurus, I must confess I began to cry and said I did not want to be a miserable refugee. We had been helping a good many of them. Gertrude Stein said, General Frotier's family are refugees and they are not miserable. More miserable than I want to be, I said bitterly.

Soon the american army came to Nîmes. One day Madame Fabre met us and said that her cook had seen some american soldiers. She must have mistaken some english soldiers for them, we said. Not at all, she answered, she is very patriotic. At any rate the american soldiers came, a regiment of them of the S. O. S. the service of supply, how well I remember how they used to say it with the emphasis on the of.

We soon got to know them all well and some of them very well. There was Duncan, a southern boy with such a very marked southern accent that when he was well into a story I was lost. Gertrude Stein whose people all come from Baltimore had no difficulty and they used to shout with laughter together, and all I could understand was that they had killed him as if he was a chicken. The people in Nîmes were as much troubled as I was. A great many of the ladies in Nîmes spoke english very well. There had always been english governesses in Nîmes, and they, the nîmoises had always prided themselves on their knowledge of english but as they said not only could they not understand these americans but these americans could not understand them when they spoke english. I had to admit that it was more or less the same with me.

The soldiers were all Kentucky, South Carolina etcetera and they were hard to understand.

Duncan was a dear. He was supply-sergeant to the camp and when we began to find american soldiers here and there in french hospitals we always took Duncan along to give the american soldier pieces of his lost uniform and white bread. Poor Duncan was miserable because he was not at the front. He had enlisted as far back as the expedition to Mexico and here he was well in the rear and no hope of getting away because he was one of the few who understood the complicated system of army book-keeping and his officers would not recommend him for the front. I will go, he used to say bitterly, they can bust me if they like I will go. But as we told him there were plenty of A.W.O.L. absent without leave the south was full of them, we were always meeting them and they would say, say any military police around here. Duncan was not made for that life. Poor Duncan. Two days before the armistice, he came in to see us and he was drunk and bitter. He was usually a sober boy but to go back and face his family never having been to the front was too awful. He was with us in a little sitting-room and in the front room were some of his officers and it would not do for them to see him in that state and it was time for him to get back to the camp. He had fallen half asleep with his head on the table. Duncan, said Gertrude Stein sharply, yes, he said. She said to him, listen Duncan. Miss Toklas is going to stand up, you stand up too and fix your eyes right on the back of her head, do you understand. Yes, he said. Well then she will start to walk and you follow her and don't you for a moment move your eyes from the back of her head until you are in my car. Yes, he said. And he did and Gertrude Stein drove him to the camp.

Dear Duncan. It was he who was all excited by the news that the americans had taken forty villages at Saint-Mihiel. He was to go with us that afternoon to Avignon to deliver some cases. He was sitting very straight on the step and all of a sudden his eye was caught by some houses. What are they, he asked. Oh just a village, Gertrude Stein said. In a minute there were some more houses. And what are those houses, he asked. Oh just a village. He fell very silent and he looked at the landscape as he had never looked at it before. Suddenly with a deep sigh, forty villages ain't so much, he said.

We did enjoy the life with these doughboys. I would like to tell nothing but doughboy stories. They all got on amazingly well with the french. They worked together in the repair sheds of the railroad. The only thing that bothered the americans were the long hours. They worked too concentratedly to keep it up so long. Finally an arrangement was made that they should have their work to do in their hours and the french in theirs. There was a great deal of friendly rivalry. The american boys did not see the use of putting so much finish on work that was to be shot up so soon again, the french said they could not complete work without finish. But both lots thoroughly liked each other.

Gertrude Stein always said the war was so much better than just going to America. Here you were with America in a kind of way that if you only went to America you could not possibly be. Every now and then one of the american soldiers would get into the hospital at Nîmes and as Doctor Fabre knew that Gertrude Stein had had a medical education he always wanted her present with the doughboy on these occasions. One of them fell off the train. He did not believe that the little french trains could go fast but they did, fast enough to kill him.

This was a tremendous occasion. Gertrude Stein in company with the wife of the préfet, the governmental head of the department and the wife of the general were the chief mourners. Duncan and two others blew on the bugle and everybody made speeches. The Protestant pastor asked Gertrude Stein about the dead man and his virtues and she asked the doughboys. It was difficult to find any virtue. Apparently he had been a fairly hard citizen. But can't you tell me something good about him, she said despairingly. Finally Taylor, one of his friends, looked up solemnly and said, I tell you he had a heart as big as a washtub.

I often wonder, I have often wondered if any of all these doughboys who knew Gertrude Stein so well in those days ever connected her with the Gertrude Stein of the newspapers.

We led a very busy life. There were all the americans, there were a great many in the small hospitals round about as well as in the regiment in Nîmes and we had to find them all and be good to them, then there were all the french in the hospitals, we had them to visit as this was really our business, and then later came the spanish grippe and Gertrude Stein and one of the military doctors from Nîmes used to go to all the villages miles around to bring into Nîmes the sick soldiers and officers who had fallen ill in their homes while on leave.

It was during these long trips that she began writing a great deal again. The landscape, the strange life stimulated her. It was then that she began to love the valley of the Rhône, the landscape that of all landscapes means the most to her. We are still here in Bilignin in the valley of the Rhône.

She wrote at that time the poem of The Deserter, printed almost immediately in Vanity Fair. Henry McBride had interested Crowninshield in her work.

One day when we were in Avignon we met Braque. Braque had been badly wounded in the head and had come to Sorgues near Avignon to recover. It was there that he had been staying when the mobilisation orders came to him. It was awfully pleasant seeing the Braques again. Picasso had just written to Gertrude Stein announcing his marriage to a jeune fille, a real young lady, and he had sent Gertrude Stein a wedding present of a lovely little painting and a photograph of a painting of his wife.

That lovely little painting he copied for me many years later on tapestry canvas and I embroidered it and that was the beginning of my tapestrying. I did not think it possible to ask him to draw me something to work but when I told Gertrude Stein she said, alright, I'll manage. And so one day when he was at the house she said, Pablo, Alice wants to make a tapestry of that little picture and I said I would trace it for her. He looked at her with kindly contempt, if it is done by anybody, he said, it will be done by me. Well, said Gertrude Stein, producing a piece of tapestry canvas, go to it, and he did. And I have been making tapestry of his drawings ever since and they are very successful and go marvelously with old chairs. I have done two small Louis fifteenth chairs in this way. He is kind enough now to make me drawings on my working canvas and to colour them for me.

Braque also told us that Apollinaire too had married a real young lady. We gossiped a great deal together. But after all there was little news to tell.

Time went on, we were very busy and then came the armistice. We were the first to bring the news to many small villages. The french soldiers in the hospitals were relieved rather than glad. They seemed not to feel that it was going to be such a lasting peace. I remember one of them saying to Gertrude Stein when she said to him, well here is peace, at least for twenty years, he said.

The next morning we had a telegram from Mrs. Lathrop. Come at once want you to go with the french armies to Alsace. We did not stop on the way. We made it in a day. Very shortly after we left for Alsace.

We left for Alsace and on the road had our first and only accident. The roads were frightful, mud, ruts, snow, slush, and covered with the french armies going into Alsace. As we passed, two horses dragging an army kitchen kicked out of line and hit our ford, the mud-guard came off and the tool-chest, and worst of all the triangle of the steering gear was badly bent. The army picked up our tools and our mud-guard but there was nothing to do about the bent triangle. We went on, the car wandering all over the muddy road, up hill and down hill, and Gertrude Stein sticking to the wheel. Finally after about forty kilometres, we saw on the road some american ambulance men. Where can we get our car fixed. Just a little farther, they said. We went a little farther and there found an american ambulance outfit. They had no extra mud-guard but they could give us a new triangle. I told our troubles to the sergeant, he grunted and said a word in an undertone to a mechanic. Then turning to us he said gruffly, run-her-in. Then the mechanic took off his tunic and threw it over the radiator. As Gertrude Stein said when any american did that the car was his.

We had never realised before what mud-guards were for but by the time we arrived in Nancy we knew. The french military repair shop fitted us out with a new mud-guard and tool-chest and we went on our way.

Soon we came to the battle-fields and the lines of trenches of both sides. To any one who did not see it as it was then it is impossible to imagine it. It was not terrifying it was strange. We were used to ruined houses and even ruined towns but this was different. It was a landscape. And it belonged to no country.

I remember hearing a french nurse once say and the only

thing she did say of the front was, c'est un paysage passionnant, an absorbing landscape. And that was what it was as we saw it. It was strange. Camouflage, huts, everything was there. It was wet and dark and there were a few people, one did not know whether they were chinamen or europeans. Our fan-belt had stopped working. A staff car stopped and fixed it with a hairpin, we still wore hairpins.

Another thing that interested us enormously was how different the camouflage of the french looked from the camouflage of the germans, and then once we came across some very very neat camouflage and it was american. The idea was the same but as after all it was different nationalities who did it the difference was inevitable. The colour schemes were different, the designs were different, the way of placing them was different, it made plain the whole theory of art and its inevitability.

Finally we came to Strasbourg and then went on to Mulhouse. Here we stayed until well into May.

Our business in Alsace was not hospitals but refugees. The inhabitants were returning to their ruined homes all over the devastated country and it was the aim of the A.F.F.W. to give a pair of blankets, underclothing and children's and babies' woollen stockings and babies' booties to every family. There was a legend that the quantity of babies' booties sent to us came from the gifts sent to Mrs. Wilson who was supposed at that time to be about to produce a little Wilson. There were a great many babies' booties but not too many for Alsace.

Our headquarters was the assembly-room of one of the big school-buildings in Mulhouse. The german school teachers had disappeared and french school teachers who happened to be in the army had been put in temporarily to teach. The head of our school was in despair, not about the docility of his pupils nor their desire to learn french, but on account of their clothes. French children are all always neatly clothed. There is no such thing as a ragged child, even orphans farmed out in country villages are neatly dressed, just as all french women are neat, even the poor and the aged. They may not always be clean but they are always neat. From this standpoint the parti-coloured rags of even the comparatively prosperous alsatian children were deplorable and the french schoolmasters suffered. We did our best to help him out with black children's aprons but these did not go far, beside we had to keep them for the refugees.

We came to know Alsace and the alsatians very well, all kinds of them. They were astonished at the simplicity with which the french army and french soldiers took care of themselves. They had not been accustomed to that in the german army. On the other hand the french soldiers were rather mistrustful of the alsatians who were too anxious to be french and yet were not french. They are not frank, the french soldiers said. And it is quite true. The french whatever else they may be are frank. They are very polite, they are very adroit but sooner or later they always tell you the truth. The alsatians are not adroit, they are not polite and they do not inevitably tell you the truth. Perhaps with renewed contact with the french they will learn these things.

We distributed. We went into all the devastated villages. We usually asked the priest to help us with the distribution. One priest who gave us a great deal of good advice and with whom we became very friendly had only one large room left in his house. Without any screens or partitions he had made himself three rooms, the first third had his parlour furniture, the second third his dining room furniture and the last third his bedroom furniture. When we lunched with him and we lunched well and his alsatian wines were very good, he received us in his parlour, he then excused himself and withdrew into his bedroom to wash his hands, and then he invited us very formally to come into the dining room, it was like an old-fashioned stage setting.

We distributed, we drove around in the snow we talked to everybody and everybody talked to us and by the end of May it was all over and we decided to leave.

We went home by way of Metz, Verdun and Mildred Aldrich.

We once more returned to a changed Paris. We were restless. Gertrude Stein began to work very hard, it was at this time that she wrote her Accents in Alsace and other political

plays, the last plays in Geography and Plays. We were still in
the shadow of war work and we went on doing some of it,
visiting hospitals and seeing the soldiers left in them, now
pretty well neglected by everybody. We had spent a great
deal of our money during the war and we were economising,
servants were difficult to get if not impossible, prices were
high. We settled down for the moment with a femme de
ménage for only a few hours a day. I used to say Gertrude
Stein was the chauffeur and I was the cook. We used to go
over early in the morning to the public markets and get in our
provisions. It was a confused world.

Jessie Whitehead had come over with the peace commission
as secretary to one of the delegations and of course we were
very interested in knowing all about the peace. It was then
that Gertrude Stein described one of the young men of the
peace commission who was holding forth, as one who knew
all about the war, he had been here ever since the peace.
Gertrude Stein's cousins came over, everybody came over,
everybody was dissatisfied and every one was restless. It was
a restless and disturbed world.

Gertrude Stein and Picasso quarrelled. They neither of
them ever quite knew about what. Anyway they did not see
each other for a year and then they met by accident at a
party at Adrienne Monnier's. Picasso said, how do you do to
her and said something about her coming to see him. No I
will not, she answered gloomily. Picasso came to me and said,
Gertrude says she won't come to see me, does she mean it.
I am afraid if she says it she means it. They did not see each
other for another year and in the meantime Picasso's little
boy was born and Max Jacob was complaining that he had
not been named god-father. A very little while after this we
were somewhere at some picture gallery and Picasso came
up and put his hand on Gertrude Stein's shoulder and said,
oh hell, let's be friends. Sure, said Gertrude Stein and they
embraced. When can I come to see you, said Picasso, let's
see, said Gertrude Stein, I am afraid we are busy but come
to dinner the end of the week. Nonsense, said Picasso, we are
coming to dinner to-morrow, and they came.

It was a changed Paris. Guillaume Apollinaire was dead.

We saw a tremendous number of people but none of them
as far as I can remember that we had ever known before.
Paris was crowded. As Clive Bell remarked, they say that an
awful lot of people were killed in the war but it seems to me
that an extraordinary large number of grown men and women
have suddenly been born.

As I say we were restless and we were economical and all
day and all evening we were seeing people and at last there
was the defile, the procession under the Arc de Triomphe,
of the allies.

The members of the American Fund for French Wounded
were to have seats on the benches that were put up the length
of the Champs Elysées but quite rightly the people of Paris
objected as these seats would make it impossible for them to
see the parade and so Clemenceau promptly had them taken
down. Luckily for us Jessie Whitehead's room in her hotel
looked right over the Arc de Triomphe and she asked us to
come to it to see the parade. We accepted gladly. It was a
wonderful day.

We got up at sunrise, as later it would have been impossible to cross Paris in a car. This was one of the last trips
Auntie made. By this time the red cross was painted off it but
it was still a truck. Very shortly after it went its honourable
way and was succeeded by Godiva, a two-seated runabout,
also a little ford. She was called Godiva because she had
come naked into the world and each of our friends gave us
something with which to bedeck her.

Auntie then was making practically her last trip. We left
her near the river and walked up to the hotel. Everybody
was on the streets, men, women children, soldiers, priests,
nuns, we saw two nuns being helped into a tree from which
they would be able to see. And we ourselves were admirably
placed and we saw perfectly.

We saw it all, we saw first the few wounded from the Invalides in their wheeling chairs wheeling themselves. It is an
old french custom that a military procession should always be
preceded by the veterans from the Invalides. They all marched
past through the Arc de Triomphe. Gertrude Stein remembered that when as a child she used to swing on the chains

that were around the Arc de Triomphe her governess had told her that no one must walk underneath since the german armies had marched under it after 1870. And now everybody except the germans were passing through.

All the nations marched differently, some slowly, some quickly, the french carry their flags the best of all, Pershing and his officer carrying the flag behind him were perhaps the most perfectly spaced. It was this scene that Gertrude Stein described in the movie she wrote about this time that I have published in Operas and Plays in the Plain Edition.

However it all finally came to an end. We wandered up and we wandered down the Champs Elysées and the war was over and the piles of captured cannon that had made two pyramids were being taken away and peace was upon us.

7

AFTER THE WAR—1919-1932

We were, in these days as I look back at them, constantly seeing people.

It is a confused memory those first years after the war and very difficult to think back and remember what happened before or after something else. Picasso once said, I have already told, when Gertrude Stein and he were discussing dates, you forget that when we were young an awful lot happened in a year. During the years just after the war as I look in order to refresh my memory over the bibliography of Gertrude Stein's work, I am astonished when I realise how many things happened in a year. Perhaps we were not so young then but there were a great many young in the world and perhaps that comes to the same thing.

The old crowd had disappeared. Matisse was now permanently in Nice and in any case although Gertrude Stein and he were perfectly good friends when they met, they practically never met. This was the time when Gertrude Stein and Picasso were not seeing each other. They always talked with the tenderest friendship about each other to any one who had known them both but they did not see each other. Guillaume Apollinaire was dead. Braque and his wife we saw from time to time, he and Picasso by this time were fairly bitterly on the outs. I remember one evening Man Ray brought a photograph that he had made of Picasso to the house and Braque happened to be there. The photograph was being passed around and when it came to Braque he looked at it and said, I ought to know who that gentleman is, je dois connaître ce monsieur. It was a period this and a very considerable time afterward that Gertrude Stein celebrated under the title, Of Having for a Long Time Not Continued to be Friends.

Juan Gris was ill and discouraged. He had been very ill and was never really well again. Privation and discouragement had had their effect. Kahnweiler came back to Paris fairly early after the war but all his old crowd with the exception of Juan were too successful to have need of him. Mildred Aldrich had had her tremendous success with the Hilltop on the Marne, in Mildred's way she had spent royally all she had earned royally and was now still spending and enjoying it although getting a little uneasy. We used to go out and see her about once a month, in fact all the rest of her life we always managed to get out to see her regularly. Even in the days of her very greatest glory she loved a visit from Gertrude Stein better than a visit from anybody else. In fact it was largely to please Mildred that Gertrude Stein tried to get the Atlantic Monthly to print something of hers. Mildred always felt and said that it would be a blue ribbon if the Atlantic Monthly consented, which of course it never did. Another thing used to annoy Mildred dreadfully. Gertrude Stein's name was never in Who's Who in America. As a matter of fact it was in english authors' bibliographies before it ever entered an american one. This troubled Mildred very much. I hate to look at Who's Who in America, she said to me, when I see all those insignificant people and Gertrude's name not in. And then she would say, I know it's alright but I wish Gertrude were not so outlawed. Poor Mildred. And now just this year for reasons best known to themselves Who's Who has added Gertrude Stein's name to their list. The Atlantic Monthly needless to say has not.

The Atlantic Monthly story is rather funny.

As I said Gertrude Stein sent the Atlantic Monthly some manuscripts, not with any hope of their accepting them, but if by any miracle they should, she would be pleased and Mildred delighted. An answer came back, a long and rather argumentative answer from the editorial office. Gertrude Stein thinking that some Boston woman in the editorial office

had written, answered the arguments lengthily to Miss Ellen
Sedgwick. She received an almost immediate answer meeting
all her arguments and at the same time admitting that the
matter was not without interest but that of course Atlantic
Monthly readers could not be affronted by having these manuscripts presented in the review, but it might be possible to
have them introduced by somebody in the part of the magazine, if I remember rightly, called the Contributors' Club. The
letter ended by saying that the writer was not Ellen but
Ellery Sedgwick.

Gertrude Stein of course was delighted with its being Ellery and not Ellen and accepted being printed in the Contributors' Club, but equally of course the manuscripts did not
appear even in the part called Contributors' Club.

We began to meet new people all the time.

Some one told us, I have forgotten who, that an american
woman had started a lending library of english books in our
quarter. We had in those days of economy given up Mudie's,
but there was the American Library which supplied us a
little, but Gertrude Stein wanted more. We investigated and
we found Sylvia Beach. Sylvia Beach was very enthusiastic
about Gertrude Stein and they became friends. She was
Sylvia Beach's first annual subscriber and Sylvia Beach was
proportionately proud and grateful. Her little place was in a
little street near the Ecole de Médecine. It was not then much
frequented by americans. There was the author of Beebie the
Beebeist and there was the niece of Marcel Schwob and there
were a few stray irish poets. We saw a good deal of Sylvia
those days, she used to come to the house and also go out
into the country with us in the old car. We met Adrienne
Monnier and she brought Valéry Larbaud to the house and
they were all very interested in Three Lives and Valéry
Larbaud, so we understood, meditated translating it. It was
at this time that Tristan Tzara first appeared in Paris. Adrienne Monnier was much excited by his advent. Picabia had
found him in Switzerland during the war and they had together created dadaism, and out of dadaism, with a great deal
of struggle and quarrelling came surréalisme.

Tzara came to the house, I imagine Picabia brought him

but I am not quite certain. I have always found it very difficult to understand the stories of his violence and his wickedness, at least I found it difficult then because Tzara when he came to the house sat beside me at the tea table and talked to me like a pleasant and not very exciting cousin.

Adrienne Monnier wanted Sylvia to move to the rue de l'Odéon and Sylvia hesitated but finally she did so and as a matter of fact we did not see her very often afterward. They gave a party just after Sylvia moved in and we went and there Gertrude Stein first discovered that she had a young Oxford following. There were several young Oxford men there and they were awfully pleased to meet her and they asked her to give them some manuscripts and they published them that year nineteen twenty, in the Oxford Magazine.

Sylvia Beach from time to time brought groups of people to the house, groups of young writers and some older women with them. It was at that time that Ezra Pound came, no that was brought about in another way. She later ceased coming to the house but she sent word that Sherwood Anderson had come to Paris and wanted to see Gertrude Stein and might he come. Gertrude Stein sent back word that she would be very pleased and he came with his wife and Rosenfeld, the musical critic.

For some reason or other I was not present on this occasion, some domestic complication in all probability, at any rate when I did come home Gertrude Stein was moved and pleased as she has very rarely been. Gertrude Stein was in those days a little bitter, all her unpublished manuscripts, and no hope of publication or serious recognition. Sherwood Anderson came and quite simply and directly as is his way told her what he thought of her work and what it had meant to him in his development. He told it to her then and what was even rarer he told it in print immediately after. Gertrude Stein and Sherwood Anderson have always been the best of friends but I do not believe even he realises how much his visit meant to her. It was he who thereupon wrote the introduction to Geography and Plays.

In those days you met anybody anywhere. The Jewetts were an american couple who owned a tenth century château near Perpignan. We had met them there during the war and when they came to Paris we went to see them. There we met first Man Ray and later Robert Coates, how either of them happened to get there I do not know.

There were a lot of people in the room when we came in and soon Gertrude Stein was talking to a little man who sat in the corner. As we went out she made an engagement with him. She said he was a photographer and seemed interesting, and reminded me that Jeanne Cook, William Cook's wife, wanted her picture taken to send to Cook's people in America. We all three went to Man Ray's hotel. It was one of the little, tiny hotels in the rue Delambre and Man Ray had one of the small rooms, but I have never seen any space, not even a ship's cabin, with so many things in it and the things so admirably disposed. He had a bed, he had three large cameras, he had several kinds of lighting, he had a window screen, and in a little closet he did all his developing. He showed us pictures of Marcel Duchamp and a lot of other people and he asked if he might come and take photographs of the studio and of Gertrude Stein. He did and he also took some of me and we were very pleased with the result. He has at intervals taken pictures of Gertrude Stein and she is always fascinated with his way of using lights. She always comes home very pleased. One day she told him that she liked his photographs of her better than any that had ever been taken except one snap shot I had taken of her recently. This seemed to bother Man Ray. In a little while he asked her to come and pose and she did. He said, move all you like, your eyes, your head, it is to be a pose but it is to have in it all the qualities of a snap shot. The poses were very long, she, as he requested, moved, and the result, the last photographs he made of her, are extraordinarily interesting.

Robert Coates we also met at the Jewetts' in those early days just after the war. I remember the day very well. It was a cold, dark day, on an upper floor of a hotel. There were a number of young men there and suddenly Gertrude Stein said she had forgotten to put the light on her car and she did not want another fine, we had just had one because I had blown the klaxon at a policeman trying to get him out of our way and she had received one by going the wrong way around a post. Alright, said a red-haired young man and immediately he was down and back. The light is on, he announced. How did you know which my car was, asked Gertrude Stein. Oh I knew, said Coates. We always liked Coates. It is extraordinary in wandering about Paris how very few people you know you meet, but we often met Coates hatless and redheaded in the most unexpected places. This was just about the time of Broom, about which I will tell very soon, and Gertrude Stein took a very deep interest in Coates' work as soon as he showed it to her. She said he was the one young man who had an individual rhythm, his words made a sound to the eyes, most people's words do not. We also liked Coates' address, the City Hotel, on the island, and we liked all his ways.

Gertrude Stein was delighted with the scheme of study that he prepared for the Guggenheim prize. Unfortunately, the scheme of study, which was a most charming little novel, with Gertrude Stein as a backer, did not win a prize.

As I have said there was Broom.

Before the war we had known a young fellow, not known him much but a little; Elmer Harden, who was in Paris studying music. During the war we heard that Elmer Harden had joined the french army and had been badly wounded. It was rather an amazing story. Elmer Harden had been nursing french wounded in the american hospital and one of his patients, a captain with an arm fairly disabled, was going back to the front. Elmer Harden could not content himself any longer nursing. He said to Captain Peter, I am going with you. But it is impossible, said Captain Peter. But I am, said Elmer stubbornly. So they took a taxi and they went to the war office and to a dentist and I don't know where else, but by the end of the week Captain Peter had rejoined and Elmer Harden was in his regiment as a soldier. He fought well and was wounded. After the war we met him again and then we met often. He and the lovely flowers he used to send us were a great comfort in those days just after the peace. He and I always say that he and I will be the last people of our generation to remember the war. I am afraid we both of us

have already forgotten it a little. Only the other day though
Elmer announced that he had had a great triumph, he had
made Captain Peter and Captain Peter is a breton admit that
it was a nice war. Up to this time when he had said to Captain Peter, it was a nice war, Captain Peter had not answered,
but this time when Elmer said, it was a nice war, Captain
Peter said, yes Elmer, it was a nice war.

Kate Buss came from the same town as Elmer, from Med-
ford, Mass. She was in Paris and she came to see us. I do not
think Elmer introduced her but she did come to see us. She
was much interested in the writings of Gertrude Stein and
owned everything that up to that time could be bought. She
brought Kreymborg to see us. Kreymborg had come to Paris
with Harold Loeb to start Broom. Kreymborg and his wife
came to the house frequently. He wanted very much to run
The Long Gay Book, the thing Gertrude Stein had written
just after The Making of Americans, as a serial. Of course
Harold Loeb would not consent to that. Kreymborg used to
read out the sentences from this book with great gusto. He
and Gertrude Stein had a bond of union beside their mutual
liking because the Grafton Press that had printed Three
Lives had printed his first book and about the same time.

Kate Buss brought lots of people to the house. She brought
Djuna Barnes and Mina Loy and they had wanted to bring
James Joyce but they didn't. We were glad to see Mina whom
we had known in Florence as Mina Haweis. Mina brought
Glenway Wescott on his first trip to Europe. Glenway impressed us greatly by his english accent. Hemingway explained. He said, when you matriculate of the University of
Chicago you write down just what accent you will have and
they give it to you when you graduate. You can have a six-
teenth century or modern, whatever you like. Glenway left
behind him a silk cigarette case with his initials, we kept
it until he came back again and then gave it to him.

Mina also brought Robert McAlmon. McAlmon was very
nice in those days, very mature and very good-looking. It was
much later that he published The Making of Americans in
the Contact press and that everybody quarrelled. But that

is Paris, except that as a matter of fact Gertrude Stein and he never became friends again.

Kate Buss brought Ernest Walsh, he was very young then and very feverish and she was worried about him. We met him later with Hemingway and then in Belley, but we never knew him very well.

We met Ezra Pound at Grace Lounsbery's house, he came home to dinner with us and he stayed and he talked about japanese prints among other things. Gertrude Stein liked him but did not find him amusing. She said he was a village explainer, excellent if you were a village, but if you were not, not. Ezra also talked about T. S. Eliot. It was the first time any one had talked about T.S. at the house. Pretty soon everybody talked about T.S. Kitty Buss talked about him and much later Hemingway talked about him as the Major. Considerably later Lady Rothermere talked about him and invited Gertrude Stein to come and meet him. They were founding the Criterion. We had met Lady Rothermere through Muriel Draper whom we had seen again for the first time after many years. Gertrude Stein was not particularly anxious to go to Lady Rothermere's and meet T. S. Eliot, but we all insisted she should, and she gave a doubtful yes. I had no evening dress to wear for this occasion and started to make one. The bell rang and in walked Lady Rothermere and T.S. Eliot and Gertrude Stein had a solemn conversation, mostly about split infinitives and other grammatical solecisms and why Gertrude Stein used them. Finally Lady Rothermere and Eliot rose to go and Eliot said that if he printed anything of Gertrude Stein's in the Criterion it would have to be her very latest thing. They left and Gertrude Stein said, don't bother to finish your dress, now we don't have to go, and she began to write a portrait of T. S. Eliot and called it the fifteenth of November, that being this day and so there could be no doubt but that it was her latest thing. It was all about wool is wool and silk is silk or wool is woollen and silk is silken. She sent it to T. S. Eliot and he accepted it but naturally he did not print it.

Then began a long correspondence, not between Gertrude

Stein and T. S. Eliot, but between T. S. Eliot's secretary and myself. We each addressed the other as Sir, I signing myself A. B. Toklas and she signing initials. It was only considerably afterwards that I found out that his secretary was not a young man. I don't know whether she ever found out that I was not.

In spite of all this correspondence nothing happened and Gertrude Stein mischievously told the story to all the english people coming to the house and at that moment there were a great many english coming in and out. At any rate finally there was a note, it was now early spring, from the Criterion asking would Miss Stein mind if her contribution appeared in the October number. She replied that nothing could be more suitable than the fifteenth of November on the fifteenth of October.

Once more a long silence and then this time came proof of the article. We were surprised but returned the proof promptly. Apparently a young man had sent it without authority because very shortly came an apologetic letter saying that there had been a mistake, the article was not to be printed just yet. This was also told to the passing english with the result that after all it was printed. Thereafter it was reprinted in the Georgian Stories. Gertrude Stein was delighted when later she was told that Eliot had said in Cambridge that the work of Gertrude Stein was very fine but not for us.

But to come back to Ezra. Ezra did come back and he came back with the editor of The Dial. This time it was worse than japanese prints, it was much more violent. In his surprise at the violence Ezra fell out of Gertrude Stein's favourite little armchair, the one I have since tapestried with Picasso designs, and Gertrude Stein was furious. Finally Ezra and the editor of The Dial left, nobody too well pleased. Gertrude Stein did not want to see Ezra again. Ezra did not quite see why. He met Gertrude Stein one day near the Luxembourg gardens and said, but I do want to come to see you. I am so sorry, answered Gertrude Stein, but Miss Toklas has a bad tooth and beside we are busy picking wild flowers. All of which was literally true, like all of Gertrude Stein's literature, but it upset Ezra, and we never saw him again.

During these months after the war we were one day going down a little street and saw a man looking in at a window and going backwards and forwards and right and left and otherwise behaving strangely. Lipschitz, said Gertrude Stein. Yes, said Lipschitz, I am buying an iron cock. Where is it, we asked. Why in there, he said, and in there it was. Gertrude Stein had known Lipschitz very slightly at one time but this incident made them friends and soon he asked her to pose. He had just finished a bust of Jean Cocteau and he wanted to do her. She never minds posing, she likes the calm of it and although she does not like sculpture and told Lipschitz so, she began to pose. I remember it was a very hot spring and Lipschitz's studio was appallingly hot and they spent hours there.

Lipschitz is an excellent gossip and Gertrude Stein adores the beginning and middle and end of a story and Lipschitz was able to supply several missing parts of several stories.

And then they talked about art and Gertrude Stein rather liked her portrait and they were very good friends and the sittings were over.

One day we were across town at a picture show and somebody came up to Gertrude Stein and said something. She said, wiping her forehead, it is hot. He said he was a friend of Lipschitz and she answered, yes it was hot there. Lipschitz was to bring her some photographs of the head he had done but he did not and we were awfully busy and Gertrude Stein sometimes wondered why Lipschitz did not come. Somebody wanted the photos so she wrote to him to bring them. He came. She said why did you not come before. He said he did not come before because he had been told by some one to whom she had said it, that she was bored sitting for him. Oh hell, she said, listen I am fairly well known for saying things about any one and anything, I say them about people, I say them to people, I say them when I please and how I please but as I mostly say what I think, the least that you or anybody else can do is to rest content with what I say to you. He seemed very content and they talked happily and pleasantly and they said à bientôt, we will meet soon. Lipschitz left and we did not see him for several years.

Then Jane Heap turned up and wanted to take some of Lipschitz's things to America and she wanted Gertrude Stein to come and choose them. But how can I, said Gertrude Stein, when Lipschitz is very evidently angry, I am sure I have not the slightest idea why or how but he is. Jane Heap said that Lipschitz said that he was fonder of Gertrude Stein than he was of almost anybody and was heart broken at not seeing her. Oh, said Gertrude Stein, I am very fond of him. Sure I will go with you. She went, they embraced tenderly and had a happy time and her only revenge was in parting to say to Lipschitz, à très bientôt. And Lipschitz said, comme vous êtes méchante. They have been excellent friends ever since and Gertrude Stein has done of Lipschitz one of her most lovely portraits but they have never spoken of the quarrel and if he knows what happened the second time she does not.

It was through Lipschitz that Gertrude Stein again met Jean Cocteau. Lipschitz had told Gertrude Stein a thing which she did not know, that Cocteau in his Potomak had spoken of and quoted The Portrait of Mabel Dodge. She was naturally very pleased as Cocteau was the first french writer to speak of her work. They met once or twice and began a friendship that consists in their writing to each other quite often and liking each other immensely and having many young and old friends in common, but not in meeting.

Jo Davidson too sculptured Gertrude Stein at this time. There, all was peaceful, Jo was witty and amusing and he pleased Gertrude Stein. I cannot remember who came in and out, whether they were real or whether they were sculptured but there were a great many. There were among others Lincoln Steffens and in some queer way he is associated with the beginning of our seeing a good deal of Janet Scudder but I do not well remember just what happened.

I do however remember very well the first time I ever heard Janet Scudder's voice. It was way back when I first came to Paris and my friend and I had a little apartment in the rue Notre-Dame-des-Champs. My friend in the enthusiasm of seeing other people enthusiastic had bought a Matisse and it had just been hung on the wall. Mildred

Aldrich was calling on us, it was a warm spring afternoon and Mildred was leaning out of the window. I suddenly heard her say, Janet, Janet come up here. What is it, said a very lovely drawling voice. I want you to come up here and meet my friends Harriet and Alice and I want you to come up and see their new apartment. Oh, said the voice. And then Mildred said, and they have a new big Matisse. Come up and see it. I don't think so, said the voice.

Janet did later see a great deal of Matisse when he lived out in Clamart. And Gertrude Stein and she had always been friends, at least ever since the period when they first began to see a good deal of each other.

Like Doctor Claribel Cone, Janet, always insisting that she understands none of it, reads and feels Gertrude Stein's work and reads it aloud understandingly.

We were going to the valley of the Rhône for the first time since the war and Janet and a friend in a duplicate Godiva were to come too. I will tell about this very soon.

During all these restless months we were also trying to get Mildred Aldrich the legion of honour. After the war was over a great many war-workers were given the legion of honour but they were all members of organisations and Mildred Aldrich was not. Gertrude Stein was very anxious that Mildred Aldrich should have it. In the first place she thought she ought, no one else had done as much propaganda for France as she had by her books which everybody in America read, and beside she knew Mildred would like it. So we began the campaign. It was not a very easy thing to accomplish as naturally the organisations had the most influence. We started different people going. We began to get lists of prominent americans and asked them to sign. They did not refuse, but a list in itself helps, but does not accomplish results. Mr. Jaccacci who had a great admiration for Miss Aldrich was very helpful but all the people that he knew wanted things for themselves first. We got the American Legion interested at least two of the colonels, but they also had other names that had to pass first. We had seen and talked to and interested everybody and everybody promised and nothing happened. Finally we met a senator. He would

be helpful but then senators were busy and then one afternoon we met the senator's secretary. Gertrude Stein drove
the senator's secretary home in Godiva.

As it turned out the senator's secretary had tried to learn
to drive a car and had not succeeded. The way in which
Gertrude Stein made her way through Paris traffic with the
ease and indifference of a chauffeur, and was at the same
time a well known author impressed her immensely. She said
she would get Mildred Aldrich's papers out of the pigeon
hole in which they were probably reposing and she did. Very
shortly after the mayor of Mildred's village called upon her
one morning on official business. He presented her with the
preliminary papers to be signed for the legion of honour.
He said to her, you must remember, Mademoiselle, these
matters often start but do not get themselves accomplished.
So you must be prepared for disappointment. Mildred answered quietly, monsieur le maire, if my friends have started
a matter of this kind they will see to it that it is accomplished.
And it was. When we arrived at Avignon on our way to
Saint-Rémy there was a telegram telling us that Mildred had
her decoration. We were delighted and Mildred Aldrich to
the day of her death never lost her pride and pleasure in her
honour.

During these early restless years after the war Gertrude
Stein worked a great deal. Not as in the old days, night after
night, but anywhere, in between visits, in the automobile
while she was waiting in the street while I did errands, while
posing. She was particularly fond in these days of working
in the automobile while it stood in the crowded streets.

It was then that she wrote Finer Than Melanctha as a
joke. Harold Loeb, at that time editing Broom all by himself,
said he would like to have something of hers that would be
as fine as Melanctha, her early negro story in Three Lives.

She was much influenced by the sound of the streets and
the movement of the automobiles. She also liked then to set
a sentence for herself as a sort of tuning fork and metronome
and then write to that time and tune. Mildred's Thoughts,
published in The American Caravan, was one of these ex-

periments she thought most successful. The Birthplace of
Bonnes, published in The Little Review, was another one.
Moral Tales of 1920-1921, American Biography, and One
Hundred Prominent Men, when as she said she created out
of her imagination one hundred men equally men and all
equally prominent were written then. These two were later
printed in Useful Knowledge.

It was also about this time that Harry Gibb came back to
Paris for a short while. He was very anxious that Gertrude
Stein should publish a book of her work showing what she
had been doing in those years. Not a little book, he kept
saying, a big book, something they can get their teeth into.
You must do it, he used to say. But no publisher will look at
it now that John Lane is no longer active, she said. It makes
no difference, said Harry Gibb violently, it is the essence of
the thing that they must see and you must have a lot of
things printed, and then turning to me he said, Alice you
do it. I knew he was right and that it had to be done. But
how.

I talked to Kate Buss about it and she suggested the Four
Seas Company who had done a little book for her. I began
a correspondence with Mr. Brown, Honest to God Brown as
Gertrude Stein called him in imitation of William Cook's
phrase when everything was going particularly wrong. The
arrangements with Honest to God having finally been made
we left for the south in July, nineteen twenty-two.

We started off in Godiva, the runabout ford and followed
by Janet Scudder in a second Godiva accompanied by Mrs.
Lane. They were going to Grasse to buy themselves a home,
they finally bought one near Aix-en-Provence. And we were
going to Saint-Rémy to visit in peace the country we had
loved during the war.

We were only a hundred or so kilometers from Paris when
Janet Scudder tooted her horn which was the signal agreed
upon for us to stop and wait. Janet came alongside. I think,
said she solemnly, Gertrude Stein always called her The
Doughboy, she always said there were only two perfectly
solemn things on earth, the doughboy and Janet Scudder.

Janet had also, Gertrude Stein always said, all the subtlety of the doughboy and all his nice ways and all his lonesomeness. Janet came alongside, I think, she said solemnly, we are not on the right road, it says Paris-Perpignan and I want to go to Grasse.

Anyway at the time we got no further than Lorne and there we suddenly realised how tired we were. We were just tired.

We suggested that the others should move on to Grasse but they said they too would wait and we all waited. It was the first time we had just stayed still since Palma de Mallorca, since 1916. Finally we moved slowly on to Saint-Rémy and they went further to Grasse and then came back. They asked us what we were going to do and we answered, nothing just stay here. So they went off again and bought a property in Aix-en-Provence.

Janet Scudder, as Gertrude Stein always said, had the real pioneer's passion for buying useless real estate. In every little town we stopped on the way Janet would find a piece of property that she considered purchasable and Gertrude Stein, violently protesting, got her away. She wanted to buy property everywhere except in Grasse where she had gone to buy property. She finally did buy a house and grounds in Aix-en-Provence after insisting on Gertrude Stein's seeing it who told her not to and telegraphed no and telephoned no. However Janet did buy it but luckily after a year she was able to get rid of it. During that year we stayed quietly in Saint-Rémy.

We had intended staying only a month or two but we stayed all winter. With the exception of an occasional interchange of visits with Janet Scudder we saw no one except the people of the country. We went to Avignon to shop, we went now and then into the country we had known so well but for the most part we wandered around Saint-Rémy, we went up into the Alpilles, the little hills that Gertrude Stein described over and over again in the writing of that winter, we watched the enormous flocks of sheep going up into the mountains led by the donkeys and their water bottles, we sat

about the roman monuments and we went often to Les Baux.
The hotel was not very comfortable but we stayed on. The
valley of the Rhône was once more exercising its spell over
us.

It was during this winter that Gertrude Stein meditated
upon the use of grammar, poetical forms and what might be
termed landscape plays.

It was at this time that she wrote Elucidation, printed in
transition in nineteen twenty-seven. It was her first effort to
state her problems of expression and her attempts to answer
them. It was her first effort to realise clearly just what her
writing meant and why it was as it was. Later on much later
she wrote her treatises on grammar, sentences, paragraphs,
vocabulary etcetera, which I have printed in Plain Edition
under the title of How To Write.

It was in Saint-Rémy and during this winter that she wrote
the poetry that has so greatly influenced the younger generation. Her Capital Capitals, Virgil Thomson has put to music.
Lend a Hand or Four Religions has been printed in Useful
Knowledge. This play has always interested her immensely,
it was the first attempt that later made her Operas and Plays,
the first conception of landscape as a play. She also at that
time wrote the Valentine to Sherwood Anderson, also printed
in the volume Useful Knowledge, Indian Boy, printed later
in the Reviewer, (Carl Van Vechten sent Hunter Stagg to
us a young Southerner as attractive as his name), and Saints
In Seven, which she used to illustrate her work in her lectures at Oxford and Cambridge, and Talks to Saints in Saint-
Rémy.

She worked in those days with slow care and concentration,
and was very preoccupied.

Finally we received the first copies of Geography and Plays,
the winter was over and we went back to Paris.

This long winter in Saint-Rémy broke the restlessness of
the war and the after war. A great many things were to happen, there were to be friendships and there were to be
enmities and there were to be a great many other things
but there was not to be any restlessness.

Gertrude Stein always says that she only has two real distractions, pictures and automobiles. Perhaps she might now add dogs.

Immediately after the war her attention was attracted by the work of a young french painter, Fabre, who had a natural feeling for objects on a table and landscapes but he came to nothing. The next painter who attracted her attention was André Masson. Masson was at that time influenced by Juan Gris in whom Gertrude Stein's interest was permanent and vital. She was interested in André Masson as a painter particularly as a painter of white and she was interested in his composition in the wandering line in his compositions. Soon Masson fell under the influence of the surréalistes.

The surréalistes are the vulgarisation of Picabia as Delaunay and his followers and the futurists were the vulgarisation of Picasso. Picabia had conceived and is struggling with the problem that a line should have the vibration of a musical sound and that this vibration should be the result of conceiving the human form and the human face in so tenuous a fashion that it would induce such vibration in the line forming it. It is his way of achieving the disembodied. It was this idea that conceived mathematically influenced Marcel Duchamp and produced his The Nude Descending the Staircase.

All his life Picabia has struggled to dominate and achieve this conception. Gertrude Stein thinks that perhaps he is now approaching the solution of his problem. The surréalistes taking the manner for the matter as is the way of the vulgarisers, accept the line as having become vibrant and as therefore able in itself to inspire them to higher flights. He who is going to be the creator of the vibrant line knows that it is not yet created and if it were it would not exist by itself, it would be dependent upon the emotion of the object which compels the vibration. So much for the creator and his followers.

Gertrude Stein, in her work, has always been possessed by the intellectual passion for exactitude in the description of inner and outer reality. She has produced a simplification by this concentration, and as a result the destruction of associational emotion in poetry and prose. She knows that beauty, music, decoration, the result of emotion should never be the cause, even events should not be the cause of emotion nor should they be the material of poetry and prose. Nor should emotion itself be the cause of poetry or prose. They should consist of an exact reproduction of either an outer or an inner reality.

It was this conception of exactitude that made the close understanding between Gertrude Stein and Juan Gris.

Juan Gris conceived exactitude but in him exactitude had a mystical basis. As a mystic it was necessary for him to be exact. In Gertrude Stein the necessity was intellectual, a pure passion for exactitude. It is because of this that her work has often been compared to that of mathematicians and by a certain french critic to the work of Bach.

Picasso by nature the most endowed had less clarity of intellectual purpose. He was in his creative activity dominated by spanish ritual, later by negro ritual expressed in negro sculpture (which has an arab basis the basis also of spanish ritual) and later by russian ritual. His creative activity being tremendously dominant, he made these great rituals over into his own image.

Juan Gris was the only person whom Picasso wished away. The relation between them was just that.

In the days when the friendship between Gertrude Stein and Picasso had become if possible closer than before, (it was for his little boy, born February fourth to her February third, that she wrote her birthday book with a line for each day in the year) in those days her intimacy with Juan Gris displeased him. Once after a show of Juan's pictures at the Galérie Simon he said to her with violence, tell me why you stand up for his work, you know you do not like it; and she did not answer him.

Later when Juan died and Gertrude Stein was heart broken Picasso came to the house and spent all day there. I do not know what was said but I do know that at one time Gertrude Stein said to him bitterly, you have no right to mourn, and he said, you have no right to say that to me. You never realised his meaning because you did not have it, she said angrily. You know very well I did, he replied.

The most moving thing Gertrude Stein has ever written is The Life and Death of Juan Gris. It was printed in transition and later on translated in german for his retrospective show in Berlin.

Picasso never wished Braque away. Picasso said once when he and Gertrude Stein were talking together, yes, Braque and James Joyce, they are the incomprehensibles whom anybody can understand. Les incompréhensibles que tout le monde peut comprendre.

The first thing that happened when we were back in Paris was Hemingway with a letter of introduction from Sherwood Anderson.

I remember very well the impression I had of Hemingway that first afternoon. He was an extraordinarily good-looking young man, twenty-three years old. It was not long after that that everybody was twenty-six. It became the period of being twenty-six. During the next two or three years all the young men were twenty-six years old. It was the right age apparently for that time and place. There were one or two under twenty, for example George Lynes but they did not count as Gertrude Stein carefully explained to them. If they were young men they were twenty-six. Later on, much later on they were twenty-one and twenty-two.

So Hemingway was twenty-three, rather foreign looking, with passionately interested, rather than interesting eyes. He sat in front of Gertrude Stein and listened and looked.

They talked then, and more and more, a great deal together. He asked her to come and spend an evening in their apartment and look at his work. Hemingway had then and has always a very good instinct for finding apartments in strange but pleasing localities and good femmes de ménage and good food. This his first apartment was just off the place du Tertre. We spent the evening there and he and Gertrude Stein went over all the writing he had done up to that time. He had begun the novel that it was inevitable he would begin and there were the little poems afterwards printed by

McAlmon in the Contact Edition. Gertrude Stein rather liked the poems, they were direct, Kiplingesque, but the novel she found wanting. There is a great deal of description in this, she said, and not particularly good description. Begin over again and concentrate, she said.

Hemingway was at this time Paris correspondent for a canadian newspaper. He was obliged there to express what he called the canadian viewpoint.

He and Gertrude Stein used to walk together and talk together a great deal. One day she said to him, look here, you say you and your wife have a little money between you. Is it enough to live on if you live quietly. Yes, he said. Well, she said, then do it. If you keep on doing newspaper work you will never see things, you will only see words and that will not do, that is of course if you intend to be a writer. Hemingway said he undoubtedly intended to be a writer. He and his wife went away on a trip and shortly after Hemingway turned up alone. He came to the house about ten o'clock in the morning and he stayed, he stayed for lunch, he stayed all afternoon, he stayed for dinner and he stayed until about ten o'clock at night and then all of a sudden he announced that his wife was enceinte and then with great bitterness, and I, I am too young to be a father. We consoled him as best we could and sent him on his way.

When they came back Hemingway said that he had made up his mind. They would go back to America and he would work hard for a year and with what he would earn and what they had they would settle down and he would give up newspaper work and make himself a writer. They went away and well within the prescribed year they came back with a new born baby. Newspaper work was over.

The first thing to do when they came back was as they thought to get the baby baptised. They wanted Gertrude Stein and myself to be god-mothers and an english war comrade of Hemingway was to be god-father. We were all born of different religions and most of us were not practising any, so it was rather difficult to know in what church the baby could be baptised. We spent a great deal of time that winter, all of us, discussing the matter. Finally it was decided that it should be baptised episcopalian and episcopalian it was. Just how it was managed with the assortment of god-parents I am sure I do not know, but it was baptised in the episcopalian chapel.

Writer or painter god-parents are notoriously unreliable. That is, there is certain before long to be a cooling of friend-ship. I know several cases of this, poor Paulot Picasso's god-parents have wandered out of sight and just as naturally it is a long time since any of us have seen or heard of our Hemingway god-child.

However in the beginning we were active god-parents, I particularly. I embroidered a little chair and I knitted a gay coloured garment for the god-child. In the meantime the god-child's father was very earnestly at work making himself a writer.

Gertrude Stein never corrects any detail of anybody's writing, she sticks strictly to general principles, the way of seeing what the writer chooses to see, and the relation be-tween that vision and the way it gets down. When the vision is not complete the words are flat, it is very simple, there can be no mistake about it, so she insists. It was at this time that Hemingway began the short things that afterwards were printed in a volume called In Our Time.

One day Hemingway came in very excited about Ford Madox Ford and the Transatlantic. Ford Madox Ford had started the Transatlantic some months before. A good many years before, indeed before the war, we had met Ford Madox Ford who was at that time Ford Madox Hueffer. He was married to Violet Hunt and Violet Hunt and Gertrude Stein were next to each other at the tea table and talked a great deal together. I was next to Ford Madox Hueffer and I liked him very much and I like his stories of Mistral and Tarascon and I liked his having been followed about in that land of the french royalist, on account of his resemblance to the Bourbon claimant. I had never seen the Bourbon claimant but Ford at that time undoubtedly might have been a Bour-bon.

We had heard that Ford was in Paris, but we had not happened to meet. Gertrude Stein had however seen copies of the Transatlantic and found it interesting but had thought nothing further about it.

Hemingway came in then very excited and said that Ford wanted something of Gertrude Stein's for the next number and he, Hemingway, wanted The Making of Americans to be run in it as a serial and he had to have the first fifty pages at once. Gertrude Stein was of course quite overcome with her excitement at this idea, but there was no copy of the manuscript except the one that we had had bound. That makes no difference, said Hemingway, I will copy it. And he and I between us did copy it and it was printed in the next number of the Transatlantic. So for the first time a piece of the monumental work which was the beginning, really the beginning of modern writing, was printed, and we were very happy. Later on when things were difficult between Gertrude Stein and Hemingway, she always remembered with gratitude that after all it was Hemingway who first caused to be printed a piece of The Making of Americans. She always says, yes sure I have a weakness for Hemingway. After all he was the first of the young men to knock at my door and he did make Ford print the first piece of The Making of Americans.

I myself have not so much confidence that Hemingway did do this. I have never known what the story is but I have always been certain that there was some other story behind it all. That is the way I feel about it.

Gertrude Stein and Sherwood Anderson are very funny on the subject of Hemingway. The last time that Sherwood was in Paris they often talked about him. Hemingway had been formed by the two of them and they were both a little proud and a little ashamed of the work of their minds. Hemingway had at one moment, when he had repudiated Sherwood Anderson and all his works, written him a letter in the name of american literature which he, Hemingway, in company with his contemporaries was about to save, telling Sherwood just what he, Hemingway thought about Sherwood's work, and, that thinking, was in no sense complimentary. When Sherwood came to Paris Hemingway naturally was afraid. Sherwood as naturally was not.

As I say he and Gertrude Stein were endlessly amusing on the subject. They admitted that Hemingway was yellow, he is, Gertrude Stein insisted, just like the flat-boat men on the Mississippi river as described by Mark Twain. But what a book, they both agreed, would be the real story of Hemingway, not those he writes but the confessions of the real Ernest Hemingway. It would be for another audience than the audience Hemingway now has but it would be very wonderful. And then they both agreed that they have a weakness for Hemingway because he is such a good pupil. He is a rotten pupil, I protested. You don't understand, they both said, it is so flattering to have a pupil who does it without understanding it, in other words he takes training and anybody who takes training is a favourite pupil. They both admit it to be a weakness. Gertrude Stein added further, you see he is like Derain. You remember Monsieur de Tuille said, when I did not understand why Derain was having the success he was having that it was because he looks like a modern and he smells of the museums. And that is Hemingway, he looks like a modern and he smells of the museums. But what a story that of the real Hem, and one he should tell himself but alas he never will. After all, as he himself once murmured, there is the career, the career.

But to come back to the events that were happening.

Hemingway did it all. He copied the manuscript and corrected the proofs. Correcting proofs is, as I said before, like dusting, you learn the values of the thing as no reading suffices to teach it to you. In correcting these proofs Hemingway learned a great deal and he admired all that he learned. It was at this time that he wrote to Gertrude Stein saying that it was she who had done the work in writing The Making of Americans and he and all his had but to devote their lives to seeing that it was published.

He had hopes of being able to accomplish this. Some one, I think by the name of Sterne, said that he could place it with a publisher. Gertrude Stein and Hemingway believed that he could, but soon Hemingway reported that Sterne had entered into his period of unreliability. That was the end of that.

In the meantime and sometime before this Mina Loy had brought McAlmon to the house and he came from time to time and he brought his wife and brought William Carlos Williams. And finally he wanted to print The Making of Americans in the Contact Edition and finally he did. I will come to that.

In the meantime McAlmon had printed the three poems and ten stories of Hemingway and William Bird had printed In Our Time and Hemingway was getting to be known. He was coming to know Dos Passos and Fitzgerald and Bromfield and George Antheil and everybody else and Harold Loeb was once more in Paris. Hemingway had become a writer. He was also a shadow-boxer, thanks to Sherwood, and he heard about bull-fighting from me. I have always loved spanish dancing and spanish bull-fighting and I loved to show the photographs of bull-fighters and bull-fighting. I also loved to show the photograph where Gertrude Stein and I were in the front row and had our picture taken there accidentally. In these days Hemingway was teaching some young chap how to box. The boy did not know how, but by accident he knocked Hemingway out. I believe this sometimes happens. At any rate in these days Hemingway although a sportsman was easily tired. He used to get quite worn out walking from his house to ours. But then he had been worn by the war. Even now he is, as Hélène says all men are, fragile. Recently a robust friend of his said to Gertrude Stein, Ernest is very fragile, whenever he does anything sporting something breaks, his arm, his leg, or his head.

In those early days Hemingway liked all his contemporaries except Cummings. He accused Cummings of having copied everything, not from anybody but from somebody. Gertrude Stein who had been much impressed by The Enormous Room said that Cummings did not copy, he was the natural heir of the New England tradition with its aridity and its sterility, but also with its individuality. They disagreed about this. They also disagreed about Sherwood Anderson. Gertrude Stein contended that Sherwood Anderson had a genius for using a sentence to convey a direct emotion, this was in the great american tradition, and that really except

Sherwood there was no one in America who could write a clear and passionate sentence. Hemingway did not believe this, he did not like Sherwood's taste. Taste has nothing to do with sentences, contended Gertrude Stein. She also added that Fitzgerald was the only one of the younger writers who wrote naturally in sentences.

Gertrude Stein and Fitzgerald are very peculiar in their relation to each other. Gertrude Stein had been very much impressed by This Side of Paradise. She read it when it came out and before she knew any of the young american writers. She said of it that it was this book that really created for the public the new generation. She has never changed her opinion about this. She thinks this equally true of The Great Gatsby. She thinks Fitzgerald will be read when many of his well known contemporaries are forgotten. Fitzgerald always says that he thinks Gertrude Stein says these things just to annoy him by making him think that she means them, and he adds in his favourite way, and her doing it is the cruellest thing I ever heard. They always however have a very good time when they meet. And the last time they met they had a good time with themselves and Hemingway.

Then there was McAlmon. McAlmon had one quality that appealed to Gertrude Stein, abundance, he could go on writing, but she complained that it was dull.

There was also Glenway Wescott but Glenway Wescott at no time interested Gertrude Stein. He has a certain syrup but it does not pour.

So then Hemingway's career was begun. For a little while we saw less of him and then he began to come again. He used to recount to Gertrude Stein the conversations that he afterwards used in The Sun Also Rises and they talked endlessly about the character of Harold Loeb. At this time Hemingway was preparing his volume of short stories to submit to publishers in America. One evening after we had not seen him for a while he turned up with Shipman. Shipman was an amusing boy who was to inherit a few thousand dollars when he came of age. He was not of age. He was to buy the Transatlantic Review when he came of age, so Hemingway said. He was to support a surrealist review when he came of age, André Masson said. He was to buy a house in the country when he came of age, Josette Gris said. As a matter of fact when he came of age nobody who had known him then seemed to know what he did do with his inheritance. Hemingway brought him with him to the house to talk about buying the Transatlantic and incidentally he brought the manuscript he intended sending to America. He handed it to Gertrude Stein. He had added to his stories a little story of meditations and in these he said that The Enormous Room was the greatest book he had ever read. It was then that Gertrude Stein said, Hemingway, remarks are not literature.

After this we did not see Hemingway for quite a while and then we went to see some one, just after The Making of Americans was printed, and Hemingway who was there came up to Gertrude Stein and began to explain why he would not be able to write a review of the book. Just then a heavy hand fell on his shoulder and Ford Madox Ford said, young man it is I who wish to speak to Gertrude Stein. Ford then said to her, I wish to ask your permission to dedicate my new book to you. May I. Gertrude Stein and I were both awfully pleased and touched.

For some years after this Gertrude Stein and Hemingway did not meet. And then we heard that he was back in Paris and telling a number of people how much he wanted to see her. Don't you come home with Hemingway on your arm, I used to say when she went out for a walk. Sure enough one day she did come back bringing him with her.

They sat and talked a long time. Finally I heard her say, Hemingway, after all you are ninety percent Rotarian. Can't you, he said, make it eighty percent. No, said she regretfully, I can't. After all, as she always says, he did, and I may say, he does have moments of disinterestedness.

After that they met quite often. Gertrude Stein always says she likes to see him, he is so wonderful. And if he could only tell his own story. In their last conversation she accused him of having killed a great many of his rivals and put them under the sod. I never, said Hemingway, seriously killed anybody but one man and he was a bad man and, he deserved it, but if I killed anybody else I did it unknowingly, and so I am not responsible.

It was Ford who once said of Hemingway, he comes and sits at my feet and praises me. It makes me nervous. Hemingway also said once, I turn my flame which is a small one down and down and then suddenly there is a big explosion. If there were nothing but explosions my work would be so exciting nobody could bear it.

However, whatever I say, Gertrude Stein always says, yes I know but I have a weakness for Hemingway.

Jane Heap turned up one afternoon. The Little Review had printed the Birthplace of Bonnes and The Valentine to Sherwood Anderson. Jane Heap sat down and we began to talk. She stayed to dinner and she stayed the evening and by dawn the little ford car Godiva which had been burning its lights all night waiting to be taken home could hardly start to take Jane home. Gertrude Stein then and always liked Jane Heap immensely, Margaret Anderson interested her much less.

It was now once more summer and this time we went to the Côte d'Azur and joined the Picassos at Antibes. It was there I first saw Picasso's mother. Picasso looks extraordinarily like her. Gertrude Stein and Madame Picasso had difficulty in talking not having a common language but they talked enough to amuse themselves. They were talking about Picasso when Gertrude Stein first knew him. He was remarkably beautiful then, said Gertrude Stein, he was illuminated as if he wore a halo. Oh, said Madame Picasso, if you thought him beautiful then I assure you it was nothing compared to his looks when he was a boy. He was an angel and a devil in beauty, no one could cease looking at him. And now, said Picasso a little resentfully. Ah now, said they together, ah now there is no such beauty left. But, added his mother, you are very sweet and as a son very perfect. So he had to be satisfied with that.

It was at this time that Jean Cocteau who prides himself on being eternally thirty was writing a little biography of

Picasso, and he sent him a telegram asking him to tell him the date of his birth. And yours, telegraphed back Picasso.

There are so many stories about Picasso and Jean Cocteau. Picasso like Gertrude Stein is easily upset if asked to do something suddenly and Jean Cocteau does this quite successfully. Picasso resents it and revenges himself at greater length. Not long ago there was a long story.

Picasso was in Spain, in Barcelona, and a friend of his youth who was editor of a paper printed, not in spanish but in catalan, interviewed him. Picasso knowing that the interview to be printed in catalan was probably never going to be printed in spanish, thoroughly enjoyed himself. He said that Jean Cocteau was getting to be very popular in Paris, so popular that you could find his poems on the table of any smart coiffeur.

As I say he thoroughly enjoyed himself in giving his interview and then returned to Paris.

Some catalan in Barcelona sent the paper to some catalan friend in Paris and the catalan friend in Paris translated it to a french friend and the french friend printed the interview in a french paper.

Picasso and his wife told us the story together of what happened then. As soon as Jean saw the article, he tried to see Pablo. Pablo refused to see him, he told the maid to say that he was always out and for days they could not answer the telephone. Cocteau finally stated in an interview given to the french press that the interview which had wounded him so sorely had turned out to be an interview with Picabia and not an interview with Picasso, his friend. Picabia of course denied this. Cocteau implored Picasso to give a public denial. Picasso remained discreetly at home.

The first evening the Picassos went out they went to the theatre and there in front of them seated was Jean Cocteau's mother. At the first intermission they went up to her, and surrounded by all their mutual friends she said, my dear, you cannot imagine the relief to me and to Jean to know that it was not you that gave out that vile interview, do tell me that it was not.

And as Picasso's wife said, I as a mother could not let a mother suffer and I said of course it was not Picasso and Picasso said, yes yes of course it was not, and so the public retraction was given.

It was this summer that Gertrude Stein, delighting in the movement of the tiny waves on the Antibes shore, wrote the Completed Portrait of Picasso, the Second Portrait of Carl Van Vechten, and The Book of Concluding With As A Wife Has A Cow A Love Story this afterwards beautifully illustrated by Juan Gris.

Robert McAlmon had definitely decided to publish The Making of Americans, and we were to correct proofs that summer. The summer before we had intended as usual to meet the Picassos at Antibes. I had been reading the Guide des Gourmets and I had found among other places where one ate well, Pernollet's Hôtel in the town of Belley. Belley is its name and Belley is its nature, as Gertrude Stein's elder brother remarked. We arrived there about the middle of August. On the map it looked as if it were high up in the mountains and Gertrude Stein does not like precipices and as we drove through the gorge I was nervous and she protesting, but finally the country opened out delightfully and we arrived in Belley. It was a pleasant hotel although it had no garden and we had intended that it should have a garden. We stayed on for several days.

Then Madame Pernollet, a pleasant round faced woman said to us that since we were evidently staying on why did we not make rates by the day or by the week. We said we would. In the meanwhile the Picassos wanted to know what had become of us. We replied that we were in Belley. We found that Belley was the birthplace of Brillat-Savarin. We now in Bilignin are enjoying using the furniture from the house of Brillat-Savarin which house belongs to the owner of this house.

We also found that Lamartine had been at school in Belley and Gertrude Stein says that wherever Lamartine stayed any length of time one eats well. Madame Récamier also comes from this region and the place is full of descendants of her husband's family. All these things we found out gradually but for the moment we were comfortable and we stayed on and left late. The following summer we were to correct proofs of The Making of Americans and so we left Paris early and came again to Belley. What a summer it was.

The Making of Americans is a book one thousand pages long, closely printed on large pages. Darantière has told me it has five hundred and sixty-five thousand words. It was written in nineteen hundred and six to nineteen hundred and eight, and except for the sections printed in Transatlantic it was all still in manuscript.

The sentences as the book goes on get longer and longer, they are sometimes pages long and the compositors were french, and when they made mistakes and left out a line the effort of getting it back again was terrific.

We used to leave the hotel in the morning with camp chairs, lunch and proof, and all day we struggled with the errors of French compositors. Proof had to be corrected most of it four times and finally I broke my glasses, my eyes gave out, and Gertrude Stein finished alone.

We used to change the scene of our labours and we found lovely spots but there were always to accompany us those endless pages of printers' errors. One of our favourite hillocks where we could see Mont Blanc in the distance we called Madame Mont Blanc.

Another place we went to often was near a little pool made by a small stream near a country cross-road. This was quite like the middle ages, so many things used to happen there, in a very simple middle age way. I remember once a country-man came up to us leading his oxen. Very politely he said, ladies is there anything the matter with me. Why yes, we replied, your face is covered with blood. Oh, he said, you see my oxen were slipping down the hill and I held them back and I too slipped and I wondered if anything had happened to me. We helped him wash the blood off and he went on.

It was during this summer that Gertrude Stein began two long things, A Novel and the Phenomena of Nature which was to lead later to the whole series of meditations on grammar and sentences.

It led first to An Acquaintance With Description, afterwards printed by the Seizin Press. She began at this time to describe landscape as if anything she saw was a natural phenomenon, a thing existent in itself, and she found it, this exercise, very interesting and it finally led her to the later series of Operas and Plays. I am trying to be as commonplace as I can be, she used to say to me. And then sometimes a little worried, it is not too commonplace. The last thing that she had finished, Stanzas of Meditation, and which I am now typewriting, she considers her real achievement of the commonplace.

But to go back. We returned to Paris, the proofs almost done, and Jane Heap was there. She was very excited. She had a wonderful plan, I have now quite forgotten what it was, but Gertrude Stein was enormously pleased with it. It had something to do with a plan for another edition of The Making of Americans in America.

At any rate in the various complications connected with this matter McAlmon became very angry and not without reason, and The Making of Americans appeared but McAlmon and Gertrude Stein were no longer friends.

When Gertrude Stein was quite young her brother once remarked to her, that she, having been born in February, was very like George Washington, she was impulsive and slow-minded. Undoubtedly a great many complications have been the result.

One day in this same spring we were going to visit a new spring salon. Jane Heap had been telling us of a young russian in whose work she was interested. As we were crossing a bridge in Godiva we saw Jane Heap and the young russian. We saw his pictures and Gertrude Stein too was interested. He of course came to see us.

In How To Write Gertrude Stein makes this sentence, Painting now after its great period has come back to be a minor art.

She was very interested to know who was to be the leader of this art.

This is the story.

The young russian was interesting. He was painting, so he said, colour that was no colour, he was painting blue pictures and he was painting three heads in one. Picasso had been drawing three heads in one. Soon the russian was painting three figures in one. Was he the only one. In a way he was although there was a group of them. This group, very shortly after Gertrude Stein knew the russian, had a show at one of the art galleries, Druet's I think. The group then consisted of the russian, a frenchman, a very young dutchman, and two russian brothers. All of them except the dutchman about twenty-six years old.

At this show Gertrude Stein met George Antheil who asked to come to see her and when he came he brought with him Virgil Thomson. Gertrude Stein had not found George Antheil particularly interesting although she liked him, but Virgil Thomson she found very interesting although I did not like him.

However all this I will tell about later. To go back now to painting.

The russian Tchelitchev's work was the most vigorous of the group and the most mature and the most interesting. He had already then a passionate enmity against the frenchman whom they called Bébé Bérard and whose name was Christian Bérard and whom Tchelitchev said copied everything.

René Crevel had been the friend of all these painters. Some time later one of them was to have a one man show at the Galérie Pierre. We were going to it and on the way we met René. We all stopped, he was exhilarated with exasperation. He talked with his characteristic brilliant violence. These painters, he said, sell their pictures for several thousand francs apiece and they have the pretentiousness which comes from being valued in terms of money, and we writers who have twice their quality and infinitely greater vitality cannot earn a living and have to beg and intrigue to induce publishers to publish us; but the time will come, and René became prophetic, when these same painters will come to us to re-create them and then we will contemplate them with indifference.

René was then and has remained ever since a devout surréaliste. He needs and needed, being a frenchman, an intellectual as well as a basal justification for the passionate exaltation in him. This he could not find, being of the immediate postwar generation, in either religion or patriotism, the war having destroyed for his generation, both patriotism and religion as a passion. Surréalisme has been his justification. It has clarified for him the confused negation in which he lived and loved. This he alone of his generation has really succeeded in expressing, a little in his earlier books, and in his last book, The Clavecin of Diderot very adequately and with the brilliant violence that is his quality.

Gertrude Stein was at first not interested in this group of painters as a group but only in the russian. This interest gradually increased and then she was bothered. Granted, she used to say, that the influences which make a new movement in art and literature have continued and are making a new movement in art and literature; in order to seize these influences and create as well as re-create them there needs a very dominating creative power. This the russian manifestly did not have. Still there was a distinctly new creative idea. Where had it come from. Gertrude Stein always says to the young painters when they complain that she changes her mind about their work, it is not I that change my mind about the pictures, but the paintings disappear into the wall, I do not see them any more and then they go out of the door naturally.

In the meantime as I have said George Antheil had brought Virgil Thomson to the house and Virgil Thomson and Gertrude Stein became friends and saw each other a great deal. Virgil Thomson had put a number of Gertrude Stein's things to music, Susie Asado, Preciosilla and Capital Capitals. Gertrude Stein was very much interested in Virgil Thomson's music. He had understood Satie undoubtedly and he had a comprehension quite his own of prosody. He understood a great deal of Gertrude Stein's work, he used to dream at night that there was something there that he did not understand, but on the whole he was very well content with that which he did understand. She delighted in listening to her words framed by his music. They saw a great deal of each other.

Virgil had in his room a great many pictures by Christian

Bérard and Gertrude Stein used to look at them a great deal. She could not find out at all what she thought about them.

She and Virgil Thomson used to talk about them endlessly. Virgil said he knew nothing about pictures but he thought these wonderful. Gertrude Stein told him about her perplexity about the new movement and that the creative power behind it was not the russian. Virgil said that there he quite agreed with her and he was convinced that it was Bébé Bérard, baptised Christian. She said that perhaps that was the answer but she was very doubtful. She used to say of Bérard's pictures, they are almost something and then they are just not. As she used to explain to Virgil, the Catholic Church makes a very sharp distinction between a hysteric and a saint. The same thing holds true in the art world. There is the sensitiveness of the hysteric which has all the appearance of creation, but actual creation has an individual force which is an entirely different thing. Gertrude Stein was inclined to believe that artistically Bérard was more hysteric than saint. At this time she had come back to portrait writing with renewed vigour and she, to clarify her mind, as she said, did portraits of the russian and of the frenchman. In the meantime, through Virgil Thomson, she had met a young frenchman named Georges Hugnet. He and Gertrude Stein became very devoted to one another. He liked the sound of her writing and then he liked the sense and he liked the sentences.

At his home were a great many portraits of himself painted by his friends. Among others one by one of the two russian brothers and one by a young englishman. Gertrude Stein was not particularly interested in any of these portraits. There was however a painting of a hand by this young englishman which she did not like but which she remembered.

Every one began at this time to be very occupied with their own affairs. Virgil Thomson had asked Gertrude Stein to write an opera for him. Among the saints there were two saints whom she had always liked better than any others, Saint Theresa of Avila and Ignatius Loyola, and she said she would write him an opera about these two saints. She began this and worked very hard at it all that spring and finally finished Four Saints and gave it to Virgil Thomson to put to music. He did. And it is a completely interesting opera both as to words and music.

All these summers we had continued to go to the hotel in Belley. We now had become so fond of this country, always the valley of the Rhône, and of the people of the country, and the trees of the country, and the oxen of the country, that we began looking for a house. One day we saw the house of our dreams across a valley. Go and ask the farmer there whose house that is, Gertrude Stein said to me. I said, nonsense it is an important house and it is occupied. Go and ask him, she said. Very reluctantly I did. He said, well yes, perhaps it is for rent, it belongs to a little girl, all her people are dead and I think there is a lieutenant of the regiment stationed in Belley living there now, but I understand they were to leave. You might go and see the agent of the property. We did. He was a kindly old farmer who always told us allez doucement, go slowly. We did. We had the promise of the house, which we never saw any nearer than across the valley, as soon as the lieutenant should leave. Finally three years ago the lieutenant went to Morocco and we took the house still only having seen it from across the valley and we have liked it always more.

While we were still staying at the hotel, Natalie Barney came one day and lunched there bringing some friends, among them, the Duchess of Clermont-Tonnerre. Gertrude Stein and she were delighted with one another and the meeting led to many pleasant consequences, but of that later.

To return to the painters. Just after the opera was finished and before leaving Paris we happened to go to a show of pictures at the Galérie Boniean. There we met one of the russian brothers, Genia Berman, and Gertrude Stein was not uninterested in his pictures. She went with him to his studio and looked at everything he had ever painted. He seemed to have a purer intelligence than the other two painters who certainly had not created the modern movement, perhaps the idea had been originally his. She asked him, telling her story as she was fond of telling it at that time to any one who would listen, had he originated the idea. He said with an intelligent inner smile that he thought he had. She was not at all sure that he was not right. He came down to Bilignin to see us and she slowly concluded that though he was a very good painter he was too bad a painter to have been the creator of an idea. So once more the search began.

Again just before leaving Paris at this same picture gallery she saw a picture of a poet sitting by a waterfall. Who did that, she said. A young englishman, Francis Rose, was the reply. Oh yes I am not interested in his work. How much is that picture, she said: It cost very little. Gertrude Stein says a picture is either worth three hundred francs or three hundred thousand francs. She bought this for three hundred and we went away for the summer.

Georges Hugnet had decided to become an editor and he began editing the Editions de la Montagne. Actually it was George Maratier, everybody's friend who began this edition, but he decided to go to America and become an american and Georges Hugnet inherited it. The first book to appear was sixty pages in french of The Making of Americans. Gertrude Stein and Georges Hugnet translated them together and she was very happy about it. This was later followed by a volume of Ten Portraits written by Gertrude Stein and illustrated by portraits of the artists of themselves, and of the others drawn by them, Virgil Thomson by Bérard and a drawing of Bérard by himself, a portrait of Tchelitchev by himself, a portrait of Picasso by himself and one of Guillaume Apollinaire and one of Erik Satie by Picasso, one of Kristians Tonny the young dutchman by himself and one of Bernard Faÿ by Tonny. These volumes were very well received and everybody was pleased.

Once more everybody went away.

Gertrude Stein in winter takes her white poodle Basket to be bathed at a vet's and she used to go to the picture gallery where she had bought the englishman's romantic picture and wait for Basket to dry. Every time she came home she brought more pictures by the englishman. She did not talk much about it but they accumulated. Several people began to tell her about this young man and offered to introduce him. Gertrude Stein declined. She said no she had had enough of knowing young painters, she now would content herself with knowing young painting.

In the meantime Georges Hugnet wrote a poem called Enfance. Gertrude Stein offered to translate it for him but instead she wrote a poem about it. This at first pleased Georges Hugnet too much and then did not please him at all. Gertrude Stein then called the poem Before The Flowers Of Friendship Faded Friendship Faded. Everybody mixed themselves up in all this. The group broke up. Gertrude Stein was very upset and then consoled herself by telling all about it in a delightful short story called From Left to Right and which was printed in the London Harper's Bazaar.

It was not long after this that one day Gertrude Stein called in the concierge and asked him to hang up all the Francis Rose pictures, by this time there were some thirty odd. Gertrude Stein was very much upset while she was having this done. I asked her why she was doing it if it upset her so much. She said she could not help it, that she felt that way about it but to change the whole aspect of the room by adding these thirty pictures was very upsetting. There the matter rested for some time.

To go back again to those days just after the publication of The Making of Americans. There was at that time a review of Gertrude Stein's book Geography and Plays in the Athenaeum signed Edith Sitwell. The review was long and a little condescending but I liked it. Gertrude Stein had not cared for it. A year later in the London Vogue was an article again by Edith Sitwell saying that since writing her article in the Athenaeum she had spent the year reading nothing but Geography and Plays and she wished to say how important and beautiful a book she had found it to be.

One afternoon at Elmer Harden's we met Miss Todd the editor of the London Vogue. She said that Edith Sitwell was to be shortly in Paris and wanted very much to meet Gertrude Stein. She said that Edith Sitwell was very shy and hesitant about coming. Elmer Harden said he would act as escort.

I remember so well my first impression of her, an impression which indeed has never changed. Very tall, bending slightly, withdrawing and hesitatingly advancing, and beautiful with the most distinguished nose I have ever seen on any human being. At that time and in conversation between Gertrude Stein and herself afterwards, I delighted in the delicacy and completeness of her understanding of poetry. She and Gertrude Stein became friends at once. This friendship like all friendships has had its difficulties but I am convinced that fundamentally Gertrude Stein and Edith Sitwell are friends and enjoy being friends.

We saw a great deal of Edith Sitwell at this time and then she went back to London. In the autumn of that year nineteen twenty-five Gertrude Stein had a letter from the president of the literary society of Cambridge asking her to speak before them in the early spring. Gertrude Stein quite completely upset at the very idea quite promptly answered no. Immediately came a letter from Edith Sitwell saying that the no must be changed to yes. That it was of the first importance that Gertrude Stein should deliver this address and that moreover Oxford was waiting for the yes to be given to Cambridge to ask her to do the same at Oxford.

There was very evidently nothing to do but to say yes and so Gertrude Stein said yes.

She was very upset at the prospect, peace, she said, had much greater terrors than war. Precipices even were nothing to this. She was very low in her mind. Luckily early in January the ford car began to have everything the matter with it. The better garages would not pay much attention to aged fords and Gertrude Stein used to take hers out to a shed in Montrouge where the mechanics worked at it while she sat. If she were to leave it there there would most likely have been nothing left of it to drive away.

One cold dark afternoon she went out to sit with her ford car and while she sat on the steps of another battered ford watching her own being taken to pieces and put together again, she began to write. She stayed there several hours and when she came back chilled, with the ford repaired, she had written the whole of Composition As Explanation.

Once the lecture written the next trouble was the reading of it. Everybody gave her advice. She read it to anybody who came to the house and some of them read it to her. Prichard

happened to be in Paris just then and he and Emily Chadbourne between them gave advice and were an audience.
Prichard showed her how to read it in the english manner
but Emily Chadbourne was all for the american manner and
Gertrude Stein was too worried to have any manner. We
went one afternoon to Natalie Barney's. There there was a
very aged and a very charming french professor of history.
Natalie Barney asked him to tell Gertrude Stein how to lecture. Talk as quickly as you can and never look up, was his
advice. Prichard had said talk as slowly as possible and never
look down. At any rate I ordered a new dress and a new hat
for Gertrude Stein and early in the spring we went to London.

This was the spring of twenty-six and England was still
very strict about passports. We had ours alright but Gertrude
Stein hates to answer questions from officials, it always worries her and she was already none too happy at the prospect
of lecturing.

So taking both passports I went down stairs to see the
officials. Ah, said one of them, and where is Miss Gertrude
Stein. She is on deck, I replied, and she does not care to
come down. She does not care to come down, he repeated,
yes that is quite right, she does not care to come down, and
he affixed the required signatures. So then we arrived in
London. Edith Sitwell gave a party for us and so did her
brother Osbert. Osbert was a great comfort to Gertrude
Stein. He so thoroughly understood every possible way in
which one could be nervous that as he sat beside her in the
hotel telling her all the kinds of ways that he and she could
suffer from stage fright she was quite soothed. She was always very fond of Osbert. She always said he was like an
uncle of a king. He had that pleasant kindly irresponsible
agitated calm that an uncle of an english king always must
have.

Finally we arrived in Cambridge in the afternoon, were
given tea and then dined with the president of the society
and some of his friends. It was very pleasant and after dinner
we went to the lecture room. It was a varied audience, men
and women. Gertrude Stein was soon at her ease, the lecture

went off very well, the men afterwards asked a great many questions and were very enthusiastic. The women said nothing. Gertrude Stein wondered whether they were supposed not to or just did not.

The day after we went to Oxford. There we lunched with young Acton and then went in to the lecture. Gertrude Stein was feeling more comfortable as a lecturer and this time she had a wonderful time. As she remarked afterwards, I felt just like a prima donna.

The lecture room was full, many standing in the back, and the discussion, after the lecture, lasted over an hour and no one left. It was very exciting. They asked all sorts of questions, they wanted to know most often why Gertrude Stein thought she was right in doing the kind of writing she did. She answered that it was not a question of what any one thought but after all she had been doing as she did for about twenty years and now they wanted to hear her lecture. This did not mean of course that they were coming to think that her way was a possible way, it proved nothing, but on the other hand it did possibly indicate something. They laughed. Then up jumped one man, it turned out afterwards that he was a dean, and he said that in the Saints in Seven he had been very interested in the sentence about the ring around the moon, about the ring following the moon. He admitted that the sentence was one of the most beautifully balanced sentences he had ever heard, but still did the ring follow the moon. Gertrude Stein said, when you look at the moon and there is a ring around the moon and the moon moves does not the ring follow the moon. Perhaps it seems to, he replied. Well, in that case how, she said, do you know that it does not; he sat down. Another man, a don, next to him jumped up and asked something else. They did this several times, the two of them, jumping up one after the other. Then the first man jumped up and said, you say that everything being the same everything is always different, how can that be so. Consider, she replied, the two of you, you jump up one after the other, that is the same thing and surely you admit that the two of you are always different. Touché, he said and the meeting was over. One of the men was so moved that he confided to me as we went out that the lecture had been his greatest experience since he had read Kant's Critique of Pure Reason.

Edith Sitwell, Osbert and Sacheverell were all present and were all delighted. They were delighted with the lecture and they were delighted with the good humoured way in which Gertrude Stein had gotten the best of the hecklers. Edith Sitwell said that Sache chuckled about it all the way home.

The next day we returned to Paris. The Sitwells wanted us to stay and be interviewed and generally go on with it but Gertrude Stein felt that she had had enough of glory and excitement. Not, as she always explains, that she could ever have enough of glory. After all, as she always contends, no artist needs criticism, he only needs appreciation. If he needs criticism he is no artist.

Leonard Woolf some months after this published Composition As Explanation in the Hogarth Essay Series. It was also printed in The Dial.

Mildred Aldrich was awfully pleased at Gertrude Stein's english success. She was a good new englander and to her, recognition by Oxford and Cambridge, was even more important than recognition by the Atlantic Monthly. We went out to see her on our return and she had to have the lecture read to her again and to hear every detail of the whole experience.

Mildred Aldrich was falling upon bad days. Her annuity suddenly ceased and for a long time we did not know it. One day Dawson Johnston, the librarian of the American Library, told Gertrude Stein that Miss Aldrich had written to him to come out and get all her books as she would soon be leaving her home. We went out immediately and Mildred told us that her annuity had been stopped. It seems it was an annuity given by a woman who had fallen into her dotage and she one morning told her lawyer to cut off all the annuities that she had given for many years to a number of people. Gertrude Stein told Mildred not to worry. The Carnegie Fund, approached by Kate Buss, sent five hundred dollars, William Cook gave Gertrude Stein a blank cheque to supply all deficiencies, another friend of Mildred's from Providence Rhode Island came forward generously and the Atlantic Monthly started a fund. Very soon Mildred Aldrich was safe. She said ruefully to Gertrude Stein, you would not let me go elegantly to the poorhouse and I would have gone elegantly, but you have turned this into a poor house and I am the sole inmate. Gertrude Stein comforted her and said that she could be just as elegant in her solitary state. After all, Gertrude Stein used to say to her, Mildred nobody can say that you have not had a good run for your money. Mildred Aldrich's last years were safe.

William Cook after the war had been in Russia, in Tiflis, for three years in connection with Red Cross distribution there. One evening he and Gertrude Stein had been out to see Mildred, it was during her last illness and they were coming home one foggy evening. Cook had a small open car but a powerful searchlight, strong enough to pierce the fog. Just behind them was another small car which kept an even pace with them, when Cook drove faster, they drove faster, and when he slowed down, they slowed down. Gertrude Stein said to him, it is lucky for them that you have such a bright light, their lanterns are poor and they are having the benefit of yours. Yes, said Cook, rather curiously, I have been saying that to myself, but you know after three years of Soviet Russia and the Cheka, even I, an american, have gotten to feel a little queer, and I have to talk to myself about it, to be sure that the car behind us is not the car of the secret police.

I said that René Crevel came to the house. Of all the young men who came to the house I think I liked René the best. He had french charm, which when it is at its most charming is more charming even than american charm, charming as that can be. Marcel Duchamp and René Crevel are perhaps the most complete examples of this french charm. We were very fond of René. He was young and violent and ill and revolutionary and sweet and tender. Gertrude Stein and René are very fond of each other, he writes her most delightful english letters, and she scolds him a great deal. It was he who, in early days, first talked to us of Bernard Faÿ. He said he was a young professor in the University of Clermont-Ferrand and he wanted to take us to his house. One afternoon he did take us there. Bernard Faÿ was not at all what Gertrude Stein expected and he and she had nothing in particular to say to each other.

As I remember during that winter and the next we gave a great many parties. We gave a tea party for the Sitwells.

Carl Van Vechten sent us quantities of negroes beside there were the negroes of our neighbour Mrs. Regan who had brought Josephine Baker to Paris. Carl sent us Paul Robeson. Paul Robeson interested Gertrude Stein. He knew american values and american life as only one in it but not of it could know them. And yet as soon as any other person came into the room he became definitely a negro. Gertrude Stein did not like hearing him sing spirituals. They do not belong to you any more than anything else, so why claim them, she said. He did not answer.

Once a southern woman, a very charming southern woman, was there, and she said to him, where were you born, and he answered, in New Jersey and she said, not in the south, what a pity and he said, not for me.

Gertrude Stein concluded that negroes were not suffering from persecution, they were suffering from nothingness. She always contends the the african is not primitive, he has a very ancient but a very narrow culture and there it remains. Consequently nothing does or can happen.

Carl Van Vechten himself came over for the first time since those far away days of the pleated shirt. All those years he and Gertrude Stein had kept up a friendship and a correspondence. Now that he was actually coming Gertrude Stein was a little worried. When he came they were better friends than ever. Gertrude Stein told him that she had been worried. I wasn't, said Carl.

Among the other young men who came to the house at the time when they came in such numbers was Bravig Imbs. We liked Bravig, even though as Gertrude Stein said, his aim was to please. It was he who brought Elliot Paul to the house and Elliot Paul brought transition.

We had liked Bravig Imbs but we liked Elliot Paul more. He was very interesting. Elliot Paul was a new englander but he was a saracen, a saracen such as you sometimes see in the villages of France where the strain from some Crusading ancestor's dependents still survives. Elliot Paul was such a one. He had an element not of mystery but of evanescence, actually little by little he appeared and then as slowly he disappeared, and Eugene Jolas and Maria Jolas appeared. These once having appeared, stayed in their appearance.

Elliot Paul was at that time working on the Paris Chicago Tribune and he was there writing a series of articles on the work of Gertrude Stein, the first seriously popular estimation of her work. At the same time he was turning the young journalists and proof-readers into writers. He started Bravig Imbs on his first book, The Professor's Wife, by stopping him suddenly in his talk and saying, you begin there. He did the same thing for others. He played the accordion as nobody else not native to the accordion could play it and he learned and played for Gertrude Stein accompanied on the violin by Bravig Imbs, Gertrude Stein's favourite ditty, The Trail of the Lonesome Pine, My name is June and very very soon.

The Trail of the Lonesome Pine as a song made a lasting appeal to Gertrude Stein. Mildred Aldrich had it among her records and when we spent the afternoon with her at Huiry, Gertrude Stein inevitably would start The Trail of the Lonesome Pine on the phonograph and play it and play it. She liked it in itself and she had been fascinated during the war with the magic of The Trail of the Lonesome Pine as a book for the doughboy. How often when a doughboy in hospital had become particularly fond of her, he would say, I once read a great book, do you know it, it is called The Trail of the Lonesome Pine. They finally got a copy of it in the camp at Nîmes and it stayed by the bedside of every sick soldier. They did not read much of it, as far as she could make out sometimes only a paragraph, in the course of several days, but their voices were husky when they spoke of it, and when they were particularly devoted to her they would offer to lend her this very dirty and tattered copy.

She reads anything and naturally she read this and she was puzzled. It had practically no story to it and it was not exciting, or adventurous, and it was very well written and was

mostly description of mountain scenery. Later on she came
across some reminiscences of a southern woman who told
how the mountaineers in the southern army during the civil
war used to wait in turn to read Victor Hugo's Les Misé-
rables, an equally astonishing thing for again there is not much
of a story and a great deal of description. However Gertrude
Stein admits that she loves the song of The Trail of the Lonesome Pine in the same way that the doughboy loved the book
and Elliot Paul played it for her on the accordion.

One day Elliot Paul came in very excitedly, he usually
seemed to be feeling a great deal of excitement but neither
showed nor expressed it. This time however he did show it
and express it. He said he wanted to ask Gertrude Stein's advice. A proposition had been made to him to edit a magazine
in Paris and he was hesitating whether he should undertake
it. Gertrude Stein was naturally all for it. After all, as she
said, we do want to be printed. One writes for oneself and
strangers but with no adventurous publishers how can one
come in contact with those same strangers.

However she was very fond of Elliot Paul and did not
want him to take too much risk. No risk, said Elliot Paul, the
money for it is guaranteed for a number of years. Well then,
said Gertrude Stein, one thing is certain no one could be a
better editor than you would be. You are not egotistical and
you know what you feel.

Transition began and of course it meant a great deal to
everybody. Elliot Paul chose with great care what he wanted
to put into transition. He said he was afraid of its becoming
too popular. If ever there are more than two thousand sub-
scribers, I quit, he used to say.

He chose Elucidation Gertrude Stein's first effort to explain
herself, written in Saint-Rémy to put into the first number of
transition. Later As A Wife Has A Cow A Love Story. He
was always very enthusiastic about this story. He liked Made
A Mile Away, a description of the pictures that Gertrude
Stein has liked and later a novelette of desertion If He Thinks,
for transition. He had a perfectly definite idea of gradually
opening the eyes of the public to the work of the writers that
interested him and as I say he chose what he wanted with

great care. He was very interested in Picasso and he became very deeply interested in Juan Gris and after his death printed a translation of Juan Gris' defence of painting which had already been printed in french in the Transatlantic Review, and he printed Gertrude Stein's lament, The Life and Death of Juan Gris and her One Spaniard.

Elliot Paul slowly disappeared and Eugene and Maria Jolas appeared.

Transition grew more bulky. At Gertrude Stein's request transition reprinted Tender Buttons, printed a bibliography of all her work up to date and later printed her opera, Four Saints. For these printings Gertrude Stein was very grateful. In the last numbers of transition nothing of hers appeared. Transition died.

Of all the little magazines which as Gertrude Stein loves to quote, have died to make verse free, perhaps the youngest and freshest was the Blues. Its editor Charles Henri Ford has come to Paris and he is young and fresh as his Blues and also honest which also is a pleasure. Gertrude Stein thinks that he and Robert Coates alone among the young men have an individual sense of words.

During this time Oxford and Cambridge men turned up from time to time at the rue de Fleurus. One of them brought with him Brewer, one of the firm of Payson and Clarke.

Brewer was interested in the work of Gertrude Stein and though he promised nothing he and she talked over the possibilities of his firm printing something of hers. She had just written a shortish novel called A Novel, and was at the time working at another shortish novel which was called Lucy Church Amiably and which she describes as a novel of romantic beauty and nature and which looks like an engraving. She at Brewer's request wrote a summary of this book as an advertisement and he cabled his enthusiasm. However he wished first to commence with a collection of short things and she suggested in that case he should make it all the short things she had written about America and call it Useful Knowledge. This was done.

There are many Paris picture dealers who like adventure in their business, there are no publishers in America who like adventure in theirs. In Paris there are picture dealers like Durand-Ruel who went broke twice supporting the impressionists, Vollard for Cézanne, Sagot for Picasso and Kahnweiler for all the cubists. They make their money as they can and they keep on buying something for which there is no present sale and they do so persistently until they create its public. And these adventurers are adventurous because that is the way they feel about it. There are others who have not chosen as well and have gone entirely broke. It is the tradition among the more adventurous Paris picture dealers to adventure. I suppose there are a great many reasons why publishers do not. John Lane alone among publishers did. He perhaps did not die a very rich man but he lived well, and died a moderately rich one.

We had a hope that Brewer might be this kind of a publisher. He printed Useful Knowledge, his results were not all that he anticipated and instead of continuing and gradually creating a public for Gertrude Stein's work he procrastinated and then said no. I suppose this was inevitable. However that was the matter as it was and as it continued to be.

I now myself began to think about publishing the work of Gertrude Stein. I asked her to invent a name for my edition and she laughed and said, call it Plain Edition. And Plain Edition it is.

All that I knew about what I would have to do was that I would have to get the book printed and then to get it distributed, that is sold.

I talked to everybody about how these two things were to be accomplished.

At first I thought I would associate some one with me but that soon did not please me and I decided to do it all by myself.

Gertrude Stein wanted the first book Lucy Church Amiably to look like a school book and to be bound in blue. Once having ordered my book to be printed my next problem was the problem of distribution. On this subject I received a great deal of advice. Some of the advice turned out to be good and some of it turned out to be bad. William A. Bradley, the friend and comforter of Paris authors, told me to subscribe to The

Publishers' Weekly. This was undoubtedly wise advice. This helped me to learn something of my new business, but the real difficulty was to get to the booksellers. Ralph Church, philosopher and friend, said stick to the booksellers, first and last. Excellent advice but how to get to the booksellers. At this moment a kind friend said that she could get me copied an old list of booksellers belonging to a publisher. This list was sent to me and I began sending out my circulars. The circular pleased me at first but I soon concluded that it was not quite right. However I did get orders from America and I was paid without much difficulty and I was encouraged.

The distribution in Paris was at once easier and more difficult. It was easy to get the book put in the window of all the booksellers in Paris that sold english books. This event gave Gertrude Stein a childish delight amounting almost to ecstasy. She had never seen a book of hers in a bookstore window before, except a french translation of The Ten Portraits, and she spent all her time in her wanderings about Paris looking at the copies of Lucy Church Amiably in the windows and coming back and telling me about it.

The books were sold too and then as I was away from Paris six months in the year I turned over the Paris work to a french agent. This worked very well at first but finally did not work well. However one must learn one's trade.

I decided upon my next book How To Write and not being entirely satisfied with the get up of Lucy Church Amiably, although it did look like a school book, I decided to have the next book printed at Dijon and in the form of an Elzevir. Again the question of binding was a difficulty.

I went to work in the same way to sell How To Write, but I began to realise that my list of booksellers was out of date. Also I was told that I should write following up letters. Ellen du Pois helped me with these. I was told that I should have reviews. Ellen du Pois came to the rescue here too. And that I should advertise. Advertising would of necessity be too expensive; I had to keep my money to print my books, as my plans were getting more and more ambitious. Getting reviews was a difficulty, there are always plenty of humorous references to Gertrude Stein's work, as Gertrude Stein always says to comfort herself, they do quote me, that means that my words and my sentences get under their skins although they do not know it. It was difficult to get serious reviews. There are many writers who write her letters of admiration but even when they are in a position to do so they do not write themselves down in book reviews. Gertrude Stein likes to quote Browning who at a dinner party met a famous literary man and this man came up to Browning and spoke to him at length and in a very laudatory way about his poems. Browning listened and then said, and are you going to print what you have just said. There was naturally no answer. In Gertrude Stein's case there have been some notable exceptions, Sherwood Anderson, Edith Sitwell, Bernard Faÿ and Louis Bromfield.

I also printed an edition of one hundred copies, very beautifully done at Chartres, of the poem of Gertrude Stein Before The Flowers Of Friendship Faded Friendship Faded. These one hundred copies sold very easily.

I was better satisfied with the bookmaking of How To Write but there was always the question of binding the book. It is practically impossible to get a decent commercial binding in France, french publishers only cover their books in paper. I was very troubled about this.

One evening we went to an evening party at Georges Poupet's, a gentle friend of authors. There I met Maurice Darantière. It was he who had printed The Making of Americans and he was always justly proud of it as a book and as bookmaking. He had left Dijon and had started printing books in the neighbourhood of Paris with a hand-press and he was printing very beautiful books. He is a kind man and I naturally began telling him my troubles. Listen, he said I have the solution. But I interrupted him, you must remember that I do not want to make these books expensive. After all Gertrude Stein's readers are writers, university students, librarians and young people who have very little money. Gertrude Stein wants readers not collectors. In spite of herself her books have too often become collector's books. They pay big prices for Tender Buttons and The Portrait of Mabel Dodge and that does not please her, she wants her books read not owned. Yes yes, he said, I understand. No this is what I propose. We will have your book set by monotype which is comparatively cheap, I will see to that, then I will handpull your books on good but not too expensive paper and they will be beautifully printed and instead of any covers I will have them bound in heavy paper like The Making of Americans, paper just like that, and I will have made little boxes in which they will fit perfectly, well made little boxes and there you are. And I will be able to sell them at a reasonable price. Yes you will see, he said.

I was getting more ambitious I wished now to begin a series of three, beginning with Operas and Plays, going on with Matisse, Picasso and Gertrude Stein and Two Shorter Stories, and then going on with Two Long Poems and Many Shorter Ones.

Maurice Darantière has been as good as his word. He has printed Operas and Plays and it is a beautiful book and reasonable in price and he is now printing the second book Matisse Picasso and Gertrude Stein and Two Shorter Stories. Now I have an up to date list of booksellers and I am once more on my way.

As I was saying after the return from England and lecturing we gave a great many parties, there were many occasions for parties, all the Sitwells came over, Carl Van Vechten came over, Sherwood Anderson came over again. And beside there were many other occasions for parties.

It was then that Gertrude Stein and Bernard Faÿ met again and this time they had a great deal to say to each other. Gertrude Stein found the contact with his mind stimulating and comforting. They were slowly coming to be friends.

I remember once coming into the room and hearing Bernard Faÿ say that the three people of first rate importance that he had met in his life were Picasso, Gertrude Stein and André Gide and Gertrude Stein inquired quite simply, that is quite right but why include Gide. A year or so later in referring to this conversation he said to her, and I am not sure you were not right.

Sherwood came to Paris that winter and he was a delight. He was enjoying himself and we enjoyed him. He was being lionised and I must say he was a very appearing and disappearing lion. I remember his being asked to the Pen Club. Natalie Barney and a long-bearded frenchman were to be his sponsors. He wanted Gertrude Stein to come too. She said she loved him very much but not the Pen Club. Natalie Barney came over to ask her. Gertrude Stein who was caught outside, walking her dog, pleaded illness. The next day Sherwood turned up. How was it, asked Gertrude Stein. Why, said he, it wasn't a party for me, it was a party for a big woman, and she was just a derailed freight car.

We had installed electric radiators in the studio, we were as our finnish servant would say getting modern. She finds it difficult to understand why we are not more modern. Gertrude Stein says that if you are way ahead with your head you naturally are old fashioned and regular in your daily life. And Picasso adds, do you suppose Michael Angelo would have been grateful for a gift of a piece of renaissance furniture, no he wanted a greek coin.

We did install electric radiators and Sherwood turned up and we gave him a Christmas party. The radiators smelled and it was terrifically hot but we were all pleased as it was a nice party. Sherwood looked as usual very handsome in one of his very latest scarf ties. Sherwood Anderson does dress well and his son John follows suit. John and his sister came over with their father. While Sherwood was still in Paris John the son was an awkward shy boy. The day after Sherwood left John turned up, sat easily on the arm of the sofa and was beautiful to look upon and he knew it. Nothing to the outward eye had changed but he had changed and he knew it.

It was during this visit that Gertrude Stein and Sherwood Anderson had all those amusing conversations about Hemingway. They enjoyed each other thoroughly. They found out that they both had had and continued to have Grant as their great american hero. They did not care so much about Lincoln either of them. They had always and still liked Grant. They even planned collaborating on a life of Grant. Gertrude Stein still likes to think about this possibility.

We did give a great many parties in those days and the Duchess of Clermont-Tonnerre came very often.

She and Gertrude Stein pleased one another. They were entirely different in life education and interests but they delighted in each other's understanding. They were also the only two women whom they met who still had long hair. Gertrude Stein had always worn hers well on top of her head, an ancient fashion that she had never changed.

Madame de Clermont-Tonnerre came in very late to one of the parties, almost every one had gone, and her hair was cut. Do you like it, said Madame de Clermont-Tonnerre. I do, said Gertrude Stein. Well, said Madame de Clermont-Tonnerre, if you like it and my daughter likes it and she does like it I am satisfied. That night Gertrude Stein said to me, I guess I will have to too. Cut it off she said and I did.

I was still cutting the next evening, I had been cutting a little more all day and by this time it was only a cap of hair when Sherwood Anderson came in. Well, how do you like it, said I rather fearfully. I like it, he said, it makes her look like a monk.

As I have said, Picasso seeing it, was for a moment angry and said, and my portrait, but very soon added, after all it is all there.

We now had our country house, the one we had only seen across the valley and just before leaving we found the white poodle, Basket. He was a little puppy in a little neighbourhood dog-show and he had blue eyes, a pink nose and white hair and he jumped up into Gertrude Stein's arms. A new puppy and a new ford we went off to our new house and we were thoroughly pleased with all three. Basket although now he is a large unwieldy poodle, still will get up on Gertrude Stein's lap and stay there. She says that listening to the rhythm of his water drinking made her recognise the difference between sentences and paragraphs, that paragraphs are emotional and that sentences are not.

Bernard Faÿ came and stayed with us that summer. Gertrude Stein and he talked out in the garden about everything, about life, and America, and themselves and friendship. They then cemented the friendship that is one of the four permanent friendships of Gertrude Stein's life. He even tolerated Basket for Gertrude Stein's sake. Lately Picabia has given us a tiny mexican dog, we call Byron. Bernard Faÿ likes Byron for Byron's own sake. Gertrude Stein teases him and says naturally he likes Byron best because Byron is an american while just as naturally she likes Basket best because Basket is a frenchman.

Bilignin brings me to a new old acquaintance. One day Gertrude Stein came home from a walk to the bank and bringing out a card from her pocket said, we are lunching to-morrow with the Bromfields. Way back in the Hemingway days Gertrude Stein had met Bromfield and his wife and then from time to time there had been a slight acquaintance, there had even been a slight acquaintance with Bromfield's sister, and now suddenly we were lunching with the Bromfields. Why, I asked, because answered Gertrude Stein quite radiant, he knows all about gardens.

We lunched with the Bromfields and he does know all about gardens and all about flowers and all about soils. Gertrude Stein and he first liked each other as gardeners, then they liked each other as americans and then they liked each other as writers. Gertrude Stein says of him that he is as american as Janet Scudder, as american as a doughboy, but not as solemn.

One day the Jolases brought Furman the publisher to the house. He as have been many publishers was enthusiastic and enthusiastic about The Making of Americans. But it is terribly long, it's a thousand pages, said Gertrude Stein. Well, can't it be cut down, he said to about four hundred. Yes, said Gertrude Stein, perhaps. Well cut it down and I will publish it, said Furman.

Gertrude Stein thought about it and then did it. She spent a part of the summer over it and Bradley as well as she and myself thought it alright.

In the meantime Gertrude Stein had told Elliot Paul about the proposition. It's alright when he is over here, said Elliot Paul, but when he gets back the boys won't let him. Who the boys are I do not know but they certainly did not let him.

Elliot Paul was right. In spite of the efforts of Robert Coates and Bradley nothing happened.

In the meantime Gertrude Stein's reputation among the french writers and readers was steadily growing. The translation of the fragments of the Making of Americans, and of the Ten Portraits interested them. It was at this time that Bernard Faÿ wrote his article about her work printed in the Revue Européenne. They also printed the only thing she has ever written in french a little film about the dog Basket.

They were very interested in her later work as well as her earlier work. Marcel Brion wrote a serious criticism of her work in Echange, comparing her work to Bach. Since then, in Les Nouvelles Littéraires, he has written of each of her books as they come out. He was particularly impressed by How To Write.

About this time too Bernard Faÿ was translating a fragment of Melanctha from Three Lives for the volume of Ten American Novelists, this to be introduced by his article printed in the Revue Européenne. He came to the house one afternoon and read his translation of Melanctha aloud to us. Madame de Clermont-Tonnerre was there and she was very impressed by his translation.

One day not long after she asked to come to the house as she wished to talk to Gertrude Stein. She came and she said, the time has now come when you must be made known to a larger public. I myself believe in a larger public. Gertrude Stein too believes in a larger public but the way has always been barred. No, said Madame de Clermont-Tonnerre, the way can be opened. Let us think.

She said it must come from the translation of a big book, an important book. Gertrude Stein suggested the Making of Americans and told her how it had been prepared for an American publisher to make about four hundred pages. That will do exactly, she said. And went away.

Finally and not after much delay, Monsieur Bouteleau of Stock saw Gertrude Stein and he decided to publish the book. There was some difficulty about finding a translator, but finally that was arranged. Bernard Faÿ aided by the Baronne Seillière undertook the translation, and it is this translation which is to appear this spring, and that this summer made Gertrude Stein say, I knew it was a wonderful book in english, but it is even, well, I cannot say almost really more wonderful but just as wonderful in french.

Last autumn the day we came back to Paris from Bilignin I was as usual very busy with a number of things and Gertrude Stein went out to buy some nails at the bazaar of the rue de Rennes. There she met Guevara, a chilean painter and his wife. They are our neighbours, and they said, come to tea to-morrow. Gertrude Stein said, but we are just home, wait a bit. Do come, said Méraude Guevara. And then added, there will be some one there you will like to see. Who is it, said Gertrude Stein with a never failing curiosity. Sir Francis Rose, they said. Alright, we'll come, said Gertrude Stein. By this time she no longer objected to meeting Francis Rose. We met then and he of course immediately came back to the house with her. He was, as may be imagined, quite pink with emotion. And what, said he, did Picasso say when he saw my paintings. When he first saw them, Gertrude Stein answered, he said, at least they are less bêtes than the others. And since, he asked. And since he always goes into the corner and turns the canvas over to look at them but he says nothing.

Since then we have seen a great deal of Francis Rose but Gertrude Stein has not lost interest in the pictures. He has this summer painted the house from across the valley where we first saw it and the waterfall celebrated in Lucy Church Amiably. He has also painted her portrait. He likes it and I like it but she is not sure whether she does, but as she has just said, perhaps she does. We had a pleasant time this summer, Bernard Faÿ and Francis Rose both charming guests.

A young man who first made Gertrude Stein's acquaintance by writing engaging letters from America is Paul Frederick Bowles. Gertrude Stein says of him that he is delightful and sensible in summer but neither delightful nor sensible in the winter. Aaron Copeland came to see us with Bowles in the summer and Gertrude Stein liked him immensely. Bowles told Gertrude Stein and it pleased her that Copeland said threateningly to him when as usual in the winter he was neither delightful nor sensible, if you do not work now when you are twenty when you are thirty, nobody will love you.

For some time now many people, and publishers, have been asking Gertrude Stein to write her autobiography and she had always replied, not possibly.

She began to tease me and say that I should write my autobiography. Just think, she would say, what a lot of money you would make. She then began to invent titles for my autobiography. My Life With The Great, Wives of Geniuses I Have Sat With, My Twenty-five Years With Gertrude Stein.

Then she began to get serious and say, but really seriously you ought to write your autobiography. Finally I promised that if during the summer I could find time I would write my autobiography.

When Ford Madox Ford was editing the Transatlantic Review he once said to Gertrude Stein, I am a pretty good writer and a pretty good editor and a pretty good business man but I find it very difficult to be all three at once.

I am a pretty good housekeeper and a pretty good gardener and a pretty good needlewoman and a pretty good secretary and a pretty good editor and a pretty good vet for dogs and I have to do them all at once and I found it difficult to add being a pretty good author.

About six weeks ago Gertrude Stein said, it does not look to me as if you were ever going to write that autobiography. You know what I am going to do. I am going to write it for you. I am going to write it as simply as Defoe did the autobiography of Robinson Crusoe. And she has and this is it.

THE GRADUAL MAKING OF

THE MAKING
OF AMERICANS

This is one of the LECTURES IN AMERICA *delivered by Miss Stein during the season 1934-35 and published by Random House in 1935. The quotations from* THE MAKING OF AMERICANS *in the text are from the abbreviated Harcourt, Brace and Co. edition.*

I am going to read what I have written to read, because in a general way it is easier even if it is not better and in a general way it is better even if it is not easier to read what has been written than to say what has not been written. Any way that is one way to feel about it.

And I want to tell you about the gradual way of making The Making of Americans. I made it gradually and it took me almost three years to make it, but that is not what I mean by gradual. What I mean by gradual is the way the preparation was made inside of me. Although as I tell it it will sound historical, it really is not historical as I still very much remember it. I do remember it. That is I can remember it. And if you can remember, it may be history but it is not historical.

To begin with, I seem always to be doing the talking when I am anywhere but in spite of that I do listen. I always listen. I always have listened. I always have listened to the way everybody has to tell what they have to say. In other words I always have listened in my way of listening until they have told me and told me until I really know it, that is know what they are.

I always as I admit seem to be talking but talking can be a way of listening that is if one has the profound need of hearing and seeing what every one is telling.

And I began very early in life to talk all the time and to listen all the time. At least that is the way I feel about it.

I cannot remember not talking all the time and all the same feeling that while I was talking while I was seeing that I was not only hearing but seeing while I was talking and that at the same time the relation between myself knowing I was talking and those to whom I was talking and incidentally to whom I was listening were coming to tell me and tell me in their way everything that made them.

Those of you who have read The Making of Americans I think will very certainly understand.

When I was young and I am talking of a period even before I went to college part of this talking consisted in a desire not only to hear what each one was saying in every way everybody has of saying it but also then of helping to change them and to help them change themselves.

I was very full of convictions in those days and I at that time thought that the passion I had for finding out by talking and listening just how everybody was always telling everything that was inside them that made them that one, that this passion for knowing the basis of existence in each one was in me to help them change themselves to become what they should become. The changing should of course be dependent upon my ideas and theirs theirs as much as mine at that time.

And so in those early days I wanted to know what was inside each one which made them that one and I was deeply convinced that I needed this to help them change something.

Then I went to college and there for a little while I was tremendously occupied with finding out what was inside myself to make me what I was. I think that does happen to one at that time. It had been happening before going to college but going to college made it more lively. And being so occupied with what made me myself inside me, made me perhaps not stop talking but for awhile it made me stop listening.

At any rate that is the way it seems to me now looking back at it.

While I was at college and doing philosophy and psychology I became more and more interested in my own mental and physical processes and less in that of others and all I then was learning of what made people what they were came to me by experience and not by talking and listening.

Then as I say I became more interested in psychology, and one of the things I did was testing reactions of the average college student in a state of normal activity and in the state of fatigue induced by their examinations. I was supposed to be interested in their reactions but soon I found that I was not but instead that I was enormously interested in the types of their characters that is what I even then thought of as the bottom nature of them, and when in May 1898 I wrote my half of the report of these experiments I expressed these results as follows:

In these descriptions it will be readily observed that habits of attention are reflexes of the complete character of the individual.

Then that was over and I went to the medical school where I was bored and where once more myself and my experiences were more actively interesting me than the life inside of others.

But then after that once more I began to listen, I had left the medical school and I had for the moment nothing to do but talk and look and listen, and I did this tremendously.

I then began again to think about the bottom nature in people, I began to get enormously interested in hearing how everybody said the same thing over and over again with infinite variations but over and over again until finally if you listened with great intensity you could hear it rise and fall and tell all that that there was inside them, not so much by the actual words they said or the thoughts they had but the movement of their thoughts and words endlessly the same and endlessly different.

Many things then come out in the repeating that make a history of each one for any one who always listens to them. Many things come out of each one and as one listens to them listens to all the repeating in them, always this comes to be clear about them, the history of them of the bottom nature in them, the nature or natures mixed up in them to make the whole of them in anyway it mixes up in them. Sometimes then there will be a history of every one.

When you come to feel the whole of anyone from the beginning to the ending, all the kind of repeating there is in them, the different ways at different times repeating comes out of them, all the kinds of things and mixtures in each one, anyone can see then by looking hard at any one living near them that a history of every one must be a long one. A history of any one must be a long one, slowly it comes out from them from their beginning to their ending, slowly you can see it in them the nature and the mixtures in them, slowly everything comes out from each one in the kind of repeating each one does in the different parts and kinds of living they have in them, slowly then the history of them comes out from them, slowly then any one who looks well at any one will have the history of the whole of that one. Slowly the history of each one comes out of each one. Sometimes then there will be a history of every one. Mostly every history will be a long one. Slowly it comes out of each one, slowly any one who looks at them gets the history of each part of the living of any one in the history of the whole of each one that sometime there will be of every one.*

Repeating then is in every one, in every one their being and their feeling and their way of realizing everything and every one comes out of them in repeating. More and more then every one comes to be clear to some one.

Slowly every one in continuous repeating, to their minutest variation, comes to be clearer to some one. Every one who ever was or is or will be living sometimes will be clearly realized by some one. Sometime there will be an ordered history of every one. Slowly every kind of one comes into ordered recognition. More and more then it is wonderful in living the subtle variations coming clear into ordered recognition, coming to make every one a part of some kind of them, some kind of men and women. Repeating then is in every one, every one then comes sometimes to be clearer to some one, sometimes there will be

* *The Making of Americans* (Harcourt, Brace & Co.), Page 128.

then an orderly history of every one who ever was or is or will be living.*

Then I became very interested in resemblances, in resemblances and slight differences between people. I began to make charts of all the people I had ever known or seen, or met or remembered.

> Every one is always busy with it, no one of them then ever want to know it that every one looks like some one else and they see it mostly every one dislikes to hear it. It is very important to me to always know it, to always see it which one looks like others and to tell it.—The Making of Americans, page 211. I write for myself and strangers, I do this for my own sake and for the sake of those who know I know it that they look like other ones, that they are separate and yet always repeated. There are some who like it that I know they are like many others and repeat it, there are many who never can really like it. Every one is one inside them, every one reminds some one of some other one who is or was or will be living. Every one has it to say of each one he is like such a one I see it in him, every one has it to say of each one she is like some one else I can tell by remembering. So it goes on always in living, every one is always remembering some one who is resembling to the one at whom they are then looking. So they go on repeating, every one is themselves inside them and every one is resembling to others and that is always interesting.†

I began to see that as I saw when I saw so many students at college that all this was gradually taking form. I began to get very excited about it. I began to be sure that if I could only go on long enough and talk and hear and look and see and feel enough and long enough I could finally describe

* *The Making of Americans.*
† *The Making of Americans,* Page 212.

really describe every kind of human being that ever was or is or would be living.

I got very wrapped up in all this. And I began writing The Making of Americans.

Let me read you some passages to show you how passionately and how desperately I felt about all this.

> I am altogether a discouraged one. I am just now altogether a discouraged one. I am going on describing men and women.*
>
> I have been very glad to have been wrong. It is sometimes a very hard thing to win myself to having been wrong about something. I do a great deal of suffering.†

I was sure that in a kind of a way the enigma of the universe could in this way be solved. That after all description is explanation, and if I went on and on and on enough I could describe every individual human being that could possibly exist. I did proceed to do as much as I could.

> Sometime then there will be every kind of a history of every one who ever can or is or was or will be living. Sometime then there will be a history of every one from their beginning to their ending. Sometime then there will be a history of all of them, of every kind of them, of every one, of every bit of living they ever have in them, of them when there is never more than a beginning to them, of every kind of them, of every one when there is very little beginning and then there is an ending, there will then sometime be a history of every one there will be a history of everything that ever was or is or will be them, of everything that was or is or will be all of any one or all of all of them. Sometime then there will be a history of every one, or everything or anything that is all them or any part of them and some-

* *The Making of Americans*, Page 308.
† *The Making of Americans*, Page 310.

time then there will be a history of how anything or everything comes out for every one, comes out from every one or any one from the beginning to the ending of the being in them. Sometime then there must be a history of every one who ever was or is or will be living. As one sees every one in their living, in their loving, sitting, eating, drinking, sleeping, walking, working, thinking, laughing, as any one sees all of them from their beginning to their ending, sees them when they are little babies or children or young grown men and women or growing older men and women or old men and women then one knows it in them that sometime there will be a history of all of them, that sometime all of them will have the last touch of being, a history of them can give to them, sometime then there will be a history of each one, of all the kinds of them, of all the ways any one can know them, of all the ways each one is inside her or inside him, of all the ways anything of them comes out from them. Sometime then there will be a history of every one and so then every one will have in them the last touch of being a history of any one can give to them.*

This is then a beginning of the way of knowing everything in every one, of knowing the complete history of each one who ever is or was or will be living. This is then a little description of the winning of so much wisdom.†

Of course all the time things were happening that is in respect to my hearing and seeing and feeling. I found that as often as I thought and had every reason to be certain that I had included everything in my knowledge of any one something else would turn up that had to be included. I did not with this get at all discouraged I only became more and more interested. And I may say that I am still more and more interested I find as many things to be added now as ever

* *The Making of Americans*, Page 124.
† *The Making of Americans*, Page 217.

and that does make it eternally interesting. So I found myself getting deeper and deeper into the idea of describing really describing every individual that could exist.

While I was doing all this all unconsciously at the same time a matter of tenses and sentences came to fascinate me.

While I was listening and hearing and feeling the rhythm of each human being I gradually began to feel the difficulty of putting it down. Types of people I could put down but a whole human being felt at one and the same time, in other words while in the act of feeling that person was very difficult to put into words.

And so about the middle of The Making of Americans I became very consciously obsessed by this very definite problem.

It happens very often that a man has it in him, that a man does something, that he does it very often that he does many things, when he is a young man when he is an old man, when he is an older man. One of such of these kind of them had a little boy and this one, the little son wanted to make a collection of butterflies and beetles and it was all exciting to him and it was all arranged then and then the father said to the son you are certain this is not a cruel thing that you are wanting to be doing, killing things to make collections of them, and the son was very disturbed then and they talked about it together the two of them and more and more they talked about it then and then at last the boy was convinced it was a cruel thing and he said he would not do it and his father said the little boy was a noble boy to give up pleasure when it was a cruel one. The boy went to bed then and then the father when he got up in the early morning saw a wonderfully beautiful moth in the room and he caught him and he killed him and he pinned him and he woke up his son then and showed it to him and he said to him see what a good father I am to have caught and killed this one, the boy was all mixed up inside him

and then he said he would go on with his collecting
and that was all there was then of discussing and this
is a little description of something that happened
once and it is very interesting.*

And this brings us to the question of grammar. So let
me talk a little about that.

You know by this time that although I do listen I do see
I do hear I do feel that I do talk.

English grammar is interesting because it is so simple.
Once you really know how to diagram a sentence really know
it, you know practically all you have to know about English
grammar. In short any child thirteen years old properly
taught can by that time have learned everything there is to
learn about English grammar. So why make a fuss about it.
However one does.

It is this that makes the English language such a vital
language that the grammar of it is so simple and that one
does make a fuss about it.

When I was up against the difficulty of putting down the
complete conception that I had of an individual, the complete rhythm of a personality that I had gradually acquired
by listening seeing feeling and experience, I was faced by
the trouble that I had acquired all this knowledge gradually
but when I had it I had it completely at one time. Now that
may never have been a trouble to you but it was a terrible
trouble to me. And a great deal of The Making of Americans
was a struggle to do this thing, to make a whole present of
something that it had taken a great deal of time to find out,
but it was a whole there then within me and as such it had to
be said.

That then and ever since has been a great deal of my work
and it is that which has made me try so many ways to tell my
story.

In The Making of Americans I tried it in a variety of ways.
And my sentences grew longer and longer, my imaginary
dependent clauses were constantly being dropped out, I struggled with relations between they them and then, I began with

* *The Making of Americans*, Page 284.

a relation between tenses that sometimes almost seemed to do it. And I went on and on and then one day after I had written a thousand pages, this was in 1908 I just did not go on any more.

I did however immediately begin again. I began A Long Gay Book, that was going to be even longer than The Making of Americans and was going to be even more complicated, but then something happened in me and I said in Composition As Explanation, so then naturally it was natural that one thing an enormously long thing was not everything an enormously short thing was also not everything nor was it all of it a continuous present thing nor was it always and always beginning again.

And so this is The Making of Americans. A book one thousand pages long, and I worked over it three years, and I hope this makes it a little more understandable to you.

As I say I began A Long Gay Book and it was to be even longer than The Making of Americans and it was to describe not only every possible kind of a human being, but every possible kind of pairs of human beings and every possible threes and fours and fives of human beings and every possible kind of crowds of human beings. And I was going to do it as A Long Gay Book and at the same time I began several shorter books which were to illustrate the Long Gay Book, one called Many Many Women another Five, another Two and another G.M.P., Matisse Picasso and Gertrude Stein, but the chief book was to be the Long Gay Book and that was in a kind of way to go on and to keep going on and to go on before and it began in this way.

When they are very little just only a baby you can never tell which one is to be a lady.

There are some when they feel it inside them that it has been with them that there was once so very little of them, that they were a baby, helpless and no conscious feeling in them, that they knew nothing then when they were kissed and dandled and fixed by others who knew them when they could know nothing inside them or around them, some get from all this that once surely happened to them to that which was then every bit that was then them, there are some when they feel it later inside them that they were such once and that was all that there was then of them, there are some who have from such a knowing an uncertain curious kind of feeling in them that their having been so little once and knowing nothing makes it all a broken world for them that they have inside them, kills for them the everlasting feeling: and they spend their life in many ways, and always they are trying to make for themselves a new everlasting feeling.

One way perhaps of winning is to make a little one to come through them, little like the baby that once was all them and lost them their everlasting feeling. Some can win from just the feeling, the little one need not come, to give it to them.

And so always there is beginning and to some then a losing of the everlasting feeling. Then they make a baby to make for themselves a new beginning and so win for themselves a new everlasting feeling.*

I knew while I was writing The Making of Americans that it was possible to describe every kind there is of men and women.

I began to wonder if it was possible to describe the way every possible kind of human being acted and felt in relation with any other kind of human being and I thought if this could be done it would make A Long Gay Book. It is naturally gayer describing what any one feels acts and does in relation to any other one than to describe what they just are what they are inside them.

And as I naturally found it livelier, I myself was becoming livelier just then. One does you know, when one has come to the conclusion that what is inside every one is not all there is of any one. I was, there is no doubt about it, I was coming to be livelier in relation to myself inside me and in relation to any one inside in them. This being livelier inside me kept on

* *A Long Gay Book* (Plain Edition), Random House, Page 13.

increasing and so you see it was a natural thing that as the Long Gay Book began, it did not go on. If it were to be really lively would it go on. Does one if one is really lively and I was really very lively then does one go on and does one if one is really very lively does one content oneself with describing what is going on inside in one and going on inside in every one in any one.

At any rate what happened is this and every one reading these things, A Long Gay Book, Many Many Women and G.M.P. will see, that it changed, it kept on changing, until at last it led to something entirely different something very short and lively to the Portrait of Mabel Dodge and the little book called Tender Buttons but all that I will talk about later. To go back to The Making of Americans and A Long Gay Book.

One must not forget that although life seems long it is very short, that although civilization seems long it is not so very long. If you think about how many generations, granting that your grandfather to you make a hundred years, if you think about that, it is extraordinary how very short is the history of the world in which we live, the world which is the world where there is a world for us. It is like the generations in the Bible, they really do not take so very long. Now when you are beginning realizing everything, this is a thing that is not confusing but is a thing that as you might say is at one time very long and at the same time not at all long. Twenty-five years roll around so quickly and in writing they can do one of two things, they can either roll around more or they can roll around less quickly.

In writing The Making of Americans they rolled around less quickly. In writing A Long Gay Book, they did not roll around at all, and therefore it did not go on it led to Tender Buttons and many other things. It may even have led to war but that is of no importance.

The Making of Americans rolled around very slowly, it was only three years but they rolled around slowly and that is inevitable when one conceives everything as being there inside in one. Of course everything is always inside in one, that anybody knows but the kind of a one that one is is all inside in one or it is partly not all inside in one. When one is beginning to know everything, and that happens as it does happen, you all know that, when one is beginning to know everything inside in one description strengthens it being all inside in one. That was for me the whole of The Making of Americans, it was the strengthening the prolonging of the existing of everything being inside in one. You may call that being younger you may not just as you feel about it but what is important about it is, that if everything is all inside in one then it takes longer to know it than when it is not so completely inside in one.

Therefore it takes longer to know everything when everything is all inside one than when it is not. Call it being young if you like, or call it not including anything that is not everything. It does not make any difference whether you are young or younger or older or very much older. That does not make any difference because after all as I say civilization is not very old if you think about it by hundreds of years and realize that your grandfather to you can very much more than make a hundred years if it happens right.

And so I say and I saw that a complete description of every kind of human being that ever could or would be living is not such a very extensive thing because after all it can be all contained inside in any one and finally it can be done.

So then in writing The Making of Americans it was to me an enormously long thing to do to describe every one and slowly it was not an enormously long thing to do to describe every one. Because after all as I say civilization is not a very long thing, twenty-five years roll around so quickly and four times twenty-five years make a hundred years and that makes a grandfather to a granddaughter. Everybody is interested when that happens to any one, because it makes it long and it makes it short. And so and this is the thing that made the change a necessary change from The Making of Americans to A Long Gay Book and then to Tender Buttons.

I will read you some few little things that will show this thing. A few things out of A Long Gay Book that show how it changed, changed from Making of Americans to Tender Buttons.

It is a simple thing to be quite certain that there are kinds in men and women. It is a simple thing and then not any one has any worrying to be doing about any one being any one. It is a simple thing to be quite certain that each one is one being a kind of them and in being that kind of a one is one being, doing, thinking, feeling, remembering and forgetting, loving, disliking, being angry, laughing, eating, drinking, talking, sleeping, waking like all of them of that kind of them. There are enough kinds in men and women so that any one can be interested in that thing that there are kinds in men and women.*

Vrais says good good, excellent. Vrais listens and when he listens he says good good, excellent. Vrais listens and he being Vrais when he has listened he says good good, excellent.

Vrais listens, he being Vrais, he listens.

Anything is two things. Vrais was nicely faithful. He had been nicely faithful. Anything is two things.

He had been nicely faithful. In being one he was one who had he been one continuing would not have been one continuing being nicely faithful. He was one continuing, he was not continuing to be nicely faithful. In continuing he was being one being the one who was saying good good, excellent but in continuing he was needing that he was believing that he was aspiring to be one continuing to be able to be saying good good, excellent. He had been one saying good good, excellent. He had been that one.†

If the accumulation of inexpediency produces the withdrawing of the afternoon greeting then in the evening there is more preparation and this will take away the paper that has been lying where it could be seen. All the way that has the aging of a younger generation is part of the way that resembles anything that is not disappearing. It is not alright as colors are

* *A Long Gay Book*, Page 23.
† *A Long Gay Book*, Page 53.

existing in being accommodating. They have a way that is identical.*

Pardon the fretful autocrat who voices discontent. Pardon the colored water-color which is burnt. Pardon the intoning of the heavy way. Pardon the aristocrat who has not come to stay. Pardon the abuse which was begun. Pardon the yellow egg which has run. Pardon nothing yet, pardon what is wet, forget the opening now, and close the door again.†

A private life is the long thick tree and the private life is the life for me. A tree which is thick is a tree which is thick. A life which is private is not what there is. All the times that come are the times I sing, all the singing I sing are the tunes I sing. I sing and I sing and the tunes I sing are what are tunes if they come and I sing. I sing I sing.‡

Suppose it did, suppose it did with a sheet and a shadow and a silver set of water, suppose it did.§

When I was working with William James I completely learned one thing, that science is continuously busy with the complete description of something, with ultimately the complete complete description of anything with ultimately the complete description of everything. If this can really be done the complete description of everything then what else is there to do. We may well say nothing, but and this is the thing that makes everything continue to be anything, that after all what does happen is that as relatively few people spend all their time describing anything and they stop and so in the meantime as everything goes on somebody else can always commence and go on. And so description is really unending. When I began The Making of Americans I knew I really did know that a complete description was a possible thing, and certainly a complete description is a possible thing. But as it

* *A Long Gay Book*, Page 86.
† *A Long Gay Book*, Page 100.
‡ *A Long Gay Book*, Page 107.
§ *A Long Gay Book*, Page 114.

is a possible thing one can stop continuing to describe this everything. That is where philosophy comes in, it begins when one stops continuing describing everything.

And so this was the history of the writing of The Making of Americans and why I began A Long Gay Book. I said I would go on describing everything in A Long Gay Book, but as inevitably indeed really one does stop describing everything being at last really convinced that a description of everything is possible it was inevitable that I gradually stopped describing everything in A Long Gay Book.

Nevertheless it would be nice to really have described every kind there is of men and women, and it really would not be very hard to do but it would inevitably not be a Long Gay Book, but it would be a Making of Americans.

But I do not want to begin again or go on with what was begun because after all I know I really do know that it can be done and if it can be done why do it, particularly as I say one does know that civilization has after all not existed such a very long time if you count it by a hundred years, and each time there has been civilization it has not lasted such a long time if you count it by a hundred years, which makes a period that can connect you with some other one.

I hope you like what I say.

And so The Making of Americans has been done. It must be remembered that whether they are Chinamen or Americans there are the same kinds in men and women and one can describe all the kinds of them. This I might have done.

And so then I began The Long Gay Book. As soon as I began the Long Gay Book I knew inevitably it would not go on to continue what The Making of Americans had begun. And why not. Because as my life was my life inside me but I was realizing beginning realizing that everything described would not do any more than tell all I knew about anything why should I tell all I knew about anything since after all I did know all I knew about anything.

So then I said I would begin again. I would not know what I knew about everything what I knew about anything.

And so the Long Gay Book little by little changed from a description of any one of any one and everything there there was to be known about any one, to what if not was not not to be not known about any one about anything. And so it was necessary to let come what would happen to come because after all knowledge is what you know but what is happening is inevitably what is happening to come.

And so this brings us to other things.

In describing English literature I have explained that the twentieth century was the century not of sentences as was the eighteenth not of phrases as was the nineteenth but of paragraphs. And as I explained paragraphs were inevitable because as the nineteenth century came to its ending, phrases were no longer full of any meaning and the time had come when a whole thing was all there was of anything. Series immediately before and after made everybody clearly understand this thing. And so it was natural that in writing The Making of Americans I had proceeded to enlarge my paragraphs so as to include everything. What else could I do. In fact inevitably I made my sentences and my paragraphs do the same thing, made them be one and the same thing. This was inevitably because the nineteenth century having lived by phrases really had lost the feeling of sentences, and before this in English literature paragraphs had never been an end in themselves and now in the beginning of the twentieth century a whole thing, being what was assembled from its parts was a whole thing and so it was a paragraph. You will see that in The Making of Americans I did this thing, I made a paragraph so much a whole thing that it included in itself as a whole thing a whole sentence. That makes something clear to you does it not.

And this is what The Making of Americans was. Slowly it was not enough to satisfy myself with a whole thing as a paragraph as a whole thing and I will tell very much more about how that came about but The Making of Americans really carried it as far as it could be carried so I think the making a whole paragraph a whole thing.

Then at the same time is the question of time. The assembling of a thing to make a whole thing and each one of these whole things is one of a series, but beside this there is the important thing and the very American thing that everybody knows who is an American just how many seconds minutes or hours it is going to take to do a whole thing. It is singularly a sense for combination within a conception of the existence of a given space of time that makes the American thing the American thing, and the sense of this space of time must be within the whole thing as well as in the completed whole thing.

I felt this thing, I am an American and I felt this thing, and I made a continuous effort to create this thing in every paragraph that I made in The Making of Americans. And that is why after all this book is an American book an essentially American book, because this thing is an essentially American thing this sense of a space of time and what is to be done within this space of time not in any way excepting in the way that it is inevitable that there is this space of time and anybody who is an American feels what is inside this space of time and so well they do what they do within this space of time, and so ultimately it is a thing contained within. I wonder if I at all convey to you what I mean by this thing. I will try to tell it in every way I can as I have in all the writing that I have ever done. I am always trying to tell this thing that a space of time is a natural thing for an American to always have inside them as something in which they are continuously moving. Think of anything, of cowboys, of movies, of detective stories, of anybody who goes anywhere or stays at home and is an American and you will realize that it is something strictly American to conceive a space that is filled with moving, a space of time that is filled always filled with moving and my first real effort to express this thing which is an American thing began in writing The Making of Americans.

THE MAKING
OF AMERICANS

Written in 1906-08, this huge volume, which in its entirety runs to nearly a thousand pages, was first published in 1925. It must be as long as CLARISSA HARLOWE *which Miss Stein has described as the "greatest of all novels." There have been several different editions and parts of the book have been translated and published in French. One of her avowed aims in writing this "history," and* A LONG GAY BOOK *which followed, was to describe every known type of human being, an ambition she permitted to languish when she discovered it really would be possible for her to do it. Another aim, she asserts in* NARRATION, *was to escape from inevitably feeling that everything had meaning as beginning and middle and ending. In* EVERYBODY'S AUTOBIOGRAPHY *Gertrude Stein has written: "We had a mother and a father and I tell all about that in* THE MAKING OF AMERICANS *which is a history of our family." The author entrusted the manuscript of this work, in seven or eight bound volumes, to her friend Mrs. Charles Knoblauch who brought it to America. Mrs. Knoblauch in turn brought it to me and it remained with me for several years, during which period I attempted with no success to awaken the interest of one publisher after another. In the actual eventual publication, alas, I was not involved.*

Once an angry man dragged his father along the ground through his own orchard. "Stop!" cried the groaning old man at last, "Stop! I did not drag my father beyond this tree."

It is hard living down the tempers we are born with. We all begin well, for in our youth there is nothing we are more intolerant of than our own sins writ large in others and we fight them fiercely in ourselves; but we grow old and we see that these our sins are of all sins the really harmless ones to own, nay that they give a charm to any character, and so our struggle with them dies away.

I am writing for myself and strangers. This is the only way that I can do it. Everybody is a real one to me, everybody is like some one else too to me. No one of them that I know can want to know it and so I write for myself and strangers.

Every one is always busy with it, no one of them then ever want to know it that every one looks like some one else and they see it. Mostly every one dislikes to hear it. It is very important to me to always know it, to always see it which one looks like others and to tell it. I write for myself and strangers. I do this for my own sake and for the sake of those who know I know it that they look like other ones, that they are separate and yet always repeated. There are some who like it that I know they are like many others and repeat it, there are many who never can really like it.

There are many that I know and they know it. They are all of them repeating and I hear it. I love it and I tell it, I love it and now I will write it. This is now the history of the way some of them are it.

I write for myself and strangers. No one who knows me can like it. At least they mostly do not like it that every one is of a kind of men and women and I see it. I love it and I write it.

I want readers so strangers must do it. Mostly no one knowing me can like it that I love it that every one is a kind of men and women, that always I am looking and comparing and classifying of them, always I am seeing their repeating. Always more and more I love repeating, it may be irritating to hear from them but always more and more I love it of them. More and more I love it of them, the being in them, the mixing in them, the repeating in them, the deciding the kind of them every one is who has human being.

This is now a little of what I love and how I write it. Later there will be much more of it.

There are many ways of making kinds of men and women. Now there will be descriptions of every kind of way every one can be a kind of men and women.

This is now a history of Martha Hersland. This is now a history of Martha and of every one who came to be of her living.

There will then be soon much description of every way one can think of men and women, in their beginning, in their middle living, and their ending.

Every one then is an individual being. Every one then is like many others always living, there are many ways of thinking of every one, this is now a description of all of them. There must then be a whole history of each one of them. There must then now be a description of all repeating. Now I will tell all the meaning to me in repeating, the loving there is in me for repeating.

Every one is one inside them, every one reminds some one of some other one who is or was or will be living. Every one has it to say of each one he is like such a one I see it in him, every one has it to say of each one she is like some one else I can tell by remembering. So it goes on always in living, every one is always remembering some one who is resembling to the one at whom they are then looking. So they go on repeating, every one is themselves inside them and every one is resembling to others, and that is always interesting. There are many ways of making kinds of men and women. In each way of making kinds of them there is a different system of finding them resembling. Sometime there will be here every way there can be of seeing kinds of men and women. Sometime there will be then a complete history of each one. Every one always is repeating the whole of them and so sometime some one who sees them will have a complete history of every one. Sometime some one will know all the ways there are for people to be resembling, some one sometime then will have a completed history of every one.

Soon now there will be a history of the way repeating comes out of them comes out of men and women when they are young, when they are children, they have then their own system of being resembling; this will soon be a description of the men and women in beginning, the being young in them, the being children.

There is then now and here the loving repetition, this is then, now and here, a description of the loving of repetition and then there will be a description of all the kinds of ways there can be seen to be kinds of men and women. Then there will be realised the complete history of every one, the fundamental character of every one, the bottom nature in them, the mixtures in them, the strength and weakness of everything they have inside them, the flavor of them, the meaning in them, the being in them, and then you have a whole history then of each one. Everything then they do in living is clear to the completed understanding, their living, loving, eating, pleasing, smoking, thinking, scolding, drinking, working, dancing, walking, talking, laughing, sleeping, everything in them. There are whole beings then, they are themselves inside them, repeating coming out of them makes a history of each one of them.

Always from the beginning there was to me all living as repeating. This is now a description of my feeling. As I was saying listening to repeating is often irritating, always repeating is all of living, everything in a being is always repeating, more and more listening to repeating gives to me completed understanding. Each one slowly comes to be a whole one to me. Each one slowly comes to be a whole one in me. Soon then it commences to sound through my ears and eyes and feelings the repeating that is always coming out from each one, that is them, that makes then slowly of each one of them a whole one. Repeating then comes slowly then to be to one who has it to have loving repeating as natural being comes to be a full sound telling all the being in each one such a one is ever knowing. Sometimes it takes many years of knowing some one before the repeating that is that one gets to be a steady sounding to the hearing of one who has it as a natural being to love repeating that slowly comes out from every one. Sometimes it takes many years of knowing some one before the repeating in that one comes to be a clear history of such a one. Natures sometimes are so mixed up in some one that steady repeating in them is mixed up with changing. Soon then there will be a completed history of each one. Sometimes it is difficult to know it in some, for what these are saying is repeating in them is not the real repeating of them, is not the complete repeating for them. Sometimes many years of knowing some one pass before repeating of all being in them comes out clearly from them. As I was saying it is often irritating to listen to the repeating they are doing, always then that one that has it as being to love repeating that is the whole history of each one, such a one has it then that this irritation passes over into patient completed understanding. Loving repeating is one way of being. This is now a description of such feeling.

There are many that I know and they know it. They are all of them repeating and I hear it. I love it and I tell it. I love it and now I will write it. This is now a history of my love of it. I hear it and I love it and I write it. They repeat it. They live it and I see it and I hear it. They live it and I hear it and I see it and I love it and now and always I will write it. There are many kinds of men and women and I know it. They repeat it and I hear it and I love it. This is now a history of the way they do it. This is now a history of the way I love it.

Now I will tell of the meaning to me in repeating, of the loving there is in me for repeating.

Sometime every one becomes a whole one to me. Sometime every one has a completed history for me. Slowly each one is a whole one to me, with some, all their living is passing before they are a whole one to me. There is a completed history of them to me then when there is of them a completed understanding of the bottom nature in them of the nature or natures mixed up in them with the bottom nature of them or separated in them. There is then a history of the things they say and do and feel, and happen to them. There is then a history of the living in them. Repeating is always in all of them. Repeating in them comes out of them, slowly making clear to any one that looks closely at them the nature and the natures mixed up in them. This sometime comes to be clear in every one.

Often as I was saying repeating is very irritating to listen to from them and then slowly it settles into a completed history of them. Repeating is a wonderful thing in living being. Sometime then the nature of every one comes to be clear to some one listening to the repeating coming out of each one.

This is then now to be a little description of the loving feeling for understanding of the completed history of each one that comes to one who listens always steadily to all repeating. This is the history then of the loving feeling in me of repeating, the loving feeling in me for completed understanding of the completed history of every one as it slowly comes out in every one as patiently and steadily I hear it and see it as repeating in them. This is now a little a description of this loving feeling. This is now a little a history of it from the beginning.

Always then I listen and come back again and again to listen to every one. Always then I am thinking and feeling the repeating in every one. Sometime then there will be for me a completed history of every one. Every one is separate then and a kind of men and women.

Sometime it takes many years of knowing some one before the repeating in that one comes to be a clear history of such a one. Sometimes many years of knowing some one pass before repeating of all being in such a one comes out clearly from them, makes a completed understanding of them by some one listening, watching, hearing all the repeating coming out from such a one.

As I was saying loving listening, hearing always all repeating, coming to completed understanding of each one is to some a natural way of being. This is now more description of the feeling such a one has in them, this is now more description of the way listening to repeating comes to make complete understanding. This is now more description of the way repeating slowly comes to make in each one a completed history of them.

There are many that I know and always more and more I know it. They are all of them repeating and I hear it. More and more I understand it. Always more and more I hear it, always more and more it has completed history in it.

Every one has their own being in them. Every one is of a kind of men and women. Many have mixed up in them some kind of many kinds of men and women. Slowly this comes clearly out from them in the repeating that is always in all living. Slowly it comes out from them to the most delicate gradation, to the gentlest flavor of them. Always it comes out as repeating from them. Always it comes out as repeating, out of them. Then to the complete understanding they keep on repeating this, the whole of them and any one seeing them then can understand them. This is a joy to any one loving repeating when in any one repeating steadily tells over and over again the history of the complete being in them. This is a solid happy satisfaction to any one who has it in them to love repeating and completed understanding.

As I was saying often for many years some one is baffling. The repeated hearing of them does not make the completed being they have in them to any one. Sometimes many years pass in listening to repeating in such a one and the being of them is not a completed history to any one then listening to them. Sometimes then it comes out of them a louder repeating that before was not clear to anybody's hearing and then it is a completed being to some one listening to the repeating coming out of such a one.

This is then now a description of loving repeating being in some. This is then now a description of loving repeating being in one.

There are many that I know and they know it. They are all of them repeating and I hear it. More and more I understand it. I love it and I tell it. I love it and always I will tell it. They live it and I see it and I hear it. They repeat it and I hear it and I see it, sometimes then always I understand it, sometime then always there is a completed history of each one by it, sometime then I will tell the completed history of each one as by repeating I come to know it.

Every one always is repeating the whole of them. Every one is repeating the whole of them, such repeating is then always in them and so sometime some one who sees them will have a complete understanding of the whole of each one of them, will have a completed history of every man and every woman they ever come to know in their living, every man and every woman who were or are or will be living whom such a one can come to know in living.

This then is a history of many men and women, sometime there will be a history of every one.

As I was saying every one always is repeating the whole of them. As I was saying sometimes it takes many years of hearing the repeating in one before the whole being is clear to the understanding of one who has it as a being to love repeating, to know that always every one is repeating the whole of them.

This is then the way such a one, one who has it as a being to love repeating, to know that always every one is repeating the whole of them comes to a completed understanding of any one. This is now a description of such a way of hearing repeating.

Every one always is repeating the whole of them. Many always listen to all repeating that comes to them in their living. Some have it as being to love the repeating that is always in every one coming out from them as a whole of them. This is now a description of such a one and the completed understanding of each one who is repeating in such a one's living.

Every one always is repeating the whole of them. Always, one having loving repeating to getting completed understanding must have in them an open feeling, a sense for all the slightest variations in repeating, must never lose themselves so in the solid steadiness of all repeating that they do not hear the slightest variation. If they get deadened by the steady pounding of repeating they will not learn from each one even though each one always is repeating the whole of them they will not learn the completed history of them, they will not know the being really in them.

As I was saying every one always is repeating the whole of them. As I was saying sometimes it takes many years of listening, seeing, living, feeling, loving the repeating there is in some before one comes to a completed understanding. This is now a description, of such a way of hearing, seeing, feeling, living, loving, repetition.

Mostly every one loves some one's repeating. Mostly every one then, comes to know then the being of some one by loving the repeating in them, the repeating coming out of them. There are some who love everybody's repeating, this is now a description of such loving in one.

Mostly every one loves some one's repeating. Every one always is repeating the whole of them. This is now a history of getting completed understanding by loving repeating in every one the repeating that always is coming out of them as a history of them. This is now a description of learning to listen to all repeating that every one always is making of the whole of them.

Now I will tell of the meaning to me in repeating, of the loving there is in me for repeating.

Always from the beginning there was to me all living as repeating. This is now a description of loving repeating as a being. This is now a history of learning to listen to repeating to come to a completed understanding.

To go on now giving all of the description of how repeating comes to have meaning, how it forms itself, how one must distinguish the different meanings in repeating. Sometimes it is very hard to understand the meaning of repeating. Sometime there will be a complete history of some one having loving repeating as being, to a completed understanding. Now there will be a little description of such a one.

Sometime then there will be a complete history of all repeating to completed understanding. Sometime then there will be a complete history of every one who ever was or is or will be living.

Sometimes there will be a complete history of some one having loving repeating to a completed understanding as being. Sometime then there will be a complete history of many women and many men.

Now there is to be some description of some one having loving repeating to a completed understanding as being. Then there will be a complete history of some.

More and more then there will be a history of many men and many women from their beginning to their ending, as being babies and children and growing young men and growing young women and young grown men and young grown women and men and women in their middle living and growing old men and growing old women and old men and old women.

More and more then there will be histories of all the kinds there are of men and women.

This is now a little description of having loving repeating as being. This is now a little description of one having loving repeating as being.

Loving repeating is one way of being. This is now a description of such being. Loving repeating is always in children. Loving repeating is in a way earth fooling. Some children have loving repeating for little things and story-telling, some have it as a more bottom being. Slowly this comes out in them in all their children being, in their eating, playing, crying, and laughing. Loving repeating is then in a way earth feeling. This is very strong in some. This is very strong in many, in children and in old age being. This is very strong in many in all ways of humorous being, this is very strong in some from their beginning to their ending. This is now some description of such being in one.

As I was saying loving repeating being is in a way earthy being. In some it is repeating that gives to them always a solid feeling of being. In some children there is more feeling in repeating eating and playing, in some in story-telling and their feeling. More and more in living as growing young men and women and grown young men and women and men and women in their middle living, more and more there comes to be in them differences in loving repeating in different kinds of men and women, there comes to be in some more and in some less loving repeating. Loving repeating in some is a going on always in them of earthy being, in some it is the way to completed understanding. Loving repeating then in some is their natural way of complete being. This is now some description of one.

There is then always repeating in all living. There is then in each one always repeating their whole being, the whole nature in them. Much loving repeating has to be in a being so that that one can listen to all the repeating in every one. Almost every one loves all repeating in some one. This is now some description of loving repeating, all repeating, in every one.

To begin again with the children. To begin again with the repeating being in them. To begin again with the loving repeating being in them. As I was saying some children have it in them to love repeating in them of eating, of angry feeling in them, many of them have loving repeating for story-telling in them, many of them have loving repeating being in them for any kind of being funny, in making jokes or teasing, many of them having loving repeating being in them in all kinds of playing. Mostly every one when they are children, mostly every one has then loving repeating being strongly in them, some have it more some have it less in them and this comes out more and more in them as they come to be young adolescents in their being and then grown young men and grown young women.

To begin again then with children in their having loving repeating being. Mostly all children have loving repeating as being in them but some have it much more and some have it much less in them. Loving repeating being is more of that kind of being that has resisting as its natural way of fighting than of that kind of being that has attacking as its natural way of winning. But this is a very complicated question. I know very much about these ways of being in men and women. I know it and can say it, it is a very complex question and I do not know yet the whole of it, so I can not yet say all I know of it.

As I was saying all little children have in them mostly very much loving repeating being. As they grow into bigger children some have it more some have it less in them. Some have it in them more and more as a conscious feeling. Many of them do not have it in them more and more as a conscious feeling. Mostly when they are growing to be young men and women they have not it in them to have loving repeating being in them as a conscious feeling.

Mostly every one has not it in them as a conscious feeling as a young grown man or young grown woman. Some have it in them, loving repeating feeling as steadily developing, this is now a history of one.

Many men and many women never have it in them the conscious feeling of loving repeating. Many men and many women never have it in them until old age weakening is in them, a consciousness of repeating. Many have it in them all their living as a conscious feeling as a humorous way of being in them. Some have it in them, the consciousness of always repeating the whole of them as a serious obligation. There are many many ways then of having repeating as conscious feeling, of having loving repeating as a bottom being, of having loving repeating being as a conscious feeling.

As I was saying mostly all children have in them loving repeating being as important in them to them and to every one around them. Mostly growing young men and growing young women have to themselves very little loving repeating being, they do not have it to each other then most of them, they have it to older ones then as older ones have it to them loving repeating being, not loving repeating being but repeating as the way of being in them, repeating of the whole of them as coming every minute from them.

In the middle living of men and women there are very different ways of feeling to repeating, some have more and more in them loving repeating as a conscious feeling, some have less and less liking in them for the repeating in, to them, of mostly every one. Mostly every one has a loving feeling for repeating in some way. Some have not any such loving even in the repeating going on inside themselves then, not even for any one they are loving.

Some then have always growing in them more and more loving feeling for the repeating in every one. Many have not any loving for repeating in many of those around them.

There are then many ways of feeling in one about repeating. There are many ways of knowing repeating when one sees and hears and feels it in every one.

Loving repeating then is important being in some. This is now some description of the importance of loving repeating being in one.

Some find it interesting to find inside them repeating in them of some one they have known or some relation to them coming out in them, some never have any such feeling in them, some have not any liking for such being in them. Some like to see such being in others around them but not in themselves inside them. There are many ways of feeling in one about all these kinds of repeating. Sometime there will be written the history of all of them.

To begin again then with some description of the meaning of loving repeating being when it is strongly in a man or in a woman, when it is in them their way of understanding everything in living and there are very many always living of such being. This is now again a beginning of a little description of it in one.

Repeating of the whole of them is then always in every one. There are different stages in being, there is being babies and children and then growing young men or women and grown young men or women and men or women in middle living and in growing old and in ending. There are many kinds of men and women and soon now there will be a beginning of a history of all of them who ever were or are or will be living. There will be then here written a history of some of them. To begin again then with loving repeating being as a bottom nature in some. To begin again with the developing of it in one.

As I was saying children have it in them to have strongly loving repeating being as a conscious feeling in so far as they can be said to have such a thing in them. It gives to them a solid feeling of knowing they are safe in living. With growing it comes to be more in some, it comes to be less in others of them. Mostly there is very little conscious loving repeating feeling in growing young men and women.

In the beginning then, in remembering, repeating was strongly in the feeling of one, in the feeling of many, in the feeling of most of them who have it to have strongly in them their earthy feeling of being part of the solid dirt around them. This is one kind of being. This is mostly of one kind of being, of slow-minded resisting fighting being. This is now a little a description of one.

Slowly then some go on living, they may be fairly quick in learning, some of such of them seem very quick and impetuous in learning and in acting but such learning has for such of them very little meaning, it is the slow repeating resisting inside them that has meaning for them. Now there will be a little a description of loving repeating being in one of such of them.

The kinds and ways of repeating, of attacking and resisting in different kinds of men and women, the practical, the emotional, the sensitive, the every kind of being in every one who ever was or is or will be living, I know so much about all of them, many of them are very clear in kinds of

men and women, in individual men and women, I know
them so well inside them, repeating in them has so much
meaning to knowing, more and more I know all there is of
all being, more and more I know it in all the ways it is in
them and comes out of them, sometime there will be a history of every one, sometime all history of all men and women
will be inside some one.

Now there will be a little description of the coming to be
history of all men and women, in some one. This is then to
be a little history of such a one. This is then now to be a
little description of loving repeating being in one.

Almost every one has it in them in their beginning to have
loving repeating being strongly in them. Some of them have
attacking being as the bottom nature in them, some of them
have resisting being as the bottom nature in them. Some of
both these kinds of them have more or less in all their living
loving repeating being in them, it works differently in them
to come out of them in these two kinds of them. Later there
will be much description of the way it comes out from them
and is in them in the different kinds of them. Now there is
to be a little description of it in one having resisting as the
way of winning fighting. This is now some description of
such a one having loving repeating being developing into
completed understanding. Now to slowly begin.

The relation of learning to being, of thinking to feeling,
of realisation to emotion, all these and many others are very
complicated questions. Sometimes there will be much description of them with the kinds of men and women with
being in them, with mixtures in them, that complicates them.
There will sometime be a history of every one. This is a sure
thing.

Now again to begin. The relation of learning and thinking
to being, of feeling to realising is a complicated question.
There will now be very little talking of such way of being.
As I was saying some have it in them to have slowly resisting
as their natural way of being can have learning and thinking
come quickly enough in them. This is then not bottom being
in them. It is bottom being in some of such of them. This is

very clear now in my knowing. Now to begin again with it as telling.

Some then who are of that kind of being who have slow resisting being as their way to wisdom have it in them to be quick in learning and in thinking and in acting. As I was saying in some this is not of the bottom nature in them, in some it is bottom nature in them for the slow resisting winning bottom to them was not put in in the making of them, in some it is in them but dull and not mixing in their living, in some it is not sensitive to action in their living, it is there in them going on inside them not connecting on with the rest of them. This is not just talking, this all has real meaning. These are all then of a kind of men and women who have resisting being as the real wisdom in them. In some of such of them they seem to be winning by acting by attacking they live so very successfully in living but nevertheless they are of the kind of them that have resisting winning as their real way of fighting although never in their living does this act in them. Careful listening to the whole of them always repeating shows this in them, what kind they are of men and women.

To begin again. This is now some description of one having loving repeating as a way to wisdom, having slowly resisting winning as the bottom being. As I was saying learning in such a one and thinking about everything can be quick enough in the beginning.

The important thing then in knowing the bottom nature in any one is the way their real being slowly comes to be them, the whole of them comes to be repeating in them.

As I was saying some can have quick learning and nervous attacking or one or the other in them with slow resisting being in them as their natural way of winning. There is every kind of mixing. There is every degree of intensification. There is every degree of hastening the resisting into more rapid realisation. There is every degree of hurrying. In short there are all degrees of intensification and rapidity in motion and mixing and disguising and yet the kind he is each one, the kind she is each one, comes to be clear in the repeating that more and more steadily makes them clear to any one looking hard at them. These kinds then are existing, the independent dependent, the dependent independent, the one with attacking as the way of winning, the other with resisting as the way of wisdom for them. I know then this is true of every one that each one is of one or the other kind of these two kinds of them. I know it is in them, I know many more things about these two kinds of them. Slowly they come to be clearer in every one, sometime perhaps it will be clear to every one. Sometime perhaps some one will have completely in them the history of every one of everything in every one and the degree and kind and way of being of everything in each one in them from their beginning to their ending and coming out of them.

This is then a beginning of the way of knowing everything in every one, of knowing the complete history of each one who ever is or was or will be living. This is then a little description of the winning of so much wisdom.

As I was saying the important thing is having loving repeating being, that is the beginning of learning the complete history of every one. That being must always be in such a one, one who has it in them sometime to have in them the completed history of every one they ever can hear of as having being.

There are so many ways of beginning this description, and now once more to make a beginning.

Always repeating is all of living, everything that is being is always repeating, more and more listening to repeating gives to me completed understanding. Each one then slowly comes to be a whole one to me, each one slowly comes to be a whole one in me, slowly it sounds louder and louder and louder inside me through my ears and eyes and feelings and the talking there is always in me the repeating that is the whole of each one I come to know around, and each one of them then comes to be a whole one to me, comes to be a whole one in me. Loving repeating is one way of being. This is now a description of such being.

Always from the beginning there was to me all living as repeating. This was not in me then a conscious being. Always more and more this is in me developing to a completed being. This is now again a beginning of a little description of such being.

In their beginning as children every one has in them loving repeating being. This is for them then their natural being. Later in conscious being some have much in them of loving repeating being, some have in them almost nothing of such feeling. There are then these two kinds of them. This is then one way of thinking of them.

There are two kinds of men and women, those who have in them resisting as their way of winning those who have in them attacking as their way of winning fighting, there are many kinds, many very many kinds of each of these two kinds of men and women, sometime there will be written a description of all the kinds of them. Now this division is accepted by me and I will now give a little more description of loving repeating being and then go on to describing how it comes to slowly give to me completed understanding, loving repeating being always in me acting, of this one and that one, and then there will be some description of resembling coming to be clear by looking at the repeating in men and women and then there will be more history of Martha Hersland and the best coming out of her all her living and the being in every one she came to know in living.

Always then from the beginning there was in me always increasing as a conscious feeling loving repeating being, learning to know repeating in every one, hearing the whole being of any one always repeating in that one every minute of their living. There was then always in me as a bottom nature to me an earthy, resisting slow understanding, loving repeating being. As I was saying this has nothing to do with ordinary learning, in a way with ordinary living. This will be clearer later in this description.

Many have loving repeating being in them, many never come to know it of them, many never have it as a conscious feeling, many have in it a restful satisfaction. Some have in it always more and more understanding, many have in it very little enlarging understanding. There is every kind of way of having loving repeating being as a bottom. It is very clear to me and to my feeling, it is very slow in developing, it is very important to make it clear now in writing, it must be done now with a slow description. To begin again then with it in my feeling, to begin again then to tell of the meaning to me in all repeating, of the loving there is in me for repeating.

Sometime every one becomes a whole one to me. For many years this was just forming in me. Now sometimes it takes many years for some one to be a whole one to me. For many years loving repeating was a bottom to me, I was never thinking then of the meaning of it in me, it had nothing then much to do with the learning, the talking, the thinking, nor the living then in me. There was for many years a learning and talking and questioning in me and not listening to repeating in every one around me. Then slowly loving repeating being came to be a conscious feeling in me. Slowly then every one sometime became a whole one to me.

Now I will tell of the meaning in me of repeating, of the loving repeating being there is now always in me.

In loving repeating being then to completed understanding there must always be a feeling for all changing, a feeling for living being that is always in repeating. This is now again a beginning of a description of my feeling.

Always then I am thinking and feeling the repeating in each one as I know them. Always then slowly each one comes to be a whole one to me. As I was saying loving repeating in every one, hearing always all repeating, coming to completed understanding of each one is to me a natural way of being.

There are many that I know and always more and more I know it. They are all of them repeating and I hear it. They are all of them living and I know it. More and more I understand it, always more and more it has completed history in it.

Every one has their own being in them. Every one is of a kind of men and women. Always more and more I know the whole history of each one. This is now a little a description of such knowing in me. This is now a little a description of beginning of hearing repeating all around me.

As I was saying learning, thinking, living in the beginning of being men and women often has in it very little of real being. Real being, the bottom nature, often does not then in the beginning do very loud repeating. Learning, thinking, talking, living, often then is not of the real bottom being. Some are this way all their living. Some slowly come to be repeating louder and more clearly the bottom being that makes them. Listening to repeating, knowing being in every one who ever was or is or will be living slowly came to be in me a louder and louder pounding. Now I have it to my feeling to feel all living, to be always listening to the slightest changing, to have each one come to be a whole one to me from the repeating in each one that sometime I come to be understanding. Listening to repeating is often irritating, listening to repeating can be dulling, always repeating is all of living, everything in a being is always repeating, always more and more listening to repeating gives to me completed understanding. Each one slowly comes to be a whole one to me. Each one slowly comes to be a whole one in me.

In the beginning then learning and thinking and talking and feeling and loving and working in me mostly was not bottom being in me. Slowly it came out in me the feeling for living in repeating that now by listening and watching and feeling everything coming out of each one and always repeating the whole one gives to me completed understanding.

There was a time when I was questioning, always asking, when I was talking, wondering, there was a time when I was feeling, thinking and all the time then I did not know repeating, I did not see or hear or feel repeating. There was a long time then when there was nothing in me using the bottom loving repeating being that now leads me to knowing. Then I was attacking, questioning, wondering, thinking, always at the bottom was loving repeating being, that was not then there to my conscious being. Sometime there will be written a long history of such a beginning.

Always then there was there a recognition of the thing always repeating, the being in each one, and always then thinking, feeling, talking, living, was not of this real being.

Slowly I came to hear repeating. More and more then I came to listen, now always and always I listen and always now each one comes to be a whole one in me.

Sometimes in listening to a conversation which is very important to two men, to two women, to two men and women, sometime then it is a wonderful thing to see how each one always is repeating everything they are saying and each time in repeating, what each one is saying has more meaning to each one of them and so they go on and on and on and on and on repeating and always to some one listening, repeating is a very wonderful thing. There are many of them who do not live in each repeating each repeating coming out of them but always repeating is interesting. Repeating is what I am loving. Sometimes there is in me a sad feeling for all the repeating no one loving repeating is hearing, it is like any beauty that no one is seeing, it is a lovely thing, always some one should be knowing the meaning in the repeating always coming out of women and of men, the repeating of the being in them. So then.

Every one is a brute in her way or his way to some one, every one has some kind of sensitiveness in them.

Some feel some kinds of things others feel other kinds of things. Mostly every one feels some kinds of things. The way some things touch some and do not touch other ones and kinds in men and women then I will now begin to think a little bit about describing. To begin then.

I am thinking it is very interesting the relation of the kind of things that touch men and women with the kind of bottom nature in them, the kind of being they have in them in every way in them, the way they react to things which may be different from the way they feel them.

I am thinking very much of feeling things in men and women. As I was saying every one is a brute in her way or his way to some one, every one has some kind of sensitiveness in them. Mostly every one has some inner way of feeling in them, almost every one has some way of reacting to stimulus in them. This is not always the same thing. These things have many complications in them.

I am beginning now a little a description of three women, Miss Dounor, Miss Charles and Mrs. Redfern. I am beginning now a little a realisation of the way each one of them is in her way a brute to some one, each one has in her way a kind of sensitiveness in being. This is now some description of each one of the three of them Miss Dounor, Miss Charles and Mrs. Redfern.

In listening to a conversation, as I was saying, repeating of each one and the gradual rising and falling and rising again of realisation is very interesting. This is now some description of the three women and as I was saying of the sensitiveness in each one of them to some things and the insensitiveness to other things and the bottom nature in them and the kinds of repeating in them and the bottom nature and the other natures mixed with the bottom nature in each one of them.

Sensitiveness to something, understanding anything, feeling anything, that is very interesting to understand in each one. How much, when and where and how and when not and where not and how not they are feeling, thinking, understanding. To begin again then with feeling anything.

Mostly every one is a brute in her way or his way to some one, mostly every one has some kind of sensitiveness in them.

Mostly every one can have some kind of feeling in them, very many men and very many women can have some understanding in them of some kind of thing by the kind of being sensitive to some kind of impression that they have in them.

Some kinds of men and women have a way of having sensation from some things and other men and women have it in them to be able to be impressionable to other kinds of things. Some men and some women have very much of sensitive being in them for the kind of thing they can be feeling, they can then be very loving, or very trembly from the abundant delicate fear in them, or very attacking from the intensity of the feeling in them, or very mystic in their absorption of feeling which is then all of them. There are some men and women having in them very much weakness as the bottom in them and watery anxious feeling, and sometimes nervous anxious feeling then in them and sometimes stubborn feeling then in them. There are some who have vague or vacant being as the bottom in them and it is very hard to know with such ones of them what feeling they have ever in them and there are some with almost intermittent being in them and it is very hard to tell with such of them what kind of thing gives to them a feeling, what kind of feeling they ever have really in them. As I was saying mostly every one sometimes feels something, some one, is understanding something, some one, has some kind of sensitiveness in them to something, to some one, mostly every one.

As I was saying some men and some women have very much of sensitive being in them for something that can give to them real feeling. They can then, some of these of them, when they are filled full then of such feeling, they can then be completely loving, completely believing, they can then have a trembling awed being in them, they can have then abundant trembly feeling in them, they can then be so full up then with the feeling in them that they are a full thing and action has no place then in them, they are completely then a feeling, there are then men and women, there are then women and men who have then this finely sensitive completed feeling that is sometime all them and perhaps Cora Dounor was one of such of them. Perhaps she was one of them and was such a one in loving Phillip Redfern. Perhaps that was the whole being she had in her then.

Each one as I am saying has it in them to feel more or less, sometime, something, almost certainly each one sometime has some capacity for more or less feeling something. Some have in them always and very little feeling, some have some feeling and much nervous being always in them, some have as a bottom to them very much weakness and eagerness together then and they have then such of them some sensitiveness in them to things coming to them but often after they are then full up with nervous vibrations and then nothing can really touch them and then they can have in them nervous vibratory movement in them, anxious feeling in them and sometimes stubborn feeling then in them and then nothing can touch them and they are all this being then this nervous vibratory quivering and perhaps Mrs. Redfern was such a one Mrs. Redfern who had been Martha Hersland and was married now to Phillip Redfern and had come to Farnham and had there seen Phillip Redfern come to know Miss Dounor and had been then warned to take care of him by the dean of Farnham Miss Charles. She never knew then, Mrs. Redfern never knew then that she would not ever again have him, have Redfern again. This never could come to be real knowledge in her. She was always then and later always working at something to have him again and that was there always in her to the end of him and of her. There will be a little more description of her written in the history of the ending of the living in her father, in the history of the later living of her brother Alfred Hersland who now just when her trouble was commencing was just then marrying Julia Dehning, in the history of her brother David Hersland her younger brother. More description of her will be part of the history of the ending of the existing of the Hersland family. There will be very much history of this ending of all of them of the Hersland family written later.

The dean Miss Charles was very different from either Miss Dounor or Mrs. Redfern. She had it in her to have her own way of feeling things touching her, mostly there was in her less reactive than self-directive action in her than there was in the two women who were just then concerning her, Miss Dounor and Mrs. Redfern.

It is hard to know it of any one whether they are enjoying anything, whether they are knowing they are giving pain to some one, whether they were planning that thing. It is hard to know such things in any one when they are telling when they are not telling to any one what they know inside them. It is hard telling it of any one whether they are enjoying a thing, whether they know that they are hurting some one, whether they have been planning the acting they have been doing. It is hard telling it of any one whether they are enjoying anything, whether they know that they are hurting any one, whether they have been planning the acting they are doing. It is very hard then to know anything of the being in any one, it is hard then to know the being in many men and in many women, it is hard then to know the being and the feeling in any man or in any woman. It is hard to know it if they tell you all they know of it. It is hard to know it if they do not tell you what they know of it in it. Miss Cora Dounor then could do some planning, could do some hurting with it, that is certain. This is perhaps surprising to some, reading. To begin then with her feeling and her being and her acting.

As I am saying she had it in her to be compounded of beautiful sensitive being, of being able to be in a state of being completely possessed by a wonderful feeling of loving and that was then the whole of the being that was being then in her and then it came to be in her that she could be hurting first Miss Charles and then Mrs. Redfern, then Miss Charles and Mrs. Redfern by planning. This is then the being in her this that I am now with very much complication slowly realising, not yet completely realising, not yet completely ready to be completely describing, beginning now to be describing. The dean Miss Charles was a very different person, she was of the dependent independent kind of them. To understand the being in her there must be now a little realisation of the way beginning is in very many persons having in them a nature that is self growing and a nature that is reacting to stimulation and that have it in them to have these two natures acting in not very great harmony inside them. Mrs. Redfern as I was saying in a long description that has been already written was a very different kind of person from Miss Dounor and Miss Charles. These are then the three of them that were struggling and each of them had in them their own ways of being brutal, hurting some one, had each of them their own way of being sensitive to things and people near them.

Sometimes I am almost despairing. Yes it is very hard, almost impossible I am feeling now in my despairing feeling to have completely a realising of the being in any one, when they are telling it when they are not telling it, it is so very very hard to know it completely in one the being in one. I know the being in Miss Dounor that I am beginning describing, I know the being in Miss Charles that I am soon going to be beginning describing, I know the being in Mrs. Redfern, I have been describing the being in that one. I know the being in each one of these three of them and I am almost despairing for I am doubting if I am knowing it poignantly enough to be really knowing it, to be really knowing the being in any one of the three of them. Always now I am despairing. It is a very melancholy feeling I have in me now I am despairing about really knowing the complete being of any one of each one of these three of them Miss Dounor and Miss Charles and Mrs. Redfern.

Miss Dounor as I was saying was to Redfern the most complete thing of gentleness and intelligence he could think of ever seeing in anybody who was living, Miss Dounor had it to have in her the complete thing of gentleness, of beauty in sensitiveness, in completeness of intelligent sensitiveness in completely loving. She was the complete thing then of gentleness and sensitiveness and intelligence and she had it as a complete thing gentleness and sensitiveness and intelligence in completely loving. It was in her complete in loving, complete in creative loving, it was then completed being, it was then completely in her completely loving Phillip Redfern. And always to the ending of his living in all the other loving and other troubling and the other enjoying of men and women in him he was faithful to the thing she had been, was and would be to him the completed incarnation of gentleness and sensitiveness and intelligence, gentle intelligence and intelligent sensitiveness and all to the point of completely creative loving that was to him the supreme thing in all living. Miss Dounor was then completely what Redfern found her to him, she was of them of the independent dependent kind of them who have sensitive being to the point of creative being, of attacking, of creative loving, creative feeling, of sometimes creative thinking and writing. She was then such a one and completely then this one and she had in her completely sensitive being to the point of attacking. She could have in her a planning of attacking and this came to be in her from the completeness of sensitive creative loving that she had then in her then when she was knowing Phillip Redfern.

Perhaps she was not of this kind of them. Perhaps she was at the bottom, of the resisting kind of them. I think she was of the resisting kind of them and so she needed to own the one she needed for loving, so she could do resisting to planning making an attacking. I am almost despairing, yes a little I am realising the being in Miss Dounor and in Miss Charles and Mrs. Redfern, but I am really almost despairing, I have really in me a very very melancholy feeling, a very melancholy being, I am really then despairing.

Miss Charles was of the kind of men and women that I speak of and have spoken of as the dependent independent kind of them. I will now tell a little about what I mean by self growing activity in such of them and reactive activity in such of them. As I was saying a long time back when I was describing the dependent independent kind of them, reaction is not poignant in them unless it enters into them the stimulation is lost in them and so sets it, the mass, in motion, it is not as in the other kind of them who have it to have a reactive emotion to be as poignant as a sensation as is the case in the independent dependent kind of them. Miss Charles then as I was saying was of the kind of them where reaction to have meaning must be a slow thing, but she had quick reactions as mostly all of them of this kind of them have them and those were her mostly attacking being as is very common in those having in them dependent independent being.

It is so very confusing that I am beginning to have in me despairing melancholy feeling. Mrs. Redfern as I was saying was of the independent dependent kind of them and being in her was never really attacking, it was mostly never active into forward movement it was incessantly in action as being in a state of most continual nervous agitation. They were then very different in their being the three of them Miss Dounor and Miss Charles and Mrs. Redfern and they had each one of them their own way of hurting the other ones in their then living, of having in them sensitiveness to some-thing.

It is hard to know it of any one whether they are en-joying anything, whether they are feeling something, whether they are knowing they are giving pain to some one, whether they were planning that thing. It is a very difficult thing to know such things in any one any one is knowing, very difficult even when they are telling that one all the feeling they have in them, a very difficult thing when they are not telling any-thing. It is a very difficult thing to tell it of any one whether they are enjoying a thing, whether they know that they are hurting some one, whether they have been planning the act-ing they have been doing. It is a very difficult thing to know anything of the being in any one, it is a very difficult thing to know the being in any one if they tell you all that they themselves know of it as they live it, if they themselves tell you nothing at all about it. It is a very difficult thing to know the being in any one. It is a very difficult thing to know whether any one is feeling a thing, enjoying a thing, knowing that they are hurting some one, planning that thing, planning anything they are doing in their living. It is a difficult thing to know the being in any one if that one tells to any one com-pletely all that that one has in them of telling, it is a very difficult thing to know the being in any one if they are not telling any one anything that they can have as telling in them. It is a very difficult thing to know it of any one the being in them, it is a very difficult thing to tell it of any one what they are feeling, whether they are enjoying, whether they are knowing that they are hurting some one, whether they had been planning doing that thing. It is a very difficult thing to know these things in anyone, it is a difficult thing if that one is telling everything they can be telling, if that one is telling nothing. It is certainly a difficult thing to know it of any one whether they have in them a kind of feeling, whether they have in them at some time any realisation that they are hurting some one, whether they had planned doing that thing.

Miss Dounor had come to live with Miss Charles, they had come to know each other in the way that it was natural for each one of them to know the other one of them. The two of them then had come to know Mrs. Redfern. They both had come then each in their way to know her and to feel her and to have an opinion of her.

Miss Dounor had this being in her. She could have some planning in her, this came from the completeness of pride in her. This now comes to be clearer, that she had as completely pride in her as sensitiveness and intelligent gentleness inside her. She had in her pride as sensitive, as intelligent, as complete as the loving being in her when she was loving Redfern. She had in her pride as sensitive, as intelligent, as complete as the being ever in her. She had always had in her a pride as complete, as intelligent, as sensitive as the complete being of her. She had in her a pride as intelligent, as sensitive as complete as the being in her. This made it that she had planning in her, this made attacking sometimes in her. This never made any action in her toward a lover, this gave to her a power of planning and this was in her and she could be wonderfully punishing some around her. This could be turned into melodrama if the intelligence in her had not been so gentle and so fine in her, this in many who are like her is a melodrama. In her it made her able to do some planning against some to punish them not for interfering but for existing and so claiming something that entirely belonged to her. What was in Redfern to him himself a weakness in him was to her a heroic thing to be defending. Pride was in her then as delicate, as gentle, as intelligent as sensitive as complete as the being in her. This is now more description of her. This is now some description of the way she could be hurting another, how she could be feeling another, how she could have planning in her, how she did have planning in her. This is now more description of her and the being in her. I am now a little understanding the whole of her, I have in me still now a little melancholy feeling.

Miss Charles was of the dependent independent kind of them as I was saying.

Everybody is perfectly right. Everybody has their own being in them. Some say it of themselves in their living, I am as I am and I know I will never be changing. Mostly every one is perfectly right in living. That is a very pleasant feeling to be having about every one in the living of every one. Mostly not very many have that pleasant feeling that everybody is as they are and they will not be very much changing in them and everybody is right in their living. It is a very pleasant feeling, knowing every one is as they are and everybody is right in their living. Miss Dounor was as she was and she was not ever changing, Miss Charles was as she was and was not ever changing. Mrs. Redfern was as she was and always she wanted to be changing and always she was trying.

Miss Dounor as I was saying was as she was all her living and was not really ever changing and she was very right in her living and she was very complete in her being and her pride was as complete in her as her being and so she could be planning her conviction of how far Mrs. Redfern should not go in presumption, how far Miss Charles should not go in her interfering, how completely Phillip Redfern was a saint in living and in her devotion and she could carry out all this in its completion. Mrs. Redfern had no understanding in desiring. Phillip Redfern always should give her always would give her always would give to every one anything she, anything they were ever asking. This was the being in him. Asking was not presumption in Mrs. Redfern, desiring was presumption and Miss Dounor could then have in her a planning or perfect attacking. Always Mrs. Redfern should have anything she could ever ask of anyone, that was a very certain thing. Always Mrs. Redfern should have, would have from Mr. Redfern anything she was ever asking of him. Always then to them to Mr. Redfern and to Miss Dounor then, always then Mrs. Redfern had everything from Redfern that she ever could ask of him. This was then a very certain thing. Always then Mrs. Redfern had the right to ask anything and always she would have anything she should ever be asking of Phillip Redfern. She had in her, Mrs. Redfern, no intelligence, no understanding, in desiring, Miss Dounor had in her then a perfect power of planning the attacking that should keep Mrs. Redfern in her place of condemnation for Mrs. Redfern had not in her any intelligence in desiring, she had a right to anything she ever could be asking and she would have it given to her then whenever she asked for anything, Mrs. Redfern was never changing in her being, always she was trying, always she was without understanding in her desiring, always Miss Dounor could completely plan an attacking when the time came for such action to restrain Mrs. Redfern in her unintelligent desiring.

Miss Dounor was then perfectly right in her being. She was never changing, she was completely loving, she was completely understanding desiring, she was complete in the pride of attacking in her complete sensitive, completely intelligent, completely gentle being, completely understood desiring. Mrs. Redfern had no understanding in desiring. Mrs. Redfern always was trying to change the being she had in her to find some way of having intelligent desiring in her, always she would have from Redfern anything she could anything she should anything she would ever ask him to be giving to her. That was the being in her.

There were three of them then, Miss Charles, Miss Dounor and Mrs. Redfern.

Miss Charles was then not permitted by Miss Dounor to interfere with the being inside her, ever at any time in their living. Miss Charles was never asking anything of any one. Miss Charles was then one of the dependent independent kind of them. Miss Charles was then one having general moral and special moral aspirations and general unmoral desires and ambitious and special unmoral ways of carrying them into realisation and there was never inside her any contradiction and this is very common in very many kinds of them of men and women and later in the living of Alfred Hersland there will be so very much discussion of this matter and now there will be a little explanation of the way it acts in the kind of men and women of which Miss Charles was one.

Some have it in them some having in them a being like Miss Charles some of such of them have it in them to have it in the beginning very strongly in them that they have generalised moral aspirations, strongly detailed moral struggles in them, and then slowly in them comes out in them that they are vigorous egotistic sensual natures, loving being, living, writing, reading, eating, drinking, loving, bullying, teasing, finding out everything and slowly they get courage in them to feel the being in them they have in them, slowly they get courage in them to live the being they have in them. Some like Miss Charles keep on having tranquilly inside them equally strongly in them moral aspiration general and detailed in them, egotistic expedient domineering as a general aspiration and as detailed living in them. Some are always struggling, some of this kind of them, some get to have in them that the moral fervor in them in the general and specific expression of them get to be the whole of them, some get to have it all fairly mixed up in them. This is now a little description of how one of them when she was a young one one of the first kind of them who slowly came to have the courage of feeling and then living the real being came to have the struggle as a beginning. Later then came the courage to be more certain of the real being. This is now a little piece of such a description of such beginning experiencing.

As I was saying in many of such ones there is the slow reacting, slow expressing being that comes more and more in their living to determine them. There are in many of such ones aspirations and convictions due to quick reactions to others around them, to books they are reading, to the family tradition, to the lack of articulation of the meaning of the being in them that makes them need then to be filled full with other reactions in them so that they will then have something. Some then spend all their living struggling to adjust the being that slowly comes to active stirring in them to the aspirations they had in them, some want to create their aspirations from the being in them and they have not the courage in them. It is a wonderful thing how much courage it takes even to buy a clock you are very much liking when it is a kind of one every one thinks only a servant should be owning. It is very wonderful how much courage it takes to buy bright colored handkerchiefs when every one having good taste uses white ones or pale colored ones, when a bright colored one gives you so much pleasure you suffer always at not having them. It is very hard to have the courage of your being in you, in clocks, in handkerchiefs, in aspirations, in liking things that are low, in anything. It is a very difficult thing to get the courage to buy the kind of clock or handkerchiefs you are loving when every one thinks it is a silly thing. It takes very much courage to do anything connected with your being unless it is a very serious thing. In some, expressing their being needs courage, for, foolish ways to every one else, in them. It is a very difficult thing to have courage to buy clocks and handkerchiefs you are liking, you are seriously liking and everybody thinks then you are joking. It is a very difficult thing to have courage for something no one is thinking is a serious thing.

As I was saying Miss Charles had in her what I am calling dependent independent being, that is being that is not in its quicker reacting poignant in its feeling, not having emotion then have the keenness of sensation as those having independent dependent being have it in them. Miss Charles was then such a one.

This is then a very common thing as I am saying. Miss Charles had in her this being. As I am saying there are two ways then of acting in a being like those I have been just describing. The acting from the personality slowly developing, the acting from the organised reaction to contemporary ideals, tradition, education and need of having, before the developing of their own being, completed aspiration. Often these keep on as they did in Miss Charles and no one is knowing which is the stronger way of being in such a one. Sometimes there is as I was saying in the beginning very much struggling and then slowly the personality comes to action and that one drops away the early filling, sometimes the early filling comes to be the later filling and in such a one then there is not any changing. This is quite interesting and will be always more and more dwelt upon. This then was the being in Miss Charles and this was the meaning of her action with Miss Dounor and Mrs. Redfern and Mr. Redfern that I have been describing.

There will be now a very little more description of the being in them, of the virtuous feeling in them, of the religious feeling in them, of the sensitiveness in them, of the worldly feeling in them, of the succeeding and failing in them, in each one of the three of them, Miss Dounor, Miss Charles and Mrs. Redfern.

Every one has their own being in them. Every one is right in their own living. This is a pleasant feeling to have in one about every one. This makes every one very interesting to one having such a feeling in them. Every one is right in their living. Each one has her or his own being in her or in him. Each one is right in the living in her or in him. Each one of these three of them were right in their living. This is now a little more description of the being in each one of them.

It is a very difficult thing to know it of any one whether they are enjoying anything, whether they are knowing they are giving pain to some one, whether they were planning that thing. It is a very difficult thing to know it of any one what is the kind of thing they are sensitive to in living, what is the bottom nature in them, whether they will in living be mostly succeeding or mostly failing. It is hard to know such things in any one when they are telling everything they have in them, when they are not telling to any one anything of what they know inside them. It is a very difficult thing the telling it of any one whether they are enjoying a thing, whether they know that they are hurting some one, whether they have been planning the acting they are doing. It is a very difficult thing then to know anything of the being in any one, it is hard then to know the being in many men and in many women, it is a very difficult thing then to know the being and the feeling in any man or in any woman. It is hard to know it if they tell you all they know of it. It is hard to know it if they do not tell you what they know of it in it. Nevertheless now almost I am understanding the being in the three of them Miss Charles, Miss Dounor and Mrs. Redfern. There will be now a very little more description of the being in them, of the virtuous feeling in them of the religious feeling in them, of the sensitiveness in them, of the worldly feeling in them, of the succeeding and failure in them, in each one of the three of them Miss Charles, Miss Dounor and Mrs. Redfern.

Miss Cora Dounor could do some planning, could do some attacking with it, that is certain. This is perhaps surprising to some reading. To begin then with her feeling and her being and her doing, and her succeeding and her failing.

She was then complete in her loving, she had complete understanding in desiring in all her relation with Phillip Redfern, she had completely then the realisation later in her that Phillip Redfern was saintly and she had then in her the complete possession of her adoration, the complete understanding and possession of her adoration of the saintly being in him, and this was then in her a complete succeeding in being and in living. This was not exactly virtuous or religious being in her this way complete understanding desiring and complete intelligent being in her and this was in her succeeding in her being and in her living. This is very certain. This was in her succeeding in her being and in her living. She had then in her complete understanding in desiring, she had then completely in her completed intelligence in adoration and this was complete being in her and it was a complete possession of her and by her and this was then completely succeeding in living. This is now very certain.

She had then complete succeeding in her living as I was saying, she had in her complete pride in her and this could be in her strong sensitive attacking but this was not completely a succeeding in her living. As I was saying Mrs. Redfern had in her no intelligence whatever in desiring, this was in her then presumption in her to Miss Dounor, not the things for which Mrs. Redfern was asking, Mrs. Redfern had the right to ask for anything or everything, it was desiring in her that was a thing Miss Dounor could rightly condemn in her and later she made it very certain to every one that Mrs. Redfern had no intelligence no understanding in desiring and then at last Mrs. Redfern reproached her and so then in a sense Miss Dounor was then failing in her being completely proud inside her. Mrs. Redfern attempting to attack her, attacking her even though failing in attacking was a failing of the complete intelligent pride in the understanding sensitive planning attacking pride in Miss Dounor and so Miss Dounor in her living was not then completely succeeding. This is certain. There was then complete succeeding in Miss Dounor in her loving in her completely understanding desiring, in her complete intelligence of adoration, in the completion of the being then in her, there was in her then some failing that Mrs. Redfern could attack her with going on attempting desiring. This is all very certain.

Miss Dounor held Miss Charles from really touching her real being, she did not hold her from really touching Redfern's being. She never recognised this failing in herself inside her but it was a failing of the completeness of pride in her and later much later when Redfern was no longer existing in living it made them separate from one another, later it in spots made Miss Dounor bitter. Miss Charles then was not succeeding in keeping Miss Dounor with her, she was winning by not then having any remembrance in her of the trouble she had had with her. Miss Dounor then was succeeding and failing in some ways as I have been saying. There was real succeeding in her as I have been saying, there was real failing in her as I have been saying. This is all very certain. This has been some description of the being in Miss Dounor and of her failing and of her succeeding.

Miss Charles was of the kind of them the kind of men and women I know very well in living. I know very well all the varieties of this kind of them. In each kind of them they are nice ones they are those that are not such nice ones, they are pleasant ones and they are unpleasant ones, they are those having that kind of being in them so lightly it hardly then makes them that kind of them, there are then some of them having that being in them that kind of being in them so concentratedly it is a wonderful thing to see them, to see a kind of being so complete in one man or in one woman. Miss Charles was of a kind of being I know very well in living, very well indeed in living, I know very well all the varieties of the kind of being that Miss Charles was in living in all the very many millions ever living having had or having that kind of being in them. Some then of a kind of being are nice ones, some of that kind of them are not very nice ones, some of that kind of them are not at all nice ones. Some of a kind of them are nice ones of that kind of them and then they have a mixture in them of other kinds of being in them and then that one is not a nice one though that one has a nice kind of one kind of being in that one. That often makes one a very puzzling one to every one. There are then all kinds of ways of being one kind of them in men and women. Some are a nice kind of a kind of them, and some are not a nice kind of that same kind of them. Sometimes being in one who is a nice one of a kind of them and then has other things mixed up in them is very perplexing and sometimes no one in such a one ever comes to an understanding of that one. Well then that is true then that of each kind of them there are nice ones and nice enough ones and not very nice ones, and not at all nice ones and very horrid ones. This can be in them with any strength or weakness of their kind of being in them, it is from the mixing and the accenting and relation of parts of their kind of nature in them. There is one thing very certain of each kind of them of each kind there is of men and women there are nice ones and then there are not at all nice ones of them. And about some mostly every one is agreeing and about some there is very much disagreeing and there are very many ways of feeling every one and every one has their own being in them. Yes every one has their own being in them and yes every one is right in living their own being in them and this is a very difficult thing to be realising and it is a very pleasant thing to have inside one when it comes to be really in one.

Miss Charles was of a kind of men and women I know very well in all the kind of ways of being they have in them. Miss Charles was one of the independent dependent kind of them. Miss Charles was one who was herself a very strong one in her being and it slowly came to be more and more filling inside her. Miss Charles was one who had it in her to have reaction in her to influences around her when she was younger, to desires in her, to tradition and mob action and to very many things then and they made moral aspiration in her they made a reformer of her, they made an aggressive attacking person of her and when she was a young one all this then almost completely filled her. She was as I was saying of the dependent independent kind in men and women and resisting, slow realisation was the bottom way of feeling and of fighting and of understanding in her. This came then slowly to be stronger in her, this made then of her one that could be feeling and understanding brilliant men and brilliant women, brilliant and sensitive men and brilliant and sensitive women, made her feel them then and choose them then, then when her resisting sensitive understanding had come to be more completely the whole filling in her, then when slow steady detailed domination came to be then really filling then inside her, then when reforming attacking was changed in her to the personal being that then was mostly all the filling in her. It was never all the filling in her always she had in her a little of the special reforming attacking which was re-action in her, quick reaction to things and conditions around her and always she had very much in her of the generalised moral attacking conviction that came from the generalisation of her attacking and that made a righteous moral person of her and this is a very common thing and later there will be endless discussing of the meaning of this kind of moral being in all kinds of men and women, the generalised conviction and the relation of it to the concrete living, feeling, being in them, but this will come later in the beginning of the under-standing of Alfred Hersland that will pretty soon now com-mence to be written.

Miss Charles was of the dependent independent kind of them. These have it in them then to have when they have quick reaction in them that is not a stirring from the depths of them these have it very often that this in them is a violent attacking, often continuous bragging, often moral reforming conviction, often nervous action in them, often incessant talk-ing, incessant action, incessant attacking in them and this is in those of them that are the pure thing of dependent inde-pendent being and attacking is not their way at all of winning fighting. There are some who have in them resisting being and they have in them attacking being as another nature in them but that is a different thing from this thing that I am now describing, from the being in Miss Charles. Miss Charles was completely dependent independent being, attacking was not her way of winning fighting, it was resisting as I was saying in telling what she did to win her fighting for Miss Dounor with Redfern. That was then when she was a young one when she was no longer a young one, when her own being was almost completely then her filling, when there was in her the generalised moral emotion that came from the reaction that filled her a good deal in her young living, reaction that made attacking being then in her, in her who had in her to have resisting as her way of winning fighting, that was then what gave to her then attempting dominating every one by attacking and this is a very common thing in those having in them dependent independent being, this is a very common thing in them in their young living when their real way of winning fighting has not come yet to be in them. I am not saying that those having in them dependent independent being cannot have in them religion and moral or reforming passion as the expression of the being in them, there are very many of them who have it in them as I was saying, the old man Hissen had it in him and there are very many of them of this kind of them and there are very many of many various kinds of them of the dependent independent kind of them that have religious or virtuous or moral or reforming passion in them as the whole expression of the being in them but these express this then by resisting fighting which is their way of winning fighting. As I was saying there are many having in them dependent independent being, and there are some of them who have it in them only when they are younger ones and some have it in them very strongly in them up to their ending, there are very many of them who have much attacking of quick reacting, much attacking in bragging, in being quickly certain of everything, of being very quick in judging everything and these then some of them are mostly all filled up with this kind of reacting attacking in them which is not in them their real way of winning fighting. This is a very important thing to know in men and women, a very important thing to know in them in knowing them, in judging of the power in them of succeeding or of failing in their living. The independent dependent kind in men and women can have quick reaction that is completely poignant, that is attacking, in them, that is their real way of winning fighting. Those having in them dependent independent nature in them have not real power in quick resisting, in attacking fighting, many of them have this filling them all their living, many of them have this filling them in their young living when their own way of winning fighting is not yet developed in them enough to fill them, some have almost nothing of this kind of acting in them some of the dependent independent kind of them. All this is very important, very very important, sometime there will be very very much description of every kind of being in every kind of men and women.

Miss Charles was of the kind of them the kind of men and women I know very well in living. I know very well all the varieties of this kind of them. Some of each kind there is of men and women are very nice ones of their kind of them, some of each kind there is of men and women are not nice ones at all of their kind of them. Miss Charles was not a very nice one, she was not a not nice one at all of her kind of them. Being nice or not a nice kind of one, a pleasant or unpleasant kind of one was not in her an important thing. This is a very certain thing. She was as I was saying in her younger living aggressive in her detailed and generalised conviction of morality and reformation and equalisation. Later in her living she went on in the direction she had been going but her methods then were from the being in her and that then mostly entirely filled her. That made her control everything, every one near her by steady resisting pressure and that was then the way of winning in her. Everything near her, every one near her, every detail of everything was then more or less completely owned by her. She was of the kind of them who own the thing they need for loving. Later as I was saying Miss Dounor left her, Miss Charles had a little owned Redfern almost and Miss Dounor many years later left her and Miss Charles went on always to her ending completely owning the college of Farnham.

There has been now enough description of Miss Charles. There has been enough description of Miss Dounor. There has been enough description of Miss Dounor and of Miss Charles. There will be now a very little more description of Mrs. Redfern.

At the time of the ending of the living of the Redferns at Farnham, Alfred Hersland was just coming to his marrying of Julia Dehning. The Redferns after the ending of their living at the college of Farnham never lived anywhere together again. Mrs. Redfern never understood this thing. Always she was expecting it to begin again their living together until after the complete ending of being in Redfern. That made her certain then that they would never live together again.

After the ending of their Farnham living the Redferns never lived anywhere together again. Mrs. Redfern never understood this thing. She never knew that she would not ever again have him. This never could come to be real knowledge in her and she always working at something to have him again and that was there always in her to the end of him and of her. First she was travelling and studying and then she was working to make some women understand something and many laughed at her and always she was full of desiring and always she was never understanding in desiring. When there was the end of her living with Redfern her brother Alfred was just coming to his marrying Julia Dehning. Martha was then travelling and studying and then she came back to be with her father and her mother was weakening then and later she was dead and Mr. Hersland lost his great fortune and Martha then took care of him. There will be now a little more description of her and then of her with him. There will be a little more description of her written in the history of the ending of the living in her father, in the history of the later living of her brother Alfred Hersland, in the history of her brother David Hersland. More description of her will be part of the history of the ending of the existing of the Hersland family. There will be very much history of this ending of all of them of the Hersland family written later.

There will be now a little more description written of her and of her living with her father when she came back to the family living back out of her trouble after the ending of the living in Phillip Redfern.

After the ending of the Redferns' living at Farnham the two of them, Mr. and Mrs. Redfern never lived anywhere together again. Mrs. Redfern never understood this thing. Always she was expecting it to begin again, their living together and always she was studying and preparing herself to be a companion to him in intellectual living. Always then she was studying and striving and travelling and working. And then he was dead and then she knew they would not live together again. Then she was certain of this thing.

That was her living then until he was dead and she went back to the ten acre place where then her father and mother were living and her mother was weakening then and a little while later then she died there and Martha finished her living staying with her father who had then lost his great fortune.

Disillusionment in living is finding that no one can really ever be agreeing with you completely in anything. Disillusionment then in living that gives to very many then melancholy feeling, some despairing feeling, some resignation, some fairly cheerful beginning and some a forgetting and continuing and some a dreary trickling weeping some violent attacking and some a letting themselves do anything, disillusion then is really finding, really realising, really being certain that no one really can completely agree with you in anything, that, as is very certain, not, those fighting beside you or living completely with you or anybody, really, can really be believing anything completely that you are believing. Really realising this thing, completely realising this thing is the disillusionment in living is the beginning of being an old man or an old woman is being no longer a young one no longer a young man or a young woman no longer a growing older young man or growing older young woman. This is then what every one always has been meaning by living bringing disillusion. This is the real thing of disillusion that no one, not any one really is believing, seeing, understanding, thinking anything as you are thinking, believing, seeing, understanding such a thing. This is then what disillusion is from living and slowly then after failing again and again in changing some one, after finding that some one that has been fighting for something, that every one that has been fighting something beside you for a long time that each one of them splits off from you somewhere and you must join on with new ones or go on all alone then or be a disillusioned one who is not any longer then a young one. This is then disillusionment in living and sometime in the history of David Hersland the younger son in the Hersland family living then in a part of Gossols where they alone of rich people were living there will be completely a history of the disillusionment of such a realising and the dying then of that one, of young David Hersland then.

This is then complete disillusionment in living, the complete realisation that no one can believe as you do about anything, so not really any single one and to some as I am saying this is a sad thing, to mostly every one it is sometime a shocking thing, sometimes a shocking thing, sometime a real shock to them, to mostly every one a thing that only very slowly with constant repetition is really a complete certain thing inside to give to them the being that is no longer in them really young being. This is then the real meaning of not being any longer a young one in living, the complete realising that not any one really can believe what any other one is believing and some there are, enough of them, who never have completely such a realisation, they are always hoping to find her or him, they are always changing her or him to fit them, they are always looking, they are always forgetting failing or explaining it by something, they are always going on and on in trying. There are a very great many of them who are this way to their ending. There are a very great many who are this way almost to their very ending, there are a great many men and women who have sometime in them in their living complete disillusion.

There is then as I am saying complete disillusion in living, the realising, completely realising that not any one, not one fighting for the same thinking and believing as the other, not any one has the same believing in her or in him that any other one has in them and it comes then sometime to most every one to be realising with feeling this thing and then they often stop having friendly feeling and then often they begin again but it is then a different thing between them, they are old then and not young then in their feeling.

Young ones sometimes think they have it in them, this thing, some young ones kill themselves then, stop living then, this is often happening, young ones sometimes, very often even, think they have in them this thing but they do not have it in them, mostly not any young one, as a complete realisation, this thing, they have it in them and it is sometimes, very often then an agony to them, some of them kill themselves or are killed then, but really mostly not any of them have really realised the thing, they may be dead from this thing, they have not realised the thing, it has been an awful agony in them, they have not really grasped the thing as having general human meaning, it has been a shock to them, it may perhaps even have killed completely very completely some of them, mostly then a young one has not really such a thing in them, this is pretty nearly certain, later there will be much description of disillusionment in the being of David Hersland who was always in his living as I was saying trying to be certain from day to day in his living what there was in living that could make it for him a completely necessary thing.

This is then a very little description of feeling disillusionment in living. There is this thing then there is the moment and a very complete moment to those that have had it when something they have bought or made or loved or are is a thing that they are afraid, almost certain, very fearful that no one will think it a nice thing and then some one likes that thing and this then is a very wonderful feeling to know that some one really appreciates the thing. This is a very wonderful thing, this is a thing which I will now be illustrating.

Disillusionment in living is the finding out nobody agrees with you not those that are and were fighting with you. Disillusionment in living is the finding out nobody agrees with you not those that are fighting for you. Complete disillusionment is when you realise that no one can for they can't change. The amount they agree is important to you until the amount they do not agree with you is completely realised by you. Then you say you will write for yourself and strangers, you will be for yourself and strangers and this then makes an old man or an old woman of you.

This is then one thing, another thing is the perfect joy of finding some one, any one really liking something you are liking, making, doing, being. This is another thing and a very pleasant thing, sometimes not a pleasant thing at all. That depends on many things, on some thing.

It is a very strange feeling when one is loving a clock that is to every one of your class of living an ugly and a foolish one and one really likes such a thing and likes it very much and liking it is a serious thing, or one likes a colored handkerchief that is very gay and every one of your kind of living thinks it a very ugly or a foolish thing and thinks you like it because it is a funny thing to like it and you like it with a serious feeling, or you like eating something and liking it is a childish thing to every one or you like something that is a dirty thing and no one can really like that thing or you write a book and while you write it you are ashamed for every one must think you are a silly or a crazy one and yet you write it and you are ashamed, you know you will be laughed at or pitied by every one and you have a queer feeling and you are not very certain and you go on writing. Then some one says yes to it, to something you are liking, or doing or making and then never again can you have completely such a feeling of being afraid and ashamed that you had then when you were writing or liking the thing and not any one had said yes about the thing. In a way it is a very difficult thing to like anything, to do anything. You can never have again either about something you have done or about something any one else has done the same complete feeling if some one else besides the first one sees it, some other one if you have made it, yourself if you have understood something, you can never again have the complete feeling of recognition that you have then. You can have very many kinds of feelings you can only alone and with the first one have the perfect feeling of not being almost completely filled with being ashamed and afraid to show something to like something with a really serious feeling.

I have not been very clear in this telling, it will be clearer in the description of master and schools in living and in working, and in painting and in writing and in everything.

It is a very queer thing this not agreeing with any one. It would seem that where we are each of us always telling and repeating and explaining and doing it again and again that some one would really understand what the other one is always repeating. But in loving, in working, in everything it is always the same thing. In loving some one is jealous, really jealous and it would seem an impossible thing to the one not understanding that the other one could have about such a thing a jealous feeling and they have it and they suffer and they weep and sorrow in it and the other one cannot believe it, they cannot believe the other one can really mean it and sometime the other one perhaps comes to realise it that the other one can really suffer in it and then later that one tries to reassure the other one the one that is then suffering about that thing and the other one the one that is receiving such reassuring says then, did you think I ever could believe this thing, no I have no fear of such a thing, and it is all puzzling, to have one kind of feeling, a jealous feeling, and not have a fear in them that the other one does not want them, it is a very mixing thing and over and over again when you are certain it is a whole one some one, one must begin again and again and the only thing that is a help to one is that there is really so little fundamental changing in any one and always every one is repeating big pieces of them and so sometimes perhaps some one will know something and I certainly would like very much to be that one and so now to begin.

All this leads again to kinds in men and women. This then will be soon now a description of difference in men and women morally and intellectually in them between concrete acting, thinking and feeling in them and generalised acting, thinking and feeling in them.

Many women and men have a completely sure feeling in them. Many men and women have certain feeling with something inside them.

Many have a very certain feeling about something inside them. Many need company for it, this is very common, many need a measure for it, this will need explaining, some need drama to support it, some need lying to help it, some are not letting their right hand know what their left hand is doing with it, some love it, some hate it, some never are very certain they really have it, some only think they love it, some like the feeling of loving it they would have if they could have it. Some have a feeling they would have it if they had their life to live over again and they sigh about it. Certain feeling in men and women is very interesting.

As I was saying in many there is the slow reacting, slow expressing being that comes more and more in their living to determine them. There are in many of such ones aspirations and convictions due to quick reactions to others around them, to books they are reading, to the family tradition, to the spirit of the age in educating, in believing, to the lack of power of articulating the being in them that makes them need then to be filled full with other reactions in them so that they will then have something. Some of such of them spend all their living in adjusting the being that comes to active condition inside them in their living to the being they have come to be in living from all being that has been affecting them in all their living, some of such of them want a little in them to create their living from the being inside them and they have not the power in them for this thing, they go on then living the being of every one that has been making them. It is a wonderful thing how very much it has to be in one, how it needs to be so strongly in one anything, how much it needs to be in one anything so that thing is a thing that comes then to be done, it is a wonderful thing how very much it needs to be in one anything, any little any big thing so that that thing will be done by that one. It is a wonderful thing as I was saying and I am now repeating, it is a wonderful thing how much a thing needs to be in one as a desire in them how much courage any one must have in them to be doing anything if they are a first one, if it is something no one is thinking is a serious thing, if it is the buying of a clock one is very much liking and everybody is thinking it an ugly or a foolish one and the one wanting it has for it a serious feeling and no one can think that one is buying it for anything but as doing a funny thing. It is a hard thing to be loving something with a serious feeling and every one is thinking that only a servant girl could be loving such a thing, it is a hard thing then to buy that thing. It is a very wonderful thing how much courage it takes to buy and use them and like them bright colored handkerchiefs when every one having good taste is using white ones or pale colored ones when a bright colored one gives to the one buying them so much pleasure that that one suffers always at not having them when that one has not bought one of such of them. It is a very difficult thing to have your being in you so that you will be doing something, anything you are wanting, having something anything you are wanting when you have plenty of money for the buying, in clocks in handkerchiefs, so that you will be thinking, feeling anything that you are needing feeling, thinking, so that you will be having aspirations that are really of a thing filling you with meaning, so that you will be having really in you in liking a real feeling of satisfaction. It is very hard to know what you are liking, whether you are not really liking something that is a low thing to yourself then, it is a very difficult thing to get the courage to buy the kind of clock or handkerchiefs you are loving when every one thinks it is a silly thing, when every one thinks you are doing it for the joke of the thing. It is hard then to know whether you are really loving that thing. It takes very much courage to do anything connected with your being that is not a serious thing. It takes courage to be doing a serious thing that is connected with one's being that is certain. In some, expressing their being needs courage, in foolish ways, ways that are foolish ones to every one else, in them. It is a very difficult thing to have courage to buy clocks and handkerchiefs you are loving, you are seriously appreciating, with which you have very seriously pleasure with enjoying and everybody is thinking then that you are joking. It is a very difficult thing to have courage for that which no one is thinking is a serious thing.

Some have a measure in living and some do not have any measure to determine them. Many in their living are determined by the measure of some one, they are to themselves to be like some one or very near to what that one is for them, they are like some one or are something like some one, they have then a measure by which they can determine what they are to be, to do in living. Such then are always followers in living, many of such of them have their own being in them, all of such of them have some being in them, all of such of them have a measure that determines them, they are themselves inside them, they need only come very near doing, being some certain thing which is established already as a standard for them by some one who did not have any standard to make her or him some one and that one is a master and the others having themselves inside them and such a one as a measure for them are schoolmen, and now there will be very little description of these things in men and women for it is something that is important in the being in David Hersland the second son. The important thing now to be discussing is concrete and abstract aspiration, concrete and generalised action in many men and women of very many kinds of them and now that will be a beginning of discussing the feeling in each one of being a bad one, of being a good one, the relation of aspiration and action, of generalised and concrete aspiration and action.

It happens very often that a man has it in him, that a man does something, that he does it very often, that he does many things, when he is a young one and an older one and an old one. It happens very often that a man does something, that a man has something in him and he does a thing again and again in his living. There was a man who was always writing to his daughter that she should not do things that were wrong that would disgrace him, she should not do such things and in every letter that he wrote to her he told her she should not do such things, that he was her father and was giving good moral advice to her and always he wrote to her in every letter that she should not do things that she should not do anything that would disgrace him. He wrote this in every letter he wrote to her, he wrote very nicely to her, he wrote often enough to her and in every letter he wrote to her that she should not do anything that was a disgraceful thing for her to be doing and then once she wrote back to him that he had not any right to write moral things in letters to her, that he had taught her that he had shown her that he had commenced in her the doing the things things that would disgrace her and he had said then when he had begun with her he had said he did it so that when she was older she could take care of herself with those who wished to make her do things that were wicked things and he would teach her and she would be stronger than such girls who had not any way of knowing better, and she wrote this letter and her father got the letter and he was a paralytic always after, it was a shock to him getting such a letter, he kept saying over and over again that his daughter was trying to kill him and now she had done it and at the time he got the letter he was sitting by the fire and he threw the letter in the fire and his wife asked him what was the matter and he said it is Edith she is killing me, what, is she disgracing us said the mother, no said the father, she is killing me and that was all he said then of the matter and he never wrote another letter.

It happens very often that a man has it in him, that a man does something, that he does it very often that he does many things, when he is a young man, when he is an old man, when he is an older man. Some kind of young men do things because they are so good then they want every one to be wise enough to take care of themselves and so they do some things to them. This is very common and these then are very often good enough kind of young men who are very good men in their living. There will soon be a little description of one of them. There are then very many men and there is then from the generalised virtue and concrete action that is from the nature of them that might make one think they were hypocrites in living but they are not although certainly there are in living some men wanting to deceive other men but this is not true of this kind of them. One of such of these kind of them had a little boy and this one, the little son wanted to make a collection of butterflies and beetles and it was all exciting to him and it was all arranged then and then the father said to the son you are certain this is not a cruel thing that you are wanting to be doing, killing things to make collections of them, and the son was very disturbed then and they talked about it together the two of them and more and more they talked about it then and then at last the boy was convinced it was a cruel thing and he said he would not do it and his father said the little boy was a noble boy to give up pleasure when it was a cruel one. The boy went to bed then and then the father when he got up in the early morning saw a wonderfully beautiful moth in the room and he caught him and he killed him and he pinned him and he woke up his son then and showed it to him and he said to him "see what a good father I am to have caught and killed this one," the boy was all mixed up inside him and then he said he would go on with his collecting and that was all there was then of discussing and this is a little description of something that happened once and it is very interesting.

Curiosity and suspicion these two things are often very interesting, this one that I am now beginning describing had these very completely in him, and always then this one had these more simply in him than any one knowing him was realising, he had inquisitiveness in him for the mere satisfaction of asking and knowing, he had suspicion in him because suspicious feeling was a pleasant feeling in him, he used inquisitiveness and suspicion in living, that is certain, no one knowing him could deny that of him, but often he was not using such things, he was just inquiring, he was just asking because his attention was caught and he liked to know everything and he liked asking and often suspicion was in him because suspicion was an easy way to be feeling for him about everything and a very pleasant feeling to have inside him. This one was of the resisting slightly engulfing kind in men and women, resisting and engulfing was equally in him. In many I have been describing engulfing is stronger than resisting, in this one resisting and engulfing was pretty nearly equally divided in him, he was thick but not too thick not too dry in his being, he could take complete impression from everything he was learning, he was always asking, he was continually suspecting, he was quite successful in living. This is now to be a little a description of the questions he was always asking, of the suspicion always in him.

Some men and women are inquisitive about everything, they are always asking, if they see any one with anything they ask what is that thing, what is it you are carrying, what are you going to be doing with that thing, why have you that thing, where did you get that thing, how long will you have that thing, there are very many men and women who want to know about anything about everything. I am such a one, I certainly am such a one. A very great many like to know a good many things, a great many are always asking questions of every one, a great many are to very many doing this with intention, a great many have intention in their asking, a great many just have their attention caught by anything and then they ask the question. Some when they are hearing any one talking are immediately listening, many would like to know what is in letters others are writing and receiving, a great many quite honest ones are always wanting to know everything, a great many men and women have a good deal suspicion in them about others and this has in them not any very precise meaning. A great many are liking to know things but do not do much asking, a great many have not any such a feeling. A great many have a very great deal of suspiciousness in them, a great many have almost not any of this being in them. This one that I am now describing was one who was always asking and mostly always every one was wondering what was this one meaning by the questions he was asking and often later this one would perhaps be using information he had had from asking questions but asking questions in him was not a thing in him that came from wanting to be using some time information he was gathering, very often asking questions in him was simply from a catching of his attention by something. Once this one asked some one he was visiting, just suddenly—and this door here does that lead into the hall or directly out into the garden—and that was all he said then about this thing and afterwards every one was thinking he would be using this against them but really then this one was wondering did the door lead to the hall or directly to a garden. If such a one, one having this kind of a way is of the resisting engulfing type and fairly successful in living and slow and sudden and quite suspicious of every one, almost certainly then every one will think it to be true of such a one that this one always is asking questions for purposes of winning, perhaps of cheating, certainly for some distant manoeuvering. This is very common. There are very many having in them rather engulfing rather resisting being who are slow and sudden, who are a little absent when any one is asking them anything, who are suspicious and quite trusting, who are often asking questions for in their being being in slow action and always more or less moving they have it that their attention is always a little wandering waiting for something inside them to do something and so then these of them are very busy having their attention caught by anything and asking questions about everything and very often every one knowing such of them are very suspicious of them and mostly these then too have constant suspicion in them as constant as the questioning in them. This is very common then with this kind of being. I am not yet through with my description of this kind of resisting engulfing men and women.

A great many men and women have very much suspicion in them of everything of every one. A great many men a great many women have steadily suspicion in them of everything of every one. A great many have this in them from the beginning of living in them. A great many very many of the resisting, dependent independent very earthy men and women have complete suspicion, little steady suspicion of everything of every one always in them. They do not have it from experiencing in them they have it in them as a natural thing, they have it in them like a child walking and certain that every step they are going to be tumbling. This is very common, very many men very many women very many having resisting being in them have it in them to be suspicious always of every one of everything. This is in them very often when they are quite kindly quite trusting, very many then having resisting being have it to have very naturally in them always in them always steadily in them from their beginning that they are suspicious of every one of everything, always suspicious always steadily suspicious inside them, this one then that I am describing has suspicion always in him, there will be now a description of several of this kind in men and women. I am now going on with my description of one, who was naturally a completely suspicious one.

Many having resisting being have it in them all their living when they are beginning and then on to their ending have it to have suspicion always naturally in them and this is a natural thing for them to have in them because they having resisting being have it in them to be knowing that always some one is doing attacking. Resisting being in them is in meaning that always some one some where is attacking, resisting being is in them in some of them, in very many men in very many women as having in them completely naturally always very much suspicion. Very many men and women have in them completely all their living very complete suspicious feeling very many men and women with resisting being. Very many men and women with attacking being have suspicion in them completely in them, sometime I will be telling very much of them. Very many men and women have hardly any kind of suspicious feeling ever in them. There are very many ways of having suspicious feeling many kinds of ways many degrees of such feeling, now I am giving a not very long description of one having in him very complete suspicious feeling, very much suspicious feeling about men, very much very complete suspicious feeling about women and this one was quite a successful one in living and this one had very much inquisitive feeling in him and this one was pretty completely resisting in his being pretty completely engulfing in his being and always very many felt it about him that every bit of asking in him and every bit of suspicion in him was really deep wisdom in him and always then he had completely resisting being in him completely engulfing being in him, complete suspicion in him, complete inquisitiveness inside him, and always then he had enthusiasm and very much feeling about something and always he was asking about everything and always he was having suspicious feeling in him and altogether he was sufficiently a wise one, and very often he was just asking because he saw something and very often he was just suspecting because he had resisting being in him. This is one then that is to me a completely interesting one. Every one is to me a completely interesting one, this one is to me very completely an interesting one. I like feeling the being in this one, sometime yes certainly sometime I will be telling all the feeling I have in the complete being in this one. As I am saying suspicious feeling is very interesting, very very interesting. Sometime later I will tell very much about one kind of them of the resisting kind of them that have it in them to have suspicious feeling as a completely interesting thing in them. I hope I will not be beginning now to tell about this kind of them. Perhaps I will tell a little about such of them in among this considerable number of men and women of the resisting kind of them I am just now describing. I really do not want to begin now about them. I will not begin now about them that is certain. I will completely understand them later and will be telling then about them. I certainly will not write anything now about them. That is now certain. I have been writing now about a considerable number of the considerable number I am now describing of the resisting kind of them. I will now begin a pretty short description of another one of them. That is to be a little description of one having rich resisting being and being a little too quick perhaps quite a little too quick in ripening. This one had in him quite some inquisitiveness in him, not any suspicion in him. This is to be now quite a short description of him.

This one then as I am saying was of the resisting kind of them, that is to say resisting was the way of winning in him, that is to say this one was in a way slow in reacting, that is to say this one in a way was needing to own those this one needed for loving, this was all true and this was all not true of this one and this one was completely of resisting being, this one was all made completely all of only resisting being. This one then really was very early a completely highly developed one, this one was very flowing in the completely creating power this one had inside him, this one was a quite inquisitive one, this one had hardly any suspiciousness in natural ordinary daily living in him, this one was really not owning the one this one needed for his loving. This one as I was saying was of the resisting kind of them, not of the engulfing kind of them, of completely sensitively resisting being and the resisting being and sensitive being was pretty nearly equal in this one, it was pretty nearly as sensitive as resisting but not quite completely so in this one it was a little more sensitive than resisting and so this one was quick in developing early in flowering and this one was always trying to be a slower one and this one really never was in living a really slow one. This one was as I was saying not a suspicious one, resisting being was not strongly enough in him as protecting to give to him a suspicious feeling toward everything and every one. This one was not really owning the one this one needed for his loving. This one could only own one this one needed for loving by getting rid of the one this one needed for loving and then this one would not be having the one this one needed for loving and then where was this one, he was where he needed the one he needed for loving and taking her back again made him then lose the power of owning this one, the only way he could own this one was by getting rid of this one or by secretly letting some other one love him, in this way then this one to himself inside him could own the one he needed for loving. He really could own the one he needed for loving by sending her away from him, he then did not have near him the one he needed for loving, to himself inside him then he could own that one by letting, by making some other one love him and mostly then he dreamed of this thing, he did this thing. This is now a clear complete description of one having resisting being.

This is now to be a description of another one having resisting being, not engulfing resisting being, just resisting being, this one was a very nice one, a very pleasant gentle, sensitive, fairly resisting, sometimes angrily resisting one, this one had some suspicion in her in living, this one could have very often an injured feeling, this one had quite a good deal of inquisitive feeling in her, this one needed to own to a considerable degree those this one needed for loving, this one had children and children were to this one a piece of her cut off from her that were as it were equal to her and she was as they were, the same in living, thinking, feeling and being. This one as I was saying was a gentle, often injured, fairly angrily resisting one, quite inquisitive, with enough suspicious feeling to be defending other ones when it was not at all her business to be interfering and so this one a very nice a completely in a way honest one could do something that was not a pretty thing for this one to be doing. This is what this one did once in her living.

This one that I have been describing had not real suspicious feeling, this one was of the resisting kind of them but this one had very much more sensitiveness than resisting being was in this one not a kind of thing to make of this one really a suspicious one. This being in this one resisting being in this one was in this one a sense of really being gently minute by minute in living and so this one when this one was adding up anything would always be adding it by one and one and one. This one had it to be very careful in living and always this one would be counting everything by one and one and one. Counting everything this one was spending by one and one and one and one and one and one was in this one resisting being was in this one recognition of real existing of everything. This one could have very much injured feeling, this one could have injured feeling very often could have it for herself for other ones for any one and this one sometimes was very mixed up in doing anything by injured feeling for one and not for another one and for that other one then and for this one herself this one inside this one then and this one then was sufficiently complicated by injured feeling inside this one and injured feeling was the only complicated thing in the being and in the living of this one. This one was as I was saying a very gentle a very sensitive one, this one was a resisting one, this one was not at all an engulfing one, this one from the mixing of a little softly resisting being and very much gentle and sensitive being had in this one suspicion only as injured feeling. Some having this kind of being and having sensitiveness not delicately and sensitively in them and resisting slightly engulfing in them are completely suspicious and completely injured always in their living and these very often have it in them to having being persecuted as a mania in them. There are very many having such being in them, later I will be telling a few little things that sometimes are happening in living in the living of this kind of men this kind of women. As I was saying this one I am now just a little describing was not at all not even a little bit an engulfing one, this one was a softly resisting one a really earthy one really feeling always in living that existing anything existing is really there in being and always this one was doing all the counting this one ever was doing by counting one and then one and then one and then one. This one as I was saying had not really suspicious being, this one as I was saying had much and quite often very warmly really injured feeling, for herself in herself, for some other one, for any other one and this injured feeling was in the being of this one the only complication. Once some one, a young cousin, this one I am describing was then coming to the beginning of the middle living in this one, once a young cousin told this one, the cousin was very fond of this one, that the cousin never wanted to be eating dinner at the house of another one another cousin of this one, that he liked very much indeed being with his cousin but he did not like it at all for a place to be dining, this was then all that was said just then. Later then the first cousin the one that said this to the one I have been describing, asked this cousin who had just come to be engaged to be married then to come and take dinner with him. This one then the cousin asked to dine by the other cousin of the one I am describing happened to mention to the one I am describing that he was going to be dining next week with this cousin. This one I am now describing had then completely inside this one an injured feeling for this one that was going to be dining with the other one that this one should be going to be dining with the other one when the other one would not dine with that one because it was not a pleasant thing and so this one I am describing told the one going to be dining with the other one what that one had said about dining with him. Then of course this one would not dine with the other one. And all this came from there being in this one I am describing a soft resisting, a gentle sensitive being with not any suspiciousness in being and not any engulfing and not any

egotism so that this one had to have in this one that everything that could be aggression or suspicion or worldliness in
living or individual feeling was in this one injured feeling, a
very little angry and a very much hurt feeling and so this one
had injured feeling quite often and very much for this one,
for some other one, for any other one.

I will describe now very little a very different kind of one
from that one I have been just describing. There will not be
then very many more of them of the considerable number left
then. There will perhaps then still be left about six of them,
six kinds of them and perhaps there will be added a few more
to make another generalisation but really there have been
already done a considerable part of the considerable number
of the resisting kind of them that I am now describing.

This one then is quite a different kind of a one from the
last one I was describing. This one as a whole one is like a
cannon-ball living on a bag of cotton, the cannon-ball lying
on a cotton bag as a complete thing was the whole of this one.
This is in a way a description of this one, there will be now
a very little more description of this one.

Children are always thinking are very often thinking that
their mothers are very lovely looking and that is very often
because mostly the child is always close up to the mother
close to her when the child is looking and mostly being close
like that as a habitual thing is to find that one a lovely thing
a lovely looking one.

This one that I was saying was a whole one which was like
a cannon-ball resting on a bag of cotton was the cotton part
finding the cannon-ball lovely looking being always so close
to that thing and the cannon-ball was finding the cotton lovely
looking that being so closely always to that thing. To explain
then. This one then was one having solid enough dull not
very lively, not lively at all fairly dry resisting bottom, a
bottom that might have been engulfing if it had been a lively
dark wet thing, but this was not true of it then at all that it
was engulfing, it was entirely not engulfing. As I was saying
many having engulfing being and not having resisting being
enough in them are very aspiring and this one then had
aspiration like what might have been engulfing in the bottom

being which was not at all engulfing. Some of this kind of
them have it as a bottom being something that is more nearly
engulfing and these then have more active aspiration as ambition, these have then more nearly some power of very
nearly engulfing something but this one was as little engulfing
as such a kind of them can be in living, just as amiable and
ideal in aspiration and aspiration in this one as I was saying
was like the cannon-ball resting on the bag of cotton, it was
completely beautiful always to all that cotton and this one
was always living near light and beauty near to the aspiration,
the cannon-ball and this one was then as I was saying amiable
in intention and clear and large worded and hesitating in expression. This one is an interesting enough one. I am knowing quite well three of these of them, one is more nearly
engulfing, one has of him the very largest size in bags of
cotton, one and this is the one I am realising in now describing was a little skimped in the cotton foundation. This is not
a funny description, I was not certain I should say anything
of the cannon-ball and the cotton, I was almost certain I
would not say anything in this description about the cannon-
ball and the cotton, it was not in me a natural way of conceiving any one, some one conceived this one as a cannon-
ball resting on a bag of cotton, I used that in my description,
this is not to me a natural way of talking, I have been using
it here as I am saying. Now I will begin describing another
one and that will be leaving only a few more to be describing
of the considerable number of them that I have been describing of the resisting kind of them. This one that I am now
beginning describing is of the resisting and sensitive and
suspicious kind of them and now I will be telling a few stories
about such of them.

It is very hard with some to be realising what kind they
are this kind of them when they are quite old ones. It is a
very difficult thing to be realising of some kinds of them one
has been knowing before the beginning of their middle living
what they are as old ones, these in living. When one is oneself a fairly old one, one will be knowing a little more perhaps
of this thing, one is knowing a little of something of this thing
from old relations one is knowing and one knowing all the

family of these then is perhaps a little knowing what these are as younger ones in living. These that I am now describing are a kind of them that when they are old ones no one is paying much attention to them. They have then as old ones the same being in them I am now describing, they are mostly not any too successfully living all their living, they have when they are old ones the same being in them, mostly then not very many then are paying much attention to them then, these when they are old ones in living, these that I am now describing.

These then that I am now describing are a kind of them that have sensitiveness that is complete suspicion in them, these are of the kind of them that are themselves completely important to themselves inside them, they have resistance in them much less than sensitiveness as suspicion in them. Suspicion in these of them comes out of the sensitiveness of them before the sensitiveness in them gives to them inside them really an emotion and so in these in living suspicion is as it were the whole of them, the complete emotion always in them. This sensitiveness in them that is in them a suspicion before it is an emotion in them from anything is always every moment in such of them. That these have it in them that sensitiveness makes for them suspicion before they have from anything a complete emotion is the reason that these mostly are not very successful in living, they are a little successful many of them and when they are older ones or old ones, no one, not any one is paying much attention to them. These then in a way are not really earthy, not really resisting, not at all engulfing, these then in a way are not certain that dead is dead, that things really are existing, these can have superstition and religion and prudence and fear and almost a crazy kind of thinking in them. This is now some stories about some of them.

I feel it and I brood over it and it comes then very simply from me, do you see how simply it comes out of me, you see, I feel it and I think about it and then I know it and I know then it is a simple thing, why are you always saying then it is a complicated one when really it is a very simple one this thing, do you see now it is a very simple thing this thing, do you see that this is a simple thing like everything why then should you make of it a complicated thing when it is a simple thing, do you see now that it is a simple thing this thing, why do you make everything a complicated thing, do you see, this is a simple thing, everything is a simple thing, you make everything a complicated thing when everything is a simple thing, do you see, it is a simple thing, you say it is a complicated thing, do you see, everything is a simple thing that is certain, do you see, that is certain. Very many are always saying this thing, it is very common, to be certain, to be really certain that some one is really feeling thinking seeing that that one is really feeling thinking seeing what that one really is seeing feeling thinking is certainly a quite rare thing. Mostly then it is a difficult thing, a patient solemn thing to be really certain that any one is really feeling seeing thinking believing what that one in the way that one really is feeling thinking seeing believing is feeling thinking seeing believing anything. These then I am now describing who are completely for themselves suspicious ones, who have it in them to have emotion in them become suspicion before it is a real emotion of anything for anything about anything in them, these have it completely to be certain that every one is doing feeling seeing the thing that one is feeling doing seeing believing when such a one is not agreeing with them, when such a one is feeling thinking believing doing anything that such a one is doing that thing for a mean or wicked or jealous or stupid or obstinate or cursed or religious reason, it is not a real feeling believing seeing realising, that this one having suspicion in him is certain. One of such a kind of one once liked very well some one and then that one forgot to give this one five cents that this one had paid for that one and then this one hated that one, had no trust in that one for this one was certain that that one knowing that this one was too sensitive to be asking did not think it necessary to pay that one, he never could believe that any one forgot such a thing. This is an extreme thing of a way of feeling that is common to all of these of them. Another one once was always certain that some one who one time told him that he would sometime later be successful in teaching meant it that he would not be successful in painting and that this was because that one was jealous of this one although that one had just met this one. This one was certain that every one sometime would do a mean thing to him and always each one to him sometime did this thing. Once one said to him I hope you will be successful in the city where you are going to earn your living. That means that you think my way of working rotten, you know very well no one making a living there is doing good work to your thinking, it would be a better thing to say what you are thinking straight out, said this one. One of such a kind of them was always asking and always getting and always he was certain that every one was doing the thing they were doing because they wanted to make of him a poor thing and some of such of them are always having difficulty with partners and others and any one and then as I am saying when they are older ones not any one pays very much attention to them. These are some and more or less like them are very many a very great many always living who have it in them that anything to them makes an emotion that is suspicion before it is real emotion in them.

In some connected with them, sensitiveness that in these I have been just describing turns into suspicion before it is sensation or emotion about a person, a thing done, or anything, in these turns into cleverness in them or self-protection in the sense of doing nothing and breaking all engagements and giving up all obligation. In some it turns before it is really a sensation into a sensual passion. This is all very interesting surely to any one really believing really being certain completely certain that different ones are different in kind from other kinds of them are really different in experiencing. This is in a way a very difficult thing to really truly believe in one, that some one really has a completely different kind of a way of feeling a thing from another one. Mostly every one in practical living needs only to be completely realising their own experiencing and then need only to be realising other ones experiencing enough to be using them, the ones experiencing. It is a very difficult thing to really believe it of another one what the other one is really feeling, it is such a very long learning anybody must be having to be really to be actually believing this thing. I do this thing. I am a rare one, I know this always more in living. I know always more in living that other ones are really believing what they are believing, feeling, what they are feeling, thinking, what they are thinking, always more and more in living I know I am a rare one. There are not very many having this very completely really in them.

To go on now then describing a little more some of these I have been last mentioning. Some of these are having their sensitiveness making of them clever, or self-protecting, or sexually wanting anything, without having really emotion from the thing from the sensitiveness in them. These are of the resisting kind of them and might to some seem to be engulfing but they are not really resisting or engulfing. Sensitiveness turns into suspicion, cleverness, self-protection, sexual action before it comes as an emotion and these mostly then never have sensitiveness in them leading to emotion by reaction to a person or thing or action. These then are interesting. To be telling then now a little more of some of them.

These then all of them have it in them that everything turns inside them to suspicion, to cleverness, to self-protection, to sexual emotion, to sensibility of a kind that is a thing that is called sentimental, before it comes to produce emotion from the thing about the thing in relation to the thing itself inside them. There is one, I knew this one quite very well once and last week again I was seeing this one and now I am quite a good deal understanding this one, this is one and in this one everything was in this one sensibility of a sentimental kind, this was in this one not very much as suspicion as I was saying it is in some, and in this one everything, nothing had any meaning excepting as arousing a feeling of sentimental sensibility that was the same thing whatever was the thing that came to this one as touching this one. This one was pretty completely to every one completely socially one and this is quite a common thing. Sometime a history of her and her two mothers and her sister will be written and I have been telling that it will be written to several of them. She was as I was saying completely such a one and as a younger one was sharp and interesting and then she was a married one and then

she was large and dull. This was after she succeeded fairly
at the beginning of her middle living in coming to be a
married one. She had not then any reaction at all in living
for she was then in her married living living with bottom
being reacting and there was no bottom being in her, living,
at all in her then and every one said it was such a surprising
thing that she should be then so completely a submissive and
indifferent and inefficient and a little a timid one then when she
had been before her being a married one so altogether an emotional and dark, expressive and clever one but it was just this
thing that I am saying that I am now pretty well understanding
that makes it a completely a natural thing, she had not ever
had anything that did not turn to sensibility before it reached
her in her and when she was a tired one and married and
fatter then there was not this then. She is an interesting one,
really she is a very interesting one, she is quite a pretty ugly
one now but not in any way now an active one as now I am
completely realising. It is an interesting history the history
of all of this kind of them. It is a very interesting thing the
history of this one. The complete family living of this one is a
thing I could make a remarkably interesting thing to any one,
that is certain. I have been telling that to this one. This one
did not like very much to hear me say that thing, it is a certain
thing that it is an interesting thing to me and I could tell it
so to every one, I have been telling it to this one that I can
make it a completely interesting thing. This one was not
liking it very well then. Sometime I will be feeling completely
the telling of it and then I will be telling it, I have told this
one that I will tell it then. This one will not know then it is
this one. That is the very nice thing in this writing. Sometime I will tell everything, everything. Mostly I do tell anything.

One of this kind of them I have been describing has it that
everything is in her as cleverness, or self-protection from any
stimulation, never an emotion about a thing. This one would,
if she could, have real emotion but it never is even a little bit
in her of herself, inside her. Sometimes it is, a moment, a
real feeling in her, something from something, when it is
made to be in her by some one by force holding her from

having it turn into cleverness, suspicion, sentimental believing, self-protection and so giving it a chance to sink into her
so that she has a reaction to it really in her. This has a few
times happened to her. This one is always feeling that some
one should do this for her. Holding her from being her way
in her so that emotion can be in her has been done for her.
She never can do this for herself, ever. She is in her feeling
certain that every one in this way should be doing for her.
She is all her living needing that some one do this thing. She
has it in her as a feeling that the world owes it to her to do
this for her. She has not ever any really grateful feeling, she
has only the emotion that some one wins in her for her. It
is an interesting game to play in her and very many do it for
her. Then they lose the power and she has to have another.
She does not know that she is certain that the world owes this
to her.

This one then would have it in her to be certain that to be
dead was not to be at all really a dead one, this was what this
one wanted to have in her as realisation, as emotion, this conviction is what this one was very certain the world owed her.
This is what this one wanted that she should have in her, have
as emotion inside her, this emotion in her is what every one
knowing should do for her inside her. Very many coming to
know her tried to give it to her, always she was wanting to
have this inside her, the conviction, the emotion that to be
dead was not to be really a dead one. This was the history of
the living in her. She had in her as I was saying to have it
that nothing gave to her really an emotion about that thing.
Every thing touching her aroused in her suspicion, cleverness
and self-protection. She wanted to have conviction and emotion that to be dead is not to be really truly a dead one. She
wanted this in her, this realisation and emotion, in her, and
then too she would be certain, she knew then she would then
be really certain completely certain that every one was a very
much better one than each one really was in living. She was
certain, pretty nearly certain that if she were really completely
certain that she was really knowing that to be dead was not
to be at all a really dead one she would then be knowing that
every one living was really a very much better one than each

one really is living and this would be a very pleasant feeling for her to be having. Always then she was needing to be completely certain that she was really knowing that to be dead was not to be really at all a dead one and always she was unconsciously feeling that the world owed it to her to give her this realisation. This was a history of her. Perhaps she never came really to have it in her, perhaps she came to have it a little in her, always some one was working in her for her, this is a history of her. This is an amusing thing, this history of this one. Sometime a very detailed history of this one will be an amusing thing to be writing, to be reading. Now I will not tell any more detail of this one.

THREE PORTRAITS
OF PAINTERS

CEZANNE

MATISSE

PICASSO

The portraits of Matisse and Picasso were originally published in the August, 1912, issue of CAMERA WORK *and later were reprinted in* PORTRAITS AND PRAYERS, *1934. Stieglitz told me that he had accepted them for publication as soon as he had looked them over, principally because he did not immediately understand them. These portraits, the earliest examples of Gertrude Stein's "difficult" work to reach the public, were much commented on and satirized. In* LECTURES IN AMERICA *she has explained: "I continued to do what I was doing in* THE MAKING OF AMERICANS, *I was doing what the cinema was doing, I was making a continuous succession of the statement of what that person was until I had not many things but one thing."*

[CEZANNE]

The Irish lady can say, that to-day is every day. Caesar can say that every day is to-day and they say that every day is as they say.

In this way we have a place to stay and he was not met because he was settled to stay. When I said settled I meant settled to stay. When I said settled to stay I meant settled to stay Saturday. In this way a mouth is a mouth. In this way if in as a mouth if in as a mouth where, if in as a mouth where and there. Believe they have water too. Believe they have that water too and blue when you see blue, is all blue precious too, is all that that is precious too is all that and they meant to absolve you. In this way Cezanne nearly did nearly in this way. Cezanne nearly did nearly did and nearly did. And was I surprised. Was I very surprised. Was I surprised. I was surprised and in that patient, are you patient when you find bees. Bees in a garden make a specialty of honey and so does honey. Honey and prayer. Honey and there. There where the grass can grow nearly four times yearly.

[MATISSE]

One was quite certain that for a long part of his being one being living he had been trying to be certain that he was wrong in doing what he was doing and then when he could not come to be certain that he had been wrong in doing what he had been doing, when he had completely convinced himself that he would not come to be certain that he had been wrong in doing what he had been doing he was really certain then that he was a great one and he certainly was a great one. Certainly every one could be certain of this thing that this one is a great one.

Some said of him, when anybody believed in him they did

not then believe in any other one. Certainly some said this of him.

He certainly very clearly expressed something. Some said that he did not clearly express anything. Some were certain that he expressed something very clearly and some of such of them said that he would have been a greater one if he had not been one so clearly expressing what he was expressing. Some said he was not clearly expressing what he was expressing and some of such of them said that the greatness of struggling which was not clear expression made of him one being a completely great one.

Some said of him that he was greatly expressing something struggling. Some said of him that he was not greatly expressing something struggling.

He certainly was clearly expressing something, certainly sometime any one might come to know that of him. Very many did come to know it of him that he was clearly expressing what he was expressing. He was a great one. Any one might come to know that of him. Very many did come to know that of him. Some who came to know that of him, that he was a great one, that he was clearly expressing something, came then to be certain that he was not greatly expressing something being struggling. Certainly he was expressing something being struggling. Any one could be certain that he was expressing something being struggling. Some were certain that he was greatly expressing this thing. Some were certain that he was not greatly expressing this thing. Every one could come to be certain that he was a great man. Any one could come to be certain that he was clearly expressing something.

Some certainly were wanting to be needing to be doing what he was doing, that is clearly expressing something. Certainly they were willing to be wanting to be a great one. They were, that is some of them, were not wanting to be needing expressing anything being struggling. And certainly he was one not greatly expressing something being struggling, he was a great one, he was clearly expressing something. Some were wanting to be doing what he was doing that is clearly expressing something. Very many were doing what he was doing, not greatly expressing something being struggling. Very many were wanting to be doing what he was doing were not wanting to be expressing anything being struggling.

There were very many wanting to be doing what he was doing that is to be one clearly expressing something. He was certainly a great man, any one could be really certain of this thing, every one could be certain of this thing. There were very many who were wanting to be ones doing what he was doing that is to be ones clearly expressing something and then very many of them were not wanting to be being ones doing that thing, that is clearly expressing something, they wanted to be ones expressing something being struggling, something being going to be some other thing, something being going to be something some one sometime would be clearly expressing and that would be something that would be a thing then that would then be greatly expressing some other thing then that thing, certainly very many were then not wanting to be doing what this one was doing clearly expressing something and some of them had been ones wanting to be doing that thing wanting to be ones clearly expressing something. Some were wanting to be ones doing what this one was doing wanted to be ones clearly expressing something. Some of such of them were ones certainly clearly expressing something, that was in them a thing not really interesting then any other one. Some of such of them went on being all their living ones wanting to be clearly expressing something and some of them were clearly expressing something.

This one was one very many were knowing some and very many were glad to meet him, very many sometimes listened to him, some listened to him very often, there were some who listened to him, and he talked then and he told them then that certainly he had been one suffering and he was then being one trying to be certain that he was wrong in doing what he was doing and he had come then to be certain that he never would be certain that he was doing what it was wrong for him to be doing then and he was suffering then and he was certain that he would be one doing what he was doing and he was certain that he should be one doing what he was doing and he was certain that he would always be one suffering and this then made him certain this, that he would always be one being suffering, this made him certain that he was expressing something being struggling and certainly very many were quite certain that he was greatly expressing something being struggling. This one was knowing some who were listening to him and he was telling very often about being one suffering and this was not a dreary thing to any one hearing that then, it was not a saddening thing to any one hearing it again and again, to some it was quite an interesting thing hearing it again and again, to some it was an exciting thing hearing it again and again, some knowing this one and being certain that this one was a great man and was one clearly expressing something were ones hearing this one telling about being one being living were hearing this one telling this thing again and again. Some who were ones knowing this one and were ones certain that this one was one who was clearly telling something, was a great man, were not listening very often to this one telling again and again about being one being living. Certainly some who were certain that this one was a great man and one clearly expressing something and greatly expressing something being struggling were listening to this one telling about being living telling about this again and again and again. Certainly very many knowing this one and being certain that this one was a great man and that this one was clearly telling something were not listening to this one telling about being living, were not listening to this one telling this again and again.

This one was certainly a great man, this one was certainly clearly expressing something. Some were certain that this one was clearly expressing something being struggling, some were certain that this one was not greatly expressing something being struggling.

Very many were not listening again and again to this one telling about being one being living. Some were listening again and again to this one telling about this one being one being in living.

Some were certainly wanting to be doing what this one was doing that is were wanting to be ones clearly expressing

something. Some of such of them did not go on in being ones
wanting to be doing what this one was doing that is in being
ones clearly expressing something. Some went on being ones
wanting to be doing what this one was doing that is, being
ones clearly expressing something. Certainly this one was
one who was a great man. Any one could be certain of this
thing. Every one would come to be certain of this thing. This
one was one certainly clearly expressing something. Any one
could come to be certain of this thing. Every one would come
to be certain of this thing. This one was one, some were quite
certain, one greatly expressing something being struggling.
This one was one, some were quite certain, one not greatly
expressing something being struggling.

[PICASSO]

One whom some were certainly following was one who was
completely charming. One whom some were certainly following was one who was charming. One whom some were following was one who was completely charming. One whom
some were following was one who was certainly completely
charming.

Some were certainly following and were certain that the
one they were then following was one working and was one
bringing out of himself then something. Some were certainly
following and were certain that the one they were then following was one bringing out of himself then something that
was coming to be a heavy thing, a solid thing and a complete
thing.

One whom some were certainly following was one working
and certainly was one bringing something out of himself then
and was one who had been all his living had been one having
something coming out of him.

Something had been coming out of him, certainly it had
been coming out of him, certainly it was something, certainly

it had been coming out of him and it had meaning, a charming meaning, a solid meaning, a struggling meaning, a clear meaning.

One whom some were certainly following and some were certainly following him, one whom some were certainly following was one certainly working.

One whom some were certainly following was one having something coming out of him something having meaning and this one was certainly working then.

This one was working and something was coming then, something was coming out of this one then. This one was one and always there was something coming out of this one and always there had been something coming out of this one. This one had never been one not having something coming out of this one. This one was one having something coming out of this one. This one had been one whom some were following. This one was one whom some were following. This one was being one whom some were following. This one was one who was working.

This one was one who was working. This one was one being one having something being coming out of him. This one was one going on having something come out of him. This one was one going on working. This one was one whom some were following. This one was one who was working.

This one always had something being coming out of this one. This one was working. This one always had been working. This one was always having something that was coming out of this one that was a solid thing, a charming thing, a lovely thing, a perplexing thing, a disconcerting thing, a simple thing, a clear thing, a complicated thing, an interesting thing, a disturbing thing, a repellant thing, a very pretty thing. This one was one certainly being one having something coming out of him. This one was one whom some were following. This one was one who was working.

This one was one who was working and certainly this one was needing to be working so as to be one being working. This one was one having something coming out of him. This one would be one all his living having something coming out of him. This one was working and then this one was working and this one was needing to be working, not to be one having something coming out of him something having meaning, but was needing to be working so as to be one working.

This one was certainly working and working was something this one was certain this one would be doing and this one was doing that thing, this one was working. This one was not one completely working. This one certainly was not completely working.

This one was one having always something being coming out of him, something having completely a real meaning. This one was one whom some were following. This one was one who was working. This one was one who was working and he was one needing this thing needing to be working so as to be one having some way of being one having some way of working. This one was one who was working. This one was one having something come out of him something having meaning. This one was one always having something come out of him and this thing the thing coming out of him always had real meaning. This one was one who was working. This one was one who was almost always working. This one was not one completely working. This one was one not ever completely working. This one was not one working to have anything come out of him. He always did have something having meaning that did come out of him. He always did have something come out of him. He was working, he was not ever completely working. He did have some following. They were always following him. Some were certainly following him. He was one who was working. He was one having something coming out of him something having meaning. He was not ever completely working.

MELANCTHA

EACH ONE AS SHE MAY

This, the second story in THREE LIVES, *published first in* 1909 *and frequently reprinted since, is probably the most generally admired, and possibly the best known, work of Miss Ste n. Richard Wright has called it "the first long serious literary treatment of Negro life in the United States." In his review of* WARS I HAVE SEEN *published in* PM, *March* 11, 1945, *the author of* BLACK BOY *further commented on this story:*

"Prompted by random curiosity while I was browsing one day in a Chicago Public Library, I took from the open shelves a tiny volume called THREE LIVES *and looked at a story in it, entitled* MELANCTHA. *The style was so insistent and original and sang so quaintly that I took the book home.*

"As I read it my ears were opened for the first time to the magic of the spoken word. I began to hear the speech of my grandmother, who spoke a deep, pure Negro dialect and with whom I had lived for many years

"All of my life I had been only half hearing, but Miss Stein's struggling words made the speech of the people around me vivid. From that moment on, in my attempts at writing, I was able to tap at will the vast pool of living words that swirled around me.

"But in the midst of my delight, I was jolted. A left-wing literary critic, whose judgment I had been led to respect, condemned Miss Stein in a sharply-worded newspaper article, implying that she spent her days reclining upon a silken couch in Paris smoking hashish, that she was a hopeless prey to hallucinations and that her tortured verbalisms were throttling the Revolution. I was disturbed. Had I duped myself into worshiping decadence?

"Believing in direct action, I contrived a method to gauge the degree to which Miss Stein's prose was tainted with the spirit of counter-revolution. I gathered a group of semi-literate Negro stockyard workers—'basic proletarians with the instinct for revolution' (am I quoting right?)—into a Black Belt basement and read MELANCTHA *aloud to them. They understood every word. Enthralled, they slapped their thighs, howled, laughed, stomped, and interrupted me constantly to comment upon the characters.*

"My fondness for Steinian prose never distressed me after that."

EACH ONE AS SHE MAY

Rose Johnson made it very hard to bring her baby to its birth.

Melanctha Herbert who was Rose Johnson's friend, did everything that any woman could. She tended Rose, and she was patient, submissive, soothing, and untiring, while the sullen, childish, cowardly, black Rosie grumbled and fussed and howled and made herself to be an abomination and like a simple beast.

The child though it was healthy after it was born, did not live long. Rose Johnson was careless and negligent and selfish, and when Melanctha had to leave for a few days, the baby died. Rose Johnson had liked the baby well enough and perhaps she just forgot it for awhile, anyway the child was dead and Rose and Sam her husband were very sorry but then these things came so often in the negro world in Bridgepoint, that they neither of them thought about it very long.

Rose Johnson and Melanctha Herbert had been friends now for some years. Rose had lately married Sam Johnson a decent honest kindly fellow, a deck hand on a coasting steamer.

Melanctha Herbert had not yet been really married.

Rose Johnson was a real black, tall, well built, sullen, stupid, childlike, good looking negress. She laughed when she was happy and grumbled and was sullen with everything that troubled.

Rose Johnson was a real black negress but she had been brought up quite like their own child by white folks.

Rose laughed when she was happy but she had not the

wide, abandoned laughter that makes the warm broad glow
of negro sunshine. Rose was never joyous with the earth-born,
boundless joy of negroes. Hers was just ordinary, any sort of
woman laughter.

Rose Johnson was careless and was lazy, but she had been
brought up by white folks and she needed decent comfort.
Her white training had only made for habits, not for nature.
Rose had the simple, promiscuous unmorality of the black
people.

Rose Johnson and Melanctha Herbert like many of the twos
with women were a curious pair to be such friends.

Melanctha Herbert was a graceful, pale yellow, intelligent,
attractive negress. She had not been raised like Rose by white
folks but then she had been half made with real white blood.

She and Rose Johnson were both of the better sort of
negroes, there, in Bridgepoint.

"No, I ain't no common nigger," said Rose Johnson, "for I
was raised by white folks, and Melanctha she is so bright
and learned so much in school, she ain't no common nigger
either, though she ain't got no husband to be married to like
I am to Sam Johnson."

Why did the subtle, intelligent, attractive, half white girl
Melanctha Herbert love and do for and demean herself in
service to this coarse, decent, sullen, ordinary, black childish
Rose, and why was this unmoral, promiscuous, shiftless Rose
married, and that's not so common either, to a good man of
the negroes, while Melanctha with her white blood and attraction and her desire for a right position had not yet been
really married.

Sometimes the thought of how all her world was made,
filled the complex, desiring Melanctha with despair. She
wondered, often, how she could go on living when she was so
blue.

Melanctha told Rose one day how a woman whom she
knew had killed herself because she was so blue. Melanctha
said, sometimes, she thought this was the best thing for herself to do.

Rose Johnson did not see it the least bit that way.

"I don't see Melanctha why you should talk like you would

kill yourself just because you're blue. I'd never kill myself Melanctha just 'cause I was blue. I'd maybe kill somebody else Melanctha 'cause I was blue, but I'd never kill myself. If I ever killed myself Melanctha it'd be by accident, and if I ever killed myself by accident Melanctha, I'd be awful sorry."

Rose Johnson and Melanctha Herbert had first met, one night, at church. Rose Johnson did not care much for religion. She had not enough emotion to be really roused by a revival. Melanctha Herbert had not come yet to know how to use religion. She was still too complex with desire. However, the two of them in negro fashion went very often to the negro church, along with all their friends, and they slowly came to know each other very well.

Rose Johnson had been raised not as a servant but quite like their own child by white folks. Her mother who had died when Rose was still a baby, had been a trusted servant in the family. Rose was a cute, attractive, good looking little black girl and these people had no children of their own and so they kept Rose in their house.

As Rose grew older she drifted from her white folks back to the colored people, and she gradually no longer lived in the old house. Then it happened that these people went away to some other town to live, and somehow Rose stayed behind in Bridgepoint. Her white folks left a little money to take care of Rose, and this money she got every little while.

Rose now in the easy fashion of the poor lived with one woman in her house, and then for no reason went and lived with some other woman in her house. All this time, too, Rose kept company, and was engaged, first to this colored man and then to that and always she made sure she was engaged, for Rose had strong the sense of proper conduct.

"No, I ain't no common nigger just to go around with any man, nor you Melanctha shouldn't neither," she said one day when she was telling the complex and less sure Melanctha what was the right way for her to do. "No Melanctha, I ain't no common nigger to do so, for I was raised by white folks. You know very well Melanctha that I'se always been engaged to them."

And so Rose lived on, always comfortable and rather decent and very lazy and very well content.

After she had lived some time this way, Rose thought it would be nice and very good in her position to get regularly really married. She had lately met Sam Johnson somewhere, and she liked him and she knew he was a good man, and then he had a place where he worked every day and got good wages. Sam Johnson liked Rose very well and he was quite ready to be married. One day they had a grand real wedding and were married. Then with Melanctha Herbert's help to do the sewing and the nicer work, they furnished comfortably a little red brick house. Sam then went back to his work as deck hand on a coasting steamer, and Rose stayed home in her house and sat and bragged to all her friends how nice it was to be married really to a husband.

Life went on very smoothly with them all the year. Rose was lazy but not dirty and Sam was careful but not fussy, and then there was Melanctha to come in every day and help to keep things neat.

When Rose's baby was coming to be born, Rose came to stay in the house where Melanctha Herbert lived just then, with a big good natured colored woman who did washing.

Rose went there to stay, so that she might have the doctor from the hospital near by to help her have the baby, and then, too, Melanctha could attend to her while she was sick.

Here the baby was born, and here it died, and then Rose went back to her house again with Sam.

Melanctha Herbert had not made her life all simple like Rose Johnson. Melanctha had not found it easy with herself to make her wants and what she had, agree.

Melanctha Herbert was always losing what she had in wanting all the things she saw. Melanctha was always being left when she was not leaving others.

Melanctha Herbert always loved too hard and much too often. She was always full with mystery and subtle movements and denials and vague distrusts and complicated disillusions. Then Melanctha would be sudden and impulsive and unbounded in some faith, and then she would suffer and be strong in her repression.

Melanctha Herbert was always seeking rest and quiet, and always she could only find new ways to be in trouble.

Melanctha wondered often how it was she did not kill herself when she was so blue. Often she thought this would be really the best way for her to do.

Melanctha Herbert had been raised to be religious, by her mother. Melanctha had not liked her mother very well. This mother, 'Mis' Herbert, as her neighbors called her, had been a sweet appearing and dignified and pleasant, pale yellow, colored woman. 'Mis' Herbert had always been a little wandering and mysterious and uncertain in her ways.

Melanctha was pale yellow and mysterious and a little pleasant like her mother, but the real power in Melanctha's nature came through her robust and unpleasant and very unendurable black father.

Melanctha's father only used to come to where Melanctha and her mother lived, once in a while.

It was many years now that Melanctha had not heard or seen or known of anything her father did.

Melanctha Herbert almost always hated her black father, but she loved very well the power in herself that came through him. And so her feeling was really closer to her black coarse father, than her feeling had ever been toward her pale yellow, sweet-appearing mother. The things she had in her of her mother never made her feel respect.

Melanctha Herbert had not loved herself in childhood. All of her youth was bitter to remember.

Melanctha had not loved her father and her mother and they had found it very troublesome to have her.

Melanctha's mother and her father had been regularly married. Melanctha's father was a big black virile negro. He only came once in a while to where Melanctha and her mother lived, but always that pleasant, sweet-appearing, pale yellow woman, mysterious and uncertain and wandering in her ways, was close in sympathy and thinking to her big black virile husband.

James Herbert was a common, decent enough, colored workman, brutal and rough to his one daughter, but then she was a most disturbing child to manage.

The young Melanctha did not love her father and her mother, and she had a breakneck courage, and a tongue that could be very nasty. Then, too, Melanctha went to school and was very quick in all the learning, and she knew very well how to use this knowledge to annoy her parents who knew nothing.

Melanctha Herbert had always had a breakneck courage. Melanctha always loved to be with horses; she loved to do wild things, to ride the horses and to break and tame them.

Melanctha, when she was a little girl, had had a good chance to live with horses. Near where Melanctha and her mother lived was the stable of the Bishops, a rich family who always had fine horses.

John, the Bishops' coachman, liked Melanctha very well and he always let her do anything she wanted with the horses. John was a decent, vigorous mulatto with a prosperous house and wife and children. Melanctha Herbert was older than any of his children. She was now a well grown girl of twelve and just beginning as a woman.

James Herbert, Melanctha's father, knew this John, the Bishops' coachman very well.

One day James Herbert came to where his wife and daughter lived, and he was furious.

"Where's that Melanctha girl of yours," he said fiercely, "if she is to the Bishops' stables again, with that man John, I swear I kill her. Why don't you see to that girl better you, you're her mother."

James Herbert was a powerful, loose built, hard handed, black, angry negro. Herbert never was a joyous negro. Even when he drank with other men, and he did that very often, he was never really joyous. In the days when he had been most young and free and open, he had never had the wide abandoned laughter that gives the broad glow to negro sunshine.

His daughter, Melanctha Herbert, later always made a hard forced laughter. She was only strong and sweet and in her nature when she was really deep in trouble, when she was fighting so with all she really had, that she did not use her laughter. This was always true of poor Melanctha who was so certain that she hated trouble. Melanctha Herbert was always seeking peace and quiet, and she could always only find new ways to get excited.

James Herbert was often a very angry negro. He was fierce and serious, and he was very certain that he often had good reason to be angry with Melanctha, who knew so well how to be nasty, and to use her learning with a father who knew nothing.

James Herbert often drank with John, the Bishops' coachman. John in his good nature sometimes tried to soften Herbert's feeling toward Melanctha. Not that Melanctha ever complained to John of her home life or her father. It was never Melanctha's way, even in the midst of her worst trouble to complain to any one of what happened to her, but nevertheless somehow every one who knew Melanctha always knew how much she suffered. It was only while one really loved Melanctha that one understood how to forgive her, that she never once complained nor looked unhappy, and was always handsome and in spirits, and yet one always knew how much she suffered.

The father, James Herbert, never told his troubles either, and he was so fierce and serious that no one ever thought of asking.

'Mis' Herbert as her neighbors called her was never heard even to speak of her husband or her daughter. She was always pleasant, sweet-appearing, mysterious and uncertain, and a little wandering in her ways.

The Herberts were a silent family with their troubles, but somehow every one who knew them always knew everything that happened.

The morning of one day when in the evening Herbert and the coachman John were to meet to drink together, Melanctha had to come to the stable joyous and in the very best of humors. Her good friend John on this morning felt very firmly how good and sweet she was and how very much she suffered.

John was a very decent colored coachman. When he

thought about Melanctha it was as if she were the eldest of his children. Really he felt very strongly the power in her of a woman. John's wife always liked Melanctha and she always did all she could to make things pleasant. And Melanctha all her life loved and respected kind and good and considerate people. Melanctha always loved and wanted peace and gentleness and goodness and all her life for herself poor Melanctha could only find new ways to be in trouble.

This evening after John and Herbert had drunk awhile together, the good John began to tell the father what a fine girl he had for a daughter. Perhaps the good John had been drinking a good deal of liquor, perhaps there was a gleam of something softer than the feeling of a friendly elder in the way John then spoke of Melanctha. There had been a good deal of drinking and John certainly that very morning had felt strongly Melanctha's power as a woman. James Herbert was always a fierce, suspicious, serious negro, and drinking never made him feel more open. He looked very black and evil as he sat and listened while John grew more and more admiring as he talked half to himself, half to the father, of the virtues and sweetness of Melanctha.

Suddenly between them there came a moment filled full with strong black curses, and then sharp razors flashed in the black hands, that held them flung backward in the negro fashion, and then for some minutes there was fierce slashing.

John was a decent, pleasant, good natured, light brown negro, but he knew how to use a razor to do bloody slashing.

When the two men were pulled apart by the other negroes who were in the room drinking, John had not been much wounded but James Herbert had gotten one good strong cut that went from his right shoulder down across the front of his whole body. Razor fighting does not wound very deeply, but it makes a cut that looks most nasty, for it is so very bloody.

Herbert was held by the other negroes until he was cleaned and plastered, and then he was put to bed to sleep off his drink and fighting.

The next day he came to where his wife and daughter lived and he was furious.

"Where's that Melanctha, of yours?" he said to his wife, when he saw her. "If she is to the Bishops' stables now with that yellow John, I swear I kill her. A nice way she is going for a decent daughter. Why don't you see to that girl better you, ain't you her mother!"

Melanctha Herbert had always been old in all her ways and she knew very early how to use her power as a woman, and yet Melanctha with all her inborn intense wisdom was really very ignorant of evil. Melanctha had not yet come to understand what they meant, the things she so often heard around her, and which were just beginning to stir strongly in her.

Now when her father began fiercely to assail her, she did not really know what it was that he was so furious to force from her. In every way that he could think of in his anger, he tried to make her say a thing she did not really know. She held out and never answered anything he asked her, for Melanctha had a breakneck courage and she just then badly hated her black father.

When the excitement was all over, Melanctha began to know her power, the power she had so often felt stirring within her and which she now knew she could use to make her stronger.

James Herbert did not win his fight with his daughter. After awhile he forgot it as he soon forgot John and the cut of his sharp razor.

Melanctha almost forgot to hate her father, in her strong interest in the power she now knew she had within her.

Melanctha did not care much now, any longer, to see John or his wife or even the fine horses. This life was too quiet and accustomed and no longer stirred her to any interest or excitement.

Melanctha now really was beginning as a woman. She was ready, and she began to search in the streets and in dark corners to discover men and to learn their natures and their various ways of working.

In these next years Melanctha learned many ways that lead to wisdom. She learned the ways, and dimly in the distance she saw wisdom. These years of learning led very straight to trouble for Melanctha, though in these years Melanctha never did or meant anything that was really wrong.

Girls who are brought up with care and watching can always find moments to escape into the world, where they may learn the ways that lead to wisdom. For a girl raised like Melanctha Herbert, such escape was always very simple. Often she was alone, sometimes she was with a fellow seeker, and she strayed and stood, sometimes by railroad yards, sometimes on the docks or around new buildings where many men were working. Then when the darkness covered everything all over, she would begin to learn to know this man or that. She would advance, they would respond, and then she would withdraw a little, dimly, and always she did not know what it was that really held her. Sometimes she would almost go over, and then the strength in her of not really knowing, would stop the average man in his endeavor. It was a strange experience of ignorance and power and desire. Melanctha did not know what it was that she so badly wanted. She was afraid, and yet she did not understand that here she really was a coward.

Boys had never meant much to Melanctha. They had always been too young to content her. Melanctha had a strong respect for any kind of successful power. It was this that always kept Melanctha nearer, in her feeling toward her virile and unendurable black father, than she ever was in her feeling for her pale yellow, sweet-appearing mother. The things she had in her of her mother, never made her feel respect.

In these young days, it was only men that for Melanctha held anything there was of knowledge and power. It was not from men however that Melanctha learned to really understand this power.

From the time that Melanctha was twelve until she was sixteen she wandered, always seeking but never more than very dimly seeing wisdom. All this time Melanctha went on with her school learning; she went to school rather longer than do most of the colored children.

Melanctha's wanderings after wisdom she always had to

do in secret and by snatches, for her mother was then still living and 'Mis' Herbert always did some watching, and Melanctha with all her hard courage dreaded that there should be much telling to her father, who came now quite often to where Melanctha lived with her mother.

In these days Melanctha talked and stood and walked with many kinds of men, but she did not learn to know any of them very deeply. They all supposed her to have world knowledge and experience. They, believing that she knew all, told her nothing, and thinking that she was deciding with them, asked for nothing, and so though Melanctha wandered widely, she was really very safe with all the wandering.

It was a very wonderful experience this safety of Melanctha in these days of her attempted learning. Melanctha herself did not feel the wonder, she only knew that for her it all had no real value.

Melanctha all her life was very keen in her sense for real experience. She knew she was not getting what she so badly wanted, but with all her breakneck courage Melanctha here was a coward, and so she could not learn to really understand.

Melanctha liked to wander, and to stand by the railroad yard, and watch the men and the engines and the switches and everything that was busy there, working. Railroad yards are a ceaseless fascination. They satisfy every kind of nature. For the lazy man whose blood flows very slowly, it is a steady soothing world of motion which supplies him with the sense of a strong moving power. He need not work and yet he has it very deeply; he has it even better than the man who works in it or owns it. Then for natures that like to feel emotion without the trouble of having any suffering, it is very nice to get the swelling in the throat, and the fullness, and the heart beats, and all the flutter of excitement that comes as one watches the people come and go, and hears the engine pound and give a long drawn whistle. For a child watching through a hole in the fence above the yard, it is a wonderful world of mystery and movement. The child loves all the noise, and then it loves the silence of the wind that comes before the full rush of the pounding train, that bursts out from the tunnel where it lost itself and all its noise in darkness, and the child loves all the smoke, that sometimes comes in rings, and always puffs with fire and blue color.

For Melanctha the yard was full of the excitement of many men, and perhaps a free and whirling future.

Melanctha came here very often and watched the men and all the things that were so busy working. The men always had time for, "Hullo Sis, do you want to sit on my engine," and, "Hullo, that's a pretty lookin' yaller girl, do you want to come and see him cookin."

All the colored porters liked Melanctha. They often told her exciting things that had happened; how in the West they went through big tunnels where there was no air to breathe, and then out and winding around edges of great canyons on thin high spindling trestles, and sometimes cars, and sometimes whole trains fell from the narrow bridges, and always up from the dark places death and all kinds of queer devils looked up and laughed in their faces. And then they would tell how sometimes when the train went pounding down steep slippery mountains, great rocks would racket and roll down around them, and sometimes would smash in the car and kill men; and as the porters told these stories their round, black, shining faces would grow solemn, and their color would go grey beneath the greasy black, and their eyes would roll white in the fear and wonder of the things they could scare themselves by telling.

There was one, big, serious, melancholy, light brown porter who often told Melanctha stories, for he liked the way she had of listening with intelligence and sympathetic feeling, when he told how the white men in the far South tried to kill him because he made one of them who was drunk and called him a damned nigger, and who refused to pay money for his chair to a nigger, get off the train between stations. And then this porter had to give up going to that part of the Southern country, for all the white men swore that if he ever came there again they would surely kill him.

Melanctha liked this serious, melancholy light brown negro very well, and all her life Melanctha wanted and respected gentleness and goodness, and this man always gave her good advice and serious kindness, and Melanctha felt such things very deeply, but she could never let them help her or affect her to change the ways that always made her keep herself in trouble.

Melanctha spent many of the last hours of the daylight with the porters and with other men who worked hard, but when darkness came it was always different. Then Melanctha would find herself with the, for her, gentlemanly classes. A clerk, or a young express agent would begin to know her, and they would stand, or perhaps, walk a little while together.

Melanctha always made herself escape but often it was with an effort. She did not know what it was that she so badly wanted, but with all her courage Melanctha here was a coward, and so she could not learn to understand.

Melanctha and some man would stand in the evening and would talk together. Sometimes Melanctha would be with another girl and then it was much easier to stay or to escape, for then they could make way for themselves together, and by throwing words and laughter to each other, could keep a man from getting too strong in his attention.

But when Melanctha was alone, and she was so, very often, she would sometimes come very near to making a long step on the road that leads to wisdom. Some man would learn a good deal about her in the talk, never altogether truly, for Melanctha all her life did not know how to tell a story wholly. She always, and yet not with intention, managed to leave out big pieces which make a story very different, for when it came to what had happened and what she had said and what it was that she had really done, Melanctha never could remember right. The man would sometimes come a little nearer, would detain her, would hold her arm or make his jokes a little clearer, and then Melanctha would always make herself escape. The man thinking that she really had world wisdom would not make his meaning clear, and believing that she was deciding with him he never went so fast that he could stop her when at last she made herself escape.

And so Melanctha wandered on the edge of wisdom. "Say, Sis, why don't you when you come here stay a little longer?"

they would all ask her, and they would hold her for an answer, and she would laugh, and sometimes she did stay longer, but always just in time she made herself escape.

Melanctha Herbert wanted very much to know and yet she feared the knowledge. As she grew older she often stayed a good deal longer, and sometimes it was almost a balanced struggle, but she always made herself escape.

Next to the railroad yard it was the shipping docks that Melanctha loved best when she wandered. Often she was alone, sometimes she was with some better kind of black girl, and she would stand a long time and watch the men working at unloading, and see the steamers do their coaling, and she would listen with full feeling to the yowling of the free swinging negroes, as they ran, with their powerful loose jointed bodies and their childish savage yelling, pushing, carrying, pulling great loads from the ships to the warehouses.

The men would call out, "Say, Sis, look out or we'll come and catch yer," or "Hi, there, you yaller girl, come here and we'll take you sailin'." And then, too, Melanctha would learn to know some of the serious foreign sailors who told her all sorts of wonders, and a cook would sometimes take her and her friends over a ship and show where he made his messes and where the men slept, and where the shops were, and how everything was made by themselves, right there, on ship board.

Melanctha loved to see these dark and smelly places. She always loved to watch and talk and listen with men who worked hard. But it was never from these rougher people that Melanctha tried to learn the ways that lead to wisdom. In the daylight she always liked to talk with rough men and to listen to their lives and about their work and their various ways of doing, but when the darkness covered everything all over, Melanctha would meet, and stand, and talk with a clerk or a young shipping agent who had seen her watching, and so it was that she would try to learn to understand.

And then Melanctha was fond of watching men work on new buildings. She loved to see them hoisting, digging, sawing and stone cutting. Here, too, in the daylight, she always learned to know the common workmen. "Heh, Sis, look out or that rock will fall on you and smash you all up into little pieces. Do you think you would make a nice jelly?" And then they would all laugh and feel that their jokes were very funny. And "Say, you pretty yaller girl, would it scare you bad to stand up here on top where I be? See if you've got grit and come up here where I can hold you. All you got to do is to sit still on that there rock that they're just hoistin', and then when you get here I'll hold you tight, don't you be scared Sis."

Sometimes Melanctha would do some of these things that had much danger, and always with such men, she showed her power and her breakneck courage. Once she slipped and fell from a high place. A workman caught her and so she was not killed, but her left arm was badly broken.

All the men crowded around her. They admired her boldness in doing and in bearing pain when her arm was broken. They all went along with her with great respect to the doctor, and then they took her home in triumph and all of them were bragging about her not squealing.

James Herbert was home where his wife lived, that day. He was furious when he saw the workmen and Melanctha. He drove the men away with curses so that they were all very nearly fighting, and he would not let a doctor come in to attend Melanctha. "Why don't you see to that girl better, you, you're her mother."

James Herbert did not fight things out now any more with his daughter. He feared her tongue, and her school learning, and the way she had of saying things that were very nasty to a brutal black man who knew nothing. And Melanctha just then hated him very badly in her suffering.

And so this was the way Melanctha lived the four years of her beginning as a woman. And many things happened to Melanctha, but she knew very well that none of them had led her on to the right way, that certain way that was to lead her to world wisdom.

Melanctha Herbert was sixteen when she first met Jane Harden. Jane was a negress, but she was so white that hardly any one could guess it. Jane had had a good deal of education. She had been two years at a colored college. She had had to leave because of her bad conduct. She taught Melanctha many things. She taught her how to go the ways that lead to wisdom.

Jane Harden was at this time twenty-three years old, and she had had much experience. She was very much attracted by Melanctha, and Melanctha was very proud that this Jane would let her know her.

Jane Harden was not afraid to understand. Melanctha who had strong the sense for real experience, knew that here was a woman who had learned to understand.

Jane Harden had many bad habits. She drank a great deal, and she wandered widely. She was safe though now, when she wanted to be safe, in this wandering.

Melanctha Herbert soon always wandered with her. Melanctha tried the drinking and some of the other habits, but she did not find that she cared very much to do them. But every day she grew stronger in her desire to really understand.

It was now no longer, even in the daylight, the rougher men that these two learned to know in their wanderings, and for Melanctha the better classes were now a little higher. It was no longer express agents and clerks that she learned to know, but men in business, commercial travelers, and even men above these, and Jane and she would talk and walk and laugh and escape from them all very often. It was still the same, the knowing of them and the always just escaping, only now for Melanctha somehow it was different, for though it was always the same thing that happened it had a different flavor, for now Melanctha was with a woman who had wisdom, and dimly she began to see what it was that she should understand.

It was not from the men that Melanctha learned her wisdom. It was always Jane Harden herself who was making Melanctha begin to understand.

Jane was a roughened woman. She had power and she liked to use it, she had much white blood and that made her see clear, she liked drinking and that made her reckless. Her white blood was strong in her and she had grit and endurance and a vital courage. She was always game, however much she was in trouble. She liked Melanctha Herbert for the things that she had like her, and then Melanctha was young, and she had sweetness, and a way of listening with intelligence and sympathetic interest, to the stories that Jane Harden often told out of her experience.

Jane grew always fonder of Melanctha. Soon they began to wander, more to be together than to see men and learn their various ways of working. Then they began not to wander, and Melanctha would spend long hours with Jane in her room, sitting at her feet and listening to her stories, and feeling her strength and the power of her affection, and slowly she began to see clear before her one certain way that would be sure to lead to wisdom.

Before the end came, the end of the two years in which Melanctha spent all her time when she was not at school or in her home, with Jane Harden, before these two years were finished, Melanctha had come to see very clear, and she had come to be very certain, what it is that gives the world its wisdom.

Jane Harden always had a little money and she had a room in the lower part of the town. Jane had once taught in a colored school. She had had to leave that too on account of her bad conduct. It was her drinking that always made all the trouble for her, for that can never be really covered over.

Jane's drinking was always growing worse upon her. Melanctha had tried to do the drinking but it had no real attraction for her.

In the first year, between Jane Harden and Melanctha Herbert, Jane had been much the stronger. Jane loved Melanctha and she found her always intelligent and brave and sweet and docile, and Jane meant to, and before the year was over she had taught Melanctha what it is that gives many people in the world their wisdom.

Jane had many ways in which to do this teaching. She told Melanctha many things. She loved Melanctha hard and made Melanctha feel it very deeply. She would be with other people and with men and with Melanctha, and she would make Melanctha understand what everybody wanted, and what one did with power when one had it.

Melanctha sat at Jane's feet for many hours in these days and felt Jane's wisdom. She learned to love Jane and to have this feeling very deeply. She learned a little in these days to know joy, and she was taught too how very keenly she could suffer. It was very different this suffering from that Melanctha sometimes had from her mother and from her very unendurable black father. Then she was fighting and she could be strong and valiant in her suffering, but here with Jane Harden she was longing and she bent and pleaded with her suffering.

It was a very tumultuous, very mingled year, this time for Melanctha, but she certainly did begin to really understand.

In every way she got it from Jane Harden. There was nothing good or bad in doing, feeling, thinking or in talking, that Jane spared her. Sometimes the lesson came almost too strong for Melanctha, but somehow she always managed to endure it and so slowly, but always with increasing strength and feeling, Melanctha began to really understand.

Then slowly, between them, it began to be all different. Slowly now between them, it was Melanctha Herbert, who was stronger. Slowly now they began to drift apart from one another.

Melanctha Herbert never really lost her sense that it was Jane Harden who had taught her, but Jane did many things that Melanctha now no longer needed. And then, too, Melanctha never could remember right when it came to what she had done and what had happened. Melanctha now sometimes quarreled with Jane, and they no longer went about together, and sometimes Melanctha really forgot how much she owed to Jane Harden's teaching.

Melanctha began now to feel that she had always had world wisdom. She really knew of course, that it was Jane who had taught her, but all that began to be covered over by the trouble between them, that was now always getting stronger.

Jane Harden was a roughened woman. Once she had been very strong, but now she was weakened in all her kinds of strength by her drinking. Melanctha had tried the drinking but it had had no real attraction for her.

Jane's strong and roughened nature and her drinking made

it always harder for her to forgive Melanctha, that now Melanctha did not really need her any longer. Now it was Melanctha who was stronger and it was Jane who was dependent on her.

Melanctha was now come to be about eighteen years old. She was a graceful, pale yellow, good looking, intelligent, attractive negress, a little mysterious sometimes in her ways, and always good and pleasant, and always ready to do things for people.

Melanctha from now on saw very little of Jane Harden. Jane did not like that very well and sometimes she abused Melanctha, but her drinking soon covered everything all over.

It was not in Melanctha's nature to really lose her sense for Jane Harden. Melanctha all her life was ready to help Jane out in any of her trouble, and later, when Jane really went to pieces, Melanctha always did all that she could to help her.

But Melanctha Herbert was ready now herself to do teaching. Melanctha could do anything now that she wanted. Melanctha knew now what everybody wanted.

Melanctha had learned how she might stay a little longer; she had learned that she must decide when she wanted really to stay longer, and she had learned how when she wanted to, she could escape.

And so Melanctha began once more to wander. It was all now for her very different. It was never rougher men now that she talked to, and she did not care much now to know white men of the, for her, very better classes. It was now something realler that Melanctha wanted, something that would move her very deeply, something that would fill her fully with the wisdom that was planted now within her, and that she wanted badly, should really wholly fill her.

Melanctha these days wandered very widely. She was always alone now when she wandered. Melanctha did not need help now to know, or to stay longer, or when she wanted, to escape.

Melanctha tried a great many men, in these days before she was really suited. It was almost a year that she wandered and then she met with a young mulatto. He was a doctor who had just begun to practice. He would most likely do well in the future, but it was not this that concerned Melanctha. She found him good and strong and gentle and very intellectual, and all her life Melanctha liked and wanted good and considerate people, and then too he did not at first believe in Melanctha. He held off and did not know what it was that Melanctha wanted. Melanctha came to want him very badly. They began to know each other better. Things began to be very strong between them. Melanctha wanted him so badly that now she never wandered. She just gave herself to this experience.

Melanctha Herbert was now, all alone, in Bridgepoint. She lived now with this colored woman and now with that one, and she sewed, and sometimes she taught a little in a colored school as substitute for some teacher. Melanctha had now no home nor any regular employment. Life was just commencing for Melanctha. She had youth and had learned wisdom, and she was graceful and pale yellow and very pleasant, and always ready to do things for people, and she was mysterious in her ways and that only made belief in her more fervent.

During the year before she met Jefferson Campbell, Melanctha had tried many kinds of men but they had none of them interested Melanctha very deeply. She met them, she was much with them, she left them, she would think perhaps this next time it would be more exciting, and always she found that for her it all had no real meaning. She could now do everything she wanted, she knew now everything that everybody wanted, and yet it all had no excitement for her. With these men, she knew she could learn nothing. She wanted some one that could teach her very deeply and now at last she was sure that she had found him, yes she really had it, before she had thought to look if in this man she would find it.

During this year 'Mis' Herbert as her neighbors called her, Melanctha's pale yellow mother was very sick, and in this year she died.

Melanctha's father during these last years did not come very often to the house where his wife lived and Melanctha. Melanctha was not sure that her father was now any longer here in Bridgepoint. It was Melanctha who was very good now to her mother. It was always Melanctha's way to be good to any one in trouble.

Melanctha took good care of her mother. She did everything that any woman could, she tended and soothed and helped her pale yellow mother, and she worked hard in every way to take care of her, and make her dying easy. But Melanctha did not in these days like her mother any better, and her mother never cared much for this daughter who was always a hard child to manage, and who had a tongue that always could be very nasty.

Melanctha did everything that any woman could, and at last her mother died, and Melanctha had her buried. Melanctha's father was not heard from, and Melanctha in all her life after, never saw or heard or knew of anything that her father did.

It was the young doctor, Jefferson Campbell, who helped Melanctha toward the end, to take care of her sick mother. Jefferson Campbell had often before seen Melanctha Herbert, but he had never liked her very well, and he had never believed that she was any good. He had heard something about how she wandered. He knew a little too of Jane Harden, and he was sure that this Melanctha Herbert, who was her friend and who wandered, would never come to any good.

Dr. Jefferson Campbell was a serious, earnest, good young joyous doctor. He liked to take care of everybody and he loved his own colored people. He always found life very easy did Jeff Campbell, and everybody liked to have him with them. He was so good and sympathetic, and he was so earnest and so joyous. He sang when he was happy, and he laughed, and his was the free abandoned laughter that gives the warm broad glow to negro sunshine.

Jeff Campbell had never yet in his life had real trouble. Jefferson's father was a good, kind, serious, religious man. He was a very steady, very intelligent, and very dignified, light brown, grey haired negro. He was a butler and he had worked for the Campbell family many years, and his father and his mother before him had been in the service of this family as free people.

Jefferson Campbell's father and his mother had of course been regularly married. Jefferson's mother was a sweet, little, pale brown, gentle woman who reverenced and obeyed her good husband, and who worshipped and admired and loved hard her good, earnest, cheery, hard working doctor boy who was her only child.

Jeff Campbell had been raised religious by his people but religion had never interested Jeff very much. Jefferson was very good. He loved his people and he never hurt them, and he always did everything they wanted and that he could to please them, but he really loved best science and experimenting and to learn things, and he early wanted to be a doctor, and he was always very interested in the life of the colored people.

The Campbell family had been very good to him and had helped him on with his ambition. Jefferson studied hard, he went to a colored college, and then he learnt to be a doctor.

It was now two or three years, that he had started in to practice. Everybody liked Jeff Campbell, he was so strong and kindly and cheerful and understanding, and he laughed so with pure joy, and he always liked to help all his own colored people.

Dr. Jeff knew all about Jane Harden. He had taken care of her in some of her bad trouble. He knew about Melanctha too, though until her mother was taken sick he had never met her. Then he was called in to help Melanctha to take care of her sick mother. Dr. Campbell did not like Melanctha's ways and he did not think that she would ever come to any good.

Dr. Campbell had taken care of Jane Harden in some of her bad trouble. Jane sometimes had abused Melanctha to him. What right had that Melanctha Herbert who owed everything to her, Jane Harden, what right had a girl like that to go away to other men and leave her, but Melanctha Herbert never had any sense of how to act to anybody. Melanctha had a good mind, Jane never denied her that, but she never used it to do anything decent with it. But what could you expect when Melanctha had such a brute of a black nigger father, and Melanctha was always abusing her

father and yet she was just like him, and really she admired
him so much and he never had any sense of what he owed
to anybody, and Melanctha was just like him and she was
proud of it too, and it made Jane so tired to hear Melanctha
talk all the time as if she wasn't. Jane Harden hated people
who had good minds and didn't use them, and Melanctha
always had that weakness, and wanting to keep in with
people, and never really saying that she wanted to be like
her father, and it was so silly of Melanctha to abuse her
father, when she was so much like him and she really liked
it. No, Jane Harden had no use for Melanctha. Oh yes,
Melanctha always came around to be good to her. Melanctha
was always sure to do that. She never really went away and
left one. She didn't use her mind enough to do things straight
out like that. Melanctha Herbert had a good mind, Jane
never denied that to her, but she never wanted to see or hear
about Melanctha Herbert any more, and she wished Melanctha wouldn't come in any more to see her. She didn't hate her,
but she didn't want to hear about her father and all that
talk Melanctha always made, and that just meant nothing to
her. Jane Harden was very tired of all that now. She didn't
have any use now any more for Melanctha, and if Dr. Campbell saw her he better tell her Jane didn't want to see her,
and she could take her talk to somebody else, who was ready
to believe her. And then Jane Harden would drop away and
forget Melanctha and all her life before, and then she would
begin to drink and so she would cover everything all over.

Jeff Campbell heard all this very often, but it did not interest him very deeply. He felt no desire to know more of
this Melanctha. He heard her, once, talking to another girl
outside of the house, when he was paying a visit to Jane
Harden. He did not see much in the talk that he heard her
do. He did not see much in the things Jane Harden said
when she abused Melanctha to him. He was more interested
in Jane herself than in anything he heard about Melanctha.
He knew Jane Harden had a good mind, and she had had
power, and she could really have done things, and now this
drinking covered everything all over. Jeff Campbell was always very sorry when he had to see it. Jane Harden was a

roughened woman, and yet Jeff found a great many strong good things in her, that still made him like her.

Jeff Campbell did everything he could for Jane Harden. He did not care much to hear about Melanctha. He had no feeling, much, about her. He did not find that he took any interest in her. Jane Harden was so much a stronger woman, and Jane really had had a good mind, and she had used it to do things with it, before this drinking business had taken such a hold upon her.

Dr. Campbell was helping Melanctha Herbert to take care of her sick mother. He saw Melanctha now for long times and very often, and they sometimes talked a good deal together, but Melanctha never said anything to him about Jane Harden. She never talked to him about anything that was not just general matters, or about medicine, or to tell him funny stories. She asked him many questions and always listened very well to all he told her, and she always remembered everything she heard him say about doctoring, and she always remembered everything that she had learned from all the others.

Jeff Campbell never found that all this talk interested him very deeply. He did not find that he liked Melanctha when he saw her so much, any better. He never found that he thought much about Melanctha. He never found that he believed much in her having a good mind, like Jane Harden. He found he liked Jane Harden always better, and that he wished very much that she had never begun that bad drinking.

Melanctha Herbert's mother was now always getting sicker. Melanctha really did everything that any woman could. Melanctha's mother never liked her daughter any better. She never said much, did 'Mis' Herbert, but anybody could see that she did not think much of this daughter.

Dr. Campbell now often had to stay a long time to take care of 'Mis' Herbert. One day 'Mis' Herbert was much sicker and Dr. Campbell thought that this night, she would surely die. He came back late to the house, as he had said he would do, to sit up and watch 'Mis' Herbert, and to help Melanctha, if she should need anybody to be with her. Melanctha Her-

bert and Jeff Campbell sat up all that night together. 'Mis'
Herbert did not die. The next day she was a little better.

This house where Melanctha had always lived with her
mother was a little red brick, two story house. They had not
much furniture to fill it and some of the windows were broken
and not mended. Melanctha did not have much money to
use now on the house, but with a colored woman, who was
their neighbor and good natured and who had always helped
them, Melanctha managed to take care of her mother and to
keep the house fairly clean and neat.

Melanctha's mother was in bed in a room upstairs, and the
steps from below led right up into it. There were just two
rooms on this upstairs floor. Melanctha and Dr. Campbell
sat down on the steps, that night they watched together, so
that they could hear and see Melanctha's mother and yet the
light would be shaded, and they could sit and read, if they
wanted to, and talk low some, and yet not disturb 'Mis' Herbert.

Dr. Campbell was always very fond of reading. Dr. Campbell had not brought a book with him that night. He had just
forgotten it. He had meant to put something in his pocket
to read, so that he could amuse himself, while he was sitting
there and watching. When he was through with taking care
of 'Mis' Herbert, he came and sat down on the steps just
above where Melanctha was sitting. He spoke about how he
had forgotten to bring his book with him. Melanctha said
there were some old papers in the house, perhaps Dr. Campbell could find something in them that would help pass the
time for a while for him. All right, Dr. Campbell said, that
would be better than just sitting there with nothing. Dr.
Campbell began to read through the old papers that Melanctha gave him. When anything amused him in them, he read
it out to Melanctha. Melanctha was now pretty silent, with
him. Dr. Campbell began to feel a little, about how she
responded to him. Dr. Campbell began to see a little that
perhaps Melanctha had a good mind. Dr. Campbell was not
sure yet that she had a good mind, but he began to think a
little that perhaps she might have one.

Jefferson Campbell always liked to talk to everybody about

the things he worked at and about his thinking about what he could do for the colored people. Melanctha Herbert never thought about these things the way that he did. Melanctha had never said much to Dr. Campbell about what she thought about them. Melanctha did not feel the same as he did about being good and regular in life, and not having excitements all the time, which was the way that Jefferson Campbell wanted that everybody should be, so that everybody would be wise and yet be happy. Melanctha always had strong the sense for real experience. Melanctha Herbert did not think much of this way of coming to real wisdom.

Dr. Campbell soon got through with his reading, in the old newspapers, and then somehow he began to talk along about the things he was always thinking. Dr. Campbell said he wanted to work so that he could understand what troubled people, and not to just have excitements, and he believed you ought to love your father and your mother and to be regular in all your life and not to be always wanting new things and excitements, and to always know where you were, and what you wanted, and to always tell everything just as you meant it. That's the only kind of life he knew or believed in, Jeff Campbell repeated. "No I ain't got any use for all the time being in excitements and wanting to have all kinds of experience all the time. I got plenty of experience just living regular and quiet and with my family, and doing my work, and taking care of people, and trying to understand it. I don't believe much in this running around business and I don't want to see the colored people do it. I am a colored man and I ain't sorry, and I want to see the colored people like what is good and what I want them to have, and that's to live regular and work hard and understand things, and that's enough to keep any decent man excited." Jeff Campbell spoke now with some anger. Not to Melanctha, he did not think of her at all when he was talking. It was the life he wanted that he spoke to, and the way he wanted things to be with the colored people.

But Melanctha Herbert had listened to him say all this. She knew he meant it, but it did not mean much to her, and she was sure some day he would find out, that it was not all,

of real wisdom. Melanctha knew very well what it was to have
real wisdom. "But how about Jane Harden?" said Melanctha
to Jeff Campbell, "seems to me Dr. Campbell you find her to
have something in her, and you go there very often, and you
talk to her much more than you do to the nice girls that stay
at home with their people, the kind you say you are really
wanting. It don't seem to me Dr. Campbell, that what you
say and what you do seem to have much to do with each
other. And about your being so good Dr. Campbell," went on
Melanctha, "You don't care about going to church much
yourself, and yet you always are saying you believe so much
in things like that, for people. It seems to me, Dr. Campbell
you want to have a good time just like all us others, and then
you just keep on saying that it's right to be good and you
ought not to have excitements, and yet you really don't want
to do it Dr. Campbell, no more than me or Jane Harden.
No, Dr. Campbell, it certainly does seem to me you don't
know very well yourself, what you mean, when you are
talking."

Jefferson had been talking right along, the way he always
did when he got started, and now Melanctha's answer only
made him talk a little harder. He laughed a little, too, but
very low, so as not to disturb 'Mis' Herbert who was sleeping
very nicely, and he looked brightly at Melanctha to enjoy
her, and then he settled himself down to answer.

"Yes," he began, "it certainly does sound a little like I
didn't know very well what I do mean, when you put it like
that to me, Miss Melanctha, but that's just because you don't
understand enough about what I meant, by what I was just
saying to you. I don't say, never, I don't want to know all
kinds of people, Miss Melanctha, and I don't say there ain't
many kinds of people, and I don't say ever, that I don't find
some like Jane Harden very good to know and talk to, but it's
the strong things I like in Jane Harden, not all her excitements. I don't admire the bad things she does, Miss Melanctha, but Jane Harden is a strong woman and I always respect
that in her. No I know you don't believe what I say, Miss
Melanctha, but I mean it, and it's all just because you don't
understand it when I say it. And as for religion, that just ain't

my way of being good, Miss Melanctha, but it's a good way for many people to be good and regular in their way of living, and if they believe it, it helps them to be good, and if they're honest in it, I like to see them have it. No, what I don't like, Miss Melanctha, is this what I see so much with the colored people, their always wanting new things just to get excited."

Jefferson Campbell here stopped himself in his talking. Melanctha Herbert did not make any answer. They both sat there very quiet.

Jeff Campbell then began again on the old papers. He sat there on the steps just above where Melanctha was sitting, and he went on with his reading, and his head moving up and down, and sometimes he was reading, and sometimes he was thinking about all the things he wanted to be doing, and then he would rub the back of his dark hand over his mouth, and in between he would be frowning with his thinking, and sometimes he would be rubbing his head hard to help his thinking. And Melanctha just sat still and watched the lamp burning, and sometimes she turned it down a little, when the wind caught it and it would begin to get to smoking.

And so Jeff Campbell and Melanctha Herbert sat there on the steps, very quiet, a long time, and they didn't seem to think much, that they were together. They sat there so, for about an hour, and then it came to Jefferson very slowly and as a strong feeling that he was sitting there on the steps, alone, with Melanctha. He did not know if Melanctha Herbert was feeling very much about their being there alone together. Jefferson began to wonder about it a little. Slowly he felt that surely they must both have this feeling. It was so important that he knew that she must have it. They both sat there, very quiet, a long time.

At last Jefferson began to talk about how the lamp was smelling. Jefferson began to explain what it is that makes a lamp get to smelling. Melanctha let him talk. She did not answer, and then he stopped in his talking. Soon Melanctha began to sit up straighter and then she started in to question.

"About what you was just saying Dr. Campbell about living regular and all that, I certainly don't understand what you meant by what you was just saying. You ain't a bit like good people Dr. Campbell, like the good people you are always saying are just like you. I know good people Dr. Campbell, and you ain't a bit like men who are good and got religion. You are just as free and easy as any man can be Dr. Campbell, and you always like to be with Jane Harden, and she is a pretty bad one and you don't look down on her and you never tell her she is a bad one. I know you like her just like a friend Dr. Campbell, and so I certainly don't understand just what it is you mean by all that you was just saying to me. I know you mean honest Dr. Campbell, and I am always trying to believe you, but I can't say as I see just what you mean when you say you want to be good and real pious, because I am very certain Dr. Campbell that you ain't that kind of a man at all, and you ain't never ashamed to be with queer folks Dr. Campbell, and you seem to be thinking what you are doing is just like what you are always saying, and Dr. Campbell, I certainly don't just see what you mean by what you say."

Dr. Campbell almost laughed loud enough to wake 'Mis' Herbert. He did enjoy the way Melanctha said these things to him. He began to feel very strongly about it that perhaps Melanctha really had a good mind. He was very free now in his laughing, but not so as to make Melanctha angry. He was very friendly with her in his laughing, and then he made his face get serious, and he rubbed his head to help him in his thinking.

"I know Miss Melanctha," he began, "It ain't very easy for you to understand what I was meaning by what I was just saying to you, and perhaps some of the good people I like so wouldn't think very much, any more than you do, Miss Melanctha, about the ways I have to be good. But that's no matter Miss Melanctha. What I mean Miss Melanctha by what I was just saying to you is, that I don't, no, never, believe in doing things just to get excited. You see Miss Melanctha I mean the way so many of the colored people do it. Instead of just working hard and caring about their working and living regular with their families and saving up all their money, so they will have some to bring up their children better, instead of living regular and doing like that and getting

children better, instead of living regular and doing like that and getting all their new ways from just decent living, the colored people just keep running around and perhaps drinking and doing everything bad they can ever think of, and not just because they like all those bad things that they are always doing, but only just because they want to get excited. No Miss Melanctha, you see I am a colored man myself and I ain't sorry, and I want to see the colored people being good and careful and always honest and living always just as regular as can be, and I am sure Miss Melanctha, that that way everybody can have a good time, and be happy and keep right and be busy, and not always have to be doing bad things for new ways to get excited. Yes Miss Melanctha, I certainly do like everything to be good, and quiet, and I certainly do think that is the best way for all us colored people. No, Miss Melanctha too, I don't mean this except only just the way I say it. I ain't got any other meaning Miss Melanctha, and it's that what I mean when I am saying about being really good. It ain't Miss Melanctha to be pious and not liking every kind of people, and I don't say ever Miss Melanctha that when other kind of people come regular into your life you shouldn't want to know them always. What I mean Miss Melanctha by what I am always saying is, you shouldn't try to know everybody just to run around and get excited. It's that kind of way of doing that I hate so always Miss Melanctha, and that is so bad for all us colored people. I don't know as you understand now any better what I mean by what I was just saying to you. But you certainly do know now Miss Melanctha, that I always mean it what I say when I am talking."

"Yes I certainly do understand you when you talk so Dr. Campbell. I certainly do understand now what you mean by what you was always saying to me. I certainly do understand Dr. Campbell that you mean you don't believe it's right to love anybody." "Why sure no, yes I do Miss Melanctha. I certainly do believe strong in loving, and in being good to everybody, and trying to understand what they all need, to help them." "Oh I know all about that way of doing Dr. Campbell, but that certainly ain't the kind of love I mean when I am talking. I mean real, strong, hot love Dr. Campbell, that makes you do anything for somebody that loves you." "I don't know much about that kind of love yet Miss Melanctha. You see it's this way with me always Miss Melanctha. I am always so busy with my thinking about my work I am doing and so I don't have time for just fooling, and then too, you see Miss Melanctha, I really certainly don't ever like to get excited, and that kind of loving hard does seem always to mean just getting all the time excited. That certainly is what I always think from what I see of them that have it bad Miss Melanctha, and that certainly would never suit a man like me. You see Miss Melanctha I am a very quiet kind of fellow, and I believe in a quiet life for all the colored people. No Miss Melanctha I certainly never have mixed myself up in that kind of trouble."

"Yes I certainly do see that very clear Dr. Campbell," said Melanctha, "I see that's certainly what it is always made me not know right about you and that's certainly what it is that makes you really mean what you was always saying. You certainly are just too scared Dr. Campbell to really feel things way down in you. All you are always wanting Dr. Campbell, is just to talk about being good, and to play with people just to have a good time, and yet always to certainly keep yourself out of trouble. It don't seem to me Dr. Campbell that I admire that way to do things very much. It certainly ain't really to me being very good. It certainly ain't any more to me Dr. Campbell, but that you certainly are awful scared about really feeling things way down in you, and that's certainly the only way Dr. Campbell I can see that you can mean, by what it is that you are always saying to me."

"I don't know about that Miss Melanctha, I certainly don't think I can't feel things very deep in me, though I do say I certainly do like to have things nice and quiet, but I don't see harm in keeping out of danger Miss Melanctha, when a man knows he certainly don't want to get killed in it, and I don't know anything that's more awful dangerous Miss Melanctha than being strong in love with somebody. I don't mind sickness or real trouble Miss Melanctha, and I don't want to be talking about what I can do in real trouble, but you know something about that Miss Melanctha, but I certainly don't see much in mixing up just to get excited, in that awful kind of danger. No Miss Melanctha I certainly do only know just two kinds of ways of loving. One kind of loving seems to me, is like one has a good quiet feeling in a family when one does his work, and is always living good and being regular, and then the other way of loving is just like having it like any animal that's low in the streets together, and that don't seem to me very good Miss Melanctha, though I don't say ever that it's not all right when anybody likes it and that's all the kinds of love I know Miss Melanctha, and I certainly don't care very much to get mixed up in that kind of a way just to be in trouble."

Jefferson stopped and Melanctha thought a little.

"That certainly does explain to me Dr. Campbell what I been thinking about you this long time. I certainly did wonder how you could be so live, and knowing everything, and everybody, and talking so big always about everything, and everybody always liking you so much, and you always looking as if you was thinking, and yet you really was never knowing about anybody and certainly not being really very understanding. It certainly is all Dr. Campbell because you is so afraid you will be losing being good so easy, and it certainly do seem to me Dr. Campbell that it certainly don't amount to very much that kind of goodness."

"Perhaps you are right Miss Melanctha," Jefferson answered. "I don't say never, perhaps you ain't right Miss Melanctha. Perhaps I ought to know more about such ways Miss Melanctha. Perhaps it would help me some, taking care of the colored people, Miss Melanctha. I don't say, no, never, but perhaps I could learn a whole lot about women the right way, if I had a real good teacher."

'Mis' Herbert just then stirred a little in her sleep. Melanctha went up the steps to the bed to attend her. Dr. Campbell got up too and went to help her. 'Mis' Herbert woke up and was a little better. Now it was morning and Dr. Campbell gave his directions to Melanctha, and then left her.

Melanctha Herbert all her life long, loved and wanted good, kind and considerate people. Jefferson Campbell was all the

things that Melanctha had ever wanted. Jefferson was a
strong, well built, good looking, cheery, intelligent and good
mulatto. And then at first he had not cared to know Melanctha, and when he did begin to know her he had not liked her
very well, and he had not thought that she would ever come
to any good. And then Jefferson Campbell was so very gentle.
Jefferson never did some things like other men, things that
now were beginning to be ugly, for Melanctha. And then too
Jefferson Campbell did not seem to know very well what it
was that Melanctha really wanted, and all this was making
Melanctha feel his power with her always getting stronger.

Dr. Campbell came in every day to see 'Mis' Herbert. 'Mis'
Herbert, after that night they watched together, did get a
little better, but 'Mis' Herbert was really very sick, and soon it
was pretty sure that she would have to die. Melanctha certainly did everything, all the time, that any woman could.
Jefferson never thought much better of Melanctha while she
did it. It was not her being good, he wanted to find in her.
He knew very well Jane Harden was right, when she said
Melanctha was always being good to everybody but that that
did not make Melanctha any better for her. Then too, 'Mis'
Herbert never liked Melanctha any better, even on the last
day of her living, and so Jefferson really never thought much
of Melanctha's always being good to her mother.

Jefferson and Melanctha now saw each other, very often.
They now always liked to be with each other, and they always
now had a good time when they talked to one another. They,
mostly in their talking to each other, still just talked about outside things and what they were thinking. Except just in little
moments, and not those very often, they never said anything
about their feeling. Sometimes Melanctha would tease Jefferson a little just to show she had not forgotten, but mostly she
listened to his talking, for Jefferson still always liked to talk
along about the things he believed in. Melanctha was
liking Jefferson Campbell better every day, and Jefferson was
beginning to know that Melanctha certainly had a good mind,
and he was beginning to feel a little her real sweetness. Not in
her being good to 'Mis' Herbert, that never seemed to Jefferson to mean much in her, but there was a strong kind of sweet-

ness in Melanctha's nature that Jefferson began now to feel
when he was with her.

'Mis' Herbert was now always getting sicker. One night
again Dr. Campbell felt very certain that before it was morning she would surely die. Dr. Campbell said he would come
back to help Melanctha watch her, and to do anything he
could to make 'Mis' Herbert's dying more easy for her. Dr.
Campbell came back that evening, after he was through with
his other patients, and then he made 'Mis' Herbert easy, and
then he came and sat down on the steps just above where
Melanctha was sitting with the lamp, and looking very tired.
Dr. Campbell was pretty tired too, and they both sat there
very quiet.

"You look awful tired to-night, Dr. Campbell," Melanctha
said at last, with her voice low and very gentle, "Don't you
want to go lie down and sleep a little? You're always being
much too good to everybody, Dr. Campbell. I like to have you
stay here watching to-night with me, but it don't seem right
you ought to stay here when you got so much always to do for
everybody. You are certainly very kind to come back, Dr.
Campbell, but I can certainly get along to-night without you.
I can get help next door sure if I need it. You just go 'long
home to bed, Dr. Campbell. You certainly do look as if you
need it."

Jefferson was silent for some time, and always he was looking very gently at Melanctha.

"I certainly never did think, Miss Melanctha, I would find
you to be so sweet and thinking, with me." "Dr. Campbell,"
said Melanctha, still more gentle, "I certainly never did think
that you would ever feel it good to like me. I certainly never
did think you would want to see for yourself if I had sweet
ways in me."

They both sat there very tired, very gentle, very quiet, a
long time. At last Melanctha in a low, even tone began to talk
to Jefferson Campbell.

"You are certainly a very good man, Dr. Campbell, I cer-
tainly do feel that more every day I see you. Dr. Campbell,
I sure do want to be friends with a good man like you, now
I know you. You certainly, Dr. Campbell, never do things like

other men, that's always ugly for me. Tell me true, Dr. Campbell, how you feel about being always friends with me. I certainly do know, Dr. Campbell, you are a good man, and if you say you will be friends with me, you certainly never will go back on me, the way so many kinds of them do to every girl they ever get to like them. Tell me for true, Dr. Campbell, will you be friends with me."

"Why, Miss Melanctha," said Campbell slowly, "why you see I just can't say that right out that way to you. Why sure you know Miss Melanctha, I will be very glad if it comes by and by that we are always friends together, but you see, Miss Melanctha, I certainly am a very slow-minded quiet kind of fellow though I do say quick things all the time to everybody and when I certainly do want to mean it what I am saying to you, I can't say things like that right out to everybody till I know really more for certain all about you, and how I like you, and what I really mean to do better for you. You certainly do see what I mean, Miss Melanctha." "I certainly do admire you for talking honest to me, Jeff Campbell," said Melanctha. "Oh, I am always honest, Miss Melanctha. It's easy enough for me always to be honest, Miss Melanctha. All I got to do is always just to say right out what I am thinking. I certainly never have got any real reason for not saying it right out like that to anybody."

They sat together, very silent. "I certainly do wonder, Miss Melanctha," at last began Jeff Campbell, "I certainly do wonder, if we know very right, you and me, what each other is really thinking. I certainly do wonder, Miss Melanctha, if we know at all really what each other means by what we are always saying." "That certainly do mean, by what you say, that you think I am a bad one, Jeff Campbell," flashed out Melanctha. "Why no, Miss Melanctha, why sure I don't mean any thing like that at all, by what I am saying to you. You know well as I do, Miss Melanctha, I think better of you every day I see you, and I like to talk with you all the time now, Miss Melanctha, and I certainly do think we both like it very well when we are together, and it seems to me always more, you are very good and sweet always to everybody. It only is, I am really so slow-minded in my ways, Miss Melanctha, for all I talk so quick to everybody, and I don't like to say to you what I don't know for very sure, and I certainly don't know for sure I know just all what you mean by what you are always saying to me. And you see, Miss Melanctha, that's what makes me say what I was just saying to you when you asked me."

"I certainly do thank you again for being honest to me, Dr. Campbell," said Melanctha. "I guess I leave you now, Dr. Campbell. I think I go in the other room and rest a little. I leave you here, so perhaps if I ain't here you will maybe sleep and rest yourself a little. Good night now, Dr. Campbell, I call you if I need you later to help me, Dr. Campbell, I hope you rest well, Dr. Campbell."

Jeff Campbell, when Melanctha left him, sat there and he was very quiet and just wondered. He did not know very well just what Melanctha meant by what she was always saying to him. He did not know very well how much he really knew about Melanctha Herbert. He wondered if he should go on being so much all the time with her. He began to think about what he should do now with her. Jefferson Campbell was a man who liked everybody and many people liked very much to be with him. Women liked him, he was so strong, and good, and understanding, and innocent, and firm, and gentle. Sometimes they seemed to want very much he should be with them. When they got so, they always had made Campbell very tired. Sometimes he would play a little with them, but he never had had any strong feeling for them. Now with Melanctha Herbert everything seemed different. Jefferson was not sure that he knew here just what he wanted. He was not sure he knew just what it was that Melanctha wanted. He knew if it was only play, with Melanctha, that he did not want to do it. But he remembered always how she had told him he never knew how to feel things very deeply. He remembered how she told him he was afraid to let himself ever know real feeling, and then too, most of all to him, she had told him he was not very understanding. That always troubled Jefferson very keenly, he wanted very badly to be really understanding. If Jefferson only knew better just what Melanctha meant by what she said. Jefferson always had thought he knew something about

women. Now he found that really he knew nothing. He did
not know the least bit about Melanctha. He did not know
what it was right that he should do about it. He wondered if
it was just a little play that they were doing. If it was a play
he did not want to go on playing, but if it was really that he
was not very understanding, and that with Melanctha Herbert
he could learn to really understand, then he was very certain
he did not want to be a coward. It was very hard for him to
know what he wanted. He thought and thought, and always
he did not seem to know any better what he wanted. At last
he gave up this thinking. He felt sure it was only play with
Melanctha. "No, I certainly won't go on fooling with her any
more this way," he said at last out loud to himself, when he
was through with this thinking. "I certainly will stop fooling,
and begin to go on with my thinking about my work and
what's the matter with people like 'Mis' Herbert," and Jefferson took out his book from his pocket, and drew near to the
lamp, and began with some hard scientific reading.

Jefferson sat there for about an hour reading, and he had
really forgotten all about his trouble with Melanctha's meaning. Then 'Mis' Herbert had some trouble with her breathing.
She woke up and was gasping. Dr. Campbell went to her and
gave her something that would help her. Melanctha came out
from the other room and did things as he told her. They together made 'Mis' Herbert more comfortable and easy, and
soon she was again in her deep sleep.

Dr. Campbell went back to the steps where he had been
sitting. Melanctha came and stood a little while beside him,
and then she sat down and watched him reading. By and by
they began with their talking. Jeff Campbell began to feel
that perhaps it was all different. Perhaps it was not just play,
with Melanctha. Anyway he liked it very well that she was
with him. He began to tell her about the book he was just
reading.

Melanctha was very intelligent always in her questions.
Jefferson knew now very well that she had a good mind. They
were having a very good time, talking there together. And
then they began again to get quiet.

"It certainly was very good in you to come back and talk to

me Miss Melanctha," Jefferson said at last to her, for now he was almost certain, it was no game she was playing. Melanctha really was a good woman, and she had a good mind, and she had a real, strong sweetness, and she could surely really teach him. "Oh I always like to talk to you Dr. Campbell," said Melanctha, "And then you was only just honest to me, and I always like it when a man is really honest to me." Then they were again very silent, sitting there together, with the lamp between them, that was always smoking. Melanctha began to lean a little more toward Dr. Campbell, where he was sitting, and then she took his hand between her two and pressed it hard, but she said nothing to him. She let it go then and leaned a little nearer to him. Jefferson moved a little but did not do anything in answer. At last, "Well," said Melanctha sharply to him. "I was just thinking," began Dr. Campbell slowly, "I was just wondering," he was beginning to get ready to go on with his talking. "Don't you ever stop with your thinking long enough ever to have any feeling Jeff Campbell," said Melanctha a little sadly. "I don't know," said Jeff Campbell slowly, "I don't know Miss Melanctha much about that. No, I don't stop thinking much Miss Melanctha and if I can't ever feel without stopping thinking, I certainly am very much afraid Miss Melanctha that I never will do much with that kind of feeling. Sure you ain't worried Miss Melanctha, about my really not feeling very much all the time. I certainly do think I feel some, Miss Melanctha, even though I always do it without ever knowing how to stop with my thinking." "I am certainly afraid I don't think much of your kind of feeling Dr. Campbell." "Why I think you certainly are wrong, Miss Melanctha. I certainly do think I feel as much for you Miss Melanctha, as you ever feel about me, sure I do. I don't think you know me right when you talk like that to me. Tell me just straight out how much do you care about me, Miss Melanctha." "Care about you Jeff Campbell," said Melanctha slowly. "I certainly do care for you Jeff Campbell less than you are always thinking and much more than you are ever knowing."

Jeff Campbell paused on this, and he was silent with the power of Melanctha's meaning. They sat there together very silent, a long time. "Well Jeff Campbell," said Melanctha.

"Oh," said Dr. Campbell and he moved himself a little, and then they were very silent a long time. "Haven't you got nothing to say to me Jeff Campbell?" said Melanctha. "Why yes, what was it we were just saying about to one another. You see Miss Melanctha I am a very quiet, slow minded kind of fellow, and I am never sure I know just exactly what you mean by all that you are always saying to me. But I do like you very much Miss Melanctha and I am very sure you got very good things in you all the time. You sure do believe what I am saying to you Miss Melanctha." "Yes I believe it when you say it to me, Jeff Campbell," said Melanctha, and then she was silent and there was much sadness in it. "I guess I go in and lie down again Dr. Campbell," said Melanctha. "Don't go leave me Miss Melanctha," said Jeff Campbell quickly. "Why not, what you want of me Jeff Campbell?" said Melanctha. "Why," said Jeff Campbell slowly, "I just want to go on talking with you. I certainly do like talking about all kinds of things with you. You certainly know that all right, Miss Melanctha." "I guess I go lie down again and leave you here with your thinking," said Melanctha gently. "I certainly am very tired to-night Dr. Campbell. Good night I hope you rest well Dr. Campbell." Melanctha stooped over him, where he was sitting, to say this good night, and then, very quick and sudden, she kissed him and then, very quick again, she went away and left him.

Dr. Campbell sat there very quiet with only a little thinking and sometimes a beginning feeling, and he was alone until it began to be morning, and then he went, and Melanctha helped him, and he made 'Mis' Herbert more easy in her dying. 'Mis' Herbert lingered on till about ten o'clock the next morning, and then slowly and without much pain she died away. Jeff Campbell staid till the last moment, with Melanctha, to make her mother's dying easy for her. When it was over he sent in the colored woman from next door to help Melanctha fix things, and then he went away to take care of his other patients. He came back very soon to Melanctha. He helped her to have a funeral for her mother. Melanctha then went to live with the good natured woman, who had been her neighbor. Melanctha still saw Jeff Campbell very often. Things began to be very strong between them.

Melanctha now never wandered, unless she was with Jeff Campbell. Sometimes she and he wandered a good deal together. Jeff Campbell had not got over his way of talking to her all the time about all the things he was always thinking. Melanctha never talked much, now, when they were together. Sometimes Jeff Campbell teased her about her not talking to him. "I certainly did think Melanctha you was a great talker from the way Jane Harden and everybody said things to me, and from the way I heard you talk so much when I first met you. Tell me true Melanctha, why don't you talk more now to me, perhaps it is I talk so much I don't give you any chance to say things to me, or perhaps it is you hear me talk so much you don't think so much now of a whole lot of talking. Tell me honest Melanctha, why don't you talk more to me." "You know very well Jeff Campbell," said Melanctha, "You certainly do know very well Jeff, you don't think really much, of my talking. You think a whole lot more about everything than I do Jeff, and you don't care much what I got to say about it. You know that's true what I am saying Jeff, if you want to be real honest, the way you always are when I like you so much." Jeff laughed and looked fondly at her. "I don't say ever I know, you ain't right, when you say things like that to me, Melanctha. You see you always like to be talking just what you think everybody wants to be hearing from you, and when you are like that, Melanctha, honest, I certainly don't care very much to hear you, but sometimes you say something that is what you are really thinking, and then I like a whole lot to hear you talking." Melanctha smiled, with her strong sweetness, on him, and she felt her power very deeply. "I certainly never do talk very much when I like anybody really, Jeff. You see, Jeff, it ain't much use to talk about what a woman is really feeling in her. You see all that, Jeff, better, by and by, when you get to really feeling. You won't be so ready then always with your talking. You see, Jeff, if it don't come true what I am saying." "I don't ever say you ain't always right, Melanctha," said Jeff Campbell. "Perhaps what I call my thinking ain't really so very understanding. I don't say, no never now any more, you ain't right, Melanctha, when you really say things to me. Perhaps I see it all to be very different when I come to really see what you mean by what you are always saying to me." "You is very sweet and good to me always, Jeff Campbell," said Melanctha." " 'Deed I certainly am not good to you, Melanctha. Don't I bother you all the time with my talking, but I really do like you a whole lot, Melanctha." "And I like you, Jeff Campbell, and you certainly are mother, and father, and brother, and sister, and child and everything to me. I can't say much about how good you been to me, Jeff Campbell, I never knew any man who was good and didn't do things ugly, before I met you to take care of me, Jeff Campbell. Good-by, Jeff, come see me to-morrow, when you get through with your working." "Sure Melanctha, you know that already," said Jeff Campbell, and then he went away and left her.

These months had been an uncertain time for Jeff Campbell. He never knew how much he really knew about Melanctha. He saw her now for long times and very often. He was beginning always more and more to like her. But he did not seem to himself to know very much about her. He was beginning to feel he could almost trust the goodness in her. But then, always, really, he was not very sure about her. Melanctha always had ways that made him feel uncertain with her, and yet he was so near, in his feeling for her. He now never thought about all this in real words any more. He was always letting it fight itself out in him. He was now never taking any part in this fighting that was always going on inside him.

Jeff always loved now to be with Melanctha and yet he always hated to go to her. Somehow he was always afraid when he was to go to her, and yet he had made himself very certain that here he would not be a coward. He never felt any of this being afraid, when he was with her. Then they always were very true, and near to one another. But always when he was going to her, Jeff would like anything that could happen that would keep him a little longer from her.

It was a very uncertain time, all these months, for Jeff Campbell. He did not know very well what it was that he really wanted. He was very certain that he did not know very well what it was that Melanctha wanted. Jeff Campbell had always all his life loved to be with people, and he had loved all his life always to be thinking, but he was still only a great boy, was Jeff Campbell, and he had never before had any of this funny kind of feeling. Now, this evening, when he was free to go and see Melanctha, he talked to anybody he could find who would detain him, and so it was very late when at last he came to the house where Melanctha was waiting to receive him.

Jeff came in to where Melanctha was waiting for him, and he took off his hat and heavy coat, and then drew up a chair and sat down by the fire. It was very cold that night, and Jeff sat there, and rubbed his hands and tried to warm them. He had only said "How do you do" to Melanctha, he had not yet begun to talk to her. Melanctha sat there, by the fire, very quiet. The heat gave a pretty pink glow to her pale yellow and attractive face. Melanctha sat in a low chair, her hands, with their long, fluttering fingers, always ready to show her strong feeling, were lying quiet in her lap. Melanctha was very tired with her waiting for Jeff Campbell. She sat there very quiet and just watching. Jeff was a robust, dark, healthy, cheery negro. His hands were firm and kindly and unimpassioned. He touched women always with his big hands, like a brother. He always had a warm broad glow, like southern sunshine. He never had anything mysterious in him. He was open, he was pleasant, he was cheery, and always he wanted, as Melanctha once had wanted, always now he too wanted really to understand.

Jeff sat there this evening in his chair and was silent a long time, warming himself with the pleasant fire. He did not look at Melanctha who was watching. He sat there and just looked into the fire. At first his dark, open face was smiling, and he was rubbing the back of his black-brown hand over his mouth to help him in his smiling. Then he was thinking, and he frowned and rubbed his head hard, to help him in his thinking. Then he smiled again, but now his smiling was not very pleasant. His smile was now wavering on the edge of scorning. His smile changed more and more, and then he had a look as if he were deeply down, all disgusted. Now his face was darker, and he was bitter in his smiling, and he began, without looking from the fire, to talk to Melanctha, who was now very tense with her watching.

"Melanctha Herbert," began Jeff Campbell, "I certainly after all this time I know you, I certainly do know little, real about you. You see, Melanctha, it's like this way with me"; Jeff was frowning, with his thinking and looking very hard into the fire, "You see it's just this way, with me now, Melanctha. Sometimes you seem like one kind of a girl to me, and sometimes you are like a girl that is all different to me, and the two kinds of girls is certainly very different to each other, and I can't see any way they seem to have much to do, to be together in you. They certainly don't seem to be made much like as if they could have anything really to do with each other. Sometimes you are a girl to me I certainly never would be trusting, and you got a laugh then so hard, it just rattles, and you got ways so bad, I can't believe you mean them hardly, and yet all that I just been saying is certainly you one way I often see you, and it's what your mother and Jane Harden always found you, and it's what makes me hate so, to come near you. And then certainly sometimes, Melanctha, you certainly is all a different creature, and sometimes then there comes out in you what is certainly a thing, like a real beauty. I certainly, Melanctha, never can tell just how it is that it comes so lovely. Seems to me when it comes it's got a real sweetness, that is more wonderful than a pure flower, and a gentleness, that is more tender than the sunshine, and a kindness, that makes one feel like summer, and then a way to know, that makes everything all over, and all that, and it does certainly seem to be real for the little while it's lasting, for the little while that I can surely see it, and it gives me to feel like I certainly had got real religion. And then when I got rich with such a feeling, comes all that other girl, and then that seems more likely that that is really you what's honest and then I certainly do get awful afraid to come to you, and I certainly never do feel I could be very trusting with you. And then I certainly don't know anything at all about you, and I certainly don't know which is a real Melanctha Herbert, and I certainly don't feel no longer, I ever want to talk to you. Tell

me honest, Melanctha, which is the way that is you really,
when you are alone, and real, and all honest. Tell me, Melanctha, for I certainly do want to know it."

Melanctha did not make him any answer, and Jeff, without
looking at her, after a little while, went on with his talking.
"And then, Melanctha, sometimes you certainly do seem sort
of cruel, and not to care about people being hurt or in trouble,
something so hard about you it makes me sometimes real
nervous, sometimes somehow like you always, like your being,
with 'Mis' Herbert. You sure did do everything that any
woman could, Melanctha, I certainly never did see anybody
do things any better, and yet, I don't know how to say just
what I mean, Melanctha, but there was something awful hard
about your feeling, so different from the way I'm always used
to see good people feeling, and so it was the way Jane Harden
and 'Mis' Herbert talked when they felt strong to talk about
you, and yet, Melanctha, somehow I feel so really near to you,
and you certainly have got an awful wonderful, strong kind
of sweetness. I certainly would like to know for sure, Melanctha, whether I got really anything to be afraid for. I certainly
did think once, Melanctha, I knew something about all kinds
of women. I certainly know now really, how I don't know anything sure at all about you, Melanctha, though I been with
you so long, and so many times for whole hours with you,
and I like so awful much to be with you, and I can always say
anything I am thinking to you. I certainly do awful wish, Melanctha, I really was more understanding. I certainly do that
same, Melanctha."

Jeff stopped now and looked harder than before into the
fire. His face changed from his thinking back into that look
that was so like as if he was all through and through him, disgusted with what he had been thinking. He sat there a long
time, very quiet, and then slowly, somehow, it came strongly
to him that Melanctha Herbert, there beside him, was trembling and feeling it all to be very bitter. "Why, Melanctha,"
cried Jeff Campbell, and he got up and put his arm around
her like a brother. "I stood it just so long as I could bear it,
Jeff," sobbed Melanctha, and then she gave herself away, to
her misery, "I was awful ready, Jeff, to let you say anything

you liked that gave you any pleasure. You could say all about
me what you wanted, Jeff, and I would try to stand it, so as
you would be sure to be liking it, Jeff, but you was too cruel
to me. When you do that kind of seeing how much you can
make a woman suffer, you ought to give her a little rest, once
sometimes, Jeff. They can't any of us stand it so for always,
Jeff. I certainly did stand it just as long as I could, so you
would like it, but I,—oh Jeff, you went on too long to-night
Jeff. I couldn't stand it not a minute longer the way you was
doing of it, Jeff. When you want to be seeing how the way a
woman is really made of, Jeff, you shouldn't never be so cruel,
never to be thinking how much she can stand, the strong way
you always do it, Jeff." "Why, Melanctha," cried Jeff Campbell, in his horror, and then he was very tender to her, and
like a good, strong, gentle brother in his soothing of her, "Why
Melanctha dear, I certainly don't now see what it is you mean
by what you was just saying to me. Why Melanctha, you poor
little girl, you certainly never did believe I ever knew I was
giving you real suffering. Why, Melanctha, how could you
ever like me if you thought I ever could be so like a red
Indian?" "I don't just know, Jeff," and Melanctha nestled to
him, "I certainly never did know just what it was you wanted
to be doing with me, but I certainly wanted you should do
anything you liked, you wanted, to make me more understanding for you. I tried awful hard to stand it, Jeff, so as you could
do anything you wanted with me." "Good Lord and Jesus
Christ, Melanctha!" cried Jeff Campbell. "I certainly never
can know anything about you real, Melanctha, you poor little
girl," and Jeff drew her closer to him, "But I certainly do admire and trust you a whole lot now, Melanctha. I certainly do,
for I certainly never did think I was hurting you at all, Melanctha, by the things I always been saying to you. Melanctha,
you poor little, sweet, trembling baby now, be good, Melanctha. I certainly can't ever tell you how awful sorry I am to
hurt you so, Melanctha. I do anything I can to show you how
I never did mean to hurt you, Melanctha." "I know, I know,"
murmured Melanctha, clinging to him. "I know you are a
good man, Jeff. I always know that, no matter how much you
can hurt me." "I sure don't see how you can think so, Melanc-

tha, if you certainly did think I was trying so hard to hurt you." "Hush, you are only a great big boy, Jeff Campbell, and you don't know nothing yet about real hurting," said Melanctha, smiling up through her crying, at him. "You see, Jeff, I never knew anybody I could know real well and yet keep on always respecting, till I came to know you real well, Jeff." "I sure don't understand that very well, Melanctha. I ain't a bit better than just lots of others of the colored people. You certainly have been unlucky with the kind you met before me, that's all, Melanctha. I certainly ain't very good, Melanctha." "Hush, Jeff, you don't know nothing at all about what you are," said Melanctha. "Perhaps you are right, Melanctha. I don't say ever any more, you ain't right, when you say things to me, Melanctha," and Jefferson sighed, and then he smiled, and then they were quiet a long time together, and then after some more kindness, it was late, and then Jeff left her.

Jeff Campbell, all these months, had never told his good mother anything about Melanctha Herbert. Somehow he always kept his seeing her so much now, to himself. Melanctha too had never had any of her other friends meet him. They always acted together, these two, as if their being so much together was a secret, but really there was no one who would have made it any harder for them. Jeff Campbell did not really know how it had happened that they were so secret. He did not know if it was what Melanctha wanted. Jeff had never spoken to her at all about it. It just seemed as if it were well understood between them that nobody should know that they were so much together. It was as if it were agreed between them, that they should be alone by themselves always, and so they would work out together what they meant by what they were always saying to each other.

Jefferson often spoke to Melanctha about his good mother. He never said anything about whether Melanctha would want to meet her. Jefferson never quite understood why all this had happened so, in secret. He never really knew what it was that Melanctha really wanted. In all these ways he just, by his nature, did, what he sort of felt Melanctha wanted. And so they continued to be alone and much together, and now it had come to be the spring time, and now they had all out-doors to wander.

They had many days now when they were very happy. Jeff every day found that he really liked Melanctha better. Now surely he was beginning to have real, deep feeling in him. And still he loved to talk himself out to Melanctha, and he loved to tell her how good it all was to him, and how he always loved to be with her, and to tell her always all about it. One day, now Jeff arranged, that Sunday they would go out and have a happy, long day in the bright fields, and they would be all day just alone together. The day before, Jeff was called in to see Jane Harden.

Jane Harden was very sick almost all day and Jeff Campbell did everything he could to make her better. After a while Jane became more easy and then she began to talk to Jeff about Melanctha. Jane did not know how much Jeff was now seeing of Melanctha. Jane these days never saw Melanctha. Jane began to talk of the time when she first knew Melanctha. Jane began to tell how in these days Melanctha had very little understanding. She was young then and she had a good mind. Jane Harden never would say Melanctha never had a good mind, but in those days Melanctha certainly had not been very understanding. Jane began to explain to Jeff Campbell how in every way, she Jane, had taught Melanctha. Jane then began to explain how eager Melanctha always had been for all that kind of learning. Jane Harden began to tell how they had wandered. Jane began to tell how Melanctha once had loved her, Jane Harden. Jane began to tell Jeff of all the bad ways Melanctha had used with her. Jane began to tell all she knew of the way Melanctha had gone on, after she had left her. Jane began to tell all about the different men, white ones and blacks, Melanctha never was particular about things like that, Jane Harden said in passing, not that Melanctha was a bad one, and she had a good mind, Jane Harden never would say that she hadn't, but Melanctha always liked to use all the understanding ways that Jane had taught her, and so she wanted to know everything, always, that they knew how to teach her.

Jane was beginning to make Jeff Campbell see much clearer. Jane Harden did not know what it was that she was really doing with all this talking. Jane did not know what Jeff was feeling. Jane was always honest when she was talking, and now it just happened she had started talking about her old times with Melanctha Herbert. Jeff understood very well that it was all true what Jane was saying. Jeff Campbell was beginning now to see very clearly. He was beginning to feel very sick inside him. He knew now many things Melanctha had not yet taught him. He felt very sick and his heart was very heavy, and Melanctha certainly did seem very ugly to him. Jeff was at last beginning to know what it was to have deep feeling. He took care a little longer of Jane Harden, and then he went to his other patients, and then he went home to his room, and he sat down and at last he had stopped thinking. He was very sick and his heart was very heavy in him. He was very tired and all the world was very dreary to him, and he knew very well now at last, he was really feeling. He knew it now from the way it hurt him. He knew very well that now at last he was beginning to really have understanding. The next day he had arranged to spend, long and happy, all alone in the spring fields with Melanctha, wandering He wrote her a note and said he could not go, he had a sick patient and would have to stay home with him. For three days after, he made no sign to Melanctha. He was very sick all these days, and his heart was very heavy in him, and he knew very well that now at last he had learned what it was to have deep feeling.

At last one day he got a letter from Melanctha. "I certainly don't rightly understand what you are doing now to me Jeff Campbell," wrote Melanctha Herbert. "I certainly don't rightly understand Jeff Campbell why you ain't all these days been near me, but I certainly do suppose it's just another one of the queer kind of ways you have to be good, and repenting of yourself all of a sudden. I certainly don't say to you Jeff Campbell I admire very much the way you take to be good Jeff Campbell. I am sorry Dr. Campbell, but I certainly am afraid I can't stand it no more from you the way you have been just acting. I certainly can't stand it any more the way you act when you have been as if you thought I was always good enough for anybody to have with them, and then you act as if I was a bad one and you always just despise me. I certainly am afraid Dr. Campbell I can't stand it any more like that. I certainly can't stand it any more the way you are always changing. I certainly am afraid Dr. Campbell you ain't man enough to deserve to have anybody care so much to be always with you. I certainly am awful afraid Dr. Campbell I don't ever any more want to really see you. Good-by Dr. Campbell I wish you always to be real happy."

Jeff Campbell sat in his room, very quiet, a long time, after he got through reading this letter. He sat very still and first he was very angry. As if he, too, did not know very badly what it was to suffer keenly. As if he had not been very strong to stay with Melanctha when he never knew what it was that she really wanted. He knew he was very right to be angry, he knew he really had not been a coward. He knew Melanctha had done many things it was very hard for him to forgive her. He knew very well he had done his best to be kind, and to trust her, and to be loyal to her, and now—and then Jeff suddenly remembered how one night Melanctha had been so strong to suffer, and he felt come back to him the sweetness in her, and then Jeff knew that really, he always forgave her, and that really, it all was that he was so sorry he had hurt her, and he wanted to go straight away and be a comfort to her. Jeff knew very well, that what Jane Harden had told him about Melanctha and her bad ways, had been a true story, and yet he wanted very badly to be with Melanctha. Perhaps she could teach him to really understand it better. Perhaps she could teach him how it could be all true, and yet how he could be right to believe in her and to trust her.

Jeff sat down and began his answer to her. "Dear Melanctha," Jeff wrote to her. "I certainly don't think you got it all just right in the letter, I just been reading, that you just wrote me. I certainly don't think you are just fair or very understanding to all I have to suffer to keep straight on to really always to believe in you and trust you. I certainly don't think you always are fair to remember right how hard it is for a man, who thinks like I was always thinking, not to think you do things very bad very often. I certainly don't think, Melanctha, I ain't right when I was so angry when I got your letter to me. I know very well, Melanctha, that with you, I never have been a coward. I find it very hard, and I never said it any different, it is hard to me to be understanding, and to know really what it is you wanted, and what it is you are meaning by what you are always saying to me. I don't say ever, it ain't very hard for you to be standing that I ain't very quick to be following whichever way that you are always leading. You know very well, Melanctha, it hurts me very bad and way inside me when I have to hurt you, but I always got to be real honest with you. There ain't no other way for me to be, with you, and I know very well it hurts me too, a whole lot, when I can't follow so quick as you would have me. I don't like to be a coward to you, Melanctha, and I don't like to say what I ain't meaning to you. And if you don't want me to do things honest, Melanctha, why I can't ever talk to you, and you are right when you say, you never again want to see me, but if you got any real sense of what I always been feeling with you, and if you got any right sense, Melanctha, of how hard I been trying to think and to feel right for you, I will be very glad to come and see you, and to begin again with you. I don't say anything now, Melanctha, about how bad I been this week, since I saw you, Melanctha. It don't ever do any good to talk such things over. All I know is I do my best, Melanctha, to you, and I don't say, no, never, I can do any different than just to be honest and come as fast as I think it's right for me to be going in the ways you teach me to be really understanding. So don't talk any more foolishness, Melanctha, about my always changing. I don't change, never, and I got to do what I think is right and honest to me, and I never told you any different, and you always knew it very well that I always would do just so. If you like me to come and see you to-morrow, and go out with you, I will be very glad to, Melanctha. Let me know right away, what it is you want me to be doing for you, Melanctha.

Very truly yours,
JEFFERSON CAMPBELL

"Please come to me, Jeff." Melanctha wrote back for her answer. Jeff went very slowly to Melanctha, glad as he was.

still to be going to her. Melanctha came, very quick, to meet him, when she saw him from where she had been watching for him. They went into the house together. They were very glad to be together. They were very good to one another.

"I certainly did think, Melanctha, this time almost really, you never did want me to come to you at all any more to see you," said Jeff Campbell to her, when they had begun again with their talking to each other. "You certainly did make me think, perhaps really this time, Melanctha, it was all over, my being with you ever, and I was very mad, and very sorry, too, Melanctha."

"Well you certainly was very bad to me, Jeff Campbell," said Melanctha, fondly.

"I certainly never do say any more you ain't always right, Melanctha," Jeff answered and he was very ready now with cheerful laughing, "I certainly never do say that any more, Melanctha, if I know it, but still, really, Melanctha, honest, I think perhaps I wasn't real bad to you any more than you just needed from me."

Jeff held Melanctha in his arms and kissed her. He sighed then and was very silent with her. "Well, Melanctha," he said at last, with some more laughing, "well, Melanctha, any way you can't say ever it ain't, if we are ever friends good and really, you can't say, no, never, but that we certainly have worked right hard to get both of us together for it, so we shall sure deserve it then, if we can ever really get it." "We certainly have worked real hard, Jeff, I can't say that ain't all right the way you say it," said Melanctha. "I certainly never can deny it, Jeff, when I feel so worn with all the trouble you been making for me, you bad boy, Jeff," and then Melanctha smiled and then she sighed, and then she was very silent with him.

At last Jeff was to go away. They stood there on the steps for a long time trying to say good-by to each other. At last Jeff made himself really say it. At last he made himself, that he went down the steps and went away.

On the next Sunday they arranged, they were to have the long happy day of wandering that they had lost last time by Jane Harden's talking. Not that Melanctha Herbert had heard yet of Jane Harden's talking.

Jeff saw Melanctha every day now. Jeff was a little uncertain all this time inside him, for he had never yet told to Melanctha what it was that had so nearly made him really want to leave her. Jeff knew that for him, it was not right he should not tell her. He knew they could only have real peace between them when he had been honest, and had really told her. On this long Sunday Jeff was certain that he would really tell her.

They were very happy all that day in their wandering. They had taken things along to eat together. They sat in the bright fields and they were happy, they wandered in the woods and they were happy. Jeff always loved in this way to wander. Jeff always loved to watch everything as it was growing, and he loved all the colors in the trees and on the ground, and the little, new, bright colored bugs he found in the moist ground and in the grass he loved to lie on and in which he was always so busy searching. Jeff loved everything that moved and that was still, and that had color, and beauty, and real being.

Jeff loved very much this day while they were wandering. He almost forgot that he had any trouble with him still inside him. Jeff loved to be there with Melanctha Herbert. She was always so sympathetic to him for the way she listened to everything he found and told her, the way she felt his joy in all this being, the way she never said she wanted anything different from the way they had it. It was certainly a busy and a happy day, this their first long day of really wandering.

Later they were tired, and Melanctha sat down on the ground, and Jeff threw himself his full length beside her. Jeff lay there, very quiet, and then he pressed her hand and kissed it and murmured to her, "You certainly are very good to me, Melanctha." Melanctha felt it very deep and did not answer. Jeff lay there a long time, looking up above him. He was counting all the little leaves he saw above him. He was following all the little clouds with his eyes as they sailed past him. He watched all the birds that flew high beyond him, and all the time Jeff knew he must tell to Melanctha what it was he knew now, that which Jane Harden, just a week ago, had told him. He knew very well that for him it was certain that he had to say it. It was hard, but for Jeff Campbell the only way to lose it was to say it, the only way to know Melanctha really, was to tell her all the struggle he had made to know her, to tell her so she could help him to understand his trouble better, to help him so that never again he could have any way to doubt her.

Jeff lay there a long time, very quiet, always looking up above him, and yet feeling very close now to Melanctha. At last he turned a little toward her, took her hands closer to his to make him feel it stronger, and then very slowly, for the words came very hard for him, slowly he began his talk to her.

"Melanctha," began Jeff, very slowly, "Melanctha, it ain't right I shouldn't tell you why I went away last week and almost never got the chance again to see you. Jane Harden was sick, and I went in to take care of her. She began to tell everything she ever knew about you. She didn't know how well now I know you. I didn't tell her not to go on talking. I listened while she told me everything about you. I certainly found it very hard with what she told me. I know she was talking truth in everything she said about you. I knew you had been free in your ways, Melanctha, I knew you liked to get excitement the way I always hate to see the colored people take it. I didn't know, till I heard Jane Harden say it, you had done things so bad, Melanctha. When Jane Harden told me, I got very sick, Melanctha. I couldn't bear hardly, to think, perhaps I was just another like them to you, Melanctha. I was wrong not to trust you perhaps, Melanctha, but it did make things very ugly to me. I try to be honest to you, Melanctha, the way you say you really want it from me."

Melanctha drew her hands from Jeff Campbell. She sat there, and there was deep scorn in her anger.

"If you wasn't all through just selfish and nothing else, Jeff Campbell, you would take care you wouldn't have to tell me things like this, Jeff Campbell."

Jeff was silent a little, and he waited before he gave his answer. It was not the power of Melanctha's words that held him, for, for them, he had his answer, it was the power of the mood that filled Melanctha, and for that he had no answer. At last he broke through this awe, with his slow fighting resolution, and he began to give his answer.

"I don't say ever, Melanctha," he began, "it wouldn't have been more right for me to stop Jane Harden in her talking and to come to you to have you tell me what you were when I never knew you. I don't say it, no never to you, that that would not have been the right way for me to do, Melanctha. But I certainly am without any kind of doubting, I certainly do know for sure, I had a good right to know about what you were and your ways and your trying to use your understanding, every kind of way you could to get your learning. I certainly did have a right to know things like that about you, Melanctha. I don't say it ever, Melanctha, and I say it very often, I don't say ever I shouldn't have stopped Jane Harden in her talking and come to you and asked you yourself to tell me all about it, but I guess I wanted to keep myself from how much it would hurt me more, to have you yourself say it to me. Perhaps it was I wanted to keep you from having it hurt you so much more, having you to have to tell it to me. I don't know, I don't say it was to help you from being hurt most, or to help me. Perhaps I was a coward to let Jane Harden tell me 'stead of coming straight to you, to have you tell me, but I certainly am sure, Melanctha, I certainly had a right to know such things about you. I don't say it ever, ever, Melanctha, I hadn't the just right to know those things about you." Melanctha laughed her harsh laugh. "You needn't have been under no kind of worry, Jeff Campbell, about whether you should have asked me. You could have asked, it wouldn't have hurt nothing. I certainly never would have told you nothing." "I am not so sure of that, Melanctha," said Jeff Campbell. "I certainly do think you would have told me. I certainly do think I could make you feel it right to tell me. I certainly do think all I did wrong was to let Jane Harden tell me. I certainly do know I never did wrong, to learn what she told me. I certainly know very well, Melanctha, if I had come here to you, you would have told it all to me, Melanctha."

He was silent, and this struggle lay there, strong, between them. It was a struggle, sure to be going on always between them. It was a struggle that was as sure always to be going on between them, as their minds and hearts always were to have different ways of working.

At last Melanctha took his hand, leaned over him and kissed him. "I sure am very fond of you, Jeff Campbell," Melanctha whispered to him.

Now for a little time there was not any kind of trouble between Jeff Campbell and Melanctha Herbert. They were always together now for long times, and very often. They got much joy now, both of them, from being all the time together.

It was summer now, and they had warm sunshine to wander. It was summer now, and Jeff Campbell had more time to wander, for colored people never get sick so much in summer. It was summer now, and there was a lovely silence everywhere, and all the noises, too, that they heard around them were lovely ones, and added to the joy, in these warm days, they loved so much to be together.

They talked some to each other in these days, did Jeff Campbell and Melanctha Herbert, but always in these days their talking more and more was like it always is with real lovers. Jeff did not talk so much now about what he before always had been thinking. Sometimes Jeff would be, as if he was just waking from himself to be with Melanctha, and then he would find he had been really all the long time with her, and he had really never needed to be doing any thinking.

It was sometimes pure joy Jeff would be talking to Melanctha, in these warm days he loved so much to wander with her. Sometimes Jeff would lose all himself in a strong feeling. Very often now, and always with more joy in his feeling, he would find himself, he did not know how or what it was he had been thinking. And Melanctha always loved very well to make him feel it. She always now laughed a little at him, and went back a little in him to his before, always thinking, and she teased him with his always now being so good with her in his feeling, and then she would so well and freely, and with her pure, strong ways of reaching, she would give him all the love she knew now very well, how much he always wanted to be sure he really had it.

And Jeff took it straight now, and he loved it, and he felt,

strong, the joy of all this being, and it swelled out full inside
him, and he poured it all out back to her in freedom, in tender
kindness, and in joy, and in gentle brother fondling. And
Melanctha loved him for it always, her Jeff Campbell now,
who never did things ugly, for her, like all the men she
always knew before always had been doing to her. And they
loved it always, more and more, together, with this new
feeling they had now, in these long summer days so warm;
they, always together now, just these two so dear, more and
more to each other always, and the summer evenings when
they wandered, and the noises in the full streets, and the
music of the organs, and the dancing, and the warm smell of
the people, and of dogs and of the horses, and all the joy of
the strong, sweet pungent, dirty, moist, warm negro southern
summer.

Every day now, Jeff seemed to be coming nearer, to be
really loving. Every day now, Melanctha poured it all out to
him, with more freedom. Every day now, they seemed to be
having more and more, both together, of this strong, right
feeling. More and more every day now they seemed to know
more really, what it was each other one was always feeling.
More and more now every day Jeff found in himself, he felt
more trusting. More and more every day now, he did not
think anything in words about what he was always doing.
Every day now more and more Melanctha would let out to
Jeff her real, strong feeling.

One day there had been much joy between them, more
than they ever yet had had with their new feeling. All the
day they had lost themselves in warm wandering. Now they
were lying there and resting, with a green, bright, light-
flecked world around them.

What was it that now really happened to them? What was
it that Melanctha did, that made everything get all ugly for
them? What was it that Melanctha felt then, that made Jeff
remember all the feeling he had had in him when Jane
Harden told him how Melanctha had learned to be so very
understanding? Jeff did not know how it was that it had
happened to him. It was all green, and warm, and very
lovely to him, and now Melanctha somehow had made it all

ugly for him. What was it Melanctha was now doing with
him? What was it he used to be thinking was the right way
for him and all the colored people to be always trying to
make it right, the way they should be always living? Why
was Melanctha Herbert now all so ugly for him?

Melanctha Herbert somehow had made him feel deeply
just then, what very more it was that she wanted from him.
Jeff Campbell now felt in him what everybody always had
needed to make them really understanding, to him. Jeff felt
a strong disgust inside him; not for Melanctha herself, to him,
not for himself really, in him, not for what it was that everybody wanted, in them; he only had disgust because he never
could know really in him, what it was he wanted, to be really
right in understanding, for him, he only had disgust because
he never could know really what it was really right to him
to be always doing, in the things he had before believed in,
the things he before had believed in for himself and for all
the colored people, the living regular, and the never wanting
to be always having new things, just to keep on, always being
in excitements. All the old thinking now came up very strong
inside him. He sort of turned away then, and threw Melanctha
from him.

Jeff never, even now, knew what it was that moved him.
He never, even now, was ever sure, he really knew what
Melanctha was, when she was real herself, and honest. He
thought he knew, and then there came to him some moment,
just like this one, when she really woke him up to be strong
in him. Then he really knew he could know nothing. He knew
then, he never could know what it was she really wanted
with him. He knew then he never could know really what it
was he felt inside him. It was all so mixed up inside him. All
he knew was he wanted very badly Melanctha should be there
beside him, and he wanted very badly, too, always to throw
her from him. What was it really that Melanctha wanted
with him? What was it really, he, Jeff Campbell, wanted she
should give him? "I certainly did think now," Jeff Campbell
groaned inside him, "I certainly did think now I really was
knowing all right, what I wanted. I certainly did really think
now I was knowing how to be trusting with Melanctha. I

certainly did think it was like that now with me sure, after all I've been through all this time with her. And now I certainly do know I don't know anything that's very real about her. Oh the good Lord help and keep me!" and Jeff groaned hard inside him, and he buried his face deep in the green grass underneath him, and Melanctha Herbert was very silent there beside him.

Then Jeff turned to look and see her. She was lying very still there by him, and the bitter water on her face was biting. Jeff was so very sorry then, all over and inside him, the way he always was when Melanctha had been deep hurt by him. "I didn't mean to be so bad again to you, Melanctha, dear one," and he was very tender to her. "I certainly didn't never mean to go to be so bad to you, Melanctha, darling. I certainly don't know, Melanctha, darling, what it is makes me act so to you sometimes, when I certainly ain't meaning anything like I want to hurt you. I certainly don't mean to be so bad, Melanctha, only it comes so quick on me before I know what I am acting to you. I certainly am all sorry, hard, to be so bad to you, Melanctha, darling." "I suppose, Jeff," said Melanctha, very low and bitter, "I suppose you are always thinking, Jeff, somebody had ought to be ashamed with us two together, and you certainly do think you don't see any way to it, Jeff, for me to be feeling that way ever, so you certainly don't see any way to it, only to do it just so often for me. That certainly is the way always with you, Jeff Campbell, if I understand you right the way you are always acting to me. That certainly is right the way I am saying it to you now, Jeff Campbell. You certainly didn't anyway trust me now no more, did you, when you just acted so bad to me. I certainly am right the way I say it Jeff now to you. I certainly am right when I ask you for it now, to tell me what I ask you, about not trusting me more then again, Jeff, just like you never really knew me. You certainly never did trust me just then, Jeff, you hear me?" "Yes, Melanctha," Jeff answered slowly. Melanctha paused. "I guess I certainly never can forgive you this time, Jeff Campbell," she said firmly. Jeff paused too, and thought a little. "I certainly am afraid you never can no more now again, Melanctha," he said sadly.

They lay there very quiet now a long time, each one thinking very hard on their own trouble. At last Jeff began again to tell Melanctha what it was he was always thinking with her. "I certainly do know, Melanctha, you certainly now don't want any more to be hearing me just talking, but you see, Melanctha, really, it's just like this way always with me. You see, Melanctha, it's like this way now all the time with me. You remember, Melanctha, what I was once telling to you, when I didn't know you very long together, about how I certainly never did know more than just two kinds of ways of loving, one way the way it is good to be in families and the other kind of way, like animals are all the time just with each other, and how I didn't ever like that last kind of way much for any of the colored people. You see Melanctha, it's like this way with me. I got a new feeling now, you been teaching to me, just like I told you once, just like a new religion to me, and I see perhaps what really loving is like, like really having everything together, new things, little pieces all different, like I always before been thinking was bad to be having, all go together like, to make one good big feeling. You see, Melanctha, it's certainly like that you make me been seeing, like I never know before any way there was of all kinds of loving to come together to make one way really truly lovely. I see that now, sometimes, the way you certainly been teaching me, Melanctha, really, and then I love you those times, Melanctha, like a real religion, and then it comes over me all sudden, I don't know anything real about you Melanctha, dear one, and then it comes over me sudden, perhaps I certainly am wrong now, thinking all this way so lovely, and not thinking now any more the old way I always before was always thinking, about what was the right way for me, to live regular and all the colored people, and then I think, perhaps, Melanctha you are really just a bad one, and I think, perhaps I certainly am doing it so because I just am too anxious to be just having all the time excitements, like I don't ever like really to be doing when I know it, and then I always get so bad to you, Melanctha, and I can't help it with myself then, never, for I want to be always right really in the ways, I have to do them.

I certainly do very badly want to be right, Melanctha, the only way I know is right Melanctha really, and I don't know any way, Melanctha, to find out really, whether my old way, the way I always used to be thinking, or the new way, you make so like a real religion to me sometimes, Melanctha, which way certainly is the real right way for me to be always thinking, and then I certainly am awful good and sorry, Melanctha, I always give you so much trouble, hurting you with the bad ways I am acting. Can't you help me to any way, to make it all straight for me, Melanctha, so I know right and real what it is I should be acting. You see, Melanctha, I don't want always to be a coward with you, if I only could know certain what was the right way for me to be acting. I certainly am real sure, Melanctha, that would be the way I would be acting, if I only knew it sure for certain now, Melanctha. Can't you help me any way to find out real and true, Melanctha, dear one. I certainly do badly want to know always, the way I should be acting."

"No, Jeff, dear, I certainly can't help you much in that kind of trouble you are always having. All I can do now, Jeff, is to just keep certainly with my believing you are good always, Jeff, and though you certainly do hurt me bad, I always got strong faith in you, Jeff, more in you certainly, than you seem to be having in your acting to me, always so bad, Jeff."

"You certainly are very good to me, Melanctha, dear one," Jeff said, after a long, tender silence. "You certainly are very good to me, Melanctha, darling, and me so bad to you always, in my acting. Do you love me good, and right, Melanctha, always?" "Always and always, you be sure of that now you have me. Oh you Jeff, you always be so stupid." "I certainly never can say now you ain't right, when you say that to me so, Melanctha," Jeff answered. "Oh, Jeff dear, I love you always, you know that now, all right, for certain. If you don't know it right now, Jeff, really, I prove it to you now, for good and always." And they lay there a long time in their loving, and then Jeff began again with his happy free enjoying.

"I sure am a good boy to be learning all the time the right

way you are teaching me, Melanctha, darling," began Jeff
Campbell, laughing, "You can't say no, never, I ain't a good
scholar for you to be teaching now, Melanctha, and I am
always so ready to come to you every day, and never playing
hooky ever from you. You can't say ever, Melanctha, now
can you, I ain't a real good boy to be always studying to be
learning to be real bright, just like my teacher. You can't say
ever to me, I ain't a good boy to you now, Melanctha." "Not
near so good, Jeff Campbell, as such a good, patient kind of
teacher, like me, who never teaches any ways it ain't good
her scholars should be knowing, ought to be really having,
Jeff, you hear me? I certainly don't think I am right for you,
to be forgiving always, when you are so bad, and I so
patient, with all this hard teaching always." "But you do forgive me always, sure, Melanctha, always?" "Always and
always, you be sure Jeff, and I certainly am afraid I never
can stop with my forgiving, you always are going to be so
bad to me, and I always going to have to be so good with
my forgiving." "Oh! Oh!" cried Jeff Campbell, laughing, "I
ain't going to be so bad for always, sure I ain't, Melanctha, my
own darling. And sure you do forgive me really, and sure you
love me true and really, sure, Melanctha?" "Sure, sure, Jeff,
boy, sure now and always, sure now you believe me, sure you
do, Jeff, always." "I sure hope I does, with all my heart,
Melanctha, darling." "I sure do that same, Jeff, dear boy, now
you really know what it is to be loving, and I prove it to you
now so, Jeff, you never can be forgetting. You see now, Jeff,
good and certain, what I always before been saying to you,
Jeff, now." "Yes, Melanctha, darling," murmured Jeff, and he
was very happy in it, and so the two of them now in the
warm air of the sultry, southern, negro sunshine, lay there
for a long time just resting.

And now for a real long time there was no open trouble
any more between Jeff Campbell and Melanctha Herbert.
Then it came that Jeff knew he could not say out any more,
what it was he wanted, he could not say out any more, what
it was, he wanted to know about, what Melanctha wanted.

Melanctha sometimes now, when she was tired with being
all the time so much excited, when Jeff would talk a long

time to her about what was right for them both to be always
doing, would be, as if she gave away in her head, and lost
herself in a bad feeling. Sometimes when they had been
strong in their loving, and Jeff would have rise inside him
some strange feeling, and Melanctha felt it in him as it would
soon be coming, she would lose herself then in this bad
feeling that made her head act as if she never knew what
it was they were doing. And slowly now, Jeff soon always
came to be feeling that his Melanctha would be hurt very
much in her head in the ways he never liked to think of, if
she would ever now again have to listen to his trouble, when
he was telling about what it was he still was wanting to
make things for himself really understanding.

Now Jeff began to have always a strong feeling that
Melanctha could no longer stand it, with all her bad suffering,
to let him fight out with himself what was right for him to be
doing. Now he felt he must not, when she was there with
him, keep on, with this kind of fighting that was always going
on inside him. Jeff Campbell never knew yet, what he
thought was the right way, for himself and for all the colored
people to be living. Jeff was coming always each time closer
to be really understanding, but now Melanctha was so bad in
her suffering with him, that he knew she could not any
longer have him with her while he was always showing that
he never really yet was sure what it was, the right way, for
them to be really loving.

Jeff saw now he had to go so fast, so that Melanctha never
would have to wait any to get from him always all that she
ever wanted. He never could be honest now, he never could
be now, any more, trying to be really understanding, for
always every moment now he felt it to be a strong thing in
him, how very much it was Melanctha Herbert always
suffered.

Jeff did not know very well these days, what it was, was
really happening to him. All he knew every now and then,
when they were getting strong to get excited, the way they
used to when he gave his feeling out so that he could be
always honest, that Melanctha somehow never seemed to
hear him, she just looked at him and looked as if her head

hurt with him, and then Jeff had to keep himself from being honest, and he had to go so fast, and to do everything Melanctha ever wanted from him.

Jeff did not like it very well these days, in his true feeling. He knew now very well Melanctha was not strong enough inside her to stand any more of his slow way of doing. And yet now he knew he was not honest in his feeling. Now he always had to show more to Melanctha than he was ever feeling. Now she made him go so fast, and he knew it was not real with his feeling, and yet he could not make her suffer so any more because he always was so slow with his feeling.

It was very hard for Jeff Campbell to make all this way of doing, right, inside him. If Jeff Campbell could not be straight out, and real honest, he never could be very strong inside him. Now Melanctha, with her making him feel, always, how good she was and how very much she suffered in him, made him always go so fast then, he could not be strong then, to feel things out straight then inside him. Always now when he was with her, he was being more, than he could already yet, be feeling for her. Always now, with her, he had something inside him always holding in him, always now, with her, he was far ahead of his own feeling.

Jeff Campbell never knew very well these days what it was that was going on inside him. All he knew was, he was uneasy now always to be with Melanctha. All he knew was, that he was always uneasy when he was with Melanctha, not the way he used to be from just not being very understanding, but now, because he never could be honest with her, because he was now always feeling her strong suffering, in her, because he knew now he was having a straight, good feeling with her, but she went so fast, and he was so slow to her; Jeff knew his right feeling never got a chance to show itself as strong, to her.

All this was always getting harder for Jeff Campbell. He was very proud to hold himself to be strong, was Jeff Campbell. He was very tender not to hurt Melanctha, when he knew she would be sure to feel it badly in her head a long time after, he hated that he could not now be honest with her, he wanted to stay away to work it out all alone, without her, he was afraid she would feel it to suffer, if he kept away now from her. He was uneasy always, with her, he was uneasy when he thought about her, he knew now he had a good, straight, strong feeling of right loving for her, and yet now he never could use it to be good and honest with her.

Jeff Campbell did not know, these days, anything he could do to make it better for her. He did not know anything he could do, to set himself really right in his acting and his thinking toward her. She pulled him so fast with her, and he did not dare to hurt her, and he could not come right, so fast, the way she always needed he should be doing it now, for her.

These days were not very joyful ones now any more, to Jeff Campbell, with Melanctha. He did not think it out to himself now, in words, about her. He did not know enough, what was his real trouble, with her.

Sometimes now and again with them, and with all this trouble for a little while well forgotten by him, Jeff, and Melanctha with him, would be very happy in a strong, sweet loving. Sometimes then, Jeff would find himself to be soaring very high in his true loving. Sometimes Jeff would find then, in his loving, his soul swelling out full inside him. Always Jeff felt now in himself, deep feeling.

Always now Jeff had to go so much faster than was real with his feeling. Yet always Jeff knew now he had a right, strong feeling. Always now when Jeff was wondering, it was Melanctha he was doubting, in the loving. Now he would often ask her, was she real now to him, in her loving. He would ask her often, feeling something queer about it all inside him, though yet he was never really strong in his doubting, and always Melanctha would answer to him, "Yes Jeff, sure, you know it, always," and always Jeff felt a doubt now, in her loving.

Always now Jeff felt in himself, deep loving. Always now he did not know really, if Melanctha was true in her loving.

All these days Jeff was uncertain in him, and he was uneasy about which way he should act so as not to be wrong and put them both into bad trouble. Always now he was, as if he must feel deep into Melanctha to see if it was real loving he would find she now had in her, and always he would stop himself, with her, for always he was afraid now that he might badly hurt her.

Always now he liked it better when he was detained when he had to go and see her. Always now he never liked to go to be with her, although he never wanted really, not to be always with her. Always now he never felt really at ease with her, even when they were good friends together. Always now he felt, with her, he could not be really honest to her. And Jeff never could be happy with her when he could not feel strong to tell all his feeling to her. Always now every day he found it harder to make the time pass, with her, and not let his feeling come so that he would quarrel with her.

And so one evening, late, he was to go to her. He waited a little long, before he went to her. He was afraid, in himself, to-night, he would surely hurt her. He never wanted to go when he might quarrel with her.

Melanctha sat there looking very angry, when he came in to her. Jeff took off his hat and coat and then sat down by the fire with her.

"If you come in much later to me just now, Jeff Campbell, I certainly never would have seen you no more never to speak to you, 'thout your apologising real humble to me." "Apologising Melanctha," and Jeff laughed and was scornful to her, "Apologising, Melanctha, I ain't proud that kind of way, Melanctha, I don't mind apologising to you, Melanctha, all I mind, Melanctha is to be doing of things wrong, to you." "That's easy, to say things that way, Jeff to me. But you never was very proud Jeff, to be courageous to me." "I don't know about that Melanctha. I got courage to say some things hard, when I mean them, to you." "Oh, yes, Jeff, I know all about that, Jeff, to me. But I mean real courage, to run around and not care nothing about what happens, and always to be game in any kind of trouble. That's what I mean by real courage, to me, Jeff, if you want to know it." "Oh, yes, Melanctha, I know all that kind of courage. I see plenty of it all the time with some kinds of colored men and with some girls like you Melanctha, and Jane Harden. I know all about how you are always making a fuss to be proud because you don't holler so much when you run in to where you ain't got any business to be, and so you get hurt, the way you ought to. And then, you kind of people are very brave then, sure, with all your kinds of suffering, but the way I see it, going round with all my patients, that kind of courage makes all kind of trouble, for them who ain't so noble with their courage, and then they got it, always to be bearing it, when the end comes, to be hurt the hardest. It's like running around and being game to spend all your money always, and then a man's wife and children are the ones do all the starving and they don't ever get a name for being brave, and they don't ever want to be doing all that suffering, and they got to stand it and say nothing. That's the way I see it a good deal now with all that kind of braveness in some of the colored people. They always make a lot of noise to show they are so brave not to holler, when they got so much suffering they always bring all on themselves, just by doing things they got no business to be doing. I don't say, never, Melanctha, they ain't got good courage not to holler, but I never did see much in looking for that kind of trouble just to show you ain't going to holler. No it's all right being brave every day, just living regular and not having new ways all the time just to get excitements, the way I hate to see it in all the colored people. No I don't see much, Melanctha, in being brave just to get it good, where you've got no business. I ain't ashamed Melanctha, right here to tell you, I ain't ashamed ever to say I ain't got no longing to be brave, just to go around and look for trouble." "Yes that's just like you always, Jeff, you never understand things right, the way you are always feeling in you. You ain't got no way to understand right, how it depends what way somebody goes to look for new things, the way it makes it right for them to get excited." "No Melanctha, I certainly never do say I understand much anybody's got a right to think they won't have real bad trouble, if they go and look hard where they are certain sure to find it. No Melanctha, it certainly does sound very pretty all this talking about danger and being game and never hollering, and all that way of talking, but when two men are just fighting, the strong man mostly gets on top with doing good hard pounding, and the man that's getting all that pounding, he mostly never likes it so far as I have been able yet to see it, and I don't see much difference what kind of noble way they are made of when they ain't got any kind of business to get together there to be fighting. That certainly is the only way I ever see it happen right, Melanctha, whenever I happen to be anywhere I can be looking." "That's because you never can see anything that ain't just so simple, Jeff, with everybody, the way you always think it. It do make all the difference the kind of way anybody is made to do things game Jeff Campbell." "Maybe Melanctha, I certainly never say no you ain't right, Melanctha. I just been telling it to you all straight, Melanctha, the way I always see it. Perhaps if you run around where you ain't got any business, and you stand up very straight and say, I am so brave, nothing can ever hurt me, maybe nothing will ever hurt you then Melanctha. I never have seen it do so. I never can say truly any differently to you Melanctha, but I always am ready to be learning from you, Melanctha. And perhaps when somebody cuts into you real hard, with a brick he is throwing, perhaps you never will do any hollering then, Melanctha. I certainly don't ever say no, Melanctha to you, I only say that ain't the way yet I ever see it happen when I had a chance to be there looking."

They sat there together, quiet by the fire, and they did not seem to feel very loving.

"I certainly do wonder," Melanctha said dreamily, at last breaking into their long unloving silence. "I certainly do wonder why always it happens to me I care for anybody who ain't no ways good enough for me ever to be thinking to respect him."

Jeff looked at Melanctha. Jeff got up then and walked a little up and down the room, and then he came back, and his face was set and dark and he was very quiet to her.

"Oh dear, Jeff, sure, why you look so solemn now to me. Sure Jeff I never am meaning anything real by what I just been saying. What was I just been saying Jeff to you. I only certainly was just thinking how everything always was just happening to me."

Jeff Campbell sat very still and dark, and made no answer. "Seems to me, Jeff you might be good to me a little to-night when my head hurts so, and I am so tired with all the hard work I have been doing, thinking, and I always got so many things to be a trouble to me, living like I do with nobody ever who can help me. Seems to me you might be good to me Jeff to-night, and not get angry, every little thing I am ever saying to you."

"I certainly would not get angry ever with you, Melanctha, just because you say things to me. But now I certainly been thinking you really mean what you have been just then saying to me." "But you say all the time to me Jeff, you ain't no ways good enough in your loving to me, you certainly say to me all the time you ain't no ways good or understanding to me." "That certainly is what I say to you always, just the way I feel it to you Melanctha always, and I got it right in me to say it, and I have got a right in me to be very strong and feel it, and to be always sure to believe it, but it ain't right for you Melanctha to feel it."

They sat there then a long time by the fire, very silent, and not loving, and never looking to each other for it. Melanctha was moving and twitching herself and very nervous with it. Jeff was heavy and sullen and dark and very serious in it.

"Oh why can't you forget I said it to you Jeff now, and I certainly am so tired, and my head and all now with it."

Jeff stirred, "All right Melanctha, don't you go make yourself sick now in your head, feeling so bad with it," and Jeff made himself do it, and he was a patient doctor again now with Melanctha when he felt her really having her head hurt with it. "It's all right now Melanctha darling, sure it is now I tell you. You just lie down now a little, dear one, and I sit here by the fire and just read awhile and just watch with you so I will be here ready, if you need me to give you something to help you resting." And then Jeff was a good doctor to her, and very sweet and tender with her, and Melanctha loved him to be there to help her, and then Melanctha fell asleep a little, and Jeff waited there beside her until he saw she was really sleeping, and then he went back and sat down by the fire.

And Jeff tried to begin again with his thinking, and he could not make it come clear to himself, with all his thinking, and he felt everything all thick and heavy and bad, now inside him, everything that he could not understand right, with all the hard work he made, with his thinking. And then he moved himself a little, and took a book to forget his thinking, and then as always, he loved it when he was reading, and then very soon he was deep in his reading, and so he forgot now for a little while that he never could seem to be very understanding.

And so Jeff forgot himself for awhile in his reading, and Melanctha was sleeping. And then Melanctha woke up and she was screaming. "Oh, Jeff, I thought you gone away for always from me. Oh, Jeff, never now go away no more from me. Oh, Jeff, sure, sure, always be just so good to me."

There was a weight in Jeff Campbell from now on, always with him, that he could never lift out from him, to feel easy. He always was trying not to have it in him and he always was trying not to let Melanctha feel it, with him, but it was always there inside him. Now Jeff Campbell always was serious, and dark, and heavy, and sullen, and he would often sit a long time with Melanctha without moving.

"You certainly never have forgiven to me, what I said to you that night, Jeff, now have you?" Melanctha asked him after a long silence, late one evening with him. "It ain't ever with me a question like forgiving Melanctha, I got in me. It's just only what you are feeling for me, makes any difference to me. I ain't ever seen anything since in you, makes me think you didn't mean it right, what you said about not thinking now any more I was good, to make it right for you to be really caring so very much to love me."

"I certainly never did see no man like you, Jeff. You always wanting to have it all clear out in words always, what everybody is always feeling. I certainly don't see a reason, why I should always be explaining to you what I mean by what I am just saying. And you ain't got no feeling ever for me, to ask me what I meant, by what I was saying when I was so tired, that night. I never know anything right I was saying."

"But you don't ever tell me now, Melanctha, so I really hear you say it, you don't mean it the same way, the way you said it to me." "Oh Jeff, you so stupid always to me and always just bothering with your always asking to me. And I don't never any way remember ever anything I been saying to you, and I am always my head, so it hurts me it half kills me, and my heart jumps so, sometimes I think I die so when it hurts me, and I am so blue always, I think sometimes I take something to just kill me, and I got so much to bother thinking always and doing, and I got so much to worry, and all that, and then you come and ask me what I mean by what I was just saying to you. I certainly don't know, Jeff, when you ask me. Seems to me, Jeff, sometimes you might have some kind of a right feeling to be careful to me." "You ain't got no right Melanctha Herbert," flashed out Jeff through his dark, frowning anger, "you certainly ain't got no right always to be using your being hurt and being sick, and having pain, like a weapon, so as to make me do things it ain't never right for me to be doing for you. You certainly ain't got no right to be always holding your pain out to show me." "What do you mean by them words, Jeff Campbell." "I certainly do mean them just like I am saying them, Melanctha. You act always, like I been responsible all myself for all our loving one another. And if it's anything anyway that ever hurts you, you act like as if it was me made you just begin it all with me. I ain't no coward, you hear me, Melanctha? I never put my trouble back on anybody, thinking that they made me. I certainly am right ready always, Melanctha, you certainly had ought to know me, to stand all my own trouble for me, but I tell you straight now, the way I think it Melanctha, I ain't going to be as if I was the reason why you wanted to be loving, and to be suffering so now with me." "But ain't you certainly ought to be feeling it so, to be right, Jeff Campbell. Did I ever do anything but just let you do everything you wanted to me. Did I ever try to make you be loving to me. Did I ever do nothing except just sit there ready to endure your loving with me. But I certainly never, Jeff Campbell, did make any kind of way as if I wanted really to be having you for me."

Jeff stared at Melanctha. "So that's the way you say it when you are thinking right about it all, Melanctha. Well I certainly ain't got a word to say ever to you any more, Melanctha, if that's the way it's straight out to you now, Melanctha." And Jeff almost laughed out to her, and he turned to take his hat and coat, and go away now forever from her.

Melanctha dropped her head on her arms, and she trembled all over and inside her. Jeff stopped a little and looked very sadly at her. Jeff could not so quickly make it right for himself, to leave her.

"Oh, I certainly shall go crazy now, I certainly know that," Melanctha moaned as she sat there, all fallen and miserable and weak together.

Jeff came and took her in his arms, and held her. Jeff was very good then to her, but they neither of them felt inside all right, as they once did, to be together.

From now on, Jeff had real torment in him.

Was it true what Melanctha had said that night to him? Was it true that he was the one had made all this trouble for them? Was it true, he was the only one, who always had had wrong ways in him? Waking or sleeping Jeff now always had this torment going on inside him.

Jeff did not know now any more, what to feel within him. He did not know how to begin thinking out this trouble that must always now be bad inside him. He just felt a confused struggle and resentment always in him, a knowing, no, Melanctha was not right in what she had said that night to him, and then a feeling, perhaps he always had been wrong in the way he never could be understanding. And then would come strong to him, a sense of the deep sweetness in Melanctha's loving and a hating the cold slow way he always had to feel things in him.

Always Jeff knew, sure, Melanctha was wrong in what she had said that night to him, but always Melanctha had had deep feeling with him, always he was poor and slow in the only way he knew how to have any feeling. Jeff knew Melanctha was wrong, and yet he always had a deep doubt in him. What could he know, who had such slow feeling in him? What could he ever know, who always had to find his way with just thinking. What could he know, who had to be taught such a long time to learn about what was really loving? Jeff now always had this torment in him.

Melanctha was now always making him feel her way, strong whenever she was with him. Did she go on to it just to show him, did she do it now because she was no longer loving, did she do it so because that was her way to make him be really loving? Jeff never did know how it was that it all happened so to him.

Melanctha acted now the way she had said it always had been with them. Now it was always Jeff who had to do the asking. Now it was always Jeff who had to ask when would be the next time he should come to see her. Now always she was good and patient to him, and now always she was kind and loving with him, and always Jeff felt it was, that she was good to give him anything he ever asked or wanted, but never now any more for her own sake to make her happy in him. Now she did these things, as if it was just to please her Jeff Campbell who needed she should now have kindness for him. Always now he was the beggar, with them. Always now Melanctha gave it, not of her need, but from her bounty to him. Always now Jeff found it getting harder for him.

Sometimes Jeff wanted to tear things away from before him, always now he wanted to fight things and be angry with them, and always now Melanctha was so patient to him.

Now, deep inside him, there was always a doubt with Jeff, of Melanctha's loving. It was not a doubt yet to make him really doubting, for with that, Jeff never could be really loving, but always now he knew that something, and that not in him, something was wrong with their loving. Jeff Campbell could not know any right way to think out what was inside Melanctha with her loving, he could not use any way now to reach inside her to find if she was true in her loving, but now something had gone wrong between them, and now he never felt sure in him, the way once she had made him, that now at last he really had got to be understanding.

Melanctha was too many for him. He was helpless to find out the way she really felt now for him. Often Jeff would ask her, did she really love him. Always she said, "Yes Jeff, sure, you know that," and now instead of a full sweet strong love with it, Jeff only felt a patient, kind endurance in it.

Jeff did not know. If he was right in such a feeling, he certainly never any more did want to have Melanctha Herbert with him. Jeff Campbell hated badly to think Melanctha ever would give him love, just for his sake, and not because she needed it herself, to be with him. Such a way of loving would be very hard for Jeff to be enduring.

"Jeff what makes you act so funny to me. Jeff you certainly now are jealous to me. Sure Jeff, now I don't see ever why you be so foolish to look so to me." "Don't you ever think I can be jealous of anybody ever Melanctha, you hear me. It's just, you certainly don't ever understand me. It's just this way with me always now Melanctha. You love me, and I don't care anything what you do or what you ever been to anybody. You don't love me, then I don't care any more about what you ever do or what you ever be to anybody. But I never want you to be being good Melanctha to me, when it ain't your loving makes you need it. I certainly don't ever want to be having any of your kind of kindness to me. If you don't love me, I can stand it. All I never want to have is your being good to me from kindness. If you don't love me, then you and I certainly do quit right here Melanctha, all strong feeling, to be always living to each other. It certainly never is anybody I ever am thinking about when I am thinking with you Melanctha darling. That's the true way I am telling you Melanctha, always. It's only your loving me ever gives me anything to bother me Melanctha, so all you got to do, if you don't really love me, is just certainly to say so to me. I won't bother you more then than I can help to keep from it Melanctha. You certainly need never to be in any worry, never, about me Melanctha. You just tell me straight out Melanctha, real, the way you feel it. I certainly can stand it all right, I tell you true Melanctha. And I never will care to know why or nothing Melanctha. Loving is just living Melanctha to me, and if you don't really feel it now Melanctha to me, there ain't ever nothing between us then Melanctha, is there? That's straight and honest just the way I always feel it to you now

Melanctha. Oh Melanctha, darling, do you love me? Oh Melanctha, please, please, tell me honest, tell me, do you really love me?"

"Oh you so stupid Jeff boy of course I always love you. Always and always Jeff and I always just so good to you. Oh you so stupid Jeff and don't know when you got it good with me. Oh dear, Jeff I certainly am so tired Jeff to-night, don't you go be a bother to me. Yes I love you Jeff, how often you want me to tell you. Oh you so stupid Jeff, but yes I love you. Now I won't say it no more now to-night Jeff, you hear me. You just be good Jeff now to me or else I certainly get awful angry with you. Yes I love you, sure, Jeff, though you don't any way deserve it from me. Yes, yes I love you. Yes Jeff I say it till I certainly am very sleepy. Yes I love you now Jeff, and you certainly must stop asking me to tell you. Oh you great silly boy Jeff Campbell, sure I love you, oh you silly stupid, my own boy Jeff Campbell. Yes I love you and I certainly never won't say it one more time to-night Jeff, now you hear me."

Yes Jeff Campbell heard her, and he tried hard to believe her. He did not really doubt her but somehow it was wrong now, the way Melanctha said it. Jeff always now felt baffled with Melanctha. Something, he knew, was not right now in her. Something in her always now was making stronger the torment that was tearing every minute at the joy he once always had had with her.

Always now Jeff wondered did Melanctha love him. Always now he was wondering, was Melanctha right when she said, it was he had made all their beginning. Was Melanctha right when she said, it was he had the real responsibility for all the trouble they had and still were having now between them. If she was right, what a brute he always had been in his acting. If she was right, how good she had been to endure the pain he had made so bad so often for her. But no, surely she had made herself to bear it, for her own sake, not for his to make him happy. Surely he was not so twisted in all his long thinking. Surely he could remember right what it was had happened every day in their long loving. Surely he was not so poor a coward as Melanctha always seemed to be thinking.

Surely, surely, and then the torment would get worse every minute in him.

One night Jeff Campbell was lying in his bed with his thinking, and night after night now he could not do any sleeping for his thinking. To-night suddenly he sat up in his bed, and it all came clear to him, and he pounded his pillow with his fist, and he almost shouted out alone there to him, "I ain't a brute the way Melanctha has been saying. It's all wrong the way I been worried thinking. We did begin fair, each not for the other but for ourselves, what we were wanting. Melanctha Herbert did it just like I did it, because she liked it bad enough to want to stand it. It's all wrong in me to think it any way except the way we really did it. I certainly don't know now whether she is now real and true in her loving. I ain't got any way ever to find out if she is real and true now always to me. All I know is I didn't ever make her to begin to be with me. Melanctha has got to stand for her own trouble, just like I got to stand for my own trouble. Each man has got to do it for himself when he is in real trouble. Melanctha, she certainly don't remember right when she says I made her begin and then I made her trouble. No by God, I ain't no coward nor brute either ever to her. I been the way I felt it honest, and that certainly is all about it now between us, and everybody always has just got to stand for their own trouble. I certainly am right this time the way I see it." And Jeff lay down now, at last in comfort, and he slept, and he was free from his long doubting torment.

"You know Melanctha," Jeff Campbell began, the next time he was alone to talk a long time to Melanctha. "You know Melanctha, sometimes I think a whole lot about what you like to say so much about being game and never doing any hollering. Seems to me Melanctha, I certainly don't understand right what you mean by not hollering. Seems to me it certainly ain't only what comes right away when one is hit, that counts to be brave to be bearing, but all that comes later from your getting sick from the shock of being hurt once in a fight, and all that, and all the being taken care of for years after, and the suffering of your family, and all that, you certainly must stand and not holler, to be certainly really brave the way I understand it." "What you mean Jeff by your talking." "I mean, seems to me really not to holler, is to be strong not to show you ever have been hurt. Seems to me, to get your head hurt from your trouble and to show it, ain't certainly no braver than to say, oh, oh, how bad you hurt me, please don't hurt me mister. It just certainly seems to me, like many people think themselves so game just to stand what we all of us always just got to be standing, and everybody stands it, and we don't certainly none of us like it, and yet we don't ever most of us think we are so much being game, just because we got to stand it."

"I know what you mean now by what you are saying to me now Jeff Campbell. You make a fuss now to me, because I certainly just have stopped standing everything you like to be always doing so cruel to me. But that's just the way always with you Jeff Campbell, if you want to know it. You ain't got no kind of right feeling for all I always been forgiving to you." "I said it once for fun, Melanctha, but now I certainly do mean it, you think you got a right to go where you got no business, and you say, I am so brave nothing can hurt me, and then something, like always, it happens to hurt you, and you show your hurt always so everybody can see it, and you say, I am so brave nothing did hurt me except he certainly didn't have any right to, and see how bad I suffer, but you never hear me make a holler, though certainly anybody got any feeling, to see me suffer, would certainly never touch me except to take good care of me. Sometimes I certainly don't rightly see Melanctha, how much more game that is than just the ordinary kind of holler." "No, Jeff Campbell, and made the way you is you certainly ain't likely ever to be much more understanding." "No, Melanctha, nor you either. You think always, you are the only one who ever can do any way to really suffer." "Well, and ain't I certainly always been the only person knows how to bear it. No, Jeff Campbell, I certainly be glad to love anybody really worthy, but I made so, I never seem to be able in this world to find him." "No, and your kind of way of thinking, you certainly Melanctha never going to any way be able ever to be finding of him. Can't you understand Melanctha, ever, how no man certainly ever really can hold your love for long times together. You certainly Melanctha, you ain't got down deep loyal feeling, true inside you, and when you ain't just that moment quick with feeling, then you certainly ain't ever got anything more there to keep you. You see Melanctha, it certainly is this way with you, it is, that you ain't ever got any way to remember right what you been doing, or anybody else that has been feeling with you. You certainly Melanctha, never can remember right, when it comes what you have done and what you think happens to you." "It certainly is all easy for you Jeff Campbell to be talking. You remember right, because you don't remember nothing till you get home with your thinking everything all over, but I certainly don't think much ever of that kind of way of remembering right, Jeff Campbell. I certainly do call it remembering right Jeff Campbell, to remember right just when it happens to you, so you have a right kind of feeling not to act the way you always been doing to me, and then you go home Jeff Campbell, and you begin with your thinking, and then it certainly is very easy for you to be good and forgiving with it. No, that ain't to me, the way of remembering Jeff Campbell, not as I can see it not to make people always suffer, waiting for you certainly to get to do it. Seems to me like Jeff Campbell, I never could feel so like a man was low and to be scorning of him, like that day in the summer, when you threw me off just because you got one of those fits of your remembering. No, Jeff Campbell, it's real feeling every moment when it's needed, that certainly does seem to me like real remembering. And that way, certainly, you don't never know nothing like what should be right Jeff Campbell. No Jeff, it's me that always certainly has had to bear it with you. It's always me that certainly has had to suffer, while you go home to remember. No you certainly ain't got no sense yet Jeff, what you need to make you really feeling. No, it certainly is me Jeff Campbell, that always has got to be remembering for us both, always. That's what's the true way with us Jeff Campbell, if you want to know what it is I am always thinking." "You is certainly real modest Melanctha, when you do this kind of talking, you sure is Melanctha," said Jeff Campbell laughing. "I think sometimes Melanctha I am certainly awful conceited, when I think sometimes I am all out doors, and I think I certainly am so bright, and better than most everybody I ever got anything now to do with, but when I hear you talk this way Melanctha, I certainly do think I am a real modest kind of fellow." "Modest!" said Melanctha, angry, "Modest, that certainly is a queer thing for you Jeff to be calling yourself even when you are laughing." "Well it certainly does depend a whole lot what you are thinking with," said Jeff Campbell. "I never did use to think I was so much on being real modest Melanctha, but now I know really I am, when I hear you talking. I see all the time there are many people living just as good as I am, though they are a little different to me. Now with you Melanctha if I understand you right what you are talking, you don't think that way of no other one that you are ever knowing." "I certainly could be real modest too, Jeff Campbell," said Melanctha, "If I could meet somebody once I could keep right on respecting when I got so I was really knowing with them. But I certainly never met anybody like that yet, Jeff Campbell, if you want to know it." "No, Melanctha, and with the way you got of thinking, it certainly don't look like as if you ever will Melanctha, with your never remembering anything only what you just then are feeling in you, and you not understanding what any one else is ever feeling, if they don't holler just the way you are doing. No Melanctha, I certainly don't see any ways you are likely ever to meet one, so good as you are always thinking you be." "No, Jeff Campbell, it certainly ain't that way with me at all the way you say it. It's because I am always knowing what it is I am wanting, when I get it. I certainly don't never have to wait till I have it, and then throw away what I got in me, and then come back and say, that's a mistake I just been making, it ain't that never at all like I understood it, I want to have, bad, what I didn't think it was I wanted. It's that way of knowing right what I am wanting, makes me feel nobody can come right with me, when I am feeling things, Jeff Campbell. I certainly do say Jeff Campbell, I certainly don't think much of the way you always do it, always never knowing what it is you are ever really wanting and everybody always got to suffer. No Jeff, I don't certainly think there is much doubting which is better and the stronger with us two, Jeff Campbell."

"As you will, Melanctha Herbert," cried Jeff Campbell, and he rose up, and he thundered out a black oath, and he was fierce to leave her now forever, and then with the same movement, he took her in his arms and held her.

"What a silly goose boy you are, Jeff Campbell," Melanctha whispered to him fondly.

"Oh yes," said Jeff, very dreary. "I never could keep really mad with anybody, not when I was a little boy and playing. I used most to cry sometimes, I couldn't get real mad and keep on a long time with it, the way everybody always did it. It's certainly no use to me Melanctha, I certainly can't ever keep mad with you Melanctha, my dear one. But don't ever be thinking it's because I think you right in what you been just saying to me. I don't Melanctha really think it that way, honest, though I certainly can't get mad the way I ought to. No Melanctha, little girl, really truly, you ain't right the way you think it. I certainly do know that Melanctha, honest. You certainly don't do me right Melanctha, the way you say you are thinking. Good-bye Melanctha, though you certainly is my own little girl for always." And then they were very good a little to each other, and then Jeff went away for that evening, from her.

Melanctha had begun now once more to wander. Melanctha did not yet always wander, but a little now she needed to begin to look for others. Now Melanctha Herbert began again to be with some of the better kind of black girls, and with them she sometimes wandered. Melanctha had not yet come again to need to be alone, when she wandered.

Jeff Campbell did not know that Melanctha had begun again to wander. All Jeff knew, was that now he could not be so often with her.

Jeff never knew how it had come to happen to him, but now he never thought to go to see Melanctha Herbert, until he had before, asked her if she could be going to have time then to have him with her. Then Melanctha would think a little, and then she would say to him, "Let me see Jeff, tomorrow, you was just saying to me. I certainly am awful busy you know Jeff just now. It certainly does seem to me this week Jeff, I can't anyways fix it. Sure I want to see you soon Jeff. I certainly Jeff got to do a little more now, I been giving so much time, when I had no business, just to be with you when you asked me. Now I guess Jeff, I certainly can't see you no more this week Jeff, the way I got to do things." "All right Melanctha," Jeff would answer and he would be very angry. "I want to come only just certainly as you want me now Melanctha." "Now Jeff you know I certainly can't be neglecting always to be with everybody just to see you. You come see me next week Tuesday Jeff, you hear me. I don't think Jeff I certainly be so busy, Tuesday." Jeff Campbell would then go away and leave her, and he would be hurt and very angry, for it was hard for a man with a great pride in himself, like Jeff Campbell, to feel himself no better than a beggar. And yet he always came as she said he should, on the day she had fixed for him, and always Jeff Campbell was not sure yet that he really understood what it was Melanctha wanted. Always Melanctha said to him, yes she loved him, sure he knew that. Always Melanctha said to him, she certainly did love him just the same as always, only sure he knew now she certainly did seem to be right busy with all she certainly now had to be doing.

Jeff never knew what Melanctha had to do now, that made her always be so busy, but Jeff Campbell never cared to ask Melanctha such a question. Besides Jeff knew Melanctha Herbert would never, in such a matter, give him any kind of a real answer. Jeff did not know whether it was that Melanctha did not know how to give a simple answer. And then how could he, Jeff, know what was important to her. Jeff Campbell always felt strongly in him, he had no right to interfere with Melanctha in any practical kind of a matter. There they had always, never asked each other any kind of question. There they had felt always in each other, not any right to take care of one another. And Jeff Campbell now felt less than he had ever, any right to claim to know what Melanctha thought it right that she should do in any of her ways of living. All Jeff felt a right in himself to question, was her loving.

Jeff learned every day now, more and more, how much it

was that he could really suffer. Sometimes it hurt so in him,
when he was alone, it would force some slow tears from him.
But every day, now that Jeff Campbell, knew more how it
could hurt him, he lost his feeling of deep awe that he once
always had had for Melanctha's feeling. Suffering was not so
much after all, thought Jeff Campbell, if even he could feel
it so it hurt him. It hurt him bad, just the way he knew he
once had hurt Melanctha, and yet he too could have it and
not make any kind of a loud holler with it.

In tender-hearted natures, those that mostly never feel
strong passion, suffering often comes to make them harder.
When these do not know in themselves what it is to suffer,
suffering is then very awful to them and they badly want to
help everyone who ever has to suffer, and they have a deep
reverence for anybody who knows really how to always suffer.
But when it comes to them to really suffer, they soon begin
to lose their fear and tenderness and wonder. Why it isn't so
very much to suffer, when even I can bear to do it. It isn't
very pleasant to be having all the time, to stand it, but they
are not so much wiser after all, all the others just because they
know too how to bear it.

Passionate natures who have always made themselves, to
suffer, that is all the kind of people who have emotions that
come to them as sharp as a sensation, they always get more
tender-hearted when they suffer, and it always does them
good to suffer. Tender-hearted, unpassionate, and comfortable
natures always get much harder when they suffer, for so they
lose the fear and reverence and wonder they once had for
everybody who ever has to suffer, but now they know themselves what it is to suffer and it is not so awful any longer
to them when they know too, just as well as all the others,
how to have it.

And so it came in these days to Jeff Campbell. Jeff knew
now always, way inside him, what it is to really suffer, and
now every day with it, he knew how to understand Melanctha
better. Jeff Campbell still loved Melanctha Herbert and he
still had a real trust in her and he still had a little hope that
some day they would once more get together, but slowly,
every day, this hope in him would keep growing always

weaker. They still were a good deal of time together, but now they never any more were really trusting with each other. In the days when they used to be together, Jeff had felt he did not know much what was inside Melanctha, but he knew very well, how very deep always was his trust in her; now he knew Melanctha Herbert better, but now he never felt a deep trust in her. Now Jeff never could be really honest with her. He never doubted yet, that she was steady only to him, but somehow he could not believe much really in Melanctha's loving.

Melanctha Herbert was a little angry now when Jeff asked her, "I never give nobody before Jeff, ever more than one chance with me, and I certainly been giving you most a hundred Jeff, you hear me." "And why shouldn't you Melanctha, give me a million, if you really love me!" Jeff flashed out very angry. "I certainly don't know as you deserve that anyways from me, Jeff Campbell." "It ain't deserving, I am ever talking about to you Melanctha. It's loving, and if you are really loving to me you won't certainly never any ways call them chances." "Deed Jeff, you certainly are getting awful wise Jeff now, ain't you, to me." "No I ain't Melanctha, and I ain't jealous either to you. I just am doubting from the way you are always acting to me." "Oh yes Jeff, that's what they all say, the same way, when they certainly got jealousy all through them. You ain't got no cause to be jealous with me Jeff, and I am awful tired of all this talking now, you hear me."

Jeff Campbell never asked Melanctha any more if she loved him. Now things were always getting worse between them. Now Jeff was always very silent with Melanctha. Now Jeff never wanted to be honest to her, and now Jeff never had much to say to her.

Now when they were together, it was Melanctha always did most of the talking. Now she often had other girls there with her. Melanctha was always kind to Jeff Campbell but she never seemed to need to be alone now with him. She always treated Jeff, like her best friend, and she always spoke so to him and yet she never seemed now to very often want to see him.

Every day it was getting harder for Jeff Campbell. It was as if now, when he had learned to really love Melanctha, she did not need any more to have him. Jeff began to know this very well inside him.

Jeff Campbell did not know yet that Melanctha had begun again to wander. Jeff was not very quick to suspect Melanctha. All Jeff knew was, that he did not trust her to be now really loving to him.

Jeff was no longer now in any doubt inside him. He knew very well now he really loved Melanctha. He knew now very well she was not any more a real religion to him. Jeff Campbell knew very well too now inside him, he did not really want Melanctha, now if he could no longer trust her, though he loved her hard and really knew now what it was to suffer.

Every day Melanctha Herbert was less and less near to him. She always was very pleasant in her talk and to be with him, but somehow now it never was any comfort to him.

Melanctha Herbert now always had a lot of friends around her. Jeff Campbell never wanted to be with them. Now Melanctha began to find it, she said it often to him, always harder to arrange to be alone now with him. Sometimes she would be late for him. Then Jeff always would try to be patient in his waiting, for Jeff Campbell knew very well how to remember, and he knew it was only right that he should now endure this from her.

Then Melanctha began to manage often not to see him, and once she went away when she had promised to be there to meet him.

Then Jeff Campbell was really filled up with his anger. Now he knew he could never really want her. Now he knew he never any more could really trust her.

Jeff Campbell never knew why Melanctha had not come to meet him. Jeff had heard a little talking now, about how Melanctha Herbert had commenced once more to wander. Jeff Campbell still sometimes saw Jane Harden, who always needed a doctor to be often there to help her. Jane Harden always knew very well what happened to Melanctha. Jeff Campbell never would talk to Jane Harden anything about Melanctha. Jeff was always loyal to Melanctha. Jeff never let Jane Harden say much to him about Melanctha, though he never let her know that now he loved her. But somehow Jeff did know now about Melanctha, and he knew about some men that Melanctha met with Rose Johnson very often.

Jeff Campbell would not let himself really doubt Melanctha, but Jeff began to know now very well, he did not want her. Melanctha Herbert did not love him ever, Jeff knew it now, the way he once had thought that she could feel it. Once she had been greater for him than he had thought he could ever know how to feel it. Now Jeff had come to where he could understand Melanctha Herbert. Jeff was not bitter to her because she could not really love him, he was bitter only that he had let himself have a real illusion in him. He was a little bitter too, that he had lost now, what he had always felt real in the world, that had made it for him always full of beauty, and now he had not got this new religion really, and he had lost what he before had to know what was good and had real beauty.

Jeff Campbell was so angry now in him, because he had begged Melanctha always to be honest to him. Jeff could stand it in her not to love him, he could not stand it in her not to be honest to him.

Jeff Campbell went home from where Melanctha had not met him, and he was sore and full of anger in him.

Jeff Campbell could not be sure what to do, to make it right inside him. Surely he must be strong now and cast this loving from him, and yet, was he sure he now had real wisdom in him. Was he sure that Melanctha Herbert never had had a real deep loving for him. Was he sure Melanctha Herbert never had deserved a reverence from him. Always now Jeff had this torment in him, but always now he felt more that Melanctha never had real greatness for him.

Jeff waited to see if Melanctha would send any word to him. Melanctha Herbert never sent a line to him.

At last Jeff wrote his letter to Melanctha. "Dear Melanctha, I certainly do know you ain't been any way sick this last week when you never met me right the way you promised, and never sent me any word to say why you acted a way you certainly never could think was the right way you should do it to me. Jane Harden said she saw you that day and you

went out walking with some people you like now to be with.
Don't be misunderstanding me now any more Melanctha. I
love you now because that's my slow way to learn what you
been teaching, but I know now you certainly never had what
seems to me real kind of feeling. I don't love you Melanctha
any more now like a real religion, because now I know you
are just made like all us others. I know now no man can ever
really hold you because no man can ever be real to trust in
you, because you mean right Melanctha, but you never can
remember, and so you certainly never have got any way to be
honest. So please you understand me right now Melanctha,
it never is I don't know how to love you. I do know now how
to love you, Melanctha, really. You sure do know that, Melanctha, in me. You certainly always can trust me. And so
now Melanctha, I can say to you certainly real honest with
you, I am better than you are in my right kind of feeling. And
so Melanctha, I don't never any more want to be a trouble
to you. You certainly make me see things Melanctha, I never
any other way could be knowing. You been very good and
patient to me, when I was certainly below you in my right
feeling. I certainly never have been near so good and patient
to you ever any way Melanctha, I certainly know that Melanctha. But Melanctha, with me, it certainly is, always to be
good together, two people certainly must be thinking each
one as good as the other, to be really loving right Melanctha.
And it certainly must never be any kind of feeling, of one
only taking, and one only just giving, Melanctha, to me. I
know you certainly don't really ever understand me now
Melanctha, but that's no matter. I certainly do know what I am
feeling now with you real Melanctha. And so good-bye now for
good Melanctha. I say I can never ever really trust you real
Melanctha, that's only just certainly from your way of not
being ever equal in your feeling to anybody real, Melanctha,
and your way never to know right how to remember. Many
ways I really trust you deep Melanctha, and I certainly do feel
deep all the good sweetness you certainly got real in you
Melanctha. It's only just in your loving me Melanctha. You
never can be equal to me and that way I certainly never can

bear any more to have it. And so now Melanctha, I always be your friend, if you need me, and now we never see each other any more to talk to."

And then Jeff Campbell thought and thought, and he could never make any way for him now, to see it different, and so at last he sent this letter to Melanctha.

And now surely it was all over in Jeff Campbell. Surely now he never any more could know Melanctha. And yet, perhaps Melanctha really loved him. And then she would know how much it hurt him never any more, any way, to see her, and perhaps she would write a line to tell him. But that was a foolish way for Jeff ever to be thinking. Of course Melanctha never would write a word to him. It was all over now for always, everything between them, and Jeff felt it a real relief to him.

For many days now Jeff Campbell only felt it as a relief in him. Jeff was all locked up and quiet now inside him. It was all settling down heavy in him, and these days when it was sinking so deep in him, it was only the rest and quiet of not fighting that he could really feel inside him. Jeff Campbell could not think now, or feel anything else in him. He had no beauty nor any goodness to see around him. It was a dull, pleasant kind of quiet he now had inside him. Jeff almost began to love this dull quiet in him, for it was more nearly being free for him than anything he had known in him since Melanctha Herbert first had moved him. He did not find it a real rest yet for him, he had not really conquered what had been working so long in him, he had not learned to see beauty and real goodness yet in what had happened to him, but it was rest even if he was sodden now all through him. Jeff Campbell liked it very well, not to have fighting always going on inside him.

And so Jeff went on every day, and he was quiet, and he began again to watch himself in his working; and he did not see any beauty now around him, and it was dull and heavy always now inside him, and yet he was content to have gone so far in keeping steady to what he knew was the right way for him to come back to, to be regular, and see beauty in every kind of quiet way of living, the way he had always wanted it for himself and for all the colored people. He knew he had lost the sense he once had of joy all through him, but he could work, and perhaps he would bring some real belief back into him about the beauty that he could not now any more see around him.

And so Jeff Campbell went on with his working, and he staid home every evening, and he began again with his reading, and he did not do much talking, and he did not seem to himself to have any kind of feeling.

And one day Jeff thought perhaps he really was forgetting, one day he thought he could soon come back and be happy in his old way of regular and quiet living.

Jeff Campbell had never talked to any one of what had been going on inside him. Jeff Campbell liked to talk and he was honest, but it never came out from him, anything he was ever really feeling, it only came out from him, what it was that he was always thinking. Jeff Campbell always was very proud to hide what he was really feeling. Always he blushed hot to think things he had been feeling. Only to Melanctha Herbert, had it ever come to him, to tell what it was that he was feeling.

And so Jeff Campbell went on with this dull and sodden, heavy, quiet always in him, and he never seemed to be able to have any feeling. Only sometimes he shivered hot with shame when he remembered some things he once had been feeling. And then one day it all woke up, and was sharp in him.

Dr. Campbell was just then staying long times with a sick man who might soon be dying. One day the sick man was resting. Dr. Campbell went to the window to look out a little, while he was waiting. It was very early now in the southern spring time. The trees were just beginning to get the little zigzag crinkles in them, which the young buds always give them. The air was soft and moist and pleasant to them. The earth was wet and rich and smelling for them. The birds were making sharp fresh noises all around them. The wind was very gentle and yet urgent to them. And the buds and the long earthworms, and the negroes, and all the kinds of children, were coming out every minute farther into the new spring, watery, southern sunshine.

Jeff Campbell too began to feel a little his old joy inside him. The sodden quiet began to break up in him. He leaned far out of the window to mix it all up with him. His heart went sharp and then it almost stopped inside him. Was it Melanctha Herbert he had just seen passing by him? Was it Melanctha, or was it just some other girl, who made him feel so bad inside him? Well, it was no matter, Melanctha was there in the world around him, he did certainly always know that in him. Melanctha Herbert was always in the same town with him, and he could never any more feel her near him. What a fool he was to throw her from him. Did he know she did not really love him. Suppose Melanctha was now suffering through him. Suppose she really would be glad to see him. And did anything else he did, really mean anything now to him? What a fool he was to cast her from him. And yet did Melanctha Herbert want him, was she honest to him, had Melanctha ever loved him, and did Melanctha now suffer by him? Oh! Oh! Oh! and the bitter water once more rose up in him.

All that long day, with the warm moist young spring stirring in him, Jeff Campbell worked, and thought, and beat his breast, and wandered, and spoke aloud, and was silent, and was certain, and then in doubt and then keen to surely feel, and then all sodden in him; and he walked, and he sometimes ran fast to lose himself in his rushing, and he bit his nails to pain and bleeding, and he tore his hair so that he could be sure he was really feeling, and he never could know what it was right, he now should be doing. And then late that night he wrote it all out to Melanctha Herbert, and he made himself quickly send it without giving himself any time to change it.

"It has come to me strong to-day Melanctha, perhaps I am wrong the way I now am thinking. Perhaps you do want me badly to be with you. Perhaps I have hurt you once again the way I used to. I certainly Melanctha, if I ever think that really, I certainly do want bad not to be wrong now ever any more to you. If you do feel the way to-day it came to me strong may-be you are feeling, then say so Melanctha to me, and I come again to see you. If not, don't say anything any more ever to me. I don't want ever to be bad to you Melanctha, really. I never want ever to be a bother to you. I never can stand it to think I am wrong; really, thinking you don't want me to come to you. Tell me Melanctha, tell me honest to me, shall I come now any more to see you." "Yes" came the answer from Melanctha, "I be home Jeff to-night to see you."

Jeff Campbell went that evening late to see Melanctha Herbert. As Jeff came nearer to her, he doubted that he wanted really to be with her, he felt that he did not know what it was he now wanted from her. Jeff Campbell knew very well now, way inside him, that they could never talk their trouble out between them. What was it Jeff wanted now to tell Melanctha Herbert? What was it that Jeff Campbell now could tell her? Surely he never now could learn to trust her. Surely Jeff knew very well all that Melanctha always had inside her. And yet it was awful, never any more to see her.

Jeff Campbell went in to Melanctha, and he kissed her, and he held her, and then he went away from her and he stood still and looked at her. "Well Jeff!" "Yes Melanctha!" "Jeff what was it made you act so to me?" "You know very well Melanctha, it's always I am thinking you don't love me, and you are acting to me good out of kindness, and then Melanctha you certainly never did say anything to me why you never came to meet me, as you certainly did promise to me you would that day I never saw you!" "Jeff don't you really know for certain, I always love you?" "No Melanctha, deed I don't know it in me. Deed and certain sure Melanctha, if I only know that in me, I certainly never would give you any bother." "Jeff, I certainly do love you more seems to me always, you certainly had ought to feel that in you." "Sure Melanctha?" "Sure Jeff boy, you know that." "But then Melanctha why did you act so to me?" "Oh Jeff you certainly been such a bother to me. I just had to go away that day Jeff, and I certainly didn't mean not to tell you, and then that letter you wrote came to me and something happened to me. I don't know right what it was Jeff, I just kind of fainted, and what could I do Jeff, you said you certainly never any more wanted to come and see me!" "And no matter Melanctha, even if you knew, it was just killing me to act so to you, you never would have said nothing to me?" "No of course, how could I Jeff when you wrote that way to me. I know how you was feeling Jeff to me, but I certainly couldn't say nothing to you." "Well Melanctha, I certainly know I am right proud too in me, but I certainly never could act so to you Melanctha, if I ever knew any way at all you ever really loved me. No Melanctha darling, you and me certainly don't feel much the same way ever. Any way Melanctha, I certainly do love you true Melanctha." "And I love you too Jeff, even though you don't never certainly seem to believe me." "No I certainly don't any way believe you, Melanctha, even when you say it to me. I don't know Melanctha how, but sure I certainly do trust you, only I don't believe now ever in your really being loving to me. I certainly do know you trust me always Melanctha, only somehow it ain't ever all right to me. I certainly don't know any way otherwise Melanctha, how I can say it to you." "Well I certainly can't help you no ways any more Jeff Campbell, though you certainly say it right when you say I trust you Jeff now always. You certainly is the best man Jeff Campbell, I ever can know, to me. I never been anyways thinking it can be ever different to me." "Well you trust me then Melanctha, and I certainly love you Melanctha, and seems like to me Melanctha, you and me had ought to be a little better than we certainly ever are doing now to be together. You certainly do think that way, too, Melanctha to me. But may be you do really love me. Tell me, please, real honest now Melanctha darling, tell me so I really always know it in me, do you really truly love me?" "Oh you stupid, stupid boy, Jeff Campbell. Love you, what do you think makes me always to forgive you. If I certainly didn't always love you Jeff, I certainly never would let you be always being all the time such a bother to me the way you certainly Jeff always are to me. Now don't you dass ever any more say words like that ever to me. You hear me now Jeff, or I do something real bad sometime, so I really hurt you. Now Jeff you just be good to me. You know Jeff how bad I need it, now you should always be good to me!"

Jeff Campbell could not make an answer to Melanctha. What was it he should now say to her? What words could help him to make their feeling any better? Jeff Campbell knew that he had learned to love deeply, that, he always knew very well

now in him, Melanctha had learned to be strong to be always
trusting, that he knew too now inside him, but Melanctha did
not really love him, that he felt always too strong for him.
That fact always was there in him, and it always thrust itself
firm, between them. And so this talk did not make things
really better for them.

Jeff Campbell was never any more a torment to Melanctha,
he was only silent to her. Jeff often saw Melanctha and he was
very friendly with her and he never any more was a brother
to her. Jeff never any more now had much chance to be loving
with her. Melanctha never was alone now when he saw her.

Melanctha Herbert had just been getting thick in her
trouble with Jeff Campbell, when she went to that church
where she first met Rose, who later was married to Sam
Johnson. Rose was a good-looking, better kind of black girl,
and had been brought up quite like their own child by white
folks. Rose was living now with colored people. Rose was
staying just then with a colored woman, who had known 'Mis'
Herbert and her black husband and this girl Melanctha.

Rose soon got to like Melanctha Herbert and Melanctha
now always wanted to be with Rose, whenever she could do
it. Melanctha Herbert always was doing everything for Rose
that she could think of that Rose ever wanted. Rose always
liked to be with nice people who would do things for her. Rose
had strong common sense and she was lazy. Rose liked Melanctha Herbert, she had such kind of fine ways in her. Then,
too, Rose had it in her to be sorry for the subtle, sweet-
natured, docile, intelligent Melanctha Herbert who always
was so blue sometimes, and always had had so much trouble.
Then, too, Rose could scold Melanctha, for Melanctha Herbert
never could know how to keep herself from trouble, and Rose
was always strong to keep straight, with her simple selfish
wisdom.

But why did the subtle, intelligent, attractive, half white
girl Melanctha Herbert, with her sweetness and her power
and her wisdom, demean herself to do for and to flatter and to
be scolded, by this lazy, stupid, ordinary, selfish black girl.
This was a queer thing in Melanctha Herbert.

And so now in these new spring days, it was with Rose

that Melanctha began again to wander. Rose always knew very well in herself what was the right way to do when you wandered. Rose knew very well, she was not just any common kind of black girl, for she had been raised by white folks, and Rose always saw to it that she was engaged to him when she had any one man with whom she ever always wandered. Rose always had strong in her the sense for proper conduct. Rose always was telling the complex and less sure Melanctha, what was the right way she should do when she wandered.

Rose never knew much about Jeff Campbell with Melanctha Herbert. Rose had not known about Melanctha Herbert when she had been almost all her time with Dr. Campbell.

Jeff Campbell did not like Rose when he saw her with Melanctha. Jeff would never, when he could help it, meet her. Rose did not think much about Dr. Campbell. Melanctha never talked much about him to her. He was not important now to be with her.

Rose did not like Melanctha's old friend Jane Harden when she saw her. Jane despised Rose for an ordinary, stupid, sullen black girl. Jane could not see what Melanctha could find in that black girl, to endure her. It made Jane sick to see her. But then Melanctha had a good mind, but she certainly never did care much to really use it. Jane Harden now really never cared any more to see Melanctha, though Melanctha still always tried to be good to her. And Rose, she hated that stuck up, mean speaking, nasty, drunk thing, Jane Harden. Rose did not see how Melanctha could bear to ever see her, but Melanctha always was so good to everybody, she never would know how to act to people the way they deserved that she should do it.

Rose did not know much about Melanctha, and Jeff Campbell and Jane Harden. All Rose knew about Melanctha was her old life with her mother and her father. Rose was always glad to be good to poor Melanctha, who had had such an awful time with her mother and her father, and now she was alone and had nobody who could help her. "He was an awful black man to you Melanctha, I like to get my hands on him so he certainly could feel it. I just would Melanctha, now you hear me."

Perhaps it was this simple faith and simple anger and simple moral way of doing in Rose, that Melanctha now found such a comfort to her. Rose was selfish and was stupid and was lazy, but she was decent and knew always what was the right way she should do, and what she wanted, and she certainly did admire how bright was her friend Melanctha Herbert, and she certainly did feel how very much it was she always suffered and she scolded her to keep her from more trouble, and she never was angry when she found some of the different ways Melanctha Herbert sometimes had to do it.

And so always Rose and Melanctha were more and more together, and Jeff Campbell could now hardly ever any more be alone with Melanctha.

Once Jeff had to go away to another town to see a sick man. "When I come back Monday Melanctha, I come Monday evening to see you. You be home alone once Melanctha to see me." "Sure Jeff, I be glad to see you!"

When Jeff Campbell came to his house on Monday there was a note there from Melanctha. Could Jeff come day after to-morrow, Wednesday? Melanctha was so sorry she had to go out that evening. She was awful sorry and she hoped Jeff would not be angry.

Jeff was angry and he swore a little, and then he laughed, and then he sighed. "Poor Melanctha, she don't know any way to be real honest, but no matter, I sure do love her and I be good if she will let me."

Jeff Campbell went Wednesday night to see Melanctha. Jeff Campbell took her in his arms and kissed her. "I certainly am awful sorry not to see you Jeff Monday, the way I promised, but I just couldn't Jeff, no way I could fix it." Jeff looked at her and then he laughed a little at her. "You want me to believe that really now Melanctha. All right I believe it if you want me to Melanctha. I certainly be good to you to-night the way you like it. I believe you certainly did want to see me Melanctha, and there was no way you could fix it." "Oh Jeff dear," said Melanctha, "I sure was wrong to act so to you. It's awful hard for me ever to say it to you, I have been wrong in my acting to you, but I certainly was bad this time Jeff to you. It do certainly come hard to me to say it Jeff, but I certainly was

wrong to go away from you the way I did it. Only you always
certainly been so bad Jeff, and such a bother to me, and making everything always so hard for me, and I certainly got some
way to do it to make it come back sometimes to you. You bad
boy Jeff, now you hear me and this certainly is the first time
Jeff I ever yet said it to anybody, I ever been wrong, Jeff, you
hear me!" "All right Melanctha, I sure do forgive you, cause
it's certainly the first time I ever heard you say you ever did
anything wrong the way you shouldn't," and Jeff Campbell
laughed and kissed her, and Melanctha laughed and loved
him, and they really were happy now for a little time together.

And now they were very happy in each other and then they
were silent and then they became a little sadder and then they
were very quiet once more with each other.

"Yes I certainly do love you Jeff!" Melanctha said and she
was very dreamy. "Sure, Melanctha." "Yes Jeff sure, but not
the way you are now ever thinking. I love you more and more
seems to me Jeff always, and I certainly do trust you more and
more always to me when I know you. I do love you Jeff, sure
yes, but not the kind of way of loving you are ever thinking
it now Jeff with me. I ain't got certainly no hot passion any
more now in me. You certainly have killed all that kind of
feeling now Jeff in me. You certainly do know that Jeff, now
the way I am always, when I am loving with you. You certainly do know that Jeff, and that's the way you certainly do
like it now in me. You certainly don't mind now Jeff, to hear
me say this to you."

Jeff Campbell was hurt so that it almost killed him. Yes he
certainly did know now what it was to have real hot love in
him, and yet Melanctha certainly was right, he did not deserve
she should ever give it to him. "All right Melanctha I ain't
ever kicking. I always will give you certainly always everything you want that I got in me. I take anything you want
now to give me. I don't say never Melanctha it don't hurt me,
but I certainly don't say ever Melanctha it ought ever to be
any different to me." And the bitter tears rose up in Jeff
Campbell, and they came and choked his voice to be silent,
and he held himself hard to keep from breaking.

"Good-night Melanctha," and Jeff was very humble to her.

"Good-night Jeff, I certainly never did mean any way to hurt you. I do love you, sure Jeff every day more and more, all the time I know you." "I know Melanctha, I know, it's never nothing to me. You can't help it, anybody ever the way they are feeling. It's all right now Melanctha, you believe me, goodnight now Melanctha, I got now to leave you, good-by Melanctha, sure don't look so worried to me, sure Melanctha I come again soon to see you." And then Jeff stumbled down the steps, and then went away fast to leave her.

And now the pain came hard and harder in Jeff Campbell, and he groaned, and it hurt him so, he could not bear it. And the tears came, and his heart beat, and he was hot and worn and bitter in him.

Now Jeff knew very well what it was to love Melanctha. Now Jeff Campbell knew he was really understanding. Now Jeff knew what it was to be good to Melanctha. Now Jeff was good to her always.

Slowly Jeff felt it a comfort in him to have it hurt so, and to be good to Melanctha always. Now there was no way Melanctha ever had had to bear things from him, worse than he now had it in him. Now Jeff was strong inside him. Now with all the pain there was peace in him. Now he knew he was understanding, now he knew he had a hot love in him, and he was good always to Melanctha Herbert who was the one had made him have it. Now he knew he could be good, and not cry out for help to her to teach him how to bear it. Every day Jeff felt himself more a strong man, the way he once had thought was his real self, the way he knew it. Now Jeff Campbell had real wisdom in him, and it did not make him bitter when it hurt him, for Jeff knew now all through him that he was really strong to bear it.

And so now Jeff Campbell could see Melanctha often, and he was patient, and always very friendly to her, and every day Jeff Campbell understood Melanctha Herbert better. And always Jeff saw Melanctha could not love him the way he needed she should do it. Melanctha Herbert had no way she ever really could remember.

And now Jeff knew there was a man Melanctha met very often, and perhaps she wanted to try to have this man to be

good, for her. Jeff Campbell never saw the man Melanctha
Herbert perhaps now wanted. Jeff Campbell only knew very
well that there was one. Then there was Rose that Melanctha
now always had with her when she wandered.

Jeff Campbell was very quiet to Melanctha. He said to her,
now he thought he did not want to come any more especially
to see her. When they met, he always would be glad to see
her, but now he never would go anywhere any more to meet
her. Sure he knew she always would have a deep love in him
for her. Sure she knew that. "Yes Jeff, I always trust you Jeff,
I certainly do know that all right." Jeff Campbell said, all right
he never could say anything to reproach her. She knew always
that he really had learned all through him how to love her.
"Yes, Jeff, I certainly do know that." She knew now she could
always trust him. Jeff always would be loyal to her though
now she never was any more to him like a religion, but he
never could forget the real sweetness in her. That Jeff must
remember always, though now he never can trust her to be
really loving to any man for always, she never did have any
way she ever could remember. If she ever needed anybody to
be good to her, Jeff Campbell always would do anything he
could to help her. He never can forget the things she taught
him so he could be really understanding, but he never any
more wants to see her. He be like a brother to her always,
when she needs it, and he always will be a good friend to her.
Jeff Campbell certainly was sorry never any more to see her,
but it was good that they now knew each other really.
"Good-by Jeff you always been very good always to me."
"Good-by Melanctha you know you always can trust yourself
to me." "Yes, I know, I know Jeff, really." "I certainly got to
go now Melanctha, from you. I go this time, Melanctha
really," and Jeff Campbell went away and this time he never
looked back to her. This time Jeff Campbell just broke away
and left her.

Jeff Campbell loved to think now he was strong again to be
quiet, and to live regular, and to do everything the way he
wanted it to be right for himself and all the colored people.
Jeff went away for a little while to another town to work there,
and he worked hard, and he was very sad inside him, and

sometimes the tears would rise up in him, and then he would work hard, and then he would begin once more to see some beauty in the world around him. Jeff had behaved right and he had learned to have a real love in him. That was very good to have inside him.

Jeff Campbell never could forget the sweetness in Melanctha Herbert, and he was always very friendly to her, but they never any more came close to one another. More and more Jeff Campbell and Melanctha fell away from all knowing of each other, but Jeff never could forget Melanctha. Jeff never could forget the real sweetness she had in her, but Jeff never any more had the sense of a real religion for her. Jeff always had strong in him the meaning of all the new kind of beauty Melanctha Herbert once had shown him, and always more and more it helped him with his working for himself and for all the colored people.

Melanctha Herbert, now that she was all through with Jeff Campbell, was free to be with Rose and the new men she met now.

Rose was always now with Melanctha Herbert. Rose never found any way to get excited. Rose always was telling Melanctha Herbert the right way she should do, so that she would not always be in trouble. But Melanctha Herbert could not help it, always she would find new ways to get excited.

Melanctha was all ready now to find new ways to be in trouble. And yet Melanctha Herbert never wanted not to do right. Always Melanctha Herbert wanted peace and quiet, and always she could only find new ways to get excited.

"Melanctha," Rose would say to her, "Melanctha, I certainly have got to tell you, you ain't right to act so with that kind of feller. You better just had stick to black men now, Melanctha, you hear me what I tell you, just the way you always see me do it. They're real bad men, now I tell you Melanctha true, and you better had hear to me. I been raised by real nice kind of white folks, Melanctha, and I certainly knows awful well, soon as ever I can see 'em acting, what is a white man will act decent to you and the kind it ain't never no good to a colored girl to ever go with. Now you know real Melanctha how I always mean right to you, and you ain't got no way like me Melanctha, what was raised by white folks, to know right what is the way you should be acting with men. I don't never want to see you have bad trouble come hard to you now Melanctha, and so you just hear to me now Melanctha, what I tell you, for I knows it. I don't say never certainly to you Melanctha, you never had ought to have nothing to do ever with no white men, though it ain't never to me Melanctha, the best kind of a way a colored girl can have to be acting, no I never do say to you Melanctha, you hadn't never ought to be with white men, though it ain't never the way I feel it ever real right for a decent colored girl to be always doing, but not never Melanctha, now you hear me, no not never no kind of white men like you been with always now Melanctha when I see you. You just hear to me Melanctha, you certainly had ought to hear to me Melanctha, I say it just like I knows it awful well, Melanctha, and I knows you don't know no better, Melanctha, how to act so, the ways I seen it with them kind of white fellers, them as never can know what to do right by a decent girl they have ever got to be with them. Now you hear to me Melanctha, what I tell you."

And so it was Melanctha Herbert found new ways to be in trouble. But it was not very bad this trouble, for these white men Rose never wanted she should be with, never meant very much to Melanctha. It was only that she liked it to be with them, and they knew all about fine horses, and it was just good to Melanctha, now a little, to feel real reckless with them. But mostly it was Rose and other better kind of colored girls and colored men with whom Melanctha Herbert now always wandered.

It was summer now and the colored people came out into the sunshine, full blown with the flowers. And they shone in the streets and in the fields with their warm joy, and they glistened in their black heat, and they flung themselves free in their wide abandonment of shouting laughter.

It was very pleasant in some ways, the life Melanctha Herbert now led with Rose and all the others. It was not always that Rose had to scold her.

There was not anybody of all these colored people, excepting only Rose, who ever meant much to Melanctha Herbert.

But they all liked Melanctha, and the men all liked to see her do things, she was so game always to do anything anybody ever could do, and then she was good and sweet to do anything anybody ever wanted from her.

These were pleasant days then, in the hot southern negro sunshine, with many simple jokes and always wide abandonment of laughter. "Just look at that Melanctha there a running. Don't she just go like a bird when she is flying. Hey Melanctha there, I come and catch you, hey Melanctha, I put salt on your tail to catch you," and then the man would try to catch her, and he would fall full on the earth and roll in an agony of wide-mouthed shouting laughter. And this was the kind of way Rose always liked to have Melanctha do it, to be engaged to him, and to have a good warm nigger time with colored men, not to go about with that kind of white man, never could know how to act right, to any decent kind of girl they could ever get to be with them.

Rose, always more and more, liked Melanctha Herbert better. Rose often had to scold Melanctha Herbert, but that only made her like Melanctha better. And then Melanctha always listened to her, and always acted every way she could to please her. And then Rose was so sorry for Melanctha, when she was so blue sometimes, and wanted somebody should come and kill her.

And Melanctha Herbert clung to Rose in the hope that Rose could save her. Melanctha felt the power of Rose's selfish, decent kind of nature. It was so solid, simple, certain to her. Melanctha clung to Rose, she loved to have her scold her, she always wanted to be with her. She always felt a solid safety in her. Rose always was, in her way, very good to let Melanctha be loving to her. Melanctha never had any way she could really be a trouble to her. Melanctha never had any that she could ever get real power, to come close inside to her. Melanctha was always very humble to her. Melanctha was always ready to do anything Rose wanted from her. Melanctha needed badly to have Rose always willing to let Melanctha cling to her. Rose was a simple, sullen, selfish, black girl, but she had a solid power in her. Rose had strong the sense of decent conduct, she had strong the sense for decent comfort. Ro-

always knew very well what it was she wanted, and she knew very well what was the right way to do it to get everything she wanted, and she never had any kind of trouble to perplex her. And so the subtle intelligent attractive half white girl Melanctha Herbert loved and did for, and demeaned herself in service to this coarse, decent, sullen, ordinary, black, childish Rose and now this unmoral promiscuous shiftless Rose was to be married to a good man of the negroes, while Melanctha Herbert with her white blood and attraction and her desire for a right position was perhaps never to be really regularly married. Sometimes the thought of how all her world was made filled the complex, desiring Melanctha with despair. She wondered often how she could go on living when she was so blue. Sometimes Melanctha thought she would just kill herself, for sometimes she thought this would be really the best thing for her to do.

Rose was now to be married to a decent good man of the negroes. His name was Sam Johnson, and he worked as a deck hand on a coasting steamer, and he was very steady, and he got good wages.

Rose first met Sam Johnson at church, the same place where she had met Melanctha Herbert. Rose liked Sam when she saw him, she knew he was a good man and worked hard and got good wages, and Rose thought it would be very nice and very good now in her position to get really, regularly married.

Sam Johnson liked Rose very well and he always was ready to do anything she wanted. Sam was a tall, square shouldered, decent, a serious, straightforward, simple, kindly, colored workman. They got on very well together, Sam and Rose, when they were married. Rose was lazy, but not dirty, and Sam was careful but not fussy. Sam was a kindly, simple, earnest, steady workman, and Rose had good common decent sense in her, of how to live regular, and not to have excitements, and to be saving so you could be always sure to have money, so as to have everything you wanted.

It was not very long that Rose knew Sam Johnson, before they were regularly married. Sometimes Sam went into the country with all the other young church people, and then he would be a great deal with Rose and with her Melanctha

Herbert. Sam did not care much about Melanctha Herbert. He liked Rose's ways of doing, always better. Melanctha's mystery had no charm for Sam ever. Sam wanted a nice little house to come to when he was tired from his working, and a little baby all his own he could be good to. Sam Johnson was ready to marry as soon as ever Rose wanted he should do it. And so Sam Johnson and Rose one day had a grand real wedding and were married. Then they furnished completely, a little red brick house and then Sam went back to his work as deck hand on a coasting steamer.

Rose had often talked to Sam about how good Melanctha was and how much she always suffered. Sam Johnson never really cared about Melanctha Herbert, but he always did almost everything Rose ever wanted, and he was a gentle, kindly creature, and so he was very good to Rose's friend Melanctha. Melanctha Herbert knew very well Sam did not like her, and so she was very quiet, and always let Rose do the talking for her. She only was very good to always help Rose, and to do anything she ever wanted from her, and to be very good and listen and be quiet whenever Sam had anything to say to her. Melanctha liked Sam Johnson, and all her life Melanctha loved and wanted good and kind and considerate people, and always Melanctha loved and wanted people to be gentle to her, and always she wanted to be regular, and to have peace and quiet in her, and always Melanctha could only find new ways to be in trouble. And Melanctha needed badly to have Rose, to believe her, and to let her cling to her. Rose was the only steady thing Melanctha had to cling to and so Melanctha demeaned herself to be like a servant, to wait on, and always to be scolded, by this ordinary, sullen, black, stupid, childish woman.

Rose was always telling Sam he must be good to poor Melanctha. "You know Sam," Rose said very often to him, "You certainly had ought to be very good to poor Melanctha, she always do have so much trouble with her. You know Sam how I told you she had such a bad time always with that father, and he was awful mean to her always that awful black man, and he never took no kind of care ever to her, and he nev* helped her when her mother died so hard, that poor Mela* tha. Melanctha's ma you know Sam, always was just real religious. One day Melanctha was real little, and she heard her ma say to her pa, it was awful sad to her, Melanctha had not been the one the Lord had took from them stead of the little brother who was dead in the house there from fever. That hurt Melanctha awful when she heard her ma say it. She never could feel it right, and I don't no ways blame Melanctha, Sam, for not feeling better to her ma always after, though Melanctha, just like always she is, always was real good to her ma after, when she was so sick, and died so hard, and nobody never to help Melanctha do it, and she just all alone to do everything without no help come to her no way, and that ugly awful black man she have for a father never all the time time come near her. But that's always the way Melanctha is just doing Sam, the way I been telling to you. She always is being just so good to everybody and nobody ever there to thank her for it. I never did see nobody ever Sam, have such bad luck, seems to me always with them, like that poor Melanctha always has it, and she always so good with it, and never no murmur in her, and never no complaining from her, and just never saying nothing with it. You be real good to her Sam, now you hear me, now you and me is married right together. He certainly was an awful black man to her Sam, that father she had, acting always just like a brute to her and she so game and never to tell anybody how it hurt her. And she so sweet and good always to do anything anybody ever can be wanting. I don't see Sam how some men can be to act so awful. I told you Sam, how once Melanctha broke her arm bad and she was so sick and it hurt her awful and he never would let no doctor come near to her and he do some things so awful to her, she don't never want to tell nobody how bad he hurt her. That's just the way Sam with Melanctha always, you never can know how bad it is, it hurts her. You hear me Sam, you always be real good to her now you and me is married right to each other."

And so Rose and Sam Johnson were regularly married, and Rose sat at home and bragged to all her friends how nice it was to be married really to a husband.

Rose did not have Melanctha to live with her, now Rose

was married. Melanctha was with Rose almost as much as ever but it was a little different now their being together.

Rose Johnson never asked Melanctha to live with her in the house, now Rose was married. Rose liked to have Melanctha come all the time to help her, Rose liked Melanctha to be almost always with her, but Rose was shrewd in her simple selfish nature, she did not ever think to ask Melanctha to live with her.

Rose was hard headed, she was decent, and she always knew what it was she needed. Rose needed Melanctha to be with her, she liked to have her help her, the quick, good Melanctha to do for the slow, lazy, selfish, black girl, but Rose could have Melanctha to do for her and she did not need her to live with her.

Sam never asked Rose why she did not have her. Sam always took what Rose wanted should be done for Melanctha, as the right way he should act toward her.

It could never come to Melanctha to ask Rose to let her. It never could come to Melanctha to think that Rose would ask her. It would never ever come to Melanctha to want it, if Rose should ask her, but Melanctha would have done it for the safety she always felt when she was near her. Melanctha Herbert wanted badly to be safe now, but this living with her, that, Rose would never give her. Rose had strong the sense for decent comfort, Rose had strong the sense of proper conduct, Rose had strong the sense to get straight always what she wanted, and she always knew what was the best thing she needed, and always Rose got what she wanted.

And so Rose had Melanctha Herbert always there to help her, and she sat and was lazy and she bragged and she complained a little and she told Melanctha how she ought to do, to get good what she wanted like she Rose always did it, and always Melanctha was doing everything Rose ever needed. "Don't you bother so, doing that Melanctha, I do it or Sam when he comes home to help me. Sure you don't mind lifting it Melanctha? You is very good Melanctha to do it, and when you go out Melanctha, you stop and get some rice to bring me to-morrow when you come in. Sure you won't forget Melanctha. I never see anybody like you Melanctha to always things so nice for me." And then Melanctha would do some more for Rose, and then very late Melanctha would go home to the colored woman where she lived now.

And so though Melanctha still was so much with Rose Johnson, she had times when she could not stay there. Melanctha now could not really cling there. Rose had Sam, and Melanctha more and more lost the hold she had had there.

Melanctha Herbert began to feel she must begin again to look and see if she could find what it was she had always wanted. Now Rose Johnson could no longer help her.

And so Melanctha Herbert began once more to wander and with men Rose never thought it was right she should be with.

One day Melanctha had been very busy with the different kinds of ways she wandered. It was a pleasant late afternoon at the end of a long summer. Melanctha was walking along, and she was free and excited. Melanctha had just parted from a white man and she had a bunch of flowers he had left with her. A young buck, a mulatto, passed by and snatched them from her. "It certainly is real sweet in you sister, to be giving me them pretty flowers," he said to her.

"I don't see no way it can make them sweeter to have with you," said Melanctha. "What one man gives, another man had certainly just as much good right to be taking." "Keep your old flowers then, I certainly don't never want to have them." Melanctha Herbert laughed at him and took them. "No, I didn't nohow think you really did want to have them. Thank you kindly mister, for them. I certainly always do admire to see a man always so kind of real polite to people." The man laughed, "You ain't nobody's fool I can say for you, but you certainly are a damned pretty kind of girl, now I look at you. Want men to be polite to you? All right, I can love you, that's real polite now, want to see me try it." "I certainly ain't got no time this evening just only left to thank you. I certainly got to be real busy now, but I certainly always will admire to see you." The man tried to catch and stop her, Melanctha Herbert laughed and dodged so that he could not catch her. Melanctha went quickly down a side street near her and so the man for hat time lost her.

For some days Melanctha did not see any more of her

mulatto. One day Melanctha was with a white man and they saw him. The white man stopped to speak to him. Afterwards Melanctha left the white man and she then soon met him. Melanctha stopped to talk to him. Melanctha Herbert soon began to like him.

Jem Richards, the new man Melanctha had begun to know now, was a dashing kind of fellow, who had to do with fine horses and with racing. Sometimes Jem Richards would be betting and would be good and lucky, and be making lots of money. Sometimes Jem would be betting badly, and then he would not be having any money.

Jem Richards was a straight man. Jem Richards always knew that by and by he would win again and pay it, and so Jem mostly did win again, and then he always paid it.

Jem Richards was a man other men always trusted. Men gave him money when he lost all his, for they all knew Jem Richards would win again, and when he did win they knew, and they were right, that he would pay it.

Melanctha Herbert all her life had always loved to be with horses. Melanctha liked it that Jem knew all about fine horses. He was a reckless man was Jem Richards. He knew how to win out, and always all her life Melanctha Herbert loved successful power.

Melanctha Herbert always liked Jem Richards better. Things soon began to be very strong between them.

Jem was more game even than Melanctha. Jem always had known what it was to have real wisdom. Jem had always all his life been understanding.

Jem Richards made Melanctha Herbert come fast with him. He never gave her any time with waiting. Soon Melanctha always had Jem with her. Melanctha did not want anything better. Now in Jem Richards, Melanctha found everything she had ever needed to content her.

Melanctha was now less and less with Rose Johnson. Rose did not think much of the way Melanctha now was going. Jem Richards was all right, only Melanctha never had no sense of the right kind of way she should be doing. Rose often was telling Sam now, she did not like the fast way Melanctha was going. Rose told it to Sam, and to all the girls and men, whe she saw them. But Rose was nothing just then to Melanctha. Melanctha Herbert now only needed Jem Richards to be with her.

And things were always getting stronger between Jem Richards and Melanctha Herbert. Jem Richards began to talk now as if he wanted to get married to her. Jem was deep in his love for her. And as for Melanctha, Jem was all the world now to her. And so Jem gave her a ring, like white folks, to show he was engaged to her, and would by and by be married to her. And Melanctha was filled with joy to have Jem so good to her.

Melanctha always loved to go with Jem to the races. Jem had been lucky lately with his betting, and he had a swell turn-out to drive in, and Melanctha looked very handsome there beside him.

Melanctha was very proud to have Jem Richards want her. Melanctha loved it the way Jem knew how to do it. Melanctha loved Jem and loved that he should want her. She loved it too, that he wanted to be married to her. Jem Richards was a straight decent man, whom other men always looked up to and trusted. Melanctha needed badly a man to content her.

Melanctha's joy made her foolish. Melanctha told everybody about how Jem Richards, that swell man who owned all those fine horses and was so game, nothing ever scared him, was engaged to be married to her, and that was the ring he gave her.

Melanctha let out her joy very often to Rose Johnson, Melanctha had begun again now to go there.

Melanctha's love for Jem made her foolish. Melanctha had to have some one always now to talk to and so she went often to Rose Johnson.

Melanctha put all herself into Jem Richards. She was mad and foolish in the joy she had there.

Rose never liked the way Melanctha did it. "No Sam I don't say never Melanctha ain't engaged to Jem Richards the way she always says it, and Jem he is all right for that kind of a man he is, though he do think himself so smart and like he owns the earth and everything he can get with it, and he sure gave Melanctha a ring like he really meant he should be married right soon with it, only Sam, I don't ever like it the way Melanctha is going. When she is engaged to him Sam, she ain't not right to take on so excited. That ain't no decent kind of a way a girl ever should be acting. There ain't no kind of a man going stand that, not like I knows men Sam, and I sure does know them. I knows them white and I knows them colored, for I was raised by white folks, and they don't none of them like a girl to act so. That's all right to be so when you is just only loving, but it ain't no ways right to be acting so when you is engaged to him, and when he says, all right he get really regularly married to you. You see Sam I am right like I am always and I knows it. Jem Richards, he ain't going to the last to get real married, not if I knows it right, the way Melanctha now is acting to him. Rings or anything ain't nothing to them, and they don't never do no good for them, when a girl acts foolish like Melanctha always now is acting. I certainly will be right sorry Sam, if Melanctha has real bad trouble come now to her, but I certainly don't no ways like it Sam the kind of way Melanctha is acting to him. I don't never say nothing to her Sam. I just listens to what she is saying, and I thinks it out like I am telling to you Sam but I don't never say nothing no more now to Melanctha. Melanctha didn't say nothing to me about that Jem Richards till she was all like finished with him, and I never did like it Sam, much, the way she was acting, not coming here never when she first ran with those men and met him. And I didn't never say nothing to her, Sam, about it, and it ain't nothing ever to me, only I don't never no more want to say nothing to her, so I just listens to what she got to tell like she wants it. No Sam, I don't never want to say nothing to her. Melanctha just got to go her own way, not as I want to see her have bad trouble ever come hard to her, only it ain't in me never Sam, after Melanctha did so, ever to say nothing more to her how she should be acting. You just see Sam like I tell you, what way Jem Richards will act to her, you see Sam I just am right like I always am when I knows it."

Melanctha Herbert never thought she could ever again be in trouble. Melanctha's joy made her foolish.

And now Jem Richards had some bad trouble with his betting. Melanctha sometimes felt now when she was with him that there was something wrong inside him. Melanctha knew he had had trouble with his betting but Melanctha never felt that that could make any difference to them.

Melanctha once had told Jem, sure he knew she always would love to be with him, if he was in jail or only just a beggar. Now Melanctha said to him, "Sure you know Jem that it don't never make any kind of difference you're having any kind of trouble, you just try me Jem and be game, don't look so worried to me. Jem sure I know you love me like I love you always, and it's all I ever could be wanting Jem to me, just your wanting me always to be with you. I get married Jem to you soon ever as you can want me, if you once say it Jem to me. It ain't nothing to me ever, anything like having any money Jem, why you look so worried to me."

Melanctha Herbert's love had surely made her mad and foolish. She thrust it always deep into Jem Richards and now that he had trouble with his betting, Jem had no way that he ever wanted to be made to feel it. Jem Richards never could want to marry any girl while he had trouble. That was no way a man like him should do it. Melanctha's love had made her mad and foolish, she should be silent now and let him do it. Jem Richards was not a kind of man to want a woman to be strong to him, when he was in trouble with his betting. That was not the kind of a time when a man like him needed to have it.

Melanctha needed so badly to have it, this love which she had always wanted, she did not know what she should do to save it. Melanctha saw now, Jem Richards always had something wrong inside him. Melanctha soon dared not ask him. Jem was busy now, he had to sell things and see men to raise money. Jem could not meet Melanctha now so often.

It was lucky for Melanctha Herbert that Rose Johnson was coming now to have her baby. It had always been understood between them, Rose should come and stay then in the house where Melanctha lived with an old colored woman, so that Rose could have the Doctor from the hospital near by to help her, and Melanctha there to take care of her the way Melanctha always used to do it.

Melanctha was very good now to Rose Johnson. Melanctha did everything that any woman could, she tended Rose, and she was patient, submissive, soothing and untiring, while the sullen, childish, cowardly, black Rosie grumbled, and fussed, and howled, and made herself to be an abomination and like a simple beast.

All this time Melanctha was always being every now and then with Jem Richards. Melanctha was beginning to be stronger with Jem Richards. Melanctha was never so strong and sweet and in her nature as when she was deep in trouble, when she was fighting so with all she had, she could not do any foolish thing with her nature.

Always now Melanctha Herbert came back again to be nearer to Rose Johnson. Always now Melanctha would tell all about her troubles to Rose Johnson. Rose had begun now a little again to advise her.

Melanctha always told Rose now about the talks she had with Jem Richards, talks where they neither of them liked very well what the other one was saying. Melanctha did not know what it was Jem Richards wanted. All Melanctha knew was, he did not like it when she wanted to be good friends and get really married, and then when Melanctha would say, "all right, I never wear your ring no more Jem, we ain't not any more to meet ever like we ever going to get really regular married," then Jem did not like it either. What was it Jem Richards really wanted?

Melanctha stopped wearing Jem's ring on her finger. Poor Melanctha, she wore it on a string she tied around her neck so that she could always feel it, but Melanctha was strong now with Jem Richards, and he never saw it. And sometimes Jem seemed to be awful sorry for it, and sometimes he seemed kind of glad of it. Melanctha never could make out really what it was Jem Richards wanted.

There was no other woman yet to Jem, that Melanctha knew, and so she always trusted that Jem would come back to her, deep in his love, the way once he had had it and had made all the world like she once had never believed anybody could really make it. But Jem Richards was more game than Melanctha Herbert. He knew how to fight to win out, bet-

Melanctha really had already lost it, in not keeping quiet and waiting for Jem to do it.

Jem Richards was not yet having better luck in his betting. He never before had had such a long time without some good coming to him in his betting. Sometimes Jem talked as if he wanted to go off on a trip somewhere and try some other place for luck with his betting. Jem Richards never talked as if he wanted to take Melanctha with him.

And so Melanctha sometimes was really trusting, and sometimes she was all sick inside her with her doubting. What was it Jem really wanted to do with her? He did not have any other woman, in that Melanctha could be really trusting and when she said no to him, no she never would come near him, now he did not want to have her, then Jem would change and swear, yes sure he did want her, now and always right here near him, but he never now any more said he wanted to be married soon to her. But then Jem Richards never would marry a girl, he said that very often, when he was in this kind of trouble, and now he did not see any way he could get out of his trouble. But Melanctha ought to wear his ring, sure she knew he never had loved any kind of woman like he loved her. Melanctha would wear the ring a little while, and then they would have some more trouble, and then she would say to him, no she certainly never would any more wear anything he gave her, and then she would wear it on the string so nobody could see it but she could always feel it on her.

Poor Melanctha, surely her love had made her mad and foolish.

And now Melanctha needed always more and more to be with Rose Johnson, and Rose had commenced again to advise her, but Rose could not help her. There was no way now that anybody could advise her. The time when Melanctha could have changed it with Jem Richards was now all past for her. Rose knew it, and Melanctha too, she knew it, and it almost killed her to let herself believe it.

The only comfort Melanctha ever had now was waiting on Rose till she was so tired she could hardly stand it. Always Melanctha did everything Rose ever wanted. Sam Johnson began now to be very gentle and a little tender to Melanctha.

She was so good to Rose and Sam was so glad to have her there to help Rose and to do things and to be a comfort to her.

Rose had a hard time to bring her baby to its birth and Melanctha did everything that any woman could.

The baby though it was healthy after it was born did not live long. Rose Johnson was careless and negligent and selfish and when Melanctha had to leave for a few days the baby died. Rose Johnson had liked her baby well enough and perhaps she just forgot it for a while, anyway the child was dead and Rose and Sam were very sorry, but then these things came so often in the negro world in Bridgepoint that they neither of them thought about it very long. When Rose had become strong again she went back to her house with Sam. And Sam Johnson was always now very gentle and kind and good to Melanctha who had been so good to Rose in her bad trouble.

Melanctha Herbert's troubles with Jem Richards were never getting any better. Jem always had less and less time to be with her. When Jem was with Melanctha now he was good enough to her. Jem Richards was worried with his betting. Never since Jem had first begun to make a living had he ever had so much trouble for such a long time together with his betting. Jem Richards was good enough now to Melanctha but he had not much strength to give her. Melanctha could never any more now make him quarrel with her. Melanctha never now could complain of his treatment of her, for surely, he said it always by his actions to her, surely she must know how a man was when he had trouble on his mind with trying to make things go a little better.

Sometimes Jem and Melanctha had long talks when they neither of them liked very well what the other one was saying, but mostly now Melanctha could not make Jem Richards quarrel with her, and more and more, Melanctha could not find any way to make it right to blame him for the trouble she now always had inside her. Jem was good to her, and she knew, for he told her, that he had trouble all the time now with his betting. Melanctha knew very well that for her it was all wrong inside Jem Richards, but Melanctha had now no way that she could really reach him.

Things between Melanctha and Jem Richards were now never getting any better. Melanctha now more and more needed to be with Rose Johnson. Rose still liked to have Melanctha come to her house and do things for her, and Rose liked to grumble to her and to scold her and to tell Melanctha what was the way Melanctha always should be doing so she could make things come out better and not always be so much in trouble. Sam Johnson in these days was always very good and gentle to Melanctha. Sam was now beginning to be very sorry for her.

Jem Richards never made things any better for Melanctha. Often Jem would talk so as to make Melanctha almost certain that he never any more wanted to have her. Then Melanctha would get very blue, and she would say to Rose, sure she would kill herself, for that certainly now was the best way she could do.

Rose Johnson never saw it the least bit that way. "I don't see Melanctha why you should talk like you would kill yourself because you're blue. I'd never kill myself Melanctha cause I was blue. I'd maybe kill somebody else but I'd never kill myself. If I ever killed myself, Melanctha it'd be by accident and if I ever killed myself by accident, Melanctha, I'd be awful sorry. And that certainly is the way you should feel it Melanctha, now you hear me, not just talking foolish like you always do. It certainly is only your way just always being foolish makes you all that trouble to come to you always now, Melanctha, and I certainly right well knows that. You certainly never can learn no way Melanctha ever with all I certainly been telling to you, ever since I know you good, that it ain't never no way like you do always is the right way you be acting ever and talking, the way I certainly always have seen you do so Melanctha always. I certainly am right Melanctha about them ways you have to do it, and I knows it; but you certainly never can noways learn to act right Melanctha, I certainly do know that, I certainly do my best Melanctha to help you with it only you certainly never do act right Melanctha, not to nobody ever, I can see it. You never act right by me Melanctha no more than by everybody. I never say nothing to you Melanctha when you do so, for I certainly never do like

it when I just got to say it to you, but you just certainly done
with that Jem Richards you always say wanted real bad to be
married to you, just like I always said to Sam you certainly
was going to do it. And I certainly am real kind of sorry like
for you Melanctha, but you certainly had ought to have come
to see me to talk to you, when you first was engaged to him so
I could show you, and now you got all this trouble come to
you Melanctha like I certainly know you always catch it. It
certainly ain't never Melanctha I ain't real sorry to see trouble
come so hard to you, but I certainly can see Melanctha it all
is always just the way you always be having it in you not never
to do right. And now you always talk like you just kill yourself
because you are so blue, that certainly never is Melanctha, no
kind of a way for any decent kind of a girl to do."

Rose had begun to be strong now to scold Melanctha and
she was impatient very often with her, but Rose could now
never any more be a help to her. Melanctha Herbert never
could know now what it was right she should do. Melanctha
always wanted to have Jem Richards with her and now he
never seemed to want her, and what could Melanctha do.
Surely she was right now when she said she would just kill
herself, for that was the only way now she could do.

Sam Johnson always, more and more, was good and gentle
to Melanctha. Poor Melanctha, she was so good and sweet to
do anything anybody ever wanted, and Melanctha always
liked it if she could have peace and quiet, and always she
could only find new ways to be in trouble. Sam often said
this now to Rose about Melanctha.

"I certainly don't never want Sam to say bad things about
Melanctha, for she certainly always do have most awful kind
of trouble come hard to her, but I never can say I like it real
right Sam the way Melanctha always has to do it. It's now
just the same with her like it is always she has got to do it,
now the way she is with that Jem Richards. He certainly now
don't never want to have her but Melanctha she ain't got no
right kind of spirit. No Sam I don't never like the way any
more Melanctha is acting to him, and then Sam, she ain't
never real right honest, the way she always should do it. She
certainly just don't kind of never Sam tell right what way

she is doing with it. I don't never like to say nothing Sam no more to her about the way she always has to be acting. She always say, yes all right Rose, I do the way you say it, and then Sam she don't never noways do it. She certainly is right sweet and good, Sam, is Melanctha, nobody ever can hear me say she ain't always ready to do things for everybody any way she ever can see to do it, only Sam some ways she never does act real right ever, and some ways, Sam, she ain't ever real honest with it. And Sam sometimes I hear awful kind of things she been doing, some girls know about her how she does it, and sometimes they tell me what kind of ways she has to do it, and Sam it certainly do seem to me like more and more I certainly am awful afraid Melanctha never will come to any good. And then Sam, sometimes, you hear it, she always talk like she kill herself all the time she is so blue, and Sam that certainly never is no kind of way any decent girl ever had ought to do. You see Sam, how I am right like I always is when I knows it. You just be careful, Sam, now you hear me, you be careful Sam sure, I tell you, Melanctha more and more I see her I certainly do feel Melanctha no way is really honest. You be careful, Sam now, like I tell you, for I knows it, now you hear to me, Sam, what I tell you, for I certainly always is right, Sam, when I knows it."

At first Sam tried a little to defend Melanctha, and Sam always was good and gentle to her, and Sam liked the ways Melanctha had to be quiet to him, and to always listen as if she was learning, when she was there and heard him talking, and then Sam liked the sweet way she always did everything so nicely for him; but Sam never liked to fight with anybody ever, and surely Rose knew best about Melanctha and anyway Sam never did really care much about Melanctha. Her mystery never had had any interest for him. Sam liked it that she was sweet to him and that she always did everything Rose ever wanted that she should be doing, but Melanctha never could be important to him. All Sam ever wanted was to have a little house and to live regular and to work hard and to come home to his dinner, when he was tired with his working and by and by he wanted to have some children all his own to be good to, and so Sam was real sorry for Melanctha, she was so

good and so sweet always to them, and Jem Richards was a
bad man to behave so to her, but that was always the way
a girl got it when she liked that kind of a fast fellow. Anyhow
Melanctha was Rose's friend, and Sam never cared to have
anything to do with the kind of trouble always came to
women, when they wanted to have men, who never could
know how to behave good and steady to their women.

And so Sam never said much to Rose about Melanctha.
Sam was always very gentle to her, but now he began less
and less to see her. Soon Melanctha never came any more to
the house to see Rose and Sam never asked Rose anything
about her.

Melanctha Herbert was beginning now to come less and
less to the house to be with Rose Johnson. This was because
Rose seemed always less and less now to want her, and Rose
would not let Melanctha now do things for her. Melanctha
was always humble to her and Melanctha always wanted in
every way she could to do things for her. Rose said no, she
guessed she do that herself like she likes to have it better.
Melanctha is real good to stay so long to help her, but Rose
guessed perhaps Melanctha better go home now, Rose don't
need nobody to help her now, she is feeling real strong, not
like just after she had all that trouble with the baby, and then
Sam, when he comes home for his dinner he likes it when
Rose is all alone there just to give him his dinner. Sam always
is so tired now, like he always is in the summer, so many
people always on the steamer, and they make so much work
so Sam is real tired now, and he likes just to eat his dinner
and never have people in the house to be a trouble to him.

Each day Rose treated Melanctha more and more as if she
never wanted Melanctha any more to come there to the house
to see her. Melanctha dared not ask Rose why she acted in this
way to her. Melanctha badly needed to have Rose always
there to save her. Melanctha wanted badly to cling to her and
Rose had always been so solid for her. Melanctha did not dare
to ask Rose if she now no longer wanted her to come and
see her.

Melanctha now never any more had Sam to be gentle to
her. Rose always sent Melanctha away from her before it was

time for Sam to come home to her. One day Melanctha had stayed a little longer, for Rose that day had been good to let Melanctha begin to do things for her. Melanctha then left her and Melanctha met Sam Johnson who stopped a minute to speak kindly to her.

The next day Rose Johnson would not let Melanctha come in to her. Rose stood on the steps, and there she told Melanctha what she thought now of her.

"I guess Melanctha it certainly ain't no ways right for you to come here no more just to see me. I certainly don't Melanctha no ways like to be a trouble to you. I certainly think Melanctha I get along better now when I don't have nobody like you are, always here to help me, and Sam he do so good now with his working, he pay a little girl something to come every day to help me. I certainly do think Melanctha I don't never want you no more to come here just to see me." "Why Rose, what I ever done to you, I certainly don't think you is right Rose to be so bad now to me." "I certainly don't no ways Melanctha Herbert think you got any right ever to be complaining the way I been acting to you. I certainly never do think Melanctha Herbert, you hear to me, nobody ever been more patient to you than I always been to like you, only Melanctha, I hear more things now so awful bad about you, everybody always is telling to me what kind of a way you always have been doing so much, and me always so good to you, and you never no ways, knowing how to be honest to me. No Melanctha it ain't ever in me, not to want you to have good luck come to you, and I like it real well Melanctha when you some time learn how to act the way it is decent and right for a girl to be doing, but I don't no ways ever like it the kind of things everybody tell me now about you. No Melanctha, I can't never any more trust you. I certainly am real sorry to have never any more to see you, but there ain't no other way, I ever can be acting to you. That's all I ever got any more to say to you now Melanctha." "But Rose, deed; I certainly don't know, no more than the dead, nothing I ever done to make you act so to me. Anybody say anything bad about me Rose, to you, they just a pack of liars to you, they certainly is Rose, I tell you true. I certainly never done nothing I ever

been ashamed to tell you. Why you act so bad to me Rose.
Sam he certainly don't think ever like you do, and Rose I
always do everything I can, you ever want me to do for you."
"It ain't never no use standing there talking, Melanctha Herbert. I just can tell it to you, and Sam, he don't know nothing
about women ever the way they can be acting. I certainly am
very sorry Melanctha, to have to act so now to you, but I
certainly can't do no other way with you, when you do things
always so bad, and everybody is talking so about you. It ain't
no use to you to stand there and say it different to me Melanctha. I certainly am always right Melanctha Herbert, the
way I certainly always have been when I knows it, to you.
No Melanctha, it just is, you never can have no kind of a way
to act right, the way a decent girl has to do, and I done my
best always to be telling it to you Melanctha Herbert, but it
don't never do no good to tell nobody how to act right; they
certainly never can learn when they ain't got no sense right
to know it, and you never have no sense right Melanctha to
be honest, and I ain't never wishing no harm to you ever
Melanctha Herbert, only I don't never want any more to see
you come here. I just say to you now, like I always been
saying to you, you don't know never the right way, any kind
of decent girl has to be acting, and so Melanctha Herbert, me
and Sam, we don't never any more want you to be setting
your foot in my house here Melanctha Herbert, I just tell
you. And so you just go along now, Melanctha Herbert, you
hear me, and I don't never wish no harm to come to you."

Rose Johnson went into her house and closed the door
behind her. Melanctha stood like one dazed, she did not know
how to bear this blow that almost killed her. Slowly then
Melanctha went away without even turning to look behind
her.

Melanctha Herbert was all sore and bruised inside her.
Melanctha had needed Rose always to believe her, Melanctha
needed Rose always to let her cling to her, Melanctha wanted
badly to have somebody who could make her always feel
a little safe inside her, and now Rose had sent her from her.
Melanctha wanted Rose more than she had ever wanted all
the others. Rose always was so simple, solid, decent, for her.

And now Rose had cast her from her. Melanctha was lost, and all the world went whirling in a mad weary dance around her.

Melanctha Herbert never had any strength alone ever to feel safe inside her. And now Rose Johnson had cast her from her, and Melanctha could never any more be near her. Melanctha Herbert knew now, way inside her, that she was lost, and nothing any more could ever help her.

Melanctha went that night to meet Jem Richards who had promised to be at the old place to meet her. Jem Richards was absent in his manner to her. By and by he began to talk to her, about the trip he was going to take soon, to see if he could get some luck back in his betting. Melanctha trembled, was Jem too now going to leave her. Jem Richards talked some more then to her, about the bad luck he always had now, and how he needed to go away to see if he could make it come out any better.

Then Jem stopped, and then he looked straight at Melanctha.

"Tell me Melanctha right and true, you don't care really nothing more about me now Melanctha," he said to her.

"Why you ask me that, Jem Richards," said Melanctha.

"Why I ask you that Melanctha, God Almighty, because I just don't give a damn now for you any more Melanctha. That the reason I was asking."

Melanctha never could have for this an answer. Jem Richards waited and then he went away and left her.

Melanctha Herbert never again saw Jem Richards. Melanctha never again saw Rose Johnson, and it was hard to Melanctha never any more to see her. Rose Johnson had worked in to be the deepest of all Melanctha's emotions.

"No, I don't never see Melanctha Herbert no more now," Rose would say to anybody who asked her about Melanctha. "No, Melanctha she never comes here no more now, after we had all that trouble with her acting so bad with them kind of men she liked so much to be with. She don't never come to no good Melanctha Herbert don't, and me and Sam don't want no more to see her. She didn't do right ever the way I told her. Melanctha just wouldn't, and I always said it to her,

if she don't be more kind of careful, the way she always had
to be acting, I never did want no more she should come here
in my house no more to see me. I ain't no ways ever against
any girl having any kind of a way, to have a good time like
she wants it, but not that kind of a way Melanctha always
had to do it. I expect some day Melanctha kill herself,
when she act so bad like she do always, and then she get so
awfully blue. Melanctha always says that's the only way she
ever can think it a easy way for her to do. No, I always am
real sorry for Melanctha, she never was no just common kind
of nigger, but she don't never know not with all the time I
always was telling it to her, no she never no way could learn,
what was the right way she should do. I certainly don't never
want no kind of harm to come bad to Melanctha, but I
certainly do think she will most kill herself some time, the way
she always say it would be easy way for her to do. I never see
nobody ever could be so awful blue."

But Melanctha Herbert never really killed herself because
she was so blue, though often she thought this would be
really the best way for her to do. Melanctha never killed
herself, she only got a bad fever and went into the hospital
where they took good care of her and cured her.

When Melanctha was well again, she took a place and
began to work and to live regular. Then Melanctha got very
sick again, she began to cough and sweat and be so weak she
could not stand to do her work.

Melanctha went back to the hospital, and there the Doctor
told her she had the consumption, and before long she would
surely die. They sent her where she would be taken care of,
a home for poor consumptives, and there Melanctha stayed
until she died.

TENDER BUTTONS

OBJECTS

FOOD

ROOMS

The poet Donald Evans founded a publishing house, principally to print his own work, called Claire-Marie, after our friend Claire-Marie Burke. Having met Gertrude Stein in the summer of 1913, and having read THE PORTRAIT OF MABEL DODGE AT THE VILLA CURONIA, THREE LIVES, MATISSE, *and* PICASSO *I suggested to Donald that he print a book of hers. The idea aroused his enthusiasm and Miss Stein, on invitation, supplied the manuscript of* TENDER BUTTONS *which Donald published in 1914. It was widely quoted and ridiculed by friends and enemies in the American press. In* LECTURES IN AMERICA *Miss Stein explains: "And so in* TENDER BUTTONS *and then on I struggled with the ridding of myself of nouns. I knew that nouns must go in poetry as they had gone in prose if anything that is everything was to go on meaning something."*

OBJECTS

A CARAFE, THAT IS A BLIND GLASS

A kind in glass and a cousin, a spectacle and nothing strange a single hurt color and an arrangement in a system to pointing. All this and not ordinary, not unordered in not resembling. The difference is spreading.

GLAZED GLITTER

Nickel, what is nickel, it is originally rid of a cover.

The change in that is that red weakens an hour. The change has come. There is no search. But there is, there is that hope and that interpretation and sometime, surely any is unwelcome, sometime there is breath and there will be a sinecure and charming very charming is that clean and cleansing. Certainly glittering is handsome and convincing.

There is no gratitude in mercy and in medicine. There can be breakages in Japanese. That is no programme. That is no color chosen. It was chosen yesterday, that showed spitting and perhaps washing and polishing. It certainly showed no obligation and perhaps if borrowing is not natural there is some use in giving.

A SUBSTANCE IN A CUSHION

The change of color is likely and a difference a very little difference is prepared. Sugar is not a vegetable.

Callous is something that hardening leaves behind what will be soft if there is a genuine interest in there being present as many girls as men. Does this change. It shows that dirt is clean when there is a volume.

A cushion has that cover. Supposing you do not like to change, supposing it is very clean that there is no change in appearance, supposing that there is regularity and a costume is that any the worse than an oyster and an exchange. Come to season that is there any extreme use in feather and cotton. Is there not much more joy in a table and more chairs and very likely roundness and a place to put them.

A circle of fine card board and a chance to see a tassel.

What is the use of a violent kind of delightfulness if there is no pleasure in not getting tired of it. The question does not come before there is a quotation. In any kind of place there is a top to covering and it is a pleasure at any rate there is some venturing in refusing to believe nonsense. It shows what use there is in a whole piece if one uses it and it is extreme and very likely the little things could be dearer but in any case there is a bargain and if there is the best thing to do is to take it away and wear it and then be reckless be reckless and resolved on returning gratitude.

Light blue and the same red with purple makes a change. It shows that there is no mistake. Any pink shows that and very likely it is reasonable. Very likely there should not be a finer fancy present. Some increase means a calamity and this is the best preparation for three and more being together. A little calm is so ordinary and in any case there is sweetness and some of that.

A seal and matches and a swan and ivy and a suit.

A closet, a closet does not connect under the bed. The band if it is white and black, the band has a green string. A sight a whole sight and a little groan grinding makes a trimming such a sweet singing trimming and a red thing not a round thing but a white thing, a red thing and a white thing.

The disgrace is not in carelessness nor even in sewing it comes out out of the way.

What is the sash like. The sash is not like anything mustard it is not like a same thing that has stripes, it is not even more hurt than that, it has a little top.

A BOX

Out of kindness comes redness and out of rudeness comes rapid same question, out of an eye comes research, out of selection comes painful cattle. So then the order is that a white way of being round is something suggesting a pin and is it disappointing, it is not, it is so rudimentary to be analysed and see a fine substance strangely, it is so earnest to have a green point not to red but to point again.

A PIECE OF COFFEE

More of double.

A place in no new table.

A single image is not splendor. Dirty is yellow. A sign of more in not mentioned. A piece of coffee is not a detainer. The resemblance to yellow is dirtier and distincter. The clean mixture is whiter and not coal color, never more coal color than altogether.

The sight of a reason, the same sight slighter, the sight of a simpler negative answer, the same sore sounder, the intention to wishing, the same splendor, the same furniture.

The time to show a message is when too late and later there is no hanging in a blight.

A not torn rose-wood color. If it is not dangerous then a pleasure and more than any other if it is cheap is not cheaper. The amusing side is that the sooner there are no fewer the more certain is the necessity dwindled. Supposing that the case contained rose-wood and a color. Supposing that there was no reason for a distress and more likely for a number, supposing that there was no astonishment, is it not necessary to mingle astonishment.

The settling of stationing cleaning is one way not to shatter scatter and scattering. The one way to use custom is to use soap and silk for cleaning. The one way to see cotton is to have a design concentrating the illusion and the illustration. The perfect way is to accustom the thing to have a lining and the shape of a ribbon and to be solid, quite solid in standing and to use heaviness in morning. It is light enough in that. It has that shape nicely. Very nicely may not be exaggerating. Very strongly may be sincerely fainting. May be strangely flattering. May not be strange in everything. May not be strange to.

DIRT AND NOT COPPER

Dirt and not copper makes a color darker. It makes the shape so heavy and makes no melody harder.

It makes mercy and relaxation and even a strength to spread a table fuller. There are more places not empty. They see cover.

NOTHING ELEGANT

A charm a single charm is doubtful. If the red is rose and there is a gate surrounding it, if inside is let in and there places change then certainly something is upright. It is earnest.

MILDRED'S UMBRELLA

A cause and no curve, a cause and loud enough, a cause and extra a loud clash and an extra wagon, a sign of extra, a sac a small sac and an established color and cunning, a slender grey and no ribbon, this means a loss a great loss a restitution.

A METHOD OF A CLOAK

A single climb to a line, a straight exchange to a cane, a desperate adventure and courage and a clock, all this which is a system, which has feeling, which has resignation and success, all makes an attractive black silver.

A RED STAMP

If lilies are lily white if they exhaust noise and distance and even dust, if they dusty will dirt a surface that has no extreme grace, if they do this and it is not necessary it is not at all necessary if they do this they need a catalogue.

A BOX

A large box is handily made of what is necessary to replace any substance. Suppose an example is necessary, the plainer it is made the more reason there is for some outward recognition that there is a result.

A box is made sometimes and them to see to see to it neatly and to have the holes stopped up makes it necessary to use paper.

A custom which is necessary when a box is used and taken is that a large part of the time there are three which have different connections. The one is on the table. The two are on the table. The three are on the table. The one, one is the same length as is shown by the cover being longer. The other is different there is more cover that shows it. The other is different and that makes the corners have the same shade the eight are in singular arrangement to make four necessary.

Lax, to have corners, to be lighter than some weight, to indicate a wedding journey, to last brown and not curious, to be wealthy, cigarettes are established by length and by doubling.

Left open, to be left pounded, to be left closed, to be circulating in summer and winter, and sick color that is grey that is not dusty and red shows, to be sure cigarettes do measure an empty length sooner than a choice in color.

Winged, to be winged means that white is yellow and pieces pieces that are brown are dust color if dust is washed off, then it is choice that is to say it is fitting cigarettes sooner than paper.

An increase why is an increase idle, why is silver cloister, why is the spark brighter, if it is brighter is there any result, hardly more than ever.

A PLATE

An occasion for a plate, an occasional resource is in buying and how soon does washing enable a selection of the same thing neater. If the party is small a clever song is in order.

Plates and a dinner set of colored china. Pack together a string and enough with it to protect the centre, cause a considerable haste and gather more as it is cooling, collect more trembling and not any even trembling, cause a whole thing to be a church.

A sad size a size that is not sad is blue as every bit of blue is precocious. A kind of green a game in green and nothing flat nothing quite flat and more round, nothing a particular color strangely, nothing breaking the losing of no little piece.

A splendid address a really splendid address is not shown by giving a flower freely, it is not shown by a mark or by wetting.

Cut cut in white, cut in white so lately. Cut more than any other and show it. Show it in the stem and in starting and in evening coming complication.

A lamp is not the only sign of glass. The lamp and the cake are not the only sign of stone. The lamp and the cake and the cover are not the only necessity altogether.

A plan a hearty plan, a compressed disease and no coffee, not even a card or a change to incline each way, a plan that has that excess and that break is the one that shows filling.

A SELTZER BOTTLE

Any neglect of many particles to a cracking, any neglect of this makes around it what is lead in color and certainly discolor in silver. The use of this is manifold. Supposing a certain time selected is assured, suppose it is even necessary, suppose no other extract is permitted and no more handling is needed, suppose the rest of the message is mixed with a very long slender needle and even if it could be any black border, supposing all this altogether made a dress and suppose it was actual, suppose the mean way to state it was occasional, if you suppose this in August and even more melodiously, if you suppose this even in the necessary incident of there certainly being no middle in summer and winter, suppose this and an elegant settlement a very elegant settlement is more than of consequence, it is not final and sufficient and substituted. This which was so kindly a present was constant.

A LONG DRESS

What is the current that makes machinery, that makes it crackle, what is the current that presents a long line and a necessary waist. What is this current.

What is the wind, what is it.

Where is the serene length, it is there and a dark place is not a dark place, only a white and red are black, only a yellow and green are blue, a pink is scarlet, a bow is every color. A line distinguishes it. A line just distinguishes it.

A RED HAT

A dark grey, a very dark grey, a quite dark grey is monstrous ordinarily, it is so monstrous because there is no red in it. If red is in everything it is not necessary. Is that not an argument for any use of it and even so is there any place that is better, is there any place that has so much stretched out.

A BLUE COAT

A blue coat is guided guided away, guided and guided away, that is the particular color that is used for that length and not any width not even more than a shadow.

A PIANO

If the speed is open, if the color is careless, if the selection of a strong scent is not awkward, if the button holder is held by all the waving color and there is no color, not any color. If there is no dirt in a pin and there can be none scarcely, if there is not then the place is the same as up standing.

This is no dark custom and it even is not acted in any such a way that a restraint is not spread. That is spread, it shuts and it lifts and awkwardly not awkwardly the centre is in standing.

A CHAIR

A widow in a wise veil and more garments shows that shadows are even. It addresses no more, it shadows the stage and learning. A regular arrangement, the severest and the most preserved is that which has the arrangement not more than always authorised.

A suitable establishment, well housed, practical, patient and staring, a suitable bedding, very suitable and not more particularly than complaining, anything suitable is so necessary.

A fact is that when the direction is just like that, no more, longer, sudden and at the same time not any sofa, the main action is that without a blaming there is no custody.

Practice measurement, practice the sign that means that really means a necessary betrayal, in showing that there is wearing.

Hope, what is a spectacle, a spectacle is the resemblance between the circular side place and nothing else, nothing else.

To choose it is ended, it is actual and more and more than that it has it certainly has the same treat, and a seat all that is practiced and more easily much more easily ordinarily.

Pick a barn, a whole barn, and bend more slender accents than have ever been necessary, shine in the darkness necessarily.

Actually not aching, actually not aching, a stubborn bloom is so artificial and even more than that, it is a spectacle, it is a binding accident, it is animosity and accentuation.

If the chance to dirty diminishing is necessary, if it is why is there no complexion, why is there no rubbing, why is there no special protection.

A FRIGHTFUL RELEASE

A bag which was left and not only taken but turned away was not found. The place was shown to be very like the last time. A piece was not exchanged, not a bit of it, a piece was left over. The rest was mismanaged.

A PURSE

A purse was not green, it was not straw color, it was hardly seen and it had a use a long use and the chain, the chain was never missing, it was not misplaced, it showed that it was open, that is all that it showed.

A MOUNTED UMBRELLA

What was the use of not leaving it there where it would hang what was the use if there was no chance of ever seeing it come there and show that it was handsome and right in the way it showed it. The lesson is to learn that it does show it, that it shows it and that nothing, that there is nothing, that there is no more to do about it and just so much more is there plenty of reason for making an exchange.

A CLOTH

Enough cloth is plenty and more, more is almost enough for that and besides if there is no more spreading is there plenty of room for it. Any occasion shows the best way.

MORE

An elegant use of foliage and grace and a little piece of white cloth and oil.

Wondering so winningly in several kinds of oceans is the reason that makes red so regular and enthusiastic. The reason that there is more snips are the same shining very colored rid of no round color.

A NEW CUP AND SAUCER

Enthusiastically hurting a clouded yellow bud and saucer, enthusiastically so is the bite in the ribbon.

OBJECTS

Within, within the cut and slender joint alone, with sudden equals and no more than three, two in the centre make two one side.

If the elbow is long and it is filled so then the best example is all together.

The kind of show is made by squeezing.

EYE GLASSES

A color in shaving, a saloon is well placed in the centre of an alley.

A CUTLET

A blind agitation is manly and uttermost.

CARELESS WATER

No cup is broken in more places and mended, that is to say a plate is broken and mending does do that it shows that culture is Japanese. It shows the whole element of angels and orders. It does more to choosing and it does more to that ministering counting. It does, it does change in more water.

Supposing a single piece is a hair supposing more of them are orderly, does that show that strength, does that show that joint, does that show that balloon famously. Does it.

A PAPER

A courteous occasion makes a paper show no such occasion and this makes readiness and eyesight and likeness and a stool.

A DRAWING

The meaning of this is entirely and best to say the mark, best to say it best to shown sudden places, best to make bitter, best to make the length tall and nothing broader, anything between the half.

WATER RAINING

Water astonishing and difficult altogether makes a meadow and a stroke.

COLD CLIMATE

A season in yellow sold extra strings makes lying places.

MALACHITE

The sudden spoon is the same in no size. The sudden spoon is the wound in the decision.

AN UMBRELLA

Coloring high means that the strange reason is in front not more in front behind. Not more in front in peace of the dot.

A PETTICOAT

A light white, a disgrace, an ink spot, a rosy charm.

A WAIST

A star glide, a single frantic sullenness, a single financial grass greediness.

Object that is in wood. Hold the pine, hold the dark, hold in the rush, make the bottom.

A piece of crystal. A change, in a change that is remarkable there is no reason to say that there was a time.

A woolen object gilded. A country climb is the best disgrace, a couple of practices any of them in order is so left.

A TIME TO EAT

A pleasant simple habitual and tyrannical and authorised and educated and resumed and articulate separation. This is not tardy.

A LITTLE BIT OF A TUMBLER

A shining indication of yellow consists in there having been more of the same color than could have been expected when all four were bought. This was the hope which made the six and seven have no use for any more places and this necessarily spread into nothing. Spread into nothing.

A FIRE

What was the use of a whole time to send and not send if there was to be the kind of thing that made that come in. A letter was nicely sent.

A HANDKERCHIEF

A winning of all the blessings, a sample not a sample because there is no worry.

RED ROSES

A cool red rose and a pink cut pink, a collapse and a sold hole, a little less hot.

IN BETWEEN

In between a place and candy is a narrow foot-path that shows more mounting than anything, so much really that a calling meaning a bolster measured a whole thing with that. A virgin a whole virgin is judged made and so between curves

and outlines and real seasons and more out glasses and a
perfectly unprecedented arrangement between old ladies and
mild colds there is no satin wood shining.

COLORED HATS

Colored hats are necessary to show that curls are worn by
an addition of blank spaces, this makes the difference between
single lines and broad stomachs, the least thing is lightening,
the least thing means a little flower and a big delay a big
delay that makes more nurses than little women really little
women. So clean is a light that nearly all of it shows pearls
and little ways. A large hat is tall and me and all custard
whole.

A FEATHER

A feather is trimmed, it is trimmed by the light and the
bug and the post, it is trimmed by little leaning and by all
sorts of mounted reserves and loud volumes. It is surely
cohesive.

A BROWN

A brown which is not liquid not more so is relaxed and yet
there is a change, a news is pressing.

A LITTLE CALLED PAULINE

A little called anything shows shudders.

Come and say what prints all day. A whole few water-
melon. There is no pope.

No cut in pennies and little dressing and choose wide soles
and little spats really little spices.

A little lace makes boils. This is not true.

Gracious of gracious and a stamp a blue green white bow
a blue green lean, lean on the top.

If it is absurd then it is leadish and nearly set in where
there is a tight head.

A peaceful life to arise her, noon and moon and moon A letter a cold sleeve a blanket a shaving house and nearly the best and regular window.

Nearer in fairy sea, nearer and farther, show white has lime in sight, show a stitch of ten. Count, count more so .that thicker and thicker is leaning.

I hope she has her cow. Bidding a wedding, widening received treading, little leading mention nothing.

Cough out cough out in the leather and really feather it is not for.

Please could, please could, jam it not plus more sit in when.

A SOUND

Elephant beaten with candy and little pops and chews all bolts and reckless reckless rats, this is this.

A TABLE

A table means does it not my dear it means a whole steadiness. Is it likely that a change.

A table means more than a glass even a looking glass is tall. A table means necessary places and a revision a revision of a little thing it means it does mean that there has been a stand, a stand where it did shake.

SHOES

To be a wall with a damper a stream of pounding way and nearly enough choice makes a steady midnight. It is pus.

A shallow hole rose on red, a shallow hole in and in this makes ale less. It shows shine.

A DOG

A little monkey goes like a donkey that means to say that means to say that more sighs last goes. Leave with it. A little monkey goes like a donkey.

A WHITE HUNTER

A white hunter is nearly crazy.

A LEAVE

In the middle of a tiny spot and nearly bare there is a nice thing to say that wrist is leading. Wrist is leading.

SUPPOSE AN EYES

Suppose it is within a gate which open is open at the hour of closing summer that is to say it is so.

All the seats are needing blackening. A white dress is in sign. A soldier a real soldier has a worn lace a worn lace of different sizes that is to say if he can read, if he can read he is a size to show shutting up twenty-four.

Go red go red, laugh white.

Suppose a collapse in rubbed purr, in rubbed purr get.

Little sales ladies little sales ladies little saddles of mutton.

Little sales of leather and such beautiful beautiful, beautiful beautiful.

A SHAWL

A shawl is a hat and hurt and a red balloon and an under coat and a sizer a sizer of talks.

A shawl is a wedding, a piece of wax a little build. A shawl.

Pick a ticket, pick it in strange steps and with hollows. There is hollow hollow belt, a belt is a shawl.

A plate that has a little bobble, all of them, any so. Please a round it is ticket.

It was a mistake to state that a laugh and a lip and a laid climb and a depot and a cultivator and little choosing is a point it.

BOOK

Book was there, it was there. Book was there. Stop it, stop it, it was a cleaner, a wet cleaner and it was not where it was wet, it was not high, it was directly placed back, not back again, back it was returned, it was needless, it put a bank, a bank when, a bank care.

Suppose a man a realistic expression of resolute reliability suggests pleasing itself white all white and no head does that mean soap. It does not so. It means kind wavers and little chance to beside beside rest. A plain.

Suppose ear rings that is one way to breed, breed that. Oh chance to say, oh nice old pole. Next best and nearest a pillar. Chest not valuable, be papered.

Cover up cover up the two with a little piece of string and hope rose and green, green.

Please a plate, put a match to the seam and really then really then, really then it is a remark that joins many many lead games. It is a sister and sister and a flower and a flower and a dog and a colored sky a sky colored grey and nearly that nearly that let.

PEELED PENCIL, CHOKE

Rub her coke.

IT WAS BLACK, BLACK TOOK

Black ink best wheel bale brown.

Excellent not a hull house, not a pea soup, no bill no care, no precise no past pearl pearl goat.

THIS IS THIS DRESS, AIDER

Aider, why aider why whow, whow stop touch, aider whow, aider stop the muncher, muncher munchers.

A jack in kill her, a jack in, makes a meadowed king, makes a to let.

FOOD

ROASTBEEF; MUTTON; BREAKFAST; SUGAR; CRANBERRIES; MILK; EGGS; APPLE; TAILS; LUNCH; CUPS; RHUBARB; SINGLE; FISH; CAKE; CUSTARD; POTATOES; ASPARAGUS; BUTTER; END OF SUMMER; SAUSAGES; CELERY; VEAL; VEGETABLE; COOKING; CHICKEN; PASTRY; CREAM; CUCUMBER; DINNER; DINING; EATING; SALAD; SAUCE; SALMON; ORANGE; COCOA; AND CLEAR SOUP AND ORANGES AND OAT-MEAL; SALAD DRESSING AND AN ARTICHOKE; A CENTRE IN A TABLE.

ROASTBEEF

In the inside there is sleeping, in the outside there is reddening, in the morning there is meaning, in the evening there is feeling. In the evening there is feeling. In feeling anything is resting, in feeling anything is mounting, in feeling there is resignation, in feeling there is recognition, in feeling there is recurrence and entirely mistaken there is pinching. All the standards have steamers and all the curtains have bed linen and all the yellow has discrimination and all the circle has circling. This makes sand.

Very well. Certainly the length is thinner and the rest, the round rest has a longer summer. To shine, why not shine, to shine, to station, to enlarge, to hurry the measure all this means nothing if there is singing, if there is singing then there is the resumption.

The change the dirt, not to change dirt means that there is no beefsteak and not to have that is no obstruction, it is so easy to exchange meaning, it is so easy to see the difference. The difference is that a plain resource is not entangled with thickness and it does not mean that thickness shows such cutting, it does mean that a meadow is useful and a cow absurd. It does not mean that there are tears, it does not mean that exudation is cumbersome, it means no more than a memory, a choice and a reëstablishment, it means more than any escape from a surrounding extra. All the time that there is use there is use and any time there is a surface there is a surface, and every time there is an exception there is an exception and every time there is a division there is a dividing. Any time there is a surface there is a surface and every time there is a suggestion there is a suggestion and every time there is silence there is silence and every time that is languid there is that there then and not oftener, not always, not particular, tender and changing and external and central and surrounded and singular and simple and the same and the surface and the circle and the shine and the succor and the white and the same and the better and the red and the same and the centre and the yellow and the tender and the better, and altogether.

Considering the circumstances there is no occasion for a reduction, considering that there is no pealing there is no occasion for an obligation, considering that there is no outrage there is no necessity for any reparation, considering that there is no particle sodden there is no occasion for deliberation. Considering everything and which way the turn is tending, considering everything why is there no restraint, considering everything what makes the place settle and the plate distinguish some specialties. The whole thing is not understood and this is not strange considering that there is no ed..cation, this is not strange because having that certainty does show the difference in cutting, it shows that when there is turning there is no distress.

In kind, in a control, in a period, in the alteration of pigeons, in kind cuts and thick and thin spaces, in kind ham and different colors, the length of leaning a strong thing outside not to make a sound but to suggest a crust, the principal taste is when there is a whole chance to be reasonable, this does not mean that there is overtaking, this means nothing precious, this means clearly that the chance to exercise is a social success. So then the sound is not obtrusive. Suppose it is obtrusive suppose it is. What is certainly the desertion is not a reduced description, a description is not a birthday.

Lovely snipe and tender turn, excellent vapor and slender butter, all the splinter and the trunk, all the poisonous darkening drunk, all the joy in weak success, all the joyful tenderness, all the section and the tea, all the stouter symmetry.

Around the size that is small, inside the stern that is the middle, besides the remains that are praying, inside the between that is turning, all the region is measuring and melting is exaggerating.

Rectangular ribbon does not mean that there is no eruption it means that if there is no place to hold there is no place to spread. Kindness is not earnest, it is not assiduous it is not revered.

Room to comb chickens and feathers and ripe purple, room to curve single plates and large sets and second silver, room to send everything away, room to save heat and distemper, room to search a light that is simpler, all room has no shadow.

There is no use there is no use at all in smell, in taste, in teeth, in toast, in anything, there is no use at all and the respect is mutual.

Why should that which is uneven, that which is resumed, that which is tolerable why should all this resemble a smell, a thing is there, it whistles, it is not narrower, why is there no obligation to stay away and yet courage, courage is everywhere and the best remains to stay.

If there could be that which is contained in that which is felt there would be a chair where there are chairs and there would be no more denial about a clatter. A clatter is not a smell. All this is good.

The Saturday evening which is Sunday is every week day. What choice is there when there is a difference. A regulation is not active. Thirstiness is not equal division.

Anyway, to be older and ageder is not a surfeit nor a suction, it is not dated and careful, it is not dirty. Any little thing is clean, rubbing is black. Why should ancient lambs be goats and young colts and never beef, why should they, they should because there is so much difference in age.

A sound, a whole sound is not separation, a whole sound is in an order.

Suppose there is a pigeon, suppose there is.

Looseness, why is there a shadow in a kitchen, there is a shadow in a kitchen because every little thing is bigger.

The time when there are four choices and there are four choices in a difference, the time when there are four choices there is a kind and there is a kind. There is a kind. There is a kind. Supposing there is a bone, there is a bone. Supposing there are bones. There are bones. When there are bones there is no supposing there are bones. There are bones and there is that consuming. The kindly way to feel separating is to have a space between. This shows a likeness.

Hope in gates, hope in spoons, hope in doors, hope in tables, no hope in daintiness and determination. Hope in dates.

Tin is not a can and a stove is hardly. Tin is not necessary and neither is a stretcher. Tin is never narrow and thick.

Color is in coal. Coal is outlasting roasting and a spoonful, a whole spoon that is full is not spilling. Coal any coal is copper.

Claiming nothing, not claiming anything, not a claim in everything, collecting claiming, all this makes a harmony, it even makes a succession.

Sincerely gracious one morning, sincerely graciously trembling, sincere in gracious eloping, all this makes a furnace and a blanket. All this shows quantity.

Like an eye, not so much more, not any searching, no compliments.

Please be the beef, please beef, pleasure is not wailing. Please beef, please be carved clear, please be a case of consideration.

Search a neglect. A sale, any greatness is a stall and there is no memory, there is no clear collection.

A satin sight, what is a trick, no trick is mountainous and the color, all the rush is in the blood.

Bargaining for a little, bargain for a touch, a liberty, an estrangement, a characteristic turkey.

Please spice, please no name, place a whole weight, sink into a standard rising, raise a circle, choose a right around, make the resonance accounted and gather green any collar.

To bury a slender chicken, to raise an old feather, to surround a garland and to bake a pole splinter, to suggest a repose and to settle simply, to surrender one another, to succeed saving simpler, to satisfy a singularity and not to be blinder, to sugar nothing darker and to read redder, to have the color better, to sort out dinner, to remain together, to surprise no sinner, to curve nothing sweeter, to continue thinner, to increase in resting recreation to design string not dimmer.

Cloudiness what is cloudiness, is it a lining, is it a roll, is it melting.

The sooner there is jerking, the sooner freshness is tender, the sooner the round it is not round the sooner it is withdrawn in cutting, the sooner the measure means service, the sooner there is chinking, the sooner there is sadder than salad, the sooner there is none do her, the sooner there is no choice, the sooner there is a gloom freer, the same sooner and more sooner, this is no error in hurry and in pressure and in opposition to consideration.

A recital, what is a recital, it is an organ and use does not strengthen valor, it soothes medicine.

A transfer, a large transfer, a little transfer, some transfer, clouds and tracks do transfer, a transfer is not neglected.

Pride, when is there perfect pretence, there is no more than yesterday and ordinary.

A sentence of a vagueness that is violence is authority and a mission and stumbling and also certainly also a prison. Calmness, calm is beside the plate and in way in. There is no turn in terror. There is no volume in sound.

There is coagulation in cold and there is none in prudence. Something is preserved and the evening is long and the colder spring has sudden shadows in a sun. All the stain is tender and lilacs really lilacs are disturbed. Why is the perfect reëstablishment practiced and prized, why is it composed. The result the pure result is juice and size and baking and exhibition and nonchalance and sacrifice and volume and a section in division and the surrounding recognition and horticulture and no murmur. This is a result. There is no superposition and circumstance, there is hardness and a reason and the rest and remainder. There is no delight and no mathematics.

MUTTON

A letter which can wither, a learning which can suffer and an outrage which is simultaneous is principal.

Student, students are merciful and recognised they chew something.

Hates rests that is solid and sparse and all in a shape and largely very largely. Interleaved and successive and a sample of smell all this makes a certainty a shade.

Light curls very light curls have no more curliness than soup. This is not a subject.

Change a single stream of denting and change it hurriedly, what does it express, it expresses nausea. Like a very strange likeness and pink, like that and not more like that than the same resemblance and not more like that than no middle space in cutting.

An eye glass, what is an eye glass, it is water. A splendid specimen, what is it when it is little and tender so that there are parts. A centre can place and four are no more and two and two are not middle.

Melting and not minding, safety and powder, a particular recollection and a sincere solitude all this makes a shunning so thorough and so unrepeated and surely if there is anything left it is a bone. It is not solitary.

Any space is not quiet it is so likely to be shiny. Darkness very dark darkness is sectional. There is a way to see in onion and surely very surely rhubarb and a tomato, surely very surely there is that seeding. A little thing in is a little thing.

Mud and water were not present and not any more of either. Silk and stockings were not present and not any more of either. A receptacle and a symbol and no monster were present and no more. This made a piece show and was it a kindness, it can be asked was it a kindness to have it warmer, was it a kindness and does gliding mean more. Does it.

Does it dirty a ceiling. It does not. Is it dainty, it is if prices are sweet. Is it lamentable, it is not if there is no undertaker. Is it curious, it is not when there is youth. All this makes a line, it even makes makes no more. All this makes cherries. The reason that there is a suggestion in vanity is due to this that there is a burst of mixed music.

A temptation any temptation is an exclamation if there are misdeeds and little bones. It is not astonishing that bones mingle as they vary not at all and in any case why is a bone outstanding, it is so because the circumstance that does not make a cake and character is so easily churned and cherished.

Mouse and mountain and a quiver, a quaint statue and pain in an exterior and silence more silence louder shows salmon a mischief intender. A cake, a real salve made of mutton and liquor, a specially retained rinsing and an established cork and blazing, this which resignation influences and restrains, restrains more altogether. A sign is the specimen spoken.

A meal in mutton, mutton, why is lamb cheaper, it is cheaper because so little is more. Lecture, lecture and repeat instruction.

BREAKFAST

A change, a final change includes potatoes. This is no authority for the abuse of cheese. What language can instruct any fellow.

A shining breakfast, a breakfast shining, no dispute, no practice, nothing, nothing at all.

A sudden slice changes the whole plate, it does so suddenly.

An imitation, more imitation, imitation succeed imitations.

Anything that is decent, anything that is present, a calm and a cook and more singularly still a shelter, all these show the need of clamor. What is the custom, the custom is in the centre.

What is a loving tongue and pepper and more fish than there is when tears many tears are necessary. The tongue and the salmon, there is not salmon when brown is a color, there is salmon when there is no meaning to an early morning being pleasanter. There is no salmon, there are no tea-cups, there are the same kind of mushes as are used as stomachers by the eating hopes that makes eggs delicious. Drink is likely to stir a certain respect for an egg cup and more water melon than was ever eaten yesterday. Beer is neglected and cocoanut is famous. Coffee all coffee and a sample of soup all soup these are the choice of a baker. A white cup means a wedding. A wet cup means a vacation. A strong cup means an especial regulation. A single cup means a capital arrangement between the drawer and the place that is open.

Price a price is not in language, it is not in custom, it is not in praise.

A colored loss, why is there no leisure. If the persecution is so outrageous that nothing is solemn is there any occasion for persuasion.

A grey turn to a top and bottom, a silent pocketful of much heating, all the pliable succession of surrendering makes an ingenious joy.

A breeze in a jar and even then silence, a special anticipation in a rack, a gurgle a whole gurgle and more cheese than almost anything, is this an astonishment, does this incline more than the original division between a tray and a talking arrangement and even then a calling into another room gently with some chicken in any way.

A bent way that is a way to declare that the best is all together, a bent way shows no result, it shows a slight restraint, it shows a necessity for retraction.

Suspect a single buttered flower, suspect it certainly, suspect it and then glide, does that not alter a counting.

A hurt mended stick, a hurt mended cup, a hurt mended article of exceptional relaxation and annoyance, a hurt mended, hurt and mended is so necessary that no mistake is intended.

What is more likely than a roast, nothing really and yet it is never disappointed singularly.

A steady cake, any steady cake is perfect and not plain, any steady cake has a mounting reason and more than that

It has singular crusts. A season of more is a season that is instead. A season of many is not more a season than most.

Take no remedy lightly, take no urging intently, take no separation leniently, beware of no lake and no larder.

Burden the cracked wet soaking sack heavily, burden it so that it is an institution in fright and in climate and in the best plan that there can be.

An ordinary color, a color is that strange mixture which makes, which does make which does not make a ripe juice, which does not make a mat.

A work which is a winding a real winding of the cloaking of a relaxing rescue. This which is so cool is not dusting, it is not dirtying in smelling, it could use white water, it could use more extraordinarily and in no solitude altogether. This which is so not winsome and not widened and really not so dipped as dainty and really dainty, very dainty, ordinarily, dainty, a dainty, not in that dainty and dainty. If the time is determined, if it is determined and there is reunion there is reunion with that then outline, then there is in that a piercing shutter, all of a piercing shouter, all of a quite weather, all of a withered exterior, all of that in most violent likely.

An excuse is not dreariness, a single plate is not butter, a single weight is not excitement, a solitary crumbling is not only martial.

A mixed protection, very mixed with the same actual intentional unstrangeness and riding, a single action caused necessarily is not more a sign than a minister.

Seat a knife near a cage and very near a decision and more nearly a timely working cat and scissors. Do this temporarily and make no more mistake in standing. Spread it all and arrange the white place, does this show in the house, does it not show in the green that is not necessary for that color, does it not even show in the explanation and singularly not at all stationary.

SUGAR

A violent luck and a whole sample and even then quiet. Water is squeezing, water is almost squeezing on lard.

Water, water is a mountain and it is selected and it is so practical that there is no use in money. A mind under is exact and so it is necessary to have a mouth and eye glasses.

A question of sudden rises and more time than awfulness is so easy and shady. There is precisely that noise.

A peck a small piece not privately overseen, not at all not a slice, not at all crestfallen and open, not at all mounting and chaining and evenly surpassing, all the bidding comes to tea.

A separation is not tightly in worsted and sauce, it is so kept well and sectionally.

Put it in the stew, put it to shame. A little slight shadow and a solid fine furnace.

The teasing is tender and trying and thoughtful.

The line which sets sprinkling to be a remedy is beside the best cold.

A puzzle, a monster puzzle, a heavy choking, a neglected Tuesday.

Wet crossing and a likeness, any likeness, a likeness has blisters, it has that and teeth, it has the staggering blindly and a little green, any little green is ordinary.

One, two and one, two, nine, second and five and that.

A blaze, a search in between, a cow, only any wet place, only this tune.

Cut a gas jet uglier and then pierce pierce in between the next and negligence. Choose the rate to pay and pet pet very much. A collection of all around, a signal poison, a lack of languor and more hurts at ease.

A white bird, a colored mine, a mixed orange, a dog.

Cuddling comes in continuing a change.

A piece of separate outstanding rushing is so blind with open delicacy.

A canoe is orderly. A period is solemn. A cow is accepted.

A nice old chain is widening, it is absent, it is laid by.

CRANBERRIES

Could there not be a sudden date, could there not be in the present settlement of old age pensions, could there not be by a witness, could there be.

Count the chain, cut the grass, silence the noon and murder flies. See the basting undip the chart, see the way the kinds are best seen from the rest, from that and untidy.

Cut the whole space into twenty-four spaces and then and then is there a yellow color, there is but it is smelled, it is then put where it is and nothing stolen.

A remarkable degree of red means that, a remarkable exchange is made.

Climbing altogether in when there is a solid chance of soiling no more than a dirty thing, coloring all of it in steadying is jelly.

Just as it is suffering, just as it is succeeded, just as it is moist so is there no countering.

MILK

A white egg and a colored pan and a cabbage showing settlement, a constant increase.

A cold in a nose, a single cold nose makes an excuse. Two are more necessary.

All the goods are stolen, all the blisters are in the cup.

Cooking, cooking is the recognition between sudden and nearly sudden very little and all large holes.

A real pint, one that is open and closed and in the middle is so bad.

Tender colds, seen eye holders, all work, the best of change, the meaning, the dark red, all this and bitten, really bitten.

Guessing again and golfing again and the best men, the very best men.

MILK

Climb up in sight climb in the whole utter needles and a guess a whole guess is hanging. Hanging hanging.

EGGS

Kind height, kind in the right stomach with a little sudden mill.

Cunning shawl, cunning shawl to be steady.

In white in white handkerchiefs with little dots in a white belt all shadows are singular they are singular and procured and relieved.

No that is not the cows shame and a precocious sound, it is a bite.

Cut up alone the paved way which is harm. Harm is old boat and a likely dash.

APPLE

Apple plum, carpet steak, seed clam, colored wine, calm seen, cold cream, best shake, potato, potato and no no gold work with pet, a green seen is called bake and change sweet is bready, a little piece a little piece please.

A little piece please. Cane again to the presupposed and ready eucalyptus tree, count out sherry and ripe plates and little corners of a kind of ham. This is use.

TAILS

Cold pails, cold with joy no joy.

A tiny seat that means meadows and a lapse of cuddles with cheese and nearly bats, all this went messed. The post placed a loud loose sprain. A rest is no better. It is better yet. All the time.

LUNCH

Luck in loose plaster makes holy gauge and nearly that, nearly more states, more states come in town light kite, blight not white.

A little lunch is a break in skate a little lunch so slimy, a west end of a board line is that which shows a little beneath so that necessity is a silk under wear. That is best wet. It is so natural, and why is there flake, there is flake to explain exhaust.

A real cold hen is nervous is nervous with a towel with a spool with real beads. It is mostly an extra sole nearly all that shaved, shaved with an old mountain, more than that bees more than that dinner and a bunch of likes that is to say the hearts of onions aim less.

Cold coffee with a corn a corn yellow and green mass is a gem.

CUPS

A single example of excellence is in the meat. A bent stick is surging and might all might is mental. A grand clothes is searching out a candle not that wheatly not that by more than an owl and a path. A ham is proud of cocoanut.

A cup is neglected by being all in size. It is a handle and meadows and sugar any sugar.

A cup is neglected by being full of size. It shows no shade, in come little wood cuts and blessing and nearly not that not with a wild bought in, not at all so polite, not nearly so behind.

Cups crane in. They need a pet oyster, they need it so hoary and nearly choice. The best slam is utter. Nearly be freeze.

Why is a cup a stir and a behave. Why is it so seen.

A cup is readily shaded, it has in between no sense that is to say music, memory, musical memory.

Peanuts blame, a half sand is holey and nearly.

RHUBARB

Rhubarb is susan not susan not seat in bunch toys not wild and laughable not in little places not in neglect and vegetable not in fold coal age not please.

SINGLE FISH

Single fish single fish single fish egg-plant single fish sight.

A sweet win and not less noisy than saddle and more ploughing and nearly well painted by little things so.

Please shade it a play. It is necessary and beside the large sort is puff.

Every way oakly, please prune it near. It is so found.

It is not the same.

CAKE

Cake cast in went to be and needles wine needles are such.

This is to-day. A can experiment is that which makes a town, makes a town dirty, it is little please. We came back. Two bore, bore what, a mussed ash, ash when there is tin. This meant cake. It was a sign.

Another time there was extra a hat pin sought long and this dark made a display. The result was yellow. A caution, not a caution to be.

It is no use to cause a foolish number. A blanket stretch a cloud, a shame, all that bakery can tease, all that is beginning and yesterday yesterday we had it met. It means some change. No some day.

A little leaf upon a scene an ocean any where there, a bland and likely in the stream a recollection green land. Why white.

CUSTARD

Custard is this. It has aches, aches when. Not to be. Not to be narrowly. This makes a whole little hill.

It is better than a little thing that has mellow real mellow. It is better than lakes whole lakes, it is better than seeding.

POTATOES

Real potatoes cut in between.

POTATOES

In the preparation of cheese, in the preparation of crackers, in the preparation of butter, in it.

ROAST POTATOES

Roast potatoes for.

ASPARAGUS

Asparagus in a lean in a lean to hot. This makes it art and it is wet wet weather wet weather wet.

BUTTER

Boom in boom in, butter. Leave a grain and show it, show it. I spy.

It is a need it is a need that a flower a state flower. It is a need that a state rubber. It is a need that a state rubber is sweet and sight and a swelled stretch. It is a need. It is a need that state rubber.

Wood a supply. Clean little keep a strange, estrange on it.

Make a little white, no and not with pit, pit on in within.

END OF SUMMER

Little eyelets that have hammer and a check with stripes between a lounge, in wit, in a rested development.

SAUSAGES

Sausages in between a glass.

There is read butter. A loaf of it is managed. Wake a question. Eat an instant, answer.

A reason for bed is this, that a decline, any decline is poison, poison is a toe a toe extractor, this means a solemn change. Hanging.

No evil is wide, any extra in leaf is so strange and singular a red breast.

CELERY

Celery tastes tastes where in curled lashes and little bits and mostly in remains.

A green acre is so selfish and so pure and so enlivened.

VEAL

Very well very well, washing is old, washing is washing.

Cold soup, cold soup clear and particular and a principal a principal question to put into.

VEGETABLE

What is cut. What is cut by it. What is cut by it in.

It was a cress a crescent a cross and an unequal scream, it was upslanting, it was radiant and reasonable with little ins and red.

News. News capable of glees, cut in shoes, belike under plump of wide chalk, all this combing.

WAY LAY VEGETABLE

Leaves in grass and mow potatoes, have a skip, hurry you up flutter.

Suppose it is ex a cake suppose it is new mercy and leave charlotte and nervous bed rows. Suppose it is meal. Suppose it is sam.

COOKING

Alas, alas the pull alas the bell alas the coach in china, alas the little put in leaf alas the wedding butter meat, alas the receptacle, alas the back shape of mussle, mussle and soda.

CHICKEN

Pheasant and chicken, chicken is a peculiar bird.

CHICKEN

Alas a dirty word, alas a dirty third alas a dirty third, alas a dirty bird.

CHICKEN

Alas a doubt in case of more go to say what it is cress. What is it. Mean. Potato. Loaves.

CHICKEN

Stick stick call then, stick stick sticking, sticking with a chicken. Sticking in a extra succession, sticking in.

CHAIN-BOATS

Chain-boats are merry, are merry blew, blew west, carpet.

PASTRY

Cutting shade, cool spades and little last beds, make violet, violet when.

CREAM

In a plank, in a play sole, in a heated red left tree there is shut in specs with salt be where. This makes an eddy. Necessary.

CREAM

Cream cut. Any where crumb. Left hop chambers.

CUCUMBER

Not a razor less, not a razor, ridiculous pudding, red and relet put in, rest in a slender go in selecting, rest in, rest in in white widening.

DINNER

Not a little fit, not a little fit sun sat in shed more mentally. Let us why, let us why weight, let us why winter chess, let us why why.

Only a moon to soup her, only that in the sell never never be the cocups nice be, shatter it they lay.

Egg ear nuts, look a bout. Shoulder. Let is strange, sold in bell next herds.

It was a time when in the acres in late there was a wheel that shot a burst of land and needless are niggers and a sample sample set of old eaten butterflies with spoons, all of it to be are fled and measure make it, make it, yet all the one in that we see where shall not it set with a left and more so, yes there add when the longer not it shall the best in the way when all be with when shall not for there with see and chest how for another excellent and excellent and easy easy excellent and easy express e c, all to be nice all to be no so. All to be no so no so. All to be not a white old chat churner. Not to be any example of an edible apple in.

DINING

Dining is west.

EATING

Eat ting, eating a grand old man said roof and never never re soluble burst, not a near ring not a bewildered neck, not really any such bay.

Is it so a noise to be is it a least remain to rest, is it a so old say to be, is it a leading are been. Is it so, is it so, is it so, is it so is it so is it so.

Eel us eel us with no no pea no pea cool, no pea cool cooler, no pea cooler with a land a land cost in, with a land cost in stretches.

Eating he heat eating he heat it eating, he heat it heat eating. He heat eating.

A little piece of pay of pay owls owls such as pie, bolsters.

Will leap beat, willie well all. The rest rest oxen occasion occasion to be so purred, so purred how.

It was a ham it was a square come well it was a square remain, a square remain not it a bundle, not it a bundle so is a grip, a grip to shed bay leave bay leave draught, bay leave draw cider in low, cider in low and george. George is a mass.

EATING

It was a shame it was a shame to stare to stare and double and relieve relieve be cut up show as by the elevation of it and out out more in the steady where the come and on and the all the shed and that.

It was a garden and belows belows straight. It was a pea, a pea pour it in its not a succession, not it a simple, not it a so election, election with.

SALAD

It is a winning cake.

SAUCE

What is bay labored what is all be section, what is no much. Sauce sam in.

SALMON

It was a peculiar bin a bin fond in beside.

ORANGE

Why is a feel oyster an egg stir. Why is it orange centre.
A show at tick and loosen loosen it so to speak sat.
It was an extra leaker with a see spoon, it was an extra licker with a see spoon.

ORANGE

A type oh oh new new not no not knealer knealer of old show beef-steak, neither neither.

ORANGES

Build is all right.

ORANGE IN

Go lack go lack use to her.
Cocoa and clear soup and oranges and oat-meal.
Whist bottom whist close, whist clothes, woodling.
Cocoa and clear soup and oranges and oat-meal.
Pain soup, suppose it is question, suppose it is butter, real
is, real is only, only excreate, only excreate a no since.
A no, a no since, a no since when, a no since when since,
a no since when since a no since when since, a no since, a no
since when since, a no since, a no, a no since a no since, a no
since, a no since.

SALAD DRESSING AND AN ARTICHOKE

Please pale hot, please cover rose, please acre in the red
stranger, please butter all the beef-steak with regular feel
faces.

SALAD DRESSING AND AN ARTICHOKE

It was please it was please carriage cup in an ice-cream, in
an ice-cream it was too bended bended with scissors and all
this time. A whole is inside a part, a part does go away, a hole
is red leaf. No choice was where there was and a second and
a second.

A CENTRE IN A TABLE

It was a way a day, this made some sum. Suppose a cod
liver a cod liver is an oil, suppose a cod liver oil is tunny, suppose a cod liver oil tunny is pressed suppose a cod liver oil

tunny pressed is china and secret with a bestow a bestow reed, a reed to be a reed to be, in a reed to be.

Next to me next to a folder, next to a folder some waiter, next to a foldersome waiter and re letter and read her. Read her with her for less.

ROOMS

Act so that there is no use in a centre. A wide action is not a width. A preparation is given to the ones preparing. They do not eat who mention silver and sweet. There was an occupation.

A whole centre and a border make hanging a way of dressing. This which is not why there is a voice is the remains of an offering. There was no rental.

So the tune which is there has a little piece to play, and the exercise is all there is of a fast. Then tender and true that makes no width to hew is the time that there is question to adopt.

To begin the placing there is no wagon. There is no change lighter. It was done. And then the spreading, that was not accomplishing that needed standing and yet the time was not so difficult as they were not all in place. They had no change. They were not respected. They were that, they did it so much in the matter and this showed that that settlement was not condensed. It was spread there. Any change was in the ends of the centre. A heap was heavy. There was no change.

Burnt and behind and lifting a temporary stone and lifting more than a drawer.

The instance of there being more is an instance of more. The shadow is not shining in the way there is a black line. The truth has come. There is a disturbance. Trusting to a baker's boy meant that there would be very much exchanging and anyway what is the use of a covering to a door. There is a use, they are double.

If the centre has the place then there is distribution. That is natural. There is a contradiction and naturally returning there comes to be both sides and the centre. That can be seen from the description.

The author of all that is in there behind the door and that is entering in the morning. Explaining darkening and expecting relating is all of a piece. The stove is bigger. It was of a shape that made no audience bigger if the opening is assumed why should there not be kneeling. Any force which is bestowed on a floor shows rubbing. This is so nice and sweet and yet there comes the change, there comes the time to press more air. This does not mean the same as disappearance.

A little lingering lion and a Chinese chair, all the handsome cheese which is stone, all of it and a choice, a choice of a blotter. If it is difficult to do it one way there is no place of similar trouble. None. The whole arrangement is established. The end of which is that there is a suggestion, a suggestion that there can be a different whiteness to a wall. This was thought.

A page to a corner means that the shame is no greater when the table is longer. A glass is of any height, it is higher, it is simpler and if it were placed there would not be any doubt.

Something that is an erection is that which stands and feeds and silences a tin which is swelling. This makes no diversion that is to say what can please exaltation, that which is cooking.

A shine is that which when covered changes permission. An enclosure blends with the same that is to say there is blending. A blend is that which holds no mice and this is not because of a floor it is because of nothing, it is not in a vision.

A fact is that when the place was replaced all was left that was stored and all was retained that would not satisfy more than another. The question is this, is it possible to suggest more to replace that thing. This question and this perfect denial does make the time change all the time.

The sister was not a mister. Was this a surprise. It was. The conclusion came when there was no arrangement. All the time that there was a question there was a decision. Replacing a casual acquaintance with an ordinary daughter does not make a son.

It happened in a way that the time was perfect and there was a growth of a whole dividing time so that where formerly there was no mistake there was no mistake now. For instance before when there was a separation there was waiting, now when there is separation there is the division between intending and departing. This made no more mixture than there would be if there had been no change.

A little sign of an entrance is the one that made it alike. If it were smaller it was not alike and it was so much smaller that a table was bigger. A table was much bigger, very much bigger. Changing that made nothing bigger, it did not make anything bigger littler, it did not hinder wood from not being used as leather. And this was so charming. Harmony is so essential. Is there pleasure when there is a passage, there is when every room is open. Every room is open when there are not four, there were there and surely there were four, there were two together. There is no resemblance.

A single speed, the reception of table linen, all the wonder of six little spoons, there is no exercise.

The time came when there was a birthday. Every day was no excitement and a birthday was added, it was added on Monday, this made the memory clear, this which was a speech showed the chair in the middle where there was copper.

Alike and a snail, this means Chinamen, it does there is no doubt that to be right is more than perfect there is no doubt and glass is confusing it confuses the substance which was of a color. Then came the time for discrimination, it came then and it was never mentioned it was so triumphant, it showed the whole head that had a hole and should have a hole it showed the resemblance between silver.

Startling a starving husband is not disagreeable. The reason that nothing is hidden is that there is no suggestion of silence. No song is sad. A lesson is of consequence.

Blind and weak and organised and worried and betrothed and resumed and also asked to a fast and always asked to consider and never startled and not at all bloated, this which is no rarer than frequently is not so astonishing when hair brushing is added. There is quiet, there certainly is.

No eye-glasses are rotten, no window is useless and yet if air will not come in there is a speech ready, there always is and there is no dimness, not a bit of it.

All along the tendency to deplore the absence of more has not been authorised. It comes to mean that with burning there is that pleasant state of stupefication. Then there is a way of earning a living. Who is a man.

A silence is not indicated by any motion, less is indicated by a motion, more is not indicated it is enthralled. So sullen and so low, so much resignation, so much refusal and so much place for a lower and an upper, so much and yet more silence, why is not sleeping a feat why is it not and when is there some discharge when. There never is.

If comparing a piece that is a size that is recognised as not a size but a piece, comparing a piece with what is not recognised but what is used as it is held by holding, comparing these two comes to be repeated. Suppose they are put together, suppose that there is an interruption, supposing that beginning again they are not changed as to position, suppose all this and suppose that any five two of whom are not separating suppose that the five are not consumed. Is there an exchange, is there a resemblance to the sky which is admitted to be there and the stars which can be seen. Is there. That was a question. There was no certainty. Fitting a failing meant that any two were indifferent and yet they were all connecting that, they were all connecting that consideration. This did not determine rejoining a letter. This did not make letters smaller. It did.

The stamp that is not only torn but also fitting is not any symbol. It suggests nothing. A sack that has no opening suggests more and the loss is not commensurate. The season gliding and the torn hangings receiving mending all this shows an example, it shows the force of sacrifice and likeness and disaster and a reason.

The time when there is not the question is only seen when there is a shower. Any little thing is water.

There was a whole collection made. A damp cloth, an

oyster, a single mirror, a mannikin, a student, a silent star, a single spark, a little movement and the bed is made. This shows the disorder, it does, it shows more likeness than anything else, it shows the single mind that directs an apple. All the coats have a different shape, that does not mean that they differ in color, it means a union between use and exercise and a horse.

A plain hill, one is not that which is not white and red and green, a plain hill makes no sunshine, it shows that without a disturber. So the shape is there and the color and the outline and the miserable centre, it is not very likely that there is a centre, a hill is a hill and no hill is contained in a pink tender descender.

A can containing a curtain is a solid sentimental usage. The trouble in both eyes does not come from the same symmetrical carpet, it comes from there being no more disturbance than in little paper. This does show the teeth, it shows color.

A measure is that which put up so that it shows the length has a steel construction. Tidiness is not delicacy, it does not destroy the whole piece, certainly not it has been measured and nothing has been cut off and even if that has been lost there is a name, no name is signed and left over, not any space is fitted so that moving about is plentiful. Why is there so much resignation in a package, why is there rain, all the same the chance has come, there is no bell to ring.

A package and a filter and even a funnel, all this together makes a scene and supposing the question arises is hair curly, is it dark and dusty, supposing that question arises, is brushing necessary, is it, the whole special suddenness commences then, there is no delusion.

A cape is a cover, a cape is not a cover in summer, a cape is a cover and the regulation is that there is no such weather. A cape is not always a cover, a cape is not a cover when there is another, there is always something in that thing in establishing a disposition to put wetting where it will not do more harm. There is always that disposition and in a way there is some use in not mentioning changing and in establishing the temperature, there is some use in it as establishing all that lives dimmer freer and there is no dinner in the middle of anything. There is no such thing.

Why is a pale white not paler than blue, why is a connection made by a stove, why is the example which is mentioned not shown to be the same, why is there no adjustment between the place and the separate attention. Why is there a choice in gamboling. Why is there no necessary dull stable, why is there a single piece of any color, why is there that sensible silence. Why is there the resistance in a mixture, why is there no poster, why is there that in the window, why is there no suggester, why is there no window, why is there no oyster closer. Why is there a circular diminisher, why is there a bather, why is there no scraper, why is there a dinner, why is there a bell ringer, why is there a duster, why is there a section of a similar resemblance, why is there that scissor.

South, south which is a wind is not rain, does silence choke speech or does it not.

Lying in a conundrum, lying so makes the springs restless, lying so is a reduction, not lying so is arrangeable.

Releasing the oldest auction that is the pleasing some still renewing.

Giving it away, not giving it away, is there any difference. Giving it away. Not giving it away.

Almost very likely there is no seduction, almost very likely there is no stream, certainly very likely the height is penetrated, certainly certainly the target is cleaned. Come to sit, come to refuse, come to surround, come slowly and age is not lessening. The time which showed that was when there was no eclipse. All the time that resenting was removal all that time there was breadth. No breath is shadowed, no breath is painstaking and yet certainly what could be the use of paper, paper shows no disorder, it shows no desertion.

Why is there a difference between one window and another, why is there a difference, because the curtain is shorter. There is no distaste in beefsteak or in plums or in gallons of milk water, there is no defiance in original piling up over a roof, there is no daylight in the evening, there is none there empty.

A tribune, a tribune does not mean paper, it means nothing more than cake, it means more sugar, it shows the state of lengthening any nose. The last spice is that which shows the whole evening spent in that sleep, it shows so that walking is an alleviation, and yet this astonishes everybody the distance is so sprightly. In all the time there are three days, those are not passed uselessly. Any little thing is a change that is if nothing is wasted in that cellar. All the rest of the chairs are established.

A success, a success is alright when there are there rooms and no vacancies, a success is alright when there is a package, success is alright anyway and any curtain is wholesale. A curtain diminishes and an ample space shows varnish.

One taste one tack, one taste one bottle, one taste one fish, one taste one barometer. This shows no distinguishing sign when there is a store.

Any smile is stern and any coat is a sample. Is there any use in changing more doors than there are committees. This question is so often asked that squares show that they are blotters. It is so very agreeable to hear a voice and to see all the signs of that expression.

Cadences, real cadences, real cadences and a quiet color. Careful and curved, cake and sober, all accounts and mixture, a guess at anything is righteous, should there be a call there would be a voice.

A line in life, a single line and a stairway, a rigid cook, no cook and no equator, all the same there is higher than that another evasion. Did that mean shame, it meant memory. Looking into a place that was hanging and was visible looking into this place and seeing a chair did that mean relief, it did, it certainly did not cause constipation and yet there is a melody that has white for a tune when there is straw color. This shows no face.

Star-light, what is star-light, star-light is a little light that is not always mentioned with the sun, it is mentioned with the moon and the sun, it is mixed up with the rest of the time.

Why is the name changed. The name is changed because in the little space there is a tree, in some space there are no trees, in every space there is a hint of more, all this causes the decision.

Why is there education, there is education because the two tables which are folding are not tied together with a ribbon, string is used and string being used there is a necessity for another one and another one not being used to hearing shows no ordinary use of any evening and yet there is no disgrace in looking, none at all. This came to separate when there was simple selection of an entire pre-occupation.

A curtain, a curtain which is fastened discloses mourning, this does not mean sparrows or elocution or even a whole preparation, it means that there are ears and very often much more altogether.

Climate, climate is not southern, a little glass, a bright winter, a strange supper an elastic tumbler, all this shows that the back is furnished and red which is red is a dark color. An example of this is fifteen years and a separation of regret.

China is not down when there are plates, lights are not ponderous and incalculable.

Currents, currents are not in the air and on the floor and in the door and behind it first. Currents do not show it plainer. This which is mastered has so thin a space to build it all that there is plenty of room and yet is it quarreling, it is not and the insistence is marked. A change is in a current and there is no habitable exercise.

A religion, almost a religion, any religion, a quintal in religion, a relying and a surface and a service in indecision and a creature and a question and a syllable in answer and more counting and no quarrel and a single scientific statement and no darkness and no question and an earned administration and a single set of sisters and an outline and no blisters and the section seeing yellow and the centre having spelling and no solitude and no quaintness and yet solid quite so solid and the single surface centred and the question in the placard and the singularity, is there a singularity, and the singularity, why is there a question and the singularity why is the surface outrageous, why is it beautiful why is it not when there is no doubt, why is anything vacant, why is not disturbing a centre no virtue, why is it when it is and why is it when it is and there is no doubt, there is no doubt that the singularity shows.

A climate, a single climate, all the time there is a single climate, any time there is a doubt, any time there is music that is to question more and more and there is no politeness, there is hardly any ordeal and certainly there is no table-cloth.

This is a sound and obligingness more obligingness leads to a harmony in hesitation.

A lake a single lake which is a pond and a little water any water which is an ant and no burning, not any burning, all this is sudden.

A canister that is the remains of furniture and a looking-glass and a bed-room and a larger size, all the stand is shouted and what is ancient is practical. Should the resemblance be so that any little cover is copied, should it be so that yards are measured, should it be so and there be a sin, should it be so then certainly a room is big enough when it is so empty and the corners are gathered together.

The change is mercenary that settles whitening the coloring and serving dishes where there is metal and making yellow any yellow every color in a shade which is expressed in a tray. This is a monster and awkward quite awkward and the little design which is flowered which is not strange and yet has visible writing, this is not shown all the time but at once, after that it rests where it is and where it is in place. No change is not needed. That does show design.

Excellent, more excellence is borrowing and slanting very slanting is light and secret and a recitation and emigration. Certainly shoals are shallow and nonsense more nonsense is sullen. Very little cake is water, very little cake has that escape.

Sugar any sugar, anger every anger, lover sermon lover, centre no distractor, all order is in a measure.

Left over to be a lamp light, left over in victory, left over in saving, all this and negligence and bent wood and more even much more is not so exact as a pen and a turtle and even, certainly, and even a piece of the same experience as more.

To consider a lecture, to consider it well is so anxious and so much a charity and really supposing there is grain and if a stubble every stubble is urgent, will there not be a chance of legality. The sound is sickened and the price is purchased and golden wheat is golden, a clergyman, a single tax, a currency and an inner chamber.

Checking an emigration, checking it by smiling and certainly by the same satisfactory stretch of hands that have more use for it than nothing, and mildly not mildly a correction, not mildly even a circumstance and a sweetness and a serenity. Powder, that has no color, if it did have would it be white.

A whole soldier any whole soldier has no more detail than any case of measles.

A bridge a very small bridge in a location and thunder, any thunder, this is the capture of reversible sizing and more indeed more can be cautious. This which makes monotony careless makes it likely that there is an exchange in principle and more than that, change in organization.

This cloud does change with the movements of the moon and the narrow the quite narrow suggestion of the building. It does and then when it is settled and no sounds differ then comes the moment when cheerfulness is so assured that there is an occasion.

A plain lap, any plain lap shows that sign, it shows that there is not so much extension as there would be if there were more choice in everything. And why complain of more, why complain of very much more. Why complain at all when it is all arranged that as there is no more opportunity and no more appeal and not even any more clinching that certainly now some time has come.

A window has another spelling, it has "f" all together, it lacks no more then and this is rain, this may even be something else, at any rate there is no dedication in splendor. There is a turn of the stranger.

Catholic to be turned is to venture on youth and a section of debate, it even means that no class where each one over fifty is regular is so stationary that there are invitations.

A curving example makes righteous finger-nails. This is the only object in secretion and speech.

To being the same four are no more than were taller. The rest had a big chair and surveyance a cold accumulation of nausea, and even more than that, they had a disappointment.

Nothing aiming is a flower, if flowers are abundant then they are lilac, if they are not they are white in the centre.

Dance a clean dream and an extravagant turn up, secure the steady rights and translate more than translate the authority, show the choice and make no more mistakes than yesterday.

This means clearness it means a regular notion of exercise, it means more than that, it means liking counting, it means more than that, it does not mean exchanging a line.

Why is there more craving than there is in a mountain. This does not seem strange to one, it does not seem strange to an echo and more surely is in there not being a habit. Why is there so much useless suffering. Why is there.

Any wet weather means an open window, what is attaching eating, anything that is violent and cooking and shows weather is the same in the end and why is there more use in something than in all that.

The cases are made and books, back books are used to secure tears and church. They are even used to exchange black slippers. They can not be mended with wax. They show no need of any such occasion.

A willow and no window, a wide place stranger, a wideness makes an active center.

The sight of no pussy cat is so different that a tobacco zone is white and cream.

A lilac, all a lilac and no mention of butter, not even bread and butter, no butter and no occasion, not even a silent resemblance, not more care than just enough haughty.

A safe weight is that which when it pleases is hanging. A safer weight is one more naughty in a spectacle. The best game is that which is shiny and scratching. Please a pease and a cracker and a wretched use of summer.

Surprise, the only surprise has no occasion. It is an ingredient and the section the whole section is one season.

A pecking which is petting and no worse than in the same morning is not the only way to be continuous often.

A light in the moon the only light is on Sunday. What was the sensible decision. The sensible decision was that notwithstanding many declarations and more music, not even notwithstanding the choice and a torch and a collection, notwithstanding the celebrating hat and a vacation and even more noise than cutting, notwithstanding Europe and Asia and being overbearing, not even notwithstanding an elephant and a strict occasion, not even withstanding more cultivation and some seasoning, not even with drowning and with the ocean being encircling, not even with more likeness and any cloud, not even with terrific sacrifice of pedestrianism and a special resolution, not even more likely to be pleasing. The care with which the rain is wrong and the green is wrong and the white is wrong, the care with which there is a chair and plenty of breathing. The care with which there is incredible justice and likeness, all this makes a magnificent asparagus, and also a fountain.

COMPOSITION
AS EXPLANATION

First delivered by the author as a lecture at Cambridge and Oxford, this essay was first published by the Hogarth Press in London in 1926 and revived in the volume called WHAT ARE MASTERPIECES. *This is one of many attempts Miss Stein has made to explain her "difficult" manner of writing. Others are sections of* THE MAKING OF AMERICANS, *some of which are included in this Collection,* HOW TO WRITE, LECTURES IN AMERICA, NARRATION, THE GEOGRAPHICAL HISTORY OF AMERICA OR THE RELATION OF HUMAN NATURE TO THE HUMAN MIND, WHAT ARE MASTERPIECES, AN ACQUAINTANCE WITH DESCRIPTION, *and the most "difficult" of her explanations,* AN ELUCIDATION, *in* PORTRAITS AND PRAYERS. *It readily can be seen that Miss Stein devoted almost as much time to exegesis as to creation.*

There is singularly nothing that makes a difference a difference in beginning and in the middle and in ending except that each generation has something different at which they are all looking. By this I mean so simply that anybody knows it that composition is the difference which makes each and all of them then different from other generations and this is what makes everything different otherwise they are all alike and everybody knows it because everybody says it.

It is very likely that nearly every one has been very nearly certain that something that is interesting is interesting them. Can they and do they. It is very interesting that nothing inside in them, that is when you consider the very long history of how every one ever acted or has felt, it is very interesting that nothing inside in them in all of them makes it connectedly different. By this I mean this. The only thing that is different from one time to another is what is seen and what is seen depends upon how everybody is doing everything. This makes the thing we are looking at very different and this makes what those who describe it make of it, it makes a composition, it confuses, it shows, it is, it looks, it likes it as it is, and this makes what is seen as it is seen. Nothing changes from generation to generation except the thing seen and that makes a composition. Lord Grey remarked that when the generals before the war talked about the war they talked about it as a nineteenth century war although to be fought with twentieth century weapons. That is because war is a thing that decides how it is to be when it is to be done. It is prepared and to that degree it is like all academies it is not a thing made by being made it is a thing prepared. Writing and painting and all that, is like that, for those who occupy themselves with it and don't make it as it is made. Now the few who make it as it is made, and it is to be remarked that the most decided of them usually are prepared just as the world around them is preparing, do it in this way and so I if you do not mind I will tell you how it happens. Naturally one does not know how it happened until it is well over beginning happening.

To come back to the part that the only thing that is different is what is seen when it seems to be being seen, in other words, composition and time-sense.

No one is ahead of his time, it is only that the particular variety of creating his time is the one that his contemporaries who also are creating their own time refuse to accept. And they refuse to accept it for a very simple reason and that is that they do not have to accept it for any reason. They themselves that is everybody in their entering the modern composition and they do enter it, if they do not enter it they are not so to speak in it they are out of it and so they do enter it; but in as you may say the non-competitive efforts where if you are not in it nothing is lost except nothing at all except what is not had, there are naturally all the refusals, and the things refused are only important if unexpectedly somebody happens to need them. In the case of the arts it is very definite. Those who are creating the modern composition authentically are naturally only of importance when they are dead because by that time the modern composition having become past is classified and the description of it is classical. That is the reason why the creator of the new composition in the arts is an outlaw until he is a classic, there is hardly a moment in between and it is really too bad very much too bad naturally for the creator but also very much too bad for the enjoyer, they all really would enjoy the created so much better just after it has been made than when it is already a classic, but it is perfectly simple that there is no reason why the contemporaries should see, because it would not make any difference as they lead their lives in the new composition anyway, and as every one is naturally indolent why naturally they don't see. For this reason as in quoting Lord Grey it is quite certain that nations not actively threatened are at least several generations behind themselves militarily so æsthetically they are more than several generations behind themselves and it is very much too bad, it is so very much more exciting and satisfactory for everybody if one can have contemporaries, if all one's contemporaries could be one's contemporaries.

There is almost not an interval.

For a very long time everybody refuses and then almost without a pause almost everybody accepts. In the history of the refused in the arts and literature the rapidity of the change is always startling. Now the only difficulty with the *volte-face* concerning the arts is this. When the acceptance comes, by that acceptance the thing created becomes a classic. It is a natural phenomena a rather extraordinary natural phenomena that a thing accepted becomes a classic. And what is the characteristic quality of a classic. The characteristic quality of a classic is that it is beautiful. Now of course it is perfectly true that a more or less first rate work of art is beautiful but the trouble is that when that first rate work of art becomes a classic because it is accepted the only thing that is important from then on to the majority of the acceptors the enormous majority, the most intelligent majority of the acceptors is that it is so wonderfully beautiful. Of course it is wonderfully beautiful, only when it is still a thing irritating annoying stimulating then all quality of beauty is denied to it.

Of course it is beautiful but first all beauty in it is denied and then all the beauty of it is accepted. If every one were not so indolent they would realise that beauty is beauty even when it is irritating and stimulating not only when it is accepted and classic. Of course it is extremely difficult nothing more so than to remember back to its not being beautiful once it has become beautiful. This makes it so much more difficult to realise its beauty when the work is being refused and prevents every one from realising that they were convinced that beauty was denied, once the work is accepted. Automatically with the acceptance of the time-sense comes the recognition of the beauty and once the beauty is accepted the beauty never fails any one.

Beginning again and again is a natural thing even when there is a series.

Beginning again and again and again explaining composition and time is a natural thing.

It is understood by this time that everything is the same except composition and time, composition and the time of the composition and the time in the composition.

Everything is the same except composition and as the composition is different and always going to be different everything is not the same. Everything is not the same as the time when of the composition and the time in the composition is different. The composition is different, that is certain.

The composition is the thing seen by every one living in the living they are doing, they are the composing of the composition that at the time they are living is the composition of the time in which they are living. It is that that makes living a thing they are doing. Nothing else is different, of that almost any one can be certain. The time when and the time of and the time in that composition is the natural phenomena of that composition and of that perhaps every one can be certain.

No one thinks these things when they are making when they are creating what is the composition, naturally no one thinks, that is no one formulates until what is to be formulated has been made.

Composition is not there, it is going to be there and we are here. This is some time ago for us naturally.

The only thing that is different from one time to another is what is seen and what is seen depends upon how everybody is doing everything. This makes the thing we are looking at very different and this makes what those who describe it make of it, it makes a composition, it confuses, it shows, it is, it looks, it likes it as it is, and this makes what is seen as it is seen. Nothing changes from generation to generation except the thing seen and that makes a composition.

Now the few who make writing as it is made and it is to

be remarked that the most decided of them are those that are prepared by preparing, are prepared just as the world around them is prepared and is preparing to do it in this way and so if you do not mind I will again tell you how it happens. Naturally one does not know how it happened until it is well over beginning happening.

Each period of living differs from any other period of living not in the way life is but in the way life is conducted and that authentically speaking is composition. After life has been conducted in a certain way everybody knows it but nobody knows it, little by little, nobody knows it as long as nobody knows it. Any one creating the composition in the arts does not know it either, they are conducting life and that makes their composition what it is, it makes their work compose as it does.

Their influence and their influences are the same as that of all of their contemporaries only it must always be remembered that the analogy is not obvious until as I say the composition of a time has become so pronounced that it is past and the artistic composition of it is a classic.

And now to begin as if to begin. Composition is not there, it is going to be there and we are here. This is some time ago for us naturally. There is something to be added afterwards.

Just how much my work is known to you I do not know. I feel that perhaps it would be just as well to tell the whole of it.

In beginning writing I wrote a book called *Three Lives* this was written in 1905. I wrote a negro story called *Melanctha*. In that there was a constant recurring and beginning there was a marked direction in the direction of being in the present although naturally I had been accustomed to past present and future, and why, because the composition forming around me was a prolonged present. A composition of a prolonged present is a natural composition in the world as it has been these thirty years it was more and more a prolonged present. I created then a prolonged present naturally I knew nothing of a continuous present but it came naturally to me to make one, it was simple it was clear to me and nobody knew why it was done like that, I did not myself although naturally to me it was natural.

After that I did a book called *The Making of Americans* it is a long book about a thousand pages.

Here again it was all so natural to me and more and more complicatedly a continuous present. A continuous present is a continuous present. I made almost a thousand pages of a continuous present.

Continuous present is one thing and beginning again and again is another thing. These are both things. And then there is using everything.

This brings us again to composition this the using everything. The using everything brings us to composition and to this composition. A continuous present and using everything and beginning again. In these two books there was elaboration of the complexities of using everything and of a continuous present and of beginning again and again and again.

In the first book there was a groping for a continuous present and for using everything by beginning again and again.

There was a groping for using everything and there was a groping for a continuous present and there was an inevitable beginning of beginning again and again and again.

Having naturally done this I naturally was a little troubled with it when I read it. I became then like the others who read it. One does, you know, excepting that when I reread it myself I lost myself in it again. Then I said to myself this time it will be different and I began. I did not begin again I just began.

In this beginning naturally since I at once went on and on very soon there were pages and pages and pages more and more elaborated creating a more and more continuous present including more and more using of everything and continuing more and more beginning and beginning and beginning.

I went on and on to a thousand pages of it.

In the meantime to naturally begin I commenced making portraits of anybody and anything. In making these portraits I naturally made a continuous present an including everything and a beginning again and again within a very small thing. That started me into composing anything into one thing. So then naturally it was natural that one thing an enormously long thing was not everything an enormously short thing was also not everything nor was it all of it a continuous present thing nor was it always and always beginning again. Naturally I would then begin again. I would begin again I would naturally begin. I did naturally begin. This brings me to a great deal that has been begun.

And after that what changes what changes after that, after that what changes and what changes after that and after that and what changes and after that and what changes after that.

The problem from this time on became more definite.

It was all so nearly alike it must be different and it is different, it is natural that if everything is used and there is a continuous present and a beginning again and again if it is all so alike it must be simply different and everything simply different was the natural way of creating it then.

In this natural way of creating it then that it was simply different everything being alike it was simply different, this kept on leading one to lists. Lists naturally for a while and by lists I mean a series. More and more in going back over what was done at this time I find that I naturally kept simply different as an intention. Whether there was or whether there was not a continuous present did not then any longer trouble me there was or there was not, and using everything no longer troubled me if everything is alike using everything could no longer trouble me and beginning again and again could no longer trouble me because if lists were inevitable if series were inevitable and the whole of it was inevitable beginning again and again could not trouble me so then with nothing to trouble me I very completely began naturally since everything is alike making it as simply different naturally as simply different as possible. I began doing natural phenomena what I call natural phenomena and natural phenomena naturally everything being alike natural phenomena are making things be naturally simply different. This found its culmination later, in the beginning it began in a center confused with lists with series with geography with returning portraits and with particularly often four and three and often with five and four. It is easy to see that in the beginning such a conception as everything being naturally different would be very inarticulate and very slowly it began to emerge and take the form of anything, and then naturally if anything that is simply different is simply different what follows will follow.

So far then the progress of my conceptions was the natural progress entirely in accordance with my epoch as I am sure is to be quite easily realised if you think over the scene that was before us all from year to year.

As I said in the beginning, there is the long history of how every one ever acted or has felt and that nothing inside in them in all of them makes it connectedly different. By this I mean all this.

The only thing that is different from one time to another is what is seen and what is seen depends upon how everybody is doing everything.

It is understood by this time that everything is the same except composition and time, composition and the time of the composition and the time in the composition.

Everything is the same except composition and as the composition is different and always going to be different everything is not the same. So then I as a contemporary creating the composition in the beginning was groping toward a continuous present, a using everything a beginning again and again and then everything being alike then everything very simply everything was naturally simply different and so I as a contemporary was creating everything being alike was creating everything naturally being naturally simply different, everything being alike. This then was the period that brings me to the period of the beginning of 1914. Everything being alike everything naturally would be simply different and war came and everything being alike and everything being simply different brings everything being simply different brings it to romanticism.

Romanticism is then when everything being alike everything is naturally simply different, and romanticism.

Then for four years this was more and more different even

though this was, was everything alike. Everything alike naturally everything was simply different and this is and was romanticism and this is and was war. Everything being alike everything naturally everything is different simply different naturally simply different.

And so there was the natural phenomena that was war, which had been, before war came, several generations behind the contemporary composition, because it became war and so completely needed to be contemporary became completely contemporary and so created the completed recognition of the contemporary composition. Every one but one may say every one became consciously became aware of the existence of the authenticity of the modern composition. This then the contemporary recognition, because of the academic thing known as war having been forced to become contemporary made every one not only contemporary in act not only contemporary in thought but contemporary in self-consciousness made every one contemporary with the modern composition. And so the art creation of the contemporary composition which would have been outlawed normally outlawed several generations more behind even than war, war having been brought so to speak up to date art so to speak was allowed not completely to be up to date, but nearly up to date, in other words we who created the expression of the modern composition were to be recognized before we were dead some of us even quite a long time before we were dead. And so war may be said to have advanced a general recognition of the expression of the contemporary composition by almost thirty years.

And now after that there is no more of that in other words there is peace and something comes then and it follows coming then.

And so now one finds oneself interesting oneself in an equilibration, that of course means words as well as things and distribution as well as between themselves between the words and themselves and the things and themselves, a distribution as distribution. This makes what follows what follows and now there is every reason why there should be an arrangement made. Distribution is interesting and equilibration is interesting when a continuous present and a beginning again and again and using everything and everything alike and everything naturally simply different has been done.

After all this, there is that, there has been that that there is a composition and that nothing changes except composition the composition and the time of and the time in the composition.

The time of the composition is a natural thing and the time in the composition is a natural thing it is a natural thing and it is a contemporary thing.

The time of the composition is the time of the composition. It has been at times a present thing it has been at times a past thing it has been at times a future thing it has been at times an endeavour at parts or all of these things. In my beginning it was a continuous present a beginning again and again and again and again, it was a series it was a list it was a similarity and everything different it was a distribution and an equilibration. That is all of the time some of the time of the composition.

Now there is still something else the time-sense in the composition. This is what is always a fear a doubt and a judgement and a conviction. The quality in the creation of expression the quality in a composition that makes it go dead just after it has been made is very troublesome.

The time in the composition is a thing that is very troublesome. If the time in the composition is very troublesome it is because there must even if there is no time at all in the composition there must be time in the composition which is in its quality of distribution and equilibration. In the beginning there was the time in the composition that naturally was in the composition but time in the composition comes now and this is what is now troubling every one the time in the composition is now a part of distribution and equilibration. In the beginning there was confusion there was a continuous present and later there was romanticism which was not a confusion but an extrication and now there is either succeeding or failing there must be distribution and equilibration there must be time that is distributed and equilibrated. This is the thing that is at present the most troubling and if there is the time that is at present the most trouble-some the time-sense that is at present the most troubling is the thing that makes the present the most troubling. There is at present there is distribution, by this I mean expression and time, and in this way at present composition is time that is the reason that at present the time-sense is troubling that is the reason why at present the time-sense in the composition is the composition that is making what there is in composition.

And afterwards.

Now that is all.

PORTRAIT OF
MABEL DODGE

AT THE VILLA CURONIA

In Chapter V of THE AUTOBIOGRAPHY OF ALICE B. TOKLAS, *printed in this Collection, Gertrude Stein relates how she met Mabel Dodge, how she visited her at the Villa Curonia in Florence where she wrote this portrait, and how Mabel had 300 copies printed and bound in assorted Florentine wallpapers. Returning to America in 1912, Mabel brought a package of these little pamphlets with her and gave them away to anybody she thought would be interested enough to say or write something about the author. It was in this manner that I became acquainted with the work of Gertrude Stein and a year later, again through Mabel, I met her. The* PORTRAIT *was reprinted in* PORTRAITS AND PRAYERS, 1943, *and again in Mabel Dodge Luhan's* EUROPEAN EXPERIENCES, 1935.

The days are wonderful and the nights are wonderful and the life is pleasant.

Bargaining is something and there is not that success. The intention is what if application has that accident results are reappearing. They did not darken. That was not an adulteration.

So much breathing has not the same place when there is that much beginning. So much breathing has not the same place when the ending is lessening. So much breathing has the same place and there must not be so much suggestion. There can be there the habit that there is if there is no need of resting. The absence is not alternative.

Any time is the half of all the noise and there is not that disappointment. There is no distraction. An argument is clear.

Packing is not the same when the place which has all that is not emptied. There came there the hall and this was not the establishment. It had not all the meaning.

Blankets are warmer in the summer and the winter is not lonely. This does not assure the forgetting of the intention when there has been and there is every way to send some. There does not happen to be a dislike for water. This is not heartening.

As the expedition is without the participation of the question there will be nicely all that energy. They can arrange that the little color is not bestowed. They can leave it in regaining that intention. It is mostly repaid. There can be an irrigation. They can have the whole paper and they send it in some package. It is not inundated.

A bottle that has all the time to stand open is not so clearly shown when there is green color there. This is not the only way to change it. A little raw potato and then all that softer does happen to show that there has been enough. It changes the expression.

It is not darker and the present time is the best time to agree. This which has been feeling is what has the appetite and the patience and the time to stay. This is not collaborating.

All the attention is when there is not enough to do. This does not determine a question. The only reason that there is not that pressure is that there is a suggestion. There are many going. A delight is not bent. There had been that little wagon. There is that precision when there has not been an imagination. There has not been that kind abandonment. Nobody is alone.

If the spread that is not a piece removed from the bed is likely to be whiter then certainly the sprinkling is not drying. There can be the message where the print is pasted and this does not mean that there is that esteem. There can be the likelihood of all the days not coming later and this will not deepen the collected dim version.

It is a gnarled division that which is not any obstruction and the forgotten swelling is certainly attracting, it is attracting the whiter division, it is not sinking to be growing, it is not darkening to be disappearing, it is not aged to be annoying. There can not be sighing. This is this bliss.

Not to be wrapped and then to forget undertaking, the credit and then the resting of that interval, the pressing of the sounding when there is no trinket is not altering, there can be pleasing classing clothing.

A sap that is that adaptation is the drinking that is not increasing. There can be that lack of quivering. That does not originate every invitation. There is not wedding introduction. There is not all that filling. There is the climate that is not existing there is that plainer. There is the likeliness lying in liking likely likeliness. There is that dispensation. There is the paling that is not reddening, there is the reddening that is not reddening, there is that protection, there is that destruction, there is not the present lessening there is the argument of increasing. There is that that is not that which is that resting. There is not that occupation. There is that particular half of directing that there is that particular whole direction that is not all the measure of any combination. Gliding is not heavily moving. Looking is not vanishing. Laughing is not evaporating. There can be the climax. There can be the same dress. There can be an old dress. There can be the way there is that way there is that which is not that charging what is a regular way of paying. There has been William. All the time is likely. There is the condition. There has been admitting. There is not the print. There is that smiling. There is the season. There is that where there is not that which is where there is what there is which is beguiling. There is a paste.

Abandon a garden and the house is bigger. This is not smiling. This is comfortable. There is the comforting of predilection. An open object is establishing the loss that there was when the vase was not inside the place. It was not wandering.

A plank that was dry was not disturbing the smell of burning and altogether there was the best kind of sitting there could never be all the edging that the largest chair was having. It was not pushed. It moved then. There was not that lifting. There was that which was not any contradiction and there was not the bland fight that did not have that regulation. The contents were not darkening. There was not that hesitation. It was occupied. That was not occupying any exception. Any one had come. There was that distribution.

There was not that velvet spread when there was a pleasant head. The color was paler. The moving regulating is not a distinction. The place is there.

Likely there is not that departure when the whole place that has that texture is so much in the way. It is not there to stay. It does not change that way. A pressure is not later. There is the same. There is not the shame. There is that pleasure.

In burying that game there is not a change of name. There

is not perplexing and co-ordination. The toy that is not round has to be found and looking is not straining such relation. There can be that company. It is not wider when the length is not longer and that does make that way of staying away. Every one is exchanging returning. There is not a prediction. The whole day is that way. Any one is resting to say that the time which is not reverberating is acting in partaking.

A walk that is not stepped where the floor is covered is not in the place where the room is entered. The whole one is the same. There is not any stone. There is the wide door that is narrow on the floor. There is all that place.

There is that desire and there is no pleasure and the place is filling the only space that is placed where all the piling is not adjoining. There is not that distraction.

Praying has intention and relieving that situation is not solemn. There comes that way.

The time that is the smell of the plain season is not showing the water is running. There is not all that breath. There is the use of the stone and there is the place of the stuff and there is the practice of expending questioning. There is not that differentiation. There is that which is in time. There is the room that is the largest place when there is all that is where there is space. There is not that perturbation. The legs that show are not the certain ones that have been used. All legs are used. There is no action meant.

The particular space is not beguiling. There is that participation. It is not passing any way. It has that to show. It is why there is no exhalation.

There is all there is when there has all there has where there is what there is. That is what is done when there is done what is done and the union is won and the division is the explicit visit. There is not all of any visit.

HAVE THEY ATTACKED MARY.
HE GIGGLED.

(*A POLITICAL CARICATURE*)

This poem originally appeared in VANITY FAIR, *June 1917.
Owing to "lack of space" thirty-five lines were omitted. When
the poem was printed as a pamphlet later in 1917, illustrated
with "a political caricature of Henry McBride by Jules Pascin,"
these lines were restored. A note in the pamphlet advises the
reader that this work has been referred to as a portrait of
Henry McBride, the noted art critic. "It is in fact," the note
continues, "a genre picture and Mr. McBride is but one of
the personages. The 'political' quality of Miss Stein's caricature will not be misapprehended by students of her work."*

Can you be more confusing by laughing. Do say yes.
We are extra. We have the reasonableness of a
woman and we say we do not like a room. We wish
we were married.
Why do you believe in me.
Including all that is sold, you mean three pictures, including
all that is sold why cannot you give me that.
I do give it to you.
Thank you, I was only joking.
But I do mean it.
Thank you very much.

PAGE II

Can you swim in a lake.
We can.
Then do so.

PAGE III

Have you an automobile.

PAGE IV

The queen has.
We asked for one.
They cannot send it now.
Cannot they.
We will see.

PAGE V

In memory of the Englishwoman.
We will buy it together.
Not that Englishwoman.
No not that time or that one.

PAGE VI

We wish to go there.
Can they accept us.
We marry.
They ask.

PAGE VII

In the middle of the exercise.
We exercise.
We are successful.

PAGE VIII

Can you speak.
The dog.
Can you bear to tear the skirt.

PAGE IX

Lighting.
We can see to the lighting.

PAGE X

Can a Jew be wild.

PAGE XI

A great many settlers have mercy. Of course they
do to me.
You are proud. I am proud of my courage.

PAGE XII

Can you find me in a home.
We can all find you in a hole. I hope not.
Then keep warm. I cannot have that announcement.
Very well then elect him. We can be suggestive.

PAGE XIII

Can you finish for me.

PAGE XIV

In the midst of refusing I have been asked to go on.
We hope so.

PAGE XV

Can you wish me to think.

PAGE XVI

In the next name you mean the wife in the next name there
is a mention of a ring. In the next name they have means.
What can you do to relate it.
Many ready papers many papers are taken there.
You mean they made the mistake.
They made the mistake of choosing that silver.
Little silver little silver.

PAGE XVII

I'm coming to grieve.

PAGE XVIII

I cannot find a real dressmaker.
Neither can I.

PAGE XIX

In the little while in which I say stop it you are not
spoiled.

PAGE XX

Can you think of lingering. You mean as to weight.
Why yes I feel that. Can you think of dwindling.
Can you.

PAGE XXI

In the midst of the fortnight what was the wish.
We did not say others. Nor did he.
Indeed he was not observed. You mean in the time.

In the day time and at night.
And in the evening.

PAGE XXII

Believe me in everything.

PAGE XXIII

I can go.
Don't remind the English.

PAGE XXIV

You mean of everything.

PAGE XXV

It is wonderful the way I am not interested.
What can you do.
I can answer any question.
Very well answer this.
Who is Mr. McBride.

PAGE XXVI

It is found out.
Not by me.

PAGE XXVII

Leave me to see.

PAGE XXVIII

I told you that you were told.

PAGE XXIX

It is outrageous to mention a hotel.

PAGE XXX

Can you please me with kisses.
In France we are found.
We are found in France.

PAGE XXXI

I cannot destroy blandishments.
That is not the word you meant to use. I meant to

say that being indeed convinced of the necessity of seeing
them swim I believe in their following. Do you believe in
their following.

PAGE XXXII

Can you think in meaning to sell well. We can all
think separately. Can you think in meaning to be checquered.
I can answer for the news. Of course you can answer for the
news.

PAGE XXXIII

In the midst of that rain.
In the midst of that rain there was a wing. And he
was not sorry. Who can be sorry there. We are.
Yes lamb.
Roger.

PAGE XXXIV

Not necessarily a deception.

PAGE XXXV

Can you speak to me.
I can speak to you.
I believe in the book about England.

PAGE XXXVI

In leaning grass in leaning grass.
Yes in leaning grass.
Can you widen rivers there.

PAGE XXXVII

Can you see Cook.
Can you hear it turn.
I used to say where.
Now it is in machinery in that machinery. They do
not deplore what the war.

PAGE XXXVIII

Can you candidly say that of him.

PAGE XXXIX

Why am I so sleepy.

PAGE XL

Can you excuse any one.

PAGE XLI

Fifty boxes of matches wax matches which burn very
well and strike very well and have no smell. Do you mean
less smell than others.

PAGE XLII

You say he is that sort of a person. He has been
here again. And asked about pitchers.

PAGE XLIII

Can he ask about pitchers.

PAGE XLIV

Officers do not kiss soldiers.
What do officers kiss.
Officers kiss the cross. Indeed they do. So do soldiers
in passing.
Pass again.
Chrysanthemum.
Was his friend a friend.

PAGE XLV

Can you see him.

PAGE XLVI

Particularly today.
Feel me.
A sentimental face.

Can they say no excuse. Can they say selfish
brothers. Do they say we are pleased to have been taught.
No they do not do so they have that very negligible quality,
the station of Lyons. We were there. And books. Yes books.

You did not understand a laundry woman. Yes women porters.
Of course women porters. Why should we be proud. Because
it is foolish. It is very foolish to be wrong. In that case may I
beg to refer to it. You may.

The French are polite.

AS A WIFE HAS A COW

A COW

A LOVE STORY

Published in Paris in 1926 with lithographic illustrations by Juan Gris, this is an excellent example of Gertrude Stein's adverbial and participial style. The reader will find a clue to the passage about the "fifteenth of October" in the opening pages of Chapter VII of THE AUTOBIOGRAPHY OF ALICE B. TOKLAS *in this Collection*

Nearly all of it to be as a wife has a cow, a love story. All of it to be as a wife has a cow, all of it to be as a wife has a cow, a love story.

As to be all of it as to be a wife as a wife has a cow, a love story, all of it as to be all of it as a wife all of it as to be as a wife has a cow a love story, all of it as a wife has a cow as a wife has a cow a love story.

Has made, as it has made as it has made, has made has to be as a wife has a cow, a love story. Has made as to be as a wife has a cow a love story. As a wife has a cow, as a wife has a cow, a love story. Has to be as a wife has a cow a love story. Has made as to be as a wife has a cow a love story.

When he can, and for that when he can, for that. When he can and for that when he can. For that. When he can. For that when he can. For that. And when he can and for that. Or that, and when he can. For that and when he can.

And to in six and another. And to and in and six and another. And to and in and six and another. And to in six and and to and in and six and another. And to and in and six and another. And to and six and in and another and and to and six and another and and to and in and six and and to and six and in and another.

In came in there, came in there come out of there. In came in come out of there. Come out there in came in there. Come out of there and in and come out of there. Came in there, come out of there.

Feeling or for it, as feeling or for it, came in or come in, or come out of there or feeling as feeling or feeling as for it.

As a wife has a cow.

Came in and come out.

As a wife has a cow a love story.

As a love story, as a wife has a cow, a love story.

Not and now, now and not, not and now, by and by not and now, as not, as soon as not not and now, now as soon now now as soon, now as soon as soon as now. Just as soon just now just now just as soon just as soon as now. Just as soon as now.

And in that, as and in that, in that and and in that, so that, so that and in that, and in that and so that and as for that and as for that and that. In that. In that and and for that as for that and in that. Just as soon and in that. In that as that and just as soon. Just as soon as that.

Even now, now and even now and now and even now. Not as even now, therefor, even now and therefor, therefor and even now and even now and therefor even now. So not to and moreover and even now and therefor and moreover and even now and so and even now and therefor even now.

Do they as they do so. And do they do so.

We feel we feel. We feel or if we feel if we feel or if we feel. We feel or if we feel. As it is made made a day made a day or two made a day, as it is made a day or two, as it is made a day. Made a day. Made a day. Not away a day. By day. As it is made a day.

On the fifteenth of October as they say, said anyway, what is it as they expect, as they expect it or as they expected it, as they expect it and as they expected it, expect it or for it, expected it and it is expected of it. As they say said anyway. What is it as they expect for it, what is it and it is as they expect of it. What is it. What is it the fifteenth of October as they say as they expect or as they expected as they expect for it. What is it as they say the fifteenth of October as they say and as expected of it, the fifteenth of October as they say, what is it as expected of it. What is it and the fifteenth of October as they say and expected of it.

And prepare and prepare so prepare to prepare and pre-

pare to prepare and prepare so as to prepare, so to prepare
and prepare to prepare to prepare for and to prepare for it
to prepare, to prepare for it, in preparation, as preparation in
preparation by preparation. They will be too busy afterwards
to prepare. As preparation prepare, to prepare, as to preparation and to prepare. Out there.

Have it as having having it as happening, happening to
have it as having, having to have it as happening. Happening
and have it as happening and having it happen as happening
and having to have it happen as happening, and my wife has
a cow as now, my wife having a cow as now, my wife having
a cow as now and having a cow as now and having a cow and
having a cow now, my wife has a cow and now. My wife has
a cow.

TWO POEMS

SUSIE ASADO

PRECIOSILLA

SUSIE ASADO *is the first item in* GEOGRAPHY AND PLAYS, 1922. PRECIOSILLA *was published in* COMPOSITION AS EXPLANATION, 1926. *Gertrude Stein writes, in* LECTURES IN AMERICA: "*The strict discipline that I had given myself, the absolute refusal of never using a word that was not an exact word all through the* TENDER BUTTONS *and what I may call the early Spanish and* GEOGRAPHY AND PLAY *(sic) period finally resulted in things like* SUSIE ASADO *and* PRECIOSILLA *etc. in an extraordinary melody of words and a melody of excitement in knowing that I had done this thing.*" *There is reason to believe that these two poems paint a portrait and make an attempt to recapture the rhythm of the same flamenco dancer.*

SUSIE ASADO

Sweet sweet sweet sweet sweet tea.
Susie Asado.
Sweet sweet sweet sweet sweet tea.
Susie Asado.
Susie Asado which is a told tray sure.

A lean on the shoe this means slips slips hers.

When the ancient light grey is clean it is yellow, it is a silver seller.

This is a please this is a please there are the saids to jelly. These are the wets these say the sets to leave a crown to Incy.

Incy is short for incubus.

A pot. A pot is a beginning of a rare bit of trees. Trees tremble, the old vats are in bobbles, bobbles which shade and shove and render clean, render clean must.

Drink pups.

Drink pups drink pups lease a sash hold, see it shine and a bobolink has pins. It shows a nail.

What is a nail. A nail is unison.

Sweet sweet sweet sweet sweet tea.

PRECIOSILLA

Cousin to Clare washing.

In the win all the band beagles which have cousin lime sign and arrange a weeding match to presume a certain point to exstate to exstate a certain pass lint to exstate a lean sap prime lo and shut shut is life.

Bait, bait, tore, tore her clothes, toward it, toward a bit, to ward a sit, sit down in, in vacant surely lots, a single mingle, bait and wet, wet a single establishment that has a lily lily grow. Come to the pen come in the stem, come in the grass grown water.

Lily wet lily wet while. This is so pink so pink in stammer, a long bean which shows bows is collected by a single curly shady, shady get, get set wet bet.

It is a snuff a snuff to be told and have can wither, can is it and sleep sleep knot, it is a lily scarf the pink and blue yellow, not blue not odour sun, nobles are bleeding bleeding two seats two seats on end. Why is grief. Grief is strange black. Sugar is melting. We will not swim.

Preciosilla

Please be please be get, please get wet, wet naturally, naturally in weather. Could it be fire more firier. Could it be so in ate struck. Could it be gold up, gold up stringing, in it while while which is hanging, hanging in dingling, dingling in pinning, not so. Not so dots large dressed dots, big sizes, less laced, less laced diamonds, diamonds white, diamonds bright, diamonds in the in the light, diamonds light diamonds door diamonds hanging to be four, two four, all before, this bean, lessly, all most, a best, willow, vest, a green guest, guest, go go go go go go, go. Go go. Not guessed. Go go.

Toasted susie is my ice-cream.

TWO PLAYS

LADIES' VOICES

WHAT HAPPENED

LADIES' VOICES *and* WHAT HAPPENED *were both printed
originally in* GEOGRAPHY AND PLAYS. *Miss Stein finds a definite
connection between geography, landscape, and playwriting
and refers to this connection again and again in her work.
For instance, in* THE AUTOBIOGRAPHY OF ALICE B. TOKLAS
she says: "A landscape is such a natural arrangement for a
battlefield or a play that one must write plays." *In* LECTURES
IN AMERICA, *Miss Stein explains* "And so all of a sudden I
began to write plays. I remember very well the first one I
wrote. I called it,* WHAT HAPPENED, A PLAY, *it is in* GEOG-
RAPHY AND PLAYS *as are all the plays I wrote at that time. I
think and always have thought that if you write a play you
ought to announce that it is a play and that is what I did.
What Happened. A Play. I had just come home from a pleasant dinner party (elsewhere she tells us this dinner was given
by Harry and Bridget Gibb) and I realized then as anybody
can know that something is always happening. Something is
always happening, anybody knows a quantity of stories of
people's lives that are always happening, there are always
plenty for the newspapers and there are always plenty in
private life. Everybody knows so many stories and what is
the use of telling another story. What is the use of telling a
story since there are so many and everybody knows so many
and tells so many. In the country it is perfectly extraordinary
how many complicated dramas go on all the time. And everybody knows them, so why tell another one. There is always a
story going on. So naturally what I wanted to do in my play
was what everybody did not always know or always tell. By
everybody I do of course include myself but always I do of
course include myself. And so I wrote,* WHAT HAPPENED, A
PLAY. *Then I wrote* LADIES' VOICES. *The idea in* WHAT
HAPPENED, A PLAY *was without telling what happened, to
make a play the essence of what happened.*"

LADIES' VOICES

CURTAIN RAISER

Ladies' voices give pleasure.

The acting two is easily lead. Leading is not in winter. Here the winter is sunny.

Does that surprise you.

Ladies voices together and then she came in.

Very well good night.

Very well good night.

(Mrs. Cardillac.)

That's silver.

You mean the sound.

Yes the sound.

ACT II

Honest to God Miss Williams I don't mean to say that I was older.

But you were.

Yes I was. I do not excuse myself. I feel that there is no reason for passing an archduke.

You like the word.

You know very well that they all call it their house.

As Christ was to Lazarus so was the founder of the hill to Mahon.

You really mean it.

I do.

ACT III

Yes Genevieve does not know it. What. That we are seeing Caesar.

Caesar kisses.

Kisses today.

Caesar kisses every day.

Genevieve does not know that it is only in this country that she could speak as she does.

She does speak very well doesn't she. She told them that there was not the slightest intention on the part of her countrymen to eat the fish that was not caught in their country.

In this she was mistaken.

ACT IV

What are ladies voices.

Do you mean to believe me.

Have you caught the sun.

Dear me have you caught the sun.

SCENE II

Did you say they were different. I said it made no difference.

Where does it. Yes.

Mr. Richard Sutherland. This is a name I know.

Yes.

The Hotel Victoria.

Many words spoken to me have seemed English.

Yes we do hear one another and yet what are called voices the best decision in telling of balls.

Masked balls.

Yes masked balls.

Poor Augustine.

WHAT HAPPENED

A FIVE ACT PLAY

ACT I

(One.)

Loud and no cataract. Not any nuisance is depressing.

(Five.)

A single sum four and five together and one, not any sun a clear signal and an exchange.

Silence is in blessing and chasing and coincidences being ripe. A simple melancholy clearly precious and on the surface and surrounded and mixed strangely. A vegetable window and clearly most clearly an exchange in parts and complete.

A tiger a rapt and surrounded overcoat securely arranged with spots old enough to be thought useful and witty quite witty in a secret and in a blinding flurry.

Length what is length when silence is so windowful. What is the use of a sore if there is no joint and no toady and no tag and not even an eraser. What is the commonest exchange between more laughing and most. Carelessness is carelessness and a cake well a cake is a powder, it is very likely to be powder, it is very likely to be much worse.

A shutter and only shutter and Christmas, quite Christmas, an only shutter and a target a whole color in every centre and shooting real shooting and what can hear, that can hear that which makes such an establishment provided with what is provisionary.

(*Two.*)

Urgent action is not in graciousness it is not in clocks it is not in water wheels. It is the same so essentially, it is a worry a real worry.

A silence a whole waste of a desert spoon, a whole waste of any little shaving, a whole waste altogether open.

(*Two.*)

Paralysis why is paralysis a syllable why is it not more lively.

A special sense a very special sense is ludicrous.

(*Three.*)

Suggesting a sage brush with a turkey and also something abominable is not the only pain there is in so much provoking. There is even more. To begin a lecture is a strange way of taking dirty apple blossoms and is there more use in water, certainly there is if there is going to be fishing, enough water would make desert and even prunes, it would make nothing throw any shade because after all is there not more practical humor in a series of photographs and also in a treacherous sculpture.

Any hurry any little hurry has so much subsistence, it has and choosing, it has.

ACT II

(*Three.*)

Four and nobody wounded, five and nobody flourishing, six and nobody talkative, eight and nobody sensible.

One and a left hand lift that is so heavy that there is no way of pronouncing perfectly.

A point of accuracy, a point of a strange stove, a point that is so sober that the reason left is all the chance of swelling.

(*The same three.*)

A wide oak a wide enough oak, a very wide cake, a lightning cooky, a single wide open and exchanged box filled with the same little sac that shines.

The best the only better and more left footed stranger.

The very kindness there is in all lemons oranges apples pears and potatoes.

(*The same three.*)

A same frame a sadder portal, a singular gate and a bracketed mischance.

A rich market where there is no memory of more moon than there is everywhere and yet where strangely there is apparel and a whole set.

A connection, a clam cup connection, a survey, a ticket and a return to laying over.

ACT III

(*Two.*)

A cut, a cut is not a slice, what is the occasion for representing a cut and a slice. What is the occasion for all that.

A cut is a slice, a cut is the same slice. The reason that a cut is a slice is that if there is no hurry any time is just as useful.

(*Four.*)

A cut and a slice is there any question when a cut and a slice are just the same.

A cut and a slice has no particular exchange it has such a strange exception to all that which is different.

A cut and only slice, only a cut and only a slice, the remains of a taste may remain and tasting is accurate.

A cut and an occasion, a slice and a substitute a single hurry and a circumstance that shows that, all this is so reasonable when every thing is clear.

(*One.*)

All alone with the best reception, all alone with more than the best reception, all alone with a paragraph and something that is worth something, worth almost anything, worth the best example there is of a little occasional archbishop. This which is so clean is precious little when there is no bath water. A long time a very long time there is no use in an obstacle that is original and has a source.

ACT IV

(*Four and four more.*)

A birthday, what is a birthday, a birthday is a speech, it is a second time when there is tobacco, it is only one time when there is poison. It is more than one time when the occasion which shows an occasional sharp separation is unanimous.

A blanket, what is a blanket, a blanket is so speedy that heat much heat is hotter and cooler, very much cooler almost more nearly cooler than at any other time often.

A blame what is a blame, a blame is what arises and cautions each one to be calm and an ocean and a masterpiece.

A clever saucer, what is a clever saucer, a clever saucer is very likely practiced and even has toes, it has tiny things to shake and really if it were not for a delicate blue color would there be any reason for every one to differ.

The objection and the perfect central table, the sorrow in borrowing and the hurry in a nervous feeling, the question is it really a plague, is it really an oleander, is it really saffron in color, the surmountable appetite which shows inclination to be warmer, the safety in a match and the safety in a little piece of splinter, the real reason why cocoa is cheaper, the same use for bread as for any breathing that is softer, the lecture and the surrounding large white soft unequal and spread out sale of more and still less is no better, all this makes one regard in a season, one hat in a curtain that in rising higher, one landing and many many more, and many more many more many many more.

ACT V

(*Two.*)

A regret a single regret makes a door way. What is a door way, a door way is a photograph.

What is a photograph a photograph is a sight and a sight is always a sight of something. Very likely there is a photograph that gives color if there is then there is that color that does not change any more than it did when there was much more use for photography.

MISS FURR
AND
MISS SKEENE

From GEOGRAPHY AND PLAYS, 1922. *This charming portrait of two ladies became celebrated after it was reprinted in* VANITY FAIR, *July 1923. Gertrude Stein identified the subjects as Miss Mars and Miss Squires, early habituées of her studio, then at 27 rue de Fleurus, Paris.*

Helen Furr had quite a pleasant home. Mrs. Furr was quite a pleasant woman. Mr. Furr was quite a pleasant man. Helen Furr had quite a pleasant voice a voice quite worth cultivating. She did not mind working. She worked to cultivate her voice. She did not find it gay living in the same place where she had always been living. She went to a place where some were cultivating something, voices and other things needing cultivating. She met Georgine Skeene there who was cultivating her voice which some thought was quite a pleasant one. Helen Furr and Georgine Skeene lived together then. Georgine Skeene liked travelling. Helen Furr did not care about travelling, she liked to stay in one place and be gay there. They were together then and travelled to another place and stayed there and were gay there.

They stayed there and were gay there, not very gay there, just gay there. They were both gay there, they were regularly working there both of them cultivating their voices there, they were both gay there. Georgine Skeene was gay there and she was regular, regular in being gay, regular in not being gay, regular in being a gay one who was one not being gay longer than was needed to be one being quite a gay one. They were both gay then there and both working there then.

They were in a way both gay there where there were many cultivating something. They were both regular in being gay there. Helen Furr was gay there, she was gayer and gayer there and really she was just gay there, she was gayer and gayer there, that is to say she found ways of being gay there that she was using in being gay there. She was gay there, not gayer and gayer, just gay there, that is to say she was not gayer by using the things she found there that were gay things, she was gay there, always she was gay there.

They were quite regularly gay there, Helen Furr and Georgine Skeen, they were regularly gay there where they were gay. They were very regularly gay.

To be regularly gay was to do every day the gay thing that they did every day. To be regularly gay was to end ever day at the same time after they had been regularly gay. They were regularly gay. They were gay every day. They ended every day in the same way, at the same time, and they had been every day regularly gay.

The voice Helen Furr was cultivating was quite a pleasant one. The voice Georgine Skeene was cultivating was, some said, a better one. The voice Helen Furr was cultivating she cultivated and it was quite completely a pleasant enough one then, a cultivated enough one then. The voice Georgine Skeene was cultivating she did not cultivate too much. She cultivated it quite some. She cultivated and she would some-time go on cultivating it and it was not then an unpleasant one, it would not be then an unpleasant one, it would be a quite richly enough cultivated one, it would be quite richly enough to be a pleasant enough one.

They were gay where there were many cultivating some-thing. The two were gay there, were regularly gay there. Georgine Skeene would have liked to do more travelling. They did some travelling, not very much travelling, Georgine Skeene would have liked to do more travelling, Helen Furr did not care about doing travelling, she liked to stay in a place and be gay there.

They stayed in a place and were gay there, both of them stayed there, they stayed together there, they were gay there, they were regularly gay there.

They went quite often, not very often, but they did go back to where Helen Furr had a pleasant enough home and then Georgine Skeene went to a place where her brother had quite some distinction. They both went, every few years, went visiting to where Helen Furr had quite a pleasant home.

Certainly Helen Furr would not find it gay to stay, she did not find it gay, she said she would not stay, she said she did not find it gay, she said she would not stay where she did not find it gay, she said she found it gay where she did stay and she did stay there where very many were cultivating something. She did stay there. She always did find it gay there.

She went to see them where she had always been living and where she did not find it gay. She had a pleasant home there, Mrs. Furr was a pleasant enough woman, Mr. Furr was a pleasant enough man, Helen told them and they were not worrying, that she did not find it gay living where she had always been living.

Georgine Skeene and Helen Furr were living where they were both cultivating their voices and they were gay there. They visited where Helen Furr had come from and then they went to where they were living where they were then regularly living.

There were some dark and heavy men there then. There were some who were not so heavy and some who were not so dark. Helen Furr and Georgine Skeene sat regularly with them. They sat regularly with the ones who were dark and heavy. They sat regularly with the ones who were not so dark. They sat regularly with the ones that were not so heavy. They sat with them regularly, sat with some of them. They went with them regularly went with them. They were regular then, they were gay then, they were where they wanted to be then where it was gay to be then, they were regularly gay then. There were men there then who were dark and heavy and they sat with them with Helen Furr and Georgine Skeene and they went with them with Miss Furr and Miss Skeene, and they went with the heavy and dark men Miss Furr and Miss Skeene went with them, and they sat with them, Miss Furr and Miss Skeene sat with them, and there were other men, some were not heavy men and they sat with Miss Furr and Miss Skeene and Miss Furr and Miss Skeene sat with them, and there were other men who were not dark men and they sat with Miss Furr and Miss Skeene and Miss Furr and Miss Skeene sat with them. Miss Furr and Miss Skeene went with them and they went with Miss Furr and Miss Skeene, some who were not heavy men, some who were not dark men. Miss Furr and Miss Skeene sat regularly, they sat with some men. Miss Furr and Miss Skeene went and there were some men with them. There were men and Miss Furr and Miss Skeene went with them, went somewhere with them, went with some of them.

Helen Furr and Georgine Skeene were regularly living where very many were living and cultivating in themselves something. Helen Furr and Georgine Skeene were living very regularly then, being very regular then in being gay then. They did then learn many ways to be gay and they were then being gay being quite regular in being gay, being gay and they were learning little things, little things in ways of being gay, they were very regular then, they were learning very many little things in ways of being gay, they were being gay and using these little things they were learning to have to be gay with regularly gay with then and they were gay the same amount they had been gay. They were quite gay, they were quite regular, they were learning little things, gay little things, they were gay inside them the same amount they had been gay, they were gay the same length of time they had been gay every day.

They were regular in being gay, they learned little things that are things in being gay, they learned many little things that are things in being gay, they were gay every day, they were regular, they were gay, they were gay the same length of time every day, they were gay, they were quite regularly gay.

Georgine Skeene went away to stay two months with her brother. Helen Furr did not go then to stay with her father and her mother. Helen Furr stayed there where they had been regularly living the two of them and she would then certainly not be lonesome, she would go on being gay. She did go on being gay. She was not any more gay but she was gay longer every day than they had been being gay when they were together being gay. She was gay then quite exactly the same way. She learned a few more little ways of being gay. She was quite gay and in the same way, the same way she had been gay and she was gay a little longer in the day, more of each day she was gay. She was gay longer every day than when the two of them had been being gay. She was gay quite in the way they had been gay, quite in the same way.

She was not lonesome then, she was not at all feeling any need of having Georgine Skeene. She was not astonished at this thing. She would have been a little astonished by this thing but she knew she was not astonished at anything and so she was not astonished at this thing not astonished at not feeling any need of having Georgine Skeene.

Helen Furr had quite a completely pleasant voice and it was quite well enough cultivated and she could use it and she did use it but then there was not any way of working at cultivating a completely pleasant voice when it has become a quite completely well enough cultivated one, and there was not much use in using it when one was not wanting it to be helping to make one a gay one. Helen Furr was not needing using her voice to be a gay one. She was gay then and sometimes she used her voice and she was not using it very often. It was quite completely enough cultivated and it was quite completely a pleasant one and she did not use it very often. She was then, she was quite exactly as gay as she had been, she was gay a little longer in the day than she had been.

She was gay exactly the same way. She was never tired of being gay that way. She had learned very many little ways to use in being gay. Very many were telling about using other ways in being gay. She was gay enough, she was always gay exactly the same way, she was always learning little things to use in being gay, she was telling about using other ways in being gay, she was telling about learning other ways in being gay, she was learning other ways in being gay, she would be using other ways in being gay, she would always be gay in the same way, when Georgine Skeene was there not so long each day as when Georgine Skeene was away.

She came to using many ways in being gay, she came to use every way in being gay. She went on living where many were cultivating something and she was gay, she had used every way to be gay.

They did not live together then Helen Furr and Georgine Skeene. Helen Furr lived there the longer where they had been living regularly together. Then neither of them were living there any longer. Helen Furr was living somewhere else then and telling some about being gay and she was gay then and she was living quite regularly then. She was regularly gay then. She was quite regular in being gay then. She remembered all the little ways of being gay. She used all the little ways of being gay. She was quite regularly gay. She told many then the way of being gay, she taught very many then little ways they could use in being gay. She was living very well, she was gay then, she went on living then, she was regular in being gay, she always was living very well and was gay very well and was telling about little ways one could be learning to use in being gay, and later was telling them quite often, telling them again and again.

A SWEET TAIL

(GYPSIES)

Like so many pieces in GEOGRAPHY AND PLAYS, 1922, *this little descriptive essay is the result of a journey to Spain by Miss Stein and Miss Toklas.*

Curves.

Hold in the coat. Hold back ladders and a creation and nearly sudden extra coppery ages with colors and a clean voice gyp hoarse. Hold in that curl with a good man. Hold in cheese. Hold in cheese. Hold in cheese.

A cool brake, a cool brake not a success not a resound a re-sound and a little pan with a yell oh yes so yet change, famous, a green a green colored oak, a handsome excursion, a really handsome log, a regulation to exchange oars, a regulation or more press more precise cold pieces, more yet in the teeth within the teeth. This is the sun in. This is the lamb of the lantern with chalk. With chalk a shadow shall be a sneeze in a tooth in a tin tooth, a turned past, a turned little corset, a little tuck in a pink look and with a pin in, a pin in.

Win lake, eat splashes dig salt change benches.

Win lake eat splashes dig salt change benches.

Can in.

Come a little cheese. Come a little cheese and same same tall sun with a little thing to team, team now and a bass a whole some gurgle, little tin, little tin soak, soak why Sunday, supreme measure.

No nice burst, no nice burst sourly. Suppose a butter glass is clean and there is a bow suppose it lest the bounding ocean and a medium sized bloat in the cunning little servant handkerchief is in between.

Cuts when cuts when ten, lie on this, singling wrist tending, singling the pin.

Lie on this, shows up the boon that nick the basting thread

thinly and night night gown and pit wet kit. Loom down the thorough narrow. It is not cuddle and molest change. It is not molest principal necessary argue not that it, not that in life walk collect piece.

Colored tall bills with little no pitch and dark white dark with rubber splendid select pistons with black powdered cheese and shirts and night gowns and ready very ready sold glass butts. The simple real ball with a cold glass and no more seat than yesterday together together with lime, lime water. This is no sight, no sight suddenly, no supper with a heat which makes morgan, morgan must be so.

If it is and more that call life with show cared beard with a belt and no pin when shine see the coat and left and last with all it was to be there why show could pause with such read mice call it why those old sea cat with a shining not mouth hole if it is a white call with the inch of that sort could see that tie west with loaf which is not the copper lasting with a bright retract lamp call negligence utterly soothing in the coiling remain collapse of this which by there a called which never see and hammer by which basket all that glance zest.

Cut in simple cake simple cake, relike a gentle coat, seal it, seal it blessing and that means gracious not gracious suddenly with spoons and flavor but all the same active. Neglect a pink white neglect it for blooming on a thin piece of steady slit poplars and really all the chance is in deriding cocoanuts real cocoanuts with strawberry tunes and little ice cakes with feeding feathers and peculiar relations of nothing which is more blessed than replies. Replies sudden and no lard no lard at all to show port and colors and please little pears that is to say six.

It can no sail to key pap change and put has can we see call bet. Show leave I cup the fanned best same so that if then sad sole is more, more not, and after shown so papered with that in instep lasting pheasant. Pheasant enough. Call africa, call african cod liver, loading a bag with news and little pipes restlessly so that with in between chance white cases are muddy and show a little tint, all of it.

Please coat.

Way lay to be set in the coat and the bust. The right hold is went hole piece cageous him. He had his sisters.

Like message copowder and sashes sashes, like pedal sashes and so sashes, like pedal causes and so sashes, and pedal cause killed surgeon in six safest six which, pedal sashes.

Peel sashes not what then called and in when the crest no mandarining clothes brush often. No might of it could sudden best set. Best set boar.

Rest sing a mean old polly case with boats and a little scissors nicely sore. All the blands are with a coat and more is coach with commas. A little arrangement is manufactured by a shoal and little salt sweats are to grow grow with ice and let it seat seat more than shadows which have butter.

Suppose, suppose a tremble, a ham, a little mouth told to wheeze more and a religion a reign of a pea racket that makes a load register and passes best. Kindness necessarily swims in a bottom with a razor which needs powder powder that makes a top be in the middle and necessarily not indicate a kind of collection, a collection of more or more gilt and mostly blue pipes pipes which are bound bound with old oil and mustard exact mustard which means that yellow is obtained. Gravious oh my cold under fur, under no rescued reading.

Able there to ball bawl able to call and seat a tin a tin whip with a collar. The least license is in the eyes which make strange the less sighed hole which is nodded and leaves the bent tender. All the class is sursful. It makes medium and egg light and not really so much.

Catch white color white sober, call white sold sacks, crimp white colored harness crimp it with ferocious white saffron hides, hurry up cut clothes with calm calm bright capable engines of pink and choice and press. Peas nuts are shiny with recent stutter which makes cram and mast a mast hoe, luck.

A winter sing, take thee to stay, say mountain to me and alabaster.

Curious alright.

Wheel is not on a donkey and never never.

A little piece of fly that makes a ling a shoulder a relief to pages.

Please putter sane show a pronounce, leave sold gats, less it measles. A little thin a little thin told told not which. Rest stead.

Appeal, a peal, laugh, hurry merry, good in night, rest stole. Rest stole to bestow candle electricity in surface. The best header is nearly peek.

Come in to sun with holy pin and have the petticoat to say the day, the last of high this that. No so.

Little tree, bold up and shut with strings the piney and little weights little weights what.

Cold a packet must soak sheer land, leave it a yield so that nuts nuts are below when when cap bags are nearly believe me it is nice and quiet I thank you.

Pluck howard in the collided cheese put and not narrow.

Little in the toilet tram.

Seize noes when the behaved ties are narrowed to little finances and large garden chambers with soled more saddled heels and monkeys and tacts and little limber shading with real old powder and chest wides and left clothes and nearly all heights hats which are so whiled and reactive with moist most leaves it sell to apart.

Sober eat it, a little way to seat. The two whiskers.

All chime. So be eat hit. No case the lines are the twist of a lost last piece of flannel.

This beam in which bought not a hill than store when stone in the point way black what slate piece by all stone dust chancely.

This wee did shut, about. A land paul with a lea in and no bell no bell pose with counters and a strike a strike to poison. Does a prison make a window net does it show plates and little coats and a dear noise.

This is a cape. A real tall is a bat, the rest is nice west, the rest in, be hine with a haul a haul not. Knot not knot. A vest a voice vest. Be able to shave, shave little pills in steady, steady three, coal pied This is hum with him, believe hit believe hit page it.

Is it necessary that actuality is tempered and neglect is rolled. A little piece. The blame which makes a coping out of a cellar and into a curtain and behind behind a frontyard is that then. Please dust.

It is so thick and thin and thin, it is thick. It is thick, thin.
A spoon, thick ahead and matches, matches wear sacks.
Stew, stew, than.

FOUR SAINTS IN
THREE ACTS

First published in transition, *June, 1929, this lyric drama was later included in* OPERAS AND PLAYS; *Plain edition, Paris, 1932, and still later in a volume by itself published by Random House, in 1934. As an opera with Virgil Thomson's music it was first performed at the Avery Memorial, Wadsworth Atheneum, in Hartford, Connecticut, February 8, 1934. On February 20th of the same year it began a four weeks' run at the Forty-fourth Street Theatre in New York (since torn down to permit the enlargement of the* N. Y. TIMES *plant) and on April 9th, after a lapse of three weeks it resumed for a short run at the Empire Theatre. In Chicago, beginning November 7, 1934, five performances were given at the Auditorium Theatre. Miss Stein, Miss Toklas, and I flew to Chicago (the ladies making their virgin flight) for this event and sat in a box together for the opening night. I think the original Negro cast officiated practically intact at all these performances.*

"In FOUR SAINTS," *Miss Stein informs us in one of her* LECTURES IN AMERICA, *"I made the saints the landscape. . . .*

> *"Magpies are in the landscape that is they are in the sky of a landscape, they are black and white and they are in the landscape in Bilignin and in Spain, especially in Avila. When they are in the sky they do something I have never seen any other bird do they hold themselves up and down and look flat against the sky.*

> *"A very famous French inventor of things that have to do with stabilisation in aviation told me that what I told him magpies did could not be done by any bird but anyway whether the magpies at Avila do do it or do not at least they look as if they do do it. They look exactly like the birds in the Annunci-*

ation pictures the bird which is the Holy Ghost and rests flat against the side sky very high.

"There were magpies in my landscape and there were scarecrows.

"The scarecrows on the ground are the same thing as the magpies in the sky, they are a part of the landscape.

"They the magpies may tell their story if they and you like or even if I like but stories are only stories but that they stay in the air is not a story but a landscape. That scarecrows stay on the ground is the same thing it could be a story but it is a piece of the landscape."

> To know to know to love her so.
> Four saints prepare for saints.
> It makes it well fish.
> Four saints it makes it well fish.

Four saints prepare for saints it makes it well well fish it makes it well fish prepare for saints.

In narrative prepare for saints.

Prepare for saints.

Two saints.

Four saints.

Two saints prepare for saints it two saints prepare for saints in prepare for saints.

A narrative of prepare for saints in narrative prepare for saints.

Remain to narrate to prepare two saints for saints.

At least.

In finally.

Very well if not to have and miner.

A saint is one to be for two when three and you make five and two and cover.

A at most.

Saint saint a saint.

Forgotten saint.

What happened to-day, a narrative.

We had intended if it were a pleasant day to go to the country it was a very beautiful day and we carried out our intention. We went to places that we had been when we were equally pleased and we found very nearly what we could find and returning saw and heard that after all they were rewarded and likewise. This makes it necessary to go again.

He came and said he was hurrying hurrying and hurrying to remain he said he said finally to be and claim it he said he said feeling very nearly everything as it had been as if he could be precious be precious to like like it as it had been that if he was used it would always do it good and now this time that it was as if it had been just the same as longer when as before it made it be left to be sure and soft softly then can be changed to theirs and speck a speck of it makes blue be often sooner which is shared when theirs is in polite and reply that in their be the same with diminish always in respect to not at all and farther farther might be known as counted with it gain to be in retain which it is not to be because of most. This is how they do not like it.

Why while while in that way was it after this that to be seen made left it.

He could be hurt at that.

It is very easy to be land.

Imagine four benches separately.

One in the sun.

Two in the sun.

Three in the sun.

One not in the sun.

Not one not in the sun.

Not one.

Four benches used four benches used separately.

Four benches used separately.

That makes it be not be makes it not be at the time.

The time that it is as well as it could be leave it when when it was to be that it was to be when it was went away.

Four benches with leave it.

Might have as would be as would be as within within nearly as out. It is very close close and closed. Closed closed to letting closed close close close chose in justice in join in joining. This is where to be at at water at snow snow show show one one sun and sun snow show and no water no water unless unless why unless. Why unless why unless they were loaning it here loaning intentionally. Believe two three. What could be sad beside beside very attentively intentionally and bright.

Begin suddenly not with sisters.

To mount it up.

Up hill.

Four saints are never three.

Three saints are never four.

Four saints are never left altogether.

Three saints are never idle.

Four saints are leave it to me.

Three saints when this you see.

Begin three saints.

Begin four saints.

Two and two saints.

One and three saints.

In place.

One should it.

Easily saints.

Very well saints.

Have saints.

Said saints.

As said saints.

And not annoy.

Anoint.

Choice.

Four saints two at a time have to have to have to have to.

Have to have have to have to.

Two saints four at a time a time.

Have to have to at a time.

Four saints have to have to have at a time.

The difference between saints forget-me-nots and mountains have to have to have to at a time.

It is very easy in winter to remember winter spring and summer it is very easy in winter to remember spring and winter and summer it is very easy in winter to remember summer spring and winter it is very easy in winter to remember spring and summer and winter.

Does it show as if it could be that very successful that very successful that he was very successful that he was with them with them with them as it was not better than at worst that he could follow him to be taking it away away that way a way a way to go.

Some say some say some say so.

Why should every one be at home why should every one be at home why should every one be at home.

Why should every one be at home.

In idle acts.

Why should everybody be at home.

In idle acts.

He made very much more than he did he did make very much of it he did not only add to his part of it but and with it he was at and in a plight.

There is no parti-color in a house there is no parti parti parti color in a house. Reflections by the time that they were given the package that had been sent. Very much what they could would do as a decision.

Supposing she said that he had chosen all the miseries that he had observed in fifty of his years what had that to do with hats. They had made hats for her. Not really.

As she was.

Imagine imagine it imagine it. When she returned there was considerable rain.

In some on some evening would it be asked was there anything especial.

By and by plain plainly in making acutely a corner not at right angle but in individual in individual is it.

A narrative who do who does.

A narrative to plan an opera.

Four saints in three acts.

A croquet scene and when they made their habits. Habits not hourly habits habits not hourly at the time that they made their habits not hourly they made their habits.

When they made their habits.

To know when they made their habits.

Large pigeons in small trees.

Large pigeons in small trees.

Come panic come.

Come close.

Acts three acts.

Come close to croquet.

Four saints.

Rejoice saints rejoin saints recommence some reinvite.

Four saints have been sometime in that way that way all hall.

Four saints were not born at one time although they knew each other. One of them had a birthday before the mother of the other one the father. Four saints later to be if to be if to be to be one to be. Might tingle.

Tangle wood tanglewood.

Four saints born in separate places.

Saint saint saint saint.

Four saints an opera in three acts.

My country 'tis of thee sweet land of liberty of thee I sing.

Saint Therese something like that.

Saint Therese something like that.

Saint Therese would and would and would.

Saint Therese something like that.

Saint Therese.

Saint Therese half in doors and half out out of doors.

Saint Therese not knowing of other saints.

Saint Therese used to go not to to tell them so but to around so that Saint Therese did find that that that and there. If any came.

This is to say that four saints may may never have seen the day, like. Any day like.

Saint Ignatius.   Meant and met.

This is to say that four saints may never have. Any day like. Gradually wait.

Any one can see that any saint to be.

Saint Therese	Saint Ignatius
Saint Matyr	Saint Paul
Saint Settlement	Saint William
Saint Thomasine	Saint Gilbert
Saint Electra	Saint Settle
Saint Wilhelmina	Saint Arthur

Saint Evelyn	Saint Selmer
Saint Pilar	Saint Paul Seize
Saint Hillaire	Saint Cardinal
Saint Bernadine	Saint Plan
	Saint Giuseppe

Any one to tease a saint seriously.

ACT ONE

Saint Therese in a storm at Avila there can be rain and warm snow and warm that is the water is warm the river is not warm the sun is not warm and if to stay to cry. If to stay to if to stay if having to stay to if having to stay if to cry to stay if to cry stay to cry to stay.

Saint Therese half in and half out of doors.

Saint Ignatius not there. Saint Ignatius staying where. Never heard them speak speak of it.

Saint Ignatius silent motive not hidden.

Saint Therese silent. They were never beset.

Come one come one.

No saint to remember to remember. No saint to remember. Saint Therese knowing young and told.

If it were possible to kill five thousand chinamen by pressing a button would it be done.

Saint Therese not interested.

REPEAT FIRST ACT

A pleasure April fool's day a pleasure.

Saint Therese seated.

Not April fool's day a pleasure.

Saint Therese seated.

Not April fool's day a pleasure.

Saint Therese seated.

April fool's day April fool's day as not as pleasure as April fool's day not a pleasure.

Saint Therese seated and not surrounded. There are a great many persons and places near together.

There are a great many persons and places near together.

Saint Therese not seated at once. There are a great many places and persons near together.

Saint Therese once seated. There are a great many places and persons near together. Saint Therese seated and not surrounded. There are a great many places and persons near together.

Saint Therese visited by very many as well as the others really visited before she was seated. There are a great many persons and places close together.

Saint Therese not young and younger but visited like the others by some, who are frequently going there.

Saint Therese very nearly half inside and half outside outside the house and not surrounded.

How do you do. Very well I thank you. And when do you go. I am staying on quite continuously. When is it planned. Not more than as often.

The garden inside and outside of the wall.

Saint Therese about to be.

The garden inside and outside outside and inside of the wall.

Nobody visits more than they do visits them.

Saint Therese. Nobody visits more than they do visits them Saint Therese.

As loud as that as allowed as that.

Saint Therese. Nobody visits more than they do visits them.

Who settles a private life.

Saint Therese. Who settles a private life.

Saint Therese.

Saint Therese. Who settles a private life.

ENACT END OF AN ACT

Saint Therese seated and if he could be standing and standing and saying and saying left to be.

Introducing Saint Ignatius.

Left to be.

She can have no one no one can have any one any one can have not any one can have not any one can have can have to say so.

Saint Therese seated and not standing half and half of it and not half and half of it seated and not standing surrounded

and not seated and not seated and nct standing and not surrounded not surrounded not not not seated not seated not
seated not surrounded not seated and Saint Ignatius standing
standing not seated Saint Therese not standing not standing
and Saint Ignatius not standing standing surrounded as if in
once yesterday. In place of situations.

Did she want him dead if now.

Saint Therese could be photographed having been dressed
like a lady and then they taking out her head changed it to a
nun and a nun a saint and a saint so. Saint Therese seated
and not surrounded might be very well inclined to be settled.

Made to be coming to be here.

How many saints can sit around. A great many saints can
sit around with one standing.

A saint is easily resisted. Saint Therese. Let it as land Saint
Therese. As land beside a house. Saint Therese. As land beside a house and at one time Saint Therese. As land beside
a house to be to this this which theirs beneath Saint Therese.

Saint Therese saints make sugar with a flavor. In different
ways when it is practicable.

Saint Therese.   Could she know that that he was not not
to be to be very to be dead not dead.

Saint Therese must be must be chain left chain right chain
chain is it. No one chain is it not chain is it, chained to not
to life chained to not to snow chained to chained to go and
and gone.

Saint Therese.   Not this not in this not with this.

Saint Therese as a young girl being widowed.

Can she sing.

Saint Therese.   Leave later gaily the troubadour plays
his guitar.

Saint Therese might it be Martha.

Saint Louise and Saint Celestine and Saint Louis Paul and
Saint Settlement Fernande and Ignatius.

Saint Therese.   Can women have wishes.

SCENE TWO

Many saints seen and in between many saints seen.
Saint Therese and Saint Therese and Saint Therese.

Seen as seen.

Many saints as seen.

She is to meet her.

Can two saints be one.

Very many go out as they they do.

And make him prominent.

Saint Therese.   Could a negro be be with a beard to see
and to be.

Saint Therese.   Never have to have seen a negro there
and with it so.

Saint Therese.   To differ between go and so.

Saint Therese and three saints all one.

Who separated saints at one time.

Saint Therese.   In follow and saints.

Saint Therese.   To be somewhere with or without saints.

Saint Therese can never mention the others.

Saint Therese to them. Saints not found. All four saints not
more than all four saints.

Saint Therese come again to be absent.

SCENE III

Could all four saints not only be in brief.

Contumely.

Saint Therese advancing. Who can be shortly in their way.

Saint Therese having heard.

In this way as movement.

In having been in.

Does she want to be neglectful of hyacinths and find violets.
Saint Therese can never change herbs for pansies and dry
them.

They think there that it is their share.

And please.

Saint Therese makes as in this to be as stems.

And while.

Saint Therese settled and some come. Some come to be near
not near her but the same.

Sound them with the thirds and that.

How many are there halving.

SCENE III

Saint Therese having known that no snow in vain as snow is not vain. Saint Therese needed it as she was. Saint Therese made it be third. Snow third high third there third. Saint Therese in allowance.

How many saints can remember a house which was built before they can remember.

Ten saints can.

How many saints can be and land be and sand be and on a high plateau there is no sand there is snow and there is made to be so and very much can be what there is to see when there is a wind to have it dry and be what they can understand to undertake to let it be to send it well as much as none to be to be behind. None to be behind. Enclosure. Saint Therese. None to be behind. Enclosure.

Saint Ignatius could be in porcelain actually.

Saint Ignatius could be in porcelain actually while he was young and standing.

Saint Therese could not be young and standing she could be sitting.

Saint Therese could be.

Saint Ignatius could be in porcelain actually in porcelain standing.

They might in at most not leave out an egg. An egg and add some. Some and sum. Add sum. Add some.

Let it in around.

With seas.

With knees.

With keys.

With pleases.

Go and know.

In clouded.

Included.

Saint Therese and attachment. With any one please.

No one to be behind and enclosure. Suddenly two see.

Two and ten.

Saint Two and Saint Ten.

SCENE IV

Did wish did want did at most agree that it was not when they had met that they were separated longitudinally.

While it escapes it adds to it just as it did when it has and does with it in that to intend to intensity and sound. Is there a difference between a sound a hiss a kiss as well.

Could they grow and tell it so if it was left to be to go to go to see to see to saw to saw to build to place to come to rest to hand to beam to couple to name to rectify to do.

Saint Ignatius Saint Settlement Saint Paul Seize Saint Anselmo made it be not only obligatory but very much as they did in little patches.

Saint Therese and Saint Therese and Saint Therese Seize and Saint Therese might be very much as she would if she very much as she would if she were to be wary.

They might be that much that far that with that widen never having seen and press, it was a land in one when altitude by this to which endowed.

Might it be in claim.

Saint Therese and conversation. In one.

Saint Therese in conversation. And one.

Saint Therese in and in and one and in and one.

Saint Therese left in complete.

Saint Therese and better bowed.

Saint Therese did she and leave bright.

Snow in snow sun in sun one in one out.

A scene and withers.

Scene three and scene two.

How can a sister see Saint Therese suitably.

Pear trees cherry blossoms pink blossoms and late apples and surrounded by Spain and lain.

Why when in lean fairly rejoin place dismiss calls.

Whether weather soil.

Saint Therese refuses to bestow.

Saint Therese with account. Saint Therese having felt it with it.

There can be no peace on earth with calm with calm. There can be no peace on earth with calm with calm. There can be no peace on earth with calm with calm and with whom whose with calm and with whom whose when they well they well they call it there made message especial and come.

This amounts to Saint Therese. Saint Therese has been and has been.

All Saints make Sunday Monday Sunday Monday Sunday Monday set.

One two three Saints.

SCENE III

Saint Therese has been prepared for there being summer.
Saint Therese has been prepared for there being summer.

SCENE IV

To prepare.
One a window.
Two a shutter.
Three a palace.
Four a widow.
Five an adopted son.
Six a parlor.
Seven a shawl.
Eight an arbor.
Nine a seat.
Ten a retirement.
Saint Therese has been with him.
Saint Therese has been with him they show they show that summer summer makes a child happening at all to throw a ball too often to please.

Those used to winter like winter and summer.
Those used to summer like winter and summer.
Those used to summer like winter and summer.
Those used to summer like winter and summer like winter and summer.

Those used to summer like winter and summer.
They make this an act One.

ACT TWO

All to you.

SCENE ONE

Some and some.

This is a scene where this is seen. Saint Therese has been a queen not as you might say royalty not as you might say worn not as you might say.

Saint Therese preparing in as you might say.

ACT ONE

Saint Therese.   Preparing in as you might say.

Saint Therese was pleasing. In as you might say.

Saint Therese Act One.

Saint Therese has begun to be in act one.

Saint Therese and begun.

Saint Therese as sung.

Saint Therese act one.

Saint Therese and begun.

Saint Therese and sing and sung.

Saint Therese in an act one.

How many have been told twenty have been here as well.

Saint Therese can know the difference between singing and women. Saint Therese can know the difference between snow and thirds. Saint Therese can know the difference between when there is a day to-day to-day. To-day.

Saint Therese with the land and laid. Not observing.

Saint Therese coming to go.

Saint Therese coming and lots of which it is not as soon as if when it can left to change change theirs in glass and yellowish at most most of this can be when is it that it is very necessary not to plant it green. Planting it green means that it is protected from the wind and they never knew about it. They never knew about it green and they never knew about it she never knew about it they never knew about it they never knew about it she never knew about it. Planting it green means that it is necessary to protect it from the sun and from the wind and the sun and they never knew about it and she never knew about it and she never knew about it and they never knew about.

Scene once seen once seen once seen.

SCENE VII

One two three four five six seven all good children go to heaven some are good and some are bad one two three four five six seven.

Saint Therese when she had been left to come was left to come was left to right was right to left and there. There and not there by left and right. Saint Therese once and once. No one surrounded trees as there were none.

This makes Saint Ignatius Act II.

ACT II

Saint Ignatius was very well known.

SCENE II

Would it do if there was a Scene II.

SCENE III AND IV

Saint Ignatius and more.

Saint Ignatius with as well.

Saint Ignatius needs not be feared.

Saint Ignatius might be very well adapted to plans and a distance.

Barcelona in the distance. Was Saint Ignatius able to tell the difference between palms and Eucalyptus trees.

Saint Ignatius finally.

Saint Ignatius well bound.

Saint Ignatius with it just.

Saint Ignatius might be read.

Saint Ignatius with it Tuesday.

Saint Therese has very well added it.

SCENE IV

Usefully.

SCENE IV

How many nails are there in it.

Hard shoe nails and silver nails and silver does not sound valuable.

To be interested in Saint Therese fortunately.
To be interested in Saint Therese fortunately.
Saint Ignatius to be interested fortunately.
Fortunately to be interested in Saint Therese.
To be interested fortunately in Saint Therese.
Interested fortunately in Saint Therese Saint Ignatius and Saints who have been changed from the evening to the morning.

In the morning to be changed from the morning to the morning in the morning. A scene of changing from the morning to the morning.

SCENE V

There are many saints.

SCENE V

They can be left to many saints.

SCENE V

Many saints.

SCENE V

Many many saints can be left to many many saints scene five left to many many saints.

SCENE V

Scene five left to many saints.

SCENE V

They are left to many saints and those saints these saints these saints. Saints four saints. They are left to many saints.

SCENE V

Saint Therese does disgrace her by leaving it alone and shone.

Saint Ignatius might be five.

When three were together one woman sitting and seeing one man leading and choosing one young man saying and selling. This is just as if it was a tube.

SCENE V

SCENE VI

Away away away away a day it took three days and that day. Saint Therese was very well parted and apart apart from that. Harry marry saints in place saints and sainted distributed grace.

Saint Therese in place.

Saint Therese in place of Saint Therese in place.

Saint Therese. Can any one feel any one moving and in moving can any one feel any one and in moving.

Saint Therese. To be belied.

Saint Therese. Having happily married.

Saint Therese. Having happily beside.

Saint Therese. Having happily had with it a spoon.

Saint Therese. Having happily relied upon noon.

Saint Therese with Saint Therese.

Saint Therese. In place.

Saint Therese and Saint Therese Saint Therese to trace.

Saint Therese and place.

Saint Therese beside.

Saint Therese added ride.

Saint Therese with tied.

Saint Therese and might.

Saint Therese. Might with widow.

Saint Therese. Might.

Saint Therese very made her in.

Saint Therese Saint Therese.

Saint Therese in in in Lynn.

SCENE VII

One two three four five six seven scene seven.

Saint Therese scene seven.

Saint Therese scene scene seven.

Saint Therese could never be mistaken.

Saint Therese could never be mistaken.

Saint Therese. How many saints are there in it.

Saint Therese.   There are very many many saints in it.

Saint Therese.   There are as many saints as there are in it.

Saint Therese.   There are there are there are saints saints in it.

Saint Therese Saint Settlement Saint Ignatius Saint Lawrence Saint Pilar Saint Plan and Saint Cecilia.

Saint Cecilia.   How many saints are there in it.

Saint Cecilia.   There are as many saints as there are saints in it.

Saint Cecilia.   How many saints are there in it.

Saint Lawrence Saint Celestine.   There are saints in it Saint Celestine Saint Lawrence there are as many saints there are as many saints as there are as many saints as there are in it.

Saint Therese.   Thank you very much.

Saint Therese.   There are as many saints there are many saints in it.

A very long time but not while waiting.

Saint Ignatius.   More needily of which more anon.

Saint Ignatius.   Of more which more which more.

Saint Ignatius Loyola.   A saint to be met by and by by and by continue reading reading read read readily.

Never to be lost again to-day.

To-day to stay.

Saint Ignatius Saint Ignatius Saint Ignatius temporarily.

Saint Jan.   Who makes whose be his. I do.

Saint Therese scene scene seven one two three four five six seven.

Saint Therese.   Let it have a place.

Saint Therese Saint Ignatius and Saint Genevieve and Saint Therese and Saint Chavez.

Saint Chavez can be with them then.

Saint Ignatius can be might it be with them and furl.

Saint Therese with them in with them alone.

Saint Plan. Can be seen to be any day any day from here to there.

Saint Settlement aroused by the recall of Amsterdam.

Saint Therese. Judging it as a place to be used negligently.

Saint Ignatius by the time that rain has come.

Saint Genevieve meant with it all.

Saint Plan. Might meant with it all.

Saint Paul. Might meant might with it all.

Saint Chavez. Select.

Saints. All Saints.

SCENE EIGHT

All Saints. All Saints At All Saints.

All Saints. Any and all Saints. All Saints. All and all Saints. All Saints. All in all Saints. All Saints. All Saints. All Saints. Saints all in all Saints. All Saints. Settled in all Saints. All Saints. Settled all in all saints. Saints. Saints settled saints settled all in all saints. All saints. Saints in all saints. Saint Settlement. Saints all saints all saints. Saint Chavez. Saint Ignatius. Settled passing this in having given in which is not two days when everything being ready it is no doubt not at all the following morning that it is very much later very much earlier with then to find it acceptable as about about which which as a river river helping it to be in doubt. Who do who does and does it about about to be as a river and the order of their advance. It is to-morrow on arriving at a place to pass before the last.

Scene eight. To Wait.

Scene one. And begun.

Scene two. To and to.

Scene three. Happily be.

Scene Four. Attached or.

Scene Five. Sent to derive.

Scene Six. Let it mix.

Scene Seven. Attached eleven.

Scene Eight. To wait.

Saint Therese. Might be there.

Saint Therese. To be sure.

Saint Therese. With them and.

Saint Therese. And hand.

Saint Therese.   And alight.

Saint Therese.   With them then. Saint Therese Saint Therese. Nestle. Saint Therese. With them and a measure. It is easy to measure a settlement.

SCENE IX

Saint Therese.   To be asked how much of it is finished.

Saint Therese.   To be asked Saint Therese Saint Therese to be asked how much of it is finished.

Saint Therese.   Ask Saint Therese how much of it is finished.

Saint Therese.   To be asked Saint Therese to be asked Saint Therese to be asked ask Saint Therese ask Saint Therese how much of it is finished.

Saint Plan.   Ask Saint Therese how much of it is finished.

Saint Therese. Ask asking asking Saint Therese how much of it is finished.

Saint Settlement ⎫
Saint Chavez   ⎬ How much of it is finished.
Saint Plan   ⎭

Saint Therese.   Ask how much of it is finished.

Saint Chavez.   Ask how much of it is finished.

Saint Therese.   Ask how much of it is finished.

Saint Therese
Saint Paul
Saint Plan
Saint Anne
Saint Cecile
Saint Plan.

Once in a while.

Saint Therese.   Once in a while.
Saint Plan.   Once in a while.
Saint Chavez.   Once in a while.
Saint Settlement.   Once in a while.
Saint Therese.   Once in a while.
Saint Chavez.   Once in a while.

Saint Cecile.   Once in a while.
Saint Genevieve.   Once in a while.
Saint Anne.   Once in a while.
Saint Settlement.   Once in a while.
Saint Therese.   Once in a while.
Saint Therese.   Once in a while.
Saint Ignatius.   Once in a while.
Saint Ignatius.   Once in a while.
Saint Ignatius.   Once in a while.
Saint Settlement.   Once in a while.
Saint Therese.   Once in a while.
Saint Therese.
Saint Therese.   Once in a while.
Saint Ignatius.   Once in a while.
Saint Ignatius.   Once in a while.
Saint Therese.
Saint Therese.   Once in a while.
Saint Therese.   Once in a while.
Saint Therese.   Once in a while.
Saint Plan.   Once in a while.
Saint Ignatius.   Once in a while.
Saint Therese.

SCENE X

Could Four Acts be Three.

Saint Therese.   Could Four Acts be three.
Saint Therese Saint Therese Saint Therese Could Four
Acts be three Saint Therese.

SCENE X

When.

Saint Therese.   Could Four Acts be when four acts could
be ten Saint Therese. Saint Therese Saint Therese Four Acts
could be four acts could be when when four acts could be ten.
Saint Therese.   When.
Saint Settlement.   Then.
Saint Genevieve.   When.

Saint Cecile.   Then.
Saint Ignatius.   Then.
Saint Ignatius.   Men.
Saint Ignatius.   When.
Saint Ignatius.   Ten.
Saint Ignatius.   Then.
Saint Therese.   When.
Saint Chavez.   Ten.
Saint Plan.   When then.
Saint Settlement.   Then.
Saint Anne.   Then.
Saint Genevieve.   Ten.
Saint Cecile.   Then.
Saint Answers.   Ten.
Saint Cecile.   When then.
Saint Answers.   Saints when.
Saint Chavez.   Saints when ten.
Saint Cecile.   Ten.
Saint Answers.   Ten.
Saint Chavez.   Ten.
Saint Settlement.   Ten.
Saint Plan.   Ten.
Saint Anne.   Ten.
Saint Plan.   Ten.
Saint Plan.   Ten.
Saint Plan.   Ten.

SCENE XI

Saint Therese.   With William.
Saint Therese.   With Plan.
Saint Therese.   With William willing and with Plan will-
ing and with Plan and with William willing and with William
and with Plan.
Saint Therese.   They might be staring.
Saint Therese.   And with William.
Saint Therese.   And with Plan.
Saint Therese.   With William.
Saint Therese.   And with. Plan.

Saint Therese ⎫
Saint Plan   ⎬
  Saint Placide ⎬ How many windows are there in it.
Saint Chavez   ⎬
  and   ⎬
Saint Settlement. ⎭

Saint Therese.   How many windows and doors and floors are there in it.

Saint Therese.   How many doors how many floors and how many windows are there in it.

Saint Plan.   How many windows are there in it how many doors are there in it.

Saint Chavez.   How many doors are there in it how many floors are there in it how many doors are there in it how many windows are there in it how many floors are there in it how many windows are there in it how many doors are there in it.

Changing in between.

Saint Therese.   In this and in this and in this and clarity.

Saint Therese.   How many are there in this.

How many are there in this.

Saint Settlement.   Singularly to be sure and with a Wednesday at noon.

Saint Chavez.   In time and mine.

Saint Therese.   Settlement and in in and in and all. All to come and go to stand up to kneel and to be around. Around and around and around and as round and as around and as around and as around.

One two three.

There is a distance in between.

There is a distance in between in between others others meet meet meet met wet yet. It is very tearful to be through. Through and through.

Saint Therese.   Might be third.

Saint Therese.   Might be heard.

Saint Therese.   Might be invaded.

Saint Therese and three saints and there.

Commencing again yesterday.

Saint Therese.   And principally, Saint Therese.

SCENE X

Saint Ignatius.   Withdrew with with withdrew.

Saint Ignatius.   Occurred.

Saint Ignatius.   Occurred withdrew.

Saint Ignatius.   Withdrew occurred.

Saint Ignatius.   Withdrew occurred.

Saint Ignatius occurred Saint Ignatius withdrew occurred withdrew.

Saint Sarah.   Having heard that they had gone she said how many eggs are there in it.

Saint Absalom.   Having heard that they are gone he said how many had said how many had been where they had never been with them or with it.

Saint Absalom.   Might be anointed.

Saint Therese.   With responsibility.

Saint Therese.   And an allowance.

Saint Settlement.   In might have a change from this.

Saint Chavez.   A winning.

Saint Cecile.   In plenty.

Saint Eustace.   Might it be mountains if it were not Barcelona.

Saint Plan.   With wisdom.

Saint Chavez.   In a minute.

Saint Therese.   And circumstances.

Saint Therese.   And as much.

Saint Chavez.   With them.

An interval.

Abundance.

An interval.

Saint Chavez.   In consideration of everything and that it is done by them as it must be left to them with this as an arrangement. Night and day cannot be different.

Saint Therese.   Completely forgetting.

Saint Therese.   I will try.

Saint Therese.   Theirs and by and by.

Saint Chavez.   With noon.

ACT III

With withdrawn.

How do you do.

Very well I thank you.

This is how young men and matter. How many nails are there in it.

Who can try.

There can be a little left behind.

Not at all.

As if they liked it very well to live alone.

With withdrawn.

What can they mean by well very well.

SCENE ONE

And seen one. Very likely.

Saint Therese.   It is not what is apprehended what is apprehended what is apprehended what is apprehended intended.

SCENE ONE

Saint Chavez.   At that time.

Saint Ignatius.   And all. Then and not. Might it so. Do and doubling with it at once left and right.

Saint Chavez.   Left left left right left with what is known.

Saint Chavez.   In time.

SCENE II

Saint Ignatius.   Within it within it within it as a wedding for them in half of the time.

Saint Ignatius.   Particularly.

Saint Ignatius.   Call it a day.

Saint Ignatius.   With a wide water with within with drawn.

Saint Ignatius.   As if a fourth class.

SCENE II

Pigeons on the grass alas.

Pigeons on the grass alas.

Short longer grass short longer longer shorter yellow grass. Pigeons large pigeons on the shorter longer yellow grass alas pigeons on the grass.

If they were not pigeons what were they.

If they were not pigeons on the grass alas what were they. He had heard of a third and he asked about it it was a magpie in the sky. If a magpie in the sky on the sky can not cry if the pigeon on the grass alas can alas and to pass the pigeon on the grass alas and the magpie in the sky on the sky and to try and to try alas on the grass alas the pigeon on the grass the pigeon on the grass and alas. They might be very well very well very well they might be they might be very well they might be very well very well they might be.

Let Lucy Lily Lily Lucy Lucy let Lucy Lucy Lily Lily Lily Lily Lily let Lily Lucy Lucy let Lily. Let Lucy Lily.

SCENE ONE

Saint Ignatius and please please please please.

SCENE ONE

One and one.

SCENE ONE

Might they be with they be with them might they be with them. Never to return to distinctions.

Might they be with them with they be with they be with them.

Saint Ignatius.   In line and in in line please say it first in line.

Saint Ignatius   When it is ordinarily thoughtful and
and   making it be when they were wishing
friends.   at one time insatiably and with re-
nounced where where ware and wear wear with them with them and where where will it be as long as long as they might with it with it individually removing left to it when it very well may well and crossed crossed in articulately minding what you do.

He asked for a distant magpie as if they made a difference.

He asked for a distant magpie as if he asked for a distant magpie as if that made a difference.

He asked as if that made a difference.

He asked for a distant magpie.

As if that made a difference he asked for a distant magpie as if that made a difference. He asked as if that made a difference. A distant magpie. He asked for a distant magpie. He asked for a distant magpie.

Saint Ignatius.   Might be admired for himself alone.

Saint Chavez.   Saint Ignatius might be admired for himself alone and because of that it might be as much as any one could desire.

Saint Chavez.   Because of that it might be as much as any one could desire.

Saint Chavez.   Because of that because it might be as much as any one could desire it might be that it could be done as easily as because it might very much as if precisely why they were carried.

Saint Ignatius.   Left when there was precious little to be asked by the ones who were overwhelmingly particular about what they were adding to themselves by means of their arrangements which might be why they went away and came again.

It is every once in a while very much what they pleased.

In a minute.

Saint Ignatius. In a minute by the time that it is graciously gratification and might it be with them to be with them to be with them to be to be windowed.

As seen as seen.

Saint Ignatius surrounded by them.

Saint Ignatius and one of two.

Saint Chavez might be with them at that time. All of them. Might be with them at that time.

All of them might be with them all of them at that time.

Might be with them at that time all of them might be with them at that time.

SCENE II

It is very easy to love alone. Too much too much. There are very sweetly very sweetly Henry very sweetly Rene very sweetly many very sweetly. They are very sweetly many very sweetly Rene very sweetly there are many very sweetly.

There is a difference between Barcelona and Avila. What difference.

SCENE

There is a difference between Barcelona and Avila.
There is a difference between Barcelona.

SCENE IV

And no more.

SCENE V

Saint Ignatius.   Left to left left to left left to left. Left right left left right left left to left.

When they do change to.

Saint Vincent.   Authority for it.

Saint Gallo.   By this clock o'clock. By this clock, by this clock by this clock o'clock.

Saint Ignatius.   Foundationally marvellously aboundingly illimitably with it as a circumstance. Fundamentally and saints fundamentally and saints and fundamentally and saints.

One Saint.   Whose has whose has whose has ordered needing white and green as much as orange and with grey and how much and as much and as much and as a circumstance.

Saint Therese.   Intending to be intending to intending to to to to. To do it for me.

Saint Ignatius.   Two and two.

SCENE V

Alive.

SCENE VI

With Seven.

SCENE VII

With eight.

SCENE VIII

Ordinary pigeons and trees.

If a generation all the same between forty and fifty as as. As they were and met. Was it tenderness and seem. Might it be as well as mean with in.

Ordinary pigeons and trees. This is a setting which is as soon which is as soon which is as soon ordinary setting which is as soon which is as soon and noon.

Saint Therese.   In face of in face of might make milk sung sung face to face face in face place in place of face to face. Milk sung.

Saint Ignatius.   Once in a while and where and where around around is a sound and around is a sound and around is a sound and around. Around is a sound around is a sound around is a sound and around. Around differing from anointed now. Now differing from anointed now. Now differing differing. Now differing from anointed now. Now when there is left and with it integrally with it integrally withstood within without with out with drawn and in as much as if it could be withstanding what in might might be so.

Many might be comfortabler. This is very well known now. When this you see remember me. It was very well known to every one.

Might and right very well to do. It is all colored by a straw straw laden.

Very nearly with it with it soon soon as said.

Having asked additionally theirs instead.

Once in a minute.

In a minute.

One two three as are are and are are are to be are with them are with them are with them with are with are with with it.

SCENE IX

Letting pin in letting let in let in in in in in let in let in
wet in wed in dead in dead wed led in led wed dead in dead
in led in wed in said in said led wed dead wed dead said led
led said wed dead wed dead led in led in wed in wed in said
in wed in led in said in dead in dead wed said led led said
wed dead in. That makes they have might kind find fined
when this arbitrarily makes it be what is it might they can it
fairly well to be added to in this at the time that they can
candied leaving as with with it by the left of it with with in
in the funniest in union.

Across across across coupled across crept a cross crept
crept crept crept across. They crept across.

If they are between thirty and thirty five and alive who
made them see Saturday.

Between thirty-five and forty-five between forty five and
three five as then when when they were forty-five and thirty
five when they they were forty five and thirty five when they
were then forty five and thirty five and thirty two and to
achieve leave relieve and receive their astonishment. Were
they to be left to do to do as well as they do mean I mean
I mean.

Left to their in their to their to be their to be there all their
to be there all their all their time to be there to be there all
their to be all their time there.

With wed led said with led dead said with dead led said
with said dead led wed said wed dead led dead led said wed.

With be there all their all their time there be there vine
there be vine time there be there time there all their time
there.

Let it be why if they were adding adding comes cunningly
to be additionally cunningly in the sense of attracting attracting in the sense of adding adding in the sense of windowing
and windowing and frames and pigeons and ordinary trees
and while while away.

ACT III

Did he did we did we and did he did he did he did did **he** did did did he did did he did be categorically and did he **did** he did he did he did he did he in interruption interruption interruptedly leave letting let it be be all to me to me out and outer and this and this with in indeed deed and drawn **and** drawn work.

Saint Ferdinand singing soulfully.

Singing singing is singing is singing is singing is singing between between singing is singing is between singing **is.**

Theirs and sign. Singing theirs and singing mine.

With a stand and would it be the same as yet awhile **and** glance a glance of be very nearly left to be alone.

One at at time makes two at a time makes one at **a time and** be there where where there there where where there.

Saint Ignatius. Might be why they were after all after **all** who came. One hundred and fifty one and a half and a half **and** after and after and after and all. With it all.

Saint Chavez. A ball might be less than one.

All together one and one.

ACT IV

How many acts are there in it. Acts are there in it.

Supposing a wheel had been added to three wheels **how many** acts how many how many acts are there in it

Any Saint at all.

How many acts are there in it.

How many saints in all.

How many acts are there in it.

Ring around a rosey.

How many acts are there in it.

Wedded and weeded.

Please be coming to see me.

When this you see you are all to me.

Me which is you you who are true true to be you.

How many how many saints are there in it.

One two three all out but me.

One two three four all out but four.

How many saints are there in it.

How many saints are there in it.

One two three four and there is no door. Or more. Or more.
Or door. Or floor or door. One two three all out but me. How
many saints are there in it.

Saints and see all out but me.

How many saints are there in it.

How many saints are there in it. One two three four all out
but four one two three four four four or four or more.

More or four.

How many Acts are there in it.

Four Acts.

Act four.

Encouraged by this then when they might be by thirds
words eglantine and by this to mean feeling it as most when
they do too to be nearly lost to sight in time in time and mind
mind it for them. Let us come to this brink.

The sisters and saints assembling and reenacting why they
went away to stay.

One at a time regularly regularly by the time that they are
in and and in one at at time regularly very fairly better than
they came as they came there and where where will they be
wishing to stay here here where they are they are here here
where they are they are they are here.

Saint Chavez.   The envelopes are on all the fruit of the
fruit trees.

SCENE II

Saint Chavez.   Remembered as knew.

Saint Ignatius.   Meant to send, and meant to send and
meant meant to differ between send and went and end and
mend and very nearly one to two.

Saint Cecile.   With this and now.

Saint Plan.   Made it with with in with withdrawn.

SCENE III

Let all act as if they went away.

SCENE IV

Saint Philip.   With them and still.

Saint Cecile.   They will they will.

Saint Therese.   Begin to trace begin to race begin to place begin and in in that that is why this is what is left as may may follows June and June follows moon and moon follows soon and it is very nearly ended with bread.

Saint Chavez.   Who can think that they can leave it here to me.

When this you see remember me.

They have to be.

They have to be.

They have to be to see.

To see to say.

Laterally they may.

SCENE V

Who makes who makes it do.

Saint Therese and Saint Therese too.

Who does and who does care.

Saint Chavez to care.

Saint Chavez to care.

Who may be what is it when it is instead.

Saint Plan Saint Plan to may to say to say two may and inclined.

Who makes it be what they had as porcelain.

Saint Ignatius and left and right laterally be lined.

All Saints.

    To Saints.

Four Saints.

    And Saints.

Five Saints.

    To Saints.

Last Act.

Which is a fact.

THE WINNER LOSES

A PICTURE OF
OCCUPIED FRANCE

This paper was originally published in the ATLANTIC MONTHLY, *November, 1940. In* EVERYBODY'S AUTOBIOGRAPHY, *Gertrude Stein wrote: "It was very exciting selling* THE AUTOBIOGRAPHY OF ALICE B. TOKLAS *as I had said I always wanted two things to happen to be printed in the* ATLANTIC MONTHLY *and in the* SATURDAY EVENING POST. . . . *I do wish Mildred Aldrich had lived to see it, she would have liked it, for they did print it, but after all I do want them to print something else to prove it was not only that they wanted." Miss Stein lived to see the fulfillment of her wishes. The* ATLANTIC *published* BUTTER WILL MELT *in February, 1937,* YOUR UNITED STATES *in October, 1937, and* THE WINNER LOSES *in November, 1940. Her wish about the* SATURDAY EVENING POST *was realized too.*

We were spending the afternoon with our friends, Madame Pierlot and the d'Aiguys, in September '39 when France declared war on Germany—England had done it first. They all were upset but hopeful, but I was terribly frightened; I had been so sure there was not going to be war and here it was, it was war, and I made quite a scene. I said, 'They shouldn't! They shouldn't!' and they were very sweet, and I apologized and said I was sorry but it was awful, and they comforted me—they, the French, who had so much at stake, and I had nothing at stake comparatively.

Well, that was a Sunday.

And then there was another Sunday and we were at Béon again that Sunday, and Russia came into the war and Poland was smashed, and I did not care about Poland, but it did frighten me about France—oh dear, that was another Sunday.

And then we settled down to a really wonderful winter.

We did not know that we were going to stay all winter. There is no way of heating this stone house except by open fires, and we are in the mountains, there is a great deal of snow, and it is cold; but gradually we stayed. We had some coal, enough for the kitchen stove, and one grate fire that we more or less kept burning day and night, and there is always plenty of wood here as we are in wooded mountains, so gradually we stayed the winter. The only break was a forty-eight-hour run to Paris to get our winter clothing and arrange our affairs and then we were back for the winter.

Those few hours in Paris made us realize that the country is a better place in war than a city. They grow the things to eat right where you are, so there is no privation, as taking it away is difficult, particularly in the mountains, so there was plenty of meat and potatoes and bread and honey and we had some sugar and we even had all the oranges and lemons we needed and dates; a little short of gasoline for the car, but we learned to do what we wanted with that little, so we settled down to a comfortable and pleasantly exciting winter.

I had not spent a winter in the country, in the real country, since my childhood in California and I did enjoy it; there was snow, and moonlight, and I had to saw wood. There was plenty of wood to be had, but no men to saw it; and every day Basket II, our new poodle, and I took long walks. We took them by day and we took them in the evening, and as I used to wander around the country in the dark—because of course we had the blackout and there was no light anywhere, and the soldiers at the front were indulging in a kind of red Indian warfare all that winter—I used to wonder how anybody could get near without being seen, because I did get to be able to see every bit of the road and the fields beside them, no matter how dark it was.

There were a number of people all around spending the winter unexpectedly in the country, so we had plenty of society and we talked about the war, but not too much, and we had hired a radio wireless and we listened to it, but not too much, and the winter was all too soon over.

I had plenty of detective and adventure stories to read, Aix and Chambéry had them left over, and I bought a quantity every week, and there was an English family living near Yenne and they had books too, and we supplied each other.

One of the books they had I called the Bible; it was an astrological book called *The Last Year of War*, written by one Leonardo Blake. I burnt my copy the day of the signing of the armistice, but it certainly had been an enormous comfort to us all in between.

And so gradually spring came, a nice early spring, and all the men in the village had leave for agriculture and they all came home for a month, and nobody was very uneasy and nobody talked about the war, but nobody seemed to think that anything was going to happen. We all dug in our gardens and in the fields all day and every day, and March and April wore away.

There were slight political disturbances and a little wave of uneasiness, and Paul Reynaud, as the village said, began to say that there were not to be any more Sundays. The post-office clerks were the first to have their Sundays taken away. The village said it as a joke, 'Paul Reynaud says that there are not to be any more Sundays.' As country people work Sundays anyway when there is work, they said it as a joke to the children and the young boys, 'Paul Reynaud says that there are not to be any Sundays any more.' By that time all the men who had had an agricultural leave were gone again, and April was nearly over.

The book of astrological predictions had predicted all these things, so we were all very well satisfied.

Beside these astrological predictions there were others, and the ones they talked about most in the country were the predictions of the curé d'Ars. Ars is in this department of the Ain, and the curé, who died about eighty years ago, became a saint; and he had predicted that this year there would be a war and the women would have to sow the grain alone, but that the war would be over in time for the men to get in the harvest; and so when Alice Toklas sometimes worried about how hot it would be all summer with the shutters closed all the evening I said, 'Do not worry, the war will be over before then; they cannot all be wrong.'

So the month of March and April went on. We dug in the garden, we had a lot of soldiers in Belley, the 13th Chasseurs and the Foreign Legion being fitted out for Norway; and then Sammy Stewart sent us an American Mixmaster at Easter and that helped make the cakes which were being made then for the soldiers and everybody, and so the time went on. Then it was more troublesome, the government changed—the book of prophecy said it would, so that was all right—and the soldiers left for Norway; and then our servant and friend Madame Roux had her only son, who was a soldier, of course, dying of meningitis at Annecy, and we forgot everything for two weeks in her trouble and then we woke up to there being a certain uneasiness.

The book of prophecy said that the month of May was the beginning of the end of the Nazis, and it gave the dates. They were all Tuesdays—well, anyway they were mostly Tuesdays—and they were going to be bad days for the Nazis, and I read the book every night in bed and everybody telephoned to ask what the book said and what the dates were, and the month began.

The dates the book gave were absolutely the dates the things happened.

The first was the German attack on the new moon, the seventh, and that was a Tuesday.

Tuesdays had begun.

Everybody was quiet; one of the farmers' wives—the richest of the farmers and our town councilor—was the only one who said anything. She always said, 'Ils avancent toujours, ces coquins-là.' 'The rascals are always coming on,' she said.

There was nothing else to say and nobody said it, and then the Germans took Sedan.

That gave us all so bad a turn that nobody said anything; they just said how do you do, and talked about the weather, and that was all—there was nothing to say.

I had been in Paris as a child of five at school, and that was only ten years after the Franco-Prussian War and the debacle which began with Sedan, and when we children swung on the chains around the Arc de Triomphe we were told that the chains were there so that no one could pass under it because the Germans had, and so the name Sedan was as terrible to me as it was to all the people around us and nobody said anything. The French are very conversational and they are always polite, but when there is really nothing to say they do not say anything. And there was nothing to say.

The next thing was that General Weygand was appointed the head of the army and he said if they could hold out a month it would be all right. Nobody said anything. Nobody mentioned Gamelin's name—nobody.

I once said to a farmer that Gamelin's nose was too short to make a good general, in France you have to have a real nose, and he laughed; there was no secrecy about anything, but there was nothing to say.

We had the habit of going to Chambéry to do our shopping once a week; we always went on Tuesdays because that suited best in every way, and so it was Tuesday, and nobody was very cheerful. We had a drink in a café, Vichy for me and pineapple juice for Alice Toklas, and we heard the radio going. 'What's the news?' we asked mechanically. 'Amiens has fallen,' said the girl.

'Let's not believe it,' I said; 'you know they never hear it straight.' So we went to the news bulletin, and there it was not written up, and we said to the girl in charge, 'You know, they are putting out false news in the town; they told us Amiens was taken.' 'No,' she said, 'but I will go and ask.' She came back; she said, 'Yes, it is true.'

We did not continue shopping, we just hurried home.

And then began the series of Tuesdays in which Paul Reynaud in a tragic voice told that he had something grave to announce.

That was that Tuesday.

And the next Tuesday was the treason of the Belgian king.

And he always announced it the same way, and always in the same voice.

I have never listened to the radio since.

It was so awful that it became funny.

Well, not funny, but they did all want to know if next Tuesday Paul Reynaud would have something grave to announce.

And he did.

'Oh dear, what a month of May!' I can just hear Paul Reynaud's voice saying that.

Madame Pierlot's little granddaughter said not to worry, it was the month of the Virgin, and nothing begun in the month of Virgin could end badly; and the book of prophecy had predicted every date, but exactly. I used to read it every night; there was no mistake, but he said each one of these days was a step on in the destruction of the Third Reich, and here we were: I still believed, but here we were, one Tuesday after another; the dates were right, but oh dear!

Of course, as they were steadily advancing, the question of parachutists and bombing became more active. We had all gotten careless about lights, and wandering about, but now we were strict about lights, and we stayed at home.

II

I had begun the beginning of May to write a book for children, a book of alphabets with stories for each letter, and a book of birthdays—each story had to have a birthday in it—and I did get so that I could not think about the war but just about the stories I was making up for this book. I would walk in the daytime and make up stories, and I walked up and down on the terrace in the evening and made up stories, and I went to sleep making up stories, and I pretty well did succeed in keeping my mind off the war except for the three times a day when there was the French communiqué, and that always gave me a sinking feeling in my stomach, and though I slept well every morning I woke up with that funny feeling in my stomach.

The farmers who were left were formed into a guard to wander about at night with their shotguns to shoot parachutists if they came. Our local policeman, the policeman of Belley, lives in Bilignin, and he had an up-to-date anti-parachutist's gun. He did not look very martial and I said to him, 'What are you going to do with it?' and he said, 'I—I am not afraid.' Well, Frenchmen are never afraid, but they do like peace and their regular daily life. So now nobody talked about the war; there was nothing to say about that. They talked about parachutists and Italy and that was natural enough—we are right here in a corner made by Italy and Switzerland.

The women did say, 'They are advancing all the time, the rascals,' but the men said nothing. They were not even sad; they just said nothing.

And so that month was almost over; and then one day, it was a Sunday, I was out walking with Basket just before lunch, and as I came up the hill Emil Rosset and the very lively servant they had, who had been with them for twenty-five years and had had a decoration and reward by the government for faithful service on a farm, and who in spite of all that is very young and lively, were standing pointing and said, 'Mademoiselle! Mademoiselle! Did you see them?' 'What?' I said. 'The airplanes—the enemy airplanes! There they go, just behind the cloud!'

Well, I just did not see them; they had gone behind the clouds.

There were eight, they told me, and were flying very feebly.

We have a range of hills right in front of the terrace; on the other side of these hills is the Rhone, and that is where they had come from.

Of course we were all really excited; enemy airplanes in a city are depressing, but in the open country, with wooded hills all around, they are exciting.

We have several very religious families in Bilignin and one with four girls and a boy, and they all go into Belley to Mass, and Madame Tavel said to me, 'I knew it'—it was her day to stay home with the animals—'I knew it: they always come on Sunday and burn the church.' She had been a young girl in French Lorraine in the last war and met her husband there, who had been a prisoner.

'But,' she said, 'of course we have to go to Mass just the same.'

It was she who later on said to her little girl, who was to go out into the fields with the cows and who was crying, Madame Tavel said, 'Yes, my little one, you are right to cry. Weep. But, little one, the cows have to go, and you with them all the same. *Tu as raison, pleures, ma petite.*'

We went over to Culoz, which is about twelve kilometres away, to see our friends and to hear the news. Culoz is the big railroad station in this part of the world where trains are made up for various directions, and there they had dropped bombs. All the veterans of Culoz turned out to see the bombs drop and they were disappointed in them; they found them to be bombs of decidedly *deuxième catégorie,* very second-rate indeed.

It was the only time we had bombs really anywhere near us, and one of the German airplanes was brought down near a friend's house not far away and a country boy seventeen years old brought in the aviators, and it was a pleasant interlude, and we could all talk again and we had something to talk about and the veterans all were very pleased for the first time in this war; one of our friends remarked that it really was a *fête pour les anciens combattants*.

The war was coming nearer. The mayor of Belley came to Bilignin to tell the mothers that two of their sons were killed.

It was sad; they were each one the only sons of widows who had lost their husbands in the last war, and they were the only ones, now the war is over we know, who were killed anywhere in this countryside.

They were both hard-working quiet fellows twenty-six years old, and had gone to school together and worked together and one of them had just changed his company so as to be near the other, and now one bomb at the front had killed them both.

That month was over and June was commencing.

I had finished the child's book and had settled down to cutting the box hedges. We have what they call a *jardin de curé*, with lots of box hedges and little paths and one tall box pillar, and I found that cutting box hedges was almost as soothing as sawing wood. I walked a great deal and I cut box hedges, and every night I read the book of prophecy and went promptly to sleep.

And none of us talked about the war because there was nothing to say.

The book of prophecy once more gave the significant days for June and they were absolutely the days that the crucial events happened, only they were not the defeat of Germany but the downfall of France.

It made me feel very Shakespearean—the witches' prophecy in *Macbeth* about the woods marching and Julius Cæsar and the Ides of March; the twentieth century was just like that and like nothing else.

And then Italy came into the war and then I was scared, completely scared, and my stomach felt very weak, because

—well, here we were right in everybody's path; any enemy that wanted to go anywhere might easily come here. I was frightened; I woke up completely upset. And I said to Alice Toklas, 'Let's go away.' We went into Belley first and there were quantities of cars passing, people getting away from Besançon, both of us and all the Belleysiens standing and looking on; and I went to the garage to have my car put in order and there were quantities of cars getting ready to leave, and we had our papers prepared to go to Bordeaux and we telephoned to the American consul in Lyon and he said, 'I'll fix up your passports. Do not hesitate—leave.'

And then we began to tell Madame Roux that we could not take Basket with us and she would have to take care of him, but not to sacrifice herself to him; and she was all upset and she said she wished we were away in safety but that we would not leave, and she said the village was upset and so were we, and we went to bed intending to leave the next morning.

I read the book of predictions and went to sleep.

The next morning I said, 'Well, instead of deciding let us go to see the *préfet* at Bourg and the American consul at Lyon.'

We went; it was a lovely day, the drive from Bourg to Lyon was heavenly. They all said, 'Leave,' and I said to Alice Toklas, 'Well, I don't know—it would be awfully uncomfortable and I am fussy about my food. Let's not leave.' So we came back, and the village was happy and we were happy and that was all right, and I said I would not hear any more news—Alice Toklas could listen to the wireless, but as for me I was going to cut box hedges and forget the war.

Well, two days after when I woke up, Alice Toklas said sooner or later we would have to go.

I did not have much enthusiasm for leaving and we had not had our passports visaed for Spain, and the American consul had told us we could, so I said, 'Let's compromise and go to Lyon again.'

The car's tire was down and Madame Roux said, 'You see, even the car does not want to leave.'

Just then Balthus and his wife came along; they had come

down from Paris, sleeping two days in their little car, and they were going to their summer home in Savoy and after, if necessary, to Switzerland, Madame Balthus being Swiss. Well, anyway we went to Lyon.

On the way back we were stopped every few minutes by the military; they were preparing to blow up bridges and were placing anti-aircraft guns and it all seemed very near and less than ever did I want to go on the road.

And at the same time when Alice Toklas would say about some place on the road, 'Look, what a lovely house that is!' I said, 'I do not want to look at it—it is all going to be destroyed.'

So just before we got to Belley, at a little village near a little lake, there were Doctor and Madame Chaboux.

'What,' said we, stopping, 'are you doing here?'

'We are paying for our year's fishing rights,' they said, 'and you?' said they. 'Well,' said we, 'we are trying to make up our minds what to do, go or stay.'

'Now,' said I, 'tell me, Doctor Chaboux, what shall I do?'

'Well, we stay,' said they. 'Yes,' said I, 'but a doctor is like a soldier—he has to stay.'

'Yes,' said they.

'But now how about us? Should we or should we not?'

'Well,' said Doctor Chaboux, reflecting, 'I can't guarantee you anything, but my advice is stay. I had friends,' he said, 'who in the last war stayed in their homes all through the German occupation, and they saved their homes and those who left lost theirs. No,' he said, 'I think unless your house is actually destroyed by a bombardment, I always think the best thing to do is to stay.' He went on, 'Everybody knows you here; everybody likes you; we all would help you in every way. Why risk yourself among strangers?'

'Thank you,' we said, 'that is all we need. We stay.'

So back we came and we unpacked our spare gasoline and our bags and we said to Madame Roux, 'Here we are and here we stay.'

And I went out for a walk and I said to one of the farmers, 'We are staying.'

'*Vous faites bien,*' he said, '*mademoiselle*. We all said,

"Why should these ladies leave? In this quiet corner they are as safe as anywhere," and we have cows and milk and chickens and flour and we can all live and we know you will help us out in any way you can and we will do the same for you. Here in this little corner we are *en famille*, and if you left, to go where?—*aller, où?*'

And they all said to me, '*Aller, où?*' and I said, 'You are right—*aller, où?*'

We stayed, and dear me, I would have hated to have left.

III

The Kiddie has just written me a letter from America and he says in it, 'We have been wondering what the end of war in France will mean for you, whether you could endure staying there or the exact opposite, whether you could endure not staying there.

So I said to Alice Toklas, 'I am cutting the hedges, even the very tall one on a ladder, and I am not reading the prediction book any more, and I am walking and I am not knowing what the news is,' and Alice Toklas began making raspberry jam—it was a wonderful raspberry year—and the long slow days passed away.

They did not really pass.

One day I said to her, 'Ten days ago when we were in Lyon,' and she said, 'Nonsense, it was three days ago.' Well, it seemed like ten, but the days all the same did pass one day at a time.

In the afternoons Basket and I always walked.

We walked in the country roads and every now and then a little girl would appear through the bushes; she was sitting with the cows and knitting, but when she heard us she came to the road. They are often blue-eyed, the little girls, as we are in the hills, and hills seem to make people's eyes blue, and she would say, 'How do you do, Mademoiselle? *Vous êtes en promenade*—you are out for a walk,' and I would say, 'Yes, it is a nice day,' and she would say, 'Yes,' and I would say, 'And you are alone,' and she would say, 'Yes, my mother was here, but she went home—perhaps she will come again.' and then she would say, 'And have you heard the airplanes?' and

I would say, 'No, have you?' and she would say, 'Oh yes,' and I would say, 'Were they German or French?' and she would say, 'I do not know,' and I would say 'Perhaps they are French,' and she would say, 'Perhaps,' and then I would say good-bye and she would say good-bye and disappear back through the bushes into the field, and it was always the same conversation and it was a comfort to us both, to each little girl and to me.

We went to Belley to buy food and the rest of the time I cut box hedges and Alice Toklas went on making raspberry jam; we had lots of raspberries; and as I did not listen to any news any more it was heavy but peaceful.

Then came the next Sunday.

I went out for a walk in the morning and stopped to talk with one of the farmers, Monsieur Tavel. 'Well,' said he, 'the battle of Lyon has commenced.' 'What?' said I. 'Are they at Lyon?' From then on they were always spoken of as 'they'; they did not have any other name. 'Yes,' he said, 'but it is all right; there are lots of soldiers there and it is all right.' 'But why is it all right?' I said. 'Well,' he said, 'because there is an old prophecy which says that the day will come when France will be betrayed by a Catholic king, not her own king but another king—that another king will be crazy, and that all the Paris region will be occupied by the enemy and, in front of Lyon, France will be saved by a very old man on a white horse.

'Well,' he said, 'the king of the Belgians was a Catholic king and he betrayed us, the king of Italy has gone mad, and the Maréchal Pétain is a very old man and he always rides a white horse. So it is all right,' said Monsieur Tavel.

Well, Lyon was awfully near and if there was going to be a great battle—well, anyway it was a bright sunny day, and I came back and I was tired and so I took out my deck chair and sat in the sun on the terrace and I went sound asleep. Then there was a half-past-twelve communiqué and I woke up just to hear that the Maréchal Pétain had asked for an armistice.

Well, then he had saved France and everything was over. But it wasn't, not at all—it was just beginning for us.

The village did not know what to say and nobody said anything; they just sighed; it was all very quiet.

We thought we could keep the shutters open and light the light, but they said no, not yet, the armistice was not signed and they, the Germans, might be anywhere.

The boys between sixteen and twenty—we have five of them in the village—were frightened lest they should be taken into the German army; they went to Belley to try to enlist in the French army, but naturally that could not be done. They came back with tears in their eyes and nervous. The peasants could not work—nobody did anything for a day or two. And then news commenced again; the man who bought the milk of Bilignin had met somebody who had seen the Germans and they had been quite kind—had given them gasoline for their car. They had been stuck somewhere without gasoline because, as the Germans advanced, the order had come that the gasoline should be poured away. Some did it and some did not. Belley is very law-abiding and so all the people who sold gasoline did.

The man who had the milk route which included Bilignin told them he would not come for the milk any more, nor would he pay them, but they could have three of his pigs. They had no way of getting them, so they asked me and I supplied the means of locomotion, and we brought back three pigs and somebody from Belley came out and butchered them and they gave us a beautiful big roast of pork, and with that and a ham we had bought and what there was to eat in the village we were very well fixed.

Everybody was getting more and more nervous and on Tuesday we went in to Belley; there was no armistice yet, but we thought we might get some soap and other things we needed.

We were in the biggest store in Belley, a sort of a bazaar, when all of a sudden the proprietor called out, 'Go to the back of the shop!' Well, naturally we didn't, and we heard a rumbling noise and there two enemy machine-gun tanks came rushing through the street, with the German cross painted on them.

Oh my, it did make us feel most uncommonly queer. 'Let's

go home,' we said, and we did not do any more shopping; we went back to Bilignin.

And there we waited.

The boys between seventeen and twenty went up into the hills; they were badly frightened and excited. Their parents did not say anything. They had each taken with them their bicycles and a large loaf of bread. Naturally that did not last long and in two days they were back again. One of them, a boy named Roger, who was working for a farmer, was so frightened he ate nothing for three days and turned green with fright. He had two brothers in the French army—that was all right, but to be a German soldier! We all tried to cheer him up, but he sat in the corner and couldn't move.

The only news we had about Belley or about anything, because the electricity and the post office were cut off, was by way of the policeman of Belley, who lives in Bilignin. He had to go back to sleep in Belley, but he always managed to get out once during the day to see his mother and give us the news—yes, the Germans were there in Belley; yes, so far they had behaved very correctly; no, nobody knew anything about the armistice.

I remember the last newspaper the postman brought to us. I went out and said, 'It is nice to see you.' 'I wish,' said he, 'that I could bring you better news, and I do not think I will come again,' and he did not, not for more than three weeks.

Basket and I had begun to walk again, the cows and the children began to go out again, and then we began to hear cannon.

Every day we heard the cannon; it seemed to be all around us, which, as it turned out, it was and in some strange way we all cheered up at the sound of the cannonade.

We all began to talk about hearing the cannon, we all began to try to locate the direction of the cannon; some of the *anciens combattants* thought it came from the Alps, others thought it came from right near by, and then one evening I smelt the brimstone, and the color of the earth in the setting sun was a very strange yellow green and there were clouds, strange clouds, the kind of clouds I had never seen before, thick yellow-green clouds rolling past the hills, and it reminded me of pictures of the Civil War, the battle of Lookout Mountain and that kind of thing—it looked like it and it smelled like it, and in a strange way it was comforting.

The policeman in his daily visit home told us that it was cannon and that it was all around us; the French had blown up the bridges of the Rhone all around us, some only about four kilometres away, and in all the places we knew so well there were machine guns and cannon and fighting and quantities of Germans; armored cars were going through Belley, and in all the villages around there were Germans and some motorcycle Germans came through our village.

And then came another bad Sunday; some of the children went in to Mass and came back with an exciting story that everybody that had any gasoline in their possession was going to be shot. Well, I had some extra gasoline besides what was in my car and I did not want to be shot. So, very nervous, I rushed off to the farmer, our neighbor, who is one of the municipal councilors of Belley, and asked what I should do. 'Do nothing,' he said; 'unless they put up a notice here in Bilignin you do not need to do anything. Besides,' said he, 'I am going to Belley to find out all about it.' And he came back and told us that what had happened was that Belley had gotten rid of all its gasoline and a German company had come along and they had had an accident and lost their gasoline tank, and they had asked at a garage for gasoline. Monsieur Barlet, our very gentle garage keeper, had said that he had none, and the Germans had not believed him and said they would shoot him if he did not produce it, and the mayor, who is also a gentle soul, but efficient, said he would put up a notice and have the town crier announce what was happening, and everybody who had any gasoline would bring it, and everybody in Belley did, and very soon the Germans had more than they needed and everybody went home with their gasoline and Monsieur Barlet was not shot. But he was and is our local hero, and he was quite pale for some days after and we all thanked him for not being shot, and he always carries around in his pocketbook the order that was posted that saved him from being shot.

That was absolutely the only unpleasant incident that happened in Belley, and that was on the Sunday when the Germans were very nervous; they were held up at the Rhone, and as the Rhone makes many bends, and the Chasseurs Alpins were fighting hard there, they thought they were caught in a trap.

IV

Well, then came Tuesday and Wednesday, and the rain poured and poured and the notice of the signing of the armistice was signed by the mayor of Belley and the German Colonel in command there, and posted up in Bilignin. I will never forget that day. It was about noon, and Basket and I went out for a walk and there in the pouring rain sadly were the five young boys of Bilignin leaning on their sticks with which they lead their oxen; they were in the middle of the road and desperate.

Nobody else was around except one farmer's wife and she said to me, 'Well, I suppose we will go on working even if we are no longer masters in our own home.'

The next day was a little better. It had stopped raining and the terms of the armistice were broadcast; we once more had electricity and we knew our little corner was not going to be occupied territory, neither the Bugey nor Lyon, and we gave a sigh of relief. Monsieur Premilieu said to me, 'Of course we are going to have bad days, many bad days, but it is better to bear them indirectly than directly.' The boys cheered up and began to eat, and we went in to Belley to shop and, well, in short to begin to move about; and besides —happy moment—we could leave our lights burning at night and the windows and the shutters open.

Even now, a good month after it is finished, every night when I go out walking and see all the lights shining I know the difference, and I cannot help feeling sorry, particularly for the English, but even a little for the Germans who are there in the dark and afraid of bombardment.

Cannonading is not agreeable, but it is bearable, but bombing from above, and not very far above, is mighty unpleasant.

The soldiers and civilians are all agreed about that.

So we went in to Belley and there they were.

All the time they were here they were not spoken of as anything except they, *eux*.

It was impossible, but there they were, and we were seeing them.

Belley is a town of about five thousand inhabitants, a small town but important, as it is the capital of a rich country, has a hospital, a seminary, many schools, a county court, a *sous-préfecture*, and a garrison.

There are also a good many convents, and so, although the population is not large it has a number of very large buildings and feels like a small capital. It was also just about the centre of all the recent fighting, and so the Germans had made it the headquarters for all the troops in this part of the country.

So when we went in to Belley—we are about a mile out of Belley, on a small country road—we saw them, quantities of soldiers in gray uniforms, trucks, motorcycles, armored cars. We could not believe our eyes, but there they were.

It was not real, but there they were; it looked like photographs in a magazine, but there they were.

I sat in the car and waited while Alice Toklas shopped and then she sat in the car and waited while I went to see Madame Chaboux and shopped. We always stayed, one of us, in the car because of the dogs and the car—even though the Germans were very polite and very correct. That is what everybody was saying. 'They are correct.'

It was strange sitting there watching the people up and down on the main street of Belley, like all country towns; there are always a good many people going up and down on the main street of a country town, and now added to it were these familiar and unfamiliar German soldiers, familiar because we had seen their photographs in illustrated papers all winter and unfamiliar because we never dreamed we would see them with our own eyes.

They did not look like conquerors; they were very quiet. They bought a great deal, all sugar things, cakes and candies, all silk stockings, women's shoes, beauty products and fancy soaps, but always everlastingly what the American soldiers in the last war called 'eats'—that is, anything sweet—and anything that looked like champagne.

They went up and down, but they were gentle, slightly sad, polite; and their voices when they spoke—they did not seem to talk much—were low, not at all resonant.

Everything about them was exactly like the photographs we had seen except themselves; they were not the least bit like we thought they would be. They admired Basket II and said to each other in German, 'A beautiful dog.' They were polite and considerate; they were, as the French said, correct. It was all very sad; they were sad, the French were sad, it was all sad, but not at all the way we thought it would be, not at all.

The French, the girls and boys and the older men and older women, who also went up and down about their own affairs, had that *retenue* that is French—they neither noticed nor ignored the Germans. In all the three weeks that the Germans were in Belley there was no incident of any kind.

When the Germans left, in Belley, in Yenne, in Lyon, and I imagine everywhere else in France, they thanked the mayors and congratulated them upon the extraordinary discipline of their populations. The Germans called it discipline, but it was not—it was the state of being civilized that the French call *retenue*. It was all not at all what we had feared and expected, and it all was very wonderful and very sad.

The days went on; everybody began to work in the fields, nobody had anything to say, and everybody was waiting, waiting for the Germans to go away—'they.'

Everybody, when I went out walking and they were with the cows, would ask a little anxiously, 'Is it eight o'clock yet?' Everybody was supposed to be at home and with the shutters closed by eight o'clock. We went into Belley quite often and it was always just that, neither more nor less than just that.

And then finally one day we went in and as we turned into the main road they whistled. We did not suppose it had anything to do with us and in a way it did not, except that nobody was supposed to be on the main roads for two days because they were leaving, and the roads were to be kept open for them. We had not stopped when they whistled, but they did not bother us; they did not, one might say, bother anyone.

And then miles and miles of them went away and they were gone.

Everybody breathed again.

Everybody began to talk again, not about anything in particular, but they all just began to talk again.

The post office was open again and everybody began to worry about everybody's husband and brother and father and nephew and son, everybody, and nobody had heard anything for so long.

Slowly they began to hear; some did not hear for a very long time, but more or less they all began to hear and they all began to write all the soldiers about coming home, and they said they were coming home and they did come home.

Gradually everybody began to realize that very few Frenchmen were dead; a great many were prisoners, but very few were dead; and a great load was lifted off France. It was not like the last war, when all the men were dead or badly wounded; practically nobody was wounded and very few were dead. Everybody forgot about being defeated, it was such a relief that their men were not dead.

The Germans had said that when they were here; they said lots and lots of Germans had been killed and very, very few French.

Later on I asked the returned French soldiers how they had succeeded in killing so many Germans and not any of them being killed themselves. They explained that there was terrific aerial bombardment, but that all the soldiers had to do was to lie down and the bombs exploded before they were hit. They said that the bombs were made to explode on buildings, not in the ground, and so civilians in a city like Auxerre were killed, but as the soldiers were in the open country they were not killed. Then, while the air bombardment was going on, the tanks broke through the French line, and opened out in a fan behind the French line; the German infantry, being in serried formation behind the tanks, were shot down and so a lot of them were killed, but as there were so many of them they finally exhausted the capacity of the French to kill them and they came through too, and so the French were made prisoners except a great many who made off into the fields and, walking twenty-five kilometers a day or finding a stray bicycle, got home.

Georges Rosset made it all very clear, his only regret was that he had lost all his accoutrement and particularly a very nice pair of socks that Alice Toklas had knitted for him out of very lovely wool. He wrote all about that before he managed to get home, but Alice Toklas said to his mother to write that she would immediately start another pair and anyway he would have a chocolate cake when he came home, and she did make a chocolate cake for him when he did come home, and he is home. They all are. The curé d'Ars had said that the women would plant the grain and the men would harvest it and here they were—they are harvesting it, and it is all harvested.

He also said that when everything was at its worst, then it would turn out to be at its best.

v

It is very true that all the old predictions are that there will be a complete disaster; one said that the cock would completely lose its feathers and that afterwards its feathers would be more beautiful than ever. The French do naturally not like that life is too easy, they like, like the phœnix, to rise from the ashes. They really do believe that those that win lose.

In the meantime the government of France had changed, but that did not worry anyone.

It was natural that, since the Third Republic had not defended them from their enemies, it would end.

As I said in *Paris France*, to the French a government is something outside which does not concern them; its business is policing, defending them from their enemies; it is to be hoped that it will not cost too much, and naturally it leaves every one to lead their own French life.

And so naturally the government had changed, but their life was to go on all the same.

Everybody was happy, because their men were alive and a good many of them had come home. There were a great many difficulties, mostly concerning themselves with the question of gasoline and the question of butter.

These were the two things that bothered everybody the most.

French farmers need bread, wine, vegetables, and butter. Meat is a luxury, not a necessity, to be eaten when had, but never thought about in between; sugar and coffee a half luxury—you can do without but you miss it; but bread and wine and vegetables and butter you must have.

There was no lack of bread, wine, and vegetable; there was a moment of hesitation about bread, but the harvest was excellent, and there was no real lack; vegetables and wine are always there, and suddenly there was a question of butter. Whether it was because the Germans made such a fuss about butter that made the French think that butter could be a luxury or what I do not know, but suddenly butter became, as everybody said, *une chose rare*.

It was a puzzle—there were the same number of cows and so there was as much milk, but where was the butter?

Of course there was the trouble about gasoline. There being no gasoline, the milkmen could not make their rounds, but even so, what with bicycles and horses, milk was gathered in. But the butter?

There was a wild flurry about butter. The most sober of the farmers' wives were fussed. Their milk was under contract to go to the dairies, and the dairy would not give them butter. Nobody in France talked about anything but butter. Well, one way or another, one did get enough butter to cook with and to eat; but everybody went somewhere else to get it and it was purchased silently; it was a whole history of intrigue and it did a great deal to make everybody forget about war and about government, and then all of a sudden everybody had butter and that was over.

Everybody breathed again; everybody could have bread, butter, wine, and vegetables, and so they forgot their troubles.

They settled down to get in their harvest. Just tonight one of the wagons, with its oxen, was coming in very late at night, about ten o'clock, loaded with wheat, and I said, 'It is late. Is the harvest all in?' 'Yes,' they said, 'yes. There is our bread.' It did not look like bread yet; it looked more like straw—but it was bread.

The only trouble left was the question of gasoline and that is still a trouble, and very complicated.

Of course there is none in France and they are trying to substitute for it charcoal, and that does very well for trucks, but it does not do for small cars, and how will there be any gasoline if the English keep blowing it up and besides not letting it pass?

The only way at present is not to use any, and to gather in what there is. Well, that seems to work all right, only it stopped all business, and so from time to time a day was given in which everybody who had any gasoline could go out. You could not buy any, but you could go out. And just now, the eighth of August, everybody says that everybody who has any gasoline can go about. 'But,' said I to Madeleine Rops, 'it did not say so in the paper.' 'Ah, my dear,' said Madeleine, 'after all you do not yet understand French logic. Nobody was allowed to *rouler*, and then all of a sudden they announced that after the twenty-fifth of August nobody is allowed to *rouler*. So, *ma chère*, that means that now everybody can *rouler*, otherwise why should they say that after the twenty-fifth it will all be *contrôlé? C'est simple*,' said Madeleine Rops. So we got out the car and went shopping into Belley, most exciting; it used to be a bit of a bore to have to go shopping into Belley, but now, as it can only be done unexpectedly, it is most exciting.

And so everybody is very busy accommodating themselves to everything, and I must say the French are really happy in combining and contriving and intriguing and succeeding, and above all in saving. This evening, in going out walking, I met the town's people bringing in as much wood as they could carry; of course there are lots of woods around here and fallen branches and everybody is carrying in some for autumn burning.

I have been talking to the young people and asking them how they like it all and they said they are very pleased. They say now they can begin to feel that they have their future to create, that they were tired of the weak vices that they were all indulging in, that if they had had an easy victory the vices would have been weaker and more of them, and now—well, now there is really something to do—they have to make France itself again and there is a future; and then there is to be lots of electricity and they want France to be self-sufficing, and they think it will be and they all think that French people were getting soft, and French people should not be soft. Well, anyway they are looking forward, and then besides they won't all just go into the bureaucracy the way they were doing; they will have to find other things to do. In short, they feel alive and like it.

The older people, once they have gotten over the shock, do not seem to mind either; nobody seems to mind, as Madeleine Rops said after having come all the way from Bordeaux to Belley. Really, you know, you would not think that it was a defeated country—not at all; they seem much more wideawake than they were.

Well, yes, they do a little regret the predictions, but still all the predictions said that the cock would lose its feathers but would come out more crowing than ever, and they all said that when the worst was there the best would follow; and then there was Sainte Odile, who said that after her blood flowed in June, four months after, France would be more glorious than ever. Well, why not?

I had my own private prediction, and that was that when I had cut all the box hedges in the garden the war would be all over. Well, the box hedge is all cut now today, the eighth of August, but the war is not all over yet. But anyway our light is lit and the shutters are open, and perhaps everybody will find out, as the French know so well, that the winner loses, and everybody will be, too, like the French, that is, tremendously occupied with the business of daily living, and that that will be enough.

THE COMING OF THE AMERICANS

This, indubitably one of the best pieces of writing yet accomplished by Gertrude Stein, is the final sixty-six ecstatic pages of WARS I HAVE SEEN, *published by Random House in 1945.*

Well that was yesterday and to-day is the landing and we heard Eisenhower tell us he was here they were here and just yesterday a man sold us ten packages of Camel cigarettes, glory be, and we are singing glory hallelujah, and feeling very nicely, and everybody has been telephoning to us congratulatory messages upon my birthday which it isn't but we know what they mean. And I said in return I hoped their hair was curling nicely, and we all hope it is, and to-day is the day.

While I was out walking to-day I talked to a little girl who looked nine but was really fourteen, her people came from the neighborhood of Rome but they had been French for some time and the children all born in France, she said they were all small, she certainly was and we talked about eating, and she said she would like an orange, and I said how about a banana do you know what a banana is oh yes she said I used to eat them, but my younger brothers and sisters they never saw a banana, and some of them cannot remember an orange, well she said sighing the time will come yes it will of course one does need bread but one does need oranges and lemons and bananas too.

To-day is only the third day of the landing and what a change, everybody openly making fun of the Germans, the girls leaning out of the window and singing the Marseillaise, and all the people in the village, so pleased because it has been said that this department the department of the Ain will be the first to be free and then the Savoy and the Haute

Savoy, and indeed the mountain boys are at it, Bourg the biggest city in the department has been completely cut off by them from contact with any one, they have cut the railroads, they guard the railroads and they have interrupted the telephone, and they have occupied quite a few important towns round about, and the few Germans that are left are getting mighty uncomfortable, the fifty who are here were called to go and fight the mountain boys and they said they did not want to and their officer harangued them and then they had to go, but there were no trains and so they requisitioned the French trucks and some autocars and away they went, I was sitting with the wife of the mayor and we saw them going off to fight and it was a very great contrast to the German army of 1940, my gracious yes. They have just told us that when the Germans started to attack the mountain boys the mountain boys just climbed a little higher, and sometimes they do not trouble to fight, they just throw stones down and call out cuckoo, cuckoo, of course to the French a cuckoo is some one who has stolen somebody else's nest. The Germans did not like being called cuckoo but what else can they do. The young people are all feeling very gay, the older ones naturally are worried but the young ones are feeling very gay.

The mayors now have to have the whole responsibility of their towns, there are no communications, so they cannot get into touch with a higher authority, and so they are the ultimate authority, and they are very capable the French mayors, even in the smallest places. Our is taking care of us very well, he has managed to get flour for bread and that is important because French people do not like to live by bread alone but without bread they cannot live at all, potatoes they say are filling but an hour after you are as hungry as before while bread is really sustaining so they must have bread and so far our mayor has managed it for us. It would be nice if ours would be the first department to be completely freed of Germans, perhaps, the mountain boys around here are very active, and it would be nice.

A buzzard has carried off one after the other three of our baby chickens, that is natural the hunters usually shoot enough buzzards every year so that they do not steal baby chickens, but after three years of not hunting, the air is full of buzzards full of buzzards.

And full of everything just now but mostly rumors. There are however some funny true stories, the mountain boys the other day came into Amberieu and one of them got into the post office and sounded the alerte, the whole population and the Germans ran away supposing it was a bombardment and the mountain boys went into the round house and blew up a quantity of locomotives and left before the Germans got back. The latest rumor is that Belley is held by the mountain boys but one thing is certain at the station here no trains pass, I was around the station this afternoon and I never saw a railroad station so dead not since in my youth I crossed the continent during the Pullman strike and what else can we do, it is the third time that we have been deprived of the telephones and this time fortunately they have left us electricity and the radio, which is a pleasure. But for how long this we do not know, anyway the landing goes on and when we hear the official French announcement that the Germans are perfectly calm, we know better, they are not, what we are afraid of now is that German deserters will try to get into the house, one did to-day, he said he was looking for a German lady, but as we are well up the mountain and not in the town it sounded fishy. Basket barks and barks as if he were a savage dog instead of a lamb which is just as well. Everything is going on that is to say nothing is going on no trains no mail no telephone, nothing coming and going except a few unfortunates, I saw one to-day who seemed a little queer, and there is a noonday hush all over the place all day long, the Germans are requisitioning more and more enormous logs to get themselves barricaded, away from the mountain boys and everybody chuckles they say much good that will do them, there are according to all calculations about three thousand of them in the whole department and as the mountain boys are killing them a few at a time it may take some time but on the other hand, they are stuck they can go up and down the road a distance of about fifty kilometers and then they have to come back again, all the youth are joining up with their friends, the police too, our friend came to see us from Belley yesterday Sunday and everything is peaceful except that everywhere the mountain boys guard the roads but they are very polite and help shove the cars when they get stuck, everybody for the moment is very polite, the mayor on his bicycle goes around gathering in food from the surrounding country to feed his population and so far has succeeded very well, the only thing that is a great trouble, is when there is a need for surgical operations and it is very difficult to get a conveyance, the men with the taxis are always getting their cars out of order to avoid going around with the Germans and they are frightened of putting them in order to take the French, but by the end of the week it is now the first Sunday since the landing everybody expects that the Germans will be gone. And they will, yes they will. My gracious they are all happy not the Germans but the population, even those who were collabo as they call them are happy why not they were collabo because they were afraid afraid of communism and afraid of Germans and then too the Germans to some French people did seem to be so strong but now well they are weak nobody uses the phrase that used to annoy us so they are still strong, and so there are no collabos because now that the Anglo-Americans have proved themselves so strong they are less afraid of communism and they are not at all afraid of Germans not at all so the rejoicing is practically universal, a little frightened still but complete. Some one has just told me about how the mountain boys in Bellegarde have taken German prisoners and have put them to work picking potato bugs off the potato plants, the only agricultural activity that every French man woman and child hates, they are looking forward to the clearance of the pests completely by the German prisoners. Everybody is delighted they say potatoes came from America and the potato pest seems to have come over these recent years from America and now because of America they have been able to take German prisoners here very far away from the Americans to be sure and these prisoners can spend their days destroying the potato bugs off the potato plants.

Are we excited yes we certainly are all around us there is fighting, the conversation in the village sounds exactly like

the communiqués of the Yugo-Slavs in their early days of
guerrilla fighting only we have we hope one great advantage,
the Germans cannot get reinforcements because all the railways are cut and all the roads guarded by the mountain boys
and anyway these days the Germans have other uses for their
men even if they could send them here which they cannot.
All day long the Germans rush forward and back through the
town they requisition all the trucks and alas with their French
drivers and then they go first in one direction and then in a
very short time back they come with guns sticking out in
every direction, the other day they stationed such cannon as
they had everywhere in the village and we all a little fearfully went down to look at them and then later in the day
they took them all away, there had been no fighting, they
had been told when they were elsewhere that the mountain
boys were here but they were not of course they were not,
that is what wears the Germans out to be continually going
where there is nobody and then when not expecting having
a truck with its German contents blown off the road suddenly, we are in the high hills and of course that kind of
thing happens easily with everybody against them and helping the others, it must be pretty awful to be surrounded but
completely surrounded by hate, it must be pretty awful really
pretty awful. One German told the baker who had been a
prisoner in the last war and so had learned a little German
that the population had better be a little careful, he himself
did not mind very much when the children called him a pig
but there were others of them that might and there might be
trouble. Sometimes there are a lot of them in the village and
sometimes very few but few or many they certainly do look
worn out, and the mountain boys do kill and wound a lot of
them there were five ambulances came over from Aix, German ones of course and big ones, to take off the wounded in
yesterday's fighting, and the German captain who was here
has just been caught at Amberieu. The mountain boys do not
stay in the towns, they keep to the hills descending into the
town to barricade all the roads and then they go back to the
hills, they are always up and down, they have cut all the telephone and telegraph wires. and so the Germans cannot com-

municate with each other and they have to go on the road, the other day just a little further along an Italian in the ditch at the side of the road killed two motor cyclists as they were going along, and then he quietly got out of the ditch and went on, how can the Germans tell which is which, they cannot, it is most exciting, nobody works except in their gardens because the railroad and the few factories that are here have stopped working there being no material and no way of sending things in or out, it is a mighty effective blockade and the Germans who are gradually getting killed can really do very little except move forward and back they should have gotten out as soon as communication with Italy was cut, because after that there was no reason for their staying here, but they are slow, they always manage to do everything just too late, just too late, thank heaven they do. I suppose they are human but they do look pretty awful, and even in their most uppish days they were awfully dead and alive more dead than alive. This is not a prejudice it is a fact.

We are excited.

Perhaps the department of the Ain will be the first department to be completely cleared of the Boches. That would be nice.

They are fighting all around us this afternoon I was raking the hay with a neighbor and we heard the sound of cannon fairly near, nobody seems to know very much of what is happening, the mayor who is usually very well informed has no time to think about things like that, he has to find calves to butcher to give us all something to eat, we ourselves are very well off because they have been bringing us fish and nice lake fish they are, the bread question not so serious for us because we do not eat much bread but terribly serious for the French population, potatoes no matter how many they eat after an hour or two leave them hungry, but since either the mountain boys or the Germans cut down trees to bar the roads that lead to the mills that grind the corn even if the mayor can get some wheat together how can it turn into bread, but there is always the Savoy, mysteriously the Savoy always has everything, some one has just given us a kilo of delicious butter from the Savoy and the mayor is hoping he really is hoping to get flour from the Savoy, the Savoy is always rich in food no matter what happens you can always get meat and fish and fowl and butter and cheese and honey from the Savoy and meat, I do not know why this is so but it is so and as we are just across the river Rhone from the Savoy we do not fare too badly, even if we are completely cut off from the rest of the world which we certainly are. To-day for the first time since the landing we had some letters from Lyon they came from the Swiss consul who has charge of American interests and they solemnly ask us to make out a paper stating if we wish or do not wish to be repatriated. It is a charming thought, ten days after the landing in France the American authorities seem to be quite certain that as soon as they like they can repatriate all Americans still in France. We giggled we said that is optimism. Naturally American authorities not really realising what it is to live in an occupied country ask you to put down your religion your property and its value, as if anybody would as long as the Germans are in the country and in a position to take letters and read them if they want to. The American authorities say they are in a hurry for these facts but I imagine that all Americans will feel the same better keep quiet until the Germans are gone just naturally play possum just as long as one can. Just that.

It is a queer state living as we are all doing, you have no news except for the radio because there are no newspapers any more and no trains no mail no telephone and even going to Belley is impossible there are twenty-three barricades between here and there a distance of seventeen kilometers. As I say we live within the village completely within it, the Germans rush forward and back there are distant sounds of cannonading, some villages have been burned and that is all anybody knows. The Germans threatened to make a curfew at six o'clock and keep all vehicles including bicycles off the road, but the mayor told the Germans it was impossible as it is too hot to take the animals to pasture before half past five it is too hot and nobody can work in the fields until four because it is too hot, and as in France fields are a considerable distance from the house and now it is haying time carts have to move around so the Germans agreed and now the curfew is at nine o'clock.

Is life real is life earnest, no I do not think so, it certainly is not real.

This kind of war is funny it is awful but it does make it all unreal, really unreal.

They must have been lonesome in the middle ages and that was natural enough because busy as they were with getting enough to eat they were pretty well cut-off from communication with everything and it is kind of lonesome in this present war which is so much like that, with trees cut down to block the roads and everything but still our friends did get over in a pony cart from Belley to see us and it was a pleasure, and besides they brought us some money which was also a pleasure because the traveling banker who used to come once a week to this town has not come and money is certainly a very great necessity these days.

To-night the Americans have just had a victory and are going to take Cherbourg and that is a pleasure. To be sure in the middle ages they did not have a wireless and although it was threatened that they would take them away from us they did not and now it would be rather late for it to happen and I do like to hear their American voices. Everything is quiet around here now, nobody seems to know just what happened but it is all quiet around here now and we even had letters from Lyon to-day.

Bread and cake cake and bread which is better, I myself think that bread when there is good butter is better than cake, bread and butter but when there is no bread and butter then there is cake Marie Antoinette was quite right about that.

Some refugees have just come here from Normandy, they are friends of the wife of the mayor, they left Normandy just seven days ago and they progressed partly by bicycle partly on foot and partly by train, it took them seven days to get here, they were a party of seven with three children and the mother just about having another baby, they stopped at night and dug themselves a trench in which to sleep on account of the bombardments they describe the railways all through the north completely blocked and the German material scattered all about, and the Germans take the little roads because the big roads are bombed all the time, it is like well like nothing, although Wells did describe it in a kind of a way, and nobody says anything except it's long c'est longue, which is I suppose the inevitable human cry, in the meantime the eagles are carrying off all the baby chickens and ducks because not having guns nobody can shoot them, we had seven baby chickens and now we have only two, and the poor hen screams and goes pale but what is the use, there is no use in screaming or going pale when nobody is allowed to shoot the eagles in the air. On the other hand the wheat the vines the potatoes all are growing well, and so if there is anybody there to eat when it is all over there will be eating for them, the refugees from Normandy said you could buy a kilo of butter for ten francs in that part of Normandy but there was nobody there to buy, there seemed to be people to sell but nobody there to buy, and it made us all sigh naturally enough although we did not want ourselves to be there to buy.

Now they have made the curfew at six o'clock of the afternoon it was just to-day and all windows that face toward the street have to close from then until seven in the morning, and everybody is pretty unhappy because domestic animals will not feed in the heat of the day and farm work in the summer is from sunrise to sunset and everybody is worried, naturally enough and nobody knows why but really I imagine it is because the Germans are afraid of the mountain boys or the parachutists, but really since it is daylight until ten o'clock why should they make it at six. Of course the French population take it very simply that it is done to annoy. They take this for granted with all the German regulations, they only do it to annoy because they think it teases. Oh dear as the French say of the allies all the time if they only would hurry up. It is their only cry hurry up. The Germans are convinced of the efficiency of the new bomb, but not any Frenchmen, one German was telling about it to some Frenchmen and one of the French said to him but you are silly if you believe that, any soldier ought to know better they all say, but the German did not take offense, he just went on believing or did he. After all any hope is a hope to a dying man. All the French population can say is of the allies is if they only would hurry up, although they do admit that two weeks after the landing a great deal has been accomplished. One village to another is full of rumors. In Belley they think we have guns all around us, here we were told that all sorts of things have happened in Belley, but so far it is all rumor, the latest rumor is that the maquis the mountain boys have caught a colonel a captain and two ladies with whom they were out walking, and that is the reason they have made the curfew at six o'clock. The hide of a German comes high, said our cook why don't they send them back, they are no use to anybody and then we could go and take the potato bugs off our potato plants. Well life in an occupied country is like that.

I am going on cleaning the weeds off the terrace so when the American army gets here it can sit comfortably on it, Alice Toklas thinks the weeds may get a chance to grow again but I hope not, anyway I am making it nice and neat, and as the terrace is not on the road side of the house, I can go on working at it after we have to stay indoors, that is to say that we cannot go out of doors on the roads.

In all these years I never had a wrist watch, watches to wear never particularly interested me, I like clocks and I am always buying them any kind of clock any kind of fountain pen, but watches seemed kind of dull, I like to know what time it is in the house but out of doors it is less interesting to know about the passage of time and in a city particularly in France you see so many clocks you hear so many clocks to be sure they do not tell the same time but no matter they do tell some time and when you are going to an appointment sometimes you go quickly because you are late by one clock and then you go slowly because you are early by another clock, but now that the curfew is at six o'clock, and I am sure to be out on the road somewhere and they do shoot you if you are out I thought it best to have a wrist watch and so out I went in our little village and asked the local jeweler lady whether she had a wrist watch, yes and a Swiss one and brand new and made for sport for women and men and I thought it perfectly lovely and I came home proudly and now I wear it with immense pride and joy and it seems to keep time and I get home in time and do not get shot by the Germans.

The maquis are beginning to fight again, there was a lull for a bit and now it has commenced again and the Germans are taking all the gazogene automobiles and they are threatening to take away some of the radios from some of the people not to prevent the people listening they do not seem to care very much about that but presumably to get ready to get their orders that may come by radio when all the telephone and telegraph lines are cut which they certainly will be soon. Everything does seem as if something is going to happen that is what everybody keeps on saying. In the meantime our mayor has most efficiently gotten meat and bread and wine and corn meal and butter and everybody is very cheerful because they stand in line for hours but they finally get something and that is a pleasure. How they love a piece of bread. They certainly do. And I am going on scraping the weeds off the terrace so as to be all ready for the American army when it comes, one boy who came to-day and brought us fish said that he had seen an English soldier with his own eyes we none of us believed him naturally but it was a pleasure to hear and he did believe it.

The Germans are very uncertain in their minds now, they decided to-day to give us the curfew at ten instead of six in the evening, it was posted up at the mairie and everybody was happy and then at half past five they sent the local policeman around to announce that they had changed their minds and it was back to six o'clock again, then a half hour afterwards they sent him around again to announce that it was changed back to ten and that is where it is now, or so we hope. But that is the way they are about everything, they come and go and they are afraid of their shadow, it is very hard to believe but it is true, and now everybody knows it, guerrilla warfare gets on their nerves it is so darn individual and being individual is what they do not like that is to say what they can not do.

It is exciting to me to hear over the radio about Lake Trasimena, when my brother and I were still at college we spent one summer some weeks in Perugia at a pension and there were lots of us there and one day some of us went off to see Lake Trasimena because there was supposed to be a whole army at the bottom well an army of ancient days naturally with gold chariots, and we thought we would like a swim in the lake, and the young men took the boatmen with them at one end of a little island in the middle of the lake and we girls went to the other end to swim, and we swam without clothes in the sunset in Lake Trasimena, and I have swum in lots of lakes and oceans but there was something special about that and now well it is being mentioned every day. And Cherbourg, when my eldest brother was coming to Paris with his family, my brother and I had been living there some years already, my eldest brother was a little nervous about the trip and he had not much confidence in the ability of my brother and myself getting to the station in time to meet his train from Cherbourg, and so for several months my eldest brother wrote letters and each one of them ended up with a post-script it is six and a half hours from Cherbourg to Paris, six hours and a half. We used to laugh about it, it was a family joke six hours and a half from Cherbourg to Paris. Well perhaps, anyway it is Cherbourg, yes it is.

Everybody is excited so very excited and all around us there are explosions, we do not know what they are whether they are cannon or bridges blowing up or avions or just thunder but there is a lot of it and everybody hears and tells of a different lot, the Germans in French local trucks, not having any of their own, rush forward and back, and nobody seems to know just why or where. When I was out yesterday, I met five Germans with guns on bicycles and they were followed by a truck from Grenoble with soldiers having mitraillettes pointing in every direction and then followed by a local taxi-cab containing two officers of a higher rank than we are accustomed to see around here, and where they were going nobody knows, do they, and then there was a private car that went to Aix, and in this was an officer who had been here and was not popular and he was in a car with two soldiers each carrying a gun and the officer was driving and the car swerved and one of the soldiers dropped his gun which went off and killed the officer. And then there was his funeral with all the officers present. Then I have been seeing a German soldier working lately in the local carpenter shop, and I asked the carpenter why, well he said he told me in his own country he was owner of a carpenter shop and had six men working under him and he said as he has nothing to do he would like to handle tools and as I am short handed I let him, he says the war has settled his hash all right, when and if he gets back to his home he certainly will find nothing there for him.

It's a funny life all right, so far we ourselves have not seen any maquis, I went on a long walk yesterday and went over a road that had been barricaded, just trees pulled to the side of the road, all the telegraph and telephone wires down, they had not fought there but it was certainly like a battle field, it is hard to tell who is maquis and who isn't, they have an arm-band but naturally when they come home to see their people and they all do they keep it in their pocket and then there are still some firm reactionaries who are convinced that all maquis are terrorists, we have some charming neighbors who are like that and it worries me because after all people get angry and things might happen to them and we are very fond of them, it kind of reminds me of the description of the marauding bands in Cooper's Spy, but that of course is the extraordinary thing about this war it is so historical not recent history but fairly ancient history, not I suppose where the armies are actually fighting but here where we are. The mayor keeps us pretty well fed, there are no more tickets because there is no contact with the authorities, there is only the mayor, there are no police but we are all peaceable and we are very well fed, we seem to have everything but sugar. We even had a lemon and an orange which should have gotten to Switzerland but did not, the bridges keep being blown up and nobody wants to go out to repair them it is too dangerous, the Germans tried to pass an armored train through the other day, but did it get there, nobody seems to know.

They just blew up the electric line between here and Chambery and now everybody is walking, they walk to Grenoble they walk to Lyon, even children of three and five walk along with their elders, and sometimes somebody lends them a bicycle and sometimes the children fall off but not often they stick on holding on to anything in front of them, and so they still move around, everybody has to go somewhere and French people always find a way, they are wonders at always finding a way. The death of Henriot killed by the militia or somebody in their uniform has been an immense excitement, it is hard to make any one who has not lived with them realise how really tormented the population has been in its opinions and Henriot did perhaps more than anybody to turn Frenchmen against Frenchmen, he was a very able propagandist, he used the method not of a politician but of a churchman, he had that education, and he knew how to appeal like a revivalist sermon, and he did do it awfully well, and he held the middle classes they could not get away from him, what said I to one friend whose mother always listened to him, what will your mother do now, oh she mourns but at least for a week she will be busy with all the funeral orations, but after that, good gracious after that what will she do. A great many of the middle classes feel like that, of course the immense majority of French people are delighted at his putting off, they breathe more freely, there was no one else in the government who had the power he had, no one else. I do not think outside of France this was realised, I do not think so.

And now he is dead and except a few of the die hards everybody is happy and relieved and everybody can now get ready for the end of the war that is to say for the evacuation of France by the Germans.

One of our friends wants to be taught to say to a parachutist who comes to her door, and upon whom she has closed the door, she wants to say to him in English through the keyhole please break down the door and come in by force and take everything you want by force in that way you will have what you need and the Germans and the government cannot blame me and now said she just how can I say that to the parachutist through the keyhole. The rest of the population just wants to be taught to say we are glad to see you, and some of them are learning to say it very nicely, every one is certain that a large party of Canadians have been parachuted somewhere in our neighborhood and that they are only waiting the arrival of an English general expected any day this is the first of July for the advance to begin. As a matter of fact the forty-odd Germans who are here and who no longer get their pay are getting more and more peaceful, they ask for work they wander around unarmed and they used never to stir without a gun on their back and never less than three together, now they wander all about the country alone and unarmed. It certainly is a change this conquering army this occupying army now wandering around hoping some one will speak to them and that some one will give them a job. It certainly does look like the beginning of the end. The breathlessness of the situation is a bit on everybody's nerves but the most selfish of all the women here did to-day in a great burst announced that it was all right there must be no bread, no money no anything and then the Germans would leave, that is the way it was going to be. There are no more trains here any more, and this Culoz where we are was a very important railroad junction for Italy, Switzerland the Savoys and Lyon, but not a train not one single or solitary train not one. No wonder the Germans are meek, here they are and here they must stay until the maquis come and take them away.

They are getting away from here, the last lot that were in Artemarre are leaving and they are trying to sell the wagons that they had attached to their horses and all that is left in the region are right here in Culoz, we still have forty odd and when will they leave very soon we are hoping, they do not do anything very disagreeable here but oh dear what a relief it will be when they are gone, as everybody says even when they are not doing anything they are an oppressive burden, they are.

The Germans still eat sausages, just like the old jokes, the Hitler regime has not changed that, they borrow a sausage machine from an old woman here who is called the old Maria, and they tell her all their troubles and how they are all going home very soon now, and the soldier who accidentally killed his adjutant and who has been crying ever since locked up in a room and he wanted to commit suicide but the officers decided instead of shooting him he would be sent to the Russian front and we all laughed and said by the time he gets there there wont be any Russian front.

And now the cook has just come up to say that the maquis are on their way and may get here at Culoz not any day but at any moment of to-day. I wonder. It is now the fourth of July and things certainly are moving.

It's the fourth of July and everybody is on the broad grin. The French black troops with regular French officers are now within eight kilometers of us, they have been parachuted in the region and the Germans scared to death are packing up their bags and moving away and everybody stands around and laughs and with reason. It is a happy day.

To-day I took a long walk and all along there were groups of people telling each other all sorts of things, some had seen Canadians and some had seen English and some had heard on the radio that this department of the Ain was going to be completely emptied of Germans by the fourteenth of July and others had seen the black troops and anyway there was a sound of cannon firing and somebody had heard one of the German soldiers say; the only thing to do to shorten this war is to kill our chiefs, and sometimes when you realise that there have been twenty-four German generals killed or imprisoned in three weeks are they doing it, are they.

There is one thing certain now it is very bad form to mention maquis or mountain boys, you speak respectfully of the French army, in two days the word maquis no longer exists it is with great pride the French army. There are such funny things the new prefect was talking of having he himself been condemned to death by the maquis and the wife of the mayor said yes he will write about it in his memoirs and then she added meditatively condemned to death we are all condemned to death.

It is very pleasant to have a new army with an old name or an old army with a new name, very pleasant.

We were in Belley yesterday and there everybody was excited the night before the maquis had come into the town and walked off with the sous-prefect with the chief of police with a thousand kilos of sugar that one of the cake shops had and lots of other material, and everybody of course was excited and upset, six of us had gone over in a taxi including our mayor, and it was very exciting and then we came home and then that evening the maquis came very near to Culoz and the Germans took out cannon to shoot at them and all to-day they were firing around the mountain and we all stood around talking and everybody said if the maquis come they bring food but if the maquis come and do not succeed then the Germans will take hostages and burn up the farms, oh dear do they want maquis or do they not want maquis, it all is very exciting we now have one hundred and sixty Germans in the town and they are not leaving, we all hoped that they would leave and that would be very comfortable for everybody and they would like to leave but Hitler likes everybody to stay where they are until they are all killed, he likes it like that, so I suppose even these few will stay until they are killed so that now that the railroad is not working any more there is no use in staying but their orders are to stay anyway. A lot get killed when there is a lot and a few get killed when there are a few but the idea is to always stay and get killed. That is the way to create the last battalion which will then be killed and we will all be happy, yes quite happy.

I had seen many things in this war a great many but I had never seen an armored train and to-day as I passed the railroad track I saw one, with the engine with a sort of tea cosy made of metal over it and behind cars with sand bags and Germans and we wondered because there was no way to go the railroad being all broken up except just to Chambery and I came home to tell about it and it was almost nine

o'clock of summer night just a little later and Basket barked
and I looked out and there was a German officer and a soldier
and they said in French they wanted to sleep and I said have
you a paper from the mayor because they are always supposed to have and he said like an old time German officer I
must see the house, certainly I said, you go around to the
back and they will open, and I called the servants and told
them to attend to them, I thought with that kind of a German it was just as well to keep our American accents out of
it, and then they were at it, the German said he wanted two
rooms for officers and mattresses for six men and he did not
want any answering back and he did not care how much he
upset the ladies of the house, and the servants said very well
sir and he left and as soon as he left the soldiers were amiable
and they carried around mattresses and they had three dogs
and we locked up as much as we could and took Basket upstairs and went to bed, finally there were fifteen men sleeping
on the six mattresses and the two dogs the third one would
not come in and in the morning after they all left we could
not find my umbrella it turned out that it was used by a poor
devil of an Italian whom they kept outside all night in the
rain to sit with the horses, and they took away a new pair of
slippers of one of the servants and they broke the lock and
stole all our peaches and they took away with them why nobody knows except to be disagreeable the two keys of the
front and back doors, and then they left but the third dog
would not go with them and he is here now, there were six
hundred of them in the village and they are supposed to be
on their way to fight the maquis, but actually they themselves
thought they were going home, they were sixteen and seventeen years of age and when they were alone any one of them
with the servants they told about how hard their life was
and what an unhappy country it was where there were
maquis, and one of them said, now the Russians are getting
in to our country we will have to go to our country we will
have to go back to Berlin to defend it and we will have to
leave you French people to defend yourselves as best you
can against the English. The servants just listened and then
when another German came in then the one who was crying

got the same brutal expression on his face as the others, oh said the servants the miserable assassins. We heard firing all this afternoon and the rumor is the maquis had mined the road they went over and caught them, anyway that is the last we saw of them and that was only yesterday. All the same said the mayor they are not quite what they were, they threatened to shoot the mayor of the next village because he had not notified the Germans that the maquis were there, but how could I said the poor mayor when they imprisoned me and, said our mayor, four months ago they would not have listened to him but now they did and let him go. The rumor to-night is that they are all quitting the country and they should go the ill-omened birds that they are, say the country people. So far we none of us have seen any maquis, nor the Canadians that are supposed to be with them, but we will they all say we will. Everybody is worried and a little confused in their minds except about the Germans that they will go, that they will only go, where does not interest anybody.

And now the unhappy description of how a very small percentage of the French population feel, I just had a violent quarrel with our nearest neighbors and I will try to tell just how they do feel.

I forget to say that when these Germans came they came in trucks big trucks pulled by horses, gasoline they have none.

There was a story written about the war the American civil war called The Crisis by Winston Churchill and it was about Saint Louis and there was the north and there was a southerner and there was a northerner and they had been friends for years but when there was a threat of civil war they said can we meet can we keep off the subjects and of course they could not. The French are like that now they are violently divided and they cannot keep off the subject. Then in the last war there was a funny story. A friend of ours Louise Hayden had been all through the war in one way and another and later when she went home to Seattle a friend said to her, my dear Louise you do not know anything about the real hardships of war, over there you were in it you were busy every minute in the midst of it but over here we had the real nervousness and anxiety of war we were not in it we could only suffer about it. Well this time the French have been like that, they could only suffer the nervousness and anxiety of wars, they were not in it, that is to say of course now they are in it but from '40 to '43 well really into the beginning of '44 they were not in it, they had all the nervousness the anxiety and the suffering and the privations of war but they were not in it, and when I first heard that story I thought it was only funny but now that I have been with a nation suffering like that I understand the point of view of the woman in Seattle.

The French not fighting had plenty of time to worry and to talk and to listen to propaganda, and they have gotten so that they do not know what they believe in but they do pretty well know what they do not believe in, I laughed the other day when I met Doctor Lenormant because he surpassed most of the Frenchmen, he was anti-Russian he was anti-Anglo-American he was anti-German, he was anti-De Gaulle he was anti-Vichy he was anti-Petain he was anti-maquis he was anti-persecutions he was anti-collabo, he was anti-bombardments he was anti-militia he was anti-monarchy he was anti-communist he was anti-everything. It is very complicated, the majority of the middle classes are anti-Russian that is to say anti-communist so they are anti-Anglo-American because they are allies of Russia, they hate the Germans but they admire them because they are so disciplined and the French are not, nobody in France wants to be disciplined but they cannot help admiring anybody who is and the Germans certainly are, and then there is always the real feeling that in spite of the German being so disciplined and so powerful you can always get rid of them but can you get rid of Russians and Anglo-Americans. In the small towns like this we live in the mutual hatreds of course are much stronger than in the big cities where they do not see each other every day, and they get so bitter that is the anti-Germans that they say to the pro-Germans I wish nothing more than that your son or your husband or your brother should disappear in that Germany you love so, but I hate the Germans the other answers and I hate you and then they hate the maquis because after the maquis have been the Germans come and they shoot and burn and destroy and everybody hates everybody and everybody denounces everybody and then the maquis come and they carry off all the property and sometimes the men themselves who have been militiamen and then everybody gets excited and sometimes they get more fanatical and anyway now that Henriot is dead who heated them up all the time to hate each other and the allies are so undoubtedly winning well there are a good many who are changing opinions, they are quite a few that are keeping still and they are quite a few who are manufacturing American and English and French flags for the day of victory and this is the fourteenth of July, and all the farmers are getting ready to join up with the French army and in a little while they will be so busy eating and drinking and discussing politics that they will all be French together. But there have been moments there most certainly have.

To-day is the fourteenth of July, in Belley they made a beautiful V for victory in flowers and they made American and English and French flags and they were up all day, and even at Cezerieu six kilometers from here they did too but here nothing could be done because we still have over a hundred German soldiers, but we all went visiting and told each other how soon how very soon we expected to be free, and we do expect it.

To-day it was a shock when it was announced that the Japanese had executed the American airmen prisoners, one does hear so many awful things that I do not know why that should have been so shocking but it was and there is no doubt about it one's country is one's country and that kind of harm seems to be so far away from our country. It is queer the world is so small and so knocked about. To-night we expected to have Germans come into the house again but they did not, they came in and out and about and they are exactly like an ants nest if you put a foreign substance in it, the Germans run around just like that. The only thing that is human about them is that they like to eat pork, that is the only human thing about them.

That was yesterday.

I was sitting with the wife of the mayor and in front of us

was the main road from everywhere to Culoz. There were
quite a few motor cycles rushing up and down with German
soldiers and then there was a lull and then there came along
hundreds of German soldiers walking, it was a terribly hot
day and in the mountains heat is even hotter than below,
and these soldiers were children none older than sixteen and
some looking not more than fourteen, as they came and I have
never seen anything like it since I saw the last lap of the
walking marathon in Chicago. Our friend Elena Genin who
lives near Belley and who is a Mexican, told us that she had
seen the German troops going into Belley and she said I said
to Joan, her daughter, this is not a German army this is a
Mexican army when I was a little girl, and I did not quite
understand but now I understand, these childish faces and the
worn bodies and the tired feet and the shoulders of aged men
and an occasional mule carrying a gun heavier than the boys
could carry and then covered wagons like those that crossed
the plains only in small and country wagons with a covering
over them and later we were told in them were the sick and
wounded, and they were being dragged by mules, it was unbelievable, and about a hundred of them more on women's
bicycles that they had evidently taken as they went along,
it was unbelievable, the motorised army of Germany of 1940
being reduced to this, to an old fashioned Mexican army, it
seemed to be more ancient than pictures of the moving army
of the American civil war. I suppose said Madame Ray
the wife of the mayor that they choose them young like that,
because children can set fire to homes and burn and destroy
without knowing what they are doing, while grown men even
the worst of them draw the line somewhere. It was a sorry
sight in every way they had been in the mountains to fight the
mountain boys who of course got away from them and killed
and wounded quite a few of them and so they revenged
themselves upon the civil population who were unarmed
shooting them and burning their houses and driving away
their cattle, they had cows and calves with them dangling
along on a string, it was absolutely unbelievable that in July
1944 that the German army could look like that, it was unbelievable, one could not believe one's eyes, and then I came

home having put my dog on the leash and when I got home there were about a hundred of these Germans in the garden in the house all over the place, poor Basket the dog was so horrified that he could not even bark, I took him up to my bedroom and he just sat and shivered he did not believe it could be true. They left the next morning and Basket has hardly barked since and I heard to-day that they shot a dog of one of the homes in the village because they said he barked, a big black dog that its owner adored, perhaps Basket will never bark again, I am trying to induce him to bark again, it is not right that a dog should be silent.

The German troops are pretty well out of all this region, the trains are stopped by the French the roads defended by the French as always somewhere in their length they go through gorges and now the only Germans left in the region are the sixty odd here in the town of Culoz in which we are living, the railway was still open between here and Chambery but yesterday it was cut, and to-day the Germans killed their last three pigs and their cow so everybody thinks that they will leave too, they are getting so polite, one woman told me that a German soldier came to her to buy a chicken, she said she could not sell because her husband was not home, but he said you know German soldiers love the French, oh yes said the woman, and said he all French people like German soldiers, oh yes said the woman and then he went away, they know they are caught in a trap and cannot get away, so when they are not demanding something they are very cajoling, the French population are naturally disgusted, the French took their defeat with their heads held well up, and they thought the Germans were strong but now when they behave like that in defeat, they are disgusted. In the last war they were out of the country before they were defeated so the French have never seen them abject in defeat as they are now, and the French the few French who really admired them when they were strong now have nothing to say for them, French people do not like people who are abject in defeat, no they do not.

As for food we are pretty well off, as alas no food goes to the big cities and the Germans are not here to take it away, and so everything that is here, remains and so we have plenty of everything except fruit, this is not a fruit country, and once or twice trucks have gone to Lyon to get fruit and now the last truck has been captured by the mountain boys and the Germans have taken the others so we have no fruit, but as we have lots of butter cheese meat fish vegetables and potatoes and now bread we cannot be said to be suffering, not much sugar but plenty of honey.

Day before yesterday we were told that the Germans we had here were all leaving, then we were told at any rate we knew that they had had butchered their three remaining pigs and their cow and their goats. That was true, and then we were told that they were leaving and actually I did see them along the road with all their cars and a mitrailleuse set up and pointing down the road, the little boys in the villages all play at that, they make their guns out of wood and very lifelike they are and they set them up on the road, I suppose some of the guns I see are what they called tommy guns in gangster stories, there seem to be quite a variety of them, anyway the hundred odd soldiers that were in the village did leave to-day leaving behind some German railroad workers and station masters. They went to say good-bye to the mayor and his wife, the mayor and his wife told me to-day, the interpreter and the captain, made some polite remarks to them and the interpreter and the captain both saying that they expected to come back to Culoz a few months after the war was over, extraordinary people they think that although they are defeated they can come back as tourists as they like, the interpreter went on to say that he supposed the war would be over by the first of September, the only thing he said necessary to do now is to kill two men. We did not know the two he meant did he mean Hitler and Mussolini, or did he mean Churchill and Roosevelt, naturally we did not ask him, in the meantime, the village was much troubled because the soldiers had told them that they were going away but that they were going to be succeeded by really bad men killers, and indeed those who had been here had been quiet and peaceful enough, and with this village on the border of the maquis land it was terribly upsetting it makes everybody feel kind of queer. Naturally enough. This enemy the new lot has not come yet but there has been a rumor that the last lot were killed before they got far, but that is very likely not so. Anyway, after the other soldiers left when I was walking up the road where they had been, I found paper covers, they had covers of German tobacco and French candles and then there was this. Half pound weight Swifts yellow American farmers cheese, distributed by Bright and Company Chicago Ill. and underneath it it said, buy war bonds and stamps regularly and then it said a natural source of vitamins and riboflavin, now what that is naturally we do not know, it seems to have come on since we knew about what they needed to have in America, but where oh where did the German army get this cheese, and it is a far cry to have them leave it here in our garden, I suppose they stole it from Red Cross supplies, what else well anyway.

And now it is coming on to the end of July and things are very mixed up, just at present there are no Germans in Culoz except a few at the station but they say there are a thousand of them just across the river, are they, we do not know but everybody says so and it is a little puzzling just a little, and in the meantime the maquis are moving around the country requisitioning cars bicycles and trucks and between the Germans and the maquis everybody is scared, over at Belley they have been carrying on very livelily there are no Germans there but there are real and false maquis and everybody is frightened, quit a bit, and of course what is the worst is that the maquis come into a village have a clash with the Germans then go back to their mountains and the Germans burn and kill the village and so everybody is frightened when they see the maquis and they are frightened when they see the Germans, in the back country just now everybody is frightened, and with cause, they are no longer frightened of bombardments, because as no trains go there is no use in bombarding, there is no doubt about it, there is always plenty to scare one, to scare every one. In the meantime the mayor is trying to find flour for bread, but naturally the trucks that are to bring it never get here, that is natural enough and in the meantime everybody in the country is ready to sell you flour, it is very confusing, very.

And just now the banker has told us that the department of the Ain that is ours and the two Savoys are going to be almost at once evacuated by the Germans, and he usually knows, in fact now that the communications are cut here to Italy to Lyon to the north and to Grenoble there really does not seem any point in keeping a lot of German troops here when they seem to need them so badly elsewhere, except of course it will give a chance for the French army of the interior to organise itself. Well we must be patient. So we all tell each other.

Our two chickens are laying two eggs a day, which is a pleasure to all concerned, the two baby chickens particularly the cock is growing apace, he is weighed every day and the cook says he is destined for the first dinner party of the first American general who comes this way. To-day I took a long walk and going through a village a woman asked me to come in as she wanted to ask me a question. When I got in she showed me a package, she said her husband had just found it in a field what was it. It was a package of malted milk tablets and I told her and she said is it good and I said yes for children have you some and she said yes she had two, well I said eat one yourself and if it is good give it to them it will do them good, I suggested that she try if first, because I thought it might be something bad that the Germans had put out to discourage the people with gifts from America, but she said, you know so many strange things happen now, yes I will try it. It was strange I walked for several hours over all the roads where one always used to meet Germans and there were none, none at all, not one, they are across the river and just now ten o'clock in the evening we and the dog Basket II jumped because there were two big explosions probably blowing up more bridges. There is another funny thing. The Germans are not paying any more. They used to hire men in town to watch the railroad cars, the empties and they used to pay the men for this, and now the last few months they have not paid, they do not pay any more, they used to be very regular about paying, for lodgings for break-ages for everything and now they do not. Is it that they want to keep what French money they have, the German author-ities, is it that the French government is not paying them any more, or is it that they know now that they are not going to continue to possess France and so why pay any one since they are going away.

It is different, last night, we noticed it the most, we kept our shutters open as long as we liked and then later I went out with Basket and I called him all these days I could not go out in the garden after ten at night and I could not call Basket because naturally one did not want to attract attention to oneself, and then later about at midnight I heard a man going down the street whistling, what a sense of freedom to hear some one at midnight go down the street whistling. It is a weight off, the weight is not all off because they are still there across the river and they might come back the Germans might come back but with all the allied victories going on it is not very likely, no not very likely, about eleven o'clock last night there was a loud explosion and this afternoon there was cannonading, all across the river, where there still are a couple of hundred Germans.

To-day the banker from Belley who comes here once a week to do business gave me a copy of a photograph of the monument for the soldiers fallen in 1914-1918 the flags of America and England were made by the young girls of the town and on the 14th of July 1944 they decorated it and the people made a pilgrimage to it all day long and in spite of Germans and police it stayed there till noon.

Everybody is much excited now what between Germans and maquis, or maquisans as they call what is known as the false maquis. There is naturally a certain amount of lawless-ness there are bands who steal, under the name of maquis and now the forces of the interior that is the regular maquis are beginning to police the country in order to keep order but even they requisition what they need, cars, bicycles, motor bicycles, tires, and there are of course exaggerated stories, to be sure anybody connected with the militia fares badly and the girls who mixed up with the Germans fare badly, as badly

as is told this we do not know, and then the German soldiers
are escaping from the discipline of the army and they come
along to get bread and provision to which they are entitled,
but as the mayor says as each lot point a tommy gun at you
you naturally give them what they want, in the meantime
every day the airplanes come not to bombard but to provision the forces of the interior and we are all expecting a
considerable battle now in this region, they say to take the
airpark at Amberieu. People turn up from Paris who have
bicycled down, they say the morale is good but food completely lacking, if they cannot find a bicycle they walk but
French people have to move around they just cannot stay
put, the roads are always full of every kind of progression.

As I was walking along this afternoon I talked to an old
man and he said there were a lot of airplanes this afternoon
and they were all American taking material to the maquis,
and they tell us to stay in the houses but not at all we were
all out with spy glasses looking for the stars and stripes, yes
said he reflectively leaning on his farming implement and I
leaning on my cane, yes he said, we depend on America to
pick us up out of our troubles, we have always been friends
we helped them when they needed us and they helped us
when we needed them, the English are all right but it is
America that we count on to take care of us to see we keep
our colonies, to be sure they will want naval stations and of
course we will be pleased to have them have them. The only
thing that worries us is that our towns which have been
bombarded will they help us to build them up, there is
Chambery it was a nice town and the people are such good
republicans, yes said I and such ardent patriots, yes he said,
we always admire them the Savoyards are like that and
Chambery was their capital and now it is destroyed or at
least a good part of it, they should have hit the station but
not the town, I know I said but there are the unfortunate
accidents of war, I know he said but he said the Americans
should rebuild Chambery, and say they do and in a year or
two it would be rebuilt by them and then when it is all ready
and Mr. Roosevelt would be still living he would come over

to see it and that would be nice. Perhaps he will I said and then we each went on our way.

To-day we were over in Belley the third of August, nineteen forty-four, and I looked anxiously to see a maquis. We still have Germans here so up to now we have had no maquis. But Belley which is maquis headquarters was unfortunately empty they had gone away to fight and I only saw one at a distance in a nice khaki suit, that is shirt and trousers, with a red cord over his shoulders so we came home satisfied we had seen a maquis, in Belley they asked us with some astonishment and do you still have Germans, we still have forty odd who are railroad men and guard the station but we were very apologetic about them, we are here in Culoz the only ones in the region who still have Germans, so naturally we are apologetic, and add they are railway workers who have nothing to do they are not soldiers. Things do happen quickly, three months ago Belley was a garrison for thousands of German soldiers and now there are none and the people of Belley talk as if they never had had any as if they only had had maquis, and we in Culoz still have them which is a disgrace.

They are funny the Germans, now when the Americans are chasing across Brittany and there is no air defence, they are flying airplanes over this back water here and bombing little villages, in an attempt to stop the maquis from receiving supplies from the parachutists but of course they do not hit either supplies or maquis only the poor little village, that has nothing to do with it, but why should they not use those airplanes where they certainly seem to need them more. I suppose it is because when the orders were given it was different and now communications being so interrupted they were not able to get new orders. Our Germans here are leaving a few at a time, now there are less than a hundred in the whole region, but the airplanes go over our heads and there is a sound of distant guns or blowing up of communications any day and every day and soon very soon they will all have gone away. And now this is a spy story, there is no answer to it, but it is a spy story.

When we had the couple of hundred Germans here, there was with them an interpreter a tall dark man who wore eye-glasses. One day he came here to arrange to have the German soldiers come here when there was an alerte. I was not here and he had a long conversation with Alice Toklas. He talked very good French without any definite accent. He said that as the lower gate was closed he had entered as a brigand over the wall, and could we give him a key to the gate. Alice Toklas said the mairie had one he could get it there, no he said he wanted one to have in his own pocket so she gave him one, and after a little gay conversation he went away. He never came back. We used to see him around the town but the soldiers never came here when there was an alerte and we never had the key back. When I came home Alice Toklas told me about the conversation and said she was puzzled, he was not like a German neither his manners, nor his French nor his looks, later on we were told in the village that he used to keep a hotel in Paris and that his wife was still there keeping it and that is the reason he spoke French so well even though he was only a simple soldier.

From time to time the mayor's wife mentioned him as asking for this or asking for that for the Germans and when German troops passed through the town they never had anything to do with those who were here permanently. Mrs. Mayor said that he was always polite and helpful the interpreter and did what he could to make everybody comfortable, and that he had allowed a taxi to help get some friends of theirs to their home, these friends had come down from Normandy just after the beginning of the fighting there. And then the Germans here left and the interpreter and the captain came to say good-bye to the mayor and his wife and the captain who could not talk much French just said a few words politely and the interpreter said, after all the war is going to be over soon it will only mean killing two men and then it is finished, and said he three months after the war I will come back here to call on you.

Then they went away and a few days after Madame the mayoress told me this story, that was only yesterday.

She said what was your impression of the interpreter and

I told her what Alice Toklas said about him that he was not very German and seemed a gentleman which was strange as he was a common soldier. Yes she said it is strange he was a common soldier, and he took his turn at guard like any of them, I do not know whether he slept and ate with them but otherwise he acted like a common soldier, excepting when he was with the captain and then it was very evident that it was the interpreter who was in command, he did not go when he was sent for by the captain until it suited him and anyway there were thousands of little signs that showed that he was the superior in rank. I told you she said about how he arranged for a taxi for our friends who came from Normandy but I never told you what happened. I was with the husband and wife and children and mother at the mairie waiting for my husband to come in and he came with the interpreter and the interpreter hesitated a moment and then came in, ah said my friend I am not mistaken we have met in Normandy, oh yes said the interpreter and you were Doctor Fisch and were in command, oh yes said the interpreter and said my friend it was I who succeeded in arranging about your having chocolate, from the chocolate factory there, oh yes said the interpreter politely and there the conversation ended, and the interpreter went and got a taxi for them and I have never seen them again.

The interpreter came to see us on business very often but after this he always stayed and talked, he never referred to the conversation but he became more intimate. He once said that he knew who the members of the maquis in the town were and the captain had wanted to seize them but said the interpreter he would not allow it they are the kind of men I admire patriots and fathers of families. Then one day he asked the mayor if he would do him a personal favor, the mayor said yes of course, he said he would like him in his capacity of mayor to write to two towns in Normandy and ask for information about a certain lady, he said she is my wife, she is a Frenchwoman and she is my wife that is to say we are not married but she is my wife. The mayor did so and as yet had no answer. When the interpreter with the other Germans left he said to the mayor if you should ever get an answer, give it to the German station master and I will get it. Naturally enough there has been no answer. He also mentioned several times that he was a Luxembourgeois, he also said that he had bred and trained horses for the race track in Paris, he never said anything to them about a hotel in Paris, and as I say when he left he said he was coming back three months after the war, and he said there need only to be two killed to put an end to the war.

After the wife of the mayor was all through telling me the story, she said you know I think he was an Englishman, sometimes his French reminded me of yours, it seemed to be you speaking, but of course we will never know, and this is a true story.

There was a young woman in a village near here and of course we were all of us very envious and she had made herself a blouse out of parachute cloth that had been sent down with supplies, now we all want parachute cloth, I would love to have a shirt waist made of parachute cloth from an American airplane, a friend of ours told us that the other day he was out on his bicycle and he was stopped by the maquis who patrol all the roads that the Germans do not patrol. These boys were in a truck and they had an American flag on it, and they said we are not like the other maquis, we are American maquis, and under the direct orders of General Eisenhower, you see even in these days the French have to get gay.

It is very funny really funny, when the mayor went to Bourg to try and get some flour for bread, in order to have the truck of flour pass first you have to get permission for it to come from the Germans and then you get permission for it to pass from the maquis, we all laughed and said the only people who do not have to give permission are the people of Vichy, the prefet and sous-prefet have all fled, there is nobody left except the mayors the maquis and the Germans, it is really very funny, the mayor on his way to Bourg saw the armored train that we had seen at Culoz lying peacefully in a mountain stream at the side of the rails, naturally it never did get to Lyon.

It is wonderful the Americans just chasing around France,

everybody used to say, if they only would hurry if they only would hurry, but now they all laugh and they all say but they are hurrying you bet your life they are hurrying up. And Saint Odile, she did say that when Rome fell it would not be the end but the beginning of the end and then she said that the Mohammedan sickle moon and the Christian cross would shine together in peace and look at Turkey, well well, as the Englishman who does the propaganda in English from Berlin always says, well well.

It is nice that the forces of the interior the French are helping things along so well, it makes all the French people content that they are taking part and everybody is happy and gay.

When bread is the staff of life then we eat bread and butter yes we do eat bread and butter.

I remember when I was young and in a book we had with illustrations there was one where the Goths and the Vandals threw around and broke all the works of art in Italy, and I remember being terribly worried about all this destruction and then one day when I felt very worried about it all about the destruction of even more ancient monuments in buried cities I suddenly said to myself well after all there are miles more of works of art that even people who are really interested in them can see in their life time so why worry. But now with Florence being destroyed and Normandy and marching on Paris they are near Chartres to-day the Americans and it does kind of make one feel funny really feel funny it seemed endless this occupation of France and now there they are the American tanks near Chartres, dear me oh dear me it does make one feel funny.

Here we are so excited and rather querulous with waiting except that our minds are pretty well taken off our troubles by our own local excitements, we still have our fifty odd Germans in the region but they are frightened and they stay where they are they were in a village near by to buy some wine and the maquis heard they were there and they came along and shot dead an officer and two soldiers and now well naturally the village is frightened the maquis go away but the Germans well they are afraid to come back but now they have an evil habit of sending over five or six airplanes from Amberieu near Bourg and they drop bombs on a village, three days ago they did this completely wiping out a village and killing most of the population and almost every day these six odd German airplanes come over our heads, and what will they do, this we do not know, but something horrible that is certain.

Besides all this and which is really most exciting are the Robin Hood activities of the maquis. Night before last they came into the town, and they visited three of the principal shops whose owners aided and abetted the Germans and from one they took his car and fifty thousand francs from another they took all his hidden provisions quantities of macaroni and oil and twenty-five thousand francs and now all the rest who have either profited or been for the Germans are naturally most nervous. The maquis are using this money to help the villagers whose homes have been burnt by the Germans. They say the friends of the Germans should pay for the victims of the Germans. And then there are the shop keepers who are on the border land between friend and enemy and they are frightened, and then there are the type of old grumblers who always find everything the young generation do frightful and naturally they have talked too much against the maquis and they are worried and then there are the decayed aristocrats, who are always hoping that a new regime will give them a chance and they are the most furious of all against the defeat of the Germans they and the decayed bourgeoisie, who feel sure that everybody but themselves should be disciplined, I had a row with one of them on the street last night and my parting word in a loud voice was that she should be more charitable, using it in the American sense of charitable in thought, and the whole population laughed because she is notoriously not in deed, and everybody thought naturally I meant that but of course I did not. Then there is a very funny thing about the church bigots, they are all for the Germans, the clergy in general in France not, distinctly not, but all the old men and women who are known in France as the frogs in holy water or the mice of the sacristy they strangely enough considering how the Germans have treated the catholics in Germany are all for the Germans. It is like in the last war all the pacifists were for Germany. I used not to understand but I am beginning to now. The feeling is that all that makes for liberty and liveliness is against those that either by weakness or by strength want to suppress the others and so the Germans who are the Germans who are the arch-disciplinarians because both of their weakness and their strength they want to stop liberty so those who want liberty suppressed because liberty is a criticism of them are pro-German.

It is funny really funny, the maquis have taken charge of Culoz, they have put up notices under the heading of the fourth republic telling the population what to do and all the time there are twenty-five German soldiers at the station as frightened as rabbits, they stay out only long enough to buy their provisions and retire back to their station, across the river there are still fifty to two hundred but nobody does seem to pay any attention, the maquis do not even take the trouble to gather them in, but they will so they say and put them to work. I like their calling it the fourth republic, the French dearly love a new form of government, they do love a change, they might have thought that the third republic was just going on but not at all there was an in between, the dictatorship or the oligarchy of Vichy so you just could not have it the third republic it has to be a fourth republic. There have been so many these last hundred and forty years, I think I have counted them once already in this book, three different varieties of monarchy, two empires three republics, one commune one oligarchy and dictatorship, and now here we are at a fourth republic and everybody is pleased. It makes them feel gay and cheerful. The German captain who left with the hundred and fifty soldiers was driven to Lyon by one of the taxis from Culoz, the taxi man came back and he said the German captain cried when he said good-bye, he said he had been so happy in Culoz and had hoped to once more see his wife and children but now he was ordered to Normandy and of course he cried and expected the French chauffeur to sympathise with him. They certainly are a funny people they certainly are.

Alice Toklas has just commenced typewriting this book, as long as there were Germans around we left it in manuscript as my handwriting is so bad it was not likely that any German would be able to read it, but now well if they are not gone they are so to speak not here, we can leave our windows open and the light burning, dear me such little things but they do amount to a lot, and it is so. They have left Florence, that is something to the good and everybody cheers up, they are now expecting it to be all over by the fifteenth of August. The French like to set a date it cheers them, but it does seem rather soon, they all also say that in this region there is an English colonel and fifteen Canadian officers, but are they, sometimes we believe it and sometimes we do not. If they are here it would be nice to see them.

There are the Germans still here some forty odd but we never see them in the village the way we used to, why not, I asked the mayor, he twinkled he said they sleep all day, because they mount guard all night, they are afraid I said like rabbits he said. Everybody is so pleased that the overbearing Germans are afraid like rabbits, everybody is pleased.

Even though the Germans are still here the maquis have taken over the victualing of our town as they have done in all the region, they are distributing lots more butter and cheese than there was. They take all that was being prepared in the dairies for the Germans. Look said the cook excitedly, it is butter done up in tinfoil, oh it was prepared for those dirty Boches for the evil birds and now we have it come quick Madame and taste it. She is keeping the tinfoil as a sacred souvenir, the first spoil from the enemy. Ah she said they made us cry since forty and now they cry. Naturally it is difficult to get medicines, even the Germans have not much of that so the maquis cannot take it from them so everybody is going back to old herb remedies. The old people are always being consulted to remember what they did when they were young, for bruises you use wild verbena pounded and for disinfecting and reducing swelling application of the petals of the Easter lily preserved in eau de vie and foot baths of boiled ivy.

Just how I do not know but the French workers in Germany commence to come back. How they get away they do not say but in the last few days three of them have come back. And they describe Germany as she is.

And just to-day we are most awfully excited because the allies have just made a landing in the south of France and we will be on their way up and it is most exciting. One woman just told me that she had two spare rooms and although it was Assumption and a holiday she was immediately starting to fix them up for the first American soldiers, and the whole population wants to learn English and quickly.

As I was saying some forced workers in Germany have made their way back, you never do know how the French do it but they always keep wandering back and apparently without very much difficulty, they decide that they want to come home and they come.

As I say their descriptions of Germany are funny. They say the civilian population still stupidly believes in victory, they have not changed but that the army is completely discouraged, and besides they are comforting themselves by shooting their officers, it would seem that Hitler has ordered that any soldier should shoot any officer or soldier whom he heard talking against the government, and say the French naturally any soldier who has a grievance has nothing to do but shoot the man against whom he has it and say it was because he spoke against the government and then instead of being punished he is congratulated. And moreover the German army is beginning to mutiny, so these French boys say, but as long as the civilians still believe in victory Germany will not give in. The thing that fills all the French in Germany with horror is the way the Germans treat the Russians, women as well as men, the Germans fear them so that they go quite crazy with brutality, that is the French explanation of the situation.

All this reminds me that one day in Paris, we had a lot of people for dinner it was about '35 and they were talking Nazi and Hitler and I said it was Hitler's intention to destroy Germany, and that was because he was an Austrian and an Austrian in his heart has a hatred for Germany so great even if unconscious that if he could he would destroy Germany and Hitler can and will. They all thought that I was only trying to be bright but not at all it is true, if Hitler had been a German he could not destroy Germans the way he does, it is like Napoleon who was an Italian and naturally was indifferent as to how many Frenchmen were killed. It is the judgment of Solomon over again, there is the call of the blood, but funnily enough the foreign monster has a glamor for the nation he is destroying that a home grown monster could not have. And so Hitler is quite comfortably waiting for the last battalion to fight and win or be killed, presumably killed but he has made them all feel like that because he is a foreigner and not a German, it is the other way to of a prophet not being recognised in his own country.

Oh well these days nobody minds death from fear of heaven or hell but there is there always is with death the cessation of life and life is interesting, and certainly it is for Hitler so why stop.

The little groups of Germans all over are still all over, ours just left yesterday, they were as inoffensive as Germans can be, but then they were really not soldiers they were mostly railroad workers and the few soldiers they had with them as guards were rather miserable specimens victims of Russian rheumatism, as they call it, and now they are gone to join up with the others across the river and the five hundred at Aix-les-Bains left to go away, but to the distress of the Aix population they have come back, the maquis have cut off all the means of communication and they are back again. The maquis say they are going to mop them up and I suppose they will. We see the maquis now, they have big trucks and all camouflaged, I saw one like that to-day the first one at a little town where I occasionally buy cake, and when I saw that truck I had a shock, have the Germans come back but no there was a little tricolor cheerfully waving from the front, and everywhere the cross of Lorraine and the tricolor painted, and it was all gay and cheerful not German at all. I heard to-day that Captain Bouvet is the chief of this region, he was a nice man, he and I in the darkest days of the war used to have long conversations on the cold winter days between Belley and Bilignin, being cheered by the battle of

London being cheered by the Russian entrance being cheered by being cheerful, and of course I did not know he was mixed up with the maquis, until just before the Germans left Belley they tried to catch him and his son-in-law but they managed to hide away not too difficult there in the mountains, and the Germans did not get them, he was a retired army officer who had specialised in the chemical side of explosives so naturally he has been wonderful in stopping all railroads and destroying bridges, and now everybody can know that he is he and it is a pleasure.

But really you can understand how the Germans could never have had colonies, when you see these isolated pieces of the German army get to be like hunted rabbits as soon as they are not winning, they are always frightened even when they are winning the most and you really had to be in a country occupied by them to realise it and if you are always about to be frightened you naturally cannot impose yourself upon primitive races. Unless there were a lot of Germans about they never moved without a gun on their back and that was before there were maquis. And this is undoubtedly true, how could they ever be a dominant race, just how could they. Everybody is so cheerful now, they are all making their little flags for the allies everybody the farmers even in the midst of the harvest, the wives are taking time to make flags. Very nice, oh so very nice, we can have our windows open, and everybody is cheerful. The poor people of Aix-les-Bains with their five hundred Germans back again, it is too bad, but it is better and the Aixois know that, that they were unable to get away, even if they have for a little while to have them back again. All the men young and old want to be in it they are all for being up and at them, they are very envious of those who already joined up are in it, and the French troops landed in the south and now oh how they all want to be with them.

This morning just before dawn we were all awakened by the rattle of tommy guns and magazine rifles, but they did not last, it seems that the two forces of the maquis did not connect and so the coup did not come off, but all through the Savoy the Germans are giving themselves up and those

across the river said that they would like to perhaps they will
and then we can be peaceful with the maquis until the Americans come, then that will finish the book the first American
tank and surely it will be coming along, one week or two
weeks the pessimists say three weeks nobody expects it to
take a month, and they are thirty kilometers from Paris it is
an anxious moment, dear Paris, we saw it escape the Germans in fourteen and now forty-four.

To-day we were for the first time in company with a real
live maquis, we were in a taxi and he came along to go to
Culoz, and we were delighted, he had the tricolor on his
shoulder and looked bronzed and capable, we are Americans
we said, yes we know he said, and we solemnly shook hands
and congratulated each other, he was a captain in the maquis,
and he had been a prisoner in Germany, had escaped two
years ago and went back to his job in the water-ways and
bridges and joined the maquis and has been working with
them ever since, we were all pleased, but everybody is pleased
these days, one can hardly realise how strange it seems to
see everybody smiling and everybody is smiling.

The maquis were pretty wonderful of course now they are
armed and more or less superior in numbers to the Germans
they attack and besides they are sure of victory but when
they first began to block the German transport system, they
were practically unarmed, they were inferior in numbers,
they were often betrayed by their compatriots and still they
managed to cut railroad lines block tunnels blow up bridges,
and besides all their other troubles they had to receive the
material sent them by airplane and get away with it and
hide and manufacture it and use it all in the face of a heavily
occupied country with enemy guards all along, and the poor
maquis many of them hungry and cold and not too favorably
regarded by many of their countrymen, it was a kind of a
Valley Forge with no General Washington but each little
band had to supply itself with its own food its own plans
and its own morale. We who lived in the midst of you salute
you.

While I was walking yesterday evening as I passed through

a village little voices came out of the dark saying are not you afraid of the curfew Madame.

On the other hand the little boys who have been playing at being maquis in odd corners and in secret now play it in the open streets, with red white and blue on their shoulders their fathers' war helmets on their heads and their wooden mitraillettes in their hands, when some one asked them what would you do if the Germans came back. No Germans can come back.

Everybody is waiting, they say it goes so fast it makes them feel as if they were at a cinema. They have completely forgotten that they used to moan and say if they would only hurry. And besides they are so very much better fed, not in the big cities alas, but here in the small towns, the maquis, are doing all the policing, they have announced formally that the Vichy government does not any longer function and that they are the government, and with the assistance of the mayor they are going to feed and police the population. Already we have had supplementary butter wine and cheese, and now they are here the people are talking wildly of supplementary white bread and sardines but that is decidedly premature, anyway the maquis are now in command it puts its notices up on the mairie it sends the town crier around with his trumpet to announce what we are all to do and everybody is pleased because it is French and easy, and conversational and all who want can gather together and talk it over. I was coming up the street I heard a man saying yes before the war of fourteen, well yes they can go back to talk about before the war of fourteen it has come now the middle of August to be as peaceable as that.

It is nice to be free my gracious yes and now we have had our little battle and it was this way. The Germans had left Culoz and they had all gathered together across the river at Vions there were then between two hundred and three hundred of them. About a week ago the maquis decided to take the bridge away from them and get them on the move but there was some difficulty about the signals, they all have to come down from their mountains and there was some mistake.

Two Germans were killed on the bridge but they were still there. Yesterday in broad daylight they got a gun up on the hill and attacked the bridge, they first had to warn away the little boys who were bathing in the pools of the Rhone and two women who came along after were wounded a little bit, and then the maquis rushed the bridge and it was most exciting, six maquis attacked eight Germans killed two and the others ran away, in the meantime eight German airplanes came along from Lyon but they did not help their comrades in distress they just went on their way to Germany and we have not been seen again. Just a little while and the Germans got away as fast as they could. The maquis put the flag on the bridge and sent round to the mayor to tell the town crier that the bridge was in the hands of the maquis and nobody should cross it, then came the night, the maquis gathered from all sides attacked the fleeing Germans and killed anywhere from fifty to eighty of them in the marshes, the nephew of our baker killed five and the butcher boy killed four, the Germans were trying to escape toward Aix-les-Bains, but there others of the maquis pushed them back and it became a regular rabbit drive, the weather was hot and the Germans were in a bad way there in the marshes, some tried to surrender but others of the group fired and the maquis killed them all, every one, and then they came back, and everybody was happy and they said everybody must put up flags so we all rushed around trying to get flags, and our general store who had been a well-known collabo unearthed from his stores a quantity of French, English and American flags we got one nice one and in the meantime the maquis had given the mayor a nice big American flag and it and the French flag were hung up in front of the mairie and we were very moved and Mrs. Mayor was teaching all the children to salute the flag to say vive la France et honneur aux maquis. It is rather wonderful when you think that a quantity of little children had never seen a flag never, the Germans never had flags and of course there were no French ones allowed, and the little children go up and touch it timidly, they never have seen a flag. What a town everybody is out on the streets all the time, and in between time they sing the Marseillaise, everybody feels so easy, it is impossible to make anybody realise what occupation by Germans is who has not had it, here in Culoz it was as easy as it was possible for it to be as most of the population are railroad employees and the Germans did not want to irritate them, but it was like a suffocating cloud under which you could not breathe right, we had lots of food, and no interference on the part of the Germans but there it was a weight that was always there and now everybody feels natural, they feel good and they feel bad but they feel natural, and that was our battle, the maquis are all down there at the bridge they do not think the Germans can come back, but they are watchful, there was firing just now but it did not last, so it was probably a false alarm, we like the maquis, honneur aux maquis.

They say that six of the wounded and killed Germans escaped into the mountain and they look for them from time to time but as they have not found them they take it for granted that they are dead and gone. It is wonderful to pass the railroad station and see the block house that the Germans had built to defend themselves already gone the barbed wire already gone and the children playing around where the Boches had so solemnly been standing with their guns all ready to shoot any one. The employees of the railroad are very busy, they are getting everything ready so that the railroad track can be all mended and that trains will be able to go as soon as France is free, well it is free but not completely free, in Lyon and Chambery the two chief towns the maquis are still fighting the Germans, but soon yes soon now we can say soon.

Everybody is so pleased with the maquis taking Vichy, it is a good joke une bonne blague à la Francaise, no it was not an allied army but the maquis who took Vichy, everybody is so pleased with the joke that they have pretty well forgotten their rancor against the government, the French certainly are sans rancune, they cannot remember their hatreds very long it is at once their weakness and their strength, but it is nice, a good joke like the maquis taking Vichy and all the government running away makes everybody gay. It is hot and dry most awfully hot and dry but as everybody knows it is good

for the fighting armies to have dry weather they put up with
it contentedly, even if the vegetables are drying up, tant pis
they say, what of it, if we are free. And now there is more
distribution of wine and butter and cheese, so why worry.

And now they have just announced on the radio that the
Americans are at Grenoble and that is only eighty kilometers
away and no opposition in between, oh if they would only
come by here. We must see them. There is no way of getting
there.

And now at half past twelve to-day on the radio a voice
said attention attention attention and the Frenchman's voice
cracked with excitement and he said Paris is free. Glory hallelujah Paris is free, imagine it less than three months since the
landing and Paris is free. All these days I did not dare to
mention the prediction of Saint Odile, she said Paris would
not be burned the devotion of her people would save Paris
and it has vive la France. I cant tell you how excited we all
are and now if I can only see the Americans come to Culoz
I think all this about war will be finished yes I do.

To-night it was just like fourth of July in my youth in the
San Joaquin valley, it was just as hot and we all went to-day
that Paris was freed to put flowers on the soldiers monument,
it had already been draped with flags and the maquis
marched down the main street of Culoz, and then everybody
stood at attention and sang the Marseillaise, it was interesting
to see who out of the population of Culoz were members of
the fighting maquis, and then there were another lot of affil-
iated but not fighting maquis. I like to call them maquis, that
was what they were, when every moment was a danger, they
had to receive arms they had to transport them and they had
to hide them and they had to do sabotage and all the time a
very considerable part of their countrymen did not at all believe in them, and there were workmen, station masters, civil
servants, tailors, barbers, anything, nobody knew but they
naturally, and some of them looked pretty tired but my everybody was happy, everybody had the flag on their shoulders
and some of the girls heaven only knows how had achieved
a whole dress made of tri-color ribbons sewn together, Paris
was taken at noon and by eight o'clock all France was putting

wreaths on their soldiers monument because of course every village has that, honneur aux maquis, and they say that Americans are at Aix-les-Bains only twenty-five kilometers away how we want to see them even a little more than the rest of the population which is saying a great deal. We found some American flag ribbon in the local country store, and we gave it to all the little boys, just as we did in the 1914-1918 war when America came into the war, we rather wondered whether it was not some left over of the same ribbon, after all there was no particular reason in this little village that the local country store should otherwise have had it, vive la France vive l'Amerique vive les allies vive Paris, and after this most exciting day. Oh I forgot, I naturally wanted my dog Basket to participate and so I took him down to the local barber and I said won't you shave him and make him elegant, it is not right when the Americans come along and when Paris is free that the only French poodle in Culoz and owned by Americans should not be elegant, so perspiring freely all of us including Basket, he had his paws shaved and his muzzle shaved and he was elegant and as such he took part in the evening's celebration and all the little children, said Basket Basket come here Basket, they do say it beautifully and then there was a blare of trumpets and naturally he was frightened and tried to run away, so I tied him with a handkerchief and the effort was not so elegant but we were all proud of ourselves just the same.

We are all exhausted to-day the next day, we were so excited we are so happy we are all exhausted, we just go around shaking hands and being exhausted.

And that is the way it is after all of us being so happy yesterday, to-day they are once more fighting in the streets of Paris, dear Paris and dear dear Paris, but Saint Odile did say it would be all right and although worried well anyway to distract our minds just now while I was in my bath, bang and the house shook I got out of my bath and another big bang, and the house shook, and there down in the valley were volumes of smoke, they were trying to hit the bridges over the Rhone, the cook was screaming and the people flocking into the grounds, and we could see the railroad bridge and it seemed to be intact, but the maquis who were guarding it, well now everybody says nobody was hurt, and it was the Boches flying home because they could not any longer stay in France in vengeance dropped bombs, we saw two lots of airplanes in the air and now they are gone I was afraid they were Americans dropping bombs but nobody believes anything bad of Americans, and perhaps not, anyway we are not as happy as yesterday but to-day is to-day and that is all there is to say.

And now to-day that Paris is really free, this is what Saint Odile did say.

Saint Odile said that the world would go on and there would come the worst war of all and the fire would be thrown down from the heavens and there would be freezing and heating and rivers running with blood and at last there would be winning by the enemy and everybody would say and how can they be so strong, and everybody would say and give us peace and then little by little there would come the battle of the mountain and that was certainly Moscow, because even in the time of Saint Odile because of its many religious houses was called the Holy Mountain and indeed it was there that the enemy received its first check, and then she said, much later there would be fighting in the streets of the eternal city, and Rome taken it was not the end but the beginning of the end (which indeed was so) and that Paris which was in the greatest danger would be saved because of the holiness of its holy women, Sainte Genevieve and now it has been saved owing to the valor of its men and its women and we are all so happy, honneur aux maquis.

It is wonderful to go down to the village square on Sunday evening and to see it full of maquis in their nice shorts and khaki shirts with the tricolor on their shoulders talking to the girls everybody smiling and only ten days ago everybody was staying in the house and the Germans were in the square, only ten days ago, what a week, and nobody is really used to it, and yet it is hard to believe that it was not always so, we have one hundred and fifty maquis stationed in our town and it is a pleasure.

Yesterday I was out on the road and there was a tremendous

thunderstorm and I went into a roadside café, there were two
men sitting at a table with F.F.I. on their breasts and I said
how do you do and Basket and I were very wet, and they
said how do you do but not quite like Frenchmen, we talked
a little more and then I knew from their accent they were
Spaniards, I said I was American and we solemnly shook
hands and we began to talk, one of them was the typical
Barcelona intellectual he reminded me of Picasso's friend
Sabartes, he and his comrade with two hundred and fifty
other Spanish refugees have been with the maquis for two
years now, since said they we cannot fight for freedom in our
own country we fight for freedom wherever we can, they
have been at it for ten years now, they know about Hemingway and when I told them that I knew Picasso they stood
up and solemnly shook hands, all over again. Then I asked
where they had come from and they said Annecy and I said
you must have seen my compatriots and they said yes and a
woman journalist interviewed them and said to them what
are you Spaniards doing here, and when they told her she
said she was glad to meet them and that they were heroes.
They were going to Artemarre to see their wives who were
refugeed there and then they were going back to Annecy. If
said I you see the journalist again tell her that I want to
see her, and I told them my name but they wont remember
but anyway it was a pleasure to send word. It is very tantalis-
ing Americans all over the place sometimes only twenty
kilometers away and we do not see them, how we want to
see them and send word to America and have news from
them. To-night I was all bitten by mosquitoes trying to get
more news of them. I went down to the Pont de la Lois which
is the only bridge left over the Rhone, it strangely enough
was not destroyed in '40 and now again it has not been destroyed. It was near there that our little battle was fought and
it was near there that the bombs were dropped the other day
or was it only yesterday. Well anyway I was talking to the
maquis that were guarding the bridge, among them a boy
I knew in Cezerieu and they told me that a car with American
officers had passed over the bridge, when I told Alice Toklas
about it tonight she said she would take her typewriting down

there and await them but when I told her about mosquitoes she weakened, well anyway, one of the train hands who was also there said that they had received orders to repair the train tracks between Chambery and Culoz and that it had to be done in three days, because he said the Americans want to use it and he promised me that when the first train carrying Americans was signaled, night or day, he would leave all and come up and let me know. Dear Americans how we do want to see them.

It's wonderful in the evening hearing the voices of the children playing, for such a long time they played quietly they were afraid to play in the streets or on the sidewalk but now they are let loose and the elders smile indulgently and all of a sudden you hear a childish voice cry pomm pomm pomm, pomm pomm pomm, pomm pomm pomm that's that, of course that is a mitraillette killing the Boches, everybody calls them Boches now, and everybody is easy very easy in their minds, except of course those who made money off the Germans, and there are some, and naturally they are nervous. The maquis of course do revenge themselves a little the French are not naturally a revengeful people but the Germans did commit such awful atrocities in the mountain regions that when the mountain boys caught the S.S. troops in Annecy naturally enough they made them parade the town with their hands in the air and then took them up into the hills and there nobody knows what did happen to them, and naturally the young ones who had seen farms burned with men women and children inside them as well as the beasts, when they take a German prisoner they cannot help giving him a kick in the behind. But the French are not a vengeful people and they will soon now that they feel their strength they will not feel revengeful.

Our friend Monsieur Godet came yesterday and said he was going to try to get through to Switzerland, he has business there, and so we are hoping that he will be able to cable to America for us and tell all our friends that we are all right, he left on his bicycle with a permit from the F.F.I. and once he gets to Saint Julien, the way we always used to drive into Switzerland, he thinks he will have no trouble. It will be nice when he comes back and brings us news of the Americans. We have asked him to bring back with him a newspaper man or a newspaper woman, or two of them, if he did that would be nice. There are American cars and officers that pass so they say from time to time but I have not seen them and of course seeing is believing, because with the population, the wish is so much the father of the thought, but they will come, bless them.

I met to-day Monsieur Burtin whose daughter is at the University of Grenoble and who kept telling him when he worried about her student activities but my dear father you do not understand, this is our war not your war, and now that the F.F.I. have covered themselves with glory she said to her father, you see we were right, to be sure people of your age are less credulous than people of our age, but this time we were right in persisting in our credulity, look at the results, they are magnificent said the father, yes said the daughter you can understand it was no work for veterans.

A little later I was talking to a young fellow who is now in Culoz but whom I had often seen in Belley where he was in the first battalion of Chasseurs before they were demobilised when the Southern zone no longer existed. I had not seen him since those days. So naturally I asked him if he had been in the movement. He said because of his health, his lungs are not very strong he had not been able to be but actually all his comrades in the battalion were in the movement, not the officers, he said, this was not an officers movement, regular army officers did not in general have the kind of intelligence that makes a maquis. No I said, all the army officers that I know who were patriots, all managed somehow to get to Africa and join the regular army, yes he said they did not have the kind of quality that makes maquis, the non-commissioned officers yes lots of them were in the movement, it was said he marvelously secret, you do not know perhaps he said that one of the leaders of the Paris F.F.I. was hidden for three months in Culoz, no I said did you know at the time, oh no he said, I knew his sister very intimately but she never mentioned it, how old is he, I said, oh about twenty-four and the Germans got on his track two of the crowd were taken by the Germans but the rest of the leaders escaped, and the two who were captured in spite of frightful tortures did not give their comrades away, after three months they heard that the Germans had lost trace of them so they all went back, and continued their work, now that it is all over his sister told me all about it. And where said I did all the arms come from that the Parisians seem to have had, oh he laughed most of those have been hidden since '40, not possibly I said, yes he said I do assure you. Well honneur aux maquis, one cannot say it too often, it is nice to have two countries to be proud of that belong to you, mine of course are America and France.

To-day the village is excited terribly excited because they are shaving the heads of the girls who kept company with the Germans during the occupation, it is called the coiffure of 1944, and naturally it is terrible because the shaving is done publicly, it is being done to-day. It is as I have often said, life in the middle ages, it certainly is most interesting and logical it certainly is.

Speaking of all this there is this about a Jewish woman, a Parisienne, well known in the Paris world. She and her family took refuge in Chambery when the persecutions against the Jews began in Paris. And then later, when there was no southern zone, all the Jews were supposed to have the fact put on their carte d'identité and their food card, she went to the prefecture to do so and the official whom she saw looked at her severely Madame he said, have you any proof with you that you are a Jewess, why no she said, well he said if you have no actual proof that you are a Jewess, why do you come and bother me, why she said I beg your pardon, no he said I am not interested unless you can prove you are a Jewess, good day he said and she left. It was she who told the story. Most of the French officials were like that really like that.

And now everybody says all the time that American officers are passing through Culoz, you can tell them they all say because of their large hats. Do American officers wear large hats, oh yes they say. Do they, I wonder, or is it only a sort of cowboy idea that the population have. Perhaps the American do wear large hats, we are so eagerly waiting to see.

What a day what a day of days, I always did say that I would end this book with the first American that came to Culoz, and to-day oh happy day yesterday and to-day, the first of September 1944. There have been six of them in the house, two of them stayed the night and then three were there besides the first three not here at Culoz but at Belley. Oh happy day, that is all that I can say oh happy day.

This is the way it happened. We go to Belley about once a month to go shopping and the bank and things like that and yesterday Thursday was the day, so we went over in a taxi, and when we got to Belley as I got out of the taxi several people said to me, Americans are here. I had heard that so often that I had pretty well given up hope and I said oh nonsense but yes they said, and then the son of the watchmaker who had been the most steadfast and violent pro-ally even in the darkest days came up to me and said the Americans are here. Really I said yes he said well I said lead me to them, all right he said they are at the hotel so we went on just as fast as we could and when we got to the hotel they tried to stop me but we said no and went in. I saw the proprietor of the hotel and I said is it true there are Americans, yes he said come on, and I followed and there we were Alice Toklas panting behind and Basket very excited and we went into a room filled with maquis and the mayor of Belley and I said in a loud voice are there any Americans here and three men stood up and they were Americans God bless them and were we pleased. We held each other's hands and we patted each other and we sat down together and I told them who we were, and they knew, I always take it for granted that people will know who I am and at the same time at the last moment I kind of doubt, but they knew of course they knew, they were lieutenant Walter E. Oleson 120th Engineers and private Edward Landry and Walter Hartze, and they belonged to the Thunderbirds and how we talked and how we patted each other in the good American way, and I had to know where they came from and where they were going and where they were born. In the last war we had come across our first American soldiers and it had been nice but nothing like this, after almost two years of not a word with America, there they were, all three of them. Then we went to look at their car the jeep, and I had expected it to be much smaller but it was quite big and they said did I want a ride and I said you bet I wanted a ride and we all climbed in and there I was riding in an American army car driven by an American soldier. Everybody was so excited.

Then we all said good-bye and we did hope to see them again, and then we went on with our shopping, then suddenly everybody got excited army trucks filled with soldiers were coming along but not Americans, this was the French army in American cars and they were happy and we were happy and tired and happy and then we saw two who looked like Americans in a car standing alone and I went over and said are you Americans and they said sure, and by that time I was confident and I said I was Gertrude Stein and did they want to come back with us and spend the night. They said well yes they thought that the war could get along without them for a few hours so they came, Alice Toklas got into the car with the driver and the colonel came with me, oh a joyous moment and we all drove home and the village was wild with excitement and they all wanted to shake the colonel's hand and at last we got into the house, and were we excited. Here were the first Americans actually in the house with us, impossible to believe that only three weeks before the Germans had been in the village still and feeling themselves masters, it was wonderful. Lieutenant-Colonel William O. Perry Headquarters 47th Infantry Division and private John Schmaltz, wonderful that is all I can say about it wonderful, and I said you are going to sleep in beds where German officers slept six week ago, wonderful my gracious perfectly wonderful.

How we talked that night, they just brought all America to us every bit of it, they came from Colorado, lovely Colorado, I do not know Colorado but that is the way I felt about it lovely Colorado and then everybody was tired out and they gave us nice American specialties and my were we happy, we were, completely and truly happy and completely and entirely worn out with emotion. The next morning while they breakfasted we talked some more and we patted each other and then kissed each other and then they went away. Just as we were sitting down to lunch, in came four more Americans this time war correspondents, our emotions were not yet exhausted nor our capacity to talk, how we talked and talked and where they were born was music to the ears Baltimore and Washington D.C. and Detroit and Chicago, it is all music to the ears so long long long away from the names of the places where they were born. Well they have asked me to go with them to Voiron to broadcast with them to America next Sunday and I am going and the war is over and this certainly this is the last war to remember.

EPILOGUE

Write about us they all said a little sadly, and write about them I will. They all said good-bye Gerty as the train pulled out and then they said, well we will see you in America, and then they said we will stop on our way back, and then they said we will see you in California and then one said, you got to get to New York first.

It is pretty wonderful and pretty awful to have been intimate and friendly and proud of two American armies in France apart only by twenty-seven years. It is wonderful and if I could live twenty-seven more years could I see them here again. No I do not think so, maybe in other places but not here.

In the beginning when the Americans were here we had officers and their companion drivers. They were companion drivers, companions and drivers drivers and companions. The French revolution said, liberty brotherhood and equality, well they said it and we are it, bless us.

Of course the driver is a little prouder when it is a colonel than when it is a lieutenant or captain, well just a little. The first one was Lieutenant-Colonel Perry of Colorado, he came with me in the taxi from Belley and Miss Toklas went with Jake in the jeep, his name was not Jake but the colonel called him Jake because he used, while sitting in the jeep waiting, to sign his name as autograph for the French who crowded around him and wanted it, just like a film star, so the colonel called him Jake.

Well Miss Toklas asked him if the other one was a soldier

like himself, they were our first Americans and we did not know how to tell one from the other as on the outside they all look alike particularly when their outside jacket is buttoned up, Miss Toklas asked him and he said with contentment oh he is a lieutenant-colonel.

After that we had lots of officers and finally I met three majors in Aix-les-Bains. I said well it's all right, but now we have had everything from a second lieutenant to a full colonel and indeed several specimens of each now I want a general. The majors at least one of them said I think I can get you one. Would you like General Patch. Would I, I said, well I guess I would. If, said he, you write him a note I am sure he would come. He gave me an old card, I had already given him my autograph on a piece of French paper money, it is hard to write on French paper money but I finally did get the habit, so I wrote the note to General Patch and of course we thought it all a joke but not at all. About ten days later, came the personal secretary of General Patch with a nice driver from Arkansas who said modestly he always drove the general, and they brought me a charming letter from the general saying he would be coming along very soon, to eat the chicken dinner I had offered him. The secretary said that the general would be coming along in about two weeks. When that time came heavy fighting began in the Vosges mountains, the general's headquarters moved away from our region, and now we are still waiting, but he surely will come, he said he would and he will.

Gradually as the joy and excitement of really having Americans here really having them here began to settle a little I began to realise that Americans converse much more than they did, American men in those other days, the days before these days did not converse. How well I remember in the last war seeing four or five of them at a table at a hotel and one man would sort of drone along monologuing about what he had or had not done and the others solemnly and quietly eating and drinking and never saying a word. And seeing the soldiers stand at a corner or be seated somewhere and there they were and minutes hours passed and they never said a word, and then one would get up and leave and the others got up and left and that was that. No this army was not like that, this army conversed, it talked it listened, and each one of them had something to say no this army was not like that other army. People do not change no they don't, when I was in America after almost thirty years of absence they asked me if I did not find Americans changed and I said no what could they change to except to be American and anyway I could have gone to school with any of them they were just like the ones I went to school with and now they are still American but they can converse and they are interesting when they talk. The older Americans always told stories that was about all there was to their talking but these don't tell stories they converse and what they say is interesting and what they hear interests them and that does make them different not really different God bless them but just the same they are not quite the same.

We did not talk about that then. We had too much to tell and they had too much to tell to spend any time conversing about conversation. What we always wanted to know was the state they came from and what they did before they came over here. One said that he was born on a race track and worked in a night club. Another was the golf champion of Mississippi, but what we wanted most was to hear them say the name of the state in which they were born and the names of the other states where they had lived.

After every war, there have only been two like that but I do not think that just to say after the other war makes it feel as it does, no I do mean after every war, it feels like that, after every war when I talk and listen to all our army, it feels like that too, the thing I like most are the names of all the states of the United States. They make music and they are poetry, you do not have to recite them all but you just say any one two three four or five of them and you will see they make music and they make poetry.

After the last war I wanted to write a long book or a poem, I never did either but I wanted to, about how Kansas differed from Iowa and Iowa from Illinois and Illinois from Ohio, and Mississippi from Louisiana and Louisiana from Tennessee and Tennessee from Kentucky, and all the rest from all the rest, it would be most exciting, because each one of them does so completely differ from all the rest including their neighbors. And when you think how ruled the lines are of the states, no natural boundaries of mountains or rivers but just ruled out with a ruler to make lines and angles and all the same each one of the states has its own character, its own accent, just like provinces in France which are so ancient. It does not take long to make one state different from another state not so very long, they are all just as American as that but they are all so different one from the other Dakota and Wyoming and Texas and Oklahoma. Well any one you like. I like them all.

After all every one is as their land is, as the climate is, as the mountains and the rivers or their oceans are as the wind and rain and snow and ice and heat and moisture is, they just are and that makes them have their way to eat their way to drink their way to act their way to think and their way to be subtle, and even if the lines of demarcation are only made with a ruler after all what is inside those right angles is different from those on the outside of those right angles, any American knows that.

It is just that, I do not know why but Arkansas touched me particularly, anything touches me particularly now that is American. There is something in this native land business and you cannot get away from it, in peace time you do not seem to notice it much particularly when you live in foreign parts but when there is a war and you are all alone and completely cut off from knowing about your country well then there it is, your native land is your native land, it certainly is.

After all the excitement of all the jeeps and all the officers and all the drivers was over we were quiet a little while and we wondered are they all gone will we not see them again, and then Culoz which is a small town but a railroad center began to have them and we began to have them.

Troop trains began to pass through the station on their way to the front.

I was coming home from a walk and an F.F.I. said to me there is a train of your compatriots standing at a siding just below, I imagine it would please you to see them, thank you I said it will and I went quickly. There they were strolling along and standing about and I said Hello to the first group and they said hello and I said I am an American and they laughed and said so were they and how did I happen to get caught here and I told them how I had passed the war here, and they wanted to know if there was snow on the mountains in winter and there was a large group of them and I told them who I was thinking some one of them might have heard of me but lots of them had and they crowded around and we talked and we talked. It was the first time I had been with a real lot of honest to God infantry and they said they were just that. We began to talk states and they wanted to know about our life under the Germans and I told them and they were interested, and they told me about where they had been and what they thought of the people they had seen and then they wanted autographs and they gave me pieces of money to write on, and one Pole who was the most extravagant gave me a hundred franc bill to sign for him, funny that a Pole should have been the most wasteful of his money, perhaps he was only going to spend it anyway, and one of them told me that they knew about me because they study my poems along with other American poetry in the public schools and that did please me immensely it most certainly did and then I left and they left.

I came away meditating yes they were American boys but they had a poise and completely lacked the provincialism which did characterise the last American army, they talked and they listened and they had a sureness, they were quite certain of themselves, they had no doubts or uncertainties and they had not to make any explanations. The last army was rather given to explaining, oh just anything, they were given to explaining, these did not explain, they were just conversational.

Then more troop trains came along and we took apples down to them and we talked to them and they talked to us and I was getting more impressed with their being different, they knew where they were and what they were and why they were, yes they did, they had poise and not any of them was ever drunk, not a bit, it was most exciting that they were like that.

The last American army used to ask questions, why do the French people put walls around their houses what are they afraid of what do they want to hide. Why do they want to stay and work this ground when there is so much better land to find. This army does not ask questions like that, they consider that people have their habits and their ways of living, some you can get along with and others you can't, but they all are perfectly reasonable for the people who use them. That is the great change in the Americans, they are interested, they are observant, they are accustomed to various types of people and ways of being, they have plenty of curiosity, but not any criticism, that is the new army. It was all very exciting.

Then one day down at the station, it was raining, I saw three American soldiers standing, I said hello what are you doing, why we just came here, they said, to stay a few days. I laughed. Is it A.W.O.L. I said or do you call it something else now, well no they said we still call it that. And said I what are you going to do, just stay a few days they said. Come along I said, even if you are A.W.O.L. you will have to be given some tea and cake so come along. They came. One from Detroit, one little one from Tennessee, one big young one from New Jersey. We talked, it seemed somehow more like that old army, their being A.W.O.L. and deciding to stay here a few days. They came back with me, and we talked. They were interested, Tennessee said honestly he was tired of ten inch shells, he just had had enough of ten inch shells. The other two seemed to be just tired, they were not particular what they were tired of, they were just tired. We talked and then in talking to them I began to realise that men from the South seemed to be quite often men who had been orphans since they were children, the men from Tennessee and from Arkansas seemed to tend to be orphans from very young, they were members of large families and the large family once having been made, they promptly became orphans, I also began to realise that there were lots of pure American families where they were lots of brothers and sisters. The last army seven to eleven in a family was rare, but now it seemed to be quite common. Not emigrant families but pure American families. I was very much interested. And now the difference

between the old army and the new began to be so real to me
that I began to ask the American army about it. In the meanwhile the three A.W.O.L.s after moving into the village and
then moving out and then moving in again did finally move
out. They came to see us before they left, they did not say
where they were going and they said it had been a pleasure
to know us.

In the meanwhile, five M.P.s had come to stay in the station to watch the stuff on the trains and see that it did not
get stolen, and with these we got to be very good friends, and
they were the first ones with whom I began to talk about the
difference between the last army and this army. Why is it, I
said.

They said, yes we know we are different, and I said and
how did you find it out. From what we heard about the other
army, that made us know we were very different, I said there
is no doubt about that, you don't drink much I said, no we
don't and we save our money they said, we don't want to go
home and when we get there not have any money, we want
to have a thousand dollars or so at least to be able to look
around and to find out what we really want to do. (Even the
three A.W.O.L.s felt like that about money.) Well I explained
what one used to complain of about American men was that
as they grew older they did not grow more interesting, they
grew duller. When I made that lecture tour in '35 to the
American universities I used to say to them, now all sorts
of things interest you but what will happen to you five years
hence when you are working at some job will things interest
you or will you just get dull. Yes said one of the soldiers yes
but you see the depression made them know that a job was
not all there was to it as mostly there was no job, and if there
was it was any kind of job not the kind of job they had expected it to be, you would see a college man digging on the
road doing anything and so we all came to find out you might
just as well be interested in anything since anyway your job
might not be a job and if it was well then it was not the
kind of a job it might have been. Yes that did a lot, they all
•aid, it certainly did do a lot.

Yes said one of the younger ones even if you were only kids

during the depression you got to feel that way about it. Anyway they all agreed the depression had a lot to do with it.

There is one thing in which this army is not different from that other army that is in being generous and sweet and particularly kind to children.

They are sweet and kind and considerate all of them, how they do think about what you need and what will please you, they did then that other army and they do now this army.

When our M.P.s had got settled completely in their box car I used to go down to see them, and one day one of the mothers in the town told me that her nine year old daughter had been praying every single day that she might see an American soldier and she never had and now the mother was beginning to be afraid that the child would lose faith in prayer. I said I would take her down to see the American soldiers and we went. Naturally they were sweet and each one of them thought of something to give her, candies chewing gum, one of them gave her one of the U.S. badges they wear on their caps and one gave her a medal that the Pope had blessed in Rome and given to the American soldiers. And she was so happy, she sang them all the old French songs, Clair de la Lune, The Good King Dagobert and On the Bridge of Avignon.

Then as we were going home I said to her, about that chewing gum you must chew it but be careful not to swallow it. Oh yes I know she said. How do you know that I asked oh she said because when there was the last war my mother was a little girl and the American soldiers gave her chewing gum and all through this war my mother used to tell us about it, and she gave a rapturous sigh and said and now I have it.

More Americans came to stay at Culoz station, this time railroad workers and it became natural to have them there, natural for them and natural for us. They used all of them to want to know how we managed to escape the Germans and gradually with their asking and with the news that in the month of August the Gestapo had been in my apartment in Paris to look at everything, naturally I began to have what you might call a posthumous fear. I was quite frightened. All the time the Germans were here we were so busy trying to live through each day that except once in a while when something happened you did not know about being frightened, but now somehow with the American soldiers questions and hearing what had been happening to others, of course one knew it but now one had time to feel it and so I was quite frightened, now that there was nothing dangerous and the whole American army between us and danger. One is like that.

As I say we were getting used to having Americans here and they getting used to being here.

In the early days when the American army was first passing by, in jeeps and trucks the Americans used to say to me but they do not seem to get used to us, we have been right here over a week and they get just as excited when they see us as if they had never seen us before. You do not understand, I said to them you see every time they see you it makes them know it is not a dream that it is true that the Germans are gone and that you are here that you are here and that the Germans are gone. Every time they see you it is a new proof, a new proof that it is all true really true that the Germans are really truly completely and entirely gone, gone gone.

Yes even now when it has become so natural to see them here there are moments when it is hard to believe it. Yes of course they are really here.

Just this evening I saw a nun who had come over from Aix-les-Bains to see some sisters here, she had been in a convent in Connecticut. She said to me you know I just saw some American soldiers in the square and I just had to speak to them I just had to.

That is the way we all were we just had to.

So there were more Americans here and naturally we talked a lot, and one day one of them Ernest Humphrey from Tennessee was here and a French friend was here, he had known the American army of '17 and he too was struck with the poise and the conversation of this army. He asked him lots of questions, about what Americans feel about France about the French country and about French girls and about American men, and said my friend after Humphrey left, they are different now, they are so easy to converse with, the last army was easy to get along with but this army is easy to converse with and as French people do believe that conversation is the finest part of civilisation, naturally what he said meant a great deal.

Is it, said the Frenchman, the cinema that has taught them to be such men of the world, to be sure it has not much effect on our young men he added.

I asked so many of them about it, we had long talks about it, they all agreed that the depression had a lot to do with it, it made people stay at home because they had no money to go out with, all the same said some of them that military service that they did before we came into the war had something to do with it, it kind of sobered everybody up, kind of made them feel what it was to get ready. Some of them said the radio had a lot to do with it, they got the habit of listening to information, and then the quizzes that the radio used to give kind of made them feel that it was no use just being ignorant, and then some of them said crossword puzzles had a lot to do with it.

The conclusion that one came to was that it had happened the American men had at last come to be interested and to be interesting and conversational, and it was mighty interesting to see and hear it. Naturally we exchanged books a lot, I have all kinds here and they gave me what they had, two I enjoyed immensely, Ernie Pyle, Here Is Your War, and Helen MacInnes, Assignment in Brittany, some of the boys passing through on the train gave me the one and the railroad boys at Chambery gave me the other, the house here is filled with English books that I have been buying as I could through the war and other odds and ends, I was interested that they were a bit tired of detectives, I like them as much as ever but that is because I am so much older and they do like Westerns and then they like adventures, and any longish American novel. They do not care for English ones, they say they can't seem to get into them. They also gave me a book on Head Hunters in the Solomon Islands which they all read. Well of course they did in the last war give me The Trail of the Lonesome Pine, they did not read much not those we knew. Undoubtedly the depression had a lot to do with that, a lot.

They asked me in Lyon to go and speak to the French on the radio. When I was there I saw lots of Americans on the streets but as I was in cars I could not speak to them but one evening I wandered out on foot and in a school near by I found a number of them. Naturally well just so naturally we talked, they were glad to see me and I was glad to see them, there were about thirty of them and we told each other a lot. One who had been a school-teacher in North Carolina walked home with me and we interested each other very much. He said I was quite right about the difference between the two armies, he said he had noticed it before he had left home but now he was sure. We said we would meet again but in a war it is always difficult to meet again, very often not possible. I do hope that we will meet again.

Of course one has to remember that many in fact most of these soldiers have not been home for almost two years. It is a long time a very long time.

When I got back from Lyon the Americans here in Culoz wanted to know what I had talked about in Lyon, I said I had been telling French people what Americans are and they said what are they, and I said this is what I told them and so I told them. They were interested.

I said that I had begun by saying that after all to-day, America was the oldest country in the world and the reason why was that she was the first country to enter into the twentieth century. She had her birthday of the twentieth century when the other countries were still all either in the nineteenth century or still further back in other centuries, now all the countries except Germany, are trying to be in the twentieth century, so that considering the world as twentieth century America is the oldest as she came into the twentieth century in the eighties before any other country had any idea what the twentieth century was going to be. And now what is the twentieth century that America discovered. The twentieth century is a century that found out that the cheapest articles should be made of the very best material. The nineteenth century believed that the best material should be only used in expensive objects and that cheap things should be made of cheap material. The Americans knew that if you wanted to make a lot of things that is things that will sell cheap you had to make them of the best material otherwise you could not turn them out fast enough, that is series manufacture because cheap material could not stand the strain. So America began to live in the twentieth century in the eighties with the Ford car and all the other series manufacturing.

And so America is at the present moment the oldest country in the world because she had her twentieth century birthday in the eighteen eighties, long before any other country had their twentieth century birthday.

There is one thing one has to remember about America. it had a certain difficulty in proving itself American which no other nation has ever had.

After all anybody is as their land and air is. Anybody is as the sky is low or high. Anybody is as there is wind or no wind there. That is what makes a people, makes their kind of looks, their kind of thinking, their subtlety and their stupidity, and their eating and their drinking and their language.

I was much taken with what one American soldier said when he was in England. He said we did not get along at all with the English until they finally did get it into their heads that we were not cousins, but foreigners, once they really got that, there was no more trouble.

The trouble of course is or was that by the time America became itself everybody or very nearly everybody could read and write and so the language which would naturally have changed as Latin languages changed to suit each country, French, Italian and Spanish, Saxon countries England and Germany, Slav countries etcetera, America as everybody knew how to read and write the language instead of changing as it did in countries where nobody knew how to read and write while the language was being formed, the American language instead of changing remained English, long after the Americans in their nature their habits their feelings their pleasures and their pains had nothing to do with England.

So the only way the Americans could change their language was by choosing words which they liked better than other words, by putting words next to each other in a different way than the English way, by shoving the language around until at last now the job is done, we use the same words as the English do but the words say an entirely different thing.

Yes in that sense Americans have changed, I think of the Americans of the last war, they had their language but they were not yet in possession of it, and the children of the depression as that generation called itself it was beginning to possess its language but it was still struggling but now the job is done, the G.I. Joes have this language that is theirs, they do not have to worry about it, they dominate their language and in dominating their language which is now all theirs they have ceased to be adolescents and have become men.

When I was in America in '34 they asked me if I did not find Americans changed. I said no what could they change to, just to become more American. No I said I could have gone to school with any of them.

But all the same yes that is what they have changed to they have become more American all American, and the G.I. Joes show it and know it, God bless them.

318.52
St514

GERTRUDE STEIN was born in Pennsylvania in 1874. Her grandparents had been German-Jewish immigrants who had prospered in the United States; her parents had been beguiled by art, languages, and educational theory. At Radcliffe, Gertrude Stein was an outstanding student of William James in psychology, and conducted laboratory experiments with Hugo Münsterberg, which led her to study the anatomy of the brain at Johns Hopkins. In 1902 she joined her brother Leo in Paris, and lived abroad until her death in 1946. Her salon in the rue de Fleurus, over which she presided with Alice B. Toklas, became the gathering place for prominent writers and painters, among them Sherwood Anderson and Hemingway, Matisse and Picasso.

Gertrude Stein remained in France during the German occupation; as F. W. Dupee says, "following World War II she became a kind of oracle and motherly hostess to American military personnel in liberated Paris."

Her philosophy of composition, which was partly indebted to the aesthetic theories of William James and Bergson's concept of time, and her experiments in writing influenced other writers of her period.

LINCOLN CHRISTIAN COLLEGE AND SEMINARY

7930 9

818
S8192S
1972